PRINCE Of STORIES

THE MANY WORLDS Of NEIL GAIMAN

Neil Gaiman and friend, a doll painted by artist Kelli Bickman. Photo by and © Kelli Bickman, 1996. All rights reserved.

PRINCE OF STORIES

THE MANY WORLDS OF NEIL GAIMAN

HANK WAGNER,
CHRISTOPHER GOLDEN,
AND STEPHEN R. BISSETTE

ST. MARTIN'S PRESS ❧ NEW YORK

To my wife, Nancy, and my daughters, Leigh, Theresa, Melissa, and Sarah. In *Stardust,* Tristran Thorne had to travel far and wide and face many perils to find his true Heart's Desire. I'm lucky that, like Dorothy Gale, I don't need to look any further than my own backyard to find mine.

—H. W.

To my mother, Roberta, who always encouraged wonder and happily fed my imagination with whatever books and comics I desired, no matter how weird she might have thought them.

—C. G.

To Joe and Murial Kubert, for opening the door that led me to a new life and my friendship with Neil, among countless others; to Neil, for obvious reasons; and to Marge, for Marge knows what and Marge knows why.

—S. R. B.

PRINCE OF STORIES. Copyright © 2008 by Hank Wagner, Christopher Golden, and Stephen R. Bissette. Foreword copyright © 2006 by Terry Pratchett. All rights reserved. Printed in the United States of America. For information, address St. Martin's Press, 175 Fifth Avenue, New York, N.Y. 10010.

www.stmartins.com

Design by Level C

ISBN-13: 978-0-312-38765-5
ISBN-10: 0-312-38765-2

First Edition: November 2008

10   9   8   7   6   5   4   3   2   1

CONTENTS

ACKNOWLEDGMENTS

The authors owe a great deal of thanks to a great many people. As such, it seems advisable to apologize in advance to whoever ought to be in the following bit of grateful blathering but somehow slipped our minds. You know who you are. We're heartily sorry, and promise never to do it again.

Thanks, first and foremost, to Neil Gaiman and Lorraine Garland for their infinite patience with trivial botherings, for good cheer and hospitality, for research and breakfast, and for saying "yes" nearly all of the time (even Lorraine, the self-proclaimed "Princess of No"). Thanks also to Neil for providing photos and a whole host of text odds and ends, and for permission to reprint them.

To Marc Resnick at St. Martin's Press, also for *his* infinite patience (and perhaps you begin to see a pattern here).

To Terry Pratchett, for graciously providing our foreword.

To Linda Addison, Mark Buckingham, Peter Crowther, Mike Dringenberg, Stephen Jones, Dave McKean, Michael Reaves, P. Craig Russell, Jill Thompson, Charles Vess, Rick Veitch, and Jane Yolen for their thoughts, contributions, and good humor in helping bring this book to life.

To Peter Coleborn; Jason Drilon and Maui Reyes; Sean Cawelti and the folks at Rogue Artists Ensemble; Amy Huey and Dark Horse Comics; Jennifer Brehl; Olga Nunes; Elise Howard; Jeanne McLellan; Richard Aquan and the expeditious wonders of HarperCollins, for allowing us to include art and visuals to help make these pages come to life. To Marlene O'Connor, for kind permission to reprint "Blood Monster" in its entirety; and to Kim Newman and Eugene Byrne for permission to reprint "Who Was Jack the Ripper?" Thanks also to Chuck Forsman and Penina Gal of the Center for Cartoon Studies for their production work on "Blood Monster"; to the Center for Cartoon Studies, for providing production facilities; and to Al Nickerson for his help with legal research.

A SLIGHTLY WORN BUT STILL
QUITE LOVELY FOREWORD

BY TERRY PRATCHETT

What can I say about Neil Gaiman that has not already been said in *The Morbid Imagination: Five Case Studies*?

Well, he's no genius. He's better than that.

He's not a wizard, in other words, but a conjurer.

Wizards don't have to work. They wave their hands, and the magic happens. But conjurers, now . . . conjurers work very hard. They spend a lot of time in their youth watching, very carefully, the best conjurers of their day. They seek out old books of trickery and, being natural conjurers, read everything else as well, because history itself is just a magic show. They observe the way people think, and the many ways in which they don't. They learn the subtle use of springs, and how to open mighty temple doors at a touch, and how to make the trumpets sound.

And they take center stage and amaze you with flags of all nations and smoke and mirrors, and you cry: "A-amazing! How does he do it? What happened to the elephant? Where's the rabbit? Did he really smash my watch?"

And in the back row we, the other conjurers, say quietly, "Well *done*. Isn't that a variant of the Prague Levitating Sock? Wasn't that one Pasqual's Spirit Mirror, where the girl isn't really there? But where the *hell* did that flaming sword come from?"

And we wonder if there may be such a thing as wizardry, after all . . .

I met Neil in 1985, when *The Colour of Magic* had just come out. It was my first-ever interview as an author. Neil was making a living as a freelance journalist and had the pale features of someone who had sat through the review showings of altogether too many bad movies in order to live off the freebie cold chicken legs they served at the receptions afterwards (and to build up his contacts book, which is now the size of the Bible and contains rather more interesting people). He was doing journalism in order to eat, which is a very good way of learning journalism. Probably the only real way, come to think of it.

He also had a very bad hat. It was a grey homburg. He was not a hat person. There was no natural unity between hat and man. That was the first and last time I saw the hat. As if subconsciously aware of the bad hatitude, he used to forget it and leave it behind in restaurants. One day, he never went back for it. I put this in for the serious fans out there: if you search really, really hard, you may find a small restaurant somewhere in London with a dusty grey homburg at the back of a shelf. Who knows what will happen if you try it on?

Anyway, we got on fine. Hard to say why, but at bottom was a shared delight and amazement at the sheer strangeness of the universe, in stories, in obscure details, in strange old books in unregarded bookshops. We stayed in contact.

[SFX: pages being ripped off a calender. You know, you just don't get that in movies anymore . . .]

And one thing led to another, and he became big in graphic novels, and *Discworld* took off, and one day he sent me about six pages of a short story and said he didn't know how it continued, and I didn't either, and about a year later I took it out of the drawer and did see what happened next, even if I couldn't see how it all ended yet, and we wrote it together, and that was *Good Omens*. It was done by two guys who didn't have anything to lose by having fun. We didn't do it for the money.

But, as it turned out, we got a lot of money.

. . . hey, let me tell you about the weirdness, like when he was staying with us for the editing, and we heard a noise and went into his room and two of our white doves had got in and couldn't get out; they were panicking around the room and Neil was waking up in a storm of snowy white feathers saying, "Wstfgl?" which is his normal ante meridian vocabulary. Or the time when we were in a bar and he met the Spider Women. Or the time on tour when we checked into our hotel, and in the morning it turned out that *his* TV had been showing him strange late-night seminaked bondage bisexual chat shows, and mine had picked up nothing but reruns of *Mr. Ed*. And the moment, live on air, when we realised that an underinformed New York radio interviewer with ten minutes of chat still to go *thought* Good Omens *was not a work of fiction* . . .

[Cut to a train, pounding along the tracks. That's another scene they never show in movies these days . . .]

And there we were, ten years on, traveling across Sweden and talking about the plot of *American Gods* (him) and *The Amazing Maurice* (me). Probably both of us at the same time. It was just like the old days. One of us says, "I don't know how to deal with this tricky bit of plot"; the other one listens and says, "The solution, Grasshopper, is in the way you state the problem. Fancy a coffee?"

A lot had happened in those ten years. He'd left the comics world shaken, and it'll never be quite the same. The effect was akin to that of Tolkien on the fantasy novel—everything afterward is in some way influenced. I remember on one U.S. *Good Omens* tour walking round a comics shop. We'd been signing for a lot of comics fans, some of whom were clearly puzzled at the concept of "dis story wid no pitchers in it," and I wandered around the shelves looking at the opposition.

That's when I realised he was good. There's a delicacy of touch, a subtle scalpel, which is the hallmark of his work.

And when I heard the premise of *American Gods* I wanted to write it so much I could taste it . . .

When I read *Coraline,* I saw it as an exquisitely drawn animation; if I close my eyes I can see how the house looks, or the special dolls' picnic. No wonder he writes scripts now; soon, I hope someone will be intelligent enough to let him direct. When I read the book I remembered that children's stories are, indeed, where true horror lives. My childhood nightmares would have been quite feature-less without the imaginings of Walt Disney, and there's a few little details concerning black button eyes in that book that make a small part of the adult brain want to go and hide behind the sofa. But the purpose of the book is not the horror, it is horror's defeat.

It might come as a surprise to many to learn that Neil is either a very nice, approachable guy or an incredible actor. He sometimes takes those shades off. The leather jacket I'm not sure about; I think I once saw him in a tux, or it may have been someone else.

He takes the view that mornings happen to other people. I think I once saw him at breakfast, although possibly it was just someone who looked a bit like him who was lying with their head in the plate of baked beans. He likes good sushi, and quite likes people, too, although not raw; he is kind to fans who are not total jerks, and enjoys talking to people who know how to talk. He doesn't look as though he's forty; that may have happened to someone else, too. Or perhaps there's a special picture locked in his attic.

Have fun. You're in the hands of a master conjurer. Or, quite possibly, a wizard.

PS: He really, really likes it if you ask him to sign your battered, treasured copy of *Good Omens* that has been dropped in the tub at least once and is now held together with very old, yellowing transparent tape. You know the one.

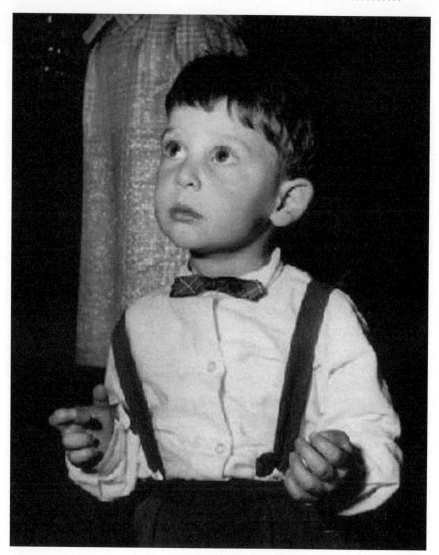

Photo courtesy of Neil Gaiman, from his collection.

||||||||||||||||||||||||||||||||||||||||||||||||||||||||||||||||||||||||

EXPLORING THE IN-BETWEEN

Who is Neil Gaiman?

Forbes magazine labeled him "the most famous author you've never heard of." His publisher, William Morrow, calls him a "pop culture phenomenon." He is listed in the *Dictionary of Literary Biography* as one of "the top ten living post-modern writers," along with Thomas Pynchon and William Burroughs.

Norman Mailer (author of *The Naked and the Dead*) said of Gaiman's best-known creation, *The Sandman*, "Along with all else, Sandman is a comic strip for intellectuals, and I say it's about time." Fantasist Harlan Ellison opined, "Neil Gaiman's work on *The Sandman* is so excellent, so much of a presentation of the new high water mark, that we realize as we read, that it is about something, that it is not merely an amusing entertainment. (Though it is that, of course . . .)"

Peter Straub (author of *Ghost Story* and *Koko*) said, "Gaiman is on a plane all his own. Nobody in his field is better than this. Gaiman is a master, and his vast roomy stories, filled with every possible shade of feeling, are unlike anyone else's."

Finally, Stephen King (author of *Salem's Lot, The Stand, Bag of Bones, The Green Mile,* and others) called him, "A treasure house of story" and stated that "we are lucky to have him in any medium."

If that's not enough, maybe the awards he's won will help paint a picture. By our count, Gaiman has received:

one International Horror Guild Award
one British Fantasy Award
one World Fantasy Award
two Mythopoeic Fantasy awards for adult literature
two British Science Fiction awards
two Nebulas
three Geffens
three Hugo awards
four Bram Stoker awards
six Locus awards
fourteen Eisner awards

To paraphrase prizefighter Rocky Marciano, somebody out there obviously likes Neil Gaiman's work.

British Fantasy Award winners 2006. Front row, left to right: Allen Ashley, Stuart Young, Joe Hill, and David Sutton. Back row, left to right: Les Edwards, Peter Crowther, Neil Gaiman, and Stephen Jones. Photo by and © Peter Coleborn.

Not enough? Okay, how about typing the word "Neil" into Google and seeing what comes up. You guessed it: The first entry is about Neil Gaiman, not about other famous Neils such as Messrs. Young, Armstrong, Sedaka, and Diamond. Type in "Neil Gaiman," as we did on the day this was written, and you're told that there are over 2.25 million items about him on the Web.

Oriented? Good.

Simply put, it is our contention that Neil Gaiman is one of the premier fantasists writing today, even perhaps *the* premier fantasist. His work, which is received with equal enthusiasm by fans and critics alike, and has been published in many languages and many countries, seems destined to take its place among the works of world-famous fantasists such as Tolkien and Borges.

Gaiman has also been on the forefront of the current generation of fantasists creating new fairy tales for a new century. For a culture that has elevated a studio erected by the long gone Walt Disney into one of the planet's most omnipresent corporate powers, Americans still use the term "fairy tale" as a pejorative in most arenas of public discourse. It takes a fantasist like Gaiman to remind us how and why fairy tales are still vital, and then prove it time and time again by writing a new one.

If the first original fairy tale of the twentieth century was L. Frank Baum's *The Wizard of Oz,* an argument can be made for the Sandman oeuvre being among the key contemporary fairy tales of the millennial shift. Like *Oz,* Gaiman's realm of his brooding hero, Dream (the Sandman), is populated with a rich diversity of citizens, who you will also meet in the pages that follow. There's Calliope, the imprisoned Muse; Mad Hettie (who hides her heart, only to forget where it might be); and many, many others, prominent among them Dream's siblings, "The Endless": the streetwise Goth-punk teen-guised Death; the rambling Delirium; along with Desire; Despair; Destruction; and Destiny.

Ah, destiny.

It's destiny—his own—that Gaiman accepted and cultivated from an early age.

Unlike many of us, Gaiman knew from childhood exactly what he wanted to do. Learning to read at the age of four, he consumed whatever was available, working his way through the entire children's section of his local library, then moving on to more adult fare. "I was the kid with the book," he has said. Gaiman read voraciously, first dipping into books by the likes of G. K. Chesterton, C. S. Lewis, J. R. R. Tolkien, and Hope Mirelees. He later sampled the works of Bradbury, Moorcock, Lafferty, Ellison, and Gene Wolfe, among many others.

In 1976, the then fifteen-year-old Gaiman met with a career counselor at his school, who asked him what he wanted to do for a living. Without hesitating he answered, "I want to write American comic books." Not knowing how to respond to the young man, the counselor simply ignored the statement, and asked if he'd ever considered a career in accountancy.

Fortunately for fans of the fantastic, Gaiman wasn't discouraged by his counselor's reaction, going on to create one of the most well-received and highly praised comic book series of all time, *The Sandman.* If Jack Kirby, Gil Kane, and others of their generation laid the foundations, and Will Eisner is credited with coining the term (and for championing the format) of the "graphic novel"; if Alan Moore, the first British writer to fulfill Gaiman's teen dream of scripting "American comic books," pioneered their treatment of mature, literary themes; well, then, Gaiman certainly was among the first of his generation to walk through the doors those who came before had opened, among the first to effectively explore and map their potential. In doing so, he's kicked that door wide open for others, encouraging the crossing of numerous boundaries and blasting many long-held but outdated ideas about publishing.

His impact on the world of comics is hard to ignore—Gaiman has even had a hand in changing the way comics are published. The graphic novel form has precursors dating back to the nineteenth century, and the collecting of individual periodical comic books into trade paperback editions had long been popular in the UK, but it had only recently become an accepted practice in the American comic book direct-sales market before Gaiman entered the field in 1987–88 (with *Violent Cases* and *Black Orchid*). Beginning in 1989, Gaiman's Sandman was the right series arriving at the right time to elevate and codify a new plateau in graphic novels. Originally published as single-issue stories, his major Sandman story arcs have

since been collected in ten volumes that fall under the growing umbrella definition of the format known as the graphic novel. Those ten volumes remain perennial best sellers, and as such have had an enormous influence on pushing graphic
novels out of comic shops and into bookstores, fueling the industrywide increase
in popularity and sales of the format.

His work on *The Sandman* opened many other doors for the suddenly popular
writer, resulting in the subsequent creation of numerous short stories, several novels,
television, other graphic novels, and a variety of films, all of which have combined to make him a Renaissance man in the realm of the written word and
storytelling.

Physically, Neil Gaiman bears a passing resemblance to his most famous character, the Sandman, always dressed in black, his unruly mop of hair always threatening to spring to life. In speech and manner, he bears an uncanny resemblance to
Dr. Gaius Baltar of *Battlestar Galactica* fame, only more controlled. He's the father
of three, a boy and two girls. He loves sushi, seeking out restaurants specializing in
that dish all across the globe. He recently acquired a dog, an Alsatian named Cabal
(after King Arthur's dog), who likes to take him for walks in the woods that
surround his home in rural Minnesota.

Over the course of his career, Gaiman has worn many hats. He began as a journalist, then moved into writing comics, graphic novels, short stories, novels, television scripts, and children's books. He's also written screenplays and directed a
film of his own, *A Short Film About John Bolton*.

Another hat he wears, with great frequency, is that of the fund-raiser and
rabble-rouser, though Gaiman has raised more funds than he has roused the rabble
(others do that without trying). He has repeatedly given back to the forums, indus-
tries, and communities he works within with an ongoing series of benefit publications, public performances, books, videos, auctions, and much, much more.
No one—except, perhaps, Cerebus creator Dave Sim—has been a more persistent
champion or raised more funds for the Comic Book Legal Defense Fund. The
CBLDF is the only legal institution that protects the comics and graphic novel
community from constant attempts to persecute and prosecute creators, publishers,
retailers, and distributors.

As Gaiman has said, in his online journal, "Now, I am a big fan of the First
Amendment, and of freedom of speech. It's without doubt my favorite thing about
America. I happen to believe that the remedy for speech and ideas you don't like is
not stopping the offending speech and punishing the speaker, but replying to it and
creating your own speech (and there's always the off switch and the marketplace)."

And the marketplace is something Gaiman knows well—as a reader, as a
writer, as an active participant in a variety of media. The marketplace of ideas is
among Gaiman's fondest devotions, in all its permutations and generations, the
oldest marketplace of them all (save, perhaps, one), the ether through which all
stories move. After all, Gaiman has made a good living in this marketplace.

Gaiman is a writer, but, first and foremost, he's a fan, a man with a passionate love of story, avidly consuming myths, television, movies, novels, short stories, animation, and comics. He stands in awe of many of his predecessors and peers, unafraid to lavish praise on the deserving.

He loves to write for writing's sake, and as a means of staying in touch with his legion of fans—his blog, now in its sixth year, has over a million unique hits each month. He recently passed the million-word mark on his popular site. This forum is the most permeable membrane between the writer and his readership, the man and his work—through it, Gaiman converses openly with his fans, communicating daily to those devoted to his work.

What can you conclude about the man based on his work? Well, it's a tricky proposition, but we're going to try to illuminate Gaiman the man in this manner. At the least, his work shows both a great deal of creativity, combined with a sense of whimsy. It also shows a great respect for what came before, and, simultaneously, a sense of awe at the possibilities the future might bring. Consideration of Gaiman's works is a complex undertaking, for among his works are not only those which he has written, but also those in which he has participated. These are the less obvious works, from a BBC miniseries to an episode of a TV series, from translating the work of Japan's greatest living animator and fantasist to a most curious short film he wrote and directed about a fellow comic book creator (or is it?), to feature films by other talents who are adapting Gaiman's works. These are the fund-raising efforts, the carrying of torches handed off by others, the trials (literally, as you shall see for yourself) and tribulations, a diverse world of works, woes, and wonders.

This is the story of that work, as best we can tell it at this point in time . . . and after all, stories are all that matter.

In the final analysis, at least in the world according to Neil Gaiman, story is paramount. Stories help us find meaning and help us to define ourselves. Telling stories is at the core of what makes us human; it's Gaiman's talent at conveying tales that touches the humanity in all of us. To Gaiman, stories can be a means of redemption, and are certainly necessary to our survival. As he notes in the last line of "Inventing Aladdin," a poem about Scheherazade, "We save our lives in such unlikely ways."

ABOUT THIS BOOK: THOUGHTS AND THEMES AND SPOILER WARNINGS!

During a Q&A session at Google, Gaiman commented that "the artist himself is probably the worst person in the world to talk about what he's done." That might be true, but not entirely, so part of this book will talk about what Gaiman has said publicly about his work, mining that treasure trove of information for insights. Gaiman is ubiquitous in terms of interviews, so we'll be citing many of his personal observations, despite his misgivings about their worth. We'll also be relying on the comments he offered during the many hours of extensive interviews we conducted with him in November 2007. We will examine his entire body of work, looking for recurring themes, analyzing characters, and looking for connections between those works. In that manner we hope to provide new readers with a primer on Gaiman's considerable output, and perhaps remind those already familiar with his canon about the intricacies and craftsmanship of those stories.

A word of warning, however. If you're one of those readers who live in fear of coming across a spoiler while reading about an author's works, DON'T READ A CHAPTER OF THIS BOOK UNTIL YOU'VE READ THE TEXTS UNDER DISCUSSION IN THAT CHAPTER. In many places we're going to provide in-depth analysis of plot points and characters, so if knowing about these in advance tends to spoil a book or story for you, forewarned is forearmed.

And one final warning: You are going to encounter many . . . unusual . . . spellings and odd turns of phrase within these pages. This is because we've left Gaiman's original spellings and idioms alone, for the most part. Bear with us on these: We can't help or change the fact that he speaks the King's English. ☺

THE QUOTABLE GAIMAN

The best thing about writing fiction is that moment where the story catches fire and comes to life on the page, and suddenly it all makes sense and you know what it's about and why you're doing it and what these people are saying and doing, and you get to feel like both the creator and the audience. Everything is suddenly both obvious and surprising ("but of course that's why he was doing that, and that means that . . .") and it's magic and wonderful and strange. You don't live there always when you write. Mostly it's a long hard walk. Sometimes it's a trudge through fog and you're scared you've lost your way and can't remember why you set out in the first place. But sometimes you fly, and that pays for everything.

—Neil Gaiman's blog, October 2007

A lot of it is because you want to talk about humanity, and you want to talk about people, but people are icebergs. So much of us is underneath. The imagination and the place that dreams come from is so huge and so important. I'm trying to write about the real world, in that I'm trying to write about whatever it is the experience that makes us human, the things that we have in common.

—Rain Taxi Review of Books
(raintaxi.com), Summer 2001

My ideal reader is me. And yes, my ideal reader comes with me and is forgiving. And will re-read. I don't know in this day and age whether it's a quixotic goal or not. Gene Wolfe, one of my favorite writers in any genre, defined good literature as that which can be read with pleasure by an educated reader and re-read with increased pleasure . . . I always try to do that with my stuff.

—Rain Taxi Review of Books
(raintaxi.com), Summer 2001

On how he became interested in mythology:

I wish I had an origin story for you. When I was four, I was bitten by a radioactive myth.
—Interview with Jesse Crispin,
Bookslut (bookslut.com), October 2006

I still love the book-ness of books, the smell of books: I am a book fetishist—books to me are the coolest and sexiest and most wonderful things there are.
—*Locus,* February 2005

On signings and fans:

When I look up at them, I ask, "Who would you like this signed for?" And they say, "Me." And I say, "Do you have a name?" and they say, "Yes! I certainly do!" "What is it?" I ask. "Alfred. No wait! It's Albert!" And I know they're thinking, "Oh, my God. He thinks I'm the biggest idiot he's ever seen at a signing." All I'm *really* thinking is, "I wish people wouldn't worry. It's fine." They aren't the first person to say "Me!" when asked their name, or even to forget their name altogether, or the first person to have rehearsed . . . something they want to say . . . and it all comes out garbled. I *never* think, "Oh, he's an idiot." Never. The people that come to my signings are good people. They are nice people and I am so grateful to them for reading my books and wanting to come see me.
—Writers Write, The Internet Writing
Journal (writerswrite.com), July 2001

PART ONE
THE EARLY YEARS

The Gaiman family roots lay in Poland, but Neil's childhood was spent entirely in England, the country to which Gaiman's grandfather emigrated from the Netherlands in 1916. His grandfather opened a grocery store on the southern coast of England, in the Hampshire city of Portsmouth, eventually expanding this business venture into a grocery store chain, where Neil's father, David Bernard Gaiman, worked. David met pharmacist Sheila Goldman, and they were wed. Neil was born November 10, 1960, in Porchester, Hampshire, and was followed by two sisters, necessitating the family move to larger quarters. They settled in 1965 in the West Sussex town of East Grinstead, where Neil lived for all but four years of his youth (1980–84).

Neil attended several Church of England schools, including his home village's Fonthill School, Ardingly College (1970–74), and Whitgift School in Croydon (1974–77). Throughout his formative years, Gaiman was a tireless reader, gravitating to the works of fantasists like James Branch Cabell, Lord Dunsany, J. R. R. Tolkien, C. S. Lewis, and G. K. Chesterton. In his teenage years he cultivated a great love for science fiction: novels and short stories by Samuel R. Delany, Michael Moorcock, Ursula K. Le Guin, Roger Zelazny, Harlan Ellison, H. P. Lovecraft, Thorne Smith, and Gene Wolfe were among his personal favorites, along with the challenging works of Jorge Luis Borges, Douglas Adams's innovative and satiric radio serial *The Hitchhiker's Guide to the Galaxy,* and the countless comic books he devoured with a passion. Gaiman's own nascent writings emerged from this steady diet of fantasy and science fiction, though it must be noted he read all genres and fields.

Once he was out of school and entering his early twenties, in the early to mid-1980s, Gaiman cut his teeth as a journalist and critic, selling many interviews, articles, and book and movie reviews to any available venue, building his professional connections and credentials as he did so. His reviews were plentiful, spanning venues from the slick newsstand UK *Penthouse* to Stefan Jaworzyn's underground *Shock Xpress* horror fanzine. Via interviews and articles, Gaiman made his first links with other writers, including novelists Ramsey Campbell (interviewed by Gaiman for the UK *Penthouse,* May 1985) and James Herbert (for *Publishing News* and the 1988 World Fantasy Convention book *Gaslight & Ghosts*). His interviews with writers, musicians, and artists also graced the pages of *Space*

Voyager, Time Out, Reflex, American Fantasy, Fantasy Empire, the British Fantasy Society, and other magazines, along with collaborative pieces for these and others, such as *The Truth,* and *Interzone.*

Gaiman struck up friendships with then rising stars such as Alan Moore (in pieces for *Knave, American Fantasy,* and *The Comics Journal*) and Clive Barker (see Gaiman's article "King of the Gory Tellers: Clive Barker" for *Today,* October 19, 1986, as well as his 1985 Barker interview in the UK *Penthouse*). His *Time Out* pieces included an article on "The Comics Explosion" (*Time Out,* 1986), and Gaiman's interviews with comics creators such as the Hernandez Brothers (*Love & Rockets*) and Dave Gibbons for other publications were critical to his future path.

Gaiman's key freelance writing venue during this period was the long popular UK adult newsstand magazine *Knave* (Galaxy Publications), which had published short fiction by Harlan Ellison, Henry Slesar, and others since the 1950s. Gaiman began freelancing for *Knave* in 1984, and his byline appeared on numerous book reviews, articles, and celebrity interviews, including interviews with popular actors like Patrick Macnee (*The Avengers*), Denholm Elliott, Divine (*Pink Flamingos*), TV comedians Rik Mayall (*The Young Ones*), Terry Jones (Monty Python), *Rocky Horror Picture Show* creator Richard O'Brien, cartoonist Gilbert Shelton, and science fiction authors Arthur C. Clarke, Frank Herbert, Harry Harrison, William Gibson, and Douglas Adams.

Gaiman's first professional short story sale was "Featherquest" for the short-lived advanced Dungeons and Dragons magazine *Imagine* (May 1984), for which he'd also written film reviews and subsequently another short story, "How to Sell the Ponti Bridge" (March 1985; reprinted in the Gaiman anthology *M is for Magic*). He also contributed three short stories to *Knave*—"We Can Get Them for You Wholesale" and "The Case of the Four & Twenty Blackbirds" (both 1984) and "Manuscript Found in a Milkbottle" (1985)—before leaving the magazine in 1986 due to an editorial change of the guard (ushering *Knave* into a more explicitly pornographic era) and into the greener pastures Gaiman had been cultivating outside of the adult magazine market.

In 1984, he wrote his first book, *Duran Duran: The First Four Years of the Fab Five* for Proteus. Gaiman delivered the definitive 126-page trade paperback volume on the English pop group, at the time the most commercially successful of the MTV-fueled (and fueling) eighties British postpunk scene bands. Written in the fifth year of the band's existence, at which point Duran Duran had sold over ten million records, the book covered the particulars of the band members— founders Nick Rhodes and John Taylor of Hollywood, Birmingham, Roger Taylor (no relation to John), Andy Taylor (ditto), and lead vocalist Simon Le Bon—and their meteoric rise. The band's hit singles of the time included "Girls on Film," "Rio," "Hungry Like the Wolf," and "The Reflex," all popularized by their videos, which played endlessly on MTV and in other venues.

Gaiman wrote in the acknowledgments, "While researching this book I discovered over seven completely wrong explanations, all of them different, for the origin of the name Duran Duran. Having checked it firsthand, I can vouch for the one given here (though the spelling is open to question)." The source? "Duran Duran took their name from the missing scientist in *Barbarella*," the 1968 Roger Vadim film based on the internationally renowned French comics series by Jean-Claude Forest (which debuted in 1962); the scientist's name was actually Durand Durand—hence, Gaiman's parenthetical note.

Such genre trivia played a bigger role in Gaiman's next book, *Ghastly Beyond Belief: The Science Fiction and Fantasy Book of Quotations*, an amusing paperback collection of absurd and simply awful dialogue and passages from science fiction, fantasy, and horror literature and movies co-authored with Kim Newman. As previously noted, Gaiman often collaborated with others on various magazine articles, and fellow journalist, critic, and novelist Kim Newman was primary among them. Born July 31, 1959, in London and growing up in Aller, Somerset, Newman's defining interest remains cinema history and horror fiction, though his own novels have struck out their own vivid strain of alternative historical fantasy. *Ghastly Beyond Belief* was Newman's first book; his second, a solo, was *Nightmare Movies: A Critical History of the Horror Film, 1968–88* (1988), an intensive history of horror films. Fellow young genre writers like Newman, Stephen Jones, and Philip Nutman were among Gaiman's circle of friends and associates, as were writers Eugene Byrne (a frequent collaborator with Gaiman and Newman on articles for *The Truth*), and Stefan Jaworzyn. With Stephen Jones, Gaiman cowrote the poem "Now We Are Sick," springboarding a satiric poetry anthology edited by Gaiman and Jones, which was published as a "sampler" in 1986, and in hardcover as *Now We Are Sick: An Anthology of Nasty Verse* in 1991. Other poets in the book include longtime Gaiman friends Kim Newman, Jo Fletcher, Terry Pratchett, Gene Wolfe, and John M. Ford. The title is a play on A. A. Milne's poetry collection *Now We Are Six* (1927). (See Gaiman's comments about A. A. Milne in his interview in this volume.)

Inspired by his ongoing comic book reading and his friendship with Alan Moore, Gaiman also began writing comics in earnest. Gaiman's first published comic scripts were four short pieces (1986–87) for the Future Shocks series for *2000 AD,* a popular weekly science fiction comic published by IPC/Fleetway which debuted in 1977 and scored with its dystopian Judge Dredd character. Future Shocks took its title from the Alvin Toffler nonfiction bestseller of the mid-seventies, and it began in *2000 AD* issue 25 as "Tharg's Future Shocks," launched by writer Steve Moore. Moore created a new format: two-to-four-page self-contained stories, usually involving time or interdimensional travel, with a twist in the tale's tail. The series proved to be popular with the readers, and has provided an ideal testing ground for new talent over the years, including Alan Moore, Peter Milligan, Alan Davis, Grant Morrison, Dave Gibbons—and Gaiman.

Two of Gaiman's *2000 AD* stories appeared in 1986—"You're Never Alone with a Phone!" in number 488 and "Conversation Piece!" in issue 489. Two others—"I'm a Believer" in issue 536 and "What's In a Name?" in issue 538—made their debuts the following year.

During this early period Neil also took part in a graphic novel anthology from Knockabout Publications entitled *Outrageous Tales from the Old Testament.* Simultaneously funny and appalling, the stories illustrate the violence and depravity inherent in many biblical tales. The cover alone promised human sacrifice, murder, the wrath of God, and "enormous boils." In addition to Gaiman, the book featured such comics superstars as Alan Moore, Dave McKean, and Dave Gibbons. Gaiman contributed six of the fourteen stories, and was the only writer to have more than one, making him the primary creative force behind this twisted bit of fun. His stories were "The Book of Judges," illustrated by Mike Matthews; "Jael and Sisera," illustrated by Julie Hollings; "Jephthah and His Daughter," illustrated by Peter Rigg; "Journey to Bethlehem," illustrated by Steve Gibson; "The Tribe of Benjamin," illustrated by Mike Matthews; and "The Prophet Who Came to Dinner," illustrated by Dave McKean.

With his pro debut in Future Shocks, Gaiman had entered the comics field, and soon grew eager to stretch his wings. The first of three original graphic novels written for his longtime friend and favorite artist, Dave McKean, *Violent Cases* (1987) soon followed. This work and the other two, *Signal to Noise* and *The Tragical Comedy or Comical Tragedy of Mr. Punch,* are discussed elsewhere in this book, as is their collaborative limited series for DC Comics, *Black Orchid.*

During this period Gaiman also wrote *Don't Panic: The Official Hitchhiker's Guide to the Galaxy Companion* (1988), his first book to be published simultaneously in the United States and the UK. Gaiman had interviewed and written about Douglas Adams for *Knave,* the UK *Penthouse, Time Out* (1988), and other venues, and *Don't Panic* was written very much in Adams's dry tongue-in-cheek style. Subsequent editions featured additional material by other writers: *Don't Panic: Douglas Adams & the Hitchhiker's Guide to the Galaxy* (1993) had new text by David K. Dickson, and *Don't Panic: Douglas Adams & the Hitchhiker's Guide to the Galaxy* (2002) featured still more new material, by M. J. Simpson. A fourth edition, the definitive North American one, was published by Titan Books in 2003. In any case, *Don't Panic* was Gaiman's final nonfiction book project. Thereafter, his own fantasies were his focus. Everything changed after his collaboration with Terry Pratchett on the comical apocalyptic novel *Good Omens: The Nice and Accurate Prophecies of Agnes Nutter, Witch* (1990).

Of course, throughout these years, young Neil had been working as a journalist. We're pleased to be able to present two early examples of that work.

THE QUOTABLE GAIMAN

As far as I'm concerned, the entire reason for becoming a writer is not having to get up in the morning. It's not writing when you don't want to, and writing late at night if you want to. I'm a fairly undisciplined writer. I'm the kind of writer who, if a deadline is looming and I'm not there yet, will go off and take a room for a couple of weeks in a cheap hotel somewhere that I don't know anybody, and do nothing but put my head down and finish the book or the project.

—Writers Write, The Internet Writing
Journal (writerswrite.com), March 1999

On his memories of Douglas Adams:

Well he *was* incredibly tall. And incredibly baffled. Not baffled in the Simon Jones or Arthur Dent way though: "I'm English and I'm truly baffled." Douglas was a combination of bafflement and bemusement, not really quite understanding how it had all happened. Which was always kind of fun. It made him very, very charming. He was a brilliant man. Completely brilliant.

—Writers Write, The Internet Writing
Journal (writeswrite.com), July 2001

III

FANTASYTIME AT
THE NEW IMPERIAL[1]

BIRMINGHAM: I4TH TO I6TH OCTOBER: FANTASYCON VIII
BY NEIL GAIMAN

Last week I attended my first convention. It was Fantasycon VIII, the annual convention of the British Fantasy Society. Conventions are a fairly new development in this country, although they've been big in the U.S. for many years. I was there to interview A Very Famous SF Writer for A Leading Men's Magazine, and felt somewhat out of place.

Outside it was raining like you wouldn't believe, and inside Ms. Jo Fletcher, cochairperson of the convention, explained what I could expect to see: "A lot of talking. And a lot of drinking, mainly. You won't find people playing all day long, games of Dungeons and Dragons, or War Gaming on the stairs, or dressed up as their favourite fantasy characters. Nobody swinging a light sword in the bar. We are *not*," she emphasizes, "*that* sort of a convention!"

That's a relief. I was worried that it might be de rigueur to arrive at the bar dressed as Red Sonja or Gandalf the Grey in order to be served.

"So this is a respectable convention, then?"

She giggled. "No. There's still too much fun for it to be a seminar. It's respected—I don't think it's respectable.

"People who are interested in the books, the films, the art-work, rather than those into games or role playing. Most people here are pros or semi pros, working in the field in one way or other.

"People who are interested aren't the sort that buy a fantasy book a year from W. H. Smiths. They are people who go to the specialist bookshops. People who dream. People who wonder. People who still live to read fairy tales. SF may be a new development," she points out, "but fantasy has been around since the world of legends began."

Isn't there, I ask nervously, something just a little odd or immature about taking so seriously what, after all, are simply fairy tales?

"NO! Absolutely not! Fairy tales are bloody and gory and . . . well, perhaps there's something immature about the people who dress up and play games. I don't go to those sort of things, so I wouldn't know. But if you just want to meet the people whose books you read and talk to the people whose films you watch, and if it happens to be in an atmosphere of booze and jollity and book covers . . . well, what's wrong with that?

"It's a gathering of like-minded people. About every aspect of fantasy. And it's very easy to become addicted to it."

With that she hands me:

1 programme
2 *Spacehunter* balloons
1 *Spacehunter* badge (3D!)
1 *Spacehunter* preview ticket
1 raffle ticket
5 assorted film/book/posters and fliers

"You've missed the Monster Club film, but it's the Cthulhu mythos panel through there in a few minutes." I nod gratefully, and, clutching my pile of freebies, I wander into the lecture room. I look at my programme. I've missed the panel on "Why Critics Revile the Sword and Sorcery Genre," and another on "What is the difference between Fantasy and Science Fiction?" (Other, I suppose, than my own rule of thumb, which I will offer here: If the book has a spaceship on the cover it's Science Fiction; if it's got someone holding a sword *or* a unicorn on the cover it's Fantasy. Voila!)

I'm just in time for the panel discussion on H. P. Lovecraft: "Is the Cthulhu Mythos Still Relevant in the 1980s?"

On the panel is Ramsey Campbell (author of *The Doll Who Ate His Mother, The Height of the Scream,* and many of the scariest short stories published in the last umpteen years); Brian Lumley, author of many Lovecraftian pastiches; Dave Carson, an Irish illustrator who draws things that scare people shitless; and Dave Reeder, small press editor.

The panel is fairly well attended. It's getting a little boring by the time the panel discussion gets to Dave Carson, who appears to be both very drunk and very hungover at the same time.

"The reason . . ." he starts, trails off, and then after a little pause, continues. "The great thing about H. P. Lovecraft is that you can draw all these nasty things with lots of tentacles. Even if they aren't in the story you can still put them in." His head collapses onto the table, the microphone is pried from his fingers, and the panel continues without him.

A member of the audience asks whether the Elder Gods might have been working *through* H. P. Lovecraft to reveal their existence to the world. Hurrah! I think. The lunatic fringe!

"Sorry," says Ramsey. "We're out of time."

Then each member of the panel gives a little wrapping-up speech. Dave Carson has been woken up. "Do you think H. P. Lovecraft has a place in the 80s?" asks Ramsey. "Who cares?" says Dave very carefully. "I just like drawing monsters."

The audience goes wild. With the exception of the gentleman who worried about the Elder Gods moving in, they don't seem to be taking this too seriously, which is a bit of a relief.

After the panel I meet Brian Lumley. What does he think the attraction of conventions like this is?

"Well," he says, in a deep voice redolent of Her Majesties Forces, "the attraction of cons . . . firstly, people who read the stuff want to see who is writing it. They wonder, perhaps, what kind of minds can put that *weird* fiction down on paper. They want to look at the books—often foreign stuff you can't get here except at specialist shops or cons. They look for insight into why their heroes write or perform, and it gives them the opportunity to meet others who like the same things they do."

How did he get into writing such fiction as *The Burrowers Beneath* and *The Transition of Titus Crow*?

"I was attracted by M. R. James, Edgar Allan Poe—the macabre writers—Lovecraft and Machen—and I wanted to have a go. That's what made me write. And I was working the late shift in Berlin, and at 2:00 A.M., when the last would-be refugee's ripped himself to death on the wire, and the last drunk's been locked up, there's not much to do; it was a good time to write."

And what does he feel the future holds for Fantasy?

"It's up and up. Stephen King—although I can't say I care much for him—has shown the way. That was where it all took off. The world's got so many problems, people are looking for a little light relief. That's what fantasy is."

I wander down to the salesroom, where oodles of obscure books, magazines, and posters are on sale. In the room I bump into Gene Wolfe, the man many people regard as the best Science Fiction/Fantasy writer currently working. His tetralogy, *The Book of the New Sun,* perhaps is the best thing anyone's ever written in the genre. I felt that by rights he should be tall and scarred, with long dark hair and a broadsword.

In reality, he's a great balding teddy bear of a man with a wicked sense of humour and a large pair of spectacles held on by elastic. He looks like a central casting American tourist. What does he think about conventions?

"I think they're a great idea!" he laughs. "The only thing that I don't understand is why they're only held to any great extent in the SF and Fantasy genres. They've been around a long time now—1939 was the first *World* SF Convention. There have been determined efforts to transfer them into the mystery field, and romance and westerns . . . they all failed. Comics have them a bit, but they are mainly fairs for vendors. What I'd like someone to explain to me is why it works with SF, and why it can't seem to work with anything else. You want to take a crack at it?'

I admit that I don't know, but privately resolve to find out before I leave. Why not footballicons? Or rockcons? Crossroadscons?

I catch the last bit of a debate on video nasties. Then to a Chinese restaurant, where I hear the Story of Bob Silverberg, the Six Girls, and the Handtowel.

After dinner everybody goes and watches *The Rocky Horror Picture Show*, except Bob Silverberg, who I interview. He says there were only three girls and people doing that kind of thing all the time in L.A. Something to do with a penthouse flat and a sauna. Hmmm. What does he think of the con?

"It's pretty small and sedate. Everyone's extremely courteous. There's no one running around in chain mail or swinging a broadsword at the bar. Most of the people weigh under 350 pounds. They're just talking and drinking. It's like cons in the U.S. 20 years ago."

That evening, in the bar downstairs, is the raffle. Due, possibly, to the fact that there are more prizes than there are people or tickets, it goes until about three in the morning, when everyone is wearing a *Blue Thunder* baseball cap and holding a book or poster of some description. I'm sitting next to Malcom Edwards, co-author of *The Complete Book of SF and Fantasy Lists*—a monumental and towering work of trivia that includes Four Books With Embarrassing Publishers' Errors; Fifteen Stories of Sex between Humans and Robots; and The Six Silliest SF Pseudonyms. Were there any lists that he didn't put in? I ask. Yup. There's the list of gay and transsexual SF writers (including one of the Big Three!) and the who-slept-with-who chain (A slept with B who was married to C who sleeps with D . . . and so forth, back to A again). From there the conversation degenerates to a fairly crude level and scurrilous anecdotes about famous British SF authors are told, and everything fades into some alcoholic haze.

The next morning it's the preview of *Spacehunter! Adventures in the Forbidden Zone,* a fairly incoherent and atrociously scripted film with useless special effects. However, if you take off the 3D glasses it has a certain surreal charm.

After the film I managed to get hold of Peter Nichols (he was in the bar; this is how you get hold of people at conventions), the editor of the prestigious *Encyclopedia of Science Fiction,* and Britain's foremost authority on SF. He told me a little of the background of conventions: "Two kind of people go to conventions. The Fans, who go to meet each other, to whom it is a social event (I won't go into the complex tribal rites of Fandom, but they're interesting and very pleasant). Then there are the people who've always been interested in SF and Fantasy, and who wander along rather shyly to see what it's like, and about half of them will never come back again. The other half really like it, and that's the first step to becoming a fan."

So why SF and Fantasy? "I've never understood it. I suppose you *know* you have something in common with someone else. People read thrillers for all sorts of different reasons. Not SF. It's a counterculture thing, not exactly underground. It's perfectly respectable, but other people interested in it often turn out to be very interesting. And it's classless, which I like—barmaids and taxi drivers and academics all mixed up together.

"Actually this is one of the most staid cons I've been to. Nobody in funny hats. No spectacular young ladies dressed up as butterflies."

What does he feel the future has in store for SF?

"SF is in a bad way, while fantasy's doing very well indeed. I'm afraid a lot of it is the fault of *Star Wars* and so on. The SF cinema set up expectations of a very juvenile kind, and pushed publishers toward the lower end of the market.

"Whereas, there's a freedom in the air in fantasy—it's much more exciting than SF; which is not to say that SF overall is in a bad state, but I do think it's harder for the average SF writer to make a living now than 30 years ago. At the same time, five of the best SF writers are writing today; Gene Wolfe is quite simply the best Science Fiction writer in the world."

He's also very enthusiastic about the direction that SF—and, more generally, horror fantasy—is going in the cinema, especially at what he describes as the "tacky end of the market."

And now it's time for the high point of the convention—the Grand Banquet and Awards ceremony. I'm sitting next to Mr. and Mrs. Ramsey Campbell (not to mention a young lady who informs me that she's FIVE, and her name is Campbell Joanne Tamsin backwards and do I want to see her dive off the stage?). Opposite me sits this prominent paperback publisher.

The meal started off with a sort of shellfishy sort of thing straight out of *Alien* or the Cthulhu mythos that sat on a bed of lettuce and stared up at me in a menacing fashion.

"Looks like the kind of thing Ramsey writes about!" I jested.

"What? You mean a real person with compelling psychological motivation trapped in forces beyond his control?" asked the publisher intensely.

It seems he was Ramsey's publisher.

Undaunted by my faux pas (and I bet Ramsey *has* written about ghastly yellow pulsating Things from time to time) I ask Mr. Campbell—who is a surprisingly jolly and amiable chap for someone with a mind so macabre—Why do people come to conventions?

"It's meeting the people they've read for years and never met, I suspect. As far as writers are concerned, it's getting for once past the business of writing alone in a room, and meeting the people out there who are buying your books. That's what I find most appealing about it anyway."

Ramsey is to be seen all over the place during the con. If he's not giving a reading of one of his stories, then he's moderating a panel or attending a meeting, not to mention riding herd on Miss Tamsin and her little brother. And he *still* manages to give the impression of spending his whole time in the bar.

Why, I ask him, are these cons solely the province of SF and fantasy?

"It goes back to the fact that those who read SF and fantasy feel paranoid about it. You are looked down on by everybody, from the booksellers who sell you the material to the people at work who see you reading that 'trash.' And of course there's the catch-22—if it's good, then of course the literary snobs say it's not SF. So you can't win. Under this kind of pressure, people get together, and it immediately becomes a subculture. We did have a lunatic fringe, but now they've mostly drifted away."

I don't understand it. Why does this incredibly nice man write the sort of stuff that scares you shitless? He explains: "Well, originally the stuff I liked myself was horror. I got into it as a natural progression from fairy tales—frightening fairy tales. The thing that really scared me was *The Princess and the Goblin* by George Macdonald. I read it at age six, and I was *terrified*. There is this sequence where creatures, malformed under the influence of the goblins, come pouring up out of the palace gardens. It's more like Lovecraft than Lovecraft. From there it was a short step to the classics." (By which he means M. R. James, Arthur Machen, and HPL, I assume.) "It's odd—I'd read the best of them and be afraid to go to bed, and afraid to shut my eyes. And yet I think that reading this fiction was less disturbing than my childhood in reality, which is to say, my mother was a clinical schizophrenic, and my father, although he was married to her and lived in the same house, didn't actually come face-to-face with her or me for twenty years. He was just a presence on the other side of the door. The footsteps that came past my room at night as I was lying awake, hoping desperately that they wouldn't stop outside my door and come into my room.

"These are the seeds of the kind of things I write.

"Another reason is to try to give back the kind of pleasure I was getting as a kid. I'd like to achieve the kind of terror and awe that you found in the best of Lovecraft, James, and Blackwood. The intensity of terror. Because of this, I suppose, I've aimed at the principle that horror fiction can't be too frightening or too disturbing. That may seem self-evident, but people *do* come up to me and say, 'Your work is too disturbing,' which I found odd. There's a lot of horror fiction that seems written to neutralize the fears it's dealing with. James Herbert does that. I don't.

"The horror story, of all fictional forms, is the one that reaches deepest into the subconscious when it's working best."

Ramsey is nominated for a British Fantasy Society Award for best short story, but is beaten by Stephen King's "Breathing Method" from the *Different Seasons* book. The awards are these sweet little cthulhupoid THINGS designed by Dave Carson, and once described (by Ramsey Campbell, I believe) as "skeletal dildos."

Gene Wolfe got one for best novel (*Sword of the Lictor*), *Blade Runner* got best film, and Fantasy Tales got best small press for the sixth year running, and withdrew from the game.

(See how familiar I am with all of this, after just 24 hours? I speak contalk like a native!)

Despite everything, though, the recession is hitting the conventions today as hard as it's hitting everything else.

Steve Jones, co-chairman of the convention and editor of Fantasy Tales, had this to say about it:

"There are people who've been at every con since they started but who couldn't get to this one. They wanted to, but many of them have been made redundant, or are going to be made redundant. And even if they do have some money, they'll spend it on the books and films as their priority; the convention comes after that, and with travel and hotel fees you're looking at perhaps 100 pounds [about U.S. $134, in 1984 dollars] for a weekend. Books and films come first, *then* the convention. And then, if there's any money left over, they buy food, children's clothes, things like that."

Brian Lumley agrees.

"Conventions are suffering right now—not because people don't want to participate, but because they haven't got the money. If they are going to keep reading the books and seeing the films they can't afford to pay the con fees and the hotel. Con attendance figures are down all over."

He gestures with a cigarette. "If the country recovers economically more people will attend the cons. It's as simple as that."

Meanwhile, the conventioneers are grabbing their cases, posters and books, and heading off into the sunset (or whatever it is they have on Sunday afternoons in Birmingham).

Feeling a bit like Allen Whicker about to depart an exotic tropical island, I asked a few of the conventioneers if they had anything to say about the con. Dave Sutton, small bebearded co-editor of *Fantasy Tales* said, "Yeah. That Winston Churchill. He needed locking up." It's in reference to a conversation we had had earlier in the day about Winston Churchill and the entire universe being pervaded by the smell of turpentine.

It's not really the kind of quote I can use to finish off an article, though.

Malcom Edwards (he's not only the compiler of those lists, but he also has a secret identity of SF editor at Gollancz) expressed it all much better when I asked him what he thought.

"Triffic!" he said. "Unbelievable. Never seen anything like it."

||||||||||||||||||||||||||||||||||||||||||||||||||||||||||||||||||||||

WHO WAS JACK THE RIPPER?[1]

SPECIAL REPORT BY NEIL GAIMAN, EUGENE BYRNE, AND KIM NEWMAN

THE SUSPECTS

Who was Jack the Ripper? It's a question that has preoccupied the makers of television documentaries for months.

Now you can make your minds up for yourselves, with this handy *Truth*

Cut-Out-And-Throw-Away guide to the Top Ten Suspects. We've listed their opportunities, and the all-important Four Ms (Means, Motive, Mm-Opportunity, and Why We Think They Did It).

For purposes of balance, and because they couldn't all have done it, unless they'd seen *Murder on the Orient Express,* we will also list each candidate's drawbacks.

I.

ALFRED, LORD TENNYSON
B 1809 D 1902
POET LAUREATE

Suspicion of this eminent Victorian poet was aroused by the recent discovery in the Bodleian of some first-draft manuscripts containing such lines as: *Come into the Garden Maud/ for the Black Bat Night has Flown/ And anyway I've got a sword/ and I'm going to make you groan* and the damning: *Half a league, Half a league,/Half a league onward/ Oh God I left my disembowelling/ knife back at the pub/ Someone had blundered*

MEANS: Ownership of a top hat and a knife drawer (see British Museum catalogue 23/17a/TENN).

Although he was 81 years old at the time of the Whitechapel murders, Tennyson was remarkably fit due to his consumption of *All Bran* (at the time an opium-based patent medicine) and his avoidance of *Big Macs* (at the time a sewage-based patent medicine). As Poet Laureate he would of course have been able to pass through the cesspits, pubs, and gutters of Whitechapel without attracting any notice.

MOTIVE: It has been suggested in Albert Goldman's biography, *Alfie! Lusty Lord Laureate!* that during high tea with her Imperial Majesty, Queen Victoria, the ukulele-playing monarch turned to Lord Alfred and said, "Lord Alfred, would you care to slice the tarts?" Tennyson misunderstood his monarch's request.

WHY NO ONE HAS SUSPECTED HIM UNTIL NOW: He was an 81-year-old Poet Laureate, and well in with the Royals.

DRAWBACKS: It has been suggested that the most conclusive evidence of Tennyson's capacity for lethal misogyny, found in Ruskin's book *More Tedious Reminiscences of an Eminent Victorian, January 1891–March 1891,* volume III, was in fact a misprint. The quote reads in full: "Fat Alfred came over with his *Bloody Idylls of the King* and gored my wife to death on the balcony. Later she served tea in the Chinese fashion."

2.

WINSTON SPENCER CHURCHILL
B. 1874, D. 1965
SCHOOLBOY, LATE PRIME MINISTER

Quote from *The Times,* October 3, 1888: "An unemployed street sweeper stated to our reporter: 'I seed this young masterguv vot looked a norful lot like the young Simon Ward a-valking by wearing a sailor suit and carrying a werry big bag of knifes, an' that was just before some gullygullets splitted Mary Kelly from weazend to stern. Stap me wittles for a bottle of gin and can ye spare a tanner for a pint of pigs trotters and herring heads for an honest man's supper?' "

MEANS: As a member of the aristocracy, Churchill could undoubtedly have bought a big bag of knives, if he had saved up his pocket money. He was not yet Prime Minister, and had a strong resemblance to Simon Ward before he got fat. One assumes that he would duck out of compulsory games (Rugger and Sodomy, Cricket and the Lash), buy a twopenny return from Harrow to Whitechapel, and be back in time for sticky buns, cocoa, and lights out. A hasty cold shower before bed would have removed any blood, and the toasting of a new boy before or during bed would have distracted attention from his big bag of knives and any little trophies he might have brought back with him.

MOTIVE: Cigar envy.

WHY NO ONE HAS SUSPECTED HIM UNTIL NOW: His father was an eminent Victorian aristocrat and politician who was well in with the Royals, and his mother was played by Anne Bancroft in the movie. As a 14-year-old Simon Ward lookalike in a sailor suit he would of course have been able to pass through the cesspits, pubs, and gutters of Whitechapel without attracting any notice.

DRAWBACKS: The only photographic, clear-cut evidence against him was dropped by air over Whitechapel in 1942. It was written in German. It has been claimed that the postcards of Simon Ward in a sailor suit cutting up Catherine Eddowes were almost certainly fakes, since the woman in the picture is Eva Braun, and the entrails are actually liverwurst.

3.

GENERAL WILLIAM BOOTH
B. 1829, D. 1912
FOUNDER OF THE SALVATION ARMY

In statements made about this time, Booth stated publicly that he wished to cleanse the streets of London of Vice and Depravity, and also that he wished to reach the hearts and minds of the poor. Taken together with his early suggestion that his new paramilitary Christian tambourine brigade be dressed in butchers' uniforms and be called the Evisceration Army, this seems pretty damn conclusive to us. Also an elderly man with a moustache clutching a huge bag of knives and a tambourine, dressed in a soldier's uniform and poke bonnet and complaining that the Devil has all the best songs would of course have been able to pass through the cesspits, pubs, and gutters of Whitechapel without attracting any notice.

MOTIVE: See above.

MEANS: Big bag of knives, used after stunning his victim with a rolled-up copy of *The War Cry.* (A pretty revealing title, eh?)

WHY NO ONE HAS SUSPECTED HIM UNTIL NOW: He was so respectable that they named the telephone box after him.

DRAWBACKS: It has been suggested (see *News of the World,* November 5, 1888, LILY'S JERSEY COMES OFF FOR RANDY GOD GENERAL) that Booth was otherwise engaged on the nights of the murders.

4.

GENERAL FORMBY

B. 1904, D. 1961

MUSIC HALL ENTERTAINER

Songs like *Mister Wu's been Chopping up the Locals* and *I'm leaning on a Lamp-post at the Corner of the Street holding a Great Big Bag of Knives in case a Certain Little Lady Comes By* have occasionally been used to indicate that the toothy, ukulele-toting chappie may well have been a homicidal Victorian loony.

It has been suggested that far from being killed by knives, most of the London prostitutes were actually bludgeoned to death with a ukulele while being held down by Gracie Fields.

MEANS: A toothy, ukulele-toting music hall singer nasally humming marginally risqué comic songs, accompanied by a woman warbling about her aspidistra in a Lancashire accent would of course have been able to pass through the cesspits, pubs, and gutters of Whitechapel without attracting any notice.

MOTIVE: Formby obviously liked hurting people and making them suffer painfully. (See his films *I Didn't Do It, Leave It To George, Trouble Brewing,* or *Let's Get Maniacal with Knives* for conclusive proof.)

WHY NO ONE HAS SUSPECTED HIM UNTIL NOW: Queen Victoria is well-known to have been a keen ukulele player, and the police at that time, in a masonic conspiracy, arranged to cover up any ukulele involvement in the Rippings in order to keep Her Majesty's name out of the papers.

DRAWBACKS: Obviously, his having been born in 1904 could be seen to disqualify him from the list of suspects. However, a master criminal like Formby would not have been deterred by a little matter like that. A masonic conspiracy of Jimmy Tarbuck and the Grumbleweeds to alter vital dates and give Formby the illusion of being above suspicion cannot be ruled out at this stage, even though we only just made it up.

5.
RUDYARD "MISTER" KIPLING
B. 1865, D. 1936
JOURNALIST AND AUTHOR

Such verses as *If you can keep your kidnes (sic) while all about you are losing theirs and blaming it on various loony members of the Royal Family, A woman is only a woman but a bag of carving knives is forever,* and perhaps that more ominous *The Colonel's Lady and Lily O'Grady are sisters under the skin* would seem to indicate that Kipling, pastry chef and author, had an unnatural interest in terminating the prostitutional population of Whitechapel with extreme prejudice.

MEANS: Despite his posting in Lahore in India, where he worked as a reporter for the *Civil and Military Gazette,* Kipling could quite conceivably have sneaked out after work clutching a big bag of knives and a toothbrush (arranging his pillows in bed to make it look as if he was still there should anyone look in on him). He could slip over the border of Afghanistan, make his way into Russia, flag down the Trans-Siberian railway, change at Prague for the Orient Express into Paris, go by boat train to Victoria, and then by cab to Whitechapel. There he would hastily eviscerate a passing demimondaine, and head back to India by alternative route to avoid suspicion, arriving back in time for breakfast the next morning. No one would suspect a thing, attributing any possible lassitude on Kipling's part to a bout of tropical fever.

Obviously a young Christopher Plummer lookalike with a heavy sun tan wearing a pith helmet and carrying a large bag of knives with travel stickers all over it would have been able to pass through the cesspits, bars, and gutters of Whitechapel without attracting any notice.

MOTIVE: Because they were there.

WHY NO ONE HAS SUSPECTED HIM UNTIL NOW: Honest face, Walt Disney filmed *The Jungle Book,* and he won a Nobel Prize for literature in 1907 in order to offset suspicion.

DRAWBACKS: Beats us. Good candidate, huh?

6.
SOOTY (ACCOMPANIED BY A PICTURE OF A TEDDY BEAR)
B. UNKNOWN, D. UNDEAD
THE PRIME SUSPECT FOR MANY RIPPEROLOGISTS.

The ancient Egyptian gods are said to have cursed Amenhotep Corbett, pyramid builder to the gentry, for building the tomb of Ramases III point downwards.

Cursed with the Unspeakable Vengeance of the Bear God Suht-ie, Corbett's right hand was transformed into a small telepathic bear. This creature was handed down through the generations, from father to son, forcing the Corbett Clan to acts of unspeakable depravity: Pontius Corbett, Genghis Corbett, Attilla the Corbett, Kublai Corbett, Adolf Corbett and Olga Corbett to name but a few.

At the time of the Ripper murders William Edward Corbett, mill owner and traveling showman, was hiding out in Whitechapel following Sooty's master-minding of the Siege of Khartoum.

MEANS: Using his magic wand, Sooty would summon passing prostitutes and whisper into their ears Egyptian words of power. Ramsbottom the Snake would play the ukulele to drown out their screams and incidentally cast suspicion on George Formby and Queen Victoria.

This evil little criminal mastermind rested secure in the knowledge that being an eight inch high glove puppet of a bear he would have been able to pass through the cesspits, bars, and gutters of Whitechapel without attracting any notice.

MOTIVE: Pure Evil.

WHY NO ONE HAS SUSPECTED HIM UNTIL NOW: He was very, very clever.

DRAWBACKS: None.

There you go. Sod the other suspects, he's your boy, Inspector. Can we claim the reward money now? Can we go home?

PART TWO

THE SANDMAN

INTRODUCTION (1988—96)

In his introduction to the 1999 stand-alone volume *The Sandman: The Dream Hunters*, Neil Gaiman neatly summarized the gist of the entire Sandman series as follows: "The king of dreams learns one must change or die and then makes his decision."

Who are we to argue with the creator of one of the most significant and memorable comic book characters in history?

Yet it is worth noting that "change or die" was in the air of the era, emerging from the very writing community Gaiman was already associated with. Among Gaiman's mentors were Clive Barker and Alan Moore; if any single theme linked the whole of Barker's seminal, influential Books of Blood short stories and his early novels and films, it was "change or die." Similarly, Moore's key early collaborative comics works—*Marvelman/Miracleman, V for Vendetta, Saga of the Swamp Thing, Watchmen*—embodied the same imperative. Transformation, transmutation, and reinvention of the self and the world fueled these vital works, as it did the whole of the Sandman series and much of Gaiman's early work.

When Gaiman began writing the series, his first concern was that it not be canceled after only a few issues. In the comic book industry of the time, critical success sometimes correlated with commercial failure, but a new trend had been set by offbeat periodicals like *Daredevil* and *Saga of the Swamp Thing*, both moribund titles (in terms of sales, fan popularity, and licensing potential) unexpectedly revived by fresh blood and new talent: Frank Miller and Klaus Janson revived Daredevil, and the already noted Alan Moore/Stephen Bissette/John Totleben/Rick Veitch team resurrected Swamp Thing. Based on their example—and directly following the success of the Swamp Thing revival and its spin-off title, *Hellblazer*, both edited by *Sandman* editor Karen Berger—there was from the beginning something special about the Sandman, something that caught readers' imaginations and captured their loyalty.

Early on, Gaiman learned an invaluable lesson, one which had the added benefit of spurring his own creativity. At first excited and eager at the prospect of working with established DC characters, he quickly became disillusioned by the problems that arose; whenever he attempted use those characters, he would encounter resistance, whether it be someone rewriting his dialogue, or coping with a retroactive continuity decision about that hero or villain. After repeatedly encountering problems of this sort, Gaiman gave up, deciding to keep major DC characters offstage and create his own continuity, respectful and mindful of the DC Universe, but also clearly another, distinct, and separate part of that landscape.

The Sandman lasted approximately eight years, spanning seventy-five issues (plus one special). Although they sold well in their original incarnations, they proved even more popular when gathered into ten distinct collections, beginning with the publication of *Preludes & Nocturnes* in 1991. Those collections, sporting introductions by some of the most significant writers of fantasy and horror of the past half century (including F. Paul Wilson, Clive Barker, Samuel R. Delany, Harlan Ellison, Steve Erickson, Gene Wolfe, Peter Straub, Stephen King, Mikal Gilmore, and Frank McConnell) have gone through numerous printings. We've chosen to discuss the series as presented in those volumes, as that's how future generations of readers are most likely to experience the magic of Gaiman's magnum opus. A brief description of each follows.

Preludes & Nocturnes presents the prologue to the series. In it, Dream, one of the Endless, escapes from a mystical prison that's contained him for seven decades. Once free, he goes on a quest to find certain talismans of great power: his helm, pouch, and ruby. The journey takes him to many planes of reality, including his own and the one controlled by Lucifer, Hell. The story clearly establishes Dream as a player in the DC Universe. It also introduces readers to Dream's sister, the irresistible Death.

The Doll's House details Dream's continuing efforts to clean up problems that arose in his realm during his long absence. Several dreams have escaped The Dreaming: the hideous Brute and Glob; the lethal Corinthian; and the dreamscape that walks like a man, Fiddler's Green. It also tells the story of a young woman named Rose Walker and her search for her little brother, Jed. As the story lines converge, Dream is forced to make a pair of decisions of great significance.

The Dream Country is the first of three Sandman short story collections. Inside, readers are introduced to Dream's former lover, Calliope, and discover that the world was not always dominated by man. Gaiman also tells the story behind the creation of Shakespeare's *Midsummer Night's Dream*. Finally, Gaiman relates the tragic final days of Element Girl, a forgotten character of the DC Universe.

Gaiman returned to his main story line in *The Season of the Mists*. Here, Lucifer, Lord of Hell, abdicates, giving the key to his realm to Dream. Dream must then decide who will succeed him. This particular story line echoes others in the series, particularly those of Destruction and Morpheus (Dream) himself.

In *A Game of You*, Barbie, a character first seen in *The Doll's House*, discovers that the strange land she dreamed of as a child actually exists, and that she is the only one who can forestall its destruction at the hands of an evil entity. Dream stays offstage during most of this epic, appearing at the end to restore order to this neglected part of his realm.

Fables & Reflections is the second short story collection in the series. Here readers are treated to tales about historical personages such as Joshua Norton (the self-proclaimed emperor of America); Marco Polo; Caesar Augustus; and Haroun al-Raschid, caliph of Baghdad. We also learn more about Morpheus's estranged son, Orpheus.

In *Brief Lives*, Dream and his little sister Delirium take to the road on a quest to locate their brother, Destruction, who has been missing for some three hundred years. They eventually achieve their goal, but Dream pays a great price for this success.

Worlds' End is the third and final short story collection within the series, featuring a group of disparate characters who are drawn together by a reality storm. All end up in a tavern called Worlds' End, where they pass the time waiting for the storm to subside by telling stories to each other.

In *The Kindly Ones,* all previous story lines converge, as Dream must deal with the repercussions of actions detailed in *Brief Lives* and *The Doll's House.* Believing that Dream is responsible for her infant son Daniel's death, Lyta Hall calls on The Kindly Ones to avenge him. Eager to comply, the bloodthirsty Furies invade The Dreaming, forcing Morpheus to make the ultimate sacrifice.

The Wake is the epilogue to this landmark series, as Dream is mourned, then reborn. Readers also learn more about Dream's friend, the immortal Hob Gadling, and about William Shakespeare, in a fitting coda to the series called "The Tempest."

It's hard to quantify the importance of Gaiman's Sandman in the overall history of comics, but its appearance on the scene is so significant that it would not be an exaggeration to suggest that comics history could be measured in terms of 'pre-' and 'post-' Sandman. The series resonates that profoundly, honoring what came before and setting an extremely high bar for subsequent efforts.

Structurally, *The Sandman* is one of the best storytelling engines ever conceived, something Gaiman proved again and again from 1988 through 1996. The character himself was pure gold: a moody, troubled soul whose personal life generated endless conflicts. As the proverbial prince of stories, Morpheus's realm—The Dreaming—is literally the repository of every story ever told, and, more significantly, of every story that could have been told. The series appropriately served as a launchpad for other characters' stories. Like Will Eisner's famous character The Spirit, The Sandman sometimes would only appear in a cameo, or—in several stories—not at all.

Gaiman's brilliance in creating this mythos is evident in his adherence to, and avoidance of, classic archetypes. He created a new pantheon of seven beings called The Endless (Dream, Death, Delirium, Desire, Destruction, Despair, and Destiny) from which the rest of human mythology can be seen to have been derived. Here he taps into archetypes, while not exactly copying them.

The Sandman (aka Master of Dreams, Morpheus, the Prince of Stories, The Lord of Sleep, Lord L'Zoril, and The Dream Lord) is in many ways a classic hero, complete with tragic flaws—in Dream's case, his romanticism, his easily bruised ego, and his self-righteousness. Throughout the series he's confronted by the consequences of his actions. As in most stories of the "hero," he receives a call to adventure, namely his capture. He embarks on a journey, first to make himself whole, then to understand his place in the world. Although he stands painfully alone, he has mentors, like his older sister Death. He also has sidekicks of sorts, such as his human friend, Hob, and his faithful raven companion, Matthew. He faces obstacles, tests, and trials before coming to realize his ultimate destiny.

Though this aspect of Sandman is rooted in classic mythology and Joseph Campbell's articulation of common mythic and religious themes, it's also important to note for contemporary Sandman and Gaiman readers that he was consciously rooting his work here, in a vein of the genre known in some quarters as "recursive fantasy." Recursive fantasy draws from existing characters, concepts, and environments—arguably, all comic books are of this ilk—but the definition is specific to works reworking elements of existing fictional precursors. Most often, this involves works using famous public-domain characters such as Frankenstein, Dracula, or Sherlock Holmes, but it's the intersecting strata of realities, including those that are fictional within the context of the fantasy's "reality," that most often is at play.

Gaiman's use of William Shakespeare's plays, and Shakespeare himself and his peers, within Sandman's metafictions is notable in this context. An obvious precursor is Tom Stoppard's *Rosencrantz and Guildenstern Are Dead* (1967), and Sandman's dense, multilayered juxtapositions of fantasy, theater, players, and the characters they play takes Stoppard's inventive concept to a whole new level. Other key predecessors Sandman fans might wish to check out include Walter De La Mare's *Henry Brocken* (1904); John Myer Myers's *Silverlock* (1949), which incorporates characters by one of Gaiman's favorite authors, G. K. Chesterton); Marvin Kaye's *The Incredible Umbrella* (1979), a baroque and inventive fusion of Mary Shelley, Sir Arthur Conan Doyle, and Edwin A. Abbott (via another Gaiman personal favorite—the libretto stylings of W. S. Gilbert!); and many others. As noted in our discussion of Gaiman's 1602 series for Marvel, Philip Jose Farmer was a premiere science fiction/fantasy author who explored and expanded this strain of fantasy, which is so relevant to *The Sandman* and other Gaiman creations.

Over the course of its publication, *The Sandman* became nothing short of a phenomenon, pulling in comic book readers in droves, but also attracting a variety of other readers, who created a subculture of their own around the book. In addition to the typical comic book readership—mostly male—the series developed a passionately loyal female readership. At the time, sales to female readers were a small fraction of the overall business of comic book retailers. Other series had appealed to that small group of female readers prior to *The Sandman*, but Gaiman's flagship series was able to do so without alienating the existing male readership.

The fan base also included many disparate subcultures—for instance, the Dream Lord and Gaiman were firmly embraced by the Goth movement, whose members appreciated the tone of the book, as well as the character's and author's fashion sensibility.

In 1996, Harper published *The Sandman: Book of Dreams,* an anthology of short stories featuring a cover by Dave McKean, a frontispiece by Clive Barker, an afterword by Tori Amos, and stories by eighteen authors in which the character appeared again, including longtime Gaiman cohorts Will Shetterly, Susanna Clarke, John M. Ford, Caitlín R. Kiernan, Steven Brust, and Gene Wolfe. However, since Gaiman's only work on the volume was as co-editor with Ed Kramer, it falls outside the parameters of this book.

More than a decade after the conclusion of Gaiman's majestic eight-year story arc, the Sandman phenomenon continues. In 1999, Gaiman collaborated with Yoshitaka Amano on the illustrated short novel *The Dream Hunters;* in 1999, he collaborated with several artists of note on *The Sandman: Endless Nights,* which features Morpheus and his siblings in seven tales. Web sites devoted to the Dream Lord abound. Indeed, the character seems more popular than ever, as witnessed by the 2006 publication of volume one of *The Absolute Sandman.* Retailing at $99.95, the six-hundred-page book reprinted the first twenty issues of the comic on high-quality paper. The art has been almost entirely recolored. Said Gaiman at the 2007 San Diego Comic-Con: "It was lovely; it's just this big, remarkable, rather intimidating book." Four volumes are planned, appearing over the next three years.

At this writing, the twentieth anniversary of the first appearance of The Sandman is fast approaching. Gaiman had hoped to commemorate the anniversary with a new story. Unfortunately, it now appears that will not come to pass.

THE QUOTABLE GAIMAN

Dreaming is such a peculiar thing. We lead these completely normal, rational lives (or we kid ourselves that we do), and then every night we close our eyes and go stark raving mad for eight hours. I love that. It's a level of reality that I've always thought is every bit as important and interesting as the life you live by day.

—Interview with Jennifer Abbots and Sarah
Brennan, bookreporter.com, June 29, 2001

Books have sexes; or to be more precise, books have genders. They do in my head, anyway. Or at least, the ones that I write do. And these are genders that have something, but not everything, to do with the gender of the main character of the story.

When I wrote the ten volumes of *Sandman,* I tended to alternate between what I thought of as male story lines, such as the first story, collected under the title

Preludes & Nocturnes, or the fourth book, *Season of Mists;* and more female stories, like *Game of You,* or *Brief Lives.*

—bn.com and Powells.com

When asked about his "open relationship" with fans:

Yes. We have an open relationship. Obviously they can see other authors if they want, and I can see other readers.

—bookslut.com, October 2006

VOLUME ONE:
PRELUDES & NOCTURNES

(1988—89)

Neil Gaiman had been working for years as a journalist and comic book writer, mostly in the United Kingdom, but with the creation of Sandman, he found lightning in a bottle. Then DC editor Karen Berger was widely known as an Anglophile who had already brought Alan Moore to the attention of American audiences. But much as she might have admired Gaiman's pitch, neither she nor the writer could possibly have expected the level of success The Sandman series would enjoy, or the fame to which it would shortly catapult its creator.

This is, perhaps, partway toward an explanation for the way that the series is firmly rooted in the history of the DC Comics universe. At the time that the first issue of The Sandman was published, there was no such thing as Vertigo, no separate imprint for the more mature titles in the company's catalog. Indeed, the success of Gaiman's title would lead it to become the flagship of Berger's effort to create that separate imprint, and the lifeblood of Vertigo for many years, with all of its various spin-offs and Gaiman-inspired series.

From the outset, the series found fertile soil in the history of the DC universe, with Gaiman brushing up against the four-color world of superheroes, and occasionally plunging in completely. But the real achievement was not in the bits that the writer borrowed from DC's history. Rather, Gaiman's creative vision was so remarkable that parts of the fictional universe were entirely reinvented, with such storytelling power that they immediately superceded all prior versions of those characters.

Thus, the hosts of House of Mystery, House of Secrets, and The Witching Hour—all old-time DC titles—essentially became Gaiman's characters in the space of a few months. And, where DC had spun tales of various characters called Sandman for half a century, Gaiman's Sandman—Morpheus, Dream of the Endless—instantly became the touchstone.

Modern comic book readers embraced this retrofitting of continuity; the world was Gaiman's to do with as he wished. In subsequent volumes, however, Gaiman abruptly veered away from the DC universe, touching it infrequently and briefly, and only when it suited his purposes.

In the first story arc, contained in *Preludes & Nocturnes,* the groundwork is carefully laid for the future of the series. The first issue introduces the missing objects of power that Morpheus will have to reclaim over the course of the next seven issues, and mentions Unity Kinkaid, a victim of the so-called sleeping sickness, who will feature prominently in *The Doll's House,* the second volume of The Sandman. The fourth issue, set in Hell, lays the keystones for *Season of Mists,* which is volume four of the series. And the final issue in this collection features Gaiman's first significant introduction of Death, one of the Endless and the sister of Dream, who would receive two miniseries of her own, and become, arguably, just as or even more popular than her brother.

Preludes & Nocturnes is also significant in that it contains the darkest and most horrific of the Sandman stories, including "24 Hours," and the whole collection—but in particular the first issue—is illustrated in a style that pays homage to classic horror comics without undermining the larger story.

The first four issues of this initial volume were illustrated by Sam Kieth and Mike Dringenberg, with Kieth and Malcolm Jones III taking over artistic duties on issues 5–8.

#1 "THE SLEEP OF THE JUST"

On June 6, 1916, Mr. Roderick Burgess comes into possession of *The Magdalene Grimoire.* Burgess hopes to use it to prevent anyone from ever dying again. Burgess and his followers attempt to summon Death with a ritual. Instead, they accidentally summon then mystically imprison Dream.

As a result, a "sleeping sickness" begins to spread around the world. Some victims cannot awaken; others cannot ever sleep.

In 1947 Roderick Burgess dies, passing the reins of his organization to his son, Alex, who becomes more and more obsessed with Morpheus.

Forty-one years later, Alex's assistant accidentally runs the wheel of Burgess's wheelchair through the circle of protection enclosing Dream's "cage," disturbing it and he escapes.

Morpheus visits Alex Burgess in a dream and learns that his pouch, helm, and ruby were stolen by Burgess's second-in-command, Ruthven Sykes years before. Morpheus punishes Burgess by giving him "eternal waking," trapping him in an endless cycle in which he dreams that he has woken, only to have the world turn into a terrifying nightmare.

#2 "IMPERFECT HOSTS"

Gaiman again dips into the history of the DC universe by incorporating into his new creation the characters Cain and Abel (yes, that Cain and Abel), formerly the hosts of two of the Silver Age DC anthology series, House of Mystery and House of Secrets. Here, the brothers live in "the Dreaming," the kingdom ruled by Morpheus, which is comprised of all of the dreams of every living thing.

Gregory, a gargoyle owned by Cain, shows up at their door carrying a weakened Morpheus—whom Cain calls the Prince of Stories.

Dream reveals that after using his remaining power on Alex Burgess, he wandered, trying to reach the gates of horn and ivory, and beyond them his castle.

The majority of Morpheus's power is invested in those three objects stolen by Ruthven Sykes, and before he can return to his throne, he must find them and restore that power. The Dreaming has fallen to ruin in Morpheus's absence. He needs his tools if he is going to restore himself, and thereby his world, fully. He summons the Hecateae, the one-who-are-three. By right he can ask them each one question, and each has to give him one answer. Questioning the maiden, the All Mother, and the crone, he ascertains the whereabouts of his powerful talismans, which have been scattered across the DC Comics universe.

As a brief preamble to future events, we also pay a visit to Arkham Asylum, where we discover that the ninety-year-old mother of John Dee, aka Dr. Destiny, visits her son, only to discover that he is mad and wretched, claiming that they have stolen his dreams away.

#3 "DREAM A LITTLE DREAM OF ME"

After John Constantine wakes from a strange dream, he hears songs about dreams. An eccentric 274-year-old woman called Mad Hettie finds John Constantine in a diner and tells him that Morpheus, the Sandman, is back, and he wants "his own."

Three days later the Sandman shows up at Constantine's flat, looking for his pouch of sand. Constantine claims to have purchased it at a garage sale. It's now in storage . . . or so Constantine thinks. He soon realizes it was stolen by a junkie ex-girlfriend named Rachel. Constantine and his friend Chas take Morpheus to Rachel's father's house.

Inside, they find a dead burglar, destroyed from within by dreams. The walls are covered by the still-living flesh of Rachel's father, who has merged with escaped dreams that have torn him apart. In Rachel's bedroom they find the girl herself, withered and ruined, her fingers dipped into the pouch of sand, lost in dreams. The power of the sand has unleashed wild dreams, wreaking havoc. Without the pouch Rachel is so desiccated that she'll die, but the Sandman must have it back. At Constantine's request, Morpheus gives her dreams of love and contentment, a happily ever after with Constantine, to carry her into death painlessly.

#4 "A HOPE IN HELL"

Morpheus descends into Hell, seeking his helm.

He encounters Nada, who has been imprisoned for ten thousand years for an unrevealed offense against him. Forgiveness will free her, but Dream says that though he still loves her, he has not forgiven her. When Morpheus encounters Lucifer, the demon mentions Destiny and Despair as Dream's siblings, other members of The Endless. Dream discovers that Lucifer now shares the rule of

Hell with Beelzebub, Lord of the Flies, and Azazel, in a triumverate. Dream informs Lucifer that he has come to retrieve his helm.

The Triumverate summon all the demons of Hell to a gathering, where Morpheus senses which one has his helm, a demon called Choronzon. Choronzon challenges Morpheus to a duel for possession of the talisman.

If Dream loses, he must become a slave of Hell for all eternity.

Choronzon begins a contest of cleverness, but Morpheus defeats him.

The Triumverate hands over the helm to Dream. Lucifer reveals that they have no intention of letting him leave, and that he cannot possibly overcome them. "What power have dreams in Hell?" Lucifer asks. But when Morpheus points out that Hell would have no power over those within if the damned could not dream of Heaven, the demons make a path for him to depart. Furious, Lucifer vows that one day he will destroy the Sandman.

In the epilogue, we see the villain, Dr. Destiny, a resident of Arkham Asylum. His mother has passed away, and a guard tosses into his cell the one thing his mother left for him—an amulet, forged to look like an eye.

#5 "PASSENGERS"

Escaping from Arkham Asylum, Dr. Destiny sees the Scarecrow (a longtime Batman villain) and tells him his plan to enslave the world and become its king. He has his amulet, and now needs to find his ruby, which he calls his "materioptikon."

Searching for the same object, the Sandman recruits Scott Free, aka Mr. Miracle of the Justice League, since the ruby was once in the league's possession. Mr. Miracle has no idea where the ruby might be, but takes the Sandman to see J'onn J'onzz, the Martian Manhunter, thinking that J'onn might know. Significantly, J'onn sees Morpheus as Lord L'Zoril, the Martian lord of dreams, indicating that Dream of the Endless is a figure of universal significance.

J'onn tells Morpheus that the ruby is stored in the Justice League's trophy room located in Mayhew, north of Gotham City. The Sandman arrives there and retrieves the ruby, only to discover that Dr. Destiny has altered it with circuitry and magic; somehow, using it causes a backlash that knocks Morpheus unconscious. Shortly thereafter, Dr. Destiny arrives and finds that the ruby has become far more powerful, having absorbed more from the Lord of Dreams. Dee goes into a diner and waits, he says, for the end of the world.

#6 "24 HOURS"

At the All-Nite Diner, Dee awaits the end of the world.

Bette Munroe is a waitress—but she fancies herself a writer who only uses her waitress job to study customers, so that she can write about small-town life. Judy is a young lesbian awaiting the arrival of her girlfriend, Donna, after they'd had a fight the night before. Marsh is a trucker who used to be a postal worker, but spent five years in prison for stealing from the post office after his wife drank herself to death. Marsh and Bette have been having a long-time affair.

Garry and Kate Fletcher are a middle-aged married couple who seem happy. A young man named Mark waits for the appointed hour for a job interview in town, but when he begins to leave, the newly powerful Dr. Destiny manipulates his mind so that he stays.

Soon, the villain begins giving them all waking dreams of wish fulfillment. All the while, the TV is showing a news report revealing that the entire area is erupting in a growing circle of madness, of suicide and violence, insanity and bad dreams. As the hours go by, Dee compels them to commit violence upon one another, then to worship him. By hour twelve, they're forced to confess their deepest secrets. In hour fourteen, Dee turns Bette, Judy, and Kate into the Oracles—the Fates—and has them tell his future.

By hour twenty-two, they are all dead. At last, at hour twenty-four, a weakened Morpheus appears.

#7 "SOUND AND FURY"

By now, Dr. Destiny's power has begun to affect hundreds of millions of people. Sleepers have terrible nightmares. Those awake are driven mad.

The badly weakened Morpheus lacks the power to defeat Dr. Destiny, and he cannot touch the ruby for fear it will drain him further. Dee must undo what he's done to the ruby first, and only then can Morpheus regain it, and his power, and try to repair the horrors that Dee has committed.

Morpheus cannot defeat him in the tangible world, so he goes into dreams, forcing Dee to follow. Dr. Destiny enters the dream world in an effort to kill his opponent. In the Dreaming, we catch a glimpse of Dream's brother Destiny, of the Endless, for the first time.

Dee's attempts to kill Morpheus, using all of the power of the ruby, result in its destruction. All of the power Dream had first placed in it, and the strength it had drained from him later, returns to Morpheus. Dee is merely mortal now, facing the wraith of one of the Endless. Dee thinks Morpheus will kill him, but instead, Dream returns him to his cell at Arkham Asylum. Once peace is restored to the dream world—and the world at large—even the inmates at Arkham sleep peacefully.

#8 "THE SOUND OF HER WINGS"

As uniformly excellent as the preceding issues are, this one is a benchmark for the series. Prior installments had the arch humor and the cleverness that are part of Gaiman's voice, but here the author settles into the wistful, melancholy mood that would flavor subsequent issues.

Sitting on a bench in New York's Washington Square Park, a depressed Dream absently feeds some pigeons. A pale Goth girl arrives, and is soon revealed to be his sister Death. She is furious at him for moping about how aimless he feels, and because he didn't bother to get in touch to let her know he was all right once he'd been freed from imprisonment.

But Death cannot spend too much time with him. She has work to do, after all. Dream accompanies her on her rounds, hearing the sound of her (unseen) wings as she carries the souls of the dead to their final destination. Being with Death, seeing the love, kindness, and acceptance with which she conducts her business, reminds Dream that he has a function to perform, that he has responsibilities. He has a kingdom to rebuild. And yet she also makes him see that life—and his return to freedom—can be cherished and celebrated.

Brother and sister part, with Death telling Dream not to be a stranger.

PEOPLE, PLACES, AND THINGS

MORPHEUS (DREAM). The Sandman, the Dream King, the Lord of Dreams. Held captive for seventy-two years, he escapes and embarks upon a quest to retrieve three objects of power stolen by his captors.

THE ENDLESS. Beings of great power, considered by some to be old gods, these seven siblings are the physical manifestations of concepts, emotions, and states of being. Within these pages, we first meet Dream, Destiny, and Death, but others are also mentioned.

RODERICK BURGESS. An occultist who perceives himself a competitor of the legendary Aleister Crowley. Using a book of occult secrets, he manages to summon and imprison Dream of the Endless.

ALEX BURGESS. The son of Roderick Burgess. When he grows old and his control over his father's former followers grows lax, a foolish accident by his assistant releases Morpheus from captivity.

DR. JOHN HATHAWAY. Curator at the British Museum, Hathaway steals a grimoire from the museum for Burgess, enabling the man to summon and capture Morpheus.

CAIN AND ABEL. Biblical brothers and characters from the original story, they are locked in an eternal cycle in which Cain repeatedly kills Abel, only to have him rise again. In between murders, they bicker constantly and help look after the Dreaming, the kingdom of the Sandman.

GOLDIE. A baby gargoyle that Cain gives to Abel as a gift.

LUCIEN. The librarian of the Dreaming, who has done his best to take care of the castle in his master's absence.

THE HECATEAE. The one-who-are-three. They are known by many names: Urth, Verthandi, and Skald; Atropos, Clotho, and Lachesis; Tisiphone, Alecto, and

Magaera—and every other combination of three witches, three faces—maiden, all mother, and crone.

JOHN CONSTANTINE. Occult magician with a bad attitude and worse luck. Constantine once had possession of Morpheus's pouch of sand, and helps him retrieve it.

MAD HETTIE. An eccentric, 274-year-old woman with certain psychic gifts.

RACHEL. Constantine's junkie ex-girlfriend. She stole Morpheus's pouch of sand, and pays a terrible price—first her sanity, and then her life.

LUCIFER MORNINGSTAR. First of the Fallen (angels), and one of the three triumverate rulers of Hell.

ETRIGAN. A rhyming demon familiar to readers of DC Comics.

NADA. A denizen of Hell—human—who has been imprisoned there at the whim of Morpheus for ten thousand years. If he would only forgive her, Nada would be free, but though he claims to still love her, he cannot forgive her.

BEELZEBUB. Lord of the Flies, and one of the triumverate rulers of Hell.

AZAZEL. The third member of Hell's ruling triumverate.

CHORONZON. A demon, he has come into possession of Morpheus's helm. When Dream challenges him to a contest with the helm as a prize, Choronzon attempts to outwit him, but finds Morpheus a formidable foe.

SCOTT FREE. Also known as Mr. Miracle, Scott Free is a member of the Justice League. He helps Dream track down his missing ruby.

J'ONN J'ONZZ. Also known as the Martian Manhunter, J'onn is a member of the Justice League. He helps Dream track down his missing ruby.

DR. DESTINY AKA JOHN DEE. Once upon a time, John Dee was a supervillain called Dr. Destiny. Now he is just another madman locked up in Arkham Asylum. When his mother dies, he comes into possession of Morpheus's ruby once more—only this time the gem is far more powerful, having drained much of the Sandman's strength. He begins to use its power to spread madness and nightmares, secreting himself away in the All-Nite Diner, where he whiles away the time by tormenting its patrons. By the time Morpheus arrives at the diner, it is too late to save them. While attempting to kill Morpheus, Dee instead destroys the ruby, returning the Dream King's power to its fullest. Showing him undeserved mercy, Dream returns Dee to Arkham.

DEATH. The sister of Dream, she is one of the Endless.

TRIVIA

- Sam Kieth, the original penciler on Sandman, quit during issue 3. In his afterword to *Preludes & Nocturnes,* Gaiman recalls that Kieth told him, "I feel like Jimi Hendrix in the Beatles. I'm in the wrong band."

- Early sketches and designs were done during the planning stages by series cover artist Dave McKean, artist Leigh Baulch, and Neil Gaiman himself.

- A panel on page 22 of issue 7 contains one of Gaiman's numerous references to *The Wizard of Oz,* as, returning to Arkham, Dr. Destiny tells one of his companions, "There's no place like home, Professor Crane." The visual accompanying this statement is priceless.

- In having Cain, in issue 2, refer to Morpheus as the "Prince of Stories," Gaiman was referencing a 1969 Velvet Underground song titled, "I'm Set Free" (a song he has said, in his blog, that "seems to have the whole plot of *Sandman* in it . . .").

- The realm of the Sandman—the Dreaming—was the subject of its own series, featuring various characters from Morpheus's kingdom, including Goldie the gargoyle, Cain, and Abel. It ran for sixty issues from 1996 to 2001, and was written and illustrated by a variety of creators, including novelist Caitlin R. Kiernan, who wrote most of the issues. Various other spin-offs and one-shots also appeared under the brand banner *The Sandman Presents.*

- The popularity of Gaiman's series caused a surge of interest in DC Comics's Golden Age Sandman, Wesley Dodds, eventually leading to a new maturereaders title for the character. *Sandman Mystery Theatre,* written by Matt Wagner and illustrated by a host of artists, ran for seventy issues between 1993 and 1999. The two Sandmen met in a one-shot written by Gaiman and Wagner entitled *Sandman Midnight Theatre.*

- Gaiman's version of the Three Witches (known by many other names, including the Fates) was spun off into two miniseries under the title *Witchcraft.*

THE QUOTABLE GAIMAN

Sandman 6 was the first time I tried to break all the rules of what had been done in comics to date, to go as far as I could go. In that story, a small bunch of people are essentially tortured to death over a twenty-four-hour period. A lot of readers said they stopped buying Sandman after issue 6 and didn't come back for ages, until they were told it was safe.

—*The Sandman Companion,* by Hy Bender

A FEW WORDS FROM
MIKE DRINGENBERG

The feelings one associates with any long friendship are never unmingled . . . they etch their way beyond the superficial like acid into a burred printing plate, softly dissolving the metal and leaving behind a trace of intimacies, the lines etched as much by the random work of the agent as by any deliberate act. As such, the final print is never the whole story, but only its shadow.

And so it is with Neil—a commingling of love, respect, and even mutual contempt, based on years of fleeting conversations and our ever presence in each other's lives. But that's only a shadow. We're both highly erratic people. I can love him as a friend, respect him as a collaborator, and hold a fair contempt for his methods, the way he goes about his work, which is quite the opposite of my own. I prefer the imminent act, but Neil will take any idea and run with it, no matter how mediocre it is. It's just a starting point with an unknown destination. The odd bits he finds along the way, the postcard sent from an obscure Amtrak station or the snapshot of the world's largest ball of twine, become his narrative.

And it all seems charming until you have to transform it into something else. At that point, exchanging the golden horde of a ragpicker into something other than itself becomes a feat worth its own tale. "If you think of a better way to lay this out, go for it," is the usual presage.

I'm very much his shadow, a little presence that holds him to the earth, and in that way keeps him honest.

VOLUME TWO:
THE DOLL'S HOUSE

(1989—90)

The title of the second volume of The Sandman—*The Doll's House*—refers to a
doll house owned by Unity Kinkaid, which she gives to her granddaughter,
Rose Walker. Yet, thematically, the title has far greater significance.

The story revolves around manipulation. Dream, his lover Nada, and the Kinkaid/
Walker family are all manipulated by Dream's sister Desire. The escaped night-
mares, Glob and Brute—characters from the 1970s version of *The Sandman* by Jack
Kirby—have even more direct control over Lyta Hall and the ghost of her husband,
Hector. Discovering that her life may be forfeit due to the meddling of the Endless,
Rose Walker rages about the injustice of these godlike beings treating mortals like
playthings—or dolls. Ironically, faced with Desire's similar belief, Dream makes it
clear that he believes the opposite is true—since the Endless are the incarnations of
human concepts, *they* are the puppets, rather than the puppeteers.

The title is an inescapable reference to legendary playwright Henrik Ibsen's *A
Doll's House,* in which the main character comes to realize that her entire life has
consisted of living to complete the picture of a perfect household, first for her
father and then for her husband, as though she is a doll in a dollhouse.

The Doll's House picks up from events in *Preludes & Nocturnes,* beginning with
the prelude "Tales in the Sand," which relates the tale of how Morpheus and
Nada, an African queen, fell in love, manipulated by Desire. The tale is the con-
nective tissue between the first and fourth volumes of the series, as Dream's
doomed relationship with Nada is the impetus for *Season of Mists.*

Rose Walker, the focal character of *The Doll's House,* is the granddaughter of
Unity Kinkaid, a victim of the sleeping sickness portrayed in *Preludes & Nocturnes.* While Unity slept, Desire fathered a child with her, but the baby was given
away. Now, years later, Unity has awoken and tracked down her long-lost daughter, and learns that she also has two grandchildren, Rose and her younger brother,
Jed. (Note that, like Brute and Glob, Jed is a holdover from Jack Kirby's 1970s version of *The Sandman,* in which he was a sort of sidekick to the title character.)

The Doll's House plants a great many seeds for the future, from Nada's story in
Season of Mists to Barbie's tale in *A Game of You;* most importantly, it sets the stage
for the series' climax, by introducing the pregnant Lyta Hall and her child, Daniel.

The story arc also expands on a theme introduced in the very first issue, which
then spans the entire series, namely that of imprisonment and liberation. The joy

and potential of liberation, having once been a captive—whether physically or emotionally, and whether of someone else's doing or one's own—flows through the series, appearing again and again. Morpheus was imprisoned for most of the twentieth century and, upon his release, finds both the world and his worldview greatly altered. Unity Kinkaid was imprisoned by the sleeping sickness, and also wakes to a new world. Jed Walker is a physical captive of his abusive cousins. Lyta Hall and her husband's ghost are captives of Brute and Glob, in a tiny, twisted version of the Dreaming, before Morpheus releases both of them.

With the inclusion of the story "Men of Good Fortune" Gaiman also continues the evolution of Morpheus as a character. In this tale, which introduces the ageless Hob Gadling, Morpheus begins to show a touch of humanity. Prior to his captivity he bristled at the suggestion that one of the Endless could ever consider a mortal man a friend. But after his release, keeping their once-a-century appointment, he sees his relationship with Hob as a genuine friendship.

The Doll's House strays from the prior volume by exploring Morpheus's role in the world and the lives of humans. While he is a vital part of the story, he is not the central character (that would be Rose Walker). Readers are made to consider that, given the nature of dreams and imagination, Morpheus is on the periphery of *all* of our tales, and only sometimes—as in the case of Rose Walker—becomes directly involved in them.

Issues 9 through 11 and 14 through 16 are illustrated by Mike Dringenberg and Malcolm Jones III, issue 12 by Chris Bachalo and Malcolm Jones III, and issue 13 by Michael Zulli and Steve Parkhouse.

#9 "TALES IN THE SAND"

In the African desert a grandfather and his grandson travel to a spot believed by their tribe to have once been the site of a great city of glass, built by their ancestors. The grandfather proceeds to tell his grandson a story. Long ago, the city was ruled by Nada, a queen unable to find a king who suited her. One day, a strange, silent man came into the city and gazed up at her tower. Seeing him, she immediately fell in love.

When she discovered that he was Kai'ckul, the Lord of Dreams, Nada ate a certain berry that helped her to visit the Dreamworld in her sleep. She saw in the Dream Lord's eyes that he loved her, too. In terror, she woke again in her own chamber. The Dream Lord followed her back to her chamber and she confessed her love again, but said that it was not for mortals to love the Endless.

Eventually she went to him, and they made love. But in the morning the sun saw what had taken place and sent a fireball down that destroyed the city of glass. Nada knew it was because of what they had done. She threw herself off the mountain and fell to her death. On the edges of the land of Death, the Dream Lord caught up with her. Again he offered to make her his queen, warning that should she decline, he would doom her to eternal suffering.

That is where the grandfather's story ends. The grandson insists that it is not a proper ending, asking his grandfather how Nada responded. The grandfather believes that Nada said no, for what else could she say?

#10 "DOLL'S HOUSE, PART ONE: THE DOLL'S HOUSE"

Using her sigil, Desire of the Endless summons her twin sister, Despair. Readers learn here that the agony Dream endured over Nada was orchestrated by Desire. Desire also tells Despair that a rare and dangerous event—a dream vortex, in the form of a mortal woman, has appeared.

In the Dreaming, Lucien has finished taking a census of all of the beings residing there, reporting to Dream that four of the major Arcana are missing—Brute, Glob, The Corinthian, and Fiddler's Green.

Rose Walker and her mother, Miranda, arrive at a nursing home in England, where they meet Unity Kinkaid, an old woman who reveals that she is Miranda's mother—Rose's grandmother. Unity was a teenage victim of the sleeping sickness discussed in *Preludes & Nocturnes*. During that time she had a baby, Miranda, who was given up for adoption.

At the Love Inn Motel in Amarillo, Texas, a man lies tied up in a bathtub. He thinks he has come here with another man to "play." But when the man, also known as the Corinthian, removes his sunglasses and takes out a knife, the victim realizes that he and his playmate have very different definitions of the word.

#11 "DOLL'S HOUSE, PART TWO: MOVING IN"

Rose Walker moves into a new apartment in Florida, a room in an old mansion. The tenants include her landlord, Hal, a young, obnoxiously peppy couple whose names are actually Ken and Barbie, a pair of bizarre women named Zelda and Chantal, aka the Spider Women, and the mysterious Gilbert, who rescues her from a trio of thugs.

Dream is concerned that, as a vortex, Rose will soon draw stray dreams to her, so he sends his raven, Matthew, to watch over her.

In Birmingham, Alabama, the Corinthian has killed again. He phones Nimrod, apparently also a serial killer, who collects trophies from his victims. Nimrod is planning a gathering of serial killers—a convention—in Georgia. The Corinthian plans to attend.

Informed by a private investigator that her brother is in Georgia (the PI found records indicating that the state placed him with a distant cousin of her father's), Rose departs to collect him. Armed with a sword cane and an old pistol, Gilbert tags along.

Rose is in Florida to search for her long-lost little brother, Jed. She hasn't seen Jed for seven years, and is thus unaware that he is currently being kept in a dank basement, his only escape coming through his dreams, where he dreams of a life with superhero parents—Hector Hall, the costumed adventurer who calls himself "the Sandman," and his wife, Lyta. But as he dreams, Morpheus finds him. Brute and Glob have severed the boy's mind from the Dreaming and are living in Jed's mind. The Dream Lord is furious.

#12 "DOLL'S HOUSE, PART THREE: PLAYING HOUSE"

Lyta Hall wakes in confusion. Pregnant, she feels she ought to have had the baby by now. She knows that this life is not right. Wandering downstairs, she finds her husband, Hector Hall, as the Sandman—with his assistants Brute and Glob—preparing to leave their home, the Dream Dome, to face another threat.

Jed is brought up from the basement where he is kept locked up by Barnaby and Clarice, his abusive guardians. In the Dream Dome—which exists inside Jed's mind—Brute and Glob realize that Morpheus is coming for them and send Hector out to confront him, convincing him that Dream is a nightmare monster. Dream breaks through into the small pocket of dreams that Brute and Glob have created for themselves in Jed's mind and pulls them all out into Clarice and Barnaby's cellar.

Brute and Glob had used a human to try to create their own Dream kingdom, their own Sandman. He went mad and killed himself, so they decided to use a ghost the next time, the spirit of Hector Hall, who was already dead. Hector then brought Lyta into the Dream Dome.

Morpheus returns Brute and Glob to the Dreaming, banishing them to "the darkness" for several hundred thousand years, then sends Hector's ghost on to the afterlife. He tells Lyta that the child she has carried unborn for two years in the Dream Dome is *his,* and that one day he will return for him. Lyta swears that this will be over her dead body.

Having run away, Jed is hitchhiking. A car pulls over to pick him up. It is driven by the Corinthian, who is traveling to the serial killers convention.

#13 "DOLL'S HOUSE, PART FOUR: MEN OF GOOD FORTUNE"

In a pub in England in 1389, Death and Dream overhear a man named Hob (Robert) Gadling as he engages in a conversation about death, insisting that people perish because they believe it's what's expected of them; he, however, has no plans to die. Dream suggests to Death that it might be interesting to make the man's assertion true. Death agrees and departs, while Dream tells Hob that he will meet the man back in the inn in one hundred years.

Dream and Hob renew their acquaintance in 1489. Come 1589, with Christopher Marlowe and William Shakespeare at a nearby table, Hob and Dream reunite. Hob has used his time wisely, becoming a wealthy knight with a wife and son.

Shakespeare wishes aloud that he could write as well as Marlowe, that he would bargain like Faustus if only he could give men stories that would inspire great dreams. Overhearing this, Morpheus makes a bargain with the ambitious playwright.

Hob and Dream continue to meet every one hundred years. In 1889, Hob tells Dream that he thinks Dream comes because he is lonely and wants friendship. Dream is offended that Hob would think he would befriend a mortal, but Hob challenges him, saying that if they meet again in the next century, it will be because they are friends.

In 1989, Hob waits for Dream in a suit and tie, smoking a cigarette. He is pleased when Morpheus arrives, not sure if he offended him the last time they met. The Dream King tells him that he has always been told it was impolite to keep friends waiting.

#14 "DOLL'S HOUSE, PART FIVE: COLLECTORS"

The serial killers convention is being held at a seedy Georgia hotel. Though the convention is supposed to have the whole hotel, there are two other guests, Rose Walker and Gilbert. When Rose called the police to inquire about her brother, Jed, they instructed her to stay put, and told the manager that he must permit her to stay.

Rose and Gilbert encounter the Corinthian on the elevator. Gilbert is terrified. He writes a name on a piece of paper and tells Rose that if things get very bad, she should say the name aloud. In the morning, there is a knock on her door. When she opens it, she is attacked by a serial killer named Funland. Rose grabs the piece of paper Gilbert had given her and calls out the name: Morpheus. The Sandman appears and rescues her.

Downstairs, the Corinthian is delivering a speech to his fellow serial killers when Morpheus enters. He is disappointed. The Corinthian was "a nightmare created to be the darkness and the fear of darkness in every human heart." Instead, during Morpheus's captivity, he wasted his time killing, inspiring all of these serial killers, becoming nothing more than they are. The disapproving Sandman *uncreates* the Corinthian. Morpheus then faces the killers, warning them that from that day forward, he will not allow them to delude themselves. They will be forced to understand what they truly are.

Outside, Gilbert has found Jed—who was in the trunk of the Corinthian's car—and brings the boy to Rose. They need to get Jed to a hospital.

#15 "DOLL'S HOUSE, PART SIX: INTO THE NIGHT"

Back at her apartment in Florida, Rose feels lost. Jed is unconscious in a local hospital, her mother is in England with her grandmother, Unity, who has been disabled by a stroke, and Gilbert seems to have vanished.

In the Dreaming, Morpheus and Matthew look down upon a growing vortex; it exists in the Dreaming, but it is also Rose Walker. Something must be done, for it threatens the Dreaming.

At the apartment house, Rose dreams. Aware of her dreaming mind and her sleeping body, she can see and feel the dreams of the others in the house, and perceive how thin the walls are between them. With a single nudge she breaks down those walls, and all of their dreams flood into one another. Ken and Barbie, Zelda and Chantal, Hal, and Rose herself are trapped at the center of a swirling vortex of dreams. The vortex grows, reaching out into the city and beyond, until Morpheus steps in and halts it.

In England, Unity Kinkaid is dying. She wakes and tells Miranda that Rose should have the doll's house that came from her own childhood home.

At the hospital in Florida, Matthew the Raven arrives to retrieve Gilbert, who has been visiting the boy. Together, the man who became a dream and the dream who tried to become a man return to the Dreaming, discussing Rose and what will happen to her. Gilbert reveals that because Rose is a vortex, Dream will have no choice but to kill her.

#16 "DOLL'S HOUSE, PART SEVEN: LOST HEARTS"

In the Dreaming, Morpheus explains to Rose that she is a vortex and that he must kill her. He reveals that vortices break down all barriers until an entire planet's dreams join together as one, and then becomes utter blackness, and destroys that world. One of Dream's functions is to prevent this from ever happening again. Once upon a time, half a universe away, he failed, and he has vowed never to do so again.

Gilbert arrives, offering his life for Rose's. Morpheus explains that this is not possible. Gilbert is a dream—a region of the Dreaming called Fiddler's Green—and he must take up his original place in the Dreaming, and Rose must die.

As Dream is about to take Rose's life, a beautiful young woman appears—the dreaming image of Unity Kinkaid. She explains that had she not fallen victim to the sleeping sickness, she would have been the vortex instead of Rose. Unity becomes the vortex in her granddaughter's place. In her bed in England, with her daughter, Miranda, looking on, Unity dies.

In the Dreaming, there is much Morpheus does not understand, but he tells Rose that her family has suffered enough. With the vortex gone, he gives her a gift—in the morning, Jed will awaken.

Later, Morpheus visits his sister Desire in her realm. There, he tells her that Rose's situation could not have been an accident and that he knows she is responsible. He also informs her that he knows he/she/it is the one who impregnated the sleeping Unity Kinkaid fifty years earlier. Had Morpheus killed Rose, he would have been killing a blood relative. Dream warns his sister that if she interferes in his affairs again, she will suffer the consequences.

PEOPLE, PLACES, AND THINGS

MORPHEUS (DREAM). Returned to his full power, the Lord of Dreams instructs Lucien to take a census of the Dreaming, and he discovers that four denizens of his kingdom are missing. He also discovers the existence of a dream vortex, which spells much trouble.

NADA. Ten thousand years ago she was queen of a great city of green glass in the midst of Africa, but she had no king. Manipulated by Desire, she falls in love with Dream and seeks him out. Upon learning his true nature, however, she realizes that only great disaster can come of their love. Still, she submits to it only to have her city destroyed as a result. Nada kills herself to avoid any further disaster, but when she continues to refuse to become queen of the Dreaming, Morpheus arranges for her to be imprisoned in Hell for eternity.

THE KING OF THE BIRDS. Nada goes to him for help locating the man she has fallen in love with, and he summons all of the birds.

THE WEAVERBIRD. It flies to the mountains of the sun to retrieve a flaming berry from a tree there. When Nada eats it she is transported to the side of her true love—to the palace of the Dream King.

HOB GADLING. In a fourteenth century tavern, he boasts that no one must die if they choose not to. Overhearing him, Dream suggests to his sister, Death, that it might be interesting to fulfill that ambition for him. Dream and Hob agree to meet in the same tavern once every century, and over the course of six hundred years, Hob becomes Dream's first mortal friend.

DEATH. A sister of Dream; one of the Endless.

LADY JOHANNA CONSTANTINE. An ancestor of John Constantine. In 1789 she attempts to capture Hob Gadling and Dream in order to learn their secrets.

WILLIAM SHAKESPEARE. Envious of the talents of his friend and fellow playwright Christopher Marlowe, Shakespeare claims aloud that he would do anything to be able to inspire men's dreams with his own tales and talent. Morpheus walks with him, and they fashion an agreement, the details of which are unknown, but the effects of which are obvious.

ROSE WALKER. Rose is a young woman who learns that she is a dream vortex, at first drawing stray dreams to her, and then, in time, beginning to break down the walls between people's individual dreams. Left unchecked she could destroy the world. Morpheus must kill her to prevent that from happening, but her grandmother, Unity Kinkaid, manages to take her place and die in her stead, leaving Rose to begin a new life with her mother and younger brother, Jed, in the Seattle area. Rose has chosen to see all of those events as a dream, unaware that she is not entirely human, but also a descendant of the Endless, since her grandmother was impregnated by Desire.

MIRANDA WALKER. Miranda and her daughter, Rose, travel to England after a mysterious summons. There they learn that Miranda was adopted as a child, and that her real mother has recently recovered from decades of illness. She was conceived and born while her mother was barely aware. Shortly after the three generations are reunited, Miranda sends Rose out to search for her son, Jed. When Rose does find him, he ends up in the hospital, but Miranda cannot go to him because her mother has had a stroke. Since her mother was impregnated by Desire, Miranda is also a member of the family of the Endless.

UNITY KINKAID. Rose's grandmother and Miranda's mother, Unity suffered from the sleeping sickness brought on by the Sandman's imprisonment. When he was freed, she woke to discover that she'd had a daughter decades before, while still afflicted. She hires private investigators to locate her daughter, and brings Miranda and Rose to England to reveal the truth to them. In time, Unity has a stroke. As she is dying, many things happen at once. She understands that her granddaughter is the dream vortex, and that the Sandman is going to kill her. But she also knows that she was meant to be the vortex, and would have been had it not been for the sleeping sickness. She offers herself in Rose's place, takes the vortex into herself, and she dies, though her spirit remains in the Dreaming.

JED WALKER. Rose's younger brother, he was separated from his mother and sister when his parents split up. When his father died, he went into the care of his grandfather, who soon also died. Eventually, Jed ended up in the care of distant cousins in Georgia, who were paid by the state to watch over him, but instead forced him to live in their basement like an animal. For a time, two errant dreams—Brute and Glob—lived in their own small dream kingdom in his mind, but when Morpheus put an end to that, Jed escaped. His freedom is short-lived, however, because he is picked up by a living nightmare called the Corinthian, who puts him in the trunk of his car and goes to a serial killers convention. When Jed is finally rescued, he ends up in the hospital. But in the end he awakens and settles down to live with his mother and sister in the Seattle area. Since his grandmother was impregnated by Desire, Jed is a member of the family of the Endless.

DESIRE. One of the Endless, at once neither male nor female and yet also both, he/she/it often schemes to trouble his/her/its older brother, Dream. Desire caused Nada and Dream to fall in love, leading to her torment and his heartbreak. Desire also impregnated Unity Kinkaid while she had the sleeping sickness.

DESPAIR. One of the Endless, the twin sister of Desire, and often her/his/its coconspirator.

HAL CARTER. The owner of an apartment house in Florida, he is briefly Rose's landlord and friend.

KEN AND BARBIE. Housemates in the apartment house where Rose lives while searching for Jed.

ZELDA AND CHANTAL. A strange pair of women who dress in white lace and are obsessed with spiders, they are either friends or lovers or sisters, or all three. They reside in the apartment house where Rose stays briefly while searching for Jed.

GILBERT. A gallant, portly gentleman who lives on the top floor of the apartment house where Rose lives briefly while searching for Jed. Gilbert accompanies her to Georgia to retrieve Jed. At the serial killers convention, he recognizes the Corinthian and encourages Rose to call for Morpheus should anything go wrong. Soon, Dream sends Matthew the Raven to retrieve him and bring him back to the Dreaming, for Gilbert is actually Fiddler's Green, a whole section of the Dreaming, who has gone AWOL. Gilbert pleads for Rose's life, to no avail. At Dream's command, he gives up his quest to live like a man and returns to the Dreaming as Fiddler's Green.

MATTHEW THE RAVEN. A raven, servant and confidant of the Dream King, Matthew was once a man but is now only a dream.

LUCIEN. A servant of Lord Morpheus, he is conducting a census when he realizes that Brute, Glob, the Corinthian, and Fiddler's Green are all missing from the Dreaming.

BRUTE AND GLOB. A pair of enterprising escapees from the Dreaming, they create the Dream Dome, a small dream kingdom of their own in the mind of Jed Walker that is cut off from the Dreaming. Taking advantage of Morpheus's absence, they attempt to create a new Dream King, one they can control.

Their creation was the second costumed adventurer to be called the Sandman. When he went mad, they recruited a new Sandman, Hector Hall. Because Hector was already dead, his ghost, still believing it was alive, became the Sandman. When their plans are ruined, Brute and Glob are upbraided by Morpheus and cast into darkness.

HECTOR HALL. Once and future superhero Hector Hall has a long history in the DC universe. But in the pages of The Sandman he is a ghost, a dead man tricked into believing himself a superhero though his spirit is actually lost in a dream inside Jed Walker's mind. He has brought his living wife, Lyta, into the Dream Dome. When Morpheus casts Brute and Glob into darkness, he sends Hector's ghost into the afterlife.

LYTA HALL. Also a part of DC universe, Lyta is Hector's wife. Pregnant with his child at the time of his death, she is drawn into the Dream Dome and her pregnancy is frozen during the time she spends there. When she is brought out of the dream, Morpheus tells her that the child is his, and that one day he will return for it. Lyta vows that this will happen over her dead body.

THE CORINTHIAN. The ultimate nightmare, he escapes from the Dreaming and becomes the inspiration for generations of serial killers. When Dream finally catches up with him, he is uncreated.

CLARICE AND BARNABY. Distant cousins of Jed and Rose's paternal grandfather, they are paid by the state to care for Jed, but instead keep the money and let him live in the basement in squalor.

NIMROD. The serial killer who organizes the serial killers convention.

FUNLAND. A pedophile and child killer, he's a volunteer at the convention, helping Nimrod. He tries to rape and kill Rose, but Morpheus prevents him from doing so.

TRIVIA

- Gilbert, aka Fiddler's Green, seems to be a visual homage to writer G. K. Chesterton, a particular favorite of Gaiman's.

- Glob and Brute are reminiscent of Croup and Vandemar, the brutal killers of *Neverwhere,* but visually, they seem to have hugely influenced the two main characters in Disney/Pixar's *Monsters, Inc.*

- Lady Constantine later appeared in a self-titled miniseries written by Andy Diggle and illustrated by Phil Noto.

- In 2001–2002, the Corinthian starred in a three-issue flashback miniseries, *The Corinthian: Death in Venice*, written by Darko Macan and illustrated by Danijel Zezelj.

- Lyta Hall starred in the spin-off graphic novel *The Furies*, written by Mike Carey and painted by John Bolton. She is featured prominently in later volumes of *The Sandman*, and has also been a character in the DC universe, on and off, for decades.

- Dream appears in writer/penciler Rick Veitch's *Swamp Thing* issue 84 (March 1989), in which longtime Swamp Thing character Matt Cable is transformed into Matthew the Raven. Gaiman and Veitch clearly worked this out—they were in constant contact at the time, in part because Gaiman (and Jamie Delano) were being groomed to take over the scripting chores on *Swamp Thing*. Veitch departed the title after issue 87 (June 1989), when a conflict erupted between the creator and DC over Veitch's plan to have Swamp Thing encounter Jesus Christ. In solidarity, Gaiman and Delano stepped away from plans for their involvement in the *Swamp Thing* monthly series.

- "Men of Good Fortune" was not only an engaging interlude amid the contemporary context of the rest of *A Doll's House*, it also initiated an innovative method Gaiman created for dealing with the sometimes unwieldy fusion of the graphic novel and serialized periodical comics. It is important to remember that, at the time, the "graphic novel" formatting of Sandman had not been codified—The Sandman was, first and foremost, a periodical composed of a serialized longer work. Building in part on precursors like the Marv Wolfman/Gene

Colan/Tom Palmer Marvel Comics series Tomb of Dracula (70 issues, 1972–79) and Alan Moore's "American Gothic" series for *The Saga of the Swamp Thing* (50 issues, 1985–87), Gaiman was struggling with the difficulties of juggling creator deadlines and sustaining reader interest in a longer serialized work published in monthly installments.

Gaiman was midway through the scripting of *A Doll's House* when he conceived of placing the story of Hob Gadling, Death, and Dream as a self-contained, self-standing single-issue chapter at its approximate midpoint. Thus, what functioned as a backstory breather in the context of the periodical schedule also served as a "keystone" chapter, too, providing both essential background and a concise narrative synthesis of the larger serialized novel's thematic points. Gaiman soon realized this device was useful, and he returned to it in subsequent serialized *Sandman* adventures.

THE QUOTABLE GAIMAN

On the genesis of "Men of Good Fortune":

Had I happened to pick a later year—say, 1594, when Shakespeare was at the height of his powers—I wouldn't have bothered to even place him in the pub. But I loved the idea of having Marlowe, who in 1589 was the finest playwright in the English language, talking to this wannabe writer, this fanboy named William Shakespeare. And Marlowe telling Shakespeare that as far as writing goes, he should stick to acting.

—*The Sandman Companion*, by Hy Bender

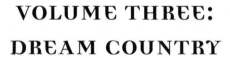

VOLUME THREE:
DREAM COUNTRY

(1990)

While *Preludes & Nocturnes* expertly laid the foundation for the new mythology Gaiman had created, and *The Doll's House* showed Gaiman's mastery of the graphic novel format, the four tales that comprise *Dream Country* are instead short stories. Gaiman's novels are sometimes large and rambling and always beautiful, but his short stories have an elegance and eloquence that might be overlooked in a larger work. This is no less true of the tales in *Dream Country*, though they are told with pictures as well as words.

This quartet of stand-alone stories explores the world of the Endless. While the fourth, "Façade," features Dream's older sister, Death, the other three examine facets of the Sandman and the extent of his reach. "Calliope" hints at a past love affair even as it reveals how much his captivity for most of the twentieth century changed him. "A Dream of a Thousand Cats" shows that he is the lord of all dreams, not merely those of humans. "Midsummer Night's Dream" details his involvement with and influence upon William Shakespeare, even as it introduces the Faerie court and hints at the complicated and long-standing relationship that Morpheus has with the king and queen of that realm.

Yet the true wonder of Morpheus as a character is that his story and mythology is both fascinating in its own right and as a vehicle for Gaiman to tell other stories and explore other ideas. "Calliope" is Gaiman's take on a classic conceit, the fundamental "be careful what you wish for" tale that has been played out since there were storytellers. Even this variation—capturing or corrupting a muse to inspire creativity and imagination, and bring success—has been done before. But Gaiman approaches the story from a different angle. Rather than focusing on the fool whose greed or ambition leads to a grim or ironic comeuppance, the story is about the object of that greed. This is Calliope's story, and the greedy fool is her antagonist.

"A Dream of a Thousand Cats" is wonderfully unique as it explores the ideas of cultural mythology, consensus reality, and the power of dreams. And yet, in a turn both sinister and whimsical, it simultaneously answers the curiosity of cat owners throughout history who have stared at their sleeping pets' nocturnal squirming and wondered about the content of their dreams.

"A Midsummer Night's Dream" suggests a theory as to the fate of William Shakespeare's son, Hamnet, cleverly dispels suspicion that Christopher Marlowe might have written Shakespeare's plays, and touches upon the melancholy of a people who realize that the world has passed them by.

All of these stories could have existed on their own, without the presence of Morpheus. Yet by weaving the character into them, Gaiman gives us a much richer world. Dream is the air we breathe, as universal as hunger, thirst, and loneliness. Morpheus touches us all, sometimes moving in the periphery of our lives, but at other times taking a more intimate role.

And in "Façade" we learn that Death is not without compassion, as Gaiman touches once again upon the outskirts of the DC universe, taking a painfully realistic approach to the fate of Element Girl. His brushes with the world of superheroes in *The Sandman* would become more infrequent as the series went on, but it is done with remarkable pathos here.

Although the stories can be read on their own, when taken as part of the entirety of the series we see the threads that Gaiman has woven through them. Imprisonment and release once again feature in this collection, especially in "Calliope," where it is more literal, and in "Façade," where it is more metaphorical.

In "Midsummer" Gaiman picks up a strand begun in *The Doll's House,* while in "Calliope" he begins to tell the story of Orpheus that will be fully realized elsewhere. The Three Witches appear again, in yet another guise. And we find further hints of the evolution of Morpheus.

#17 "CALLIOPE"

(ILLUSTRATED BY KELLEY JONES AND MALCOLM JONES III)

Suffering from a terrible case of writer's block, desperate novelist Richard Madoc resorts to supernatural means to cure his malady, trading a trichinobezoar (a knot of hair found in the stomach of a girl who compulsively ate her own hair, believed to be able to cure the sick) to the aged writer, Erasmus Fry, for the muse Calliope, whom Frye captured in Greece many years ago.

Bringing Calliope home, Richard rapes her, then sits down to write, completely cured of his writer's block. Calliope, meanwhile, makes supplication and calls to the three-who-are-one, and, in their guise from Greek mythology, they appear. She pleads with them but they can't intercede personally, instead suggesting that one of the Endless might be able to help her.

Calliope and Morpheus were once lovers; in fact, she bore him a son, Orpheus. Their relationship ended badly, but she begs for them to send anyone to help her, even him. Unfortunately, Dream is also a prisoner at this time.

Madoc enjoys extraordinary success over the course of the next three years. Then, in 1989, he comes home one day to find Morpheus waiting for him in his living room. Dream tells Madoc that if it is ideas he wants, it is ideas that he will have.

Attending a party afterwards, Madoc experiences a torrential flood of ideas that drives him mad. He draws the images in his head on a wall with his fingers, wearing his fingers down to bloody claws. He is found staggering in the street by a friend whom he begs to go to his house and free Calliope. When the man arrives there, and calls out to the darkened house that whoever is there is free, he finds the house is now empty.

Free at last, Calliope tells Morpheus she is surprised that he came to her. He obviously was changed by his imprisonment, no longer hating her for the events in their past. When she asks that he release Madoc from his torture now that she is free, Morpheus agrees.

PEOPLE, PLACES, AND THINGS

MORPHEUS (DREAM). The Lord of Dreams, the Dream King, is known by many names and many faces. The ancient Greeks knew him as Oneiros.

RICHARD MADOC. Lacking ideas and conscience, the writer trades an item of some mystical value to aged author Erasmus Fry in exchange for possession of Calliope, one of the muses of ancient Greece. While keeping her prisoner he finds success greater than he's ever hoped for, but when Morpheus asks him to free Calliope and he refuses, the Sandman gives him enough ideas to drive him mad. At last he has no choice but to set her free.

ERASMUS FRY. An octogenarian author who owes his success to the imprisoned Calliope. Concluding that he no longer has any use for her, he trades her to Madoc.

CALLIOPE. The youngest of the nine muses of Greek myth, she was captured in 1927 by Erasmus Fry and forced to become his personal muse. In ancient times she was romantically involved with Oneiros (Morpheus), bearing him a son, Orpheus, whose tale is told elsewhere. Orpheus died, and for millennia, Oneiros hated Calliope. But his own recent imprisonment has softened his heart toward her, and after Fry trades her to Richard Madoc, Morpheus forces the latter to release her.

THE THREE WITCHES. In their aspects from Greek myth, the three-who-are-one appear at Calliope's summoning. They cannot help free her, but apparently they do manage to get word to Morpheus, who eventually comes to her aid.

#18 "A DREAM OF A THOUSAND CATS"

(ILLUSTRATED BY KELLEY JONES AND MALCOLM JONES III)

As his owners go up to bed, a kitten is called outside by a larger cat. All of the cats in the area are assembling to hear an address by a female cat whose presence has elicited great excitement. When they have gathered, she begins to speak.

She tells them that she was once a plaything of humans, who fooled herself into thinking that she was in control of her own life. She found that wasn't the case when her owner, Paul, cruelly killed the litter of kittens she had just borne.

Seeking understanding and justice, she prayed to the King of Cats. Later, in a dream, she visited the cave of the Cat of Dreams.

The Dream Lord—a huge black cat—told the cat to look into his eyes. There, she tells the gathered felines, she saw the world the way it once was, a time when cats were giant and ruled the land, and used tiny humans as their pets and playthings. But one human gathered the others and convinced them that dreams shaped reality. In time, enough humans simultaneously dreamed the dream of a different world that they were able to alter reality, so that the time of cats had never even existed, and never would.

Since then the cat has traveled the world, spreading the word that cats must dream the world anew to change it, to return to the paradise they once had. If enough cats dream at once, it will happen, she says, and she will spread the word until enough believe, or until she dies.

When she departs the gathering, the kitten catches up to her and tells her that she believes. "Then there is hope, child," the cat says.

PEOPLE, PLACES, AND THINGS

THE KITTEN. An ordinary kitten, she goes out late one night to a convocation of cats who have gathered to hear a speech.

THE CAT. A wandering cat has come to an ordinary suburban neighborhood to share a secret and to speak about her dream for the future with her fellow felines.

THE CAT OF DREAMS. Dreaming cats who encounter Morpheus would see him as the Cat of Dreams.

#19 "A MIDSUMMER NIGHT'S DREAM"

(ILLUSTRATED BY CHARLES VESS AND MALCOLM JONES III)

On June 23, 1593, William Shakespeare leads his theatrical troupe into the countryside. Morpheus has commissioned him to write the play *A Midsummer Night's Dream,* and to perform it here in the middle of nowhere. When the troupe is ready, Auberon and Titania, king and queen of Faerie, step into this world from their own realm, accompanied by their entire court.

At the intermission the hobgoblin Robin Goodfellow takes the place of the actor who has been performing the role of Puck. The leading man, Richard Burbage, makes the mistake of asking Auberon for gold in payment for their entertainment, which he hands over with grim intent. Titania takes Shakespeare's disgruntled son, Hamnet, aside and speaks sweetly to him about the beauty and magic of her realm.

Morpheus tells Titania and Auberon that during their time on Earth, the Fay have given him much amusement and entertainment, and he wished to pay them back. Though they might never return to this realm, thanks to his efforts through Shakespeare, humanity will remember them always. They thank him for his gift.

When Auberon and Titania and their court depart, Robin Goodfellow—the trickster, Puck—stays behind. In the morning, Shakespeare's troupe wakes, disoriented. Richard Burbage finds that the pouch of gold he received in payment is filled with flowers instead. Hamnet tells his father he had a strange dream about a woman who wanted him to go home with her. A final note reveals that Hamnet died in 1596, three years later, at the age of eleven, and that the whereabouts of Robin Goodfellow are unknown.

PEOPLE, PLACES, AND THINGS

MORPHEUS (DREAM). The Dream King, Lord of Dreams, the Sandman.

WILLIAM SHAKESPEARE. In 1589, the Dream King met Shakespeare in a tavern. Overhearing the playwright bemoaning the tragedy that his talents did not live up to his ambitions to inspire the dreams of mankind, Morpheus made a bargain with him. In exchange for inspiration, Shakespeare would write two plays for

Morpheus. The first of them is *A Midsummer Night's Dream,* which he has Shakespeare's troupe perform for the king and queen of Faerie and their court as a gift. The second, we learn later in the series, is *The Tempest* (see *The Wake*).

HAMNET SHAKESPEARE. The eight-year-old son of William Shakespeare, he is precociously aware of how little attention his father pays to him. His mother has sent him to spend the summer with his father, and he has been put to use in a female role in the production of *A Midsummer Night's Dream.* Queen Titania finds him beautiful and asks if he'd like to come and live with her in Faerie. In the morning Hamnet believes it was only a dream, but three years later he is dead, begging the question of whether his spirit rested in peace, or somehow ended up in Faerie.

AUBERON. King of Faerie and husband to Titania, he feels vaguely that he ought to be offended by *A Midsummer Night's Dream,* but instead he appreciates this strange gift that Morpheus has given them. The Fay (the people of Faerie) had left the human realm years before and never intended to return. This afternoon, when they come through to watch Shakespeare's play, is the last time they will visit the human world.

TITANIA. Queen of Faerie, she becomes intrigued by Hamnet Shakespeare and tempts him with thoughts of returning home with her.

ROBIN GOODFELLOW. The trickster Puck of *A Midsummer Night's Dream* is the fool of the Faerie court. When the rest leave the human world forever, Robin Goodfellow remains behind, hungry for mischief. His presence will be felt in *The Kindly Ones,* later in the series.

#20 "FAÇADE"

(ILLUSTRATED BY COLLEEN DORAN AND MALCOLM JONES III)

Once upon a time, Urania Blackwell was employed by "the Company" (presumably the CIA). On a mission, she found herself in a tomb in Egypt—the very same tomb where Rex Mason once touched the Orb of Ra and found himself transformed into the DC universe hero Metamorpho. "Rainie" Blackwell also came into contact with the orb, and she became Element Girl, able to alter her physical makeup on a chemical and molecular level, including molding her features any way she wishes. She will not transmute herself into flesh; she tried it once and it smelled like rotten meat. The easiest thing for her to do is create a face out of silicate, which dries and falls off after a while.

She now lives in a small apartment surrounded by masks that hang on the walls. The masks are the faces she has created for herself in the past, now fallen away and hardened. Nobody calls and nobody comes to visit, and the best she can hope for is a weekly phone call with her contact at the Company, the man who makes sure that her pension check arrives.

Lost and alone, she is joined in the room by Death of the Endless, who observes that people are always holding onto old identities, old faces and masks, long after they've served their purpose, but that they've got to learn to throw things away eventually.

Rainie confesses that she's thought about killing herself but is not sure she even *can* die. When Rainie realizes who she's talking to, she is excited, thinking that Death has come for her.

Seeing Rainie's desperation, Death decides to help. She reminds Rainie that Ra made her this way, and Ra can undo what he has done. Ra is not only in the orb Rainie touched in Egypt, but in the sun itself. All she has to do is talk to him. At the window, Rainie does precisely that. She calls out, asking for Ra to end it for her, and she sees that the sun is also a mask, and behind it is a beautiful face. Then she is changed into a statue of sand or salt, which sifts down into a pile of grains on the floor, beside one of Rainie's cast-off faces.

PEOPLE, PLACES, AND THINGS

URANIA BLACKWELL. "Rainie" Blackwell was a member of the Company before being exposed to the Orb of Ra, which transformed her into a metamorphae—a shape-changer able to alter the chemical composition of her body. Living in an apartment building, alone and lonely, relying on her pension because she's unable to work for the Company anymore, Rainie wants to die but can't figure out a method of suicide that would actually end her life.

DELLA KARIAKIS. An old friend of Rainie's from the Company, Della invites her out to lunch in order to have someone with whom she can share the secret that she is pregnant. At lunch, the silicate face that Rainie has created for herself hardens and falls off, horrifying Della.

DEATH. Death of the Endless has come to the building to retrieve a woman who has died there, but on her way out she hears Rainie crying and enters her apartment. She assures Rainie that even a metamorph will die eventually, but that she hasn't come for Rainie yet. Taking pity on Rainie, she tells her to ask Ra to end her life. Looking out at the sun, Rainie does so, and Ra complies.

TRIVIA

- Urania Blackwell, aka Element Girl, was introduced in the 1960s DC comic *Metamorpho, The Element Man* (17 issues, 1965–68), written by Bob Haney and illustrated by the most prominent female cartoonist of DC's Silver Age, Ramona Fradon. Metamorpho was originally introduced in *The Brave and the Bold* issues 57 and 58 (1964), and the lovely, green-haired Urania was among the comic's excellent supporting cast. Though Metamorpho reappeared years later (as a backup series in *Action Comics* issues 413 through 418, and as a regular in *Batman and the Outsiders* and *Justice League Europe*, among others), Element Girl had been almost completely forgotten until Gaiman detailed the moving final chapter in Urania's life in this issue of *The Sandman*.

- The Shakespeare play that Gaiman uses as the foundation of issue 19, "A Midsummer Night's Dream," revolves around the wedding of the Amazonian queen Hippolyta and Duke Theseus of Athens, and takes places simultaneously in an earthly forest and in the world of Faerie. The play opens with a young woman named Hermia running off with her lover, Lysander, to avoid marrying Demetrius, whom her father has chosen as her husband. Demetrius and a girl named Helena give chase. Meanwhile, Oberon and Titania, the king and queen of Faerie, arrive in the forest outside of Athens, where Titania plans to remain until after the wedding of Hippolyta and Theseus. Perturbed with his queen, Oberon enlists the aid of the trickster, Puck, who provides an ointment which, when put into Titania's eyes, will make her fall in love with the first creature she sees. Oberon intends to distract his wife and, thus, win their argument.

  With a single error on Puck's part, the entire cast is thrust into a sex farce of false identity, love potions gone wrong, and embarrassing situations. This includes a troupe of actors performing a play in a clearing (one of whom has his head turned into a donkey's—who is of course the one Titania is bewitched into loving).

  In the end, Theseus and Hippolyta arrive for their wedding and arrange a multiple ceremony, in which Demetrius marries Helena, and Hermia takes Lysander as her husband. All those who experienced the bizarre night choose to believe it was all a dream.

- *A Midsummer Night's Dream* was adapted to comics for the first time in *Classics Illustrated* issue 87 (September 1951), featuring art by Alex Blum; it was reprinted by Acclaim as Classics Illustrated number 9 (1997). Another graphic novel adaptation was published in Pocket Classics Vol. 7: *William Shakespeare's "A Midsummer Night's Dream"* (1984). Gaiman may well have seen future Stardust collaborator Charles Vess's early work in the illustrations Vess did for the Donning/Starblaze edition of *A Midsummer Night's Dream* in 1988. Gaiman first met Vess in person in 1989 at Comic-Con International convention in San Diego.

THE QUOTABLE GAIMAN

On "A Dream of a Thousand Cats":

So I thought, why not do a story about cats changing reality, with a light touch—similar to Fritz Leiber's 1958 story "Space Time for Springers"? I decided it should be based around the idea that cats once ruled the world—and whether that happens to be true or not, it's the story cats tell other cats.

—*The Sandman Companion,* by Hy Bender

||||||||||||||||||||||||||||||||||||||||||||||||||||||||||||||||||||||||

VOLUME FOUR:
SEASON OF MISTS

(1990—91)

*S**eason of Mists* is Gaiman's second opus in the Sandman series (*The Doll's House* being the first). It ranges from Destiny's garden to the Silver City, where the angels reside, from the Dreaming to Hell, and includes appearances from gods and mystical figures from various myths and legendary pantheons.

And, yet, for all of that, it doesn't really *feel* like an opus.

Rather, Gaiman continues to weight the scales in favor of intimacy, taking the vast metaphysical structure of the mythology he's created and telling a story about intimacy, regret, recrimination, and epiphany.

As the story opens and the Endless gather—minus one sibling—it is like the reunion of any dysfunctional family. Although Desire has been instigating trouble for Dream for so long that his frustration boils over, her accusations about his abuse of his former lover, Nada, still sting. And when Death, the sibling to whom Dream is closest, agrees with Desire, he is shocked and shamed.

The result is the next phase in a humanization of Morpheus that began in the first volume of *The Sandman* and continues throughout the series. That isn't to say that Dream becomes more ordinary. But from his acceptance of Hob Gadling's friendship and his treatment of Rose Walker in *The Doll's House,* to the fear and doubt and compassion he shows in *Season of Mists,* it is clear that the distance previously held between Dream and humanity is narrowing.

Much of the first half of the series is about him fulfilling his role as one of the Endless—ancient beings, predating the concept of godhood—realizing that, although his lofty station might give him reason to be haughty, and to perceive the needs of humanity as beneath his own, in truth it gives him a responsibility to them as well. It is out of self-centered arrogance and caprice that Morpheus banished Nada to eternal torment in Hell (traits which also cause him to mistreat his own son, as we shall see later). Such behavior seems unsurprising from one of the Endless as compared to the gods of legend. But from the modern Morpheus that callousness is shocking.

In *Season of Mists,* Morpheus is still adjusting, his attitudes seemingly falling somewhere between the callous disregard of the other Endless and the compassionate practicality of his sister Death. When she admonishes him for his treatment of Nada, he is ashamed, and sets out to free her. Yet even that is only the beginning of this episode of his evolution. Upon arriving in Hell, he discovers that Lucifer has had an epiphany as well—tired, he doesn't want to rule Hell anymore. For his own benefit, and perhaps also as the perfect way to torment Morpheus for past wrongs (see *Preludes & Nocturnes*), he hands over a key symbolizing ownership of, and the responsibility for, Hell to the Dream King.

While others covet the key, Morpheus is burdened by it. Out of all the beings of power, only he does not want the key, because he has no interest in ruling Hell. When the angels inform him that God—the Creator—wants the key, he sees it as the perfect way out. After all, he cannot be faulted by those who wanted Hell if the one who created it wants it back. What his decision might otherwise have been, we can never know, but it is in the sleepless night he spends on his throne contemplating that dilemma that Morpheus seems most human. And when he frees Nada at last, only to have her refuse him one final time, the reader cannot be surprised when his initial pique quickly softens to gentle acceptance and benevolence. Morpheus is changing.

The theme of imprisonment and liberty recurs here once again. Gaiman touched on this many times throughout the series. Morpheus himself was imprisoned and released, of course, and past volumes echoed that arc. In *Season of Mists* the theme is returned to again and again. Nada, of course, is imprisoned in Hell and finally given release not only from her suffering but from the life and memory she leaves behind upon her reincarnation.

Lucifer's abdication of the throne of Hell is certainly also an escape from confinement—in this case, responsibility. Lucifer and dead English schoolboy Charles Rowland both make it clear that Hell is of one's own making. The damned damn themselves and are punished, because it fulfills their expectations. Lucifer banishes the damned and the demons, and in so doing releases himself from a Hell largely of his own making. He went along with the Creator's plan, but now he is leaving all of that behind. The sight of him relaxing—and smiling—on a beach at the end of this volume is the perfect picture of the liberty that release from confinement (even of one's own creation) brings.

Edwin Paine, one of the dead driven from Hell, returns to the English boarding school he once attended and to the attic where he was murdered. He thinks himself trapped there with his bones. But upon his own death, fellow student Charles Rowland convinces him that there is no reason to remain behind, that that's part of growing up. You don't have to stay anywhere forever, particularly in the role prescribed for you by others.

By the time The Sandman comes to its conclusion, six volumes from now, it is this theme that will echo most powerfully and make the ending not at all surprising to anyone who has been paying close attention.

The presence of Loki is significant here for several reasons. In the pages of The Sandman, his escape will have major repercussions in later volumes. But, more important to the overall examination of Gaiman's works, the appearance of Loki, Odin, and Thor—and to a lesser extent the pantheons of other mythologies—is an early example of the author exploring some of the themes, ideas, and mythological characters that would appear later in his breakthrough novel, the New York Times bestseller *American Gods*.

Issue 21 is illustrated by Mike Dringenberg and Malcolm Jones III; issues 22 and 23, by Kelley Jones and Malcolm Jones III; issue 24, by Kelley Jones and P. Craig Russell; issue 25, by Matt Wagner; issue 26, by Kelley Jones and George Pratt; issue 27 by Kelley Jones and Dick Giordano; and issue 28, by Mike Dringenberg and George Pratt.

#21 "SEASON OF MISTS: A PROLOGUE"

In a place that is not of the world, Destiny of the Endless walks through his garden, book in hand. When the Three Witches—in this guise, the Grey Ladies, the Fates—appear to Destiny, making dire predictions about the oldest battle beginning again. Destiny has no choice but to call for a family gathering.

None of the Endless want to be there, especially Dream. Destiny has summoned them because they are meant to be in this place at this time. Desire—having already caused a great deal of trouble for Dream—baits him with snide remarks about his love life, especially his history with Calliope and with Nada, who has endured thousands of years of punishment in Hell because she would not obey him.

Furious, Dream storms out of the chamber and retires to a balcony overlooking Destiny's garden.

Death joins him outside where they discuss Desire's comments. To Dream's astonishment, Death agrees that his treatment of Nada was far too harsh a punishment for the crime of simply having enough sense to say no to him.

Because he trusts her, Dream takes Death's admonishment to heart. He therefore decides that he must travel to Hell to free Nada. The events foreseen by the Fates have been set in motion.

#22 "SEASON OF MISTS: CHAPTER ONE"

Lucien and Matthew the Raven are chatting in Lucien's library, which contains all the stories ever conceived, written and unwritten. Summoned to Morpheus's throne room, they discover the entire palace staff. Morpheus tells them that he has to go away, and that he might be gone quite a while.

Dream explains to those gathered there that ten thousand years past he loved a woman, but when the relationship ended badly, with her suicide, he condemned her to Hell until such time as he might forgive her. He now intends to go to Hell to free her. Given that the last time he visited Hell he made the powerful Lucifer look foolish in front of his minions, this could be a very dangerous, even fatal, trip.

At the home of Hippolyta Hall, Dream appears in the room of her unnamed newborn. Lyta is furious at him just for being there, blaming him for the death of her husband. But Morpheus has only come to visit, telling her there is much she doesn't understand. It has been a very long time since a child had gestated in the realm of dreams. Before he departs he informs Lyta that her baby's name is Daniel.

Next, Morpheus visits the dreams of his one mortal friend, the undying Hob Gadling, bringing a bottle of wine so rare that it probably exists only in dreams. After they share a toast, he departs, leaving Hob the rest of the wine.

Back at Morpheus's palace, Lucien pleads with Dream to reconsider. Explaining that there sometimes is no choice, Morpheus opens a passage out of his realm, and steps through.

#23 "SEASON OF MISTS: CHAPTER TWO"

Morpheus arrives at the main gate of Hell, which stands open. Once inside, he transports himself to the cliffs into which Nada's cell was carved. He discovers that she has been removed, but then his senses reveal to him that it is not merely Nada who is gone.

Hell is empty. The damned souls of humanity and the demons (the "never-born") have all departed. Only Lucifer remains, and when Dream calls to him, he appears. Lucifer explains to Morpheus that he has quit and has sent all of the denizens of Hell away.

The First of the Fallen does not care where the denizens of Hell have gone—Heaven, Earth, limbo, some other realm. He doesn't even know what he'll do next, except explore possibilities, perhaps learn to dance or play the piano, or just relax on a beach somewhere.

Finally, he asks Morpheus to cut off his wings, and the Dream Lord agrees. It is painful, but Lucifer endures it. As he cuts, Morpheus asks what became of Nada, but Lucifer claims he does not know—that she is out there, somewhere, with all of the others he's banished.

Once they are outside the bounds of Hell, Lucifer gives Morpheus its key, making him sole monarch of that damned place. Having sworn to destroy the Dream King, Lucifer doesn't know if this will destroy his enemy, but he is certain it won't make his life any easier.

#24 "SEASON OF MISTS: CHAPTER THREE"

In a cavern underneath the world, the god Loki, bound beneath a snake whose jaws drip a constant trickle of venom, is visited by his father, Odin.

Odin reminds Loki that he is there because he is too cunning and malevolent to be unconfined, that he will not be freed until Ragnarok (the Norse myths' version of Armageddon) comes. But Odin has a new plan. He suggests that he and Loki might leave entirely, that Asgard might be destroyed when Ragnarok comes, but if they are simply not there when it happens, they will survive. Lucifer has left Hell. It stands empty, a possible sanctuary, a protectorate of the Dream King. They can claim it. Loki agrees to help, and the two recruit the dull-witted Thor to their cause.

In his chambers, Dream is approached by one of the guardians of the gates to the Dreaming, and is told that he has many visitors. Odin, Loki, and Thor have come from Asgard. Anubis, Bast, and Bes have come from the Egyptian pantheon. A Japanese myth called Susano-O-No-Mikoto also enters and announces himself. Azazel, the Merkin, and Choronzon represent the former hordes of Hell. A personal slave of Kilderkin, a Lord of Order—represented in this place by a simple cardboard box—carries his master. Shivering Jemmy of the Shallow Brigade is a princess of Chaos in the form of a little girl in clown makeup, carrying a balloon. They all want the key to Hell.

Remiel and Duma, the angels from the Silver City, are there to observe.

Dream welcomes them all and tells them that their suites are being prepared. Tonight there will be a banquet, and tomorrow they will talk.

#25 "SEASON OF MISTS: CHAPTER FOUR"

At St. Hilarion's School For Boys, in England, Charles Rowland comes out of a dream to find himself on the floor of a dusty attic, attended to by another boy whose name is Paine. Rowland tries to piece together his memory of how he came to be here. Forced to remain at the school over the holidays, Rowland was woken one morning by three dead boys—Cheeseman, Barrow, and Skinner. In a school full of dead boys, Rowland followed instructions, but there was no dinner served (the dead don't need to eat). He snuck down to the kitchen that night only to be attacked by the bullies. They began to torture him, but he fell unconscious, and they departed. Edwin Paine found Rowland and helped him, taking the living boy up to the attic.

Now in that attic, Rowland asks Paine what it was like when he died, for Paine is a ghost. Paine admits it was not very pleasant, since he went to Hell.

Paine explains that he is there because his bones are still there, in a trunk in the corner that barely covers the arcane symbols drawn on the floor by the students who sacrificed him in a misguided attempt to raise demons.

On Sunday, Rowland dies. But he and Paine have become friends, and when Death comes to collect him, Rowland refuses to go with her. Frustrated and overwhelmed by the chaos that Lucifer's closing of Hell has caused, Death can't be bothered with him. She tells him that she'll be back for him when things are "less crazy," and departs.

Once Death is gone, Rowland makes to leave the attic. Paine is afraid. He doesn't want to leave his bones behind. But Rowland urges him on, and Paine relents. It's part of growing up, he realizes: "You always have to leave something behind you." They debate the qualities of Hell. Rowland believes that it is self-inflicted—echoing Lucifer's statements earlier in the story—while Paine believes that Hell *is* a place, but that no one has to stay anywhere, even in Hell, forever.

#26 "SEASON OF MISTS: CHAPTER FIVE"

Lord Cluracan of Faerie and his sister, Nuala, arrive at the palace of the Dream King. Auberon and Titania, the king and queen of Faerie, have sent Cluracan to lobby Morpheus to keep Hell empty. In exchange, the rulers of Faerie would give Dream many things, and as an example, Cluracan gives Nuala to him.

At the banquet, each of the envoys approach Morpheus, requesting private audiences. He promises to see them all in his chambers that night.

One by one, the envoys visit Dream's chambers, each with their own promises, entreaties, or threats.

Bast, for instance, says she knows where his prodigal brother, Destruction, is, and will tell him in exchange for Hell. Azazel offers Nada but also the demon Choronzon, who once challenged Morpheus in Hell. If Dream refuses, Azazel will consume Nada, so the last fragment of her essence will be inside him forever.

Morpheus sends them all away with a promise that he will make his decision and announce it the next day. He sits alone in his chambers, holding the key, wishing he could simply throw it away.

#27 "SEASON OF MISTS: CHAPTER SIX"

As he prepares to go announce his decision, Dream is visited in his chambers by Remiel and Duma, the angels. Remiel has a message from the Creator; Hell is the reflection of Heaven, and without it, Heaven has no meaning. To Remiel's horror, he and Duma have been instructed to take control of Hell, and never again return to the Silver City or be in the presence of the Creator.

Morpheus, Remiel, and Duma appear before the gathered delegations and Dream announces his decision, much to the fury of his other guests. When it is pointed out that Morpheus does not have to accede to the wishes of the creator of Hell, he notes that he is not the one who created Heaven or Hell, and if its creator wishes to have it back, that is not his affair.

Enraged, Azazel tells Morpheus that he will devour Nada's soul. Morpheus reminds him that he offered his hospitality—including his protection—to all of his visitors, which includes both those he knew about and those he did not. That means he will not allow Nada or Choronzon to be harmed. Azazel challenges him, but has made a mistake, attacking Morpheus in the heart of the Dreaming.

Reality conforms to *his* wishes, here. Azazel is captured within a glass jar and placed with a number of other trinkets inside an old trunk.

#24 "SEASON OF MISTS: CHAPTER 8"

In Hell, Remiel watches the demons return, while silent Duma looks away. Soon the damned will also return.

At dinner—in the aspect that Nada first fell in love with—Dream sits across from her. One last time, he suggests that she could remain in the Dreaming as his queen, but again she refuses. Nada tells him that he could give it all up and be with her, but Dream cannot abandon his responsibilities. All that remains is to discuss what will become of her now.

Cluracan and Nuala make ready to depart, but Cluracan reveals that Nuala cannot come with him. She was a gift from Titania, and Morpheus has accepted that gift. They both risk the ire of the queen of Faerie if Nuala does not stay. Morpheus agrees, but removes the glamour that makes Nuala regal and beautiful. He dislikes "little magics."

Nada appears, ready to depart as well. Dream wishes she would not leave so soon, but she has decided. He offered her two choices, and she has chosen to be reincarnated. She will not remember him, but he will always remember her, and when she is reborn as a baby, he goes to her and tells her that she is always welcome in the Dreaming, no matter what body she wears.

On a beach on the Australian coast, Lucifer sits and watches the sunset, which he deems "bloody marvelous."

The tale ends as it began, with Destiny walking in his garden, reading from his book, and as he closes it, the story concludes.

PEOPLE, PLACES, AND THINGS

MORPHEUS (DREAM). The Sandman. The Dream King. The Lord of Dreams. Aside from Destiny, he is the one of the Endless most conscious of his responsibilities. When Desire castigates him for his treatment of Nada—whom he consigned to Hell after she spurned him—he seeks the counsel of Death. But when Death surprises him by agreeing, with their sister Dream sets out to free Nada.

DESTINY. The eldest of the Endless, he wanders his garden, reading from his book. He casts no shadow, and leaves no footprints. Approached by the Fates with dire predictions about what's to come, he realizes he must gather the Endless, causing the argument that sets events in motion.

DEATH. The second eldest of the Endless, she admonishes Dream for his treatment of Nada, prompting him to vow to go to Hell and free her. Lucifer's banishment of the dead from Hell makes her duties quite chaotic for a time.

DELIRIUM. The youngest of the Endless, she is a curious, tragic figure. Once she was Delight.

DESPAIR. The twin of Desire.

DESIRE. The twin of Despair, she/he/it seems to love nothing better than causing trouble for Dream. Though she manipulated him into falling in love with Nada in the first place, she/he/it takes issue with his treatment of her.

LUCIFER. The First of the Fallen, Lucifer Morningstar was once the angel Samael, before he rebelled against the Creator and was cast out of Heaven and the Silver City of the angels. Prompted partially by the news that Morpheus is coming to Hell to free Nada, he decides to quit his post as ruler of Hell. He sends the demons and the damned souls out of Hell, locks all of the gates, and gives the key to Morpheus to do with as he wishes. His travels take him to the beaches of Australia, and in time, to many other places as well (see *The Kindly Ones*).

NADA. Once the queen of an ancient African city, she was manipulated by Desire and fell in love with Dream. Morpheus, in turn, fell in love with her, and asked her to be his queen. Realizing that only tragedy could come from love between a mortal and one of the Endless, Nada refused him. Spurned, Dream consigned her to suffering in Hell until such time as he might forgive her. Ten thousand years later he frees her at last, and she is reincarnated into a new life, with no memory of her prior existence, or of the Sandman.

THE THREE WITCHES. They have many faces and here appear as the Grey Ladies, or the Fates, with a dire warning for Destiny of the Endless.

MATTHEW THE RAVEN. A loyal servant of Morpheus, he was once a man, but is now a dream.

LUCIEN. The librarian of the Dreaming, as well as Dream's most trusted servant.

CAIN. Son of Eve, brother and slayer of Abel, and a resident of the Dreaming, he is sent to Hell with a message from Morpheus, safe because the Creator marked him and commanded that no one ever kill him.

LYTA HALL. A former superhero and the widow of Hector Hall, she lived for a time in the Dreaming. While pregnant, she carried her child the entire time she inhabited that sphere. Since the child gestated in the Dreaming, Morpheus has claimed the boy as his own, and even given him a name—Daniel. One day, he has told Lyta, he will return for Daniel.

HOB GADLING. Dream's only mortal friend.

DUMA. The angel of silence, one of the two to whom the Creator entrusts the key to Hell and the duty to oversee its functions.

REMIEL. The other angel sent to oversee the disposition of the key to Hell, only to find that the Creator has entrusted it to him and Duma, and given them the responsibility to rule Hell.

AZAZEL. Formerly a member of the ruling triumverate of Hell, this demon was driven out by Lucifer. The demons in Limbo support his bid to take over, and Azazel goes to the Dreaming to get the key. He offers Dream vengeance on Choronzon and the soul of Nada. When Dream gives the key to the angels, Azazel attempts to destroy Morpheus, but his efforts are useless in the Dreaming. Morpheus captures him and puts him away in a jar, intending to give Azazel eons to ponder his errors.

THE MERKIN. A demon of Hell, cast out to Limbo, who aids Azazel's plans.

CHORONZON. A demon who once challenged Morpheus for possession of his helm, he is betrayed by Azazel and offered as a prize to the Dream King in exchange for the key to Hell. But Morpheus refuses and rescues Choronzon from Azazel's cruelty.

CLURACAN. An envoy sent by the king and queen of Faerie, Lord Cluracan comes to the Dreaming in hopes of persuading Morpheus to leave Hell empty, and to not give the key to anyone.

NUALA. The sister of Cluracan, she is given to Morpheus as a gift from Queen Titania of Faerie.

ODIN. The one-eyed king of the gods of Asgard, he travels to the Dreaming, hoping to persuade Morpheus to give him the key to Hell.

LOKI. The trickster god of Norse myth, he accompanies Odin. He has been kept for twelve hundred years in a cavern under the world, tied down, with the venom of a serpent dripping down onto his body and into his eyes. While in the Dreaming, he uses magic to swap places with another, but is discovered by Morpheus. Dream makes a bargain with him, that he will put a dream image of Loki in that cavern, allowing Loki to be free in exchange for some favor, but precisely what that might be is not revealed.

THOR. Norse god of storms, he is a drunk and a boor.

KILDERKIN. A lord of Order, sent to attempt to get the key to Hell from Morpheus.

SHIVERING JEMMY. A princess of Chaos, who tries to threaten Morpheus into surrendering the key to Hell.

ANUBIS. A god of Egypt, Anubis travels to the Dreaming, hoping to receive the key to Hell.

BAST. A god of Egypt, Bast travels with Anubis to the Dreaming. She tells Dream she knows the location of his prodigal brother, and is willing to divulge it in exchange for the key.

BES. Part of the delegation from the Egyptian pantheon.

SUSANO-O-NO-MIKOTO. Representing only himself and not his pantheon, this god of Nippon comes to the Dreaming in hopes of acquiring Hell to add to his mother's existing underworld.

CHARLES ROWLAND. A young boy at an English boarding school, Charles is left behind over the Christmas holiday because his father has been taken hostage by Iraqi forces. When Lucifer sends the dead out from Hell, the school's own dead return, and for a time Charles walks among them, and he is befriended by the dead form of Edwin Paine, a boy who'd attended the school many decades before. When Charles dies, and Death comes to collect him, he refuses to accompany her, and he and Edwin go off together to have adventures until she comes back to claim them.

EDWIN PAINE. When the dead are banished from Hell, Edwin Paine returns to the earthly plane, and to the school where he was murdered in an occult ritual. There he befriends the still-living Charles Rowland. After Charles dies, the two go off to have adventures together, until Death can return to claim them at last.

CHEESEMAN, BARROW, AND SKINNER. School bullies, dead boys, and the murderers of Edwin Paine.

TRIVIA

- The version of Lucifer first introduced in *Season of Mists* (the changes in the character are significant enough to set him apart even from the portrayal in earlier volumes of *The Sandman*) was spun off into his own series. Written by Mike Carey, the spin-off ran seventy-five issues, with the vast majority of art chores by Peter Gross, Dean Ormston, and Ryan Kelly.

- Gaiman returned to the characters of Charles Rowland and Edwin Paine in the two bookend issues of DC/Vertigo's crossover event *The Children's Crusade,* christening them "The Dead Boy Detectives." The characters went on to headline a four-issue miniseries written by Ed Brubaker and illustrated by Bryan Talbot, and a graphic novel by Jill Thompson. They also made brief appearances in the series *The Books of Magic,* another spin-off from a separate Gaiman project at Vertigo.

- Bast is featured in a 2003 three-issue miniseries, *Bast: Eternity Games,* written by Caitlin R. Kiernan and penciled by Joe Bennett.

THE QUOTABLE GAIMAN

On Lucifer's appearance:

My mental picture was of David Bowie, back when he was a nineteen-year-old hippie. A junkie angel with a cruel slyness—but still an angel, soft and beautiful.
—*The Sandman Companion,* by Hy Bender

IIIIIIIIIIIIIIIIIIIIIIIIIIIIIIIIIIIIIIIIIIIIIIIIIIIIIIIIIIIIIIIIIIIIIIIII

VOLUME FIVE:
A GAME OF YOU

(1991—92)

In the fifth volume of The Sandman—*A Game of You*—Neil Gaiman continued to weave a tapestry of interconnected narrative and thematic threads. As he did in previous volumes, Gaiman returns to a previously peripheral character and brings her to center stage. In this case, it's Barbie, the Florida blonde from the pages of *A Doll's House,* who is now divorced from the shallow husband—Ken—she was partnered with there.

Barbie has left Florida for New York, where she lives in an apartment building populated almost entirely by women. Besides a female landlord, there's a pre-operative transsexual named Wanda, a bookish witch called Thessaly, and a young lesbian couple named Hazel and Foxglove. In such a female-centric story, it comes as no surprise that the lone male in the building, George, is a vessel of malicious intent sent by the villain of the piece, the Cuckoo.

Within the Dreaming, there are shoals—distant islands of dreams, whole archipelagos of scattered dream worlds and fantasy realms. Once, long ago, Morpheus made a deal with a woman named Alianora that required the creation of one such shoal, called "the Land." Part of that deal was that when she summoned him back, he would uncreate the Land and grant her a boon. But Alianora died.

As a child, Barbie began dreaming of the Land while sleeping. She didn't invent the place, but she visited there and had continuing adventures, every night. Due to her contact with the dream vortex in *The Doll's House,* however, Barbie stopped dreaming altogether, cutting her off from the Land—and sealing it off from the rest of the Dreaming. The Cuckoo, a fragment of a dream trapped in the Land, did not like being trapped, and conspired to find a way to retrieve a talisman called the Porpentine. Joined with an obelisk called the Hierogram, it would destroy the Land and free the Cuckoo to fly to other realms.

Though Morpheus will eventually set all to rights, Barbie is drawn into the Land. Hazel and Foxglove follow, with the help of the witch, Thessaly, who is furious that the Cuckoo's servants tried to harm her.

A Game of You is populated with wonderfully drawn characters, including a prominent example of an ordinary lesbian couple that was rare in mainstream popular entertainment at the time. Hazel's discovery that she has gotten pregnant from a drunken one-night stand is portrayed with such innocence, and her relief at Foxglove's acceptance and forgiveness so poignant, that these characters become just as interesting and vital as the protagonist. Wanda's struggle with gender identity is rendered with respect and wonderful humor, so that instead of becoming either caricature or political statement, she is a human being.

In the course of preparing this book, we asked Gaiman if Hazel and Foxglove were based on real-life models, people he knew in his own life, and what the reception to those characters was at the time of the story's publication.

"Well, bits of Hazel's behaviour—her utter innocence about heterosexual sex and reproduction—was borrowed from a lesbian friend," Gaiman explains, "who did indeed call me up to ask how to find out if she was pregnant, because she'd let a boy into her bed, but they couldn't have actually done it because he was drunk. . . ." And there were bits of lots of people I knew in London at the time in them and in Wanda.

"The 'I don't like dogs' lady [Maisie Hill] was on a tube train. She had a plastic policeman's hat on, and was in her midtwenties.

"The reaction was, as far as I remember, one of vague disgruntlement. But that had more to do with people wanting more Dream and less New York grunge. At DC I had a fight with editorial over the use of the word 'dyke,' which was what all my lesbian friends called each other, and Alisa Kwitney had to go downtown and ask real lesbians if it was offensive or not—and it's still in there, so I imagine that the answer was no."

The recurring themes in *A Game of You* manifest as the story's revelations unfold. This story arc, perhaps more than any of the others, is layered with themes that ripple in both directions, back toward the beginning and onward toward the end of the tale. Hazel's view of bad dreams is fascinating. Believing that the truly frightening aspect of them is that they come from inside us, she maintains that having bad dreams is an act of self-betrayal. In other words, the wounds inflicted by nightmares are self-inflicted. The similarity to Lucifer's take on Hell is inescapable.

Gaiman also returns here to the overarching theme of *A Doll's House,* the question of whether humans are simply toys in the hands of some larger force. In *A Game of You,* Barbie's loyal dream friends turn out to be her own inventions, created to populate the preexisting Land, based on her favorite childhood toys.

The theme of imprisonment and freedom recurs as well, though in this case it is the imprisonment of the antagonist, the Cuckoo. As merciless as the Cuckoo is portrayed, and though Barbie considers killing it, when it is finally freed, its joy is infectious. It is a childlike thing, and it only ever wanted to be free to fly. The Cuckoo's liberty is a by-product of Barbie's request that Morpheus send them all home, safe and sound, which also means freeing Hazel, Foxglove, and Thessaly from being imprisoned in this now vacant corner of the Dreaming.

Together, those three also make their own sort of witch trio, a reflection of the Three Witches/The Fates/The Furies (and, later, The Kindly Ones). When Thessaly draws down the moon, using menstrual blood to conduct a very female ritual to summon it, it also appears as a three-faced goddess. The Three Witches are nearly always maiden, mother, and crone. In this case, Foxglove represents the maiden, pregnant Hazel the mother, and Thessaly (cute, but actually quite ancient), the crone.

There is another parallel to the trio of Foxglove, Hazel, and Thessaly, however. Gaiman frequently includes references to *The Wizard of Oz* in The Sandman, and its influences are omnipresent in *A Game of You*. Barbie is Dorothy, of course, although she has two sets of companions. In the Land, they are Luz, Prinado, and Wilkinson. Barbie actually compares the magical path they follow to the yellow brick road. But in the real world—and then traveling the moon's path to join her in the Land—Foxglove, Hazel, and Thessaly are the Tin Man, Scarecrow, and Lion of the piece. The Cuckoo may be both witch and wizard combined, and there are myriad other points of comparison. Suffice to say that Oz's influence is felt throughout the piece, particularly when Barbie says that she's going to take "the Dorothy option," and wish them all home.

The story itself—a woman who discovers that her dream world is real and must travel there to preserve it or set things right—is not unique. Gaiman's execution, characters, and themes are, as always, what make his story so effective. In addition to Oz, *The Chronicles of Narnia* comes to mind, though Narnia was never like this. A careful reader cannot fail to notice Gaiman's thank-you to Jonathan Carroll in the afterword. The novelist—whose first novel, *The Land of Laughs,* covered similar territory—apparently encouraged Gaiman to forge ahead with plans for *A Game of You*. In that afterword, Gaiman reflects that Carroll taught him "one of the purposes of a writer is to write it new," presumably meaning that though the stories traveled some of the same paths, originality was what mattered.

The issue of identity also comes frequently into play in this six-issue arc. Thessaly's true identity is not known by her neighbors. Wanda is struggling with identity issues defined by her efforts to live as a woman. Foxglove does not use her real name, which is Donna. Barbie once lived with Ken in her dream house in Florida, and now regularly reinvents herself with makeup, never wanting to be the same person twice. While some of them seem to be hiding their true identity, and others searching for it, there seems to be a strong argument for the idea that they are all doing both.

Finally, one theme that comes up in this arc echoes not other themes in *The

Sandman, but a different Gaiman work entirely. As the Cuckoo tells Barbie, little girls dream different dreams than little boys. Among the things girls dream is that "your parents are not your parents," an idea that Gaiman followed up to great effect in his young adult novel *Coraline*.

Issues 32, 33, 35, and 37 of *The Sandman* are illustrated by Shawn McManus; issue 34, by Colleen Doran, George Pratt, and Dick Giordano; and issue 36 by McManus, Bryan Talbot, and Stan Woch.

#32 "A GAME OF YOU, CHAPTER ONE: SLAUGHTER ON FIFTH AVENUE"

In the Dreaming, Morpheus has sensed something amiss. One of the skerries—distant islets in the shoals of dream—is dying.

On the subway, Barbie tells Wanda again that she doesn't dream at all. She used to dream every night, a series of stories about another land, but something happened to her dreams one strange night (as seen in *A Doll's House*), shortly before she ended her relationship with her ex, Ken, and she doesn't dream anymore.

Nearby, Martin Tenbones—a huge, shaggy, doglike creature—sets off in search of Princess Barbara, hoping that Murphy (the god of the Land) will protect him. When Barbie and Wanda come around the corner and see Martin Tenbones, Barbie recognizes him immediately, and speaks his name. Martin sees her and calls out to his princess, just before the police, considering the creature a danger, open fire.

Before he dies Martin Tenbones tells Barbie that the Cuckoo threatens the Land, and that he has come for her help. Martin insists that she take the Porpentine—a gem-encrusted amulet—which he carries around his neck.

Back in her apartment, a tearful Barbie stares at the Porpentine in astonishment, recognizing it—and Martin—as things that she had thought existed only in her long-ago dreams. When she mentions "the Cuckoo" out loud, she has a momentary vision of a flock of dark birds in her apartment, but they quickly fade. In the hallway, a tenant named George sits on the stairs. A bird lands in his hands. He picks it up, opens his mouth, and slides it down his gullet. George either always was, or has become, one of the Children of the Cuckoo, and he means to harm Princess Barbara.

#33 "A GAME OF YOU, CHAPTER TWO: LULLABIES OF BROADWAY"

A fellow tenant named Hazel pays a visit to Barbie's apartment in search of advice. Though Hazel is a lesbian, she recently had a drunken fling with a male coworker, and thinks she might be pregnant.

Later, Barbie falls asleep and finds her way through a set of curtains, and into the Land, where a trench-coated rodent named Wilkinson is waiting.

While everyone else in the building sleeps, George opens his chest, exposing his rib cage, and releasing a quartet of birds that has been hiding there. Wanda, Hazel, and her girlfriend Foxglove have terrifying nightmares. Hazel's, in particular, is deeply disturbing. Foxglove's real name is revealed to be Donna, and we discover that two years earlier she was the girlfriend of a woman named Judy, who died at the hands of Dr. Destiny when he got his hands on Morpheus's ruby (as seen in *Preludes & Nocturnes*).

The birds are bringing these nightmares, but when one of them attempts to do the same to a tenant named Thessaly, she wakes and grabs it from the air. She understands what it is, and it incinerates in her hands. Thessaly is clearly more than she appears. Armed with a very sharp knife, she goes upstairs to visit George.

In the Land, Princess Barbara is reunited with her friends, the parrot, Luz, and the organ grinder's monkey, Prinado, and tells them of Martin Tenbones's death. The princess has to reach a place called the Brightly Shining Sea, which will mean avoiding the Black Guard and getting past the citadel of the Cuckoo.

#34 "A GAME OF YOU, CHAPTER THREE: BAD MOON RISING"

Thessaly gathers Hazel, Foxglove, and Wanda—all of them recovering from their bad dreams, and they go to check on Barbie.

Inside Barbie's apartment they find her unconscious. Thessaly asks Wanda to carry Barbie up to George's apartment while she gets some things. When Thessaly enters George's apartment, the others ask where George is, and Thessaly explains that he's in the bathtub—she killed him.

Wanda tries to leave the room but discovers that Thessaly has taken control of her and her companions.

Thessaly cuts off George's face and hangs it on the wall. She removes his eyes and tongue and puts them in place on the hanging face, summoning George to speak to her. At Thessaly's command, George admits that he is a servant of the Cuckoo. The Children of the Cuckoo were trying to consume the other residents in the building to make one of them destroy the Porpentine. Thessaly wants to know where to find the Cuckoo, and George says it can be found in Barbie's dream.

There are two ways into the dreams of another: through the Dream King, or by the moon's road.

Thessaly calls upon the moon—a variation of the three-who-are-one, the Fates or Furies or Witches and commands them to take her, Foxglove, and Hazel into Barbie's dream. Wanda must remain—she cannot travel this way, because she isn't physically a woman—and is angry and frustrated. But Thessaly assures her that her duty is vital, that someone must protect Barbie's body.

#35 "A GAME OF YOU, CHAPTER FOUR: BEGINNING TO SEE THE LIGHT"

In the Land, Barbie, learns that though she dreams herself, she did not create the Land. It existed before her, and she simply comes there when she dreams.

In the Dreaming, Lucien has come with a map of the skerries to show Morpheus which one is crumbling. This particular skerry was involved in an ancient compact, but Morpheus had thought the skerry, and the compact, to have dissipated long ago.

Barbie and her friends find themselves on a cliff overlooking a town near the Brightly Shining Sea. Luz flies down to the town to seek out the resistance and bring back help.

Back in New York, George tells Wanda that Thessaly has done something dangerous. Drawing down the moon is not only spiritual, but physical. She might have caused havoc with the tides and the weather.

In the Land, Luz returns, commanding the Black Guard; he has betrayed them to the Cuckoo. Wilkinson tries to protect Barbie but is killed, and Barbie is captured. The Black Guard takes Barbie to the Cuckoo's citadel.

#36 "A GAME OF YOU, CHAPTER FIVE: OVER THE SEA TO SKY"

The Cuckoo explains that she is a version of Barbie at that age. Barbie's friends from the Land are versions of her favorite childhood toys, and one of them is a doll, Princess Barbie.

Wielding some kind of hypnotic influence over Barbie, the Cuckoo persuades her to agree that she, the Cuckoo, has a right to live, and that it would be all right if the Cuckoo had to kill her.

The Cuckoo is going to leave the Land, but can't do so until it dies. She drags Barbie out along the causeway to the Isle of Thorns, a tiny bit of land upon which sits an obelisk scrawled with strange characters, the Hierogram.

Even as the Cuckoo reaches the Isle of Thorns with Barbie and Luz, Thessaly arrives with Foxglove and Hazel in tow. The Cuckoo makes them think that Luz is the Cuckoo. Thessaly kills the bird. By then the Cuckoo has taken control of the minds of the three women. She wakes Barbie and explains that once she has destroyed the Hierogram and the Porpentine, the Land will die, and she can finally leave the nest and fly.

Back in George's apartment, Wanda talks to the old woman, whose name is Maisie Hill. Maisie had a grandson who, like Wanda, wanted to become a woman, but was murdered before that could happen.

The mind-controlled Barbie takes off the Porpentine and smashes it against the Hierogram, destroying both.

In New York, the weather worsens, as a hurricane veers toward New York City.

On the Isle of Thorns, Morpheus appears. By the terms of an ancient compact, the destruction of the Porpentine and Hierogram have summoned him and called this skerry—this tiny island of the Dreaming—to its final judgment. The Cuckoo is confused; she doesn't understand what she's done. But Morpheus realizes that Barbie is the one who summoned him. When he notices that she and the others are not in control of their own minds, he frees them from the Cuckoo's control. Barbie realizes that Morpheus is in fact Murphy, the god that all her friends talked about.

Dream turns from them to uncreate the Land. It is an old land, and it is time for it to rest, he says. Then the Land seems to shrink, and all of the creatures of the Land, past and present, march along the causeway and vanish into the Dream King's cloak, until only a woman named Alianora remains. He refers to her as his "old love," the one with whom he'd made that ancient compact. Then she, too, enters his cloak.

In New York, the hurricane destroys the apartment building, with Wanda inside.

#37 "A GAME OF YOU, CHAPTER SIX: I WOKE UP AND ONE OF US WAS CRYING"

In the Dreaming, Barbie appeals to Morpheus to do something about the Cuckoo. Morpheus agrees that she is dangerous, but not necessarily evil. It is partly Barbie's fault that she was trapped here, unable to fly the way cuckoos are supposed to. The events of *A Doll's House,* during which Barbie was drawn into Rose's dream vortex and subsequently ceased dreaming, trapped the Cuckoo in the Land.

Though Morpheus is angry with Thessaly, at Barbie's request, he sends them all home, safe and sound. The Cuckoo realizes that this means she is free, and she runs to the edge of a cliff, leaps off, and transforms into a huge, beautiful bird.

Days later, Barbie emerges from the bathroom in a diner, where she meets Wanda's aunt. Thessaly, Foxglove, and Hazel survived the collapse of the old building during the hurricane that killed Wanda, and Barbie is in Kansas for her funeral.

Wanda's aunt tells her that it's too bad she missed the wake, in which Alvin was displayed in an open casket. They had cut his hair and put him in a suit. Barbie is horrified, because Wanda had always been so proud of her hair.

At the funeral, she is asked to stand at the back. She stays when they all leave—save Aunt Dora, who waits to drive her to the bus station. Before she leaves the grave, Barbie takes out her lipstick and crosses off the name "Alvin" on the headstone, writing "Wanda" there in bright pink.

As Aunt Dora drives, Barbie remembers the dream she'd had on the bus the day before. She'd dreamed of Wanda, looking perfectly beautiful, like Glinda in the movie version of *The Wizard of Oz,* with nothing artificial about her—a beautiful girl, and so happy. Wanda is with a girl Barbie doesn't know—Death, of the

Endless. Death whispers in Wanda's ear, and then Wanda sees Barbie somehow, and waves to her, smiling.

PEOPLE, PLACES, AND THINGS

MORPHEUS (DREAM). The King of Dreams. The Sandman. Once upon a time, he made a compact with a woman named Alianora, creating a dream world just for her. In time she died without summoning him to fulfill the compact, which required him to uncreate the Land and grant a boon. When Barbie summons him instead, it is she who is granted the boon.

BARBIE. Raised in Florida, she lived there even as an adult, with her husband Ken. But after divorcing Ken, she resettled in an apartment house in New York. All her life, Barbie had dreamed sequentially, returning each night to a dream kingdom called the Land, where she was the princess. But shortly before her relationship with Ken ended, Barbie's dream world was disrupted by her proximity to a dream vortex, and she stopped dreaming. Since that time, the Cuckoo, a being who lives in the Land, has taken over. When the Cuckoo attempts to force Barbie to destroy the Land, Morpheus appears to fulfill the terms of the compact he made with Alianora. A hurricane destroys her apartment in New York City, but Barbie survives. After attending the funeral of her friend Wanda, she moves on.

ALIANORA. A mysterious woman, long dead, whom Morpheus once loved, and for whom he created the Land.

WANDA. Born Alvin Mann ("a man"), Wanda is Barbie's best friend in New York. A preoperative transsexual, Wanda lives as a woman and is accepted as such by her friends. When Barbie is in trouble, trapped in her dream world, and the witch Thessaly goes to help her by drawing down the moon and traveling the moon's road, essentially sneaking into the Dreaming, Wanda cannot go with her because she is not biologically a woman. Raised in Kansas and scorned by her family, she is infuriated by this. She knows inside who she is. When a hurricane destroys their apartment building, Wanda is killed. But Barbie has a dream of her in which Wanda is truly a girl, happy and beautiful and elegant, a representation of her inner spirit, who then travels on with Death to whatever awaits.

FOXGLOVE (DONNA) CAVANAGH. Her name was once Donna, but she now calls herself Foxglove. She and her girlfriend, Hazel, live in the same building as Barbie and consider her a friend. When things go horribly wrong, and Thessaly gives them the opportunity to enter Barbie's dream to help her, Foxglove goes along.

HAZEL MCNAMARA. Pregnant from a drunken one-night stand with a coworker, Hazel doesn't know how to tell Foxglove. When the truth is revealed, she is stunned by Foxglove's forgiveness and understanding. When Barbie is drawn into the Land, and Thessaly gives Hazel, with Foxglove, the opportunity to help, she doesn't hesitate.

THESSALY. The last surviving Thessalian witch, Thessaly is very angry when George—a servant of the Cuckoo—attempts to fill her with nightmares and turn her into a puppet. She leads the others into Barbie's dream, not to save Barbie, but to teach the Cuckoo a lesson.

GEORGE. A servant of the Cuckoo, he sends nightmares after the women in the apartment building. Thessaly murders him, then nails his face, eyes, and tongue to the wall and forces him to answer her questions.

PRINADO. Prinado the monkey is a loyal friend to Barbie; he is murdered by creatures called the Tweeners while trying to help her. When Morpheus uncreates the Land, however, he is resurrected and drawn back into the fabric of the Dreaming.

LUZ. Another of Barbie's friends in the Land, the bird named Luz becomes the unwitting servant of the Cuckoo and betrays her. Thessaly ends up killing him. However, when Morpheus uncreates the Land, he is resurrected and drawn back into the fabric of the Dreaming.

WILKINSON. A trench coat–wearing rat, Wilkinson is a loyal friend and protector of Barbie in her dream world. He is murdered by the Black Guard after Luz's betrayal. When Morpheus uncreates the Land, however, he is resurrected and drawn back into the fabric of the Dreaming.

MARTIN TENBONES. A massive, shaggy, doglike creature who was Barbie's constant companion in her dream world, two years after she stopped dreaming about it he is sent out into the real world to find her, but is shot dead by the police. When Morpheus uncreates the Land, however, he is resurrected and drawn back into the fabric of the Dreaming.

THE TANTOBLIN. Though he only met Barbie once, this goblin creature was loyal to her, and a part of the resistance against the Cuckoo, and he died trying to bring a message to the friends of Princess Barbara. It is presumed that when Morpheus uncreates the Land, he is resurrected and drawn back into the fabric of the Dreaming.

THE CUCKOO. Perhaps a part of Barbie's childhood self, or a dream thing that she did not create the way she did the others that populate the Land. When Barbie is cut off from the Land, the Cuckoo is trapped there. In order for it to be free, to fly away to other worlds, the Cuckoo takes over the Land and manages to bring Barbie back, so that the talismans keeping the very old dream world from crumbling can be destroyed. When at last Morpheus appears to fulfill his ancient compact, and he uncreates the Land, the Cuckoo is allowed to leave, and flies free at last, full of joy. Barbie could have chosen to kill it, but instead set it free.

MAISIE HILL. An old, homeless woman, Maisie senses something very wrong with the moon and the weather, and finds herself in front of Barbie's apartment building. When the storm knocks her down, Wanda comes out to help her, and takes her upstairs to George's apartment. When the hurricane tears the building apart, Maisie is killed, but she falls on top of Barbie, shielding her from the worst. Because Maisie is there, Barbie survives.

DEATH. One of the Endless; older sister of Dream. When Wanda dies, she comes to claim her, and in a dream Barbie sees that, in spirit, Wanda is the woman she always knew herself to be.

NUALA. A girl from Faerie, given as a gift to Morpheus, she is now a servant in the Dreaming. When sent to monitor Barbie, Nuala warns her that something bad is going to happen. Dream approves.

LUCIEN. A servant in the Dreaming; Morpheus's trusted right-hand man.

TRIVIA

- Thessaly starred in two four-issue miniseries of her own, *The Sandman Presents: The Thessaliad* and *Thessaly: Witch for Hire,* both by Bill Willingham and Shawn McManus.

- Gaiman's dedication for this volume reads: "'Facts are engraved Hierograms for which the fewest have the key.' For two of the few: Jonathan Carroll and Tori Amos."

THE QUOTABLE GAIMAN

I spent more than half a year with Barbie and Wanda and Hazel and Foxglove and Thessaly and the rest of them wandering around in my head. Some nights, I still miss them.
—Afterword, *A Game of You*

||||||||||||||||||||||||||||||||||||||||||||||||||||||||||||||||||||

VOLUME SIX:
FABLES & REFLECTIONS

(1993)

Though Gaiman's magnum opus contained several huge story arcs, the series worked equally well when the author focused on stand-alone tales that illuminated Morpheus as a character, or his world, or merely the impact that he had on the lives of others with whom he came into contact. Like *Dream Country,*

Fables & Reflections contains a number of those engrossing, well-wrought short stories. Some shed new light on the Sandman mythos and set the stage for things to come; others merely feature the Prince of Stories in a supporting role. All, though, focus on the complexities of humanity, and all celebrate the very notion of story (indeed, each tale includes someone *telling* a story within it).

Originally Gaiman wanted to call this volume *Accounts and Reflections,* but the powers that be at DC nixed that idea. His thinking, he has said, was that the book contained a set of stories about intersecting elements, which he titled *"Convergence"* ("The Hunt," "Soft Places," and "A Parliament of Rooks"), and a set of historical tales he titled *"Distant Mirrors"* ("Three Septembers and a January," "Thermidor," and "August"), and that the word "accounts" would represent the totaling of both subjects, or them coming together, and the recounting of ancient tales. But DC felt that title would make readers think of chartered accountancy.

Over the course of The Sandman's run, Gaiman adopted the habit of joining forces with an artist for a short piece before setting them loose to work on major story arcs. Shawn McManus worked on most of *A Game of You* (issues 32–37, which was published between the *"Convergence,"* issues 29–31, and *"Distant Mirrors,"* 38–40, story lines). Later, Jill Thompson and Vince Locke illustrated *Brief Lives* (issues 41–49), while Bryan Talbot and Mark Buckingham labored on *Worlds' End* (issues 51–56). As was also his practice, Gaiman made an effort to write to a particular artist's strengths, which explains the variety and diversity of these engrossing tales.

Once more, Gaiman displays a tendency to reach back while simultaneously looking forward. In "Three Septembers and a January" we get further insight into the contentious relationship between Dream and his twin sisters, Despair and Desire. In "Thermidor" and "Orpheus" readers meet Dream's son, and are reacquainted with Lady Johanna Constantine and Calliope. "Orpheus" is also key in showing Dream's inflexibility, even toward his own son, an inflexibility that proves disastrous later on in his saga. The story also features the first appearance of the prodigal Endless brother, Destruction, in a speaking role.

The series' continuing leitmotif of imprisonment and being set free also features heavily in several of these tales. Todd Faber is imprisoned by doubt but freed by Morpheus's words; Joshua Norton is trapped by despair but freed by madness; and Caius is caged by the trappings and burdens of leadership, and has to go to extremes to feel a moment's peace. Ironically, though, imprisonment, in the sense of being captured, is portrayed as something to be desired in "Ramadan," as imprisonment is equated with the preservation of beauty and wonder.

Additional aspects of the three witches also put in appearances. As though they were his own nightmares and muses during the years he spent on the series, Gaiman can't seem to go very long without weaving them back into the story of Morpheus. In "A Fear of Falling," Todd, in his dream, sees three witches before he ascends to a roof and falls off; in "The Hunt" they take the aspect of Princess (the maiden), Gypsy (the mother), and Baba Yaga (the crone).

VERTIGO PREVIEW #1 "FEAR OF FALLING"

(ILLUSTRATED BY KENT WILLIAMS AND SHERILYN VAN VALKENBURGH)

This very short tale (ten pages), which opens the volume, is the story of an anxious playwright who scales a mountain in a dream and discovers Morpheus and Matthew the Raven waiting for him at the summit. There they have a discussion about the playwright's dual fears—of heights and of falling—which conceal the man's immediate concern, that his new play might flop. Providing the revelation that it might not be such a bad thing to fall, Dream forces him to confront his fears. As the playwright says at the story's end, when you dream of falling, sometimes you wake up, sometimes you die, but sometimes when you fall, you fly.

PEOPLE, PLACES, AND THINGS

TODD FABER. A playwright whose fears are getting the better of him, Todd meets Morpheus in a dream one evening. The Dream Lord's conversation with the playwright allows him to trust his storytelling instincts.

DREAM. In this tale Dream, acting as an adviser to one of his mortal servants (as all writers undoubtedly are), is rendered as wise and imperious. Just this side of cryptic, Dream's words give Todd Faber the confidence to trust his storytelling instincts.

#31 "THREE SEPTEMBERS AND A JANUARY"

(ILLUSTRATED BY SHAWN MCMANUS)

This story begins in September 1859, as Dream is summoned to San Francisco by his sister Despair, who has been working her depressing magic on one Joshua Abraham Norton, who is accordingly contemplating suicide. Backed by Desire and Delirium, Despair challenges her brother to offer an antidote to despair, which Dream does, granting Norton the gift of madness. Norton promptly proclaims himself the first and only Emperor of the United States, and becomes San Francisco's unofficial mascot for the next few decades. Gaiman gives us three more glimpses into Norton's life, visiting him in September 1864 (when he meets a young newspaperman named Sam Clemens), September 1875 (when Norton is tempted by Desire), and January 1880 (when the Emperor is visited by Death).

This tale echoes, in some respects, "Men of Good Fortune," in which Morpheus is able to visit Hob Gadling at different eras of his life, observing humanity over long periods, from a perspective only available to one of the Endless.

PEOPLE, PLACES, AND THINGS

DESPAIR. Dream's sister, she provides him with a challenge in the form of a despairing man, one Joshua Abraham Norton. She asks him what he, with his "little dreams," can do to redeem Norton.

DREAM. In this tale Dream enters into a wager with his contentious sister Despair as to whether dreams can save someone from despair. In the case of Joshua Abraham Norton, dreams proved to be a lifesaver, allowing the man to embrace madness instead of death.

JOSHUA ABRAHAM NORTON. The self-proclaimed Emperor of America, Norton walked the streets of San Francisco during the last part of the nineteenth century, providing the citizenry with entertainment and much food for thought. Although he was quite mad (a gift given to him by Dream), he touched many lives.

DELIRIUM. Another of Dream's sisters, she also appears in "Three Septembers and a January." Her presence nearby may have inspired Mark Twain to write about a certain celebrated frog.

SAMUEL CLEMENS. Also known by his pen name, Mark Twain. Working as a journalist, Clemens encounters Joshua Abraham Norton in San Francisco, who proclaims Clemens "official spinner of tales and teller of stories to these United States of America, for the duration of his mortal lifetime."

THE KING OF PAIN. An emissary of Dream's sister Desire, he offers Norton anything he wants. Norton is content to live out his life serving as Emperor.

DESIRE. Attempting to help her twin win her wager with Dream, Desire sends an emissary, the King of Pain, to tempt Norton. Norton cannot be tempted, because, in his madness, he already has everything he wants or needs.

DEATH. As always, Death is there in the end, ready to usher Norton off this mortal coil. Norton exclaims, "I must confess, I have always wondered what lay beyond life, my dear." Death responds, "Yeah, everyone wonders. And sooner or later everybody gets to find out."

#29 "THERMIDOR"

(ILLUSTRATED BY STAN WOCH AND DICK GIORDANO)

Returning to Dream's story, Lady Johanna Constantine accepts a commission from the Dream King to rescue his son Orpheus (or, more accurately, Orpheus's head) from Paris during the French revolution. In order to escape from Maximilien Robespierre's prison, Johanna asks Orpheus to sing his haunting song; the song first speaks of blood, then of freedom.

PEOPLE, PLACES, AND THINGS

DREAM. Although Dream is estranged from his son Orpheus, that does not mean he does not still care for him. When Orpheus is abducted from his island sanctuary, Morpheus commissions Lady Johanna Constantine to retrieve him from revolutionary France.

LADY JOHANNA CONSTANTINE. Adventuress and ancestor of John Constantine, she first met Dream in 1789 (see "Men of Good Fortune"). Five years later Dream sends her on a mission to spirit the disembodied, living head of his son Orpheus out of revolutionary France. To do so she engages in a battle of wits with the most powerful man in France, Maximilien Robespierre.

#38 "THE HUNT"

(ILLUSTRATED BY DUNCAN EAGLESON AND VINCE LOCKE)

A doting grandfather tells his granddaughter a tale from the old country, a tale of Vassily, a young man of the People, who falls in love with a duke's daughter after seeing her picture in a miniature carried by a wandering tinker. In order to obtain the picture, he robs the tinker of her stock, at the same time obtaining a book that had been stolen from a librarian who is very anxious that his master, Lord Morpheus, not come to hear of the incident. In exchange for the book, the young man asks the librarian to give him the girl of his dreams. Vassily's wish is granted, but things don't turn out the way you might expect.

PEOPLE, PLACES, AND THINGS

THE GRANDFATHER. It is he who tells his granddaughter the story of "The Hunt." He implies at the end of the story that he is actually Vassily, the hero of the piece.

VASSILY. The protagonist of "The Hunt," he is a young man of the People, a race of shape-changers who can shift from men to wolves. Vassily meets an old woman peddler in the forest, and is kind to her. He eventually scares her off, because she perceives his true nature, but not before she leaves him a quest—and her peddler's bag. The quest is to find the duke's youngest daughter, with whom he has fallen in love after merely glimpsing her picture. The bag contains many trinkets, among them a special book.

BABA YAGA. A witch, she assists Vassily in his quest to find the duke's daughter, Natasha.

NATASHA. The duke's daughter, who is everything Vassily had dreamed of. Despite this, upon encountering her in the flesh Vassily realizes that she is not really the woman for him. Rather, he was meant to be with one of his own people, a fellow lycanthrope, with whom he can run and hunt.

LUCIEN. Librarian of the Dreaming, it is his job to care for the myriad tomes that comprise Dream's library. When he discovers that one of those volumes, *The Merrie Comedies of the Redemption of Doctor Faustus,* by Christopher Marlowe, is missing, he tracks it down, finding it in Vassily's possession. Lucien brings Vassily into the Dreaming, where he introduces him to his master, Morpheus. In return for the book, Dream grants the young man his wish.

DREAM. Lord of the Dream realm, he steps in to solve Lucien's dilemma by granting Vassily's wish, teaching the young man that reality is often less ideal than the dream.

#30 "AUGUST"
(ILLUSTRATED BY BRYAN TALBOT AND STAN WOCH)

This is a story about Caius Octavius, better known as the emperor Augustus (patron of Virgil, Ovid, Livy, and Horace), who, because of a dream, spends one day a year in the marketplace of Rome disguised as a beggar, a penniless mendicant. Accompanied by a young actor, who assists him with this disguise, he uses the time away from his court merely to think and to reflect on life.

PEOPLE, PLACES, AND THINGS

LYCIUS. A twenty-two-year-old dwarf, he is an actor whose skill with makeup enables his emperor, Caius, to mingle anonymously with his subjects.

CAIUS. Caius Octavius, who later took the name Caius Julius Caesar Octavius, who later came to be known as Emperor Augustus. Once a year he disguises himself as a beggar and, accompanied by Lycius, he walks among his people. During this time he reflects on his life and the burdens placed upon him by his position. Caius acts in this manner because of a meeting he had some years earlier with Morpheus, who had come to him in a dream.

DREAM. Accompanied by the raven formerly known as Aristeas of Mamora, Morpheus visits Caius in a dream to tell him he can avoid the nightmares that have been plaguing him by dressing as a beggar and going out to the marketplace once a year. There he can plan his course, "when the gods will not be watching."

#39 "SOFT PLACES"
(ILLUSTRATED BY JOHN WATKISS)

"Soft Places" finds the young Marco Polo separated from his father Niccolo's caravan, wandering in the desert of Lop. There he meets his future cell mate, Rustichello of Pisa, and Fiddler's Green, the physical embodiment of the dream of a place (see *A Doll's House*). Dream's servant tells the two men, "Time at the edge of The Dreaming is softer than elsewhere, and here in the soft places it swoops and whorls on itself. In the soft places where the border between dreams and reality is eroded, or has not yet formed . . . Time. It's like throwing a stone into a pool. It casts ripples. Hoom. That's where we are. Here. In the soft places, where the geographies of dream intrude upon the real."

PEOPLE, PLACES, AND THINGS

MARCO POLO. In the year 1273, the famous adventurer is separated from the rest of his party, and is wandering across the desert. On the vast expanse he encounters a soft place, where he finds a friend from the future, a servant of Dream, and, finally, the Dream Lord himself.

RUSTICHELLO OF PISA. A friend from Marco's future, he will share a cell with him, and go on to chronicle Marco's adventures. Oddly, he relates a story to Marco that Marco relates back to him years in the future.

FIDDLER'S GREEN. Coming out to the soft place to think, Fiddler's Green (the 1992 version) encounters Marco Polo and Rustichello of Pisa, and palavers with them.

#1 "THE SANDMAN SPECIAL: ORPHEUS"

(ILLUSTRATED BY BRYAN TALBOT AND MARK BUCKINGHAM)

The most notable story in this volume is a lengthy retelling of the legend of Orpheus and Eurydice, which reveals how he lost his bride, and then his head. The tale contains a fascinating sequence in which Orpheus introduces his future bride to his Endless family: his aunts Teleute (Death), Aponoia (Despair), and Mania (Delirium), his "uncle-aunt" Epithumia (Desire), and his uncles Oletheros (Destruction) and Potmos (Destiny).

PEOPLE, PLACES, AND THINGS

ORPHEUS. According to mythology, Orpheus was one of the chief poets and musicians of antiquity, and the inventor of the lyre. With his music and singing, he could charm wild beasts, coax the trees and rocks to dance, and even divert the courses of rivers. As one of the pioneers of civilization, he is said to have taught humanity the arts of medicine, writing, and agriculture. Orpheus's father was Oeagrus, a Thracian king (or, according to another version of the story, the god Apollo); his mother was the muse Calliope.

In Gaiman's Sandman mythology, Orpheus the Balladeer is the son of Dream, the result of his marriage to Calliope. Orpheus becomes estranged from his father after the Dream Lord refuses to assist him in his quest to rescue Eurydice from the underworld. His quest to save her ends tragically; his head is severed from his body but remains alive. His father ensures his son's safety by leaving him with caretakers on the island of Naxos, where, with the exception of a few decades (see "Thermidor," above) he remains until Dream visits him during the course of the story told in *Brief Lives*.

DREAM. Disagreeing with Orpheus's plan to rescue Eurydice from the underworld, Morpheus tells him he will no longer have anything to do with him if he proceeds. When Orpheus does just that, Morpheus cuts all ties with his son. When Orpheus is dismembered, Morpheus acts more bemused than concerned.

ARISTAEUS. A centaur, and Orpheus's friend, the latter's lust for Eurydice inadvertently leads to her death.

CALLIOPE. A muse, she is Orpheus's mother and one of Dream's former lovers (see *Dream Country*).

EURYDICE. Orpheus's bride, she dies tragically on her wedding day. While fleeing from Aristaeus she encounters a venomous snake, which bites her fatally on her leg. Distraught at her death, Orpheus descends into the underworld to rescue her. His music softens the hearts of Hades and Persephone, who agree to allow Eurydice to return with him to earth on one condition: He must walk in front of her and not look back until they both reach the upper world. In his anxiety he forgets that both of them need to be in the upper world at the same time. He turns to look at her prematurely, and dooms her to the underworld, this time forever.

THE ENDLESS. Dream and his brothers and sisters; several of Orpheus's aunts and uncles play a key role in his story. Death comes to her nephew's wedding to shepherd Eurydice into the afterlife, and also allows him to visit the underworld. His uncle Destruction helps him to locate his aunt Death so that he can petition her to bring Eurydice back from the dead.

THE BACCHEAE. The sisters of the frenzy, they tear Orpheus apart, leaving him to survive as a disembodied head.

#40 "THE PARLIAMENT OF ROOKS"

(ILLUSTRATED BY JILL THOMPSON AND VINCE LOCKE)

Daniel, Lyta Hall's son (whom she was last seen carrying back in *A Doll's House*), is now an adventurous toddler who gets into all sorts of mischief. Here he finds his way into Cain and Abel's little corner of the Dreaming, where he's told stories by the bickering brothers and another ancient storyteller, Eve (yes, that Eve). Thompson's "Li'l Endless" version of the cosmic entities (picture Death and Dream as the

DC Comics' characters Sugar and Spike) illustrating Abel's simplified version of his own story, proved very popular with fans. Eve tells the story of Adam's three wives: Lilith; the Nameless One; and herself. As for Cain, he begins the session with the story that gives the issue its title (and which is completed by his brother later), that tells of the mystery of the black birds, who gather around to listen to one of their number before flying off together or killing him.

PEOPLE, PLACES, AND THINGS

LYTA HALL. Former resident of the Dreaming, the widowed Lyta is doing her level best to raise Daniel, her infant son.

DANIEL HALL. The son of Hector and Lyta Hall, Daniel has a special purpose, revealed later in the Sandman series (see *The Kindly Ones* and *The Wake*). Like Little Nemo, one of Gaiman's favorite comic strip characters, the infant Daniel has adventures in the Dreaming. On this particular night he encounters Eve, Cain, and Abel, who tell him stories. Cain tells the tale of the Parliament of Rooks, Eve tells the story of Adam's three wives, and Abel relates the story of how he and Cain came to reside in the Dreaming.

#50 "RAMADAN"

(ILLUSTRATED BY P. CRAIG RUSSELL)

In "Ramadan," a story told, illustrated, and even lettered in the Arabic tradition, the troubled Haroun al-Raschid (Aaron the Upright), caliph of Baghdad when Islamic culture was at its zenith, summons the Dream Lord so he can bargain for a special place in eternity. He asks Dream to purchase the city from him, and to take it into dreams. In exchange he wants it to never die. Morpheus keeps his end of the bargain "after a fashion," as al-Raschid appears in many of the *Tales of the Arabian Nights* as a wise and just ruler.

The monthlong religious fast of Ramadan falls in the ninth month of the Muslim lunar year.

PEOPLE, PLACES, AND THINGS

HAROUN AL-RASCHID. The caliph of ancient Baghdad. In order to preserve the majesty and grandeur of the Baghdad he knows, he strikes a deal with Dream. Dream preserves the city in a bottle; both the city and the caliph live on in the *Tales of the Arabian Nights.*

DREAM. Here Morpheus fills the role of a godlike creature with which the caliph bargains to preserve the beautiful city he loves. After some discussion, Dream agrees to his proposal.

TRIVIA

- In the creators' biographies at the end of the volume, Gaiman's entry reads, "This is Neil Gaiman. You shouldn't believe a word he says."

- In "The Hunt," Gaiman based Vassily's speech patterns on those of his own grandparents.

- When "Ramadan" was originally published as *The Sandman* issue 50, it sold more than 250,000 copies, making it the most successful issue in the series.

THE QUOTABLE GAIMAN

On identifying with the playwright Todd Faber from "Fear of Falling":

All of a sudden I'd gone from writing a little comic book to being somebody whose work was being looked at by everyone. And I was learning that fear of success could be every bit as crippling as fear of failure, a notion that had never occurred to me before.

—*The Sandman Companion,* by Hy Bender

||||||||||||||||||||||||||||||||||||||||||||||||||||||||||||||||||||||

A FEW WORDS FROM
P. CRAIG RUSSELL

Right now I'm knee-deep into my seventh collaboration with Neil Gaiman (*The Dream Hunters,* at 120 pages) spanning a fifteen-year period. It began with what seemed to me at the time as just another assignment, as inker over Kelley Jones on an issue of Sandman. A few years later Neil approached me about providing the finished art for Sandman number 50. The script for it was simply the finest original I'd ever been offered. I've said numerous times that I'd never have spent so much time adapting "classics" (always a sure deal in looking for quality material) if I had scripts of such quality dropped in my lap on a regular basis.

I've worked on two of Neil's original scripts for comics, and five doing the script adaptation myself from his previously written short stories or novels. With an original script there's no question of editing. I use every word he's written, adding panels where I see an opportunity to expand or amplify for the sake of visual storytelling, but dropping not a word. The adaptations from his published prose are always a little trickier, a little more nerve-wracking, as one never uses every written word in an adaptation. So I sit and cross out lines, paragraphs, pages at a time (sometimes I feel like the wicked witch from *The Wizard of Oz*—"these things must be done delllicately"), always aware that this author whose prose I'm manhandling is, unlike Oscar Wilde or Rudyard Kipling, still very much alive. He keeps sending me projects, so I guess I haven't cut too deep.

||||||||||||||||||||||||||||||||||||||||||||::||||||||||||||||||

VOLUME SEVEN:
BRIEF LIVES

(1994)

Many consider *Brief Lives* to be the highpoint of Gaiman's tenure on The Sandman, pointing to this story arc as the one in the series where Gaiman hits his stride. While *The Doll's House* may be the early peak of the author's exploration of the world in which Morpheus exists, and *Season of Mists* represents the firm establishment of the Dreaming and what it means to be Dream King, *Brief Lives* provided Sandman readers with a long-awaited sojourn into the family bonds that tie together the siblings of the Endless. It is a major turning point in the series, a juncture at which secrets hinted at in earlier volumes are revealed, and where actions are taken that make subsequent developments inevitable.

The premise of *Brief Lives* (which originally appeared in issues 41 through 49 of *The Sandman*) can be boiled down to one sentence: Dream and Delirium take to the road on a quest to find their long-lost brother, Destruction, who abandoned his realm without explanation some three hundred years earlier. The arc focuses on the theme of change, and on the question of whether a conceptual being, embodying a necessary part of the human experience, can ever really change, or are they doomed to follow the same patterns throughout eternity? Given that Delirium was once Delight, the answer seems self-evident, but it actually prompts a more complex philosophical query: What constitutes genuine change?

Gaiman does not provide answers, but those are in many ways tangential to the tale. Even the Endless search for meaning, he seems to suggest. In some ways, even those who are eternal never quite find the answers to their own wonderings. At one point Delirium asks her brother, "What's the name of the word for things not being the same always . . . there must be a word for it. The thing that lets you know time is happening. Is there a word?"

"Change," replies Dream.

And it is in *Brief Lives* that many things change, and many things start to change. Change is in the air, whether it be the change that comes with death, as in the case of the old ones who appear in these pages, or in changing one's mind, as in Dream's realization that he needs to reconcile with his estranged son, Orpheus, after many millennia. And change is coming as a result of Dream's actions in *Brief Lives:* His tender act of compassion toward his son (disguised as an act of expediency) sets a series of events in motion that eventually leads to Morpheus's demise.

But all of this doesn't happen at once; it's what happens along the way that provides the meat of the story. Rich in memorable incident, *Brief Lives* is also filled with humor, humanity, and pathos. First of all, it's a story about the road, calling to mind such classic books as John Steinbeck's *Travels with Charlie* and Jack Kerouac's *On the Road,* and movies such as Frank Capra's *It Happened One Night.* The story is alternately dark—dealing with the unexpected deaths of several long-lived beings, and Morpheus's estrangement from his son, Orpheus—and hilarious, as when it deals with Delirium's driving skills or Destruction's antagonistic relationship with his talking dog, Barnabas (recalling Blood, from Harlan Ellison's classic apocalyptic tale, "A Boy and His Dog"). As indicated by the title of Peter Straub's afterword to the collection, "On Mortality and Change," it's about coping with a shifting emotional and spiritual terrain. Like Gaiman's later work *Anansi Boys,* it's also a story about surviving your family—or not, as the case may be.

A contributing factor to why many consider this the definitive Sandman story arc is artist Jill Thompson's involvement. She had previously worked on the series in the stand-alone story "A Parliament of Rooks," and may be *the* definitive Sandman artist. Her simple, cartoony style subtly propels the narrative forward, without letting showy or overly detailed imagery get in the way.

Another factor that makes this story arc memorable is Todd Klein's fabulous lettering. Although he lettered every issue of the series, his work here stands out. Forced to render copious amounts of dialogue in the unique styles he perfected (Dream's white-on-black word balloon scheme, and Delirium's multicolored, wavy scribbles), his contribution to the success of the nine issues that comprise *Brief Lives* cannot be underestimated—Gaiman doesn't call him a "letterer's letterer" without good reason.

Yet another thing that makes *Brief Lives* so memorable is the presence of the irrepressible Delirium. To begin with, she's quite a contrast to the dark, dour, inflexible Dream, day to his night. An eternal optimist, she's not afraid to give vent to her emotions, something Dream finds difficult, almost abhorrent. Her sense of whimsy, coupled with her constant disorientation, makes her almost irresistible—Gaiman obviously took special joy and care in writing her dialogue.

One can see that with *Brief Lives* Gaiman is turning a significant storytelling corner; having slowly laid the groundwork for the endgame, he's now reached a point where that final story will begin to unfurl. This is a bittersweet moment for

Gaiman's readers, a time of mixed emotions, for, even as the series approaches its zenith, it's also approaching its end.

Brief Lives is illustrated by Jill Thompson and Vince Locke.

#41 "BRIEF LIVES, CHAPTER ONE"

The tale opens as an old man named Andros makes his way to a temple, on the way passing the grave of Lady Johanna Constantine (1760–1859). Inside, he engages in a conversation with the disembodied head of Orpheus, who still lives after all these millennia.

Meanwhile, in New York City, Delirium enters a nightclub looking for her sister Desire, who reveals herself to Delirium after a few moments. They retire to Desire's realm, where Delirium asks her sister to help her find their prodigal brother, Destruction. Desire refuses her. Delirium then seeks the aid of her sister Despair, who also refuses her, despite the fact that, as revealed in a flashback, she is quite fond of her boisterous brother, who was never afraid to display affection, even to one as ugly as her.

Delirium then retires to her realm to think.

#42 "BRIEF LIVES, CHAPTER TWO"

Chapter 2 begins with storm clouds gathering in the Dreaming, reflecting Morpheus's distress at breaking up with an unnamed paramour. He's quite dramatic about the whole thing, even going so far as to tell Lucien that he would appreciate it if the palace staff would refrain from even mentioning *her* name to him. His staff worriedly and sometimes bemusedly discusses his dilemma, even as Dream continues to brood.

Showing exquisite timing, Delirium arrives at the palace seeking his help in finding Destruction. As much to distract himself from his problems as to humor the adamant Delirium, he agrees to accompany her on her quest. Thus, they set out to speak with Destruction's friends, acquaintances, and lovers.

#43 "BRIEF LIVES, CHAPTER THREE"

Walking among us are those called "the old ones," humans who somehow survive for millennia. Apparently, merely by setting out to find their lost brother, Dream and Delirium create a ripple in the fabric of the cosmos, and the old ones begin to die in strange ways. Fifteen-thousand-year-old Bernie Capax, for instance, has a building literally fall on him.

Dream and Delirium begin their travels in Dublin, procuring the services of the former god Pharamond, now known as Mr. Farrell, of Farrell Travel. Farrell delightedly agrees to see that all their travel needs are met.

Meanwhile, another old one, named Etain, barely escapes her apartment before it is destroyed in a freak natural gas explosion. Sensing strange things are happening, she decides to go to ground.

On an unnamed island, Destruction paints the landscape outside his villa. His companion, Barnabas, analyzes the portrait, criticizing the perspective, the colors, and Destruction's amateurish technique. Destruction dismisses his comments, saying, "What the hell would you know? You're a dog." Entering a room in his villa that's been locked as long as Barnabas can remember, Destruction consults his "early warning system," which tells him "big" trouble is coming. Dream and Delirium are coming closer.

#44 "BRIEF LIVES, CHAPTER FOUR"

In the North Lands, an old one named the Alder Man is alerted to the disturbance in the cosmos by an unnatural display of the Northern Lights in the midsummer sky. Heeding the warning, he drops out of sight by transforming into a bear and biting off his shadow, which is still cast in the shape of a man. His shadow takes his place in the world, and the Alder Man lumbers off into the forest.

Dream and Delirium arrive at Bernie Capax's house, where a wake is being held. They speak to Bernie's son Danny, who, upon his father's death, discovered his old man had many hidden facets.

Dream, Delirium, and Ruby DeLonge, the chauffer Farrell had arranged for them, retire to a hotel. While Ruby smokes in bed, Delirium "lets herself go," trying to locate other people on her list of Delirium's friends and associates. Capax is definitely dead, Etain has left this plane entirely, and the Alder Man has changed somehow. The only one she can locate is the "dancing woman," Ishtar. Meanwhile, Dream checks in with Lucien, then recalls one of the last times he saw his brother Destruction, circa 1685. At that time Destruction expressed doubts to his brother as to whether he was still needed on this plane.

Dream's reverie is interrupted by the shouts of firemen; while he was reflecting on the past, Ruby had fallen asleep, and her lit cigarette started a fire that has consumed the entire hotel, killing her. Dream is disturbed by this, telling Delirium that Capax's and Ruby's deaths cannot be coincidental.

#45 "BRIEF LIVES, CHAPTER FIVE"

After focusing briefly on Ishtar's current situation, the story veers (literally) to Dream and Delirium, as Delirium haphazardly pilots the car Farrell has rented for them. They are pulled over by a policeman, who is rude to Delirium. Because she considers him nasty, she plants a suggestion in his mind that he will feel as if he is covered by insects for the rest of his life. When Dream asks her if that was entirely necessary, she tells him to back off, saying that she doesn't tell him how to conduct *his* business. To avoid further problems, Dream summons Matthew the raven (who drove when he was a human) to advise Delirium on her driving.

The trio catches up with Ishtar at Suffragette City, the strip club where the former goddess dances. Dream speaks with her between shows, but she is unable to shed any light on her former lover's whereabouts. After Dream departs, Ishtar dances one last incredible dance, ending her existence in a bright flash that destroys the club and kills everyone inside, except for her fellow stripper Tiffany, who gets a second chance at making her life work.

#46 "BRIEf LIVES, CHAPTER SIX"

This chapter opens with a visit to Destruction's hideaway, where he is now realizing that a visit from members of his family is becoming inevitable. He both eagerly anticipates and dreads their coming.

Dismayed by the damage they seem to be causing, Dream calls off the search and retires to the Dreaming to reflect on what has happened. Seeking an answer, he visits Lady Bast, who had told him previously (see *Season of Mists*) that she knew Destruction's location. She informs him that she was lying then, that she really has no idea where his brother is.

Returning to the Dreaming, he takes a moment to dress Mervyn down a bit (Mervyn had told Lucien that he could set his flaky boss straight, unaware that Morpheus was listening), then speaks to Lucien, who informs him that he could not determine exactly why so many had died since the Dream Lord began his search.

Dream is then visited by Death, who is furious with him for upsetting Delirium by abandoning the search for Destruction. Dream agrees to speak with their little sister, and enters her realm. Seeing her dismay, he agrees to continue.

#47 "BRIEf LIVES, CHAPTER SEVEN"

The search proceeds, with Dream and Delirium visiting their older brother Destiny. Entering a maze/labyrinth at a carnival, they soon find themselves in the Garden of Destiny, where you can see your past by looking behind you. Delirium glances back and sees her younger self, looking much happier and more like a goddess than the homeless waif she resembles now.

Destiny will not tell them where Destruction is. If Dream wants that kind of advice, he says, he needs to seek an oracle. When Dream protests that no run-of-the-mill oracle will do when it comes to the Endless, Destiny reminds him that there is a family member who fits the bill. Realizing that Destiny is referring to Orpheus, Dream is overcome with emotion.

Although he dreads their meeting, he keeps his promise to his sister and visits Orpheus. In a conversation that is not presented, he learns that Destruction is on a nearby island.

Arriving at Destruction's hideaway, the two are greeted warmly by their brother, who marvels at how they've changed. Looking at Delirium, he tells her she's grown. He says the same thing to Dream, who dismisses the observation out of hand, unable to admit to himself the drastic impact the experiences of the past century have had on him.

Destruction then invites them to dinner, saying they have much to discuss.

#48 "BRIEF LIVES, CHAPTER EIGHT"

Dream, Delirium, and Destruction sit down for a meal, and have a long talk— about the past, about the family, and about responsibility. Dream and Delirium do their level best to bring Destruction back into the fold, but he resists. They part at the story's end, with Destruction ascending into the heavens, and Dream and Delirium returning to their own realms.

Dream's heart is heavy, not only because of his brother's decision, but because of a promise he made to Orpheus in exchange for the information on Destruction's location. Dream, you see, promised Orpheus that he would return to the temple and kill him.

#49 "BRIEF LIVES, CHAPTER NINE"

The last chapter in *Brief Lives* constitutes a milestone in the Sandman series— everything that has come before has been leading to this point, and everything that comes after occurs as a result of the events described here. Simply put, Morpheus takes his son Orpheus's life in a tender act of mercy.

PEOPLE, PLACES, AND THINGS

ANDROS. Caretaker/caregiver to Orpheus, who has survived hundreds of years despite having his head separated from his body. It is Andros's life's work to care for Dream's son, as it was his father's and grandfather's before him. In fact, his ancestors have performed this task for generations, originally commissioned by Dream after Orpheus's death. Andros is freed from his responsibilities at the end of *Brief Lives* due to Dream's actions. He and his son-in-law Kris bury Orpheus's head in an unmarked grave at the Dream Lord's request.

ORPHEUS. Morpheus's son by Calliope, he survived an attack by the Baccheae, but only as a disembodied head. With the exception of a brief period in the eighteenth century, he's spent his life on an Adriatic island, cared for by members of the same family for generations. Orpheus is an oracle, meaning he is uniquely able to provide advice or wisdom to those who seek his counsel. When his father fails to locate Destruction through other means, he is forced to seek his estranged son's help. Orpheus provides the information, but only in exchange for a boon from his father—he asks Dream to end his life. Dream reluctantly agrees, and does so, spilling the blood of a family member, setting in motion a harrowing series of events that lead to the demise of his current incarnation.

DELIRIUM. Despite her muddled state, Dream's younger sister demonstrates surprising determination once she resolves to locate her errant brother, Destruction. Her entreaties rejected by Desire and Despair, she cajoles Dream into helping her find him. They are successful in locating him, but cannot convince him to return to the fold.

DESIRE. When she says no to Delirium, Desire knows that that won't be the end of the matter. In a conversation with Despair, she indicates that she's afraid Delirium may involve their elder siblings, Destiny, Death, and Dream, but she doesn't indicate why. Although she should be pleased with how things eventually work out, having tried to get Dream to spill family blood in the past (see *The Doll's House*), and because of a grudge she holds against her brother (see "Three Septembers and a January"), she instead shows regret upon learning that Dream has taken Orpheus's life.

DESPAIR. Another of the Endless, she is also approached by Delirium for assistance; like her twin, Desire, she also says no. Despair secretly hopes Delirium succeeds in her quest because she misses her brother Destruction, who is the only one of her siblings who ever kissed her.

DESTRUCTION. A more appropriate name for Destruction might be Change, because that's what he brings about, by breaking things down and tearing things apart. Although one might expect someone who embodies Destruction to be aggressive and angry, he's exactly the opposite: a caring, gentle soul who seems to be a stabilizing force among the Endless.

Destruction gave up his responsibilities some three hundred years prior to the start of *Brief Lives,* having decided that mankind was on the verge of achieving such proficiency in the art of destruction that it no longer needed him. Breaking all ties with his siblings, he dropped out of sight to pursue his passion for the arts, taking joy in creating art and poetry that his companion, Barnabas the talking dog, enjoys disparaging.

Although he greets Delirium and Dream warmly when they arrive on his doorstep, he takes their appearance as an omen that it's time to move on, to go even deeper under cover.

DREAM. Moody and testy from having just ended an affair (with Thessaly, of all people, we learn later in *The Kindly Ones*), Morpheus agrees to assist Delirium in the search for Destruction, not with any expectation that they'll actually find him, but in the hopes that it will provide him with a much needed distraction from his romantic failures. Their colorful odyssey takes Dream and Delirium from the Dreaming to Dublin, to America, and to an island in the Adriatic Sea.

At first Dream goes through the motions, at one point even abandoning the search. But, after speaking with Death, he recommits to the quest, deciding to do whatever is necessary to find his brother. With that decision he has sealed his fate. Exhausting all other avenues, he's forced to seek assistance from his estranged son,

Orpheus, who, as an oracle, knows exactly where his uncle is hiding. To provide this information, Orpheus exacts a terrible price.

Dream's reunion with his brother is a bittersweet affair, as their meeting achieves nothing other than to remind Dream that he, too, misses Destruction, and that, while it is possible for some to abdicate their responsibilities, it's just not in the cards for him. Although he himself has told Delirium, "You can stop being anything," he doesn't mean it—his life revolves around work and duty.

After his meeting with Destruction, Dream returns to Orpheus's temple to fulfill his promise to his son by taking his life. Dream returns to his kingdom quite shaken, but with a new appreciation of his realm and those who serve him.

LUCIEN, NUALA, MERVYN, MATTHEW, ABEL, TARAMIS. Dream's servants and companions in the Dreaming. They are all made anxious by his melancholy after his breakup.

THE DREAMING. Morpheus's realm, his Xanadu, it reflects his whims, desires, and, significantly, his moods. When he is suffering the agonies of his romantic breakup, it rains for days, only to let up when he makes his decision to accompany Delirium on her quest. Then the sun shines, and a rainbow glimmers overhead.

THE OLD ONES. Long-lived humans, they walk among the populace unnoticed, usually content to just get by. As readers are told in Chapter 3, there are less than ten thousand individuals who have personal memories of saber-toothed tigers, less than a thousand who walked the streets of Atlantis, less than five hundred who remember the human civilizations that predated the dinosaurs, and "roughly seventy people who were alive before the earth had begun to congeal from gas and dust."

BERNIE CAPAX. One of the old ones, he's handled legal matters for Destruction in the past. Coincidentally, Capax dies in an accident just before Death and Delirium, following Destruction's trail, come to visit, after living to the ripe old age of fifteen thousand. Encountering Death, he asks, "But I did okay, didn't I? I mean, I got what, fifteen thousand years, that's pretty good, isn't it? I lived a pretty long time." Death replies, "You lived what anybody gets, Bernie. You got a lifetime. No more. No less."

ISHTAR. Also known as Belili and Astarte (Easter), she was formerly a Babylonian goddess of love, sex, and war. She is also one of Destruction's former lovers. Dream and Delirium find her performing in a sleazy dance club called Suffragette City. Touching on a concept Gaiman first introduced in *Season of Mists,* and that he expounds upon in more detail in his novel *American Gods,* she ruminates about the nature of gods, saying they start as dreams, then walk out of those dreams into the land, where they are worshipped. "And then one day there's no one left to worship. And in the end, each little god and goddess takes its last journey back into dreams. And what comes after, not even we know."

MR. FARRELL. Also known as Pharamond, he's yet another former god, and is now in the travel business. Farrell uses his contacts to make Dream's earthly travel arrangements.

RUBY ELISABETH DELONGE. An employee of Mr. Farrell, she acts as Dream and Delirium's chauffer. She is killed in a hotel fire that she started by smoking in bed.

THE LADY BAST. The cat-headed goddess who sought the key to Hell from Dream in *Season of the Mists*. Dream seeks her out because of her oracular nature, but she is unable to provide him with any leads as to Destruction's whereabouts.

BARNABAS. A talking dog, his main function seems to be keeping Destruction in line. When Destruction abandons Earth for other planes of existence, Barnabas's former "master" gifts him to Delirium.

ETAIN AND THE ALDER MAN. Two others Dream and Delirium seek for ideas about their brother's whereabouts. Realizing something is up when she narrowly escapes a gas explosion that destroys her apartment, Etain flees this reality. The Alder Man drops out of sight in a unique manner, by turning himself into a bear and biting off his shadow.

THE CORINTHIAN. Dream's lethal servant appears in a flashback involving Destruction in 1685, England.

DEATH. She appears a couple of times in *Brief Lives,* first collecting Bernie Capax, then appearing to chastise her brother Dream for disappointing their sister Delirium by abandoning his search for Destruction.

DESTINY. The last of the Endless with whom Dream speaks while seeking Destruction. Although he will not tell Dream where their brother is to be found, he does tell him he needs an oracle. When Dream points out that there are no oracles who can tell of their family, Destiny reminds him that he thought of one when he spoke to Bast. He also reminds him that there is an oracle who is *of* the family. That oracle is none other than Orpheus.

TRIVIA

- Dave McKean's cover for this collection features an eerie visage composed of dozens of photographs of human faces, a format suggested by Gaiman. Not common at the time, the technique has been used more and more by others in subsequent years.

- In Chapter 1, Delirium visits a bondage bar seeking Desire; there's a humorous moment when she mistakes a Goth chick for her sister Death. Another neat thing about that particular set piece is the music that plays in the background (the lyrics can be seen floating in the air over the heads of the patrons): It's Gaiman's friend Tori Amos's song "Tear In Your Hand," from her album *Little Earthquakes.*

- The first part of an interesting bit of symmetry occurs in Chapter 7 of *Brief Lives,* as, in a single panel late in the story, readers are given their first glimpse of Daniel as Morpheus, albeit from behind, as he faces the bloodied and distraught Corinthian. That panel is reproduced (although not exactly) in the final chapter of *The Kindly Ones.*

- *Brief Lives* is also the name of a collection of short biographies written by John Aubrey in the last decades of the seventeenth century. Aubrey initially began collecting biographical material to assist Oxford scholar Anthony Wood. In time, Aubrey's researches went beyond mere assistance to Wood and became a project in its own right. A quote from Aubrey serves as the epigraph for this collection.

- Destruction, speaking to his siblings, references *The Wizard of Oz,* saying, "Well, it looks like neither of you is interested in the dinner I made. Is there anything else you were after? Brains? A heart? A ride in a balloon?"

- Peter Straub's afterword closes with the following: "If this isn't literature, nothing is."

THE QUOTABLE GAIMAN

What you need to know before you start: there are seven beings that aren't gods, who existed before humanity dreamed of gods and will exist after the last god is dead. They are called The Endless. They are embodiments of (in order of age) Destiny, Death, Dream, Destruction, Desire, Despair and Delirium.

Approximately three hundred years ago, Destruction abandoned his realm. That's all you need.

—"Not an Introduction," *Brief Lives*

||||||||||||||||||||||||||||||||||||||||||||||||||||||||||||||||||||||||

A CONVERSATION WITH
JILL THOMPSON

Question: How did you first meet Neil, and how did you come to work with him the first time?

JILL THOMPSON: I met Neil at the San Diego Comic-Con around 1990 or so. I can't recollect the exact year. But that sounds about right. I was working as the penciler on Wonder Woman at the time. Anyway, I had just finished doing the famed "nude Death" commission for a fan named Kim Metzger. Nothing sala-cious or anything. Just perky Death, if she were sitting on an ivy-covered wall in the nude. I tried to keep it tasteful, y'know? Anyway, I eventually made my way over to the DC booth or something, where I was introduced to Neil. The first thing he mentioned was that he had just seen the most lovely sketch I had done of Death . . . in the nude. I was so embarrassed. But apparently that was not the first piece of art by me that Neil had seen. He was familiar with my work on Wonder Woman and thought I would do a good job on a story arc.

Q: What were the goals you set for yourself when you first decided you wanted to be an artist?
JT: I wanted to draw comics. My first goal was to draw the X-Men. I wanted to pencil the book and have Terry Austin ink me. Hmm. I guess I wanted to be John Byrne. As I have matured, I have altered my comics goals from penciler to illustra-tor, and finally to creator. I mean, I enjoy collaborating with other writers and artists, but now I get the most satisfaction from creating my own work. Writing it, illustrating it, and orchestrating nearly everything.

Q: Who are your greatest influences as an artist?
JT: They change all the time. I'd say I've been most influenced by Charles Schulz, Bob Bolling, Dan DeCarlo, John Buscema, John Byrne, Wendy Pini, Steve Rude, P. Craig Russell, the Hernandez brothers . . . That really covers my teen and art school years. As I started working in the comics industry, I was influ-enced by nearly everyone I met. Mike Mignola, Steve Purcell, Dave Gibbons . . .

I remember the first time I really appreciated the art of Jack Kirby. I had never liked it when I was younger. Or the first time I was bowled over by Alex Toth. My God, you can learn so much by going back and rereading things you've read be-fore. I really think I'm influenced by what I see around me, nowadays. Shadow and form. Nature, urban architecture. I think it's best to just sit back and watch things. Watch people. That can be very inspiring.

Q: Sandman is a milestone in comics and a cultural touchstone. While work-ing on Brief Lives, did you have an awareness of it as a "big deal," and if not, did it ever feel that way to you?
JT: I felt it was a big deal to work on *Sandman* because it was a comic that I loved reading. Working as a professional comic artist was a big deal to me because I was drawing for a living. But I guess I realized that *Sandman* might be a huge deal for my career when I was walking to Artist's Alley at another San Diego Comic-Con. I remember walking past some retailer tables, and I heard someone say, "That's Jill Thompson. She draws *Sandman*."

I was shocked and honored that someone recognized me in a huge crowd, and they made mention of my work as well. And I wasn't even sitting at a table that had a place card with my name on it or anything.

Q: *How did the Little Endless come about?*

JT: It was in the script of "A Parliament of Rooks." Neil called for Abel to tell a story to Matthew about a time when Dream and Death went walking. Neil had originally art-directed for them to look like Sugar and Spike from the old DC comic, because he wanted them to look supercute. I think I called him or asked if it was okay if I drew them like "Hello Kitty," or more Kawaii. Supercute. Big heads, wee bodies . . . Japanese style.

After the issue was published, fans would ask me for sketches of them. It made me think of what the other members of the family might look like if they were drawn in the same style. I drew it really quickly and faxed it to Neil, who thought it was a hoot. Then, at some point, I painted a version of the sketch. That is the frontispiece at the beginning of *The Little Endless Storybook*. I sewed some stuffed dolls once, of Dream and Death, gave them to Neil, and then made two more. Those were auctioned off at a convention, and Paul Dini owns them.

It took over ten more years for them to make their way to their own little book. But fans demanded it, and their perserverence seems to have paid off.

Q: *Are there any Gaiman-related projects in your future?*

JT: You'd have to ask Neil that. He pulls the trigger on all of the Gaiman-related projects. I'd love to collaborate with him on a story.

Q: *What's on tap for you next? Any Scary Godmother projects to look forward to?*

JT: July of 2008 will see the first of four ninety-three-page, full-color painted graphic novels for HarperCollins, written and illustrated by me. They are called *Magic Trixie*, and they should be great fun for all ages. They'll be in the digest/chapterbook size with a soft cover. But they are chockfull of sequential art. You'll be able to find them in the kids' book section of your favorite bookstore. Hopefully, with the covers facing out so everyone can see them! Perhaps there will be a point-of-purchase display like there was with the *Akiko* novels by Mark Crilley.

I also have plans to collaborate with Evan Dorkin and Sarah Dyer on more of those dogs and cats stories. I believe Evan has named the series *Burden Hill*. That's the name of the town all the dogs live in. And, I'm going to collaborate with Josh Elder of *Mail Order Ninja* fame on a supercool Superman story. Painted? Yes.

As for *Scary Godmother*, I'd love to tell more stories set on the fright side. Or make more animated specials or stage more theatrical productions. As it stands, I've been very busy with *Magic Trixie* these days, writing and illustrating and everything. And, unfortunately, I have no hands-on control over TV or animation. But the ones we have are great, and I'm so very proud of them. Maybe there will be a *Magic Trixie* show or something. Live action might be interesting to try. I love set and costume design, and I'd love to create something physically tangible.

VOLUME EIGHT:
WORLDS' END

(1994)

After finishing the *Brief Lives* story arc, Gaiman seemed ready to take a breather from the core tale of *The Sandman*, switching to stories in which the Dream Lord was a presence, rather than at the heart of, the tales Gaiman had to tell. The fiftieth issue of The Sandman featured "Ramadan," the story of Haroun al-Raschid and the city of Baghdad (see chapter on *Fables & Reflections* for details). Then, in issues 51 through 56 he provided a small anthology of short stories, all told under the overarching title of *Worlds' End*.

These tales are indeed a perfect showcase for Gaiman's passion for stories, of his talent for creating them, and his love for the very telling of them. As such, it makes a nice companion to the first two Sandman-inspired short story collections, *Dream Country* and *Fables & Reflections*. It can be distinguished from those volumes, however, by the fact that it works best as a collection, its framing device amplifying and feeding off of the stories it bookends.

The structure of *Worlds' End* recalls that of Geoffrey Chaucer's *The Canterbury Tales*. These stories, written in the fourteenth century (two of them in prose, the others in verse), are contained inside a framing tale, and are told by a group of pilgrims making their way from Southwark to Canterbury to visit a shrine. The structure has been used again and again in modern tales—examples can be found in Peter Straub's *Ghost Story* (the stories told by the Chowder Society), Stephen King's tales of the gentleman's club located at 249B East 34th Street in Manhattan (for example, "The Man Who Would Not Shake Hands"), and Gaiman's own short story "October in the Chair."

#51 "A TALE OF TWO CITIES"

There are two stories within this issue: a framing sequence commencing the entire story arc (illustrated by Bryan Talbot and Mark Buckingham), and the title story (illustrated by Alec Stevens). The framing sequence is quite elegant. When two coworkers wreck their car in a freak snowstorm, the only place they can find shelter is a mysterious, antiquated inn called Worlds' End. Here they wait out the storm, listening to stories from the many travelers also stuck there. Worlds' End is apparently one of those "soft places" beyond space and time (perhaps the king of all soft places), where all eras, realities, realms, and planes intersect. Some travelers between the worlds go there willingly, but others find themselves driven there by reality storms, caused by events that disturb the very fabric of the cosmos. That is the case with most of the guests in the inn on this particular night. Finding themselves cut off from familiar environs, they pass the time telling stories.

"Tale" is the vaguely Lovecraftian story of a sleeping man trapped in a dream city—or is he awake and merely stumbling through the dream of a sleeping city? As one character states, "Perhaps a city is a living thing. Each city has its own personality, after all."

"So?" replies Robert.

"So, if a city has a personality, maybe it also has a soul. Maybe it dreams."

Gaiman fans will note that the essay he wrote as an introduction to the *SimCity 2000* game touches on many of the themes developed in "A Tale of Two Cities."

PEOPLE, PLACES, AND THINGS

BRANT TUCKER. Driving along one June evening with his coworker Carole in the passenger seat, Brant is amazed when it starts to snow. A creature right out of mythology darts across the road in front of him, causing him to swerve and crash the car. Their car totaled, the two make their way into the surrounding countryside, stumbling upon a tavern called Worlds' End. There they are given aid, and treated to a number of stories by the patrons, a colorful bunch dressed in the styles of many other realities and eras. Worlds' End, you see, is akin to a soft place, a nexus of realities where the denizens of each can mingle.

CHARLENE MOONEY. Charlene is sleeping when Brant goes off the road. Dazed, she manages to make it to the Worlds' End inn, where, after being treated for her injuries, she enjoys the stories the other patrons have to tell.

CHIRON. A centaur, he is at Worlds' End when Brant and Charlene stumble in. The finest physician in twelve realms, he tends to Charlene, reviving her and bandaging her wounds.

THE WORLDS' END INN. An inn (not a bar, an inn) at the nexus of all realities, it caters to a wildly diverse clientele, including humans, centaurs, mages, and faerie folk. As the innkeeper tells Brant, it's a free house, not part of any kingdom or empire. "When a world ends, there's always something left over. A story, perhaps, or a vision, or a hope. This inn is a refuge, after the lights go out. For a while."

ROBERT. The protagonist of "A Tale of Two Cities," Robert works in a drab job, and leads a drab life in a drab city. A solitary man, he likes to daydream as he walks aimlessly about his city. One day he finds himself on a train that is transporting only one other soul besides him, Dream. Exiting the train, he finds that he has been incorporated into the city's dream. He wanders the city, seeing only a couple of people throughout his strange trip, eventually stumbling on a doorway that he uses to exit the strange dream world.

MR. GAHERIS. He spins the tale about Robert and the city, having met him in Scotland some years after the events of the story took place. Robert tells him that he is not afraid of being pulled back into the city's dream. He's not afraid of a city that's sleeping, he says; he's terrified that someday cities might start waking up.

DREAM. When Robert boards an underground train, unlike any other he has ever seen before, he encounters another passenger inside, an odd-looking man dressed entirely in black. The stranger simply stares at him, with "Dark Eyes, like pools of night." The silent stranger is Morpheus. As an aside, Dream is seen disembarking from this very same train early on in *The Kindly Ones.*

#52 "CLURACAN'S TALE"

(ILLUSTRATED BY JOHN WATKISS)

This story tells of the mission of Cluracan (first seen during the *Season of Mists* storyline), Ambassador of the Queen of Faerie to the mortal world. It demonstrates the truth behind the belief that it's not a good idea to cross the fair folk. Cluracan is an antihero in the mold of George MacDonald Fraser's Sir Harry Flashman, a spineless, self-centered bastard who always seems to prosper at other people's expense.

PEOPLE, PLACES, AND THINGS

CLURACAN. Ambassador of Faerie, he is sent to the city of Aurelia by Queen Titania on a diplomatic mission, as an envoy to a summit that the folk of the plains are holding. During the summit Cluracan offends Innocent XI, psychopomp of the Universal Aurelian Church, and is imprisoned. Freed by Dream at the behest of his sister, Nuala, Cluracan proceeds to create havoc in Aurelia, undermining the power of the psychopomp.

INNOCENT XI. The powerful and evil religious leader that Cluracan deposes through a campaign of innuendo and gossip.

DREAM. Responding to his servant Nuala's entreaties on behalf of her imprisoned brother, Dream visits Cluracan in his cell, freeing the envoy from his iron bonds, and releasing him from prison by opening the iron door, something Morpheus specializes in.

#53 "HOB'S LEVIATHAN"

(ILLUSTRATED BY MICHAEL ZULLI AND DICK GIORDANO)

"Hob's Leviathan" tells the story of a thirteen-year-old girl who, disguised as a boy, sails the seas, first on *The Spirit of Whitby,* then the *Pyramus,* and finally, the

Sea Witch. Once aboard that last vessel, Jim, as she is known to the crew, encounters Dream's human mate, Hob Gadling, who owns the ship. She also witnesses a sight that would drive many to madness, as the ship crosses paths with a massive sea serpent (in a scene that may have been paying homage to a similar one in C. S. Lewis's *The Voyage of the Dawn Treader*).

PEOPLE, PLACES, AND THINGS

JIM/MARGARET. The narrator of "Hob's Leviathan," a thirteen-year-old girl disguised as a boy, who, in 1912, signs aboard the sailing ship *Sea Witch*. On that voyage she spends many hours in the company of Hob Gadling, and sees an awesome sight, an actual sea serpent. Anxious to tell someone about what she has seen, she stays quiet on the advice of her new friend, Mr. Gadling. Afforded the opportunity to relate her tale to the patrons of the Worlds' End inn, she leaps at the chance, saying she's been holding it in for two years.

HOB GADLING. Dream's friend, first introduced in "Men of Good Fortune." Alive for over five hundred years at the time this story takes place, he is the owner of the *Sea Witch,* a ship that carries tea and cotton from Bombay to Liverpool. Gadling grows fond of Jim on the voyage, eventually tumbling onto "his" secret, which Hob does not reveal to the rest of the crew and passengers.

Jim (Margaret) is bursting to tell someone, anyone, of what she saw on the voyage, but Gadling advises her not to. When Hob's actions give Jim an inkling that he is perhaps a man who also has something to conceal, she asks Gadling: "How old *are* you, sir?"

Gadling replies, "Old enough to have learned to keep my mouth shut about seeing a bloody great snake in the middle of the ocean."

THE INDIAN GENTLEMAN. A stowaway on the *Sea Witch,* the cost of his passage is taken care of by Hob Gadling, who perhaps has recognized a kindred spirit. He relates a story within the story told by Jim, a tragic tale of an Indian king who partook of the fruit of the tree of life. Readers learn later in the series that the Indian gentleman is indeed that very same king. He is, apparently, also a very good friend of Lucien's (see *The Wake*).

#54 "THE GOLDEN BOY"

(ILLUSTRATED BY MICHAEL ALLRED)

Here Gaiman resurrects Prez, an obscure character who first appeared in the 1970s, courtesy of Joe Simon and Jerry Grandenetti. Prez Rickard was the first teenage president of the United States. In this tale of idealism clashing with cynicism in another America, Prez works for what is good and right, struggling all the while against the evil machinations of Boss Smiley, who literally has a smiley face for a head. This story is a bit corny, but in a good, Frank Capraesque (think *Mr. Smith Goes to Washington* or *Meet John Doe*) or Horatio Alger kind of way.

PEOPLE, PLACES, AND THINGS

THE SEEKER. Wandering in the rooms above the Worlds' End inn, Brant Tucker comes across an oriental-looking man, who describes himself as a seeker and a follower. It is he who tells the tale of the "Golden Boy." At the end of the story he tells Brant that he walks the worlds, following Prez, seeking him, walking ahead, "spreading his word." In other words, he acts as a prophet for Prez, much as John the Baptist did for Jesus.

PREZ RICKARD. An idealistic teenager who from birth was destined to become president of the United States, Prez first catches the attention of the public by fixing the clocks of a town called Steadfast. Though offered power by the god/devil-like Boss Smiley, Prez says he will become president on his own. He does just that (benefiting from the youth vote, and from changes in the law that allow citizens age eighteen and over, rather than thirty-five, to run for president), and sets about changing things for the better, against the wishes of Boss Smiley. Due to Smiley's machinations, a disillusioned Prez fades into obscurity after finishing his second term, his ultimate fate the subject of several urban legends.

Readers learn of his true fate here. After his death Prez encounters Boss Smiley in the afterworld, learning that he has been the evil one's pawn all along. Just when it seems all hope is lost, Prez is rescued by Dream, who gives him the ability to walk between the worlds, traveling from America to America, helping the helpless and sheltering the weak, a cosmic Tom Joad.

BOSS SMILEY. A veritable god in the America in which Prez Rickard grew up, he's literally the devil in the details. Furious that Prez will not serve him, Smiley has the young man's love, Kathy, assassinated, an act that breaks Prez's will. When Prez dies, Smiley tries to claim his soul, but is frustrated by Dream.

DEATH. Dream's sister makes an appearance in this story, speaking with Prez at the moment of his passing. When he sees her he asks, "Have we met before?" "Once," she replies (in keeping with the statement made by Destruction in "The Song of Orpheus," that Death is present at both the beginning and the end of our lives).

DREAM. Here again, Dream exercises almost godlike powers in rescuing Prez from Boss Smiley, and enabling him to travel between the worlds, to fight for the American ideals (dreams?) of truth, justice, equality, and freedom. Prez gives Dream a gift, a pocket watch that had previously belonged to his father.

#55 "CEREMENTS"

(ILLUSTRATED BY SHEA ANTON PENSA AND VINCE LOCKE)

The penultimate story concerns the great necropolis Litharge, a city that exists to render respectful last rites to the dead. Litharge is so efficient at this task that even the Endless trust their dead to it.

"Cerements" is truly labyrinthine. Remember that it is a story within a story already, as a segment of The Sandman series. In that story you find yourself in an inn where people are telling . . . stories. When you consider that characters inside the story being told then also start telling stories, and that one of those stories features Destruction telling a story . . . well, you might get a headache.

PEOPLE, PLACES, AND THINGS

LITHARGE. A legendary necropolis, it is a city devoted to the disposal of the bodies of the dead. Inhabitants of the city are renowned for their wide knowledge of funeral customs. Readers will visit Litharge one more time before the series ends, in *The Wake*.

PETREFAX. The narrator of "Cerements," he tells a tale containing three other tales (those of Mig, Scroyle, and Master Hermas), all having to do with the funeral trade and Litharge. Petrefax is a journeyman, having been elevated from the station of prentice, someone who is in the process of learning the art and craft of body disposal.

KLAPROTH. Petrefax's master, he teaches him about the art of body disposal.

MIG, SCROYLE, AND MASTER HERMAS. Three expert practitioners in the burial arts, they teach Petrefax about the craft by telling him stories around a campfire.

DESTRUCTION. Dream's prodigal brother is featured in Scroyle's tale, in the guise of "The Traveler." There he tells Scroyle of the history of Litharge, and of its importance: "It's important to have places like this. Once the spirit's flown and the spark of life has gone, then the rituals of farewell are needed. They have other functions, too, those rites. It is a fearful thing to be haunted by those who loved us once. It is a fearful thing to haunt those one loves."

#56 "WORLDS' END"

(ILLUSTRATED BY BRYAN TALBOT, MARK BUCKINGHAM, DICK GIORDANO, STEVE LEIALOHA, GARY AMARO, AND TONY HARRIS)

After all the preceding tales are told, the guests are granted a spectacular vision of the event that is powerful enough to create a storm to shake all their worlds, one that we later learn is Dream's funeral procession.

PEOPLE, PLACES, AND THINGS

BRANT TUCKER. Brant, who listens to these stories but doesn't add one of his own, goes back to his own reality when the reality storm abates. We learn that we've been eavesdropping on him all along, as he tells his story, which contains all the others, to a bartender on this plane of existence.

CHARLENE MOONEY. Having spent all this time listening to stories, Charlene complains that all she's heard so far are boys' stories, including "Jim's" (she even goes on to point out the phallic nature of the sea serpent rising out of the sea).

Protesting that she doesn't have a story of her own to tell, Charlene relates one without intending to. Reflecting on the meaning of her story helps her reach the decision to give up her empty life in our reality and take a job in the kitchen at Worlds' End.

THE REALITY STORM. Reality storms occur when things happen that are so momentous that they "ripple," unsettling everything. They can be triggered by an event of great moment and consequence, an occurrence that reverberates across time and space and myth. It's a reality storm that has stranded so many travelers at the Worlds' End inn this particular night, one caused by the passing of one of the Endless, Dream.

DREAM. Although Morpheus does not appear in this segment, his presence is certainly felt, as it is his death which has triggered the reality storm which rages outside the Worlds' End Inn.

THE ENDLESS. The rest of the Endless, sans Destruction, make cameos in this segment—their ghostly figures appear in the sky, part of a funeral procession for their deceased brother, Morpheus.

TRIVIA

- The dedication reads: "This book's for Maddy, pink and tiny, born one hour and ten minutes ago, who has spent most of the intervening time sucking vigorously on my fingers in the mistaken belief that they provide a source of nutrition. I give you all your tomorrows, and these small stories. With my love, Neil Gaiman."

- In his book *Alice in Sunderland, Worlds' End* artist Bryan Talbot wrote, "[i]n St. Bede's Terrace [where he and his family live, in Sunderland, UK] there are occasional street bonfire parties held by the residents. . . . It's a small world. One neighbor claims to grow up with writer Neil Gaiman and another goes to school and plays in the first band of artist and Gaiman collaborator Dave McKean. I draw some of Neil's comics, notably a few of his tales of the Sandman, the King of Dreams. Dave does the covers. Both Neil and Dave grow up at the other end of the country. And there's only twenty-three houses in the terrace. Yep, small world."

- The collection's epigraph comes from Gaiman favorite G. K. Chesterton's 1904 novel, *The Napoleon of Notting Hill:* " 'For you and me, and all brave men, my brother,' said Wayne, in his strange chant, 'there is good wine poured in the inn at the end of the world.' "

- In his introduction, Stephen King says: "Gaiman's characters are always more than bugs running around in a tin can, to be skewered or let loose at the writer's whim. He takes each one on his or her own terms, so we feel their pride, their terror, their cunning, and their sadness."

- As with all of Gaiman's work, numerous "Easter eggs" have been inserted throughout the pages of *Worlds' End.* We'll mention a couple of the ones we find especially cool, both from "Hob's Leviathan." The first involves the ships Jim serves on. The first ship upon which Jim sets sail is called *The Spirit of Whitby.* Horror fans will recognize Whitby as a *Dracula* reference—it was the destination of the *Demeter,* the ill-fated vessel that transported Count Dracula to England in Bram Stoker's book. The second ship is called the *Pyramus;* the story of the ill-fated lovers Pyramus and Thisbe was told in Boccaccio's *Decameron,* and was later retold by Geoffrey Chaucer. It was probably the basis of *Romeo and Juliet,* and was also referenced in Shakespeare's *A Midsummer Night's Dream.* The second grace note is the line that opens the story, "Call me Jim." This obviously evokes "Call me Ishmael," the first line of Herman Melville's *Moby Dick.* Gaiman has said in interviews that "Hob's Leviathan" is him doing Kipling, and it feels to us like he's channeling Robert Louis Stevenson and Joseph Conrad as well.

- The first Hob Gadling story, "Men of Good Fortune," was named after a Lou Reed song. Reed's song "Heroin" is said to have had an influence on the story told in "Hob's Leviathan."

- Author Steven Brust, a contributor to *Sandman: Book of Dreams,* appears as a patron of the Worlds' End inn. He also makes an appearance in one of the epilogues to *The Wake,* at the Renaissance festival that serves as the backdrop for the story "Sunday Mourning."

- Petrefax received his own miniseries in 2000, in the four-issue *The Sandman Presents: Petrefax,* written by Mike Carey and illustrated by Steve Leialoha.

- The Joe Simon DC Comics oddities Brother Power, the Geek, and Prez were embraced by Gaiman for *Sandman* and a *Swamp Thing Annual* (see our entry on *Midnight Days,* later in this volume). Simon is a revered Golden Age comics writer/artist and frequent Jack Kirby collaborator, cocreator of the Simon/Kirby *Sandman,* and best known as cocreator (with Kirby) of Captain America. For DC Comics, Simon created the hippie-era oddity *Brother Power, the Geek* (1968, 2 issues), which crashed and burned. He followed this up with *Prez* (1974, 4 issues), in which long-haired, eighteen-year-old Prez Rickard is elected president of the United States, a concept undoubtedly inspired by the movie *Wild in the Streets* (1968, American-International Pictures). Simon and artist Jerry Grandenetti pitted Prez against such bizarre villains as Boss Smiley—the man with the smiley-button head Gaiman resurrects here—and a legless vampire. *Prez* lasted only two issues longer than Brother Power, and appeared in only one other comic, *Supergirl* issue 10, later in the seventies, until Gaiman revived the character for *Sandman* issue 54. Gaiman's resurrection of Prez led to one more appearance in the excellent Vertigo one-shot *Prez: Smells Like Teen President* (1994), scripted by Ed Brubaker and beautifully drawn by Eric Shanower. Brubaker and Shanower's Prez was an affectionate but sorrowful, somber "road movie" contrasting the idealistic counterculture values of the 1960s with the reality of the 1990s.

THE QUOTABLE GAIMAN

Well, I love doing short stories because of the variety they provide, and I saw *Worlds' End* as my last chance to explore a bunch of different genres in *Sandman*. I'd previously found it arduous to begin every story from scratch, however, so this time I used an inn to provide framing sequences.

—*The Sandman Companion*, by Hy Bender

||||||||||||||||||||||||||||||||||||||||||||||||||||||||||||||||||||

VOLUME NINE:
THE KINDLY ONES

(1996)

When Neil Gaiman began to write this story arc in 1993 (the first issue had a cover date of February 1994), he had been working on The Sandman for approximately five years. Although the opening pages of *The Kindly Ones* marked the beginning of the end, the series would continue for more than two years.

Numbering thirteen installments, *The Kindly Ones* was by far the longest story line in the series. Fans grew a bit impatient that the story was taking so long, and some complained about Marc Hempel's unconventional art style. Gaiman himself has commented on this, stating that the arc, while jarring to traditional comics fans when presented in a monthly format, works much better when collected together and read as a complete work.

Although chronologically representing the penultimate story arc, *The Kindly*

Ones is, for all intents and purposes, the climax of Sandman. While no prior sequence had seemed like a direct continuation of a preceding one, *The Kindly Ones* is a climactic metasequel of sorts that features characters and pulls together plot lines from all previous story arcs. As the late professor Frank McConnell writes in his introduction: "Gaiman has said repeatedly that *The Sandman* would conclude when the story begun in the first issue was completed. To many who have followed the book through its five-year development, that often seemed a heroic, but rather rash, claim. *The Kindly Ones* ends with monthly issue #69, and with that issue, he makes good his promise."

Or, as the Kindly Ones say at the end of the story:

"There. For good or bad. It's done."

The core of *Brief Lives*—what was originally published as The Sandman issues 47 through 49—laid the bedrock for all that culminates in *The Kindly Ones*. That said, the whole of the series to this point weighs heavily on this arc. *The Kindly Ones* is rich with subplots, but the main story concerns the abduction of three-year-old Daniel Hall. Daniel, you may recall, is the child of Lyta and the late Hector Hall. As depicted in *The Doll's House,* the Halls were residents of the Dreaming for a good portion of Lyta's pregnancy. Because of this, Morpheus considers Daniel "his," and when the child is kidnapped, Lyta believes the Dream King to be the culprit. After the real captors trick her into believing that Daniel has been killed, Lyta seeks out the Kindly Ones, avenging spirits who specialize in tormenting and slaying those who have killed family members. Having taken the life of Orpheus (see *Brief Lives*) in what amounted to a mercy killing, Dream makes an especially appealing target for the harpies, who embark on a campaign of terror in the Dreaming.

Meanwhile, Nuala, a faerie princess who was gifted to Morpheus (see *Season of Mists*), reluctantly returns to her homeland; Delirium searches for her lost pet dog, Barnabas (given to her by her brother Destruction at the conclusion of *Brief Lives*); Lucifer, who abdicated as ruler of Hell (also in *Season of Mists*), opens Lux, a Los Angeles nightclub; and Rose Walker (*A Game of You*), the young American woman who was once a dream vortex, travels to England to get her heart back from her dead grandmother.

One can surely conclude from even the brief summary provided above that *The Kindly Ones* is a sprawling, ambitious, complex work. Gaiman successfully pulls together the disparate threads of the tale he has been telling for half a decade, moving toward the conclusion he had envisioned from the first. Marc Hempel's art is vibrant and dynamic, and, in retrospect, perfectly appropriate to convey the madness and strangeness of Gaiman's endgame. The stories are full of nods to past issues, and packed with the wonderful literary references Gaiman so effortlessly weaves into his works.

Speaking with Despair toward the end of *Brief Lives,* Desire says of her brother Dream, "It's almost sad, in a way. He was a wreck just waiting for a place to happen." A bit flip, but perceptive nonetheless. At its core, *The Kindly Ones* is the story of that wreck, the tragic tale of Morpheus's ultimate downfall, a collapse made inevitable by his inability to adapt to changing circumstances. Trapped by outside forces at the beginning of the saga, the Dream Lord is now trapped in a cage of his own making, its bars forged out of his sense of duty, secured by the lock of his rigid, unbending nature. Faced with the choice of changing or dying, he chooses death.

When it comes to the subject of Dream's passing, perhaps it's best to let Mikal Gilmore have the last word. Commenting on the Dream Lord's demise in his perceptive introduction to *The Wake,* he writes: "In the end, Morpheus' heart could not be fixed or healed; it could not simply be set right by his own will, or therapy, or medication, (gods—or their equals—do not get to opt for therapy or medication) and Morpheus, in these tales, has come to understand the futility of living with a heart that cannot be fixed—especially living endlessly with such a heart."

The Kindly Ones was originally published in single-issue form as *Vertigo Jam* 1 (illustrated by Kevin Nowlan) and *The Sandman* issues 57 through 69 (illustrated by Marc Hempel).

VERTIGO JAM #1 "THE CASTLE" (PROLOGUE TO THE KINDLY ONES)

In this tale, a dreamer takes a tour of Dream's castle, conducted by Lucien. Lucien takes special pride in the library, pointing out that even the dreamer has a book in it, titled *The Bestselling Romantic Spy Thriller I Used to Think About on the Bus that Would Sell a Billion Copies and Mean I'd Never Have to Work Again.* Over the course of the tour, the dreamer (whose eyes we see out of) meets Mervyn Pumpkinhead, Nuala of Faerie, Matthew the Raven, Cain and Abel, and, finally, Dream himself.

Dream asks the dreamer if he has learned anything on his visit, to which the dreamer replies no. Dream says, "Well, all of you come here, sooner or later. This place is the heart of your dreaming, after all."

Just as Dream is asking him whether he'd like to stay a bit longer, the dreamer receives a call from the hotel operator, waking him up. He forgets what he just dreamed almost immediately.

#57 "THE KINDLY ONES, PART ONE"

The story opens with the three Fates chatting about their work, as they sit and spin people's destinies, stopping every so often to casually snip a thread to end someone's life. It then segues to Lyta Hall's apartment, where she's discussing with her friend Carla how hard it is to raise her son, Daniel, on her own. She also discusses how fiercely protective of Daniel she is, telling Carla she'd kill anyone who hurt him.

Meanwhile, in the Dreaming, Matthew the Raven drops in to visit Morpheus in his castle, stopping first to chat with Mervyn, Nuala, and Lucien. He comes upon Dream as he is re-creating the Corinthian. Matthew asks Dream about a comment that Delirium made in *Brief Lives,* that there had been eleven or twelve more ravens before him. Dream tells him there have been even more than that, but won't answer Matthew's questions about their fates. Concluding that he won't learn anything more, Matthew returns to Eve's cave.

The chapter concludes on a sour note, as Lyta, at a nightclub called Lux (owned by Lucifer, who also plays the piano there) to discuss a job offer, suddenly has a terrible feeling that something is wrong at home. Hurrying back to her apartment, she discovers to her horror that Daniel is gone.

#58 "THE KINDLY ONES, PART TWO"

Lyta Hall sits in a chair in her apartment, mute, staring off into space, traumatized by Daniel's disappearance. Questioned by two policemen, Lieutenant Luke Pinkerton and his partner, Gordy Fellowes, she responds that she knows of no one with an undue interest in her son. ("No. Nobody real," she mutters.) All she knows is that when she came home, her babysitter was asleep on the couch and her child was gone.

Simultaneously, Cluracan arrives at Dream's castle. Although told to keep to a certain path, he strays from it, entering a room with a mirror that contains an image of Dream that we later learn is Daniel. While in that room, he vomits up a wild hart (a stag), his Nemesis, which turns to attack him. Cluracan is saved at the last moment by his sister, Nuala.

Cluracan catches up with his sister, and describes his visits to Aurelia and to the Worlds' End inn. It turns out that when he told Queen Titania what he had seen while at the inn (see *Worlds' End* for details), she sent him to the Dreaming to retrieve Nuala. They go to Morpheus to see if he will release her. To her dismay (for she loves him), the Dream Lord acquiesces, but not before giving her a gift. Touching the charm around her neck, he tells her that she has only to call and he will appear, ready to grant her a boon.

In the real world, Lyta is descending into madness. In a dream, she walks to her cellar, where she meets the three Fates, who call her "granddaughter." They tell her that they will see her again.

#59 "THE KINDLY ONES, PART THREE"

Loki and Puck reappear; sitting in an empty room, they feed logs into the fireplace, discussing past exploits. Readers learn that they are in fact Daniel's kidnappers, and are planning on feeding him to the flames.

The story then cuts to a distressed Hob Gadling standing at the grave of his latest lost love, who was killed by an automobile while crossing the street. Hob pours his heart out to her, the first woman he had been with since Peggy died in the Blitz

(Peggy may be the grown-up Margaret, who *Sandman* readers met in the guise of Jim in "Hob's Leviathan"). Leaving the cemetery, he sees Dream, who wants to talk. They retire to a tavern to chat, but Dream quickly grows tense, and leaves.

The story briefly cuts away to look in on the Endless. Destiny walks through his garden, catching a glimpse of himself in the distance; Desire closes herself off inside her realm; Despair notes that Desire's sigil has gone dark; and Delirium transforms into 111 (coincidentally, the number of her hotel room in *Brief Lives*) perfect, tiny, multicolored fish, then back again before setting off to find her dog, Barnabas, who has gone missing.

As this chapter concludes, Lyta Hall is told by the police that they've found a charred body that could be Daniel. Clutching the photograph of the corpse in her hand, she reflects on Dream's intrusion into her life, and on his promise that he would one day come for Daniel. Tipping over into madness, she realizes that she knows exactly what she must do.

#60 "THE KINDLY ONES, PART FOUR"

The angel Remiel visits Lucifer to ask if he's ever thought about returning to rule over Hell. Lucifer just laughs in his face.

Elsewhere, Lyta Hall begins a long, strange trip to find the Kindly Ones. At the beginning of this phase of her journey she meets a young hero trying to free his true love from a tower, a queen who has been turned into a cyclops, and a cat/woman on her way to challenge a shape-changing ogre.

Cut to Rose Walker's apartment, one floor below Lyta's. Rose awakes from a sex dream (where she's interrupted by a Peeping Tom, Abel) to find Lyta's friend Carla at the door. It turns out that Rose is the babysitter who fell asleep while watching Daniel; she is in Los Angeles to visit a sick friend. Carla tells Rose that the police would like to speak to her, and she is puzzled to find that the card they gave her is totally blank.

As Lyta moves forward, she comes to a house occupied by two sisters dressed as brides, Stheno and Euryale. They ask if she wants an apple, then direct her to a garden. Coming upon the tree, she meets Geryon, a three-headed serpent, who intimates that this is the biblical tree of life, as opposed to the tree of knowledge, whose fruit Adam and Eve sampled. Although they advise against it, Lyta takes a bite of the apple.

In the Dreaming, Morpheus adds some finishing touches to the Corinthian, in preparation for his revival.

#61 "THE KINDLY ONES, PART FIVE"

Chapter 5 begins as Stheno and Euryale contemplate a sleeping Lyta. Lyta awakes to discover that she has snakes in her hair; the longer she stays with the sisters, the more she'll come to resemble their dead sister, Medusa.

Rose visits Zelda (see *The Doll's House*), who is dying from AIDS. Rose is paying for Zelda's care, and keeping a vigil over her friend. Zelda dozes, and awakes with a message for Rose from her grandmother: She must go back to where Unity used to sleep; if she goes there, Unity will give her her heart back.

In the Dreaming, Morpheus speaks with the new Corinthian. Dream asks him and Matthew to run an errand for him: Find Daniel and bring him back to the Dreaming.

In Faerie, Titania speaks with Nuala, and asks if Dream had ever spoken of her, or if he had happened to give Nuala any messages for her. Nuala says no. Titania fingers the gift Dream gave Nuala, and asks, "If I were to ask you for it, what would you say?" Nuala replies that it was a gift, and not in her power to give.

In Los Angeles, Carla attempts to locate Detectives Fellowes and Pinkerton, but it seems as if they don't exist. After Daniel tries to communicate with her through the photograph of his "corpse," Loki appears to her as Pinkerton. Fearing she is on the verge of stumbling upon the truth, he immolates her. As he walks away he says to himself, "I am Loki. And I will be under an obligation to no one."

#62 "THE KINDLY ONES, PART SIX"

Chapter 6 focuses entirely on Rose Walker, and on her trip to England and the nursing home where her grandmother, Unity, had slept. While there she meets the owner, Paul McGuire, and Jack Holdaway, an attorney from the law firm that handles her family's affairs. Wandering through the nursing home, she meets three older women, Amelia Crupp, Magda Treadgold, and Helena. Amelia tells her a story called "The Flying Children."

This trio is yet another incarnation—either actual or symbolic—of the Three Witches: mother, maiden, and crone.

Leaving the ladies, she encounters McGuire, who tells her that the nursing home is just down the road from the Ashdown Forest, the basis for A. A. Milne's Hundred Acre Wood. He also tells her that the original Piglet toy was lost in that wood by Christopher Robin Milne, and how, as a boy, he and his mother would walk the woods looking for Piglet.

Later, McGuire takes her into his comatose lover's room. His lover turns out to be Alex Burgess, whose affliction was caused by Morpheus. Alex has been asleep for five years. Next to him in his bed lies a Piglet toy. Rose leaves her grandmother's ring next to Alex for luck.

#63 "THE KINDLY ONES, PART SEVEN"

Thessaly arrives in Los Angeles, looking for Lyta, who she finds in an alley. Thessaly places her in a protective circle. Although appearing to be out of it in our world, Lyta still seeks the Furies in the surreal land in which she's been traveling.

In the Dreaming, Morpheus is visited by Odin, who has discovered that it was not Loki who was returned to his prison beneath the earth, and has concluded that Dream must have had something to do with it. Dream does not deny this. Odin tells Dream that his plan to place Loki in his debt will most certainly backfire.

Cut to Delirium, still looking for her dog, Barnabas. Walking into her brother Destiny's garden, she notices that the statue of Dream has its head in its hands, as if it is mourning. She asks if she should go comfort him, but Destiny advises against it.

Lyta finds the Furies at last, and tells them that she wants revenge against Morpheus for killing her husband and for stealing and killing her son. The Furies tell her that that's not enough, that they are only empowered to avenge blood debts. They tell her she's mistaken about Morpheus killing her son, and that even if he had killed Daniel, they could do nothing about it.

They can, however, seek revenge against Morpheus for killing *his* own son . . .

#64 "THE KINDLY ONES, PART EIGHT"

Dream has a contentious meeting with his sister Delirium, who questions his unwavering devotion to duty.

In England, Rose Walker sleeps with Jack Holdaway, an impulsive act she comes to regret later, when she learns that he is married. In Los Angeles, Matthew and the Corinthian examine Carla's charred corpse. Here the Corinthian is especially useful, because he can see through Carla's eyes. Placing her orbs inside his empty eye sockets, he learns that she was killed by Loki. He also divines that Daniel is no longer in the waking world.

Dream's castle receives a visitor—the three-who-are-one. Although they are only seen as shadows, we know that the Furies have arrived in the Dreaming. Meeting resistance from the castle's three gatekeepers, they kill one of them, the Gryphon. After this display of power, Dream instructs the remaining two guards to let them pass.

They ascend into the main hall, and identify themselves after Dream mistakenly assumes it is Lyta Hall. They are far more than Lyta Hall. They are the Kindly Ones, the Erinyes. They are vengeance and unending hatred. "We are," they tell him, "your doom." They are here with a warning: Submit, or they will destroy everything he has ever loved or cared for.

#65 "THE KINDLY ONES, PART NINE"

Rose visits Fawney Rig, ancestral home of the Roderick family. Touring the manor with Paul McGuire, she enters the library, which is as unique in its way as Dream's. Left to her own devices, she descends into the basement, into the very room where

Dream was formerly imprisoned. There she meets Desire, who reveals to Rose that he is her grandfather. Rose opens up to Desire, telling her how she hates love, because it makes you vulnerable. She continues until McGuire opens the door to find her sleeping on the floor. Laying next to her is an art deco lighter shaped like a heart.

Matthew and the Corinthian visit Svartalfheim, where they find Loki. The Corinthian subdues the trickster, and tortures him brutally until he gives up Daniel.

In the Dreaming, the Furies attack and kill Gilbert (Fiddler's Green) by thrusting a wooden lance through his heart. Seeking to forestall further attacks, Dream travels to Lyta Hall's side, only to discover that he cannot cross the mystical circle that Thessaly has constructed. Their discussion, held standing over the prone body of Lyta, is revealing, as readers learn that it was Thessaly who was the cause of Morpheus's distress at the beginning of *Brief Lives*.

#66 "THE KINDLY ONES, PART TEN"

Freeing Daniel, the Corinthian confronts Loki's partner, Puck, who was hiding in the rafters. Rather than battling Dream's servant, Puck simply decides to return to Faerie. After the Corinthian departs, Odin and Thor appear to return Loki to his place of eternal torture beneath the earth.

The Furies continue to slay denizens of the Dreaming, this time slaughtering Abel, then moving on to Mervyn Pumpkinhead. When Lucien asks Dream why he doesn't simply restore the things the Kindly Ones destroy, Morpheus tells him they won't leave until he is destroyed, by his own hand or another's. "Removing" Lyta Hall proving "impractical," the Dream Lord is now "considering" what to do.

Learning that Dream is in trouble, Nuala summons him to Faerie with her charm, in order to warn him. He tells her that he was already aware of the danger of the Dirae (as she calls the Furies), and that no real harm can occur as long as he remains in the Dreaming . . . which, they realize, he has not.

#67 "THE KINDLY ONES, PART ELEVEN"

The Corinthian returns to the Dreaming with Daniel in tow, encountering Cain as he makes his way toward the castle. Cain tells him that things have changed since he's been away, that the Dreaming is under attack. He also tells the killer a secret: A raven created the world. When Noah sent him out to find land, it had all been washed away, so he created it. "He shat the dry land and he pissed the fresh water," says Cain. "Then he flew off, laughing fit to burst. So the world was there for the dove to find."

Nuala and Dream continue their discussion. When Nuala says that it seems as if he wants to be punished for killing Orpheus, Dream is silent. Before he departs he tells her he still owes her a boon. She tells him that she wants him to stay, and to love her, but now . . . she'd prefer it if he would just go.

In Los Angeles, Rose Walker learns that Zelda has died. In the Dreaming, Lucien, Cain, the Corinthian, and Daniel wait for Morpheus to return. Destiny wanders in his garden, reading from his book.

Traveling by horse-drawn coach, then by an art deco train, Dream finally arrives back in his realm, where he is immediately confronted by the Kindly Ones, who strike him in the face with a whip composed of scorpions, scarring him as Alianora had foretold. Although this angers Dream, he remains composed.

As this chapter draws to a close, the Kindly Ones have again disappeared. Dream prepares for their final meeting.

#68 "THE KINDLY ONES, PART TWELVE"

As this chapter opens, Dream is contemplating an emerald as he talks to Matthew. Daniel plays contentedly on the floor at Dream's feet. Finally, dressed in his cloak and his helm, Dream, accompanied by Matthew, leaves the castle to confront his destiny.

Cut to Delirium, outside Club Lux, asking Lucifer's aide and companion Mazikeen to let her enter. Cut to Matthew and Dream traveling to the final battlefield. Cut to Rose Walker, informing Hal (her former landlord in Florida who is now famous as the television personality known as Vixen) of Zelda's death.

Matthew and Dream converse as they wait for the Kindly Ones on the borders of nightmare. When Matthew asks about the ravens that preceded him, Dream replies that some, tiring of their existence, were allowed to enter Death's realm. One was returned to humanity. Two stayed in the Dreaming, Lucien, the first raven, being one of those.

Finally, the Kindly Ones arrive. Speaking with them, Dream determines that they will not settle for anything other than his death. He asks Matthew to return to the castle with his pouch and his helm, and to ask Death to come meet him. Matthew does as his master has bid.

#69 "THE KINDLY ONES, PART THIRTEEN"

Death comes to Dream. Reenacting the scene on the park bench depicted in "The Sound of Her Wings," she sits down next to him on top of a rocky crag. Dream tells her he is tired, very tired. Death does her best to dissuade him from the course he's chosen, but he will not be swayed. Death eventually realizes that there is nothing she can do except help her brother. She asks Dream to take her hand, and he does so.

Dream's passing is felt everywhere, most notably in Faerie by Titania, and on Earth by Delirium (just as she's reunited with Barnabas) and Lucifer. In Los Angeles, Hal and Rose Walker attend Zelda's funeral. In England, Alex Burgess awakens and asks for Paul McGuire. In Thessaly's flat, Lyta comes back to herself.

In the Dreaming, Daniel sits on the castle floor, holding the same emerald Morpheus was holding before he left to confront the Kindly Ones. The emerald flashes, then changes shape in his hand, becoming a pendant on a chain. Daniel also changes—into the new Dream. Unlike Morpheus, he dresses in white; the only color displayed is the green of the emerald that hangs around his neck.

PEOPLE, PLACES, AND THINGS

THE KINDLY ONES. Also known as The Furies, The Ladies, the Fates, the Eumenides, the Dirae, the Erinye, or the three-who-are-one, it's their function to avenge blood killings. Empowered by Lyta Hall's fury, and justified by Dream's killing of his own son, Orpheus, the Kindly Ones launch an assault on the Dreaming, leading to the death of the current incarnation of Dream.

LYTA HALL. Mother of Daniel, she mistakenly believes that Dream is behind the kidnapping and apparent death of her son. Driven insane by her loss and her hatred of Dream, she seeks out the Kindly Ones to ask that they avenge her son's death, unleashing their power on Morpheus.

DANIEL. Early on in the Sandman saga Morpheus somewhat ominously says to Lyta Hall, "The child you have carried so long in dreams. That child is mine. Take good care of it. One day I will come for it." Morpheus himself does not come for Daniel; rather, he sends his emissary, the Corinthian, to rescue the child from Loki and Puck and bring the boy back to the Dreaming. After Morpheus passes, Daniel, through the power of the green emerald, becomes the new Dream.

THE GRYPHON, MERVYN, GILBERT, AND ABEL. All servants of Dream, they all are killed by the Kindly Ones when those three ancient beings invade the Dreaming.

MATTHEW. Eve's raven, and also Dream's, Matthew stays with Dream in the moments before he confronts the Kindly Ones. He also accompanies the Corinthian on his mission to find Daniel.

NUALA. At the request of her brother, Cluracan, Dream releases her from his service. To formally thank her for the three years she has served him, Dream touches her pendant and gives her a gift: "If in need, hold the stone with both hands, and call me. I will come to you; you may have one boon."

Dream comes to regret this gift, as Nuala, discovering he is in danger, calls to him at an inopportune time. Duty-bound, Dream comes and tells her he is already aware of the situation. When he asks her what she'd like from him, she replies, "I wanted you to love me." Utterly surprised, Dream says that though he cannot grant her wish, he could give her a dream of his love. "I already have that, my lord," says Nuala.

DREAM. Morpheus spends a good part of *The Kindly Ones* going through what Elizabeth Kübler-Ross labeled the five stages of grief: denial, anger, bargaining, depression, and, finally, acceptance. His acceptance leads to a meeting with his sister Death, and ultimately, his demise. Dream lives on, however, in the body of Daniel.

THE CORINTHIAN. Re-created by Dream to find the missing Daniel, the "dark mirror of humanity" faithfully performs that function, bringing Daniel safely to the Dreaming.

LUCIFER. In *The Kindly Ones* we see that Lucifer is fulfilling some of the goals he set for himself in *Season of the Mists*. He has, for instance, opened up a restaurant in Los Angeles called Lux, where he plays the piano for his customers, amusing himself by occasionally causing the deaths of some of them.

LOKI AND PUCK. (Aka Lieutenant Luke Pinkerton and Gordy Fellowes.) Doing what they do best, Loki and Puck kidnap Daniel, and chaos ensues. After the Corinthian rescues Daniel from their clutches, Loki is returned to his eternal punishment by Odin and Thor, and Puck returns to Faerie.

HOB GADLING. After departing the cemetery where the latest of his long string of lovers has been buried, the long-lived Hob is met by Dream, who, troubled, seeks out his old friend. They retire to a bar (called Faith, Hope and Charity) to chat. Dream does not find what he is seeking, however.

ROSE WALKER. During the course of *The Kindly Ones*, Rose unsuccessfully babysits for Daniel; travels to England; meets her grandfather, Desire (Desire raped Unity Kincaid when she suffered from the sleeping sickness); engages in a brief affair; and loses a friend, Zelda, to AIDS. We learn she's been spending her time since the end of *The Doll's House* researching a book she's writing about the quest for the triple goddess (maiden, mother, and crone) in TV sitcoms.

STHENO AND EURYALE. Two sisters (who look a lot like the spider women duo from *The Doll's House*) Lyta speaks with on her journey to discover the whereabouts of the Kindly Ones. They ask her if she'd like to remain with them to replace their lost sibling. In Greek mythology, Euryale and Stheno were two of the three Gorgons, three vicious sisters with brass hands, sharp fangs, and hair of living, venomous snakes. The Gorgons were able to turn any creature to stone with their gaze. Stheno and Euryale were immortal, but Medusa, the other sister, was mortal.

GERYON. A three-headed creature that Lyta encounters in her travels to see the Kindly Ones. In mythology Geryon was slain by Hercules as part of his twelve labors.

THESSALY. The sorceress who first appeared in *A Game of You*. In *The Kindly Ones* we learn that she is another of Dream's ex-lovers; in fact, she is the one who had just broken Morpheus's heart at the beginning of *Brief Lives*. Finding Lyta on the streets, Thessaly brings her home and places her in a mystical circle of protection, and stands guard over her. When Dream considers taking Lyta's life to stop her madness, Thessaly stops him.

CELIA CRIPPS. Rose sits next to her on the plane back to the United States, and they discuss their tastes in literature. Celia mentions an aunt, Ethel Cripps, the former mistress of Burgess, and John Dee's mother (see *Preludes & Nocturnes*).

THE DREAMSTONES. In a conversation with Matthew the Raven, Dream tells the bird that he's been contemplating a green emerald, one of the twelve Dreamstones he created very long ago. The greatest of them, the one he put most of himself into, was the Ruby. "There were others," he says. "A Rose–Quartz I gave to poor Alianora, a Fire-Opal, a Black Pearl, a Topaz . . ." Some were scattered. Some destroyed. The green emerald is the least of them, an eagle stone Dream created for the great birds, which they used for a while, then returned. Dream gives the jewel to the toddler Daniel; later it seems to transform the boy into the new incarnation of Dream.

DEATH. Of course, if Dream is destined to die, he must be visited by his older sister. After determining that the Kindly Ones will not be satisfied with anything short of his death, he summons her. They speak briefly, intimately for a while, until Death says, "Destruction simply left. Took down his sigil, said he wasn't responsible for the realm of destruction anymore, that it was no longer his affair, and took off into the forever. You could have done that."

"No," Dream replies, "I could not."

"No," she says. "You couldn't, could you?"

In a panel ironically reminiscent of Michelangelo's *God's Creation of Adam*, Dream gives Death his hand, and is gone.

ALEX BURGESS. The effects of Dream's passing are felt everywhere. For instance, Alex Burgess (see *Preludes & Nocturnes*), asleep for the past five years, wakes up, asking for his lover, Paul McGuire.

TRIVIA

- After Thessaly rescues Lyta from a back alley, she's seen reading a book about Richard Dadd. Dadd (1817–86) was an English painter famous for his depictions of fairies and other supernatural subjects, which he rendered with obsessively minuscule detail. Most of the works for which he is best known were created while he was incarcerated in a psychiatric hospital. One of his works is called *Contradiction: Oberon and Titania*.

- When next we see her, she is reading a book about John Bauer (1882–1918), a Swedish painter and illustrator, best known for his illustrations for the yearly fairy tale book *Bland tomtar och troll* (*Among Gnomes and Trolls*). Still later, Thessaly is reading a book titled *When Real Things Happen to Imaginary People*.

- When Dream is contemplating what's to come, he travels throughout the world, at one point stopping to feed pigeons, and at another, to watch a performance of *A Midsummer Night's Dream,* echoing actions seen in issues 8 and 19. Other panels in this story arc may look familiar, as they are re-creations of ones from earlier stories, such as when Dream tells Lyta that Daniel is his, and when the Corinthian encounters Daniel/Morpheus for the first time.

- On the plane ride home Rose is reading a volume from the Burgess library titled *Here Comes a Candle,* a novel by some "dead white male," about an artist who dreams of a woman. Meeting her in the flesh, he locks her up in his cellar; every night, he goes down to the cellar and she tells him what to paint. Rose thinks they're "screwing," but it's an old book, and thus not very explicit. Explicit or not, it sounds a lot like the story of Calliope told in issue 17.

- The first panel of each issue includes a cord, symbolizing the thread of fate that is eventually going to be cut. The cords are accompanied by text that comments on where the story line is at that moment.

- Part 6 of *The Kindly Ones* tells the story of Rose Walker's trip to England. During that episode she is told a folktale about revenge by an old woman, Amelia Crupp, in a nursing home. The pages that carry that story are drawn by Charles Vess.

- A dream sequence illustrated by Shawn McManus for Vertigo's *The Dreaming* issue 39 is a visual reference to *The Kindly Ones*.

- If you look carefully at page six of Part 9 (on the floor, to the right of Desire) you can see a paperback copy of Stephen King's *IT,* still laying where Dream's guard Barney left it on page twenty-six of the very first issue of The Sandman.

- The Corinthian's revival echoes that of Duncan Idaho in Frank Herbert's *Dune Messiah*. Reading that novel before he read *Dune,* Gaiman was struck by how Duncan was revived with some, but not all, of his memories.

THE QUOTABLE GAIMAN

I still do not know how successful *The Kindly Ones* was, how close I got or how far I came from what I set out to say. Still, it's the heaviest of all of these volumes, and thus, in hardback at least, could undoubtedly be used to stun a burglar; which has always been my definition of real art.

—Afterword, *The Kindly Ones*

VOLUME TEN:
THE WAKE

(1997)

The three issues of The Sandman that comprise *The Wake* explore themes of mortality, mourning, reconciliation, change, and facing the future. It stands as an epilogue to the entire series, its mood being restrained, reflective, but overall, quietly celebratory. The first half of the collection is a story arc that chronicles the wake for Dream's incarnation of Morpheus, who died at the end of *The Kindly Ones*. Numerous characters from the series make appearances, mingle, and express their feelings about what has occurred. In the last installment of this three-issue story, a series of speakers, ending with Death, appear to eulogize Morpheus. Even as all of these events take place, Daniel, the new aspect of Dream who first appeared at the end of *The Kindly Ones,* starts to build (and rebuild) relationships with the varied inhabitants of the Dreaming.

There is a wonderful warmth and grace in how Gaiman deals with Dream's passing, the mourning of his friends, family, and associates, and the welcoming of a new family member into the ranks of the Endless that makes this tale resonate with readers. *The Wake* is one of the most touching and carefully constructed sequences in the entire Sandman saga.

Probably the most moving aspect of this arc is the new Dream's combination of world weariness and naïveté. In the tradition of his old incarnation, the new Dream understands that he has responsibilities, but he has little practical idea of how to go about fulfilling them. The fear he feels at meeting his family for the "first" time shows that Dream is now more human. His humanity, and his change in perspective, are especially evident in the mercy he shows toward Lyta Hall, in forgiving her for her involvement in the Kindly Ones affair, something Morpheus could never have done. Besides being more human, he has also become more humane.

Now, after the three issues which comprised *The Wake,* most fans would probably have been satisfied with one epilogue, but Gaiman saw fit to provide three. The first, "Sunday Mourning," brings readers up-to-date on the doings of Hob Gadling. The second, "The Exiles," is a sequel to "Soft Places." The third, "The Tempest," tells the story of the second play William Shakespeare wrote for Dream. Each, in its own way, explores the themes mentioned above, while also providing a sense of closure.

And thus, the saga ended.

Fans who followed the series felt a deep sense of loss when it concluded, but were given some good advice in the words of Matthew the Raven. Summing up the message of *The Wake,* he says to Daniel: "When the dead are gone, you mourn, and go on living."

Readers who cherished the monthly series felt like a special part of their lives was ending. But Gaiman and Matthew both know that, like Dream, stories endure. To quote the raven again: "The king is dead. Long live the king."

#70 "THE WAKE, CHAPTER ONE: WHICH OCCURS IN THE WAKE OF WHAT HAS GONE BEFORE"

(ILLUSTRATED BY MICHAEL ZULLI)

Here the call goes out from parts unknown, informing the Endless that one of their number, Dream, has passed from this plane of reality. Gathering together in Litharge (see *Brief Lives*), the remaining Endless (sans Destruction) create a golem to descend into the catacombs beneath the city to gather Dream's cerement and the funeral rites. Meanwhile, upon falling asleep, all those who have known Morpheus begin to enter the Dreaming to attend his funeral.

Morpheus's servants must adjust to the departure of their former master and the arrival of their new one. Daniel, the new incarnation of Dream, is also adjusting to his new station and surroundings; everything is at once familiar and strange to him. He begins to repair the damage done by the Kindly Ones by restoring Abel and Mervyn to life; he tries to revive Gilbert, who refuses the gift, feeling it would cheapen his death.

Matthew seems to be the only one in the Dreaming who is not breathing a sigh of relief. Rather, he is grieving for Morpheus, a grief amplified by the guilt he feels at leaving Dream to face the Kindly Ones alone, even if it was at his master's request.

In Faerie, and on Earth, various characters who appeared in previous story arcs dream in preparation for entering the Dreaming for Morpheus's funeral. Nuala dreams. Rose Walker and Richard Madoc dream, as do Lyta Hall, Alex Burgess, and Hob Gadling. Beings of great power, like Queen Titania, Duma, and the Lady Bast enter portals to Dream's realm.

#71 "THE WAKE, CHAPTER TWO: IN WHICH A WAKE IS HELD"

(ILLUSTRATED BY MICHAEL ZULLI)

Characters who have appeared in the Sandman comic continue to arrive, mingling as they wait for the proceedings to get under way. There are some impromptu eulogies given, as various characters reminisce about Morpheus. As Gaiman writes, "Everybody's here. You're here."

Daniel remains in the castle; it seems he cannot attend the wake. "Not according to the book of the ceremony, no," Lucien tells him. "The family may not greet you, nor formally recognize you, until the funeral matters are over with and done."

#72 "THE WAKE, CHAPTER THREE: IN WHICH WE WAKE"

(ILLUSTRATED BY MICHAEL ZULLI)

The ceremonies finally get under way, and Morpheus, who appears to be lying on a table underneath the cerement Eblis has spread across it, is formally eulogized by his family and friends. At their conclusion, Morpheus's "body" is placed on a ship, which sails into the sky. With a brilliant flash, Morpheus takes his place among the stars.

Back in the Dreaming, Daniel continues to go about his new duties. After having a heart-to-heart talk with Matthew, and forgiving his mother, Lyta Hall, for her actions, he goes to meet his family again for the first time.

PEOPLE, PLACES, AND THINGS

THE ENDLESS. Sans Destruction, they gather at a crossroads in the shadow of the Quinsy Mountains to prepare for their brother's funeral. Visiting the necropolis Litharge, they create a golem, whom they name Eblis O'Shaughnessy, to descend into the catacombs of the city to collect the funeral rite and Morpheus's cerements. They then enter the Dreaming and begin to prepare. Once those tasks are accomplished, they speak about him at his funeral.

EBLIS O'SHAUGHNESSY. A golem created by the Endless as their envoy, he's given life by Death, and named by Delirium. Eblis descends into the catacombs beneath Litharge to gather the cerement cloth and the book of the ceremony. He remains in the Dreaming afterward as a new servant for Dream.

DANIEL. The new incarnation of Dream, he is clearly not Morpheus, although he obviously retains Morpheus's knowledge and powers. Still driven by a strong sense of responsibility, the new Dream is more flexible and less judgmental than his predecessor. He's also a bit unsure of himself, admitting to Matthew the Raven, "This is very new to me, Matthew. This place. This world. I have existed since the beginning of time. This is a true thing. I am older than worlds and suns and gods. But tomorrow I will meet my brother and sisters for the first time. And I am afraid."

MORPHEUS. The former incarnation of Dream, he "died" in *The Kindly Ones*. Now his friends and acquaintances gather together to remember the being they knew and, perhaps, loved. After his funeral Morpheus is given an air burial, placed on a ship that conveys his essence to the stars.

THE GRYPHON, ABEL, MERVYN, AND GILBERT. All denizens of the Dreaming, they were all early casualties in the war between the Kindly Ones and Dream, losing their lives to the Furies. Abel, Mervyn, and Gilbert are all resurrected by Daniel as he goes about restoring order to the Dreaming. Gilbert, also known as Fiddler's Green, rejects Daniel's gift, however, telling him that it would cheapen his death. It is not necessary for Dream to resurrect the Gryphon; he merely sends a request to the island of Arimaspia for a replacement. Abel sums up what's happened on the way to the ceremony. Asked by a confused Eblis O'Shaughnessy (he's been told Dream has died, but has just met Daniel in the castle), "Then what died? Who are you mourning?" Abel, whose job, after all, is to tell secrets, replies, "A puh-point of view."

MATTHEW. Morpheus's raven, he is so distraught at his friend's death that he initially considers asking Daniel to let him follow Morpheus into the great beyond. After much anguished reflection, he decides to stay in the Dreaming to help Daniel cope with being the new Dream Lord.

HOB GADLING. Dream's long-lived mortal friend, with whom he met at least once every century, attends the funeral in his dreams, sitting next to Mad Hettie, who seems surprised to see him.

LYTA HALL. Despite playing a role in Morpheus's death, a disheveled Lyta is also present at his funeral. Afterward, she meets with Daniel, who gives her the gift of forgetfulness, and promises to protect her for the rest of her days.

CLURACAN AND THE NEMESIS. A citizen of Faerie, Cluracan attends the funeral in his role as ambassador of that land. Once in the Dreaming, he is confronted by his Nemesis, who he himself gave birth to in *The Kindly Ones*. Although it's his reason for being, the Nemesis is not trying to destroy Cluracan at that moment, because it would not be good manners to do so at a wake. He does vow, however, to do so once the proceedings are over.

LUCIEN. Dream's librarian, the first man, and Dream's first raven, he provides what amounts to a synopsis of the entire series when Matthew asks him, "Why did it happen? Why did he let it happen?" Lucien replies, "Let it, Matthew? I think he did a little more than let it happen . . . Charitably . . . I think . . . sometimes one must change or die. And, in the end, there were, perhaps, limits to how much he could let himself change."

TITANIA, CALLIOPE, THESSALY, NADA, AND ALIANORA. The queen of Faerie, a muse, a sorceress, a reincarnated African queen, and the former owner of the Land (see *A Game of You*), respectively, they've all been romantically involved with Morpheus at one time or another. All are drawn to this complex being's wake and funeral, out of love and nostalgia.

BHARTARI RAJA. An "old, old" friend of Lucien's, he first appeared in *Brief Lives* in the story "Hob's Leviathan," relating his tale of the immortal Indian king. He tells

Matthew that he's currently living under the name of Silas Tomken Cumberbatch, "like Winnie the Pooh and Mister Saunders."

SUPERMAN, BATMAN, AND J'ONN J'ONZZ. Key players in the DC Comics universe, they have all crossed paths with Morpheus during their crime-fighting careers. Tellingly, Superman appears in the Dreaming in his alias of Clark Kent, suggesting that this is how he really sees himself.

JOHN CONSTANTINE, THE PHANTOM STRANGER, DR. OCCULT, AND MISTER E. Just as the superheroes attending the funeral gather together to talk shop, so do DC's main mystery men. Constantine (see *Preludes & Nocturnes*) says, "Nice trench coat" to Dr. Occult. The Stranger consults his pocket watch. These are also the four individuals who aid Timothy Hunter in Gaiman's *The Books of Magic*.

THE EULOGIES. Speeches about and remembrances of Morpheus are delivered by countless entities. Readers get to hear firsthand those given by Destiny, the Lady Bast, Desire, Despair, Wesley Dodds, Dumas, Delirium, and Matthew. In addition, they get to see brief glimpses of those delivered by the Alder Man, Odin, Nada, and Pharamond.

ORPHEUS. Morpheus's deceased son, his spirit watches as his father's "corpse" is conveyed by ship to its resting place among the stars.

DESTRUCTION. Morpheus's brother doesn't attend the funeral, but he does secretly visit Daniel as it progresses. They talk of many things, ending as Destruction says, "I wasn't going to come, and then I thought, sod it. I'll stop by, give you a little advice. You've never been inclined to listen to advice in the past, but, well: Things change, don't they?"

"Yes, they do," replies Daniel.

"Wise lad," comments Destruction.

#73 "SUNDAY MOURNING"

(ILLUSTRATED BY MICHAEL ZULLI)

"Sunday Mourning" chronicles the immortal Hob Gadling's day at a Renaissance festival with his latest girlfriend, Gwen, who works there. Miserable, and feeling every year of his advanced age (635), he grouses that no one there has any idea of what the Renaissance era in England was *really* like ("Nobody in England had even *heard* of the Renaissance until it had been over for centuries"); then he gets into an argument about English slaving practices with Gwen (something he knows about firsthand, unfortunately).

Then he gets drunk.

Hob, of course, has appeared several times in the series since first surfacing in "Men of Good Fortune." Here readers see how disillusioned with living he has become. Later he enters a condemned building, where he encounters Death of the Endless, who tells him of the death of Morpheus (although he attended the funeral, it was while he was dreaming). She offers to let him die as well, now that he no longer has his agreement with Morpheus to fulfill. But, after reflecting on it for a few moments, Hob turns her down, choosing to go on living. His mood improved, he leaves the fair with Gwen, eager to see what the future will bring.

Hob's anguish over whether to choose a poetic death over a degrading life is one of the great moments in the series.

#74 "EXILES"

(ILLUSTRATED BY JOHN J. MUTH)

"Exiles" is a sequel of sorts to "Soft Places" (see *Fables & Reflections*). It tells the story of Master Li. A former man of respect and means, he is exiled by his emperor when his son brings disgrace on his house. Like Morpheus, he cannot forgive his son's trespasses; nor can he ignore his responsibilities. Traveling across a desert accompanied by a kitten he rescued, he wanders into a soft place, a place where different realities intrude upon one another. There he meets Morpheus, who tells him a story about a father and son, a recasting of his falling out with Orpheus. Moving on after his meeting with Dream, Li encounters many strange visions before meeting Dream again, only this time in the form of Daniel. Intrigued by the man, Daniel asks him if he would like to serve him as a counselor. Li, a man who takes his responsibilities as seriously as the former Dream did, declines, stating that he must obey his former master, and tells Daniel that he must travel to the village of Wei, as the emperor has commanded. Eventually he reaches that village, where he lives out the remainder of his life in exile.

#75 "THE TEMPEST" (WITH ADDITIONAL MATERIAL BY WILLIAM SHAKESPEARE)

(ILLUSTRATED BY CHARLES VESS)

The final story of the series, and of the collection, is "The Tempest," a companion piece to "A Midsummer Night's Dream" from the third collection, *Dream Country*. "The Tempest" is more contemplative than the first tale, and features less of the original play, though it echoes the latter cleverly in several ways, and actually quotes it a few times.

"The Tempest" focuses on the relationship between Dream and William Shakespeare. It is a story about the act of writing and the telling of tales, about family, and about the life you actually lead versus the life you might have led. It's also a story about responsibilities and obligations, how sometimes they come to define you, and how sometimes they consume you.

PEOPLE, PLACES, AND THINGS

WILLIAM SHAKESPEARE. Weighed down by life, stuck in a dead-end marriage, and unhappy with his daughter's choice for a husband, he deals with the pressure by drinking with Ben Jonson, and by pouring his heart and soul into the last play he'd pen by himself, *The Tempest*. Upon finishing the play Will is visited by his patron, Morpheus, who invites him to the Dreaming, where they discuss life and stories. After his last encounter with Morpheus, he returns home, dying a few years later.

THE TEMPEST. The last play Shakespeare was to write on his own, believed to have been penned around 1611. One commonly held view of the play is that it constitutes the Bard's farewell to the stage. A story about sin, atonement, and most important, reconciliation, the play begins as King Alonso of Naples, accompanied by his entourage, sails home to Italy after attending his daughter's wedding. Encountering a violent storm, they abandon ship and are washed ashore on a strange island inhabited by the mage Prospero, the creator of the tempest. Prospero is, in fact, the rightful duke of Milan who, twelve years prior, had been put to sea to die with his three-year-old daughter, Miranda, by his brother Antonio, an ally of Alonso.

Prospero and Miranda live in a cave that is also inhabited by a sprite, Ariel, and a deformed monster, Caliban, who resents Prospero because he believes he is the rightful ruler of the island. Once the castaways hit the island, things start to happen. Caliban plots with members of Alonso's entourage to murder Prospero; Miranda and Alonso's son, Ferdinand, fall in love; Ariel rebukes Alonso for his previous crimes against Prospero; and numerous plots against Prospero are hatched (and all fail, thanks to Prospero's magic).

The play ends with all offenders repenting their misdeeds. Prospero regains his title and position, Ariel calms the tempest, and everyone leaves the island, with the exception of Caliban.

TRIVIA

- The very first line on the very first page of *Preludes & Nocturnes* reads "Wake up sir, we're here." The last line of issue 72 is "You woke up."

- The book's dedication reads as follows: "This book is for Dave McKean, as a small token of thanks. I do not know what *Sandman* would have been without Dave, as our public face—creating the covers, the typefaces, the design, all that—and as my hardest critic. It was a long, strange journey, and it was the better for having a friend by my side on the way."

- À la Stan Lee and Jack Kirby making appearances at the wedding of their creations Reed Richards and Susan Storm, Gaiman and Zulli appear at Morpheus's funeral.

- Gaiman's personal assistant, Lorraine Garland, and Emma Bull of Flash Girls fame also appear.

- Characters from the DC universe who never appeared in the series show up at Morpheus's funeral. For instance, one panel features the villainous Darkseid (sitting in the same row as Emperor Norton from "Two Septembers and a January").

- Superman appears, chatting with Batman and J'onn J'onzz (the Martian Manhunter) about dreams he's had about having an ant's head and turning into a gorilla. These of course are references to the classic Silver Age "Red Kryptonite" Superman stories from the fifties and sixties.

- The barge sequence at the end of the third issue was originally only two pages long; Zulli was permitted to expand the sequence to four pages for the collection.

- The painting hanging behind Destiny on the last page of issue 72 is by Giorgione, a Renaissance artist. Placed there by Michael Zulli as a nod to the upcoming last issue, it is called *The Tempest*. It is considered the first great psychological painting, because of its attempt to depict the subconscious.

- After Master Li encounters Morpheus, he continues on his journey through the soft place, where he encounters a weird, laughing sailor in a glass case, crosses a bridge, and finally comes upon an arcade attraction that lets patrons attempt to secure prizes by manipulating a large mechanical claw. According to Gaiman, that sequence is one of the few places in the series where he used actual imagery from one of his own dreams.

- In "The Tempest," Shakespeare and Ben Jonson spontaneously compose a bit of doggerel on November 5, 1612, in celebration of Guy Fawkes Day—"Remember, remember, the fifth of November, gun powder, treason, and plot . . . ," Shakespeare begins. "I see no reason why gunpowder treason should ever be forgot," concludes Jonson. Shakespeare then tells it to a boy, guessing that it will last a hundred years. It lasts longer than that. Fans of Gaiman's mentor Alan Moore should certainly recognize these words from Moore's *V for Vendetta*.

- *The Tempest* has been adapted for film (and television) more than fifteen times since 1908, including *Forbidden Planet* (1956), and for comics at least three times before *Sandman* issue 75, including *Pocket Classics 11: William Shakespeare's "The Tempest"* (1984). Among Gaiman's favorite filmmakers is British director Peter Greenaway, and among Greenaway's most baroque and opulent films is his adaptation of *The Tempest*, entitled *Prospero's Books* (1991). The framed poster for the film hangs in Gaiman's master bathroom.

THE QUOTABLE GAIMAN

The Ten Volumes of *Sandman*, of which this is the last, comprise a story about stories. But in looking back over the nine years between my starting *Sandman* and writing this, what comes to mind are not stories, but friends. Some of whom I have met, some of whom I have still to meet.

To the friends of Sandman, and to my friends, my thanks.

—Afterword, *The Wake*

I'd originally planned on doing "The Tempest" about a year after "A Midsummer Night's Dream." But I later realized that because the play is all about stories and endings, it would be an appropriate subject for the last issue of the series.

—*The Sandman Companion,* by Hy Bender

THE SANDMAN: THE DREAM HUNTERS

(1999)

*T*he *Dream Hunters* gave Gaiman a chance to work with Yoshitaka Amano (famed designer of the Final Fantasy game series), whose work first caught the author's attention when the artist did the painting of Dream that began the festivities surrounding the celebration of the tenth anniversary of the first issue of The Sandman.

Shortly after he saw that poster, Karen Berger, who edited his run on The Sandman, called to ask Gaiman whether he'd be interested in writing a Sandman story as a tenth-anniversary project. "I asked," Gaiman writes in his afterword, "if she would be willing to allow me to retell an old Japanese story in my own way, and she said she would."

Gaiman's desire to tell such a story probably had its origins in the research he did in preparing to translate Miyazaki's film *Princess Mononoke* into English. The origins of the story told in *The Dream Hunters,* however, are less clear.

Gaiman's afterword states that he first encountered the tale, "The Fox, the Monk, and the Mikado of All Night's Dreaming" in the Reverend B. W. Ashton's *Fairy Tales of Old Japan,* and was struck at the similarities between the story and elements of his Sandman series. He went on to write that he then asked Amano and his assistants if they could find him any other versions of the story in an English translation. They found, he reported, a similar tale in one of Y. T. Ozaki's collections of Japanese tales, which he retooled to fit into his Sandman continuity.

But, it has been reported, no such tale is to be found in Ozaki's work. Further doubt is cast on this story because of a passage in Gaiman's introduction to *Endless Nights*, written in 2003, where he describes *Dream Hunters* as "an illustrated book which contained a retelling of an old Japanese folktale I completely made up."

Gaiman has been completely open about this perceived conflict since the publication of *The Dream Hunters*. When asked about it for this book, Gaiman replied:

> So Amano was illustrating *Dream Hunters* and I got a worried call from [Vertigo editor] Jenny Lee, saying that the book was going to run short and could I do anything to fill a few pages at the end. So I wrote an afterword, about how this really *was* an old Japanese folktale, and [I] expected it to be treated with as much respect as my claims on the box of the first Sandman statue, that [artist] Kelly Jones and [sculptor] Randy Bowen and I had been allowed into the vaults beneath the British Museum to copy it.
>
> And then it turned out that we didn't have the pages to fill after all, and the afterword was printed in small official-looking type.
>
> Which somehow made it no longer part of the story, and nobody ever doubted that I was telling the truth about this being an old Japanese folktale which happened to have Morpheus, a raven, and even Cain and Abel in it.

Gaiman was amused to discover claims on the graphic novel's Wikipedia entry that *The Dream Hunters* "takes elements from Chinese folktales and can also be found in *Strange Stories From a Chinese Studio*, by Pu Songling," which was written in the seventeenth century and first published in the eighteenth. Of course, the contributor of that bit of Wikiwisdom is incorrect. Whatever the similarities, *The Dream Hunters* was a pure Gaiman concoction.

The final product is a thing of beauty, a short story well told, accompanied by artwork that can only be described as breathtaking, an illustrated novel that remains true to both the timeless Japanese tales that inspired it and the motifs that made the Sandman series so popular. Gaiman's prose is enchanting, and Amano's renderings, from the ink brush–painted endpapers to the luminous page layout (including Amano's gatefold painting of Morpheus in a sea of reds, oranges, and violets, the original of which hangs in a place of honor in Gaiman's home), casts a spell over viewers that's hard to break.

The story, at the time representing Gaiman's first Sandman story in three years, was titled "The Fox, the Monk, and the Mikado of All Night's Dreaming." The central characters are the Fox and the Monk. The Sandman, referred to here as the King of All Night's Dreaming, plays only a peripheral role.

The elegant story is so brief and so straightforward that we will abandon our usual format so as not to be repetitive. Here then is a brief summary of *The Dream Hunters*.

A fox and a badger make a somewhat malicious wager: Whichever of them drives a Buddhist monk from his isolated temple can claim it as their own. Because the monk is a clever man capable of seeing through their deceit, both of them fail miserably. The badger flees in disgrace, and is not mentioned again in the story.

The monk makes a great impression on the fox, which falls in love with him. Taking the form of a beautiful woman, she visits the monk and apologizes to him for her rude behavior. Bemused, the monk permits her to remain as his guest, provided that she agrees not to play any of her "foolish fox tricks" on him again.

Meanwhile, in a house in Kyoto, a rich onmyoji, a master of Yin-Yang, is consumed by fear. He visits three witches and asks for their aid, and they instruct him in how to alleviate his fear. The end result would be that the aforementioned monk would have evil dreams for three nights running. He would end up trapped inside a dream, and his body would sleep continuously until it dies.

One night, the monk's guest overhears a group of creatures discussing the plans of their master to kill the monk in his dreams. Determined to save the monk from this horrible fate, she petitions Morpheus, who appears to her as an enormous black fox. He listens to her plight, and advises her. She then formulates a plan to take the monk's place on the third night.

The plan is successful, but the monk is distraught that the fox now lies at death's door. Leaving his temple in hopes that he may find some means of awakening her, he encounters an old man named Binzuru Harada, the first of Buddha's disciples, who first thrashes him soundly for abandoning his temple, then instructs him in how to find Morpheus. After a journey through the Dreaming (during which he encounters what appear to be Japanese analogs of Cain and Abel) he arrives at the palace. A raven (one of Matthew's predecessors) guides him to Morpheus, who grants him an audience.

Morpheus tells him of the fox's sacrifice, and notes that if he is successful in rescuing her, all her efforts will have been in vain. The monk remains steadfast in his resolve, and goes to meet the fox, who is trapped inside a mirror in her human form. Initially she resists, but he is insistent. Before they are forced to part forever, Dream grants them a few moments of intimacy.

As the monk takes her place, he advises her, "Seek not revenge, but the Buddha." The fox decides she will follow this advice, but only after she has her revenge. She awakens, and the monk dies several days later.

Once again taking human form, the fox tracks down the Onmyoji. Seducing him, she tells him he can't touch her until he abandons his wealth and power. Driven mad by his lust, he burns down both his house and that of the witches, killing them, his family, and his servants. When he returns to inform the fox that he has done as she asked, she has him disrobe; instead of making love to him, she reverts to her true form and bites out one of his eyes, leaving him disfigured, penniless, powerless, and quite mad.

In the Dreaming, Morpheus and his Raven ponder the events that have unfolded and consider their significance. Morpheus opines, "Lessons were learned. Events occurred as it was proper for them to do. I do not perceive that my attention was wasted." The narration ends by noting that since that time, people who dream of the distant regions where the Baku (Dream Eaters) graze can often see the fox and the monk walking together far off in the distance.

TRIVIA

- As a postscript to Gaiman's afterword, Amano writes about Gaiman, "I was impressed by the sincerity of his attitude, and perhaps his tenacity toward his work is something I share. It was almost destined that our paths would cross. This is only the beginning."

- In 2000, *The Dream Hunters* was nominated for a Hugo Award and won an Eisner Award. Yoshitaka Amano was a guest of honor at Dragon Con that year, where he received the Dragon Con Award and Julie Award for his work on *The Dream Hunters*.

- Gaiman told the authors he did this tenth anniversary project as "a gift to Karen Berger," his steadfast DC/Vertigo editor, who first invited him into the fold. Gaiman's deal was consistent with that instituted in his business arrangements with DC since the 1980s, including revisions initiated by DC itself in the interim.

- In his career of more than thirty-five years to date, Yoshitaka Amano has made his mark as an artist in many media: illustration, anime, video games, theater, painting, lithography, stained glass, kimono design, ceramics, and more. He worked at Tatsunoko Productions from 1967–81, designing characters for anime, including Gatchaman (G-Force), The Time Bokan series, Tekkaman, and Kashaan. Since 1982, his illustrations have graced collections of the short stories of Rampo Edogawa (the complete works in sixty-five volumes!), Baku Yumemakura's Chimera novels, works by Michael Moorcock, the Wagner "paper operas" *Tristan and Isolde* and *The Flying Dutchman*, and magazines like *Science Fiction* and the celebrated literary magazine *Shishi-O* (1985–92). His manga and illustration work also includes *Demon City Shinjuku* and Hideyuki Kikuchi's *Vampire Hunter D* (1983), and Amano handled the character design for the anime feature adaptation (1985), with which he was dissatisfied. Shifting gears to work with completely new gaming technologies in 1987, Amano developed design concepts for the *Final Fantasy* gaming series, which he continued through *Final Fantasy IV* (1994). After this he continued to create design and conceptual work for many other games. Amano has also created character and concept designs for other media, including the partly 3D animated short film *1001 Nights* (1998), the revamp of *Vampire Hunter D* (2000), multigenre presentations of his own creation *Hero* (2001), album cover paintings, and more. He established a New York City studio in 1997, and has enjoyed many international exhibitions of his work in all media.

THE QUOTABLE GAIMAN

For all that is felicitous in this volume, I thank my collaborators, living and dead, and my friends.

—Afterword, *The Dream Hunters*

||||||||||||||||||||||||||||||||||||||||||||||||||||||||||||||||||||||||||

DEATH: THE HIGH COST OF LIVING

(1993)

DEATH: THE TIME OF YOUR LIFE

(1996)

From the moment she first appeared in the pages of The Sandman issue 8, readers loved the Dream King's older sister. It might seem strange to the uninitiated that anyone could feel so fondly about Death, and yet—as written by Neil Gaiman—her charm is unmistakable. At the end of *Death: The High Cost of Living*, Sexton Furnival notes that "it would be really neat if Death was somebody, and not just nothing, or pain, or blackness. And it would be really good if Death could be somebody like Didi. Somebody funny, and friendly, and nice, and maybe just a tiny bit crazy."

Those sentiments are an echo of thoughts shared by thousands of readers. Death is not the enemy. She simply *is*. Life is defined by the omnipresent knowledge that it must, eventually, end. Yet death remains one of the great taboos of conversation. Few like to discuss it, and far fewer seem able to make their peace with its inevitability.

With her appearances in Sandman, and two solo miniseries (*Death: The High Cost of Living* and *Death: The Time of Your Life*), Neil Gaiman has created a version of Death that is not only a comfort, but a friend. The job of spiriting our souls away when we die is her purpose, but Death is full of compassion, humor, and gentle wisdom. In *Sandman,* she seems always to ease the souls of the recently departed into melancholy acceptance or resignation.

In a landmark episode of his series *The Twilight Zone,* Rod Serling worked with screenwriter George Clayton Johnson to present a similarly tender persona for Death. The story, "Nothing in the Dark," featured Robert Redford as Death, both tricking an old woman afraid of dying into letting him into her home and simultaneously leading her toward a bittersweet acceptance of her fate. Fredric March also played a gentle Death, seeking the meaning of mortality and discovering romance, in the famed 1934 film *Death Takes a Holiday* (remade in 1971, and again—as *Meet Joe Black*—in 1998).

The simplicity of the character design for Gaiman's version of Death lent itself to her popularity among readers. As originally designed by Mike Dringenberg (based, according to Gaiman, on a friend of the artist's named Cinnamon), Death manifests as an almost pixyish girl in her late teens, clad all in black, face pale white, and wearing a silver ankh around her neck. The image is that of the ultimate Goth girl, even in a post-Goth world.

On her face, around her right eye, Death has a tattoo that is reminiscent of the Egyptian symbol called a *wadjet,* also known as the Eye of Horus, or the Eye of Ra. Though it represented the sun, the Eye of Horus also symbolized indestructibility, and was thought to assist in the rebirth of the dead. Given that Gaiman's charismatic Death is also shown to be present at the birth of all humans, there is a powerful cyclical symbolism inherent in the symbol: birth, death, and rebirth, with Gaiman's sweet, philosophizing Death welcoming souls to life, and guiding them gently to the afterlife.

In the overall hierarchy of the mythology Gaiman created for *The Sandman* and its related DC/Vertigo publications, Death is the second eldest of the Endless (only Destiny is older). Dream (Morpheus) seeks her counsel and company fairly often, and they share a closeness he does not have with any of his other siblings. In *The Books of Magic,* Gaiman indicates that Death and Destiny will be the last beings surviving in the universe, but that she will then have to claim Destiny's life before reality itself comes to an end.

DEATH: THE HIGH COST OF LIVING

For the first solo flight of Death of the Endless, the three-issue miniseries *The High Cost of Living,* Gaiman enlisted penciler Chris Bachalo and inker Mark Buckingham. The premise has a beautiful simplicity: Once a century Death spends a day as a mortal, simply living life, to better understand the nature of mortality. Instead of finding this requirement a curse, she views it as a gift, and spends the day almost relentlessly upbeat, interacting with people and taking joy from life.

Though Gaiman includes a villain and a seemingly typical threat in the story—in the form of an eerie, magical blind man called the Eremite—this plot turns out to be of little consequence. The story is clearly about Death and her interactions with a suicidal boy named Sexton, and about the impact the day they spend together has on both of them.

In this miniseries Gaiman also loops in threads from The Sandman, using the long-lived Mad Hettie and, more importantly, lesbian couple Hazel and Foxglove, who will come to play a larger role in Gaiman's epic as *The Sandman* nears its end.

#1 "DEATH: THE HIGH COST OF LIVING, THE SPIRIT OF THE STAIRWAY"

An ancient homeless woman—the enigmatic Mad Hettie, a regular in The *Sandman* and *Hellblazer* comics—kills a bird in order to see the future in its entrails, and confirms her suspicions that "she" is coming back. Hettie vows not to "miss her this time."

Elsewhere, a teenage boy named Sexton Furnival is writing a suicide note. Sexton doesn't believe in love, and doesn't see any purpose in life, so he figures he might as well be dead.

Later, wandering the city, Sexton ends up in the junkyard, where he stands atop an old fridge. When it gives way underneath him, he slides down a mountain of junk, and the fridge lands on top of him, trapping him there. Death comes to his rescue, introducing herself as "Didi."

Didi takes him back to her apartment and explains that the photo of her family isn't real, that she herself is really only three hours old. When she tells him she's Death, he leaves, slamming the door on his way out.

Sexton thinks of all the things he should have replied to Didi's absurd assertion, but when he gets outside, Mad Hettie is waiting for him. Hettie makes Sexton take her up to Didi's apartment. Once inside, she reveals that she "missed" Death one hundred years ago, the last time she was "nobody special" for a day. But she needs Death to find her heart, and if Death refuses, she'll cut off Sexton's nose, just for a start.

#2 "DEATH: THE HIGH COST OF LIVING, A NIGHT TO REMEMBER"

In Washington Square Park, Death and Sexton set out to find Mad Hettie's heart.

Elsewhere, a creepy old blind guy (the Eremite) tells his lackey, Theo, that "she" is coming. He can feel her. Theo is supposed to bring Death back to his master, and if that's not possible, at least bring him the ankh she wears around her neck.

Sexton and Didi arrive at a club only to run into Hazel McNamara in line.

Readers learn that the pregnant Hazel's partner Foxglove has given up writing and is playing music at the club, the Undercut. On the stage, Foxglove performs a song called "Donna's Dream," which is about what happened to her ex-girlfriend, Judy (in the pages of *Sandman* she was murdered by Dr. Destiny in a diner). In the audience Sexton talks to a guy from a record label who's there to check out the show. The man knows Sexton's father, and because Sexton likes Foxglove, the exec takes an interest in her.

Theo arrives and persuades Didi to go with him. Sexton knows him from school and tries to convince her that Theo's bad news, but she won't listen. The three of them leave together. Theo takes them to the Eremite under the ruse of taking them to a party, then quickly rips the ankh from around Death's neck. But Theo double-crosses the Eremite, refusing to give up the ankh. In a quick burst of violence, the Eremite kills him and takes the ankh, then leaves Didi and Sexton locked in the stone cellar.

#3 "DEATH: THE HIGH COST OF LIVING"

Trapped in the basement, the still-skeptical Sexton questions Didi about her identity. She tells him that once a century, Death takes on mortal flesh to better understand the "bitter tang of mortality." It's the price she must pay for being the divider of the living from life.

After a while they fall asleep, but soon Mad Hettie comes to the rescue. Hettie read about their plight in some tea leaves.

Didi and Sexton have breakfast in a diner, where the Eremite finds them. He's frustrated that they escaped and baffled as to how they managed it, because he has the ankh, Death's sigil of power, Didi tells him it has power, but not the kind he thinks. When the diner's owner makes the Eremite leave, Didi and Sexton go out the back. On the street Didi buys a new ankh from a man selling jewelry on the sidewalk.

Didi tells Sexton that she enjoyed her day. He's dubious. What's to enjoy about being locked up and terrorized? But she enjoys it all, the good bits and the bad bits, because it's all part of life. She gives Sexton a Russian nesting doll, asking him to pass it on to Hettie (it contains her heart). Then she stands at the edge of a fountain, breathing the air and feeling the wind, and says, "No, please, I . . . ," and dies, falling into the water.

Elsewhere, Didi is met by her own self, Death—somehow they both exist at once—and she asks herself how the day was. "*Wonderful.*" She wishes it didn't have to end. "It always ends," Death tells herself. "That's what gives it value."

Sexton is back at his apartment, talking to Billy, a neighbor. He says what's crazy is that he *almost* believed Didi. He's been thinking a lot about Death, and he hopes that Death really is someone like Didi.

Mad Hettie gets her heart back, but she's already looking for somewhere else to hide it.

"DEATH: THE HIGH COST OF LIVING,
DEATH TALKS ABOUT LIFE" (1994)

This tale first appeared as a special seven-page story in a Vertigo giveaway, then in the collection *Death: The High Cost of Living*. In the story, Death of the Endless frankly discusses AIDS and its prevention. The highlight of the segment is a demonstration of how to use a condom, using a banana provided by a sheepish John Constantine as a prop.

PEOPLE, PLACES, AND THINGS

DEATH (DIDI): The second eldest of the Endless, she is the embodiment and manifestation of the concept of Death, present at the birth of every man and woman, and there to guide them to the afterlife upon their demise. Once a century she takes human form to better understand the bittersweet nature of mortality. In the twentieth century she becomes a girl named Didi, whose family was killed in an accident, and she befriends a suicidal teenager named Sexton and spends her one day with him.

SEXTON FURNIVAL. Sexton, a teenage boy, is contemplating suicide when his mother interrupts him and sends him out of the house so that she has no interruptions while she cleans. He nearly dies in a foolish accident, but is saved by a girl named Didi, who turns out to be Death incarnate. He spends an odd day—full of danger and wonder—with her, and through her openness and appreciation of the small things in life begins to appreciate his own.

SYLVIA FURNIVAL. Sexton's mother, she gets the urge to clean her house and sends Sexton away so that she can do so without interruption.

MAD HETTIE. An eccentric, filthy, centuries-old homeless woman, Mad Hettie once hid her heart away. She needs Death to find it for her, and tracks Death down on the one day that she is mortal. Mad Hettie believes that by threatening Sexton, she has convinced Death to locate her heart, but in the end realizes that Death had her heart all along. Now she has to hide it again.

MRS. ROBBINS. A neighbor who lives in the same building as Didi, she helps Mad Hettie to free Didi and Sexton after they are captured by the Eremite.

THE EREMITE. The word literally means a hermit, particularly an individual who has become reclusive as part of some religious devotion. Little is revealed about the Eremite, save for the fact that he wishes to acquire from Death the secrets of life and death—apparently in an effort to die himself one day. He acquires Death's ankh—her sigil—but apparently it only symbolizes her power, and she can imbue that power in another ankh simply by willing it. The Eremite does not get the answers he seeks.

THEO. A dangerous kid whom Sexton knows from school, Theo is sent by the

Eremite to bring Death back and/or steal her ankh. When he refuses to hand it over, the Eremite kills him.

HAZEL MCNAMARA. A pregnant woman who used to be a chef at a restaurant owned by Sylvia Furnival, Hazel gets Didi and Sexton into a club where her girlfriend, Foxglove, is performing.

FOXGLOVE. Hazel's girlfriend, Foxglove is a writer and musician. Thanks in part to a conversation Sexton has with a music executive, she gets a record deal.

DEATH: THE TIME OF YOUR LIFE

Once again joined by Chris Bachalo on pencils and Mark Buckingham on inks, Gaiman pulls together threads introduced in the previous miniseries into a tale of love and death. Structurally, however, this miniseries bears a greater resemblance to classic Gaiman *Sandman* stories, as Death herself binds the story together, rather than being a character who is an active protagonist.

Instead, Gaiman returns yet again to Hazel and Foxglove—and to their son, Alvie—for a story about the way life can change love. Desperation and sadness and forgiveness can all be found within these pages. Though it purports to be a story about death, *The Time of Your Life* seems to be far more concerned with living, a rumination on the things we choose as priorities and the sacrifices we make in life.

"Alvie" is, of course, an anagram for "Alive." From a writer of Gaiman's caliber, this cannot be coincidence.

#1 "DEATH: THE TIME OF YOUR LIFE, THINGS YOU JUST DO WHEN YOU'RE BORED"

In February, Hazel runs outside her house carrying the unmoving form of her baby, Alvie, and lays him on the grass. A dark figure approaches from behind and she turns, surprised at the (unrevealed) identity of her visitor.

Months later, in November, Foxglove is in a hotel in New York City, preparing for an appearance on *David Letterman*. She is visited by her manager, Larry, who takes her out for breakfast. The conversation turns to Foxglove's desire to come out, to publicly acknowledge that she is a lesbian. Larry is very resistant.

On his plane back to L.A., Larry has a heart attack and dies. Before her appearance with Letterman, Foxglove is in her dressing room and Larry's ghost appears to her. He tells her that she has to do what Hazel tells her, even if it sounds crazy. His features begin to burn, and then he vanishes. She thinks she must have been dreaming.

After the show Hazel calls and asks her to come home, and Foxglove gets annoyed. She's going to a movie premiere and then is headed to Europe the next morning. She can't come home right now.

Back at home Hazel hangs up the phone, saddened. Death is there with her. Hazel must go with her. She doesn't have any choice.

#2 "DEATH: THE TIME OF YOUR LIFE, IMAGINARY SOLUTIONS"

At the premiere of the crappy movie for which she has done the theme song, Foxglove nods off and dreams that she is a butterfly. When she wakes up she is asked to step outside by her bodyguard and tour manager, Boris, who tells her of Larry's death. She remembers what he said in her "dream" about listening to Hazel, and freaks out.

Boris tries to talk Foxglove into continuing with her work, but she insists she has to get back to L.A.—to Hazel. In the midst of all of this she receives a message from a reporter, who has been told by a woman from Foxglove's record label in France that Foxglove was sleeping with her all through her last European tour.

In Death's realm Hazel begins to tell Death the story of her relationship with Foxglove, explaining that nothing's been the same since Foxglove got her recording contract.

On the plane back to L.A., Foxglove talks to Vito, the "date" Larry had set up for Foxglove for the premiere. She's freaked out because she's been calling and calling home, but nobody answers. She's wracked with guilt about having cheated on Hazel.

When Foxglove, Boris, and Vito get home, they find that Hazel and Alvie are not there. Foxglove believes she knows where they've gone, and prepares to do a ritual to bring herself into the realm of Death to retrieve them.

#3 "DEATH: THE TIME OF YOUR LIFE"

That night, when Alvie stopped breathing in his crib and Hazel carried him out into the rain, it was Death who appeared to her. Hazel understands what Death is, that she's come for Alvie. Hazel wants to make a deal. Foxglove performs a blood rite that will allow her to walk the moon's road into the realm of Death.

Foxglove, Boris, and Vito cross over into a limbo on the borders of Death's realm, where Boris and Foxglove get into a conversation about names and identity, and who we choose to be. This theme resonates throughout the miniseries.

Meanwhile, Death tells Hazel that Foxglove is coming. She assures Hazel that she isn't dead, and that Alvie isn't dead "yet."

When Foxglove arrives, Death and Hazel explain that on that rainy night, Hazel had made a deal with Death. Hazel had promised that if Alvie could live a while longer, she and Fox and Alvie would all go to see Death, and that one of them would stay in Death's realm. She hoped that when Death saw how much they all loved each other, Death would let them all live.

Confronted with the pureness of Hazel's love, Foxglove confesses that she has cheated on her many times. She says she doesn't think she loves Hazel anymore. Hazel thinks she's being silly. If Foxglove followed her into Death, of *course* she loves her. Hazel doesn't care what she's done; all she wants is to not have to share her anymore, to just be together again the way they used to be.

Boris had promised Larry he would take care of Foxglove. It's his job, and his vow. Foxglove says her life is crap; *she'll* stay. But Boris won't let her. He stays in her place, and Death accepts him as sweetly as she does everyone eventually.

Time passes. A couple of years later, Vito has won an Oscar, Foxglove's hair has grown long and changed color, and Hazel wears big glasses. Foxglove has given up being a rock star—the rocker just vanished and has become a legend. Now they're just raising Alvie and being together, living a simple life.

PEOPLE, PLACES, AND THINGS

DEATH. The second eldest of the Endless, she is the embodiment and manifestation of the concept of Death, present at the birth of every man and woman, and there to guide them to the afterlife upon their demise. She usually doesn't make deals, but remembers Hazel fondly from the day she spent as a mortal a few years earlier. When Hazel's son, Alvie, dies, Death agrees to give him more time, but when that time is up, Hazel, Foxglove, and Alvie must come visit Death together, and one of them will be required to stay behind.

HAZEL. When Hazel met Foxglove, it was love at first sight. They've been together ever since, despite Hazel becoming pregnant during a drunken bit of foolishness with a coworker one night. Now that Foxglove has become a famous singer-songwriter, they've had to hide the fact that they are lesbians, lovers, and the mothers of Alvie, much to Hazel's frustration. She misses the way things used to be and doesn't want to share Foxglove anymore.

ALVIE. Hazel's son. When Alvie dies, Hazel makes a bargain with Death: If Alvie can live a while longer, at the end of that time, Hazel, Foxglove, and Alvie will visit Death, and one of them will remain with her, agreeing to die.

FOXGLOVE. Though her real name is Donna Cavanagh, to the rest of the world she is a famous rock singer called Foxglove. Fame has caused her to travel the world, and those travels make her lonely. Far from home, she has had numerous affairs, despite her supposedly monogamous relationship with Hazel. Foxglove's success has caused obvious strain between the two women. When Hazel told her what happened to Alvie, Foxglove didn't really believe her. But when the ghost of her manager, Larry, tells her to listen to Hazel, she realizes something terrible must have happened, and rushes home. Though Foxglove doesn't think she loves Hazel anymore, she follows her into the realm of Death, proving herself wrong. Her life is in turmoil, and she offers to remain behind in exchange for Alvie's life, but her bodyguard, Boris, has promised to look after her, and stays in her place. Foxglove leaves her rock star status behind, and she and Hazel live happy, anonymous lives as Alvie's parents.

LARRY. Foxglove's manager. When he has a heart attack and dies, he comes back from Death as a ghost—perhaps as a dream—to warn her to do as Hazel tells her.

BORIS. His real name is Endymion, and he is Foxglove's tour manager and bodyguard. He promised Larry he would look after her, so when he travels to the gray lands on the border of the land of Death and realizes that someone must stay behind in order for the others to live, he volunteers. He made a promise, and he means to keep it.

VITO. A handsome young model, Vito is hired by Larry to be Foxglove's "date" at a movie premiere. It is all an act, since Foxglove is a lesbian. Vito is there only to be a stand-in to blunt rumors about Fox's sexual preference. But when Foxglove's life turns to chaos, Vito extends his friendship to her in a way strangers so rarely do, eventually even going into the realm of Death with her.

TRIVIA

- The character design for Death came from a sketch Mike Dringenberg had done, based on a woman he knew named Cinnamon, but Death's Goth style emerged later. On the same day Gaiman first saw Dringenberg's sketch, he and artist Dave McKean spotted an American waitress in a restaurant, dressed in black and wearing the silver ankh that became Death's signature.

- Writer-artist Jill Thompson crafted a manga-style graphic novel in 2003 entitled *Death at Death's Door*. It told the events from *The Sandman: Season of Mists* from Death's perspective.

- In addition to her frequent presence in and impact on *The Sandman*, Death played a significant role both in Gaiman's *Books of Magic* miniseries and several issues of the monthly *Books of Magic* series not penned by Gaiman. She has made minor cameo appearances in several other comic books as well, including *The Legion of Super-Heroes* and *Ambush Bug Nothing Special* number 1.

THE QUOTABLE GAIMAN

Q. You're about to make your directing debut with Death. *Are you directing that because, of all your works, that's the one that would hurt more than any of them if botched?*

GAIMAN: I'm not sure about more than any of them, but more than most. *Death* is so tonal. I'm so proud of *The High Cost of Living,* the graphic novel that it's based on, that I know that most of what works about Death is tone of voice and the way that it's told. If somebody made a bad *Neverwhere* movie I can go, "Well, there's the novel. It's decent." If somebody made *Death* and they screwed it up, it would hurt. She's like my kid. If anyone's going to screw it up I'd rather it were me.

—Interview on SciFi.com, August 6, 2007

|||||||||||||||||||||||||||||||||||||||||||||||||||||||||||||||||||||

THE SANDMAN: ENDLESS NIGHTS

(2003)

An anthology in the tradition of *Dream Country, Fables & Reflections,* and *Worlds' End, Endless Nights* differs in that its seven chapters are each devoted to a different sibling in the family of the Endless. In some tales the Endless play central roles; in others, due to their very natures, they inform the story but do not necessarily take an active role in the proceedings.

Endless Nights was conceived by Gaiman as a celebration/commemoration of the tenth anniversary of the first appearance of The Sandman. It was a project he eagerly embraced, as it gave him a chance to explore the nature of his creations, the Endless, and provided him with the opportunity to work with seven artists he admired, all of whom he handpicked. It's obvious to anyone reading his introduction that he enjoyed himself. "Writing these stories," he states, "was like coming home."

The stories will be discussed in order of their appearance. We'll depart from our format in this chapter, since adding a section on people, places, and things would be redundant.

"DEATH AND VENICE"

(ILLUSTRATED BY P. CRAIG RUSSELL)

This story was written in Venice, a week after September 11, 2001, when Gaiman found himself "pondering the nature of time and of death." Its title echoes Thomas Mann's *A Death in Venice,* but its subject matter evokes Poe's "Masque of the Red Death." "Death and Venice" tells two stories: a third-person account of a sixteenth-century count who has managed to keep his estate and his guests frozen in time, safe from illness, aging, and Death; and a first-person account of a soldier who has grown cynical about life because of his violent profession.

The problem of living forever, the count finds, is that you get bored, so he is forced to find increasingly bizarre ways of entertaining himself and his guests. The soldier, Sergei, finds himself drawn to the island where Death patiently waits for entry to the count's centuries-long party. The soldier opens the door for Death, ending the festivities for the count and his fellow revelers. After leaving the island, the soldier, who has seen Death in action, dedicates his life to her, "sending people to her" by taking their lives.

"WHAT I'VE TASTED OF DESIRE"
(ILLUSTRATED BY MILO MANARA)

Gaiman had admired Manara's work for years; he considers the artist's work on the graphic novel *Indian Summer,* written by Hugo Pratt, one of the high points of comics history. In his introduction he states that the notion that Manara would draw him a tale of Desire was one of the things that "carried" him into writing *Endless Nights.*

In this tale (inspired by a historical anecdote mentioned by George MacDonald Fraser, author of *The Flashman Papers*), a maiden is transformed by Desire into a crafty seductress, enabling her to lure the man of her dreams into her bed. When her husband, who is chief of their clan, is killed by a group of barbarians, she exacts a terrible revenge upon them, all without lifting a finger against them.

"THE HEART OF A STAR"
(ILLUSTRATED BY MIGUELANXO PRADO)

Chronologically, this piece is the earliest Sandman story Gaiman has ever told. Here, the author states, he found it "pleasurable to explain a few things." Besides providing insight into the animosity between Dream and Desire, it also features Delirium's previous incarnation, Delight. This tale is also notable for the appearances of the living stars Rao (Krypton's sun), Sol (Earth's sun), and Sto-Oa (Oa's sun), all integral parts of the DC Comics universe. Gaiman would go on to use the concept of a star taking human form in his delightful fairy tale *Stardust.*

The heart of the star referred to in the title belongs to Sto-Oa, who long ago lost his to Killalla of the Glow, a denizen of the planet Oa (famous as the home of the Guardians and their servants, the Green Lantern Corps, in the DC universe). Sto-Oa meets Killalla at a parliament of stars that the young woman is attending as the guest of her paramour, Dream. Killalla breaks Dream's heart by falling in love with the star, and abandoning him. At first thankful to Desire for granting him the "gift" of Killalla, Dream now holds her responsible for his heartbreak and misery.

"FIFTEEN PORTRAITS OF DESPAIR"

(ILLUSTRATED BY BARRON STOREY AND DESIGNED BY DAVE MCKEAN)

This segment consists of fifteen bizarre pieces of art featuring the grotesque Despair, each complemented by disturbing vignettes about people who have stumbled into her realm. Bleak, disturbing, and unrelenting, most readers will probably feel lucky that there are only fifteen (Gaiman has said that the original concept was "*Twenty-Five* Portraits of Despair.")

The author used similar templates in his work on the Sandman Tarot, and in the text he created for Tori Amos's *Strange Little Girls* Tour Book.

"GOING INSIDE"

(ILLUSTRATED BY BILL SIENKIEWICZ)

Dream recruits five mentally ill people to rescue his sister Delirium from a dangerous situation she has inadvertently gotten herself into in her realm. This chapter is told in a blend of computer-generated images and drawings that is simply stunning. Sienkiewicz is at his lunatic best in this visit deep inside Delirium's realm.

"DESTRUCTION ON THE PENINSULA"

(ILLUSTRATED BY GLENN FABRY)

Essentially a science fiction story in which Destruction plays a minor role, this tale is narrated by Rachel, an archeologist who dreams of the end of the world—until she is invited on a dig where all the "artifacts" discovered appear to come from a dangerous future. Destruction takes a job on-site, helping to avert disaster on a couple of occasions. (When Rachel asks him if he's had any experience with ruins, he replies, "I've certainly made my share of them.") He also comes to dominate the archeologist's sexually charged dreams.

When representatives of the government show up, hoping to exploit the dangerous technology that's been turning up, Rachel quits the dig in protest. It turns out that she's gotten out just in the nick of time, as the entire site is obliterated in a flash of light shortly after she leaves. Now Rachel's dreams are no longer haunted by Armageddon, but of the man she knows as Joe, who understands more about destruction than anyone else in the universe.

"ENDLESS NIGHTS"

(ILLUSTRATED BY FRANK QUITELY)

In this beautifully drawn segment (of Quitely, Gaiman says, "I always knew he was good. I didn't know he was *this* good."), readers are taken on a journey through Destiny's vast realm. Destiny, we are told, is chained to a book that contains "the Universe"—everything that has happened, or will happen, to anyone you've ever met, heard of, or never heard of. While Gaiman's incarnation of Destiny could never be a classic protagonist, he would be perfectly suited to play host for an anthology series. He is privy, after all, to every story ever told.

TRIVIA

- Gaiman's dedication reads: "For Jenette, for Paul, and especially for Karen, for trusting me." This refers to Jenette Kahn, Paul Levitz, and editor Karen Berger, the powers that be at DC Comics at the time Berger hired Gaiman to write *The Sandman*.

- Barron Storey, artist of the unforgettable "Fifteen Portraits of Despair," is a prominent artist, illustrator, and teacher whose work is seminal to contemporary artists and cartoonists like Bill Sienkiewicz, Kent Williams, George Pratt, Bill Koeb, Dan Clowes, and frequent Gaiman collaborator Dave McKean. Still, he and his work remain essentially unknown to comics and graphic novel readers. An incredibly prolific and eternally challenging creator, winner of the New York Society of Illustrators Gold Medal (1976) and New York Society of Illustrator's Instructor of the Year (2001), Storey currently teaches at the California College of Art in San Francisco, at San Jose State University, and at Pixar Studios. His illustrations and covers have graced *Time, Boys' Life, Reader's Digest, National Geographic,* and many book covers, and his paintings are showcased in New York's American Museum of Natural History, the Air and Space Museum on the National Mall, and the Smithsonian's National Portrait Gallery. His work in *Endless Nights* represents his first appearance in an American mainstream comics publication.

THE QUOTABLE GAIMAN

When I was done with *Sandman*, people asked me if I would ever come back to those characters. Would I ever tell more stories about Morpheus, the King of Stories, or about his family, the Endless?

"Sure," I said. "One day."

This volume exists because there were artists I wanted to work with, and stories I wanted to tell, and because sometimes you look up and realize that one day is now.

—Introduction, *Endless Nights*

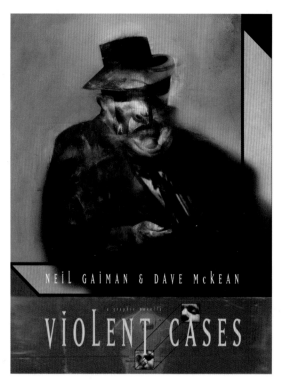

Cover art from *The Day I Swapped My Dad For Two Goldfish* © by Dave McKean

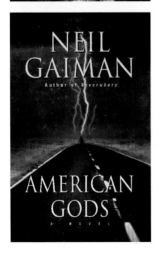

Original U.S. release hardcover art from Avon for *Neverwhere* (1997) reprinted courtesy of William Morrow, an imprint of HarperCollins Publishers.

Original U.S. release hardcover art from Avon for *American Gods* (2001) reprinted courtesy of William Morrow, an imprint of HarperCollins Publishers.

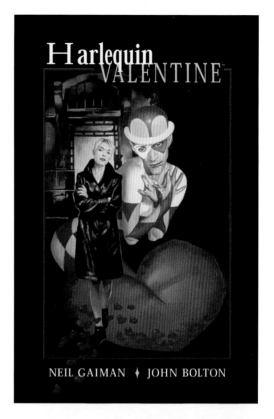

LEFT: Gaiman's description: "About three? Down at the bottom of the garden in Purbrook, in Hampshire, on the swing." Photo courtesy of Neil Gaiman, from his collection.

BELOW LEFT: Gaiman's description: My sister, my mother, her mother, and me. September 1963." Photo courtesy of Neil Gaiman, from his collection.

BOTTOM: Gaiman's description: "Douglas Adams and me in 1983. I'm 22, still smoking and wearing colours. Douglas is playing guitar while we wait for the photographer, John Copthorne, to finish setting up. (Douglas is playing Marvin's "How I Hate the Night" song.)" Photo courtesy of Neil Gaiman, from his collection.

OPPOSITE TOP: Neil Gaiman and Charles Vess at World Fantasy Convention, 1991, holding the World Fantasy Awards they won for Best Short Story for *The Sandman* issue #19, "A Midsummer Night's Dream." After their stunning, unprecedented victory, the rules were amended to prevent a comic book from ever winning the award again. Photo by and © Beth Gwinn

OPPOSITE LEFT: Gaiman's description: "I think this was taken the day before Maddy was born in August 1994. I'd decided I wasn't going to get a haircut or shave until she turned up. Or something like that. I'd grown some pumpkins for practically the first time." Photo courtesy of Neil Gaiman, from his collection.

OPPOSITE RIGHT: Gaiman's description: "Me and Clive Barker circa 1996. Two very scary people in leather jackets. Look! We are so scary!" Photo by and © Beth Gwinn.

Neil Gaiman and *Warrior*
magazine founder Des Skinn.
Photo by and © Peter Coleborn

Cover art from *The Wolves In The Walls* © 2003 by Dave McKean

Creatures of the Night is a trademark of
Neil Gaiman. *The Price*™ © 2004 Neil
Gaiman. *Daughter Of Owls*™ © 2004 Neil
Gaiman, artwork © 2004 Michael Zulli.
Published by Dark Horse Comics, Inc.
"Dark Horse Comics® & the Dark Horse
logo are registered trademarks of Dark
Horse Comics, Inc."

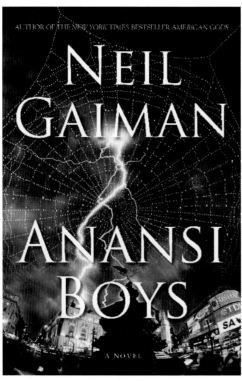

LEFT: Original U.S. release hardcover art from Avon for *Anansi Boys* (2005) reprinted courtesy of William Morrow, an imprint of HarperCollins Publishers.

BELOW LEFT: Original U.S. release hardcover art from Avon for *Fragile Things* (2006) reprinted courtesy of William Morrow, an imprint of HarperCollins Publishers.

BELOW: Cover art from *M Is for Magic* © 2007 by Teddy Kristiansen

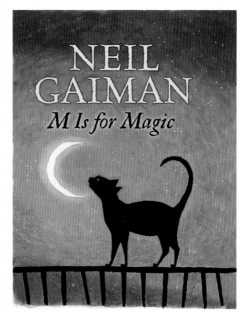

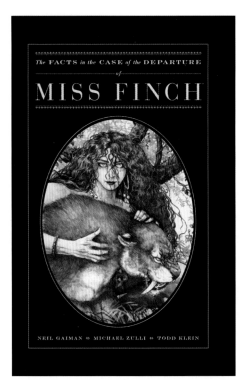

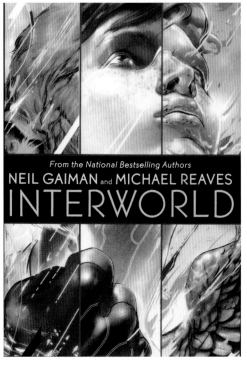

Cover art for *Interworld* © 2007 by James Jean

The Facts in the Case of the Departure of Miss Finch™ text © 2007 Neil Gaiman, art © 2007 Michael Zulli. Miss Finch is a trademark of Neil Gaiman. Published by Dark Horse Comics, Inc. "Dark Horse Comics® & the Dark Horse logo are registered trademarks of Dark Horse Comics, Inc."

Cover art for *The Dangerous Alphabet* © 2007 by Gris Grimly

"THE FLOWERS OF ROMANCE" FROM WINTER'S EDGE #1

(1998)

This tale, beautifully painted by John Bolton, begins with a Pan-like satyr, alone on a tiny island, reminiscing about the days when naiads and dryads were plentiful, and neither they nor human women could resist his goatish "stink" and the charm of his grin. He's old now, with no lovers left, and his horns are withered and cracked. Old and dying in the winter of the world he'd known, he invokes a promise made to his kind at the dawn of the world, and Desire appears.

She'd thought he was gone with the rest of his kind. "Other things desire," she says, but he and his kind "were nothing *but* desire." She explains that soon Death will come for him, and he will go to Dream's realm to die, as all of his kind do. First, though, he asks a boon of her, which the reader does not hear. It is evident soon enough, however. Despite the winter, an archaeologist and his girlfriend come out to camp on the island. The satyr plays his pipes, and in the night she comes to him. For those precious moments he is young again, and has a lover.

Soon, the archaeologist finds her—in a little patch of spring, where flowers have now grown on the spot where the satyr had been. He has passed from the world now, but not until receiving one small boon from Desire.

"A WINTER'S TALE" FROM WINTER'S EDGE #2

(1999)

In this story, which originally appeared in the Vertigo anthology comic *Winter's Edge* number 2, illustrated by Jeff Jones, Gaiman gives a glimpse at the early days, as it were, of Death. At first Death was welcomed. But in time that changed. People greeted her as though dying were "an admission of failure." For a while she stopped taking lives, and nothing would die, and things became very unpleasant. Later, the second eldest of the Endless became bitter—"hard and cold and brittle inside," as she says—when Death began to be something that inspired terror and despair. The tale also touches on the events that led to Death's decision to take on human life for one twenty-four-hour period every hundred years—to taste life and then lose it, so that she can experience that loss—contributing to the changes in her persona that have occurred between ancient and modern times.

Given Gaiman's love of Shakespeare, the title is likely a nod to the Bard's *The Winter's Tale.*

||||||||||||||||||||||||||||||||||||||||||||||||||||||||||||||||||

"HOW THEY MET THEMSELVES" fROM WINTER'S EDGE #3

(2000)

Illustrated by Michael Zulli, this tale of Desire of the Endless is considered one of the "lost" Sandman stories, as it appeared only in the Vertigo anthology comic book *Winter's Edge* issue 3. In the year 1862, a woman named Lizzie—despairing that her husband is having an affair—takes a dose of laudanum and descends into what might be dream or memory or vision. Three people ride in a train car, and Lizzie imagines she could be any one of them: a sickly woman; her painter/poet husband (who claims she, his former model, is his muse); and the scruffy unpublished poet who accompanies them. When they are joined by a fourth—a man with the oddest eyes—a conversation ensues. The man, clearly, is Desire of the Endless, and he/she expresses concern that the woman might be too ill for the snowy day picnic the three have planned.

Each of them sees Desire in their own way: the husband as a young woman; the woman as a young man; and the poet, Algy, as a little of both, but someone he would enjoy having tie him up and whip his buttocks. When they get off the train Desire explains that all the land around them belongs to him/her, and that there is a place nearby where the weather is always fair, and it is said that anyone who goes there will meet their true love.

The husband and wife meet doppelgängers of themselves in the woods, while Algy, the poet, concocts a paean to Desire, confessing that he just wants her to hurt him. "Oh," she replies in his mind, "I always do that." The artist realizes that he is his *own* true love.

Lizzie never wakes from the haze of laudanum and realization, and when her husband returns home, he finds her dead. As he had promised in her dream memory of that train ride, he puts his poems into her coffin to be buried with her, but ten years later he returns to dig them up again. She had been his muse, but she is not at all surprised that time has changed that.

In the wood in the realm of Desire, she'd seen a doppelgänger of herself and of her husband, and she'd seen Algy, and even after death has claimed her, she wonders which of them had been her own true love.

||||||||||||||||||||||||||||||||||||||||||||||||||||||||||||||||||||||||||

PART THREE
THE GRAPHIC NOVELS

As Guy Delcourt said to me during a conversation in Copenhagen in September 1993, the windfall success of Watchmen and Dark Knight, including widespread public acceptance and licensed foreign editions (which Delcourt issued in France), wasn't followed by anything of equal substance, and the wind soon went out of the sales (pun intended) on an international scale.

It was Neil's Sandman-collected trades that saved the day. Despite the episodic nature of the first issues collected (as Neil has noted, Sandman grew from a periodical to the multi-chapter graphic novel form over time), Neil's Sandman was a coherent work of great merit, substance, and growing popularity. The first trade collections hit just in time, at the beginning of the 1990s. Sandman's invented mythos, the adult quality of the work itself, the sophistication of Neil's scripts and collaborative artists, Dave McKean's then-innovative covers and book design work, and the satisfying reading experience the Sandman collections offered—significantly shorn of the "comic book universe" continuity baggage that came with collections that publishers like DC and Marvel were pushing—were instrumental in expanding the graphic novel market.

The careful cultivation and cross-marketing of the Sandman comic book series in conjunction with the release of the first collected "graphic novel" trade paperback editions was instrumental not only in building Sandman readership, but also in pushing the graphic novel as a format into bookstores. The Sandman collections thrived within the direct sales market, but more important they sold well in bookstores and other markets. This diversified the medium and format beyond the narrow parameters of genre (primarily superheroes) that had previously alienated all but indoctrinated readers of those genres. You didn't have to be a Batman or Spider-Man fan. There was nothing in any way childish about the look, feel, read, or packaging of Sandman. Sandman crossed party lines, if you will, and by doing so carved out sorely needed new audiences—and shelf space. Sandman spoke to a new generation, and not only to those frequenting comic shops.

In the meantime, the direct-sales market had become an incestuous, collector-oriented, comics-as-junk-bond-driven marketplace that stymied rather than nurtured new readers. Sandman reached outside that marketplace, and did so with lasting success, ensuring the survival of the title, the Vertigo imprint, and graphic novels at precisely the right time. By the time the direct market implosion hit in 1996, Sandman was a proven seller in bookstores and other venues, and it continues to sell well (e.g., the high-ticket Absolute Sandman collections, launched in 2007).

Now, I'm not saying Neil and Sandman *accomplished this alone. There were many, many other factors, of course, including the emergence of English-translated manga in the 1990s. The amazing diversity of quality graphic novels that emerged throughout the '90s to the present made the difference—but Neil and* Sandman *were instrumental in nurturing and sustaining market growth at a time when the direct-sales market wasn't.* Sandman *thankfully emerged just as bookstores were experimenting with what was to them a new genre, a new niche: graphic novels.* Sandman *fueled that niche being accepted, established, and growing, and was fundamental to its adoption and success. That cannot and should not be forgotten.*

—Stephen R. Bissette

Now that graphic novels are the "hot new format" and a new norm in the book industry, it's important we remember its sometimes difficult birth pangs, and how hard the series of experiments, battles, skirmishes, and marketing gambles were—failed, successful, and everything in between—that led to what we now have in bookstores everywhere in the twenty-first century. With a few notable exceptions, Art Spiegelman's *Maus* prominent among those, the midwife of the format was the American direct-sales comic book market, comprised of comics shops, that thrived for about two decades between the direct-sales market's emergence in the 1970s and the market implosion of the mid-1990s.

By 2000, most mainstream bookstores had launched their respective graphic novels sections—and that was due in part to Neil Gaiman and *Sandman* in the 1990s.

There were precursors, of course: Innovative artists like Frans Masereel, Lynd Ward, and others had created woodcut and woodblock "wordless novels" in the early 1900s. Book-format comics had long thrived in Europe (*Tintin, Asterix,* etc.) and other international markets, where book-format comics had become the standard while America maintained its addiction to the pamphlet-format comic book for generations.

In America, it was Will Eisner's *A Contract With God* (1978) that codified the term "graphic novel," which Marvel quickly adopted for their line of thin (sixty-eight pages, more or less) graphic novels. These were hardly "novels" in any traditional sense of the word, but it was a start. During the same period, there were the Heavy Metal collections of European comics in trade paperback form, including the work of Jean "Moebius" Giraud, culminating in the breakthrough *New York Times* bestseller listing of the Heavy Metal/Simon & Schuster graphic novel adaptation of *Alien* (1979).

The late Byron Preiss pioneered mainstream bookstore marketing of original graphic novels and anthologies, most often adaptations of existing science fiction novels and short stories, with erratic success. In the comic book direct-sales marketplace, trade paperback–collected editions of many comics series were widely available throughout the 1980s, but these were hardly "novels," either; publishers experimented with various slim trade paperback formats, like DC Comics's multivolume Prestige Format for *The Dark Knight Returns* and Gaiman's and Dave McKean's own *Black Orchid*.

It was Dave Sim's massive five-hundred-page *Cerebus* "phone book" collection that broke the twenty-five-dollar "glass ceilings" for page count, content, and pricing, a trailblazing breakthrough that DC Comics/Time Warner immediately embraced for *Watchmen* and *The Dark Knight Returns* hardcover and paperback collected editions.

In the wake of this embrace of new formats and more expansive graphic novel formats, the repackaged trade-edition collections of Gaiman's *Sandman* sold in both the direct-sales comic book market and in mainstream bookstores; it was the ideal fusion of content, product, packaging, and marketing, and dramatically launched Sandman into higher visibility, and to wider audiences and new markets, to the benefit of all. *Sandman* was the right graphic novel series arriving at precisely the right time.

The rest, as they say, is history.

Of course, Gaiman's excursions and experiments in the graphic novel format—most notably and most successfully with Dave McKean—did not begin or end with *Sandman*. In the section that follows we will explore and examine the other remarkable works of art and fiction that he has written in this format, some of which are among the most imaginative and breathtaking examples not only of Gaiman's work in the medium, but in its history.

VIOLENT CASES

(1987)

The first volume of what some refer to as Gaiman's "memory trilogy" (consisting of *Violent Cases, Signal to Noise,* and *Mr. Punch*), *Violent Cases* is significant for two reasons: It was one of Gaiman's first ventures into the world of comics and graphic novels, and it marked the first time he collaborated with the gifted Dave McKean, beginning a vital creative association that still exists today.

In 1986, Gaiman and McKean were working for a magazine called *Borderline.* Gaiman was a young journalist; McKean was still attending art college. After they met and hit it off, Gaiman suggested they work together on what became *Violent Cases,* based on a short story he had written as part of the Milford Writer's Workshop.

"We were intoxicated by the potential of the medium, by the then-strange idea that comics weren't exclusively for kids anymore (if they ever had been); that the possibilities were endless," writes Gaiman, in his introduction to the U.S. edition from Tundra Publishing.

As McKean has said in interviews, *Violent Cases* was where Gaiman and he "planted our flag," establishing the duo as a creative force to be reckoned with. McKean's art enhances Gaiman's story; the artist adds nice touches throughout, such as patterning the look of the anonymous narrator on Gaiman. From the very beginning, Gaiman and McKean found themselves in sync, their individual artistic choices combining to produce superior work that neither was likely to do on his own.

Per Gaiman's introduction to a later edition: "One of the things that had impressed me most about the work of Dave's I'd seen so far," says Gaiman, "leaving aside his simple ability to draw the pants off most of his contemporaries, was his sense of storytelling and design. I knew that if I was going to write something for him to draw, I was going to let him tell the story, let him discover the panel progressions."

The duo finished the story in early 1987. Gaiman mentor/inspiration Alan Moore wrote the introduction for the black-and-white first edition, published in the UK by Titan Books. Because the graphic novel was never properly distributed in the United States, Gaiman and McKean were "excited" when Tundra Publishing expressed interest in publishing a U.S. edition in 1991; printed in full color, this version was, in Gaiman's words, "*Violent Cases* as it was meant to be."

Violent Cases is constructed around its narrator's disturbing childhood memory; as such, it is vivid but ultimately unreliable, as, looking back as an adult, the storyteller has trouble remembering exact details, even to the point of substantially revising his description of one of the characters, Al Capone's osteopath, midstory. McKean's illustrations are stark but oddly beautiful, giving the tale an air of reality tinged by dreams; the depth of meaning and symbolism cement the strange mix of truth and supposition at the core of Gaiman's story.

A challenging, clever work, *Violent Cases,* while notable in its own right, only hints at the outstanding work Gaiman and McKean would produce together in the years to follow.

Oh, the title? Well, it's a story about memory, but it's also a story about gangsters, and, as everybody knows, old-time gangsters are infamous for carrying tommy guns in violin (violent) cases.

PEOPLE, PLACES, AND THINGS

THE NARRATOR. Appearing in the first panel of the story, he bears a striking resemblance to the adult Gaiman. Beginning his tale on a disturbing note—"I would not want you to think I was a battered child. However . . ."—he takes readers back to his childhood, when he was four, when his father "did something" to his arm. After what he refers to as "the accident," he has to wear his arm in a sling.

The narrator's father (who, in other scenes, exhibits borderline abusive behavior) brings the boy to an osteopath for treatment, a man the narrator is later told treated none other than Al Capone when the man lived in America. As the osteopath continues to treat him, the boy asks him to tell him about gangsters. The osteopath obliges.

After he finishes his course of treatments, the boy encounters the osteopath again a few months later, after ducking out of a birthday party held at a hotel. A little bit drunk, the man tells the boy about the horrific events that occurred in 1929 after "Al's big party." Their time together ends when the osteopath is escorted out of the bar by four men, who indicate that they've been calling him for a long time. The narrator remembers one of the men tipping his hat to him: "I was delighted and waved vigorously at all four of them until they were out of sight."

THE OSTEOPATH. Initially, the narrator relies on his father's description of the osteopath as an older man, not very tall, with a big nose ("An Eagle's Nose"), and a full head of hair. He spoke English with a middle European accent. His father said, concluding, "He looked like a red Indian chief, a Polish red Indian chief."

The narrator remembers an owl-like man with glasses, chubby and friendly. Describing the man he encountered a few months later, however, he modifies that description, saying he looked like Humphrey Bogart's partner in *The Maltese Falcon* (Miles Archer, played by Jerome Cowan).

The osteopath immigrated to the United States with his family at the beginning of the twentieth century, becoming a chiropractor around the time the United States entered World War I. In the twenties he was hired as a masseuse by Al Capone. His proximity to the gangster put him in the wrong place at the wrong time, as he witnessed some things that he wished he hadn't.

After World War II he moved to Portsmouth, England, where he practiced for almost twenty years. Apparently, the things he saw still could place certain people in danger, as, around 1965, he disappeared, after being accosted in a hotel bar by a large bald man accompanied by three menacing hoods carrying baseball bats.

TRIVIA

- One of the nicer touches in the book involves a number of movie posters hanging on the walls of the hotel bar where the narrator last sees the osteopath. Readers encounter, in rapid succession, posters from the films *Public Enemy, The Man Who Knew Too Much, They Died with Their Boots On,* and, finally, *The Maltese Falcon* (which may explain the Jerome Cowan reference).

- Stars are also a motif in the book. A magician who appears in the story wears a robe featuring a pattern of stars and moons. A star appears in the osteopath's glasses when he tells the narrator that he will see him "before he goes." Starlike glints appear in people's smiles, or when the sun hits the metal of a hubcap in a certain way. A star also plays an important part in an anecdote the narrator tells later in the story, a flashback (or flash-forward, depending on your perspective) of when he was sixteen, when the entire area he was in was illuminated by a brilliant flash of light.

THE QUOTABLE GAIMAN

And while one's feelings for one's children (and, by the same token, for one's parents) must always be mixed, and while it is unwise to show favoritism, *Violent Cases* was our first child, and it commands from both of us a love and loyalty that's all its own.

—Introduction, *Violent Cases*

||||||||||||||||||||||||||||||||||||||||||||||||||||||||||||||||||||||

A CONVERSATION WITH DAVE McKEAN

Question: Give us the real scoop on Neil Gaiman—he can't be as agreeable as he seems.

DAVE MCKEAN: No, he's passive-aggressive. It's all, "Oh sure, we could do that, whatever you like, I'm easy really, it's entirely up to you, I'm just happy to be along for the ride, really, really, I don't want to make a fuss." But when pressed you start to be aware of the little "of courses." "Of course, I'm just trying to make it better. Of course, I've been writing an awfully long time, and people, a lot of people, most people, actually, everybody, and everybody who might exist in the near future (not so near actually) likes what I write, but, of course, if you can do better . . . it just won't be supported by the millions, multimillions, quillions, puckillions of people who visit my Web site every minute of every day to ask for any tiny crumb of a word or thought or pure-liquid-gold inspiration that I might be able to bestow on them in their drab little existences . . . of course, none of those people, or animals, will support your side of the argument, because they know the *power* of my imagination, and it's all-encompassing correctness in all things concerning storytelling, and writing things down, and things like that . . . but, you know, I'm easy, really. Do what you want."

Q: *Any funny stories you can tell, special, memorable moments, etcetera?*
DM: Well there's the fatwa story, or the third leg, or the crayfish in jelly . . . so many.

In the very beginning, I remember seeing Neil in Forbidden Planet in London before a meeting for *Borderline* (the magazine that never happened that we were both working on). I showed him an illustration I had done for a story called "Going to California." We talked about all sorts during the twenty-minute walk to the *Borderline* office (borrowed without the owner's knowledge), and had pretty much decided to do *Violent Cases* instead by the time we arrived. Actually, come to think of it, I just kind of said, "Okay." I hadn't read it, I didn't know Neil, I was busy doing other things, I was still in art school, but I just kind of said, "Okay."

I realized the same thing happened when we went to see Karen Berger and Dick Giordano in a hotel in London and pitched them *Black Orchid*. Neil pitched; I sat and smiled, and tried not to make it too obvious that I didn't really know who or what Black Orchid was. I'm not sure we had an appointment, or if they even wanted to see anyone. And, they just kind of said, "Okay." Like me.

And, I'm sure, many other people, Charles Vess, Matthew Vaughan, Robert Zemeckis, Penn Gillette (who really should know when he's being hypnotized), Norman Mailer, Lisa Henson, Henry Selick, have all just kind of said "okay" when Neil smiled at them and asked them to do something.

He's a bit evil, really.

I also like to dig out the photos of Neil pretending to be impaled with a broom handle, posing as Batman in his flat in Forest Hill for *Arkham Asylum*. Call them my little insurance policy against damnation.

Q: *What was the collaborative process like on early projects like* Black Orchid, Violent Cases, Signal to Noise, *and* Mr. Punch?
DM: All quite different, although our basic rule that Neil has final cut on the words, me on the pictures has been consistent.

Neil wrote a short story for *Violent Cases* and I turned it into a narrated comic.

Black Orchid was more like a film script. I don't think it was broken down into pages or panels; I remember doing that in doodle form in my sketchbooks first.

Signal to Noise was very different, as it started with a bunch of writing, several false starts, and a few fractured paragraphs that I shaped into a first chapter. After that Neil picked up the tone of voice and ran with it. The chapters had to be delivered to *The Face* magazine on the first week of the month to be printed and in the shops by the fourth. Also, the story had to have a beginning (the director finds out he's going to die) and an end (he dies), but an infinitely expandable or contractible middle (depending on whether the drugs work, remission, sudden downturn, whatever). The editors just didn't know in how many issues the story would run. I showed the final thing to Barron Storey, a trusted friend in America, who wrote me a very clear-sighted critique, and some of those notes went into the expanded book version, and all of his notes and many others have gone into the screenplay for the as yet unmade film.

Mr. Punch was written at a difficult time in Neil's private life, and so was brilliant but unfocussed in first draft. I had a long talk with him in a hotel lobby in New York till four A.M., and the second draft was great. Neil originally told me he wanted the series of murders to be the spine of the story, but for some reason, that Greenaway-like system was lost, and the relentless tick-tick of the murders was diffused. But out of those meanderings came all the family memories. *Mr. Punch* was good fun to do, and is my favorite of our comics together. I think we can do better; I'd still like to try.

Incidentally, I did the music for the BBC Radio 4 version of *Mr. Punch* last year, and it reminded me how powerful, and how slippery, as a narrative, it is. It would make an interesting film.

Q: When you first started working with Neil did you ever imagine that you'd still be collaborating over two decades later?

DM: I like ongoing collaborations. I've worked with a few people over the years, and for one reason or another fallen out, or drifted apart, so there's something about growing up with someone over a long period of time that is, well, irreplaceable. There's no substitute for time. So, the answer is "yes."

Q: How were the covers for the various issues of Sandman created? Was there a specific process? How do you see that body of work in relation to the rest of your work?

DM: The process changed over the seven years as I got more confident, more willing to play, and as Neil got more and more crushed by deadlines. When the series started I could read the scripts. By the end I was lucky to get a sentence outline. But by then, the relationship between the cover and interiors had become more of a feeling, an atmosphere, or a filter that colored the story, rather than a literal depiction of what happens inside.

It feels like a diary to me. From the collages I was doing in art school, to discovering photography through Matt Mahurin, and design through Vaughan Oliver (and many other influences, but these are two big obvious ones), and on to sculptural work, Xerox experiments, computer compositing and three-D rendering. They were a regular "note to self," one a month, for a long time.

Unfortunately, publishers generally have become more and more dominated by marketing departments, who are reactive rather than proactive, so it became very difficult to look forward. *Sandman* was a really great example, that if you give creators an opportunity and let them run, you never know where it will lead.

Q: Do you think you would have done as much work in the area of children's literature if not for your relationship with Neil?
DM: Actually, yes. I've always put of lot of my personal life into my own stories, books, and films, and so with the birth of my two children, I would have inevitably been led into children's books, and dealing with the experience of parenthood in my work. The rhythm of good picture-book writing has really affected my own short stories. Obviously, it's great to have Neil's stories to illustrate, and because they have all (so far) been completely personally written little stories, I think usually written very quickly and directly in an afternoon, and not driven by publishing deadlines, editorial policy, or market forces, they remain some of my favorite things Neil has ever written.

Q: Was the experience of working together on MirrorMask as difficult as Neil made it out to be in interviews?
DM: Yes. It was an unsettling collision of forces and expectations. I have very little writing experience, but when I do write, it is with a completely different style and methodology to Neil. On reflection, I think we both panicked in the same way we did with *Black Orchid*; too eager to please, too willing to write to brief, or what we perceived the brief to be. Also, neither of us believed it would ever happen, which is a lousy attitude to write anything. Also, it should have been developed a lot more than it was. So yes, it was painful to realize we couldn't work together in the same room; even the same floor was tough (you can't write *and* listen to Radio4 chat shows at the same time, I don't care what anyone says). It was painful for me feeling like I was spoiling the party, being so critical all the time, but I just didn't get it. And I needed to "get it" if I was going to spend two years making it, and explaining it to actors, animators, and eventually journalists. And then the production side was hell on earth. And then I was so disappointed with the end result, I nearly ran away rather than face our first audiences in Sundance.

So, yes. Difficult.

Q: *How has working with Neil affected you as an artist/creator? How do you think you've influenced him?*

DM: Very hard to say. First of all, he's a very good friend. I hope we've been a good team, filling in the blanks in each other's personalities. I think I've become much more aware of the craft of writing, and the fact that writing and drawing the book is only part one of the story. Watching Neil's awareness of the bigger picture, the *career* picture, was new to me. And I realize that if you want to carry on writing and drawing, and not spending all your time doing another job to make enough money to live, then yes, you do have to have a wider view.

Drawing pictures every day is pretty lonely, which most of the time I enjoy. But it is a great comfort for me to know that I will be doing something with Neil again. Don't know what at the moment, but something will come up. It makes you feel like you are part of a team, and it gives you a little more confidence to face the daily battle of creating things from scratch, and getting them past the suits and into the real world.

Q: *Can you talk a little bit about your influences/inspirations?*

DM: All sorts: painters, architects, places, food, people, films and music, and all sorts. When I started my influences were obvious and superficial: American illustration from the sixties and seventies, and then the conceptual illustrators from the eighties, surrealism, the secessionists, the English postwar artists, Polish posters and Russian animation, Ralph Steadman, Jim Dine, Woody Allen, Miles Davis, and Franz Kafka.

In comics I loved Bill Sienkiewicz's collision of art styles, and Moebius's drawing, and Alan Moore's writing, and the freedom of expression in mainland Europe.

And then I got to a point where I stopped looking at everyone else's work and started looking at my own. Since then, I think the people who've had the biggest impact on me are Lorenzo Mattotti, Egon Schiele, the Quay Brothers, Joel Peter Witkin, and Anthony Minghella.

And these days everything is so diffused. Anouar Brahem, Alexandr Sokurov, Patrick Bokanowski, Franciszek Starowieyski, Wojciech Has, Buster Keaton, Louise Bourgoise, Venice, Heston Blumenthal have all had deep impacts on me, but they softly diffuse into everything, rather than sit on the surface looking out of place.

Q: *Are there any dream projects in the back of your mind that you think you'd like to work on with Neil in the future?*

DM: Both of us love musicals. Or rather, we hate most musicals (Andrew Lloyd bleedin' Webber), but really love them when they work, when they become this other parallel version of the real world—that is extraordinarily moving. When Sondheim "brings it all together, piece by piece," there's something really deep in us that music and words and pictures in perfect balance touches.

So, a musical, on film or onstage. So long as I don't have to sing.

THE QUOTABLE GAIMAN

After reading the foregoing interview:

I think I want all that on my tombstone. It can be written small. I don't mind.

||||||||||||||||||||||||||||||||||||||||||||||||||||||||||||||||||||||||

SIGNAL TO NOISE

(1992)

The phrase "signal to noise" derives from the idea of the signal-to-noise ratio, an electrical engineering concept that has come to be used in other fields; it is defined as the ratio of a signal power to the noise power corrupting the signal.

In less technical terms, the signal-to-noise ratio compares the level of a desired signal (such as music) to the level of background noise: the higher the ratio, the less obtrusive the background noise. You could also say that it refers to the ratio of useful information to false or irrelevant data.

In Gaiman and McKean's graphic novel of the same name, it refers to the difficulty of conveying the ideas in your head accurately and completely to an audience. The signal of the title refers to the story that its protagonist wishes to tell; the noise refers to his creativity being challenged by the fact of his imminent demise.

Readers get to experience both stories, walking behind the director as he pieces the film together in his mind—crafting the script, building a cast, and finally constructing the final version of the movie—even as he moves toward his final fate. The film will end, and the director's story will end; the villagers, however, will not pass on, at least not yet, but be left to deal with the problems of living.

Gaiman's story is haunting; his narration conveys a sense of loss and regret and melancholy that is almost palpable. The story provides a tantalizing glimpse into the creative process, where the final, tangible product is never as good as what was in the creator's head. McKean's art, combining photography, pencil and brush drawing, and digital imagery, is simply stunning. Words and illustrations merge to create an artistic hybrid whose messages, overt and covert, resonate in readers' minds long after they turn the last page.

Author Jonathan Carroll (*The Land of Laughs, Outside the Dog Museum*) gets to the heart of things in his introduction: "*Signal to Noise* does not entertain. It scratches, it provokes, it frightens. It tells you things you don't want to know but then twists you inside out by saying, look harder and see the poignance, the beauty of lights dancing on life's edge, truth that is as simple and direct as death."

PEOPLE, PLACES, AND THINGS

THE DIRECTOR. As the story opens, a famous film director has just been told that, because of a malignant tumor, he only has a few months to live. He begins to make a film in his head, assembling the actors, setting up the shots, struggling to "complete" it before he passes. His film will tell the story of a European village as the last hour of A.D. 999 approached; the drama in his film stems from the fact that the villagers are convinced that midnight will bring an ending to all they know. His personal dilemma differs from theirs in that he knows his time is almost up; they fear the end, but have no idea when it's coming.

Tragically, the film he's imagined will never be seen.

TRIVIA

- Gaiman dedicates this graphic novel as follows: "This one's for Emma Bull and Will Shetterly. And Fourth Street." Bull (author of *Bone Dance*) and Shetterly (author of *Dogland*) are husband and wife. Bull, together with Gaiman's personal assistant, Lorraine Garland, formerly performed folk music together as the Flash Girls.

- *Signal to Noise* was originally serialized in a magazine called *The Face* in 1989, and was expanded and revised into a full-blown graphic novel in 1992.

- A stage version of *Signal to Noise* was presented by Chicago's NOWtheatre in February 1999 as a joint benefit for the theater group and the Comic Book Legal Defense Fund. The graphic novel was adapted for the stage by Robert Toombs and Marc Rosenbush (the latter also directed). Promotional materials stated: "True to Gaiman's original, the play presents a richly textured, intensely theatrical experience with something for everyone: paper storms, flagellants, numerology, star-crossed lovers, a slightly mad hunchback, the Four Horsemen of the Apocalypse, giant puppets, and more."

THE QUOTABLE GAIMAN

On attending the preview of the stage version of *Signal to Noise*:
It was very interesting going to see a stage adaptation of something you've written, especially when a good 50 percent of the words you're hearing on the stage are not the words you wrote. I'm really looking forward to going back, if I can, and seeing it before the end of the run. Because what I saw was essentially the dress rehearsal, the preview. It was the first time they'd done everything on the stage, with the lighting cues, etc. As it began, the actors were rather nervous. But it warmed up as it went, and it seems to be getting quite good reviews.

—Interview with Lucy Snyder, SFSite,
February 14, 1999

THE TRAGICAL COMEDY OR COMICAL TRAGEDY Of MR. PUNCH: A ROMANCE

(1994)

The final installment of Gaiman and McKean's loose-knit "memory trilogy" evolved from something as simple and as sinister as a Punch and Judy show. Most readers are probably at least familiar with the concept of a Punch and Judy show: a puppet show consisting of a sequence of short scenes, each depicting an interaction between two characters, most typically the anarchic Punch and one other character, usually his wife, Judy. The show is traditionally performed by a single puppeteer, known as a professor, who conducts Punch through a series of confrontations with a number of foils besides his spouse, including his baby, Joey the Clown, a policeman, a doctor, a beadle, a crocodile, a skeleton, a hangman, and the Devil himself.

Punch and Judy shows have been popular for centuries; some have traced their roots back to the sixteenth century and the Italian commedia dell'arte. Punch is a classic example of the trickster figures of mythology, like Loki, coyote, Robin Goodfellow, or Anansi—all of which Gaiman has used at some point in his career. In other words, while Punch is a character who usually causes chaos, he's a character that we secretly and perversely can't help liking. In the British Punch and Judy show, Punch wears a jester's costume and is a hunchback with a hooked nose and a curved, jutting chin. He carries a huge stick, which he uses enthusiastically to club the other characters in the show. Punch speaks in a distinctive, squawking voice that is produced by a contrivance known as a swazzle or swatchel, which the professor holds in his mouth to transmit Punch's maniacal cackle.

Mr. Punch tells the story of a young boy who has a strange relationship with Punch, beginning with an encounter on a South Sea beach when he was seven. The narrator goes on to describe subsequent encounters with the trickster, as Gaiman again explores the familiar topics of memory, childhood, family, violence, and betrayal. "The path of memory is neither straight nor safe, and we travel down it at our own risk," the narrator tells readers early on in *Mr. Punch*. "It is easier to take short journeys into the past, remembering in miniature, constructing tiny puppet plays in our heads." He concludes in the traditional manner of Punch and Judy shows: "That's the way to do it."

Gaiman certainly recalls what it's like to be a child, on the edges of the adult world. For instance, the narrator's strongest memories are of the deaths of relatives, since those events tend to stand out. The narrator also reminds us how scary it is to be small; as he says, adults are threatening creatures "who joke about throwing you in the sea, or in the rubbish bin, who think nothing of making strange comments in jest ('I'll eat you up') or in anger ('I'll take you back and get another little boy')."

Once again, McKean's illustration elevates the visuals beyond the values present in typical comic book art. His innovative use of photographic elements adds depth and a sense of realism (and, for that matter, surrealism). Sharp, inventive, utterly enthralling, McKean's work in *Mr. Punch* represents some of the best of his career so far. The design of the book is simply innovative and unique; presenting the Punch and Judy puppets as the only "real" elements (apart from backgrounds and props) is a masterstroke. Punch is a terrifying figure, all pointy angles and bulging eyes. His word balloons, featuring lettering in fonts larger than the others, stands out against smears of white as he laughs and taunts. The other characters are, for the most part, painted, except in limited instances.

PEOPLE, PLACES, AND THINGS

THE NARRATOR. As an adult, the narrator feels ill after witnessing Punch bludgeon Judy to death during a puppet show given in his village. His narration reveals a possible reason for this reaction as he tells us of his first encounter with Punch on a South Sea beach. Out fishing with his grandfather, the then seven-year-old boy decides to take a walk and happens upon a Punch and Judy booth. Not knowing what to make of it, the boy stands outside until Punch (resembling a demented Marty Feldman as Igor in *Young Frankenstein*) and his wife appear. In short order, Punch inquires after their baby, who an obliging Judy brings onstage. The baby starts squalling, however, and Punch flings it off the stage. Frightened by this sudden act of violence, the boy flees. Whether this really happened or not is left unclear.

A year later the boy, who has just gotten over a childhood disease, is sent away to stay with his grandparents in Portsmouth while his parents await the birth of their third child. It is here that the boy meets Mr. Swatchell, a Punch and Judy professor, and the murderous Mr. Punch re-enters the boy's life.

The boy becomes Mr. Swatchell's bottler (a position his grandfather, Arthur, once held), the person whose task it is to "take round the collecting tin for the Punch and Judy show." A good bottler, the professor tells him, starts the back chat with the puppets from the audience, and ensures that no children sneak around the back of the booth.

The antics of Punch and Judy are echoed in a violent tableau the boy witnesses one night. Out with his grandfather, the boy is told to wait in the car for a moment. Having to use the bathroom, the boy emerges from the car and enters the building his grandfather went into. There he sees a woman (who he recognizes as the mermaid from the arcade his grandfather operates when she runs past him) arguing with three men (notably, he cannot or will not identify them). He then watches as she is beaten by one of the men with a slat of wood.

Making his way out of the building, he comes upon his grandfather sitting alone ("If there had been three men, two of them were gone"). After collecting himself, Arthur tells the boy, "You didn't see anything."

The boy is sent home the next day.

GRANDFATHER AND GRANDMOTHER. Also known as Arthur and Ruby. Once successful enough to own a "huge black Daimler," a car accident leaves Arthur impaired ("He was never the same," says the boy). He now runs a run-down seaside arcade, complete with old slot machines, a mirror maze, a fortune-teller, and a singing mermaid. Arthur seems to have some sort of relationship with the woman who plays the mermaid, most likely romantic.

UNCLE MORTON. A hunchback (like Punch), he's the boy's favorite relative, because he was the first adult the boy could look in the eye. Morton's deformity may come from a disease like polio or tuberculosis, or it may have resulted from him being "thrown downstairs when he was a baby." Or maybe, one cousin offers, that was Morton's twin?

The boy overhears his uncle, who works at the arcade, chatting with the mermaid, but only catches a snatch of conversation spoken by his uncle: "—after what bloody happened with the last one? Keeping that quiet was no picnic, believe you me."

MR. SWATCHELL. An old acquaintance of Arthur's, he is a Punch and Judy professor, but not very happy about it. "Punch and Judy men die in the gutter," he tells the impressionable young boy. But he has great respect for the show, which he calls, "The greatest, wisest play there is: the comical tragedy, the tragical comedy, of Mr. Punch."

THE MERMAID. Arthur employs this young woman who plays the part of a mermaid in what he labels an "attraction," even though she doesn't earn money for the arcade. The young woman tells the boy's uncle Morton that Arthur loves her ("He told me so.").

TRIVIA

- Gaiman's acknowledgment reads: "Thank you to my parents and Aunts and Uncles, whose memories, both of Punch and Judy, and of my family history, I have so recklessly and shamelessly plundered and twisted to my own purposes." An example of this "plundering" comes at the point in the story where the boy is told a story about his grandfather being a peddler when he first came to England, selling Sunlight Soap. "Only it wasn't *real* Sunlight Soap." The story about Arthur being pummeled by some villagers he had swindled was true, according to Gaiman; it happened to *his* grandfather.

- The dedication to *Mr. Punch* reads as follows: "For Holly Gaiman, who is now too old to be thrown out of the window and for Yolanda McKean, who is just the right age."

- Gaiman's use of the ironic subtitle *A Romance* (possibly inspired by a novel by Gaiman's favorite author, G. K. Chesterton, namely *The Man Who Was Thursday: A Nightmare*) is very interesting. According to the *American Heritage College Dictionary,* one definition of romance is "a fictitiously embellished account or explanation."

- In 2005, an audio dramatization of *Mr. Punch,* scripted by Gaiman, was broadcast by BBC Radio 3.

THE QUOTABLE GAIMAN

I took refuge in a junk shop, to get out of the rain. And in the junk shop they had Sidney de Hempel's book *How to Do Punch and Judy,* sitting on a pile of junk. I picked it up, said, 'How much is this?' and the little old lady in this junk shop—she looked at it and said, 'Fifteen quid.' And I thought about it for a second, and I paid my money. Took the book home, my fifteen-quid-circa-1917-book on how to do Punch and Judy. And when I finished it . . . it ends with this wonderful little description of the plot: The baby starts crying, Punch throws the baby out the window and kills it; Judy comes up and complains; he kills her; a policeman comes to arrest him; he kills the policeman; he has a fight with a crocodile; the doctor comes to heal him; he kills the doctor; they come to hang him; he kills the hangman; the devil comes to take him off to hell; he kills the devil. And the last line was: 'And Mister Punch then goes off to spread joy and happiness to children all over the land.'"

—"Feature Focus on Mr. Punch,"
by Peter Hogan, *Previews,* 1994

||||||||||||||||||||||||||||||||||||||||||||||||||||||||||||||||||||

A CONVERSATION WITH ROGUES

DISCUSSING THE THEATRICAL ADAPTATION OF *MR. PUNCH* WITH THE ROGUE ARTISTS ENSEMBLE

Rogue Artists Ensemble is a Los Angeles–area organization that bills itself as "a collective of multi-disciplinary artists who create *Hyper-theater,* an innovative hybrid of theater traditions, puppetry, mask work, dance, music, and modern technology. Through a collaborative development process, with an emphasis on design and storytelling, the Rogues create original, thought-provoking performances."

The group prides itself on providing "unique audience experiences." In 2007, one of those was an extraordinary production of Gaiman and McKean's *The Comical Tragedy or Tragical Comedy of Mr. Punch.* According to *Variety,* the show was "an otherworldly phantasmagoria. Under Sean T. Cawelti's protean direction, the show is a feast for the senses." Though *Variety* pointed out several flaws in the show, the review was overwhelmingly positive, concluding thus:

> Cawelti's direction triumphantly mixes traditional puppeteering, shadow puppets, masks, video projections and more into a thriving whole. Joel Daavid's spooky set combines nuance and utility. John Nobori's waves of sound and Melissa Domingo's washes of light make a thrilling combination. Joyce Hutter's puppets are magnificently eerie creations, and Patrick Rubio's masks are quite effective, particularly a huge and fierce roaring Grandpa face. Finally, Patrick Heyn and Brian White's video design is outstanding, adding another aesthetic level of achievement and tying the entire show together.

The members of the Rogue Artists Ensemble were kind enough to allow the presentation within these pages of designs and photographs, and also to elaborate on their efforts to bring Mr. Punch to life.

Question: *Why did Rogue Artists Ensemble choose* Mr. Punch?

SEAN T. CAWELTI
ARTISTIC DIRECTOR, ROGUE ARTISTS ENSEMBLE
DIRECTOR/ADAPTOR OF *MR. PUNCH*

In many Rogue projects, we use the art of puppetry to allow us to tell stories from different perspectives and views. Often, the puppets, masks, and other *Hypertheatrical* storytelling conventions are added on to an existing story. Our board chair happened to see the graphic novel while working on another project, when a designer brought it in as a bit of inspiration. We received a call shortly after, urging us to seek out the graphic novel, as even at that early stage it was apparent that there was a bit of potential there. As soon as we read *Mr. Punch* we all realized we had found a rare bit of inspiration: a story with puppets already integrally incorporated. In *Mr. Punch,* we enter a man's fragmented memory, where he is unable to discern between what is actual, what is a puppet show, and what may have been fabricated or synthesized after the fact. The group was very keen on adapting such a challenging work, and it felt immediately like the perfect project for us to tackle. Having just created a living comic strip onstage in *The Victorian Hotel,* we were excited to work on combining the storytelling conventions of theater and graphic novels.

MEGAN OWINGS
MANAGING DIRECTOR, ROGUE ARTISTS ENSEMBLE

In *Mr. Punch,* there is definitely a deep appreciation for the transformative nature of puppets and their importance in history. Rogue Artists Ensemble was built on the concept that theater is a way to reflect the most precious and obscure parts of the human psyche, which *Mr. Punch* embraces, too. We also felt that the graphic novel is a small study in *Hyper-theatrical* concepts in the way that it blends artistic mediums.

JENNY OWINGS
ENSEMBLE MEMBER, ROGUE ARTISTS ENSEMBLE

I believe that all of the Rogues can identify with the alienation, imagination, and surreal qualities of the piece. For our particular brand of art, we draw on our childhood fascinations, fears, and dreams all the time. Discussing our memories together is always an interesting journey, and it is usually these explorations that act as a catalyst for new designs, stories, and creations. Neil's graphic novel *Mr. Punch* captures the incongruities and beauty of those memories and that odyssey. It is not the sedate and archaic exploration of a fabled past but a tumultuous jumble of sensations and emotions. It does not carry the weight of an adult's cynicism or wear the rose-colored glasses of "bygone days." I like to think that the Rogues try to emulate that perspective in our own art, capturing the essence of experiences with sight, sound, and movement. It is not forced through a filter; it simply exists, as it is, in its own time and space.

How was the audience response?

CAWELTI:

Mr. Punch was a truly visceral experience for audiences, and affected them in a profound and highly emotional way. Our adaptation was at times more like watching a graphic novel come to life than watching a play, so some audiences were puzzled by the cryptic nature of the story and had difficulty following along. We chose to remain faithful to the novel's nonlinear approach to the story of the boy, which was a challenge for some audience members. However, we used video projection to display what looked like panels from the graphic novel, and that helped to reorient the audience. The mermaid and her story were always an audience favorite, and having a real child actor as the central character in the story gave the entire performance a sense of authenticity. We are eager to remount *Mr. Punch* and have taken great lengths to continue developing the project to enable an even greater number of audience members to appreciate the story we are telling.

MEGAN OWINGS:

It was definitely mixed. There are those who loved every minute of it, those who were very disturbed by it, and others who were just confused. But that is the point of theater, to provoke a reaction and a thought process and connect with an audience on many different levels. *Mr. Punch* has been our most successful piece to date, based on the fact that it inspired so much dialogue between us and our audience.

CARI TURLEY
COMMUNICATIONS DIRECTOR, ROGUE ARTISTS ENSEMBLE
ACTOR/ASSISTANT MASK DESIGNER/ASSISTANT STAGE MANAGER
FOR *MR. PUNCH*

The audience response was virtually unanimous. Everyone claimed it was visually stunning, and remarked how well we'd adapted the two-dimensional drawings of Dave McKean into a full, three-dimensional world. The only criticism we heard was that the story was hard to follow, which we as a group agree with and are working to change for the remount. With the graphic novel the reader has a chance to reread certain passages, and go at his or her own pace, but that's not the case when watching a play. Regardless of that issue, however, audiences across-the-board were excited by the show—especially those who were already familiar with the graphic novel. It gave people the chance to sit in the same room with Gaiman and McKean's characters, hear their voices, and even touch them. The puppets looked identical to McKean's drawings, the set was torn straight from the pages of the book, and even the human characters looked exactly like the illustrations, with the help of some innovative mask design. For audience members even a little familiar with the graphic novel, we heard it was a stunning experience.

JENNY OWINGS:

There was a wide range of responses! I had many relatives and friends come to see it, and they all had very different responses to the piece. The older members of our audience had a very emotional response to the piece, empathizing not only with the little boy, but the grown man that boy would one day become. The younger people seemed to focus more on the other stimuli, such as the sounds, the puppets, and the projections. I think they reveled in the experience as it related to them, in that moment, rather than the emotional journey that was unfolding.

Was it a difficult production?

CAWELTI:

Mr. Punch was the single most challenging production I have ever worked on. Fueled by an intense passion and desire to make something truly original and unique, the project took the combined talents of nearly fifty artists. The design for *Mr. Punch* was inspired by the graphic novel but still retained the group's aesthetic, which proved difficult to balance. As a director, it was challenging to work with a child actor in such a large role as well as deal with the innumerable *hyper-theatrical* elements that were critical to the success of the production. We were determined to create several moments of synchronicity that would feel to the audience that the performance had paused and actually become a panel from the graphic novel. These scenes combined several elements (puppets, masks, surround sound, digital media, special effects, and more) and were incredibly challenging to stage. They often took days to perfect, even though they lasted just a few minutes in performance. The cast's tenacity and belief in the project was unmatched and made the entire process a joy beyond what words can express.

MEGAN OWINGS:

Of course—every production is a new adventure! While we have an established process, this can be altered based on the difficulty of the source material and the number of collaborating artists. With *Mr. Punch,* the challenge was staying true to the original content and artistic merit while also making it feel like our own production. It was a trick paying homage to the beauty of the novel and honoring its authors without just creating a photocopy of it. The worst thing, in our minds, would have been to create mediocre mockery of the original novel. We had to be mindful at all times of what we were creating and be willing to make adjustments and compromises to save the original integrity of the piece.

TURLEY:

It was a very challenging production, but a labor of love all the way. Gaiman's text and McKean's visuals are both so distinct that it was difficult to remain faithful to them while infusing our own aesthetic. After all, what would be the artistic merit of simply copying them? We had to find a way to honor the original artists and still make a distinctly "Rogue" production. I think we succeeded, ultimately, but it was definitely a struggle.

JENNY OWINGS:

Overall, I think that tackling this project was one of the most difficult things we have had to do as a group. It was difficult in the sense that there are so many layers to the story. There are defining, passionate moments and action sandwiched between very delicate and nuanced states of mind. As a designer, it is a veritable playground for the imagination, but it is also a challenge to mediate between the essence and overlying mood of the piece in conjunction with what is implied. I think the director had the hardest job in trying to tell the story as it was meant to be told, while simultaneously navigating the audience through a spectrum of actual occurrences and childhood hyperbole. The production really allowed us to stretch the limits of our capabilities and think outside of the box from a technical and creative standpoint.

||||||||||||||||||||||||||||||||||||||||||||||||||||||||||||||||||||

NEIL GAIMAN ON DAVE McKEAN
BY NEIL GAIMAN

I was twenty-six when I first met Dave McKean. I was a working journalist who wanted to write comics. He was twenty-three, in his last year at art college, and he wanted to draw comics. We met in the offices of a telephone sales company, several members of which, we had been told, were going to bankroll an exciting new anthology comic. It was the kind of comic that was so cool that it was only going to employ untried new talent, and we certainly were that.

I liked Dave, who was quiet and bearded and quite obviously the most artistically talented person I had ever encountered.

That mysterious entity which Eddie Campbell calls "the man at the crossroads," but everyone else knows as Paul Gravett, had been conned into running advertising in his magazine *Escape* for the Exciting New Comic. He came to take a look at it himself. He liked what Dave was drawing, liked what I was writing, asked if we'd like to work together.

We did. We wanted to work together very much.

Somewhere in there we figured out that the reason the Exciting New Comic was only employing untried talent was that no-one else would work with the editor. And that he didn't have the money to publish it. And that it was part of history . . . Still, we had our graphic novel to be getting on with for Paul Gravett. It was called *Violent Cases*.

We became friends, sharing enthusiasms, and taking pleasure in bringing each other new things. (I gave him Stephen Sondheim, he gave me Jan Svenkmayer. He gave me Conlan Nancarrow, I gave him John Cale. It continues.)

I met his girlfriend, Clare, who played violin and was starting to think that, as she came up to graduation from university, she probably didn't want to be a chiropodist.

People from DC Comics came to England on a talent-scouting expedition. Dave and I went up to their hotel room, and they scouted us. "They don't really want us to do stuff for them," said Dave, as we walked out of the hotel room. "They were probably just being polite."

But we did an outline for *Black Orchid* and gave them that and a number of paintings anyway, and they took them back to New York with them, politely. That was fifteen years ago. Somewhere in there Dave and I did *Black Orchid* and *Signal to Noise,* and *Mr. Punch,* and *The Day I Swapped My Dad for Two Goldfish.*

And Dave's done book covers and interior work for Jonathan Carroll and Iain Sinclair and John Cale and CD covers for a hundred bands.

This is how we talk on the phone: we talk, and we talk, and we talk until we're all talked out, and we're ready to get off the phone. Then the one who called remembers why he called in the first place, and we talk about that.

Dave McKean is still bearded. He plays badminton on Monday Nights. He has two children, Yolanda and Liam, and he lives with them and with Clare (who teaches violin and runs Dave's life and never became a chiropodist) in a beautiful converted Oast House in the Kent countryside.

When I'm in England I go and stay with them, and I sleep in a perfectly round room.

Dave is friendly and polite. He knows what he likes and what he doesn't like, and will tell you. He has a very gentle sense of humour. He likes Mexican Food. He will not eat sushi, but has on several occasions humoured me by sitting and drinking tea and nibbling chicken in Japanese Restaurants.

You get to his studio by walking across an improvised log bridge over a pond filled with Koi Carp. I read an article once in the *Fortean Times,* or possibly *The Weekly World News* about Koi exploding, and I have warned him several times of the dangers, but he will not listen. Actually, he scoffs.

When I wrote *Sandman* Dave was my best and sharpest critic. He painted, built, or constructed every *Sandman* cover, and his was the face *Sandman* presented to the world.

I never minded Dave being an astonishing artist and visual designer. That never bothered me. That he's a world-class keyboard player and composer bothers me only a little. That he drives amazing cars very fast down tiny Kentish back roads only bothers me if I'm a passenger after a full meal, and much of the time I keep my eyes shut anyway. He's now becoming a world-class film and video director, that he can write comics as well as I can, if not better, that he subsidises his art (still uncompromised after all these years) with highly paid advertising work which still manages, despite being advertising work, to be witty and heartfelt and beautiful . . . well, frankly, these things bother me. It seems somehow wrong for so much talent to be concentrated in one place, and I am fairly sure the only reason that no-one has yet risen up and done something about it is because he's modest, sensible, and nice. If it was me, I'd be dead by now.

He likes fine liqueurs. He also likes chocolate. One Christmas my wife and I gave Dave and Clare a hamper of chocolate. Chocolates, and things made of chocolate, and chocolate liqueur, and even chocolate glasses to drink the liqueur from. There were chocolate truffles in that hamper, and Belgian chocolates, and this was not a small hamper. I'm telling you, there was six months of chocolate in that hamper.

It was empty before New Year's Day.

He's in England, and I'm in America, have been for ten years, and I still miss him as much as I miss anyone. Whenever the opportunity to work with Dave comes up, I just say yes.

I was amused, when *Coraline* came out recently, to find people who only knew Dave for his computer-enhanced multimedia work were astonished at the simple elegance of his pen-and-ink drawings. They didn't know he could draw, or they'd forgotten.

Dave has created art styles. Some of what he does is recognisable enough as his that art directors will give young artists samples of Dave McKean work and tell them to do that—often a specific art style that Dave created to solve a specific problem, or a place he went as an artist for a little while, decided that it wasn't where he wanted to be, and moved on.

(For example, I once suggested to him, remembering Arcimbaldo and Josh Kirby's old Alfred Hitchcock paperback-cover paintings, that the cover of *Sandman: Brief Lives* could be a face made up of faces. This was before Dave owned a computer, and he laboriously photographed and painted a head made of smaller faces. He's been asked to do similar covers many times since by art directors. And so have other artists. I wonder if they know where it came from.)

People ask me who my favourite artist is to work with. I've worked with world-class artists, after all, heaps of them. World-class people. And when they ask me about my favorite, I say Dave McKean. And then people ask why. I say, because he surprises me.

He always does. He did it from the first thing we did together, and a couple of weeks ago I looked at the illustrations he's done for our new graphic novel for all ages, *The Wolves in the Walls.* He's combined paintings of people, amazing, funny-scary line drawings of wolves, and photographs of objects (jam, tubas, and so on) to create something that is once again not what I expected, nothing like what I had in my head, but better than anything I could have dreamed of, more beautiful and more powerful.

I don't think there's anything Dave McKean cannot do as an artist. (There are certainly things he doesn't want to do, but that's not the same thing at all.) After sixteen years, some artists are content to rest on their laurels (and Dave has shelves-full of Laurels, including a World Fantasy Award for best artist). It's a rare artist who is as restless and as enthusiastic as he was when he was still almost a teenager, still questing for the right way to make art.

MELINDA

(2004)

Over the years Neil Gaiman has been known to produce all sorts of imaginative oddities to send to friends, family, and associates at the holidays. Some years there have been strange scrolls (*The Dangerous Alphabet*) or exquisite pamphlets (a scene excised from *American Gods*). Once, in 2004, that "holiday card" took the form of an entire book.

Hill House Publishers—which had done limited editions of other Gaiman works—produced *Melinda* in a beautiful edition, a showcase for the art of Dagmara Matuszak, which includes stark, black-and-white illustrations, and color plates that were printed separately and laid by hand into each copy of the book.

Melinda is difficult to categorize. Its relatively few words are written as poetry, and tell the tale of a girl living alone in a postapocalyptic city. And yet, as presented, with each page a single, breathtaking illustration—and given the age of its protagonist—it might easily be considered a children's picture book—were it not for the grim subject matter and bleak tone. If there is hope in *Melinda,* it comes from the girl's imagination and perseverance, and the end of the tale is no ending at all, except that Gaiman runs out of words, and Matuszak pictures. It's difficult to imagine this as a book for children.

Thus, we present it here, among the graphic novels, for though it is both poem and picture book, it is most certainly also a graphic novel, and rests comfortably with the other works in this section.

Melinda wanders the ruin of a city, with feral animals and machines running down: "Now, where the future rots and rusts, only Melinda, and the dust."

It may be that whatever caused the cataclysm isn't widespread—Melinda believes that one day she will return here with soldiers at her back who will do her bidding and reclaim the city—but it is a desolate and lonely existence. And what little evidence Gaiman provides certainly implies that hope for the future may be fruitless, since gigantic spheres with spiderlike legs amble over the cityscape from time to time.

"The road was empty," Gaiman writes. "Only domes that trundled thoughtfully along intent on something, and they pass like beetles made of steel and glass."

Whether these things are robot conquerors, aliens, or military creations is unclear, and matters little to the tale, or to the young girl living in the ruins.

Gaiman has said that there is more to the story—that this may only be Part 1—but what has appeared of the tale thus far is quite dark indeed.

TRIVIA

- Fifteen hundred copies of *Melinda* were printed. Gaiman received four hundred and Matuszak one hundred. The remaining one thousand copies were numbered and signed by Gaiman, and retailed at ninety dollars.

- Hill House also offered an art triptych, showcasing three of the color illustrations Matuszak did for the book, signed by the artist and the author, which sold for seventy-five dollars. Along with the three images and the signature card was a card with a quote from the text: "Now, where the future rots and rusts, only Melinda, and the dust." All materials were matted and framed, and only two hundred triptychs were offered for sale.

THE QUOTABLE GAIMAN

[*Melinda*] was meant to be a sort of Christmas Card and got out of hand (which was, in hindsight, not a bad thing) . . . It's an art object much more than it's a book. It's probably *Melinda Part One* in reality, as I need to write the next bit of the story.

—journal.neilgaiman.com

I met Dag a couple of years ago in Krakow, having seen her artwork as part of a small exhibition of art inspired by stuff I'd written, and I knew on seeing it that I wanted to work with her. *Melinda* started as a conversation between us about me writing something that she could do as a comic, but she then took what I wrote and pushed it to some very strange places.

—journal.neilgaimain.com

ᴘ ᴀ ʀ ᴛ ꜰ ᴏ ᴜ ʀ
THE COMICS

I don't think editors, publishers, and readers would have been as receptive to Neil or Neil's collaborative work without the foundations Alan Moore poured, but Neil's affecting fusion of myth, theology, fairy tales, and the common banalities of being human with a cunning fidelity to the various historical comic book universe continuities was (and remains) beguiling. Thus, Neil immediately embraced and refined much of what Alan had established as a vital new orientation to writing comics, and improved upon it. Neil and Alan have since gone in their own directions, and that's interesting to chart, and they have remained good friends in the bargain.

But Neil also tapped his personal inner life in ways previous mainstream comics writers had always resisted; with precious few exceptions, only the underground comix creators and cartoonists like Eddie Campbell had openly courted autobiography as a viable genre. Neil's initial forays in American comics built upon Moore's path in obvious ways, but more telling was his collaboration with Dave McKean on Violent Cases in 1987, meshing autobiography, memory, and fantasy with refreshing introspection and skill.

Neil was also very lucky, and very sharp in guiding what part of that luck he could. Sandman was the golden ship, and a voyage many chose to join him on. It was in many ways an accident of history, but the fact that Neil was finding and evolving his own voice via Sandman (1989–96) even as his growing readership was finding their own, and finding Neil en route—and decided to take that trip with Neil—was one of those generational shifts in the arts we live for. I don't think it's too grandiose to say that Neil offered his voice and vision to a readership eager for a comic that spoke for and to their own era. Neil and Sandman provided that.

Neil's comics work is seminal to the 1990s, and will continue to resonate for generations to come. Without Alan Moore and Karen Berger, there would have been no Vertigo Comics, but without Neil, Vertigo might have withered on the vine. Neil and Vertigo were literally made for one another. It's too bad they've grown apart, in terms of possible new work, but c'est la vie; that's the industry's fault, really. The attitude of "we made you" is never conducive to growing with a maturing artist, and there's no reason on earth for Neil to do anything but grow. That Neil has engaged with other (not per se "better," but certainly different) media is inevitable. As a novelist, screenwriter, filmmaker, and so on, Neil continues to evolve and explore, and his audience is moving with him. That's a loss *to comics, though Neil still works in the medium when opportunity permits; but as with so many other creators, the comics industry hasn't exactly made it viable for Neil to stay engaged. That's not his fault, or his worry: It's all writing, and Neil is, after all, a writer first and foremost.*

—Stephen R. Bissette

For American comics readers, Gaiman was (along with Grant Morrison, Garth Ennis, Warren Ellis, and others) part of the "third wave" of British talent to dramatically impact the industry and medium. Barry Windsor Smith was first in the seventies—essentially a one-man wave with his Marvel freelance work. Smith's art on Conan the Barbarian was the most prominent example, along with his transformative work with the Studio.

The 1980s brought the second wave: writers Alan Moore, John Wagner, Alan Grant, etc., and artists John Bolton, Dave Gibbons, Brian Bolland, David Lloyd, Kevin O'Neill, and their generation. That said, it was arguably Alan Moore's work that fundamentally changed things in ways his immediate peers hadn't and didn't—and it was Moore's legacy Gaiman initially and quite consciously carried on and expanded upon.

Like Moore, Gaiman excelled in terms of ingenious revamps, reinventions, and resurrections of old characters and concepts, recognizing and fanning dim flames others had disposed of as so much charcoal. But that was just the tip of the iceberg, as his individualistic approach to *Sandman* proved.

Furthermore, Gaiman's ability to tailor his own scripts to draw the best out of his collaborative artists was a great strength, and he did so with greater diplomacy and attention to fair business practices than any before him (and, alas, too few after).

Gaiman also had a primal, invigorating orientation to fantasy—its power, purpose, and urgency—that was revelatory. While every voice and vision of Gaiman's generation of British comics writers and artists was and is distinctive and influential, each in their own way, it is Gaiman's work in comics that has had the greatest impact upon other creators in other media—novelists, filmmakers, musicians, etc.—even as Gaiman himself moved into those media and venues with his creative work outside of comics.

He also contributed to the field in another unique way, and with greater passion and vigor than any of his British wave peers. To date Gaiman has done more active fundraising for, and donated more of his time, energy, and work to, the Comic Book Legal Defense Fund than almost any single other comics creator (only Dave Sim, creator of Cerebus, can match Gaiman's dedication to the cause).

Gaiman entered comics at a time when the industry and art form suffered almost constant persecution and legal prosecution from a number of sources. It was enduring a cultural backlash against the maturation of the comics art form, from the popular perception of it as a medium best suited to providing children's entertainment, as "funnybooks," and thus in need of constant regulation to repress adult concepts, themes, and imagery. Almost from his first year of work in the American comics industry, Gaiman dedicated himself to supporting and raising awareness of, and funds for, the CBLDF. This is a part of his legacy too rarely acknowledged or understood, but it reflects Gaiman's ongoing passion for the medium, its potential, and his audience that transcends an assessment of his published work alone.

BLACK ORCHID

(1988)

B*lack Orchid*, Neil Gaiman's first graphic novel for an American publisher—
originally serialized in three separate volumes, then collected as a three-chapter
graphic novel—initiated the long-term relationship with DC Comics, editor
Karen Berger, and what would soon become Berger's Vertigo imprint at DC. It
was here that Gaiman would launch his breakthrough creation, Sandman.

To understand the importance of *Black Orchid* one must understand what
doors the project opened for Gaiman for the long term. On the heels of the
United Kingdom comics publisher Escape's successful debut of *Violent Cases* in
1987, Neil and his close friend Dave McKean were among the young UK talents
vying for the attention of *Saga of the Swamp Thing* editor Karen Berger. With
the ongoing success of Swamp Thing, Berger's plans for expansion and further
experimentation at DC Comics would soon blossom from the vaguely defined
"mature readers/sophisticated suspense" titles (*Hellblazer, Swamp Thing*) into
the Vertigo line. Given the success of *Swamp Thing* and *Watchmen* writer Alan
Moore, Berger paid a great deal of attention to other writers, creators, and icono-
clasts in the UK comics industry. A youthful and highly ambitious Neil Gaiman
was among that circle.

Gaiman and Dave McKean presented themselves as a collaborative team, prof-
fering *Violent Cases* as a sample of their capabilities while making it clear that they
were eager to work within the DC universe. Gaiman in particular was attuned to
the ripe potential in the dramatic resurrections, reinventions, and recontextualizing of the venerable DC concepts and characters Moore had popularized in short
order, beginning with his collaborative work on *Swamp Thing*.

Like Moore, Gaiman's avid reading of DC Comics throughout his youth and
his arcane knowledge of its labyrinthian nooks and crannies, fueled a passion for
reviving and reinvigorating its most alien and abandoned denizens. Also like
Moore, Gaiman did so with an eye toward fresh associative and unsuspected fa-
milial links, much as sixties science fiction author Philip José Farmer had tied together previously unlinked family trees of popular characters from history,
literature, and the pulps with startling revisionist novels like *Tarzan Alive!*

Among Neil and Dave's pitches was a revival and redefinition of an essentially
forgotten 1973 DC character named Black Orchid, which Gaiman cleverly folded
into the *Swamp Thing* universe helmed by editor Karen Berger.

The original *Black Orchid* debuted in 1973 in *Adventure Comics* issues 428
through 430, the creation of DC Comics veteran writer/artist/editor Sheldon Mayer,

under the helm of then editor Joe Orlando. Mayer scripted Black Orchid's enig-matic three issues without an origin story, adding to the somewhat Gothic allure of this unusual costumed superheroine, who never revealed her true identity. Her modus operandi: infiltrating and working for criminal organizations in human guise and, once inside, taking them out as the Black Orchid. She was capable of flight, feats of superhuman strength, apparent invulnerability to bullets, and more. Graced with Tony DeZuniga's art, the Black Orchid stood out amid the round-robin experimentation of *Adventure Comics*, the first new superhero char-acter to debut in that title since the Golden Age.

Mayer and DeZuniga's team effort with the character carried over into a single backup story in *The Phantom Stranger* issue 31 (1974), launching a series of Black Orchid stories (by other creators, including Michael Fleischer) that continued for ten issues. Thereafter Orchid was reduced to inconsequential guest star status in various titles. Her background and true identity remained an unresolved riddle, relegating her to limbo until Gaiman and McKean's pitch fourteen years later. So complete was the character's anonymity by that point that DC's initial response to Gaiman's suggestion was confusion, thinking Gaiman had referred to Blackhawk Kid.

Adopting and refining aspects of his mentor Alan Moore's aesthetic and revi-sionist orientation to the DC universe, Neil proposed a synthesis of known elements—Marv Wolfman's corporate Lex Luthor; the leaner, meaner, post–Frank Miller Batman of the mideighties; and the newly forged (in the pages of *Swamp Thing*) fusion of the long-scattered seeds of a hierarchy of sentient botanical/ele-mental beings in the DC rogue's gallery—with the great unknown of the Black Orchid. Coaxing an origin from both the Mayer/DeZuniga originals and a story from the first narrative arc of the Alan Moore/Stephen Bissette/John Totleben *Saga of the Swamp Thing*, Gaiman ingeniously linked the various DC vegetable characters via a singular backstory.

Thus, a shared past was created. Gaiman detailed how the human incarnations of Swamp Thing (Alec Holland) and Batman femme fatale Poison Ivy (Pamela Isley) had studied alongside Orchid's creator Philip Sylvian under botanist Dr. Jason Woodrue, also know as the Floronic Man. Gaiman's simple but utterly original synthesis of tangled, previously unaligned narrative threads into a singu-lar unifying tapestry impressed Karen Berger as one of the young writer's strengths. This ingenuity neatly dovetailed into DC's grand experimentation of the 1980s and her need for an imaginative team of cartographers charting a cohesive genre foundation for what would soon become the Vertigo line.

Drawing from a broader pop cultural canvas, Neil also adapted potent iconog-raphy from Jack Finney's SF classic novel *The Body Snatchers* (first filmed in 1956 by Don Siegel as *Invasion of the Body Snatchers*) to his and McKean's needs. The malignant "pod people" of Finney's extraterrestrial invasion scenario fueled Gaiman and McKean's new origin story for the benevolent Orchid—and her "sisters." Rather than Finney's invasive pod people supplanting human life, though, Gaiman and McKean's Orchids cohabited with mankind, and only supplanted themselves, as necessary. Hybrids of human DNA and the actual flowers, capable of drawing all they need to live and grow from the atmosphere, the Orchids are nurtured in a protective greenhouse, and blossom into violet beauties. Upon the death of their sole active sister, who has been operating as the crime-fighting Black Orchid in the human world, one of the hybrids will awake to take her place.

As in Finney's SF classic, the pods/Orchids merge collective and individual sentience. Though "sleeping," they share the active Orchid's experiences and memories—to a point; complete transfer requires direct contact between sisters ("singing," as Gaiman's first-person script puts it). Deprived of such direct transfer when the active Orchid is brutally slain by Lex Luthor's "chairman," a pair of awakened Orchids—one adult, one child—struggle to piece together the secret of their identity/identities. It's a classic personal quest approach, steeped in buried memories, horrific trauma, and loss. As the Orchids unravel the riddle of their origins, the reader discovers the same, in what were originally three volumes of DC's mideighties trade paperback miniseries.

Like Gaiman and McKean's *Violent Cases, Black Orchid* is rooted in organized crime, childhood trauma—past (via Black Orchid's shared memory of her previous incarnation's violent death) and present (via Suzy's abduction, which initially suggests pedophilia, then threatened trauma, via Lex Luthor's plans to vivisect her)—and the desire to transcend both, finding alternatives and seeking escape into a better life. As Gaiman said at the time, "I wanted to do a pacifist fable," establishing himself in American comics with his first work as a creator of parables and fairy tales. Like all good fairy tales (and Black Orchid and the child Suzy are often rendered explicitly as fairies), the wellsprings of this narrative emerge from primal fears.

Following *Black Orchid,* there were plans afoot for Neil Gaiman and *Hellblazer* writer Jamie Delano to take over the scripting of *Swamp Thing* after the departure of writer/artist Rick Veitch. These plans were scuttled when DC refused to publish Veitch's controversial "Swamp Thing Meets Jesus" issue slated for *Swamp Thing* issue 88, which prompted Veitch's early resignation from the title. Gaiman and Delano stepped away from the title in solidarity—without jeopardizing ongoing relations with DC/Vertigo on other projects.

According to Veitch, Gaiman was even more involved with *Swamp Thing* at that time than anyone knew.

> Neil was . . . involved with helping me plot the ending to my *Swamp Thing* time travel story which was aborted when DC decided not to publish the completed *Swamp Thing* #88, where Swampy met Jesus. Neil, even then the wandering writer, visited me in Vermont while I was developing the story line and we came up with the ultimate confrontation between Swampy and Arcane in which the techno-sorcerer arrives at the birth of Alec and Abby's

baby to take it for himself. Swampy shows up and Arcane blasts him with every ounce of evil he's dragged up from hell. But Swampy, by observing Jesus a few issues earlier, has learned to let all evil pass through him, and thus not only defeats Arcane, but cures him of his evil ways.

Neil was scheduled to take over *Swamp Thing,* in a rotating schedule with Jamie Delano, when I was done, but both resigned from the project in solidarity after the *Swamp Thing* #88 debacle.[1]

PEOPLE, PLACES, AND THINGS

BLACK ORCHID I/SUSAN LINDEN. The character of Black Orchid appears in three incarnations in the graphic novel. The active Black Orchid in the opening sequence of the first chapter is Susan Linden, a courageous female crime fighter who has infiltrated Lexcorp. She is unmasked at the end of a Lexcorp board meeting, unceremoniously shot point-blank in the head, doused with gasoline, and left to burn in a deliberately set fire. Unable to escape in time, she is also prevented from fully transferring her memories to her successor.

The Black Orchid incarnation of Susan Linden was a superhuman vegetable/human hybrid derived partly from genetic components of the all-too-human Susan Linden, who had grown up in and escaped from an abusive household, only to eventually marry a gangster named Carl Thorne. After divorcing and escaping from Thorne, Linden fled to live and work with her friend Dr. Philip Sylvian. When a vengeful Thorne assassinated Linden, Sylvian extracted a sample of the human Linden's blood and used its genetic material to breed the hybrid Black Orchid simulacrums in Linden's image.

BLACK ORCHID II/SUSAN II. Awakening in Dr. Sylvian's Black Orchid greenhouse after the sudden death of Susan Linden/Black Orchid, Susan II struggles with vague impressions of Susan I's identity and death, and the fragments of her incomplete memory transference. Troubled by these shards of memory, driven by instinct, and shorn of guidance when Thorne kills Sylvian, her only companion is the childlike fellow Orchid simulacrum Suzy. Susan II is thrust into a quest for knowledge of her true nature, and for safe haven for her and her kind, knowing she is being stalked by the lethal forces that killed her predecessor.

Despite the fact that Susan II saves Thorne's life at one point, he, still vengeful, joins the ranks of those threatening her and her younger sister, Suzy. Susan II still follows her instinct, braving the bowels of Arkham Asylum and the swamps of Louisiana to track down two of Sylvian's former colleagues, Pamela Isley/Poison Ivy and Alec Holland/Swamp Thing.

During their brief rendezvous, Swamp Thing unexpectedly provides Susan II with the means of propagating her kind by reaching into her Orchid "flesh" and plucking fertilized seeds. In a remote corner of the Brazilian forests, Susan II and Suzy sow those seeds for a new generation of Black Orchid successors.

At the eleventh hour, Susan II's revulsion at the destructive and self-destructive capacities of the human race finds an unexpected ally among the Chairman's entourage.

SUZY. In what seems to be an unprecedented accident, a second Black Orchid "blossom" awakens to sentient life, in adolescent form. With the appearance, maturity, and sensibility of a preteen female child, Suzy (as she elects to call herself) is a more vulnerable and—free of the more adult concerns that trouble Susan II—more psychically open incarnation of Black Orchid. She also stirs protective maternal instincts in Susan II—Suzy calls her "Mommy"—though Susan II is slow to awaken to the attendant responsibilities (leaving Suzy alone in a tree, for instance, where she is easy pickings for one of the novel's many predatory adults, who sells her to Lexcorp operatives for dissection). Once she has rescued Suzy, Susan II develops a more parental relationship, and in the end Suzy and Susan II choose to fly from their Brazilian Black Orchid garden and seek their fortunes in the world, soaring into the sunset.

DR. PHILIP SYLVIAN. Dr. Philip Sylvian, the shy, reclusive botany expert who created the Black Orchid, grew up next door to Susan Linden. As they matured and approached intimacy, Susan's abusive father lashed out, and Susan fled, though she maintained mail contact with (but distance from) Sylvian over the years. Once in college, he, Alec Holland, and Pamela Isley were classmates; they all studied under Dr. Jason Woodrue. Woodrue later turned to crime and transformed into the murderous Floronic Man, a vegetable being intent on usurping mankind's rule and asserting an age of plant dominion.

Sylvian developed his own strain of research in accord with theories he and Holland had discussed. His goal of developing a plant/human hybrid capable of surviving the planetary environmental apocalypse he considered inevitable culminated in his creation of the Black Orchid.

He is there when the new Black Orchid, Susan II, awakens, after her immediate predecessor is slain by Lexcorp, and he begins to explain the riddle of her origins and being, and mentions his former classmates. However, Sylvian is killed by Linden's insanely jealous gangster ex-husband before Sylvian can teach her anything about her hybrid existence.

CARL THORNE. Carl Thorne is an arms dealer and black marketeer who spent seven years in prison. When he emerges from prison he is a man out of time, in more ways than one.

Lex Luthor, Carl's former employer, becomes infuriated when Thorne kills Sylvian and destroys his laboratory and the Orchids—research of great interest and potential value to Lexcorp. Thorne is targeted for immediate assassination, but escapes death due to Susan II/Black Orchid's intervention. In spite of this, he shows no gratitude, instead directing his rage toward her.

Years earlier, when his wife divorced and fled from him, she became the focus of his maniacal obsession. When he discovers, after his release from prison—and long after her death—that Susan "lives on" via Dr. Sylvian's hybrid Black Orchids, his homicidal fixation flares anew, and he targets Sylvian, and any and all surviving Orchids, and ultimately finds him on Susan II and Suzy's trail. Nothing short of their complete annihilation will satisfy him, though he stands to gain nothing from their deaths. His need to control (via obliteration) any and every trace of the Susan he once possessed is all-consuming, even to the point of complete self-destruction.

LEX LUTHOR, ALEC HOLLAND/SWAMP THING, PAMELA ISLEY/POISON IVY. Three characters that were not created by Neil Gaiman, Lex Luthor, Alec Holland/Swamp Thing, and Pamela Isley/Poison Ivy, are also central to Black Orchid. Lex Luthor is the infamous nemesis of Superman, here presented as a corporate CEO/criminal mastermind. In their original human forms, Alec Holland and Pamela Isley are, for the first time, posited as college science student classmates, here associated with Gaiman's character of Dr. Philip Sylvian. In their better known DC incarnations, Swamp Thing and Poison Ivy, they are linked by Gaiman with the nascent Green universe Alan Moore invented in the mideighties in the pages of *Swamp Thing*. Swamp Thing is the monster "hero" created by Len Wein and Berni Wrightson in 1971, while Poison Ivy is best known as a villain in Batman's rogues gallery able to manipulate and utilize lethal mutant plant life in her crimes.

TRIVIA

- Gaiman's first script submission to DC editor Karen Berger was a short *Swamp Thing* piece entitled "Jack-in-the-Green." It is set in medieval, plague-ridden England and features an early incarnation of Swamp Thing, Jack-in-the-Green, a variation on the Green Man archetype of Celtic and UK myth and lore. The script wasn't accepted, but it did open the door to the *Black Orchid* project. In 1999, the "Jack-in-the-Green" script was revived and illustrated by the artist team that had worked with Alan Moore on *Swamp Thing*, Stephen Bissette and John Totleben, and published in the Vertigo Gaiman anthology *Midnight Days*.

- A Vertigo Black Orchid series scripted by a fellow member of Alan Moore's circle of friends, Dick Foreman, was launched in 1993, lasting two years (twenty-two issues and one Annual).

- In 1989, Neil Gaiman sent Karen Berger and *Swamp Thing* writer/artist Rick Veitch an essay entitled "Notes Towards a Vegetable Theology," a meditation on the "vegetable universe" of the DC comic book pantheon, building upon the bedrock laid in his *Black Orchid* graphic novel. The essay remained unpublished and unavailable online, until now.

THE QUOTABLE GAIMAN

It was absolutely terrifying. This was the first mainstream comic I'd written, the first David had ever painted. When we asked DC whether they thought it would sell, they said, "You're two guys no one's ever heard of, doing a character nobody's ever heard of. She's a female character, and nobody buys books about female characters. So, no, we don't think it's going to sell.

> —Interview for
> "The Second British Invasion,"
> by Michael Berry, 1991, www.sff.net/people/
> mbarry/gaiman.htm

||||||||||||||||||||||||||||||||||||||||||||||||||||||||||||||||

NOTES TOWARDS A VEGETABLE THEOLOGY[1]

BY NEIL GAIMAN

I) NON SEQUITUR MUSINGS ON THE GENERAL DC RELIGIOUS SET-UP

In the beginning, if there ever was a beginning, God created a number of things, including the universe, and, to some degree, let them get on with it.

The first revolt came among the angels, when God decided to fill the universe with life, with free will and individual consciousness and conscience. After that the tale grows a little muddy.

There was a garden—that much is certain. And in the garden, the first man and the first woman tasted forbidden fruit, and were cast out into the world. Their children were a gardener—the first murderer, a slaughterer of animals—and the first victim; the stories continue from there.

Did this happen once, or many times? On this planet or another? At the end of time, or, in an infinite inhabited universe, is this happening for ever until the last day?

On this, as with so many other things, secrets are kept, and mysteries are held.

Genesis mentions two trees in the Garden: The Tree of Life, and the Tree of Knowledge of Good and Evil. It was of the latter that Mankind ate, and it was from fear that we would taste the fruit of the Tree of Life that God expelled us from the

Garden, and set the angel Uriel to guard the Tree and the Garden with a flaming sword.

The Norse had a tree as well, Yggdrasil, the world-tree, whose top was in Asgard, whose trunk was on Earth and whose roots were below, holding the whole thing together, never to be breached until the twilight of the Gods and the battle of Ragnarok.

Intelligent life spread out across the multiverse. Life-forms with powers in dimensions that we could never hope to perceive. Life-forms that we would regard as demons and devils and gods (and, indeed, so regarded and regard themselves).

Even here on Earth we see spirits and ghosts, aliens and heroes, powers incarnate and people never born of man and woman.

THE EARTH POWERS

A GAEA

The Greatest of the Earth Powers—the embodiment of the Earth, is Nature, Gaea, Mother Earth—call it what you will. Gaea is also one of the Titans—she was the Mother of the Titans, as I recall, however, I'm still not entirely sure to what extent the DC Greek Gods, Titans etc, *are* Gods and Titans: what exactly is Ares's relationship to War, for example, or Athena's to Wisdom? I tend to feel that Nature/Gaea is a whole lot more than a woman with a toga and a nice smile; however, Gaea the Greek Goddess might well be a minor aspect of Gaea the force for growth and survival and life on this planet.

All living things owe their creation to Gaea, and she regards all of them as her children. However, the plants were first, and are the oldest, and it is for the plants she has a special affection. The plants, and the most infuriating and unruly of her offspring—man.

B) ERL-KINGS

Foremost among the Earth Powers, as far as that personification of the life cycle on this Earth that we call Nature is concerned, are the Erl-Kings. Brought out of the Earth through fire and flame at a time of trouble, the Erl-Kings (Jack-in-the-Green; Swamp Thing; Walker in the Rushes; Great Url; Walber; the Leaf King; Father of Grass; Brede, and the rest of them) are plant elementals of tremendous power. Kings when the Earth was just a world of algae and fern, as animal life arose on the planet Nature created a champion for both worlds, a rough mockery and mimicry of animal life in green.

It has been hypothesised that the reason for the cycle of burning and rebirth, the reason why each Erl-King borrowed its consciousness from a living thing, was to teach them humility, and a love of humanity along with the rest of all created things; for next to the galaxy of life-forms, humanity can seem pitiful. But humanity has a special destiny.

The first Erl-King arose before life on Earth came out of the seas, when the world was given over to plants, when the Earth was a garden. They prevented the darkness from encroaching into the word of sanity and order, of growth and normal decay. But nothing is perfect: there are forces of chaos and destruction. Some Erl-Kings have spoiled in creation—Solomon Grundy was one of these.

It is quite possible that the destiny of the Erl-Kings was to create Swamp Thing and Abby's child: A human-appearing consciousness, an elemental who could be the spokesman for humanity and the green, reconciling the two at the time they need it most.

There is never more than one Erl-King at one time.[2]

c) NOTES ON THE GREEN

The Green is, as I see it, the collected mind of plants on this earth. It's not quite a place or dimension, not quite a consciousness (although it can be both).

All plants have, to some extent, perception. Few have what we would term intelligence (only a few old trees, such as Redwoods and ancient oaks); however, the collected awareness of species of plants, individual plants, and the plants in a certain geographic area constitute the place known as the Green.

There are specific intelligences within the Green. The Parliament of Trees is one. There are others.

d) THE WALKERS IN THE GREEN

I) DRYADS.

The second arm of the Earth Powers are the Walkers in the Green. They are another form of life—far less prevalent on this Earth than formerly.

There are two kinds of Walker. The first are the *Dryads* of myth, plant-women, elementals whose natural environment is the Green. They are free-floating consciousnesses within the Green. They can emerge from the Green onto the Earth, in a physical form; but to do this they need to form a symbiotic relationship with a plant in this dimension, from whom they borrow the physical mass to create a body. This leaves them vulnerable to the destruction of their tree, or plant—if it is destroyed while the Dryad is using it as her link with this plane, then the Dryad is also destroyed.

Once much more prevalent than currently, most of the Walkers left this dimensional plane for an all-plant-elemental dimension many, many years ago. (This is the world that Woodrue came from, from which he was expelled.)

II) FOREST LORDS.

The other form of Walker in the Green are the *Forest Lords.*

From the dawn of time until about two thousand years ago, the Earth was covered with Forests: England, for example, had ARDEN and ANDERIDA; HERCYNIA covered Europe, CIMINIAN covered Italy, and so forth.

Each of these forests had a lord, a Dweller in the Green, with responsibilities for thousands of square miles of forest. At the heart of each of these forests was a sacred grove. The Grove and the Lord had some kind of symbiotic relationship. Essentially, the Lords, not entirely friendly beings of huge and preternatural powers, were bound to the Grove: plants in the grove partook of the might of the Forest Lord, and, once the grove was destroyed, the Forest Lord went also. Forest Lords have huge and inexplicable powers, part of which are manifested into, and bound up with, their Sacred Groves: A plant or tree taken from a sacred grove can give one some access to the powers of the Forest Lord.

These were the rulers of Thicket, Weald, and Copse, Lords of Oak and Ash and Thorn.

The power of the Forest Lords is now much reduced: a grove of olives in Greece is all that keeps the Greek Forest Lord in existence; other Lords have died. Few of them fought back. With the upcoming deforestation of the world, though, it is more than possible that they might be retaliating. There could also be a number of Forest Queens.

They have meddled, and still meddle, in human affairs to some degree. But they are Great Slow Kings; after millions of years, their time frame had become that of a forest; when mankind began wantonly to destroy, it took the Forest Lords a while to slow down enough and perceive and react on what, to them, was a micro-level. In their precious time frame a year to them was what to us would be a few minutes.

Currently the Forest Lords are divided into factions: those who believe their time is over, and those who believe they should wipe every wood-hewing, air-polluting, house-building human off the face of the Earth. (It is not impossible that the latter faction had something to do with Woodrue's attack on humanity in *Swamp Thing* #23—it was, after all, his initial contact with the Green that drove him mad.)

I like the idea that an earlier attack on humanity (or contemplated attack on humanity) by the Forest Lords was defeated, or postponed, by a previous Erl-King.

E) PLANTS

It should be noted that Plants per se can have medicinal or restorative properties. They can also poison, drug, and induce altered states of consciousness, raise or lower perception, promote healing, and do all other things that we know that plants can do, and, this being the DC universe, they can do slightly more.

However, Plants do not have "magical" properties as such, so plants display powers or effects from elsewhere—normally from Walkers in the Green.

An example of this would be something like the God-Plant which created the Cheetah in Wonder Woman—a rare and worshipped plant with genuine magical powers of transformation. It needs blood and worship, and confers power on its chosen in exchange. On this basis it could be assumed that the plant comes from the sacred grove of an African Forest King. Thus if that plant were destroyed, another plant from the same grove could grant similar powers. And indeed, the Forest Lord himself could grant such powers, if it suited him.

Also some trees and plants in ancient sacred groves have gained a certain amount of mobility and sentience, borrowed from Forest Lords—these tend to take on the same attitude to humanity that The Forest Lord in question has (i.e. friendly or not).

ƒ) THE MAY QUEENS.

The third arm of the three ancient Earth Powers: always female, as the Erl-Kings are always male. Always flowers, always beautiful.

The May Queens are related to the Erl-Kings: both are children of the Earth Mother. But while the Erl-Kings were created by the Earth as her champions, as a buffer between the darkness of eternal sterility and cold, a buffer against entropy, the May Queens were brought forth originally as a symbol of growth in the dark times.

They can be possessed of huge strength, and flight abilities, and of the ability to communicate with specific plants. Some of them have abilities to do things to plants—inducing growth, inducing change—which scientifically could be seen as impossible.

Unlike the Erl-Kings, they are not elementals. Also, they do not have an unbroken line of succession; when Nature needs a May Queen she begins to manipulate things to bring one, or a number, forth. As with Erl-Kings, May Queens need a dead human consciousness to start from. Unlike Erl-Kings, May Queens have no immortality to retreat into: they live, act, and are gone.

Poison Ivy is a May Queen that went rotten—like Solomon Grundy is an Erl-King gone rotten.[3] I assume that the original Thorn, who has recently been displaying inexplicable plant powers, is also a rotten May Queen.

There have been waves of May Queens earlier in history. Currently there are only Black Orchid, Poison Ivy, and (possibly) the Original Thorn.

OVERALL PICTURE

What I've tried to do here is align the various vegetable set-ups within the DC universe, and throw in a few things to make it fun and codifiable, while still leaving room open for other people to create within it.

As I see it, perhaps the most important character is that of Gaea/Nature (call her/it what you will): This is the force that's the hidden destiny behind the events that have occurred to Swamp Thing, and to Black Orchid.

However, as I said, Nature is not a character who should be personified by some wisely-smelling blonde woman in a toga clutching an olive branch—or, for that matter, be personified at all. Doing that winds up reducing Nature to just another comic-book Goddess (or God), with comprehensible motivations. An aspect of Gaea may well be perceived as being the mother of Titans, but Gaea has to predate anthropomorphism.

It's a nice conceit to think that possibly the baby Orchid and the Swamp Thing baby might grow up and get together . . . the ultimate reconciliation of flesh with flowers.

Anyway, as far as I can see, this gives a fairly complete framework within which new Plant-related characters and events can occur, and which gives perspective to older ones.

On a final note, this set-up only applies here on Earth. Whether the same thing holds true for, say, Rann, or Thanagar, or Krypton, is another matter. What is obvious is that there are a number of planets on which vegetable life-forms have achieved dominance; possibly on some of them is a dimension called the Red, in which that bizarrity, an animal intelligence, perhaps even an animal Erl-King, could be found.

Anyway, this is the set-up I propose. Hope it meets with approval across the Atlantic . . .

Best,

Neil.

||||||||||||||||||||||||||||||||||||||||||||||||||||||||||||||||||||||||

THE BOOKS OF MAGIC

(1990—91)

In the tapestry of Gaiman's work, *The Books of Magic* is a unique design, connected inextricably to much of the author's other work—both in novels and comics—and to the DC and Vertigo comic book universes. (Note, however, that DC's "mature readers" were not officially separated from the mainstream universe until the establishment of the Vertigo imprint, which did not come until 1993.)

Published in 1990 and 1991, *The Books of Magic* was comprised of four extra-long issues, illustrated by some of the greatest artists in the comic book industry. The artists—John Bolton, Scott Hampton, Charles Vess, and Paul Johnson—drew a single issue each.

The story concerns a young English boy named Timothy Hunter, who has within him the potential to become the greatest magician of the modern age. Other practitioners of magic and beings of supernatural power have sensed his existence or recognized the potential in him. Tim might choose magic, or turn his back on that path and live a mundane life. Should he pursue magic, he might turn out to be a force for great good or great evil. As such, there are those who want to kill him before he can fulfill his potential.

In order to protect Timothy Hunter, and to give him the opportunity to make an informed decision about magic and his future, four individuals with powerful supernatural power of their own band together and go visit the boy. Those four include the Phantom Stranger, John Constantine, Mister E, and Doctor Occult, all of whom were previously existing DC Comics characters, though the latter two were relatively obscure prior to their appearance here. Constantine nicknamed the four of them "the Trench Coat Brigade," a reference that caught on, eventually leading to the phrase being used as the title of a miniseries featuring the same characters.

Though Mister E thinks it might be best just to kill Timothy, the Phantom Stranger insists that the boy must be educated so that he can make the choice as to whether or not he wants magic in his life. The Trench Coat Brigade agrees to provide a kind of tutorial for Timothy Hunter, which includes both information and a kind of tour of the supernatural elements of the DC/Vertigo universe. The Phantom Stranger will take Tim into the past and show him the creation of the universe and the rise of magic. John Constantine will give him a tour of the present, where he meets many magical characters. Doctor Occult takes Timothy on a journey through Faerie and other magical realms that exist side by side with the world he's always known. And Mister E is meant to take Timothy into the future of magic, to give him a glimpse of what may come.

Along the way Tim meets multitudes of magical characters from the DC universe, and from Gaiman's *The Sandman*. The Trench Coat Brigade does battle with an occult organization called the Brotherhood of the Cold Flame—who wish the boy ill—and a price is put on Timothy's head. The Spectre saves him from an assassin. Constantine leaves Tim in the care of Zatanna, who takes him to a Halloween party attended by many of the supernatural bad guys in the DC universe, and nearly gets him killed. The boy is tricked by the queen of Faerie and nearly forced to spend the rest of eternity there as her slave. And Mister E, meant to be one of his mentors, turns out to be totally insane, and takes him on a journey so far into the future that they reach the end of time; Mister E tries to kill Tim, only to be thwarted by the arrival of Destiny and Death, the last two beings in the universe.

For Gaiman—and for readers—it was a propitious time for this story to be told. Gaiman had already put his stamp on the mature end of the DC universe with the stories he was telling in *The Sandman,* but with the creation of the Vertigo imprint still two years away, the wall that would eventually separate Vertigo from the DC universe had not yet solidified. Therefore, Timothy could encounter the Endless and Gaiman's version of the queen of Faerie while also meeting characters like Doctor Fate and the Spectre, who are more strictly denizens of the DC universe.

For those intrigued by the world Gaiman created for *The Sandman, The Books of Magic* holds significant ties, including appearances by Dream, Death, and Destiny. While the Phantom Stranger is showing him the past, Timothy sees the Silver City of the angels and witnesses the fall of the angels who rebelled against god—including Lucifer Morningstar. This is clearly meant to be the same origin story that Gaiman put forth in *The Sandman.* Gaiman also provides a nod to his signature comics work when, in the third issue of *The Books of Magic,* Queen Titania of Faerie is shown being served by Hamnet, the son of William Shakespeare. In "A Midsummer Night's Dream," the issue of *The Sandman* that won the World Fantasy award, Gaiman implied that Titania eventually drew Hamnet into Faerie to serve her.

In that same issue of *The Books of Magic,* drawn by Charles Vess, the groundwork is laid for *Stardust,* a future Gaiman/Vess collaboration. The marketplace in Faerie is visualized in much the same manner as in the later work, and a gate that exists in both the human and fairy worlds is a precursor to the hole in the wall between worlds in *Stardust.*

A thrilling, and sometimes chilling, adventure, *The Books of Magic* is also a magical journey. Gaiman has acknowledged the influence of his nine-year-old self and the wonders he discovered in books about magic at that age. In the introduction to the collection, fantasy writer Roger Zelazny dissects the miniseries in relation to Joseph Campbell's *Hero with a Thousand Faces,* and the hero's journey is clearly a significant part of what Gaiman has created in these pages.

And yet it should be noted that, though such lofty comparisons apply, Gaiman's fond nostalgia for stories of magic seems more intrinsic to the tale than the dry purpose of Campbell's myth-making theses. Whereas Gaiman came to his years of writing *The Sandman* with a certain gravitas, *The Books of Magic* is almost a romp in comparison. Yes, there is horror and unpleasantness here, and an emphasis on the cost of magic; the price of getting anything for nothing (whether through magic or, in Faerie, as a gift) is resonant.

But there is also the inescapable sense that Gaiman is having a fine old time writing the tale of Timothy Hunter. The deus ex machina ending—featuring Death of the Endless—is a perfect example, as are the ways in which he has woven in his other DC/Vertigo works. But the best ones come in the humor of John Constantine and the ghost of Boston Brand (Deadman), and through the travelogue feeling that arises in the second and part of the third issues of the miniseries. Gaiman's presentation of the menagerie of magical characters in the DC universe is a kind of who's who, executed with a combination of love, respect, and cheek.

Finally, no conversation about *The Books of Magic* would be complete without at least a mention of Harry Potter. For several years, as the Potter craze took on a life of its own, there were mutterings among various fans, and even in newspaper reports, suggesting that J. K. Rowling stole certain elements from *The Books of Magic* in her creation of Harry Potter. The similarities are certainly there. Timothy Hunter is a young, dark-haired English boy with round glasses who has the potential to be the greatest wizard in the world. But such coincidences are not at all uncommon in fiction, and are usually attributable to shared frames of reference and shared influences between the authors. In this case, Gaiman has firmly defended Rowling, suggesting that both were "stealing from T. H. White," the author of *The Once and Future King*.

Even so, it does seem likely that the success of Harry Potter may have interfered with any chance Timothy Hunter may have had to make it to the world of feature films.

PEOPLE, PLACES, AND THINGS

TIMOTHY HUNTER. A young English boy, Tim has the potential to be the greatest magician that the modern world has seen. This nascent possibility has made him the focus of great powers, both for good and evil, and drawn the attention of most of the supernatural beings in the world, and many beyond it. Worried that such power might be twisted toward evil, the Phantom Stranger gathers three other occult figures—John Constantine, Mister E, and Doctor Occult—to discuss what is to be done about Timothy Hunter.

Though Mister E thinks the simplest solution is to kill the boy, at the Stranger's urging the four eventually agree that they must mentor the boy, and introduce him to the world of magic so that he can make an informed decision about whether or not he wants magic in his life.

When they first approach him, Tim tries to run, thinking they mean him harm. But once they have explained the situation—and Dr. Occult has turned Tim's yo-yo into an owl (which becomes his pet)—Tim agrees to go along with the plan. Each of the four mystics will take him on a tour of a specific part of the magical world.

However, other forces mean him harm. While Tim is being introduced to magical figures in the present day, an assassin attempts to kill him, and he is only saved by the timely intervention of the Spectre. Later, when Dr. Occult gives him a tour of Faerie, he is tricked by its queen, Titania, and only sheer luck and happenstance provide him a way to escape her trickery. Yet the greatest threat to Timothy Hunter is in Mister E, the fourth of his supposed mentors, whose role is to take him into the future to see what will become of magic in the world. Unfortunately, Mister E is insane, and he takes Tim to the end of time, where he attempts to murder him. Concerned, the other three mystics send Yo-Yo (the owl) into the future to help, and the owl buys Tim enough time so that two of the Endless, Death and Destiny, arrive before Mister E can finish the job.

Returned to his own time and place, Tim approaches his three remaining mentors to tell them that he is safe. Yo-Yo has been turned back into a toy yo-yo. The Phantom Stranger reminds him that he has to choose, now, whether he wants magic in his life, and Tim declines. The boy goes home, and the Phantom Stranger reveals to Constantine and Dr. Occult that despite what he's said, Tim made his choice in the affirmative before they ever set off.

Back at home, playing with his yo-yo, Tim realizes that the ordinary world seems flat and boring now that he knows about magic. By concentrating, and believing, he transforms the toy back into Yo-Yo, his pet owl, choosing the destiny that magic will bring him.

JOHN CONSTANTINE. A womanizing, chain-smoking British magician—but not of the stage variety. Constantine is the latest in a long line of mystics in his lineage, all of whom have a tendency to draw trouble to them, endangering all those they care about, or who care about them, sometimes with dreadful purpose.

It is Constantine's task to give Timothy Hunter a tour of the world of magic in the present day, to introduce him to powerful figures in the magical hierarchy and to some of the fundamental concepts governing magic. He begins by taking Tim to Madame Xanadu and the Spectre. But Tim is being pursued by assassins, and the plot against him makes Constantine's job both more difficult and somewhat simpler, drawing him into more abrupt contact with other key members of the magical world, such as Dr. Fate—who brings a message from the Phantom Stranger—and with Baron Winter and Jason Blood.

The message Dr. Fate brings is a summons. The other three mystics are in battle against the Brotherhood of the Cold Flame, and they need his help. Unwilling to leave Tim undefended, Constantine brings him to stay with Zatanna, and later returns just in time to rescue them both from a roomful of dark magicians and other supernatural beings who mean to collect the bounty on Tim's head.

THE PHANTOM STRANGER. One of the most powerful mystic figures in the universe, the Phantom Stranger is also one of the most mysterious. Though there are many theories about his origins, no one seems to know the true story. Some say he is an angel who remained neutral when Lucifer rebelled, but there are other stories.

The Phantom Stranger gathers Constantine, Mister E, and Dr. Occult to discuss the future of Timothy Hunter, and persuades them all to mentor him, and to introduce him to the world of magic so that he might be set on a heroic path rather than one of darkness. The Stranger is the first to give Timothy a tour, and brings him into the past, all the way to the moment of Creation. With the Stranger he witnesses the Silver City—the home of the angels—the rebellion against God, and the fall of Lucifer and his cohorts. The Stranger shows him the world in its earliest forms, and a parallel version of the world full of demons. He gives Tim a tour of mystical history, from ancient Atlantis up through the great civilizations of the world, and to a chamber where they meet a young Merlin, and his friend Iason (Jason Blood).

Finally, the Stranger introduces him to mystics of the past, including Sargon the Sorcerer and Zatara, both of whom were stage magicians, using their public performances as a façade to disguise their command of true magic. But both men are dead, and they try to dissuade Timothy from choosing to follow in their footsteps, telling him that the price of magical power is much too high.

MISTER E. As a boy, Eric was badly abused by his father, who warped him with his belief that humanity was, by its very nature, evil. His father put out Eric's eyes with a sharpened spoon, believing he was saving his son from temptation. As an adult, calling himself Mister E, he took to hunting monsters, and he developed magical senses and the ability to walk forward through time.

Mister E first believes that they should kill Timothy Hunter to avoid any possibility that his nascent magical power might one day be used for evil. When the Phantom Stranger, John Constantine, and Dr. Occult disagree, he goes along with their plan instead. He is the fourth and last of them to take a hand in Timothy's magical education. Mister E is supposed to take Timothy on a tour of the future, showing him the influence magic will have—or may have—on the world. But he shows Tim mainly variations on the future where the boy himself has become an evil wizard, and has caused terrible evil, and he walks him forward past the point of safety, thousands and thousands of years into the future, and finally a hundred billion years, to the end of time, where he attempts to murder Tim.

Fortunately, suspecting something has gone wrong, the others have sent Tim's owl, Yo-Yo, into the future to help. Yo-Yo arrives just in time to interfere, and buys Tim a few seconds. By then, two of the Endless—Destiny and Death—arrive. They are supposed to be the only two things left in the universe, and must deal with this anomaly. Mister E is made to walk back, step by step, across a hundred billion years. Death gives Tim back his yo-yo—now only a toy again—and then returns him to his own time.

DOCTOR OCCULT. Dr. Occult is a powerful magician, historically a supernatural detective, who has somehow become bonded with his former partner, a woman named Rose. The two now share the same body, and possibly the same spirit as well. The details of this symbiosis are unclear, though at times—in Faerie, particularly—Rose physically replaces Dr. Occult.

Upon his first meeting with Timothy Hunter, Occult transforms the boy's yo-yo into an owl in order to demonstrate magic. When it is his turn as Tim's tutor, he guides the boy on a tour of some of the magical realms that adjoin the earthly plane, including Gemworld, Skartaris, and, most significantly, Faerie.

It is also Dr. Occult who, sensing that Tim must be in trouble in the far future with Mister E, sends Yo-Yo into the future to help him.

YO-YO. Dr. Occult transforms Timothy Hunter's yo-yo into an owl—whom the boy names Yo-Yo. The owl is a faithful companion. When Mister E attempts to kill Tim, Yo-Yo buys the boy vital seconds that help to save his life.

MERLIN. The greatest wizard of his age, and the chief adviser to King Arthur, Merlin meets Timothy Hunter while the Phantom Stranger is giving the boy a tour of the history of magic. Merlin's best friend and blood brother is Iason, who will one day be known as Jason Blood.

DR. FATE. In the past, Timothy meets Dr. Fate at a time when Kent Nelson carried the mantle, and the obligations, that come with that name. Later, while traveling with John Constantine, Tim encounters a different version of Dr. Fate, at a time when two people shared the helm and powers and name.

SARGON THE SORCERER. One of the great magicians of his era, John Sargent performed onstage as Sargon the Sorcerer to hide his true magical power in plain sight. When the Phantom Stranger takes Tim on a tour of magical history, they encounter Sargon, who warns Tim that the price of magic is too high.

ZATARA. The father of the better known Zatanna, Zatara was a famed stage magician in his day. Like Sargon, he used this identity to hide his true magic. Zatara is also dead, and Timothy encounters him on his trip through the past with the Phantom Stranger.

DEADMAN (BOSTON BRAND). The ghost of a circus acrobat, Boston Brand can inhabit and control the body of any living person. He does so several times to warn Timothy of the rising threat against him, and twice saves the boy's life.

MADAME XANADU. A cartomancer, Madame Xanadu reads the future in Tarot cards.

THE SPECTRE (JIM CORRIGAN). Jim Corrigan is the ghost of a 1930s police detective who is joined with a power called the Spectre, who is the wrath of God. When an assassin attempts to kill Timothy Hunter, the Spectre saves the boy's life.

JASON BLOOD. Once the best friend of Merlin and known as Iason, Jason Blood is physically bonded with the demon Etrigan. He is a dinner guest of Baron Winter's when John Constantine and Timothy Hunter drop in unexpectedly.

DR. THIRTEEN. Dr. Terence Thirteen does not believe in the supernatural and spends his life debunking psychics, mediums, and tales of ghosts and other creatures. He picks up Constantine and Timothy hitchhiking and gives them a ride.

ZATANNA. The daughter of Zatara and a hugely famous stage magician, Zatanna has a romantic history with John Constantine. When he needs someone to look after Tim for a while, he takes the boy to Zatanna. Thinking that she is helping by introducing him to many of the world's magical practitioners, she takes him to a Halloween party attended mainly by dark magicians and other unpleasant supernatural beings. There is a price on Timothy's head, and he and Zatanna are nearly killed at the party, until Constantine shows up and intimidates them all into leaving Zatanna and Tim alone. While she is far more powerful than Constantine, his reputation makes him someone even the most wicked sorcerer would like to avoid.

SNOUT. A goblin or other magical creature (his species is never identified), Snout attempts to frame Timothy Hunter for theft in the marketplace in Faerie. Caught at his deception, Snout is forced by the warden of the market to give up one of his possessions each to Tim, Dr. Occult, and Yo-Yo.

LORD GLORY. The warden of the market in Faerie.

THE MUNDANE EGG. In a market in Faerie, Tim is nearly tricked into becoming the slave of a creature called Snout, but instead he, Occult, and Yo-Yo each get to choose one of Snout's possessions for themselves. Tim chooses a Mundane Egg. When Tim is later tricked by Queen Titania into taking a gift from her—which should require him to stay in Faerie as her servant for eternity—he can only escape by giving her something of equal value in return. The Mundane Egg, which will one day birth a world, is the object he trades. Previously, all of them were thought to have already hatched.

BABA YAGA. A terrible crone, she captures Timothy by luring him off the path in Faerie, when he is briefly parted from Dr. Occult. Yo-Yo helps to free Tim, and then Dr. Occult arrives in time to defeat Baba Yaga.

TITANIA. The queen of Faerie, she tricks Timothy into taking a valuable gift from her. In exchange, he will have to remain in Faerie forever, as her servant, unless he can give her a gift of equal value. Having acquired the Mundane Egg, Tim gives it to her as a gift, and she is forced to allow him to leave.

DREAM. Morpheus, the King of Dreams, is one of the Endless—a family of seven ancient beings who embody concepts. Timothy encounters him when Dr. Occult brings him, briefly, to Morpheus's realm, the Dreaming.

DESTINY. The first and eldest of the Endless, Destiny carries the book in which is written the story of all creation from beginning to end. When Mister E takes Tim to the end of time, they bear witness to the death of Destiny.

DEATH. The second eldest of the Endless, Death will be the last being in the universe, and then shall cause its death as well. When Mister E takes Tim to the end of time, she forces him to walk back through time, moment by moment, across a hundred billion years, while she sends Tim back instantaneously.

TRIVIA

- Timothy Hunter appeared in the Vertigo Comics crossover series *The Children's Crusade,* most notably in the *Arcana* special event annual (1993).

- *The Books of Magic* became an ongoing monthly comic book series, with the first fifty issues written by John Ney Rieber, and the latter twenty-five by Peter Gross. The series ran for seventy-five issues, from 1994 to 2000, and also spawned two other monthly series (*Hunter: The Age of Magic,* 25 issues, 2001–2003, and *Books of Magick: Life During Wartime,* 15 issues, 2004–2005), and multiple miniseries, including *The Names of Magic, The Books of Faerie,* and *The Books of Faerie: Auberon's Tale.*

- Beginning in 2003, HarperCollins published a series of novels by Carla Jablonski adapting *The Books of Magic.* Six novels were published in the series, the first of which adapted Gaiman's original *The Books of Magic* miniseries.

- The massive success of Gaiman's tale led, as his work in comics often did, to a ripple effect throughout the worlds of DC and Vertigo. The Gaiman version of Doctor Occult appeared multiple times in later DC universe stories and in a one-shot from Vertigo. Mister E earned his own four-issue miniseries in 1991. And the two were reunited with the Phantom Stranger (a perennial character shared by DC and Vertigo) in the miniseries *The Trenchcoat Brigade.*

- With his gathering of all of DC's sorcery and magic-related characters, Gaiman consciously expanded upon a similar gathering initiated by Alan Moore's scripts for *Swamp Thing Annual* issue 2, "Down Amongst the Dead Men," and *Swamp Thing* issue 50.

- Gaiman always wanted to do a Phantom Stranger project with DC, but due to other creators having "dibs" on the character that predated Gaiman joining DC's freelance stable, that unfortunately never came to pass.

THE QUOTABLE GAIMAN

On suggestions that J. K. Rowling "ripped off" Timothy Hunter to create Harry Potter:

Last year, initially *The Scotsman* newspaper—being Scottish and J. K. Rowling being Scottish—and because of the English tendency to try and tear down their idols, they kept trying to build stories which said J. K. Rowling ripped off Neil Gaiman. They kept getting in touch with me and I kept declining to play because I thought it was silly. . . . And I said to [Rowling] that I thought we were both just stealing from T. H. White: very straightforward.

—Interview with *January* magazine, August 2001

SWEENEY TODD AND
OTHER TABOOS

(1990—92)

*T*aboo was a trade-paperback format, cutting-edge horror comics anthology cocreated by *Saga of the Swamp Thing* artists Stephen Bissette and John Totleben in response to an invitation from *Cerebus* creator Dave Sim to publish any project the team wished to create. From the beginning, it was an anthology with a philosophy and manifesto: to show the unshowable; to publish the unpublishable; to push the horror genre and comics medium further than it had ever gone before.

After three years of work, *Taboo* issue 1 was self-published by Bissette's SpiderBaby Grafix & Publications in 1988, with considerable behind-the-scenes business advice and initial financial support from Sim and his short-lived venture, Aardvark-One International. *Taboo* issues 2 and 3 were also self-published by SpiderBaby Grafix. For its fourth volume (1990), Bissette forged a copublishing deal to continue *Taboo* with *Teenage Mutant Ninja Turtles* cocreator Kevin Eastman's new publishing entity, Tundra Publishing, Inc. SpiderBaby and Tundra copublished *Taboo* issues 4 through 7 and *Taboo Especial* before dissolving their association just prior to Tundra's collapse in 1993. *Taboo*'s final two volumes, issues 8 and 9, were published by Kitchen Sink Press (1995) with editor Phil Amara alone credited, though both volumes were indeed prepared with Bissette (who chose to forego credit).

Taboo remains renowned as the gestation venue for a number of significant comics and graphic novel projects, including Charles Burns's *Black Hole* (which began with Burns's story "Contagious" in *Taboo* issue 1), Jeff Nicholson's *Through the Habitrails* (serialized in *Taboo* issues 5 through 9), Tim Lucas's *Throat Sprockets* (which Lucas completed as a novel, *Throat Sprockets,* 1994), and most notably, Alan Moore and Eddie Campbell's From Hell (created for *Taboo,* and originally serialized in *Taboo* issues 2 through 7) and Alan Moore and Melinda Gebbie's Lost Girls (also created for *Taboo,* launched and serialized in *Taboo* issues 5 through 7).

Given the international lineup of writers and artists showcased in *Taboo* and the relationship of Gaiman and cocreator and editor Bissette, as well as the involvement of many of their mutual friends, it was no surprise to find Gaiman contributing stories to the anthology beginning in 1990. Appropriate to the ongoing experimental nature of the anthology, Gaiman's contributions are all quite unusual, including a story written by Neil and Mary Gaiman's then five-year-old daughter Holly.

"BABYCAKES" (TABOO #4, 1990)

Neil Gaiman and Michael Zulli were just beginning their long-term creative collaborative relationship when they worked together on the four-page "Babycakes." A fablelike contemporary spin on Jonathan Swift's infamous satiric pamphlet "A Modest Proposal" (1729, in which Swift recommended solving the Irish famine by urging the Irish to eat their own children), "Babycakes" opens with the mysterious disappearance of all animals from existence, leaving mankind "lost, for a time, and then someone pointed out that just because we didn't have animals any more, that was no reason . . . to change our diets, or to cease testing products that might cause us harm. After all, there were still babies." This provides a short-term solution, until all the babies disappear . . .

Michael Zulli, best known at this time for his collaboration with writer Stephen Murphy on their ambitious, metaphoric, ecological SF-fantasy epic Puma Blues (1986–89), was a constant *Taboo* contributor since the story "Mercy" in *Taboo* number 2 (1989). "Babycakes" was published in *Taboo* about one year prior to its inclusion in the benefit anthology comic *Born to be Wild* (October 1991), edited by Valarie Jones, who also edited Miracleman issues 21 through 24. Sales of *Born to be Wild* benefited PETA (People for the Ethical Treatment of Animals), ostensibly on behalf of CETA (Creators for the Ethical Treatment of Animals), and included contributions by Bill Sienkiewicz, Grant Morrison, Steve Rude, Todd McFarlane, and others. Prior to publication, Valarie Jones wrote, "[I]t is not intended as a hard-line polemic proselytizing for that group. The contributors expressed varied opinions on the subject of animal rights and, as editor, I have tried to allow individuals to voice their thoughts in the hope that yet more information will help readers clarify their own opinions in the matter of animal rights."[1]

"BLOOD MONSTER" AND "HOLLY'S STORY" (TABOO #6, 1992)

Taboo issue 6 featured Neil Gaiman and Nancy (now Marlene) O'Connor's portrait of domestic bliss, "Blood Monster," and then five-year-old Holly Gaiman's "Holly's Story," dreamily delineated by Michael Zulli. The two stories framed the issue's contents, as both stories were meditations on families, parents, and children, and their relationships.

"Blood Monster" was written after Gaiman visited the home of *Taboo* editor/publisher Bissette, and suggested that Bissette's then wife Nancy (now Marlene) O'Connor illustrate the story. Marlene happily took on the task, "casting" Bissette and their two children, Maia and Daniel, as the husband and children in the story, and a friend of the family as the wife. "Blood Monster" is reprinted herein; see the Acknowledgments for more information.

"Holly's Story" was written by Gaiman's daughter Holly, with her father typing from Holly's dictation. Zulli was delighted by the story and proposed illustrating it for *Taboo,* adhering strictly to Holly's script directions, and occasionally relying on phone conversations with Holly to sort out various details. The result is a delirious, delightful, and disturbing fairy tale–like adventure, told and visualized with great imagination.

"SWEENEY TODD" (PENNY DREADFUL, TABOO #6; PROLOGUE, TABOO #7, 1992)

Gaiman and Zulli's planned serialized graphic novel *Sweeney Todd* remains a tantalizing proposition. Inspired by *From Hell,* the expansive serialized historical fiction created especially for *Taboo* by his mentor, Alan Moore, and Eddie Campbell, Gaiman and his creative partner Zulli wished to create a similarly expansive, exploratory genre work likewise rooted in one of London's great bogeymen, the fictional "Demon Barber of Fleet Street." Work began in 1991, yielding two published introductory works before *Taboo* ceased publication.

Originally shrink-wrapped with *Taboo* issue 6 was the rare sixteen-page promotional "Sweeney Todd Penny Dreadful" by Neil Gaiman and Michael Zulli, a unique booklet detailing the legacy of the character and concept, and introducing their never-completed serialized graphic novel, *Sweeney Todd.* This featured the only publication to date of Gaiman's "Sweeney Todd: A Brief Introduction." Appropriate to *Sweeney Todd*'s nineteenth-century roots, the booklet was designed to emulate the format of the nineteenth-century British penny dreadfuls, cheaply produced and affordably priced (usually costing a "half penny," hence their moniker) contemporaries of the American "dime novels" and precursor to the twentieth-century pulps. This promotional item was initially shipped with pre-ordered copies only (meaning, copies pre-ordered via the comic book direct-sales market distributors, prominent among them Diamond Comics and Capital Comics); less than nine thousand were pre-ordered, making the "Penny Dreadful" a truly rare collectible in Gaiman's body of work.

The first and only installment of Neil Gaiman and Michael Zulli's *Sweeney Todd* was the highlight of the final SpiderBaby/Tundra issue of *Taboo,* marking the end of the grand experiment the very year *Taboo* won the comics industry's Eisner Award for Best Anthology (after being nominated three years in a row). Also terminated prematurely were the ongoing series—Moore and Campbell's *From Hell* (continued and concluded by Kitchen Sink); Moore and Gebbie's *Lost Girls* (completed and published by Top Shelf in 2007); Jeff Nicholson's *Through the Habitrails* (completed and self-published by Nicholson as a graphic novel); they were joined by David Thorpe and Aidan Potts's Afterlife interlude, "Marquis My Love" (intended as the launch of another series, which was also featured in *Taboo* issue 9, the final volume). Unlike all but one of the other Taboo serialized graphic novels (Afterlife), *Sweeney Todd* was never continued or completed; the first chapter was never scripted, and save for a promotional poster issued by SpiderBaby/Tundra in 1992 (see Trivia), nothing further was ever published.

The demise of *Taboo* certainly was a key factor in the abrupt termination of *Sweeney Todd* just as it was out of the starting gate, but there were other factors. Gaiman and Zulli had ceased work on the serialized venture before *Taboo*'s publishing partner Tundra Publishing had changed hands, reportedly purchased by the venerable Wisconsin-based underground and alternative comics publisher Kitchen Sink Press.

Unease with some aspects of Tundra's handling of the first American edition of *Violent Cases* was a factor, as was Tundra's simultaneous publication of *Taboo* with the serialization of Moore and Campbell's *From Hell,* among others, and the Tundra collected editions of *From Hell*—which understandably confused retailers and buyers, and undercut *Taboo*'s circulation. Tundra management, presuming (sans negotiation) that Tundra would also have a claim on *Sweeney Todd,* only complicated the situation. In any case, even before SpiderBaby Grafix and Tundra finally parted ways, it was far simpler for Gaiman and Zulli to simply let sleeping Sweeneys lie than to involve themselves further.

"I think if *Taboo* had continued it would have continued," Gaiman replied, when asked about the story for this book. "I wound up doing a bit in *American Gods* that was sort of setting up for it. It's certainly not impossible that I'd want to go back to that material some time. And I couldn't see me doing it without Michael [Zulli]. But I don't know how we'd do it."

In "A Brief Introduction," Gaiman outlined his and Zulli's intentions for the novel:

> *Sweeney Todd* is about Manners, and Mirrors, and Meat. It's about razors, and women, and men. It's about death, and about London. It's about the past, and about the legacy from the past that we carry with us forever. . . . Each time the story of *Sweeney Todd* has been told it gains some elements, loses others. . . . Each generation tells and re-tells the story of Sweeney. We get, if you will, the Sweeneys we deserve. Shock-headed, long-fingered Sweeneys, crafty and scheming; bull-necked, shave-headed Sweeneys, Hyde to the earlier Sweeney's Jekyll; Irish, Scots, and French Sweeneys. Bald or blond or brilliant, maligned or malicious, the Sweeneys open their cut-throat razors and get into line. Ours is waiting for you now . . . there are roots and archetypes; and these we will trace and explore in the coming work. And there are dark magics that run beneath the tales, like a hidden river, like a sewer beneath a city street, and this too we shall touch on as we go.

A hint as to the structure Gaiman and Zulli were gravitating to is implied in the "Brief Introduction" and published prologue: "Take one hesitant step into Sweeney's world, and you've entered a shop full of mirrors, all of them distorting, lying, untruthful—or at best, unreliable. These are not mirrors in which it would be safe to shave." Gaiman and Zulli referred to their planned *Sweeney Todd* as a "gallery of mirrors," each reflecting different versions of the murderous barber Todd and Mrs. Lovett, his baker confederate/confidant making pies from Todd's victims, and their various supporting players.

"To investigate Sweeney—indeed to investigate a distant gallery of Sweeney Todds and Mrs. Lovetts—Mister Zulli and I shall be using the medium of a journalist in Victorian London, Master Edmund Wyld," Gaiman wrote. "It is he who will explore the past for us: along his way he will uncover clandestine wars and secret societies, strange magics and old religions, maps to forgotten cities, lost legacies, and dangerous birthrights. We will walk streets and alleys that run with offal and mud, lose ourselves in the rookeries and bordellos of old London, and find ourselves . . . perhaps . . . reflected in the stained glass of Mr. Todd's mirror, or the gleaming silver blade of his razor."

"*Sweeney Todd* is the story of a city, and of a street," Gaiman concluded in the penny dreadful's final page. "It's a story about stories. Urban legends and legendary towns; dead kings and virgin queens. It's about food. It's about patterns, and reflections, and professionals. And perhaps along the way you'll learn more than is comfortable about pies, and pearls, and the past."

Though his motives and methods vary from version to version of the tale throughout two centuries, Sweeney Todd is most often portrayed as a barber who cuts the throats of his victims for greed or for vengeance, or for both. In most versions, his partner in crime is Mrs. Lovett, a baker who disposes of the bodies of Todd's victims by making mincemeat of them and baking them into pies that she sells from their Fleet Street establishment. Gaiman and Zulli's *Sweeney* was to reflect all these possible incarnations, embracing the mercurial nature of the historic character: another exploration of myth, its function and its role, this time as embodied in the archetypal tale of *Sweeney Todd*.

The rather tangled history of *Sweeney Todd*—by all evidence a fictional character, possibly derived from the seventeenth-century "Ballad of the Seven [or Five] Lady Barbers of Drury Lane," though that lineage is questionable—is discussed in Gaiman's "A Brief Introduction" in *Taboo's Penny Dreadful*. "Sweeney lived, or he didn't," Gaiman notes. "A version of the tale was told in the 1820s, set in France, but there is evidence that the French had pirated it from a 1795 English tale; at any rate it is apparent that elements of the tale were the stuff of common London urban legend before the appearance of the 1840s play and tale."

Among the earliest published versions of the story (which Gaiman quotes throughout the *Penny Dreadful*) were George Dibdin Pitt's play (1842) and penny dreadful novelization *The String of Pearls; or, The Fiend of Fleet Street* (1847), and People's Periodical and Family Library's eighteen-part *The String of Pearls; or the Sailor's Gift; A Romance of Peculiar Interest* (1846–47), attributed to Thomas Pecket Prest. Frederick Hazleton's novel *Sweeney Todd, The Demon*

Barber of Fleet Street (1862) was one of the many versions to follow, published around the same year his play (also one of many by others) was first performed. A longer penny dreadful version was published in the 1880s, sans author credit, incorporating elements from Hazleton ("extensively plagiarized" is how Gaiman put it), along with a retelling in the penny dreadful *Boy's Standard* under the title "The Link Boys of Old London." In the twentieth and twenty-first centuries, there are a number of film versions, from a silent 1926 comedy to 2007's Tim Burton adaptation of the 1979 Stephen Sondheim–Hugh Wheeler musical, *Sweeney Todd: The Demon Barber of Fleet Street*. Noting that the 1974 Christopher Bond play "and the Sondheim musical are both highly recommended, those familiar with the story that they tell should not expect to see it reprised in our tale." Gaiman elaborates further:

> Sweeney Todd and Mrs. Lovett between them embody two basic human needs. The need to look good, and the need to eat. Journalists and whores both claim themselves the oldest professionals; but barbers and cooks were there early. And journalists and whores, barbers and cooks there will be in abundance in *Sweeney Todd;* and thieves and highwaymen, cut-throats and revolutionaries, mud-larks and aristocrats, poets and vicars, pirates and pie-men. Also plagues, ditches, sewers and hidden rivers. And recipes.

> *Sweeney Todd: The Demon Barber of Fleet Street: Prologue: Shaving; His Troubles With Women, a Folly; Chickens and Hens; The Mulberry Tree; Getting Lost in Failing Light; Temple Bar; Three Peacock Feathers; Stains; Going to America; Beware Falling Masonry* . . . That is the full title of the single published installment of Gaiman and Zulli's *Sweeney Todd,* an engaging 26-page prologue (and it is a prologue, not Chapter 1, as some sources erroneously report) that reads as a self-standing short story. Gaiman features himself in a semi-autobiographical sojourn (with Titan Comics' Mike Lake) that carries the reader with the author and his traveling companion to the fenced-in remnant of Temple Bar.

As Gaiman noted in the first page of the penny dreadful:

> The entrance to Fleet Street was signified for many years by Temple Bar, a Christopher Wren arch, built in 1670 on the site of previous gates, the first of which was probably erected four hundred years before the Knights Templar; and the entrance to Fleet Street is the entrance to the City of London, the anomalous city within a city. Temple Bar still exists, although it is no longer in London. You may see it if you wish, although barbed wire discourages those who might approach too close.

Gaiman and Zulli get us as close to Temple Bar as one can get, circa 1990, but in a roundabout manner—via their leisurely but increasingly ominous, atmospheric account of Gaiman and Lake's excursion, the storytellers are circling their own entryway to the narrative itself. In fact, many pages are spent at the wrong artifact: after exploring an ancient monument that turns out not to be Temple Bar, Gaiman and Lake are redirected and find the actual monument, fenced and impregnable. Lake finds three peacock feathers in the brush; "They're beautiful," Gaiman says, "But that's really weird . . ." "I feel scared," Gaiman thinks as he ponders the structure. "It's history out of context. There's nothing here to tell us what it is . . . to render it tame and harmless. Instead it's sitting in the middle of nowhere, like an unexploded bomb. The gate to the city." Only after Gaiman and Lake leave in the gathering dusk does Zulli render the spectral forms of Sweeney Todd and Mrs. Lovett, materializing in the mist at Temple Gate.

The prologue, then, literally set the stage; but the curtain never opened afterward.

In "A Brief Introduction," Gaiman wrote: "You never know what you'll find when you go looking for something. *Sweeney Todd* began for us as a small, elegant chance to retell a familiar tale, and has grown and shifted with each new jigsaw piece until now it squats monstrous and dark and still, waiting to be told."

That is as true today as it was eighteen years ago; *Sweeney Todd* still sits "like an unexploded bomb."

TRIVIA

- At Gaiman and Zulli's request, Bissette lettered "Babycakes." The creative team donated their collective payment for the story's appearance in *Taboo* to PETA.

- Michael Zulli did many, many sketches, pen-and-ink drawings, and full oil paintings of Sweeney Todd and the characters Gaiman and Zulli planned to feature in the serialized graphic novel. While a few of these pieces remain in Gaiman's personal collection, the rest were sold to collectors of Zulli's art, with the lion's share going to Kevin Eastman's personal collection. As this collection has been sold off over the past decade, precious little remains accessible from this fertile period of collaborative work.

- An oversized five-color *Sweeney Todd* poster, designed and painted by Michael Zulli, was printed by SpiderBaby/Tundra in 1992. Gaiman and Zulli signed a portion of the print run, and the rest were left unsigned; these were to be used as a promotional giveaway for distributors, but were never shipped from Tundra (Zulli eventually salvaged the remaining backstock of both the signed and unsigned posters)—which was another bone of contention in the final weeks of the fraying Taboo/Tundra relations. This truly handsome promotional piece features Sweeney Todd, bloodied razor in hand, impassively standing behind his most recent victim, who is writhing in Todd's infamous barber's chair.

- Gaiman and Zulli's *Sweeney Todd* has retained a mystique since its aborted launch. Iain Sinclair's *London Orbital* (2002)—the "middle circle" of his "London walk" trilogy (*Lights Out for the Territory*, 1997; *Sixty Miles Out*, 1999)—featured what Gaiman referred to on his blog as "a lovely sequence" on the Gaiman/Zulli *Sweeney Todd*.

THE QUOTABLE GAIMAN

I'm not sure what will happen with Sweeney, really. We may finish it as a *From Hell*–sized comic, or I might write it as a novel and ask Michael to illustrate each chapter, or something else might happen.

—journal.neilgaiman.com

||||||||||||||||||||||||||||||||||||||||||||||||||||||||||||||||||

"BLOOD MONSTER"

(1992)

A RARE, FOUR-PAGE COMICS STORY FROM *TABOO* #4, 1992, ILLUSTRATED BY MARLENE O'CONNOR, REPRODUCED IN ITS ENTIRETY

("Blood Monster" is in the color inserts in this book.)

"Blood Monster" was originally written and drawn for *Taboo*, the horror anthology cofounded by Stephen Bissette and John Totleben and co-edited and co-published by Bissette and his first wife, Marlene (then named Nancy) O'Connor under the SpiderBaby Comix & Publications imprint. Though Marlene's artwork appeared in *Taboo* issues 3 and 4, she ceased co-editing and copublishing with *Taboo* issue 3 (1990). "Blood Monster" was published in *Taboo* issue 6 (1992), which also featured Gaiman and Michael Zulli's *Sweeney Todd Penny Dreadful* and Zulli's comics adaptation of then five-year-old Holly Gaiman's "Holly's Story."

Gaiman wrote "Blood Monster"—his first original script for the anthology series—after visiting Bissette and O'Connor in 1990–91, specifically tailoring the script for Marlene and requesting that she illustrate it for *Taboo*. This was O'Connor's first comics narrative. In an e-mail to the authors, she notes, "To me, 'Blood Monster' speaks to the pain of not being seen, not being heard, and the anger that comes from that. It is also about how small children, though without worldly power, are sometimes smarter than adults." In this, "Blood Monster" anticipates core themes of Gaiman's later works, prominent among them *The Wolves in the Walls.*

Marlene O'Connor currently lives in Southern Vermont with her partner, Kathy Carr. She can be visited at marleneoconnorart.com. Marlene adds, "I would like to thank Steve Bissette and our kids Maia and Danny, as well as our friend Karen Lennon, for being the models for the characters in 'Blood Monster.' And thank you to Neil for this story, a subtle and complex tale of many layers."

This is the story's first publication since its original publication in *Taboo* issue 6. There is only one revision (one word balloon has been corrected), and the artist supervised the final scans used for this printing.

|||||||||||||||||||||||||||||||||||||||||||||||||||||||||||||||||||||||||||

BEING AN ACCOUNT OF THE LIFE AND DEATH OF THE EMPEROR HELIOGABOLUS: A 24 HOUR COMIC[1]

(1990)

The 24 Hour Comic was "invented"—his own term—by Scott McCloud, the creator of *Zot!* and other comics and graphic novels, who is globally renowned as the author of *Understanding Comics* (1992), the definitive analysis of the comics medium that has become a standard media text in universities, libraries, and schools around the world. In his introduction to *24 Hour Comics* (2004, About Comics, featuring Gaiman's story in its only book-format reprint), McCloud described how he invented the 24-hour comic in the summer of 1990, as a challenge for his friend and fellow cartoonist (and coauthor of this book) Stephen Bissette. At the time, McCloud and Bissette had reputations as being among the "slowest artists in comics." If only as a personal challenge to remedy their self-images, McCloud challenged Bissette to "each do a complete 24-page comic in a single day." Five days apart, with both (unaware the other had done so) adding an additional page—a cover—thus, McCloud and then Bissette each drew "a complete 25-page, 24-hour comic" on August 31 and "August 36th," respectively.

The rules were simple. McCloud writes:

The Goal: To create a complete 24 page comic in 24 continuous hours. That means *everything:* story, finished art, lettering, colors (if you want 'em),

paste-ups, everything! Once pen hits paper, the clock starts ticking. [Twenty-
four] hours later, the pen lifts off the paper, never to descend again. Even
proofreading has to occur in the 24 hour period. . . . No sketches, designs,
plot summaries or any other kind of direct preparation can precede the 24
hour period. Indirect preparations such as assembling tools, reference materials, food, music etc. is fine. . . . Pages can be any size, any material. . . . The
24 hours are continuous. You can take a nap if you like, but the clock will
continue to tick. If you get to 24 hours and you're not done, either end it
there ("the Gaiman variation") or keep going until you're done ("the [Kevin]
Eastman [cocreator of the Teenage Mutant Ninja Turtles] variation"). I consider both of these "Noble Failure Variants" and true 24 hour comics in
spirit; but you must sincerely intend to do the 24 pages in 24 hours at the
outset.[2]

As cartoonist Nat Gertler notes, "Considering that teams of people (a writer, a
pencil artist, an ink artist, and a letterer) are generally needed to keep a monthly
comic book on track, completing a 24 hour comic seems nigh-miraculous."[3]

Circulating photocopies of their 25-page 24-hour comics to their friends
that fateful fall, McCloud and Bissette were delighted to find that the 24-hour
comic challenge had "gone viral." The first cartoonist to rise to the challenge
was Cerebus creator/self-publisher Dave Sim, who completed "Bigger Blacker
Kiss" (a title reference to Howard Chaykin's then current adult comic series
Black Kiss) during October 26–27, 1990. The prolific Rick Veitch (*Swamp
Thing, Bratpack, Army@Love*, etc.) was next, who modified the challenge to fit
his own interest in chronicling his dreams in comics form, yielding twenty-four
self-standing dream comics, each drawn in a single hour on different days; this
spawned Veitch's self-published comics and graphic novel series *Rarebit Fiends*
(1992–2008).

Gaiman was among the initial circle of 24-hour comics creators, and the
first-ever writer to take on the challenge, wielding what cartooning skills he had
in 1990. Gaiman was the fifth creator on Earth "to pick up the bug," McCloud
wrote. "Neil was just getting rolling on his groundbreaking *Sandman* series at
the time. . . . Though he couldn't make the 24-page mark, he still managed to
turn in one of the most literate and funny of all the 24-hour comics, filled with
several memorable I-don't-know-how-to-draw-this-so-I'll-draw-something-else-
instead panels. Neil's effort gave birth to the so-called 'Gaiman variation': If you
get to 24 hours and you're not done, end it there"[4]

"Being an Account of the Life and Death of the Emperor Heliogabolus" is what
it says it is, but it is also a delightful stream-of-consciousness exercise in autobiography and biography. From its first page, Heliogabolus indulges Gaiman's personal
memories and connections to his subject: his first hearing of Heliogabolus via Gilbert and Sullivan, his aunt Diane, etc. Heliogabolus is indeed among Gaiman's
semiautobiographic works, despite his assertion on the first panel of page two,

"But this isn't about me." Of course, much of it is, though all the while Gaiman offers a rich, inventive overview of the life and reign of Emperor Heliogabolus (A.D. 204–22), whose antics make those of the infamous Caligula seem tame by comparison, a fact Gaiman riffs on with glee: "Sometimes I think its peculiar that Heliogabolus is so little known. I mean, everyone knows that Caligula made his horse, Incitatus, a senator. Only he didn't. According to Seutonius, Caligula was only said to be planning to make the horse a consul. Heliogabolus, on the other hand, DID make his horse a consul." Gaiman's crude but always expressive art also makes the most horrific details (e.g., Heliogabolus reading human entrails) bemusing, enhancing the black comic invention of the whole.

There's clear evidence in Gaiman's Heliogabolus of the still intimate "inner circle" nature of the challenge at that time; these little in-jokes may confuse contemporary or uninitiated readers. Note, for instance, that among the "I-don't-know-how-to-draw-this" visual detours Gaiman embraced was a non-sequitur panel showing a zombie instead of a horse, with a handwritten note and arrow alongside that reads, "This is also not a horse. It's a rotting zombie especially for Steve Bissette." After Gaiman faxed a copy of the comic to Bissette upon its completion, Bissette responded with a fax to Gaiman offering two "replacement panel" drawings, one of a horse and one of a zombie; these were later included in the 1993 Chicago Convention mini-comic publication of "Heliogabolus."

Though the 24-hour comics weren't originally intended for publication, after the completion of the first-ever 24-hour comics, McCloud and Bissette agreed to publish their efforts in Bissette's anthology series, *Taboo*. McCloud's "A Day's Work" appeared in *Taboo Especial* (1991) and Bissette's "A Life in Black and White" in *Taboo* issue 7 (1992). Prior to this Sim had begun to preview and/or publish the initial 24-hour comics as backup features in the monthly Cerebus. This spread word of the 24-hour comic challenge to thousands of readers and fellow cartoonists, and the challenge quickly spread from there.

Gaiman's 24-hour comic was initially published in Cerebus issue 147 (1991). It was subsequently published as a one-shot minicomic special (1992), designed by Larry Marder (*Beanworld*) for the Chicago-based comic retail chain Moondog's, in conjunction with a special signing event, for which Gaiman originally wrote, as an introduction, the following chapter. Gaiman's 24 hour comic was included in the definitive collected edition, *24 Hour Comics* (About Comics, 2004), edited by McCloud, which also features Bissette's "A Life in Black and White." Those readers interested in the chronology leading up to Gaiman's effort should also see *24 Hour Comics All-Stars* (*About Comics*, 2005), which includes McCloud's historic first-ever 24-hour comic "A Day's Work" and Dave Sim's "Bigger Blacker Kiss." The complete 1992 edition of "Heliogabolus" is posted online.[5]

No less an authority than McCloud, inventor of the challenge, wrote: "Word for word, 'Heliogabolus' is probably the best written of the 24-hour comics. This will surprise no one, considering the author. What's particularly interesting though is the way it's forever losing and then rediscovering its structure—as if Neil was continually forgetting where he was, until every few pages, he surfaced, groundhog-like, took it all in and then burrowed back down.

"Most remarkable of all is the simple fact that he drew it at all," McCloud notes, citing it as "the first comic drawn by comics' most celebrated writer in over 14 years. And the last, as far as I know." True enough. Though Gaiman's mentor, Alan Moore, was also a cartoonist, having written and drawn his own early comics and the regionally published comic strip "Maxwell, the Magic Cat" (under the pen name 'Jill De Ray'), "Heliogabolus" is Gaiman's only conventionally published narrative comic effort as writer and artist. As Gaiman notes in the following text, "I swore I would never take an artist for granted again."

But, why don't we let him tell it . . .

||||||||||||||||||||||||||||||||||||||||||||||||||||||||||||||||||||

"IT'S PRONOUNCED HE'LL-LEO-GABBLE-US."

BEING AN ACCOUNT OF A FAILED ATTEMPT TO PRODUCE 24 PAGES IN 24 HOURS.

Scott McCloud should have been born a long time ago. (This is relevant. Bear with me.) This is because Scott is a great inventor and discoverer. He invented *Zot!*, and the *Frying Pan*. He discovered and invented 1990s comics with his seminal *Destroy!* He discovered Ivy Ratafia, and married her to boot. If he'd been born a long time ago, before all the things we take for granted were invented, he would have invented string and rubber bands and electric lights and hats. Currently he's working on a book which will explain to the world what comics are and why, and about time, too. Scott is, of course a Genius. Only a Genius could have invented the 24 Hour Comic.

These are the 24 Hour Comic Rules as I understand them:

1. You have to write, draw, letter (and, I suppose, if you've got any time left over, colour and set to music) a 24-page comic, in 24 Hours. No preliminary work. No plotting, sketching, roughing. Nothing. The clock starts ticking hour 1, minute 1. Just 24 hours to create a 24-page story.

2. Well, that's pretty much it.

You should do one. Honest. Or at least try to.

Now, I draw a lot of comics. No one ever sees them but me; no one is *meant* to see them. Every time I write a comic I take some sheets of paper, fold them over, and as

I go I draw and doodle out what I'm asking the artist to do. When I finish the strip I put the doodle comic in a file. But I haven't drawn a comic since I was sixteen.

(The comics I did when I was sixteen were mostly drawn in history lessons; this was because I sat next to Geoff Notkin in history, and I'd pencil and he'd ink.) I haven't drawn since, not really. After all, I'm surrounded by people who can really draw and do, at the drop of a pen. But the idea of the 24 hour comic somehow grabbed me. I saw Steve Bissette's, and Scott McCloud's. I saw Dave Sim's and damn it, I wanted to do one of these.

I drew a trial page, a one-page story in an hour, and gave it to Dave McKean. He faxed back to me a three-page lesson on drawing, on his way out the door to go to Dublin.

We set a date for it. As I recall, Dave McKean, Steve Bissette, and Neil Gaiman were all going to do 24 hour comics on the same day. Dave fell by the wayside; he'd suddenly had to go to Dublin in Ireland, to color *Hellblazer* 50. So that left me and Steve.

I got a pad of paper and bought lots of pens and pencils, and, as late afternoon struck, I began my comic.

Heliogabolus was one of those historical persons whom I had always vaguely wanted to write about. There was a measure of wilfulness, perversion and eccentricity I found intriguing—too much so, perhaps, for a mainstream comic.

The comic wasn't plotted, planned, or outlined. It just happened. I would take a piece of paper, draw some panel borders, letter it and then draw it. Then I'd start on the next one.

Somewhere about 4:00 A.M. I phoned Steve Bissette, in Vermont. It was about 11 P.M. his time. "My hand hurts," I told him. "My hand hurts and it's all stupid and it's a pointless story and I can't draw and I ought to be in bed and I'll never make 24 pages at this rate and I don't know why I ever let you idiots talk me into this."

"Yeah? Go to bed," said Bissette.

"It's 4:00 A.M. and my hand hurts and I've just drawn this page with crocodiles on it and I'm pissed off and . . . what did you say?"

"Forget it," said Steve Bissette cheerfully. "I've done 10 pages of mine, but hell, I'm giving up and going to bed. You should too."

"Never!" I muttered, a trifle hysterically.

It got better after that. My hand still hurt, but that didn't matter because I was so tired I couldn't think. I blundered on. Somewhere in there it became apparent that I wasn't going to make 24 pages, which meant that I wound up losing a few Heliogabolus facts I'd wanted to share with the world. When you read the following comic you will find no mention of how he was too scared to review the troops, and made his grandmother come down with him whenever he had to talk to the army, or of the Women's Senate he created (not quite the feminist gesture it might appear: they were permitted only to pass laws relating to fashion and cosmetics). You'll find no mention of the first time I heard the rose-petal story (Alan Moore told it to me once, over dinner at a convention, I think).

Well, if it was a 14-page 24-hour comic then that was what it was. There wasn't much I could do about that.

Somehow, when I got near the end, the disparate threads knotted themselves together: Everything made sense, with that desperate, flat clarity that things attain after 36 hours without sleeping.

So I got to the end okay, and the end was a real end, and it came after about 23 hours and 40 minutes. All that time I had spent drawing and writing, with the exception of occasional food and bathroom breaks.

I swore I would never take an artist for granted again, and got the thing photocopied. And stayed up another eight hours, in that condition of almost-pain that lack of sleep can cause, to stop my sleeping schedule being more messed up than it already was and finally went to bed.

I sent photocopies to people I wanted to see it—people like Eddie Campbell, Dave McKean, Rick Veitch, Scott McCloud, and Dave Sim. Eddie liked it. Rick liked it. Dave McKean liked it. Scott liked it. Dave Sim asked if he could publish it in *Cerebus*. I had to think about this for a while: I didn't mind my friends seeing what I'd drawn. But real money-paying people? Ah well, strange things happen in the back of *Cerebus*. I doubted anyone would notice.

Mostly when I do signings these days, we limit the number of things people get signed. They bring the two or three things I've done that are their real favorites. *Hellblazer* 27, *Sandman* 8 or 17 or 19 or 31. Some bring *Cerebus* 147, and when that happens, somewhere behind the dark glasses, I glow with pride. Anyway, here's my 24 hour comic (failed). I hope you like it. One day I'll probably draw something else. My thanks to Dave Sim, and Steve Bissette, to Dave McKean, and of course to Scott McCloud, who is a genius, and should have lived a long time ago.

—Neil Gaiman, 4 October 1992

TRIVIA

- Note that to date none of the original circle of 24-hour comic creators have ever done another—including Gaiman. As noted in Gaiman's introduction to the 1992 edition of his effort, the original cartoonist McCloud challenged—Bissette—began a second effort the very evening Gaiman began his own, but never completed more than ten pages. This was the case with a couple of others who attempted it. At the time, Dave Sim noted, "It's like running a long-distance marathon—once you've done it, you've nothing more to prove to anyone." This truism is no longer the case, as a new generation has grown up with the challenge as an annual socializing event. Since the late 1990s, many young cartoonists who have taken up the challenge have done many 24-hour comics.

- Every year since 1990 cartoonists around the world have created their own 24-hour comics, and continue to do so. There's a Web site dedicated to the phenomenon, 24hourcomics.com, and a global "24 hour comics day" celebrated annually, yielding hundreds of new 24-hour comics. The challenge also spread into other creative mediums. After a friend told New York City–based Crux Productions director Tina Fallon about the 24-hour comics, Fallon launched the 24-hour plays, debuting the challenge at the annual Fringe Festival in the early 1990s. The concept soon spread beyond Fallon and Crux, and 24-hour plays are now a worldwide phenomenon, which in turn spawned the 48-hour film project (48hourfilm.com), the 24-hour animation Web site, the 24-hour Web site challenge, and so on.

MIRACLEMAN #17—24

(1992)

*M*iracleman is a difficult subject; it is both a high point and a tragic unre-solved chapter in Gaiman's comics scripting career. While Gaiman's two-year tenure on the title and character is easily summarized, there is no simple way to summarize the history of the character, before or since. *Miracleman* has one of the most tangled histories and legacies in contemporary comics. Given the labyrinthine nature of most comics continuities, that is really saying something.

For instance, what is the character's name? Because Gaiman's issues were published only under the American title *Miracleman,* that is the name we will use herein. But the character's original name was Marvelman, and to trace that we must return to Gaiman's native country of England.

BACKGROUND

Since the late 1930s many American comics have reached the United Kingdom via a variety of small UK publishers. Len Miller & Son, Ltd. was a London-based publisher of pulps, magazines, and comics that functioned in this manner, taking advantage of the British ban on importing printed matter by arranging to publish British black-and-white (with color covers) editions of American comic books, from the 1940s until 1966. According to comics historian Denis Gifford, after World War II, "when the dollar situation cut short the supply of American comic books, minor British publishers leapt aboard the bandwagon. . . . Not only the Yankee format was imitated but their characters, too. Superheroes abounded . . . and the most successful of them all [was] Mick Anglo's *Marvelman* (1954) for L. Miller & Son."[1]

Miller had enjoyed enormous profits repackaging Fawcett Publications's popular

Golden Age *Captain Marvel* and its spinoff Marvel Family titles (*Mary Marvel,
Captain Marvel, Jr.,* etc.). Fawcett's decision to cancel the line of *Captain Marvel*
titles—surrendering in 1953 to ongoing legal pressure from National Periodicals
(DC Comics)—left Miller high and dry, without the cash cow that the Fawcett
reprints had provided.

Enter Maurice "Mick" Anglo, aka Michael Anglo, who had created *Wonder-
man* (1948) for Paget Publications, *Captain Zenith Comic* (both 1950) for Martin
& Reid Ltd., *Captain Universe* for Arnold Book Company (1953), and many,
many others. Anglo was already packaging *Space Commander Kerry* and *Space
Commando Comics* for Len Miller (both 1953) when Miller hired Anglo to make
minor changes to America's *Captain Marvel* and create an immediate successor/
clone. Anglo changed Captain Marvel's black hair to blond; altered his costume;
changed his secret identity from radio reporter Billy Batson to boy newspaper reporter Michael Moran; and the magic word that changed Moran to superhero
became the new Marvelman's atomic-age "Kimota!" (say it backward). Thus, Anglo re-created Captain Marvel and his family: Marvelman was joined by Kid
Marvelman (whose mortal alter ego was Johnny Bates) and Young Marvelman
(the superhuman incarnation of Dicky Dauntless). Captain Marvel's nemesis Dr.
Sivana was changed to Dr. Gargunza, and the evil Black Adam became Young
Nastyman. Anglo and his studio of freelancers kept the series going in a trio of
titles into the sixties.

The weekly titles *Marvelman* and *Young Marvelman* were joined by the
monthly *Marvelman Family* in 1956, and the series annuals flourished throughout
the rest of the 1950s in Britain, Spain, Italy, and Brazil (where Marvelman was
known as "Jack Marvel"), until the popularity of superheroes waned. The weekly
publishing schedules slowed to monthly, and Mick Anglo left the series in 1959,
after which Miller continued with reprints. The British line ended with *Marvelman* issue 370 and *Young Marvelman* issue 370 (both February 1963).

Anglo launched his own Anglo Features imprint, and among the four titles he
published were his redrawn versions of old *Marvelman* comics under the new
moniker *Captain Miracle* (1960), joined by *Miracle Junior*. This effort ended
within nine months (including a title change to *Invincible* with its sixth issue),
after which Anglo reportedly again revamped existing *Marvelman* stories under
the title *Miracleman*. This, too, did not last, relegating Marvelman to limbo for
almost two decades, during which almost every conceivable superhero archetype
underwent enormous changes.

In the early 1980s, Mick Anglo was approached by British magazine and comics publisher/packager Dez Skinn. "He contacted me and he wanted to revive
[Marvelman]," Anglo told interviewer George Khoury, "and I said go ahead and
do what you like, as far as I was concerned."[2] What legal rights actually changed
hands remains undocumented and unresolved; however, Skinn claimed to have
acquired the necessary permission, and Anglo's interview indicates this may have

been true at the time (at least a verbal permission), though the Marvelman property had little perceived market value in 1981, which is certainly no longer the case.

Scripted by Alan Moore—who had expressed his enthusiasm for reviving the character in a 1981 interview in the *Journal of the Society of Strip Illustrators,* prompting Skinn's interest—Marvelman was resurrected in Dez Skinn's innovative new black-and-white comic magazine *Warrior* (26 issues, March 1982–January 1985). Moore's scripts were initially illustrated by *Warrior* art director Garry Leach. Leach inked penciler Alan Davis's sketches for the Marvelman chapter published in *Warrior* issues 6 and 7, and thereafter Davis worked with Moore on the series until there was a falling out between the creators; their final collaboration appearing in *Warrior* issue 21.

Shorn of its most popular feature, *Warrior* ended a mere five issues later. But while it existed, *Warrior* touted itself as publishing primarily creator-owned comics, a rare commodity in the British comics industry outside of the underground comix scene. After the cancellation of *Warrior,* many of the unfinished serialized adventures were published (and completed) by various U.S. comic publishing companies, though many remained compromised by questionable proprietorships—the most famous being, of course, Marvelman.

The collaborative Marvelman stories by Moore, Leach, and Davis not only reinvigorated Marvelman as a viable British comics icon, but (along with Frank Miller's tenure on Marvel's *Daredevil* in the United States) became a catalyst for an international resurgence in the superhero genre itself.

Moore launched the series with an urgency unusual in its day: When terrorists attack a nuclear power plant during its opening, which was being covered by aging reporter Michael Moran, the ensuing violence causes Moran to accidentally read aloud the word "atomic" backward: "Kimota!" The word spoken, Moran transforms into Marvelman, setting in motion the premise Moore had outlined in his original proposal: "[W]ithout deviating in fact from the naive and simplistic Marvelman concept of the Fifties, I want to transplant it into a cruel and cynical Eighties." (Source: "Alan Moore's Original Proposal," quoted from Khoury, *Kimota!,* pg. 24).

To do so, Moore, Leach, and Davis made Michael Moran a more vulnerable, troubled, middle-aged man plagued by dreams, the fragmented remnants of a past superheroic existence wiped from his memory by devastating events in 1961 that left him a broken man. They made Dr. Emil Gargunza a truly Machiavellian scientific genius who had bred the Marvelman family in a series of top-secret, covert, government-funded experiments, and destroyed the superheroic clan when they attacked Gargunza's nuclear fortress in 1961; and they changed Johnny Bates/Kid Marvelman into an amoral now-adult megalomaniac with wealth, power, and superpowers he keeps hidden; with the full knowledge of what he was and is; and with no concern for anyone's well-being save his own. The resulting series ingeniously deconstructed the very concept of superheroes, ultimately questioning what effect the appearance of genuinely godlike beings might have on mankind, a theme Moore subsequently explored further in *Watchmen* (1986–87).

Ironically, another character name change became necessary when Skinn published a one-shot reprint of Mick Anglo Marvelman stories entitled *Marvelman Special* issue 1, which sported the cover copy, "Back in their own title—after 20 years!" (This special was eventually reprinted by Eclipse Comics in the United States as *Miracleman 3-D* issue 1.) Enforcing their trademarked company moniker, Marvel Comics threatened legal action over Skinn's use of the name Marvelman.[3] Given Marvel's corporate legal clout, he backed down; when Eclipse Comics later launched its color comic book reprinting of the Moore/Leach/Davis *Warrior* stories beginning in 1985, Marvelman became Miracleman in the United States.

With the involvement of Alan Moore, Eclipse Comics launched *Miracleman*, by reprinting the published *Warrior* chapters in color, engaging Moore to complete the truncated story line, and continue the series. In the era of monthly comic books, the series was troubled: despite its success, it was plagued with constant delays and sporadic publication dates. Nevertheless, *Book One, Miracleman: A Dream of Flying* came together. The *Warrior* reprint material concluded in *Miracleman* issue 6 (February 1986), which also featured the first new episode, sporting art by Moore's new collaborator, Chuck Beckum (now known as Chuck Austen), who also delineated the two chapters in issue 7 (issue 8 was entirely composed of Mick Anglo–produced reprint material). Rick Veitch illustrated the controversial *Miracleman* issue 9, which featured the graphic birth of Miracleman's child Winter, and the final chapter of the *Book Two, Miracleman: The Red King Syndrome* series arc in issue 10.

Book Three, Miracleman: Olympus was launched in *Miracleman* issue 11 (1987). Having significantly expanded the Miracleman mythos—including the arrival of two races of aliens, the Warpsmiths and the Qys, to Earth; the emergence of Miraclewoman; and the revelation that several native superhumans already live on Earth—*Miracleman: Olympus* was Moore's final work on the character and concept, a magnum opus that took three years to complete in six issues, all illustrated by Moore's former *Swamp Thing* collaborator John Totleben. This was the only Moore *Miracleman* arc to be illustrated by a single artist, and Totleben's truly visionary collaboration with Moore yielded an unprecedented landmark for its genres—superhero and science fiction comics—and the comics art form as a whole.

Miracleman issue 15's genuinely apocalyptic resolution of the Miracleman showdown with the demonic Johnny Bates/Kid Miracleman resonated into subsequent entries (in which Neil Gaiman took over writing chores). Bates is beaten only after Warpsmith Aza Chorn teleports a shard of wreckage into Kid Miracleman's body, forcing him to transform back into his mortal form, which allows Miracleman to execute Bates. Having utterly demolished London, killed the

Warpsmith, revealed to all that superbeings live among us, and dramatized Moran's final decision to remain Miracleman permanently, Moore and Totleben set the stage for the breathtakingly beautiful but decidedly frighteningly totalitarian utopia then imposed upon mankind by Miracleman in issue 16.

That completed, Moore passed the baton—and his share of the rights to the Miracleman property—over to his personal choice for successor, the pre-*Sandman* Neil Gaiman, whose tenure began with *Miracleman* issue 17 (1990).

GAIMAN'S MIRACLEMAN

To say the Alan Moore/John Totleben *Miracleman: Olympus* was a tough act to follow would be a gross understatement, but Gaiman and his artist collaborator, Mark Buckingham, rose to the challenge with *Book Four, Miracleman: The Golden Age* (issues 17–22, 1990–91) and the beginning of *Book Five, The Silver Age.* Gaiman planned three books, consisting of six issues each, but *The Golden Age* was the only one completed and collected, though it was to have been followed by *The Silver Age* and *The Dark Age.* The last published issue of *Miracleman* to date remains issue 24 (1992), only two chapters into *The Silver Age* and halfway through Gaiman's planned story arc.

Gaiman's first Miracleman story actually appeared in the Eclipse Comics five-issue miniseries *Total Eclipse* (1988), a cross-company crossover involving all of Eclipse's characters. Each issue was comprised of a serialized main story written by Marv Wolfman (who had scripted DC Comics's twelve-issue crossover epic *Crisis on Infinite Earths,* 1985) and drawn by Bo Hampton. Among the shorter self-standing stories by various creators featuring Eclipse characters in each issue was *Total Eclipse* issue 4's ten-pager "Screaming" (reprinted in *Miracleman* issue 21), scripted by Gaiman and illustrated by Mark Buckingham.

"Screaming" is essentially a confession a young man shares with his lover as bedroom conversation after his first sexual experience. As a boy he'd missed going to London with his best friend due to a seaside family outing he had to attend; his friend went anyway, and was killed by Johnny Bates/Kid Miracleman during the ravaging of London. He recalls seeing a documentary of the London atrocities, and recognizing his friend among the victims; he remembers when, at age "nine or ten," he met Miracleman in the forest and spoke to him, asking if Miracleman would save him if there were a nuclear war ("He said, no promises, but he'd try. If he could"). Pondering whether Miracleman indeed was "looking out for me," and the nature of miracles, the boy turns out the light and asks his lover, "What do you think about that, then?" only to find that she is sound asleep. "Screaming" features Gaiman's initial reference to "the Kubrick movie, *Veneer,*" a fictional Stanley Kubrick (*Dr. Strangelove, 2001: A Space Odyssey, A Clockwork Orange, The Shining,* etc.) feature built around graphic documentary footage of the Miracleman/Kid Miracleman destruction of London.

"Screaming" is also a tidy precursor to *The Golden Age* in scope and intent. Gaiman deftly executed *The Golden Age* as a sort of narrative sleight of hand, eschewing the obvious and leapfrogging the chronological narrative of Moore's three books. Mark Buckingham drew each chapter in a distinctively different style, a collaborative experiment that was wholly successful, though consistency-obsessed comics fans bristled at this during the series' original publication.

MIRACLEMAN: BOOK FOUR: THE GOLDEN AGE (1990—91)

Set a few years into the future, *The Golden Age* probes the completely transformed society under Miracleman's utopian dynasty, via self-contained character studies of mortals and their fleeting brushes with the godlike superbeings who reign. This effectively kept Miracleman off center stage to explore the volatile emotional, psychological, cultural, and societal issues suggested by the traumatizing London apocalypse and subsequent international reinvention and renaissance of society Moore had delineated. Gaiman and Buckingham's strategy may have prompted some critical disdain as it was published, but read today in the context of the entire *Miracleman* saga it decidedly enhances and expands the impact of Moore's science fiction epic. The cumulative effect is to evoke the impact of an imposed utopia— however benevolent the intentions of the ruling superbeings—on the inevitably messy, mundane, but deeply felt foibles and frailties of human beings living in the inescapable shadows of the ruling deities—the utter impossibilities of perfection. *The Golden Age* is consistently introspective, illuminating, and often surprisingly moving, yielding at least one brilliant masterpiece, "Notes from the Underground," issue 19 (1990), and laying the groundwork for themes and formats, in the case of "Winter's Tale," issue 20 (1991) that Gaiman would explore further in future works.

The chapters of *The Golden Age* are deceptively simple in concept, and easy to synopsize; as with all Gaiman's work, any capsule summary misses the resonance of the read.

"A PRAYER AND HOPE . . ."

This first chapter follows four pilgrims seeking an audience with Miracleman, which requires an unimaginable climb into the spires of Olympus. This becomes a spiritual journey, an endurance test, and an ordeal, and claims the sanity and life of one before the remaining three reach their goal. One of them tries to assassinate Miracleman, and failing that, commits suicide; another asks to be given the chance to become an artist and is granted her wish; the third begs for the life of his daughter, who was brain damaged in the battle between Miracleman and Kid Miracleman. Miracleman simply says no before departing, leaving the forlorn father to climb back down to Earth.

"TRENDS" AND "SCREAMING"

These short pieces are positioned here in the reprint volume. "Screaming" has been discussed. "Trends" (from *Miracleman* issue 18, 8 pages) is vital because it introduces, via an ongoing schoolyard conflict, a covert religious movement that worships Johnny Bates/Kid Miracleman as a new messiah (the silver icon of their cult, worn in the manner Christians wear crosses, is the sculpted image of Bates transfixed by the teleported steel shard).

"SKIN DEEP"

This is a tale of a self-exiled caretaker of windmills who is visited by Miraclewoman and becomes her lover ("She was perfect . . . it was perfect."). He becomes obsessed with her perfection. Her ultimate gift to him, though, is to dash this obsession by returning to her human alter ego for their last night of lovemaking ("[Y]ou have to understand. This is me, too. There's no such thing as perfection—not the perfection you imagine."). No longer adrift from humanity, he opens himself to the world. Gaiman told interviewer George Khoury that this story "was really me trying to retell the story of Cupid and Psyche".[4]

"NOTES FROM THE UNDERGROUND"

This tale was inspired by a reference to Andy Warhol that Alan Moore used in the concluding chapter of *Miracleman: Olympus*. In a potent story that is by turns delightful, disturbing, and haunting, Gaiman posited a realm inhabited by eighteen simulacrums of Andy Warhol, to which the reanimated Dr. Emile Gargunza is consigned. The interaction between Andek, "the sixth Andy Warhol," who narrates the tale, and the resurrected Gargunza is engaging: Andek is entranced by Gargunza's celebrity and oblivious to his true nature; he craves the doctor's attention like a child, and seeks a deeper relationship he can neither articulate nor express for fear of rejection—which comes, inevitably, when Gargunza's escape attempt is foiled by the alien Mors, overseer of this odd experiment in human reproduction. Responding to Gaiman's impeccable, at times uncanny, script, this chapter yielded Buckingham's most imaginative artwork of the series; he emulates Warhol imagery while forging his own distinctive fusion of sequential panels and inventive rendering techniques (much of it drawn with colored pencil on blackboard). Gaiman said of this chapter, "The Warhol one is one of the best stories I've done. . . . The whole Warhol story is pretty damn obviously the story of Persephone. I even made a point of sticking the pomegranate into it."[5]

"WINTER'S TALE"

This is a science fiction meditation on parents and children and extended families told by Rachel, who is a rather frumpy, unhappy screenwriter living with her partner, Jack, and his son, Glen. The occasion is the eve of Wintersday, the world's celebration of Miracleman's child Winter's tenth birthday, which brings Rachel's child, Mist, to their home to visit. Mist, however, isn't a normal little girl—she is a "superchild," born via artificial insemination with Miracleman's sperm, and she is spending the night en route to Winter's party the next day. "Where's the party?" Rachel asks. "Paraguay," Mist replies matter-of-factly, "to begin with, but after that it's going to move around a bit."

The powers and intelligence the parahuman Mist manifests with ease makes for a rather awkward evening, capped with her casual mention to Rachel that Jack is planning on leaving her for another woman, and taking Glen with him. That, coupled with the obvious distance Rachel feels from her own child—who is, in so many ways, not a child, since she is capable of so much more than any mortal adult—and her dream of traveling away with Mist, make this parable particularly poignant.

"Winter's Tale" is as remarkable a chapter as "Notes from the Underground." It effectively pinpoints the dynamic between the characters of various common Achilles' heels in such extended families. Rachel's plight is unique, but her disappointment that parenting fails to be the "fix-all" balm she'd hoped for ("There's a cold place inside me, and I thought a child would melt it.") is an all-too-universal situation for many adults. Further, the superhuman Mist also provides a potent metaphor for both the latent capabilities of succeeding generations to be capable of so much more than the prior ("They know more than we do. They've traveled further. They've seen so much more than we have.") and the chasm parents feel when confronted with their children's ease with technologies and cultural shifts unfathomable to the older generation.

The chapter also features what arguably is Gaiman's first children's book: the delightful fourteen-page *Winter's Tale,* showcased within the adult *Miracleman* chapter "Winter's Tale." The story emulates the tenor, rhythm, and format of a true children's book almost perfectly, and tells a completely original story. Admittedly, the juxtaposition of short comics sequences within *that* book—as Rachel's reading of the children's book is interrupted by both Glen and Mist's comments—makes the faux children's book inseparable from its context. Arguably, the lovingly orchestrated elements of the *Miracleman* mythos (Winter, the Warpsmiths Aza Chorn and Kana Blur, the aliens Qys, etc.) function quite nicely apart from the whole.

"SPY STORY"

This tale is set in an artificial city inhabited only by spies. Its narrative charts the tentative "moment of clarity" that opens the door for its protagonist's awakening and re-entry into mainstream society, free of her addiction to subterfuge and espionage (and all that that worldview entails). Evelyn Cream, the sapphire-toothed assassin Alan Moore introduced in the first *Warrior* chapters of Marvelman/Miracleman, makes a critical cameo appearance. Of this chapter, Gaiman says, "I just love the idea of the rehabilitation of spies. It was trying to do *The Prisoner* [Patrick McGoohan's famous 1968 cult British TV series] upside-down but instead of looking at all these spies taken off to this village and imprisoned, it's much more like all these spies have been taken off to this village where they are just playing this giant game of spies. And there is the possibility of rehabilitation, if they abandoned the game when they understand the game; they come out and join everything else".[6]

Discerning readers will also notice parallels to one of Gaiman's favorite novels, G. K. Chesterton's 1908 classic of paranoia, *The Man Who Was Thursday: A Nightmare.*

"CARNIVAL"

The concluding chapter of *The Golden Age* is an Altmanesque multicharacter summary of all Gaiman's themes and observations on how "the Golden Age was not so golden. . . . The only thing that gave it magic and meaning was humanity and what humanity meant."[7] This tapestry features many of the key characters from the previous chapters arriving in London for the events Rachel described in the opening two pages of "Winter's Tale": London's Day, August 17, initiating the five-day mourning of "those taken by the Adversary," culminating in celebratory carnival on the sixth day. "I knew from the start that I was going to end it in a huge party," Gaiman recalls, "with fireworks and everybody going up in the sky in balloons, which seemed to be the most glorious way that anybody could end any story."[8]

Missing from the trade paperback collected edition of *Miracleman: Book Four: The Golden Age* is the enigmatic coda to each single comic book issue, "Retrieval" 1 through 6—short, textless, two-page glimpses of a mysterious process involving cellular growth, artificial gestation of fetal life, and ravaged bodies preserved from the London apocalypse and manipulated by Miracleman with alien technology—that set up events in the Silver Age. In the end, it is revealed that the process has used genetic material from the deceased Dicky Dauntless/Young Miracleman to create a new body for his mind to occupy. Presumably, this would have been included in the planned *Book Five, Miracleman: The Silver Age* collected edition.

MIRACLEMAN: APOCRYPHA (1991—92)

Eager to exploit the ongoing success of the series (reportedly the best-selling series in Eclipse's lineup), and increasingly frustrated by its continuing scheduling difficulties, Eclipse decided to publish a three-issue miniseries entitled *Miracleman: Apochrypha* (1991–92) after the conclusion of *The Golden Age,* hoping these could be packaged and published comparatively quickly, because they featured multiple artistic teams.

Framed by terse but evocative sequences by Gaiman and Buckingham that placed *Apocrypha* within the chronological cap between *The Golden Age* and *The Silver Age* arcs, the three issues featured stories by other writers and artists. The *Apocrypha* stories were: "Miracleman & The Magic Monsters," by Steve Moore and Stan Woch; "The Scrapbook," by Sarah Byam and Norm Breyfogle; "Limbo," by Matt Wagner; "Prodigal," by Kurt Busiek and Christopher Schenck; "Stray Thoughts," by Stefan Petrucha and Broderick Macaraeg; "The Janitor," by Dick Foreman, Alan Smith, and Peter Williamson; and the Bradburyesque "Wishing on a Star," by Steve Moore and Alex Ross.

There were also two tales involving Johnny Bates/Kid Miracleman's backstory—the horrific "The Rascal Prince," by James Robinson and Kelley Jones, and the somber "A Bright and Sunny Day," by Fred Schiller and Val Mayerick, which pinpoints the beginning of Bates's disenchantment with and animosity toward Miracleman—as well as the Bates religious cult narrative "Gospel," by Steven Grant and Darick Robertson.

These are presented as stories from various comic books created and published within the world of Miracleman, which Miracleman himself reads to reflect upon how mankind sees and fantasizes about their ruler and his kind. Gaiman cleverly contextualizes these self-contained stories as fictions, freeing himself and the series from any continuity gaffes, restraints, or detours they might otherwise create. Also, by presenting them as artifacts of the post–*Miracleman: Olympus* new world, but relics of a period predating the era of *Miracleman: The Golden Age,* Gaiman's framing device allows these metafictions to further delineate aspects of the Golden Age.

Gaiman and Buckingham's framing pages also evocatively dramatized Miracleman and Miraclewoman's sexual and emotional relationship, providing a much needed snapshot of their inner lives after two years of *The Golden Age*'s calculated distance from these characters.

MIRACLEMAN: BOOK FIVE: THE SILVER AGE AND BEYOND (1992)

Miracleman: Book Five: The Silver Age began with *Miracleman* issue 23 (June 1992). Jumping further into the future, Gaiman turned his narrative's focus to the Miracleman family, specifically the revival of Dicky Dauntless, aka Young Miracleman. Overtly building upon hints Alan Moore had dropped during his tenure on the series, issue 24's "When Titans Clash!" highlighted Young Miracleman's ongoing difficulties awakening in and adjusting to the new, utopian world—literally, a world apart from the lad's 1950s sensibilities. The process is traumatizing, due in part to his screening of the Stanley Kubrick film *Veneer,* which Gaiman first referred to in "Screaming," and through which Young Miracleman sees the horrors of Bates/Kid Miracleman's devastation of London.

Dicky's confusion over Bates/Kid Miracleman's transformation, and Miracleman and Miraclewoman's worry that Dicky himself might similarly change, are only parts of the problem. There's also the matter of Young Miracleman's apparent homosexuality, and his long-standing devotion and attraction to Miracleman. Miraclewoman encourages Miracleman to help Dicky confront his sexual orientation via open acceptance and expression of mutual love, but this backfires: When the patriarchal Miracleman kisses Dicky on the lips, Young Miracleman reacts violently and flees. The series ended on this cliffhanger, leaving readers dangling.

This adventurous confrontation with gay sexuality was still daring in nonunderground, mainstream comics venues in 1992, and predated Gaiman's exploration of gay characters in *Sandman* and other works. The issue provoked much controversy, already fanned by fan ambivalence and/or animosity toward *The Golden Age*. As to the issue of whether Dicky is (was) indeed gay or not, Gaiman today says, "Well, it's interesting. The only authority we have for Young Miracleman's sexuality is Miraclewoman. In the only solo Young Miracleman story of Alan's, we see Young Miracleman with a major crush on a girl, getting her jewels which melt."[9]

Far more upsetting to fans, though, was the inadvertent termination of the series; speculation raged in the fan press. Gaiman's script for issue 25 was completed, and Buckingham and inker D'Israeli had finished and delivered the artwork; as Buckingham told interviewer George Khoury, "certainly #25 was done and waiting for something to happen with it. Then Eclipse folded."[10] Eclipse Comic's final publication was its spring 1993 catalogue, which featured a complete bibliography of its publications; the company ceased operations in 1994 and declared bankruptcy. Before the bankruptcy auction, Eclipse editor-in-chief and partner Cat Yronwode, to her credit, returned the original art for *Miracleman* issue 25 to Gaiman and Buckingham.

What was in *Miracleman* issue 25? In *Kimota!* Gaiman told interviewer George Khoury: "[T]he next thing that happened was we get Young Miracleman waking up in human form as Dick[y] Dauntless on the side of a mountain. . . . He's sort of trekking through the Himalayas with a friend that he makes, and the old man that he meets in a cave. Basically . . . *The Silver Age* was very consciously designed as one of these 'Heroes with a Thousand Faces' kind of stories. . . . [T]hey all have the same pattern in which the young prince leaves his kingdom, learns things and evidently returns. So that would have been the overall shape of *The Silver Age*."[11] Issue 25 was also to have featured the return of Johnny Bates/Kid Miracleman as "a sort of seeping psychic presence from the underworld. . . . [I]n *The Dark Age*, I would have him back."[12] Pages from the issue were published in *Kimota!*[13] In the subsequent arc *The Dark Age*, Gaiman tells us, "the world would have started off bad, and got badder quickly."[14]

Unfortunately, no other publisher could take up publication of the issue, nor resume any publication of *Miracleman* in any form. After Eclipse declared bankruptcy, and especially after the auction of their material assets in 1996, the whole of *Miracleman* became entangled in a massive copyright dispute that essentially froze the property to the present day.

The only uncontested fact about what followed is that in 1996 former *Spider-Man* and *Hulk* artist, *Spawn* creator, Image Comics cofounder, and Todd McFarlane Productions proprietor Todd McFarlane purchased Eclipse's material assets in a bankruptcy auction. What McFarlane paid, and what he actually acquired and owns, is still questionable. Some sources report McFarlane paid $25,000 to $40,000 (see wikipedia.org/wiki/Miracleman), but Gaiman recalls that "the bankruptcy judge didn't want to be bothered with chopping up properties into bits and on the bankruptcy [auction] day, McFarlane simply offered $50,000 for the lot. . . . So, that's how he got Eclipse."[15]

Whatever the sum actually paid, McFarlane's involvement and actions since the auction, and subsequent legal claims and assertions of those claims via the publication and manufacture of Miracleman-related works (see Trivia following), has immeasurably complicated an already convoluted chain of ownership.

For readers seeking more information, the only book on the subject remains *Kimota! The Miracleman Companion* by George Khoury,[16] which we have already cited herein. However, Khoury's admittedly comprehensive book should not and cannot stand as the definitive—much less final—word on the subject, given its own confused account of the alleged ownership of the property and division of that ownership. After the publication of *Kimota!* Marvelman/Miracleman artist Alan Davis publicly clarified his own views of the ownership of the character and the work he had collaborated on. In a November 5, 2001, open letter to the online *CBR News: The Comic Wire,* Davis asserted that Khoury's account of the Marvelman/Miracleman title and character ownership issues were inaccurate. Davis also wrote, "I do want to make it clear that I still own the rights to the *Marvelman* pages I drew . . . I did not give or sell anything to Eclipse."[17]

Given the number of artists who worked on Marvelman/Miracleman from 1982 to 1992, the issue of ownership on that collaborative body of work alone is hardly a simple matter. But, added to that, Maurice "Mick" Anglo still claims some form of ownership, having created the character Marvelman in 1954; *Warrior* publisher Dez Skinn claims to have published Marvelman in *Warrior* with permission, and claims partial ownership of the character and property; the now-defunct American publisher of the series, Eclipse Comics, had legal claim to the Miracleman trademark, and claimed a partial ownership of the entire property; Alan Moore passed on his respective share of the ownership of the work and property to Gaiman; the respective creators of the *Warrior* and Eclipse-published Marvelman/Miracleman series, including Gaiman, have a legitimate claim to owning copyright to their portion of the collaborative body of work; and, as of 1996, McFarlane—who never had any prior creative or business involvement with Miracleman, in any form—claims to now own Eclipse's partial rights to the property, though whatever those may have been or may be has never been documented or disclosed in any public venue.

This has, in the public arena, come down to an ongoing ethical and legal battle between Gaiman and McFarlane that came to a head in 2001–2002.

The character of Michael Moran appeared in the *Spawn* spin-off title *Hellspawn* in 2001, beginning with issue issue 6. Moran's appearance as a supporting character (a reporter) was to culminate in the reintroduction of Miracleman himself in *Hellspawn* issue 13; the Ashley Wood *Miracleman* cover was painted and the issue was promoted for distribution. By that time, *Hellspawn* issue 15 was already being solicited in distributor catalogues, promising a resolution to the story arc, beginning with issue 13. But before *Hellspawn* issue 13 was released, Gaiman's objections, and the filing of the Marvels and Miracles LLC lawsuit against McFarlane, resulted in the pulling of the planned reintroduction of Miracleman, and another cover and story line supplanted issue 13's contents, as were the contents of the subsequent issues.

McFarlane also began to produce Miracleman-related products through his comics and toy companies beginning in 2000, including lithograph posters, statues, and action figures, all claiming (apparently total) copyright and trademark to Miracleman for Todd McFarlane Productions, Inc.

Gaiman responded with a statue he sanctioned from Bowen Designs Studio in 2003. This was, as advertised, designed "by Neil Gaiman" and sculpted by famed limited-editions figure sculptor Randy Bowen; the painted statue stands thirteen inches tall overall, and was limited to one thousand pieces. At the time of the release Gaiman publicly commented, " "What we've actually done is, Marvels and Miracles [LLC] has licensed *Miracleman* to Randy Bowen on the basis that I really like Randy's stuff—he did all the nicest Sandman statues—so he's going to be doing a Miracleman statue. Mainly just to go, 'No no no, Miracleman doesn't look like that. He doesn't clench!' The Todd one is terribly clenched."[18]

The conflict over Miracleman ownership between Gaiman and McFarlane, was not resolved in the final legal verdict in the October 2002 *Gaiman vs. McFarlane* trial (see more information on this trial in the section on Spawn and Angela), or by the critical decisions following that verdict that could have resolved the matter.

Following the verdict in Gaiman's favor concerning the damages portion of the trial, ICV2.com reported:

Gaiman decided to keep his copyright interest in characters he created for Todd McFarlane's *Spawn* comic—Medieval Spawn, and Cagliostro—rather than seeking breach of contract damages from McFarlane. . . . Under the option Gaiman chose, the rights for *Miracleman* that McFarlane purchased from Eclipse remain in McFarlane's hands. . . . What will Gaiman ask for in a deal? He's still likely to ask for the rights to *Miracleman* as part of any settlement. He's made it clear that he wants to acquire unencumbered rights to the property, reprint the old issues, and create new materials (see "Marvel Snags Neil Gaiman"). Gaiman created Marvels and Miracles LLC, one of the plaintiffs in the suit, to own and manage the rights to *Miracleman,* and has promised that after creators are compensated, proceeds will go to benefit two favorite industry charities—the Comic Book Legal Defense Fund and ACTOR. It seems unlikely that he would not pursue that goal now.[19]

However, since 2002, Todd McFarlane Productions has further complicated matters, not only with the products noted above, but also with subsequent publications. A character derivative of Miracleman, named "Man of Miracles," appeared in *Spawn* issue 150 (October 2005). In 2006, McFarlane Toys' *Spawn: Evolutions* line of action figures offered a Man of Miracles action figure, a slightly redesigned variation on the Miracleman character sporting the distinctive "MM" logo. The packaging read "Copyright 2006 TMP (Todd McFarlane Productions) International."

Through Marvels and Miracles LLC, Gaiman continues to work to resolve the convoluted Marvelman/Miracleman legal issues. "M&M LLC is basically just me and Bucky [Mark Buckingham] and exists to try and untangle the MM copyright/rights situation and, if possible, get the material from *Miracleman*s 1–24 back into print, with royalties being paid to the creators," Gaiman explains. "Dunno if this is ever going to happen now, but that was the goal."[20]

According to Gaiman, "Actually, it looks as if the rights to Marvelman were held by Mick Anglo all that time—it was always copyrighted to him, not to Len Miller, and Dez admits he had no rights in Marvelman and did nothing to obtain them. Mick Anglo was legally pursuing Eclipse all the years I was writing it, although they never mentioned this to me. . . . [T]hey were working out a deal with him that then died when Eclipse died."[21]

In 2007, Anglo's Marvelman/Miracleman rights were sold to Emotiv & Company. As of this writing, there is no resolution. An Emotiv & Company representative simply stated, "[T]his is an ongoing situation that will probably still take years to fix."[22] Gaiman notes, "I know they bought the rights to Marvelman from Mick Anglo for four thousand pounds, and have been working hard to establish his ownership of the property. . . . I've chatted to the guys who bought the MM rights . . . and wish them well."[23]

As to whether any portion of the *Warrior* and Eclipse *Marvelman/Miracleman* body of work will ever see print again, Gaiman says, "I don't know whether the existing stuff will get reprinted, honestly. It depends on the Mick Anglo people."[24] Asked whether Marvel Comics's recent involvement may play a role, Gaiman says only, "It remains to be seen."[25]

At the time of this writing, this matter—and the hope of reprinting, and perhaps completing, Gaiman's portion of the series—remains in limbo.

TRIVIA

- Gaiman is a lifetime fan of Lou Reed, who was part of the 1960s New York City band Velvet Underground and the original Warhol studio scene, and Gaiman's script for *The Golden Age*'s "Notes from the Underground" struck a nerve for Reed. "I had dinner with Lou Reed once in New York," Gaiman told interviewer George Khoury, "and he was complaining that I had ripped him off for the Warhol episode; that I had ripped off *Songs of Drella* [the concept album by Reed and John Cale, 1990]. I said that I never stole a word that I know of but I had that CD playing all the time and the whiny, slightly bitchy tone of it brought Warhol to life for me in a way that the Victor Bockris biography never did [*The Life and Death of Andy Warhol* by Victor Bockris, 1989][26]. . . . Listening to *Songs of Drella,* I said, 'Okay, I know what his voice sounds like.' "[27]

- In the final issue of *Miracleman* to see print to date—issue 24, dated August 1993—editor Andy Willett announced another forthcoming spin-off title, *Miracleman Triumphant!,* to be scripted by frequent Eclipse freelance writer Fred Burke "with plot input by Neil Gaiman," though Gaiman denied any involvement when interviewed by George Khoury[28] According to Willett, *Miracleman Triumphant!* was intended to "fill in the ten-year lacuna between the Golden and Silver Ages" in Gaiman's run. "Having read the script," editor Willett concluded, "I can safely say that this is going to be a doozy." The series was never published in any form, though the first issue was reportedly completed and turned in to Eclipse, with art by Mike Deodato, Jr.

- Though the partnership of Marvel Comics, Gaiman, and Gaiman's company Marvels and Miracles, LLC, was unprecedented, this wasn't the first crossover between Marvel Comics and the character Marvelman/Miracleman. Marvel Comics and the Alan Moore Miracleman crossed paths in print once: In the British Marvel UK tabloid *Daredevils* issue 7 (1981), the Alan Moore (script) and Alan Davis (art) series *Captain Britain* featured a page in which Marvelman is named and—apparently—shot to death! When this Captain Britain story arc (from *Daredevils* issues 6–8) was eventually reprinted in America by Marvel Comics in *X-Men Archives Featuring Captain Britain* issue 4 (October 1995), the page was reprinted in color, with Marvelman (now "Miracleman") and his "death" intact.

THE QUOTABLE GAIMAN

Apocrypha was one of those things where there were a lot of people who wanted to do Miracleman stories and I loved the idea of just doing a book of imaginary stories and you got some great writers; you got Kurt Busiek and so forth. . . .

The idea of [Book Six, Miracleman:] The Dark Age is that it would have been set another 300 or 400 years on, maybe even as much as a thousand years on, and a lot of things changed. The children have gone. All the Miraclechildren grew up one day and left. You would have somebody who was claiming to be Mike Moran, who may or may not be, who has turned up a thousand years later. And then things get from bad to worse when [Johnny] Bates comes in. It's strange; I know generally how The Dark Age would have gone exactly, how the very last episode would go. . . . I knew the point I was heading to from the very, very beginning, which was going to be the very final episode called "Two Voices." And it's two people having a conversation on a fairly ruined planet while they wait for the last sun to come up. . . .

At one point in time, we settled the dispute, Todd and I. And one part of the dispute was he agreeing to give me the rest of the rights to Miracleman, so I would have owned Miracleman completely with Mark Buckingham. Todd sent me some of the film for Miracleman and what they had in their files, which wasn't very much, but that was that. And when I asked him for some more documentation, I never heard anything more. . . . [G]iven the time span of creating Miracleman, it would be very nice if I could finish that story before I die.[29]

|||||||||||||||||||||||||||||||||||||||||||||||||||||||||||||||||||||||||||

A CONVERSATION WITH MARK
BUCKINGHAM

JANUARY 9TH, 2008

Question: I wonder if you'd be willing to comment about your experience working with Neil? If you are willing, and could touch on how it came about, your best memory of it, your thoughts about Neil as a creator, and any amusing anecdote, we'd be in your debt.

Q: How did you first come to work with Neil?
MARK BUCKINGHAM: I think I first became aware of Neil in 1986. He was writing for a new British anthology title called Borderline. Dave McKean was drawing

a couple of strips in it . . . and my friend Matt [D'Israeli, the artist] was drawing a strip, too. I went along to the panel which launched the project in September '86 at the UK Comic Art Convention. I got my hands on a photocopy
dummy for number 1. Hoping to follow Matt's example, I took along art samples and a project proposal of my own. I had a very encouraging chat with both
Dave McKean and Leigh Balsch. Neil was around, too, but we never got to
speak. I went away filled with enthusiasm and set to work on developing my
strip. Unfortunately the *Borderline* project was canceled before anything saw
print.

A few months later I started attending meetings of the SSI [Society for Strip
Illustration]. Once again it was Matt who had got there first and encouraged me to
come along. They used to meet once a month at the Sketch Club in Chelsea, London. I joined as an associate member (I hadn't been published yet) in January
1987. Neil Gaiman and Dave McKean also joined as associates at the same meeting. I was pretty shy at first . . . but I did hang around with both of them a lot at
meetings, and was really inspired by the work they were doing together on *Violent
Cases,* and the work for DC that started to develop.

That summer, having finally got myself in print through charity comic *Strip
Aids* (and a little penciling for Harrier Comics), I landed a job drawing strips and
illustrations for a new humor magazine called *The Truth.* By happy accident, most
of the articles I illustrated were written by Kim Newman, Eugene Byrne, and. . . .
Neil Gaiman. Although the work didn't require me to talk much with the writers,
it did give me an extra excuse to chat more with Neil at the monthly SSI meetings,
which really helped our friendship to grow.

At the time I had come to the conclusion that I wasn't cut out for action adventure strips and was focusing my attention on a more cartoony style. However, with
encouragement from Don and Lionel [editors of *Strip Aids*] I took another crack at
a more realistic superhero/action style for their new project *Heartbreak Hotel.* I
wrote and drew a four-page strip called the *Wild Side of Life.* I took a copy of it
along to the SSI Christmas party. Whilst I sat at the bar sharing a drink with Neil
I showed him the finished artwork. I was really pleased when he told me how
much he liked it. What really surprised me, though, was what he said next. He
told me that he could write far more than Dave had time to draw. He said that
Alan Moore was going to hand over the writing of Miracleman to him, and that
he needed an artist. What I just shown him would be perfect, and would I like to
draw it. I said yes. I couldn't quite believe it . . . and Neil reminds me that I kept
saying that I'd understand if he found a real artist to draw it. That was the moment my comic career truly began.

Q: An auspicious beginning.

MB: Neil went to extraordinary lengths to help me build my career in those first
few months. He spoke to me about *Sandman* that night as well. A few weeks later

he met with Karen Berger and showed her some samples of my work. She didn't think I was quite ready as a penciler . . . but maybe as an inker?

Two months later, with that in mind, Neil arranged a meeting between myself and Richard Piers Rayner at a meeting of the SSI. Neil was keen to help me get more experience, so I'd be ready for Miracleman when the time came. Richard had just been hired to draw *Hellblazer,* but he hadn't penciled any of it yet. He sent me some assorted art photostats from his self-published project. I inked a few in a hurry and mailed them to Karen. She wasn't impressed and looked elsewhere for an inker.

I was devastated and went to the next SSI meeting convinced my career would never get off the ground. Neil and Dave McKean were incredibly supportive and encouraged me not to give in. Neil said, "Do another set of samples . . . take your time . . . razzle-dazzle them!" I got back in touch with Richard who, by that point, had penciled the first five or six pages of Hellblazer number 10. I only inked a page and a half . . . but I really took my time over them, pouring all my effort into the cleanest and slickest brushwork I could manage. Then I sent them to Karen . . . and showed copies to Neil and Dave.

A few days later I was back at my parents' home for the Easter holidays, April 1988, when the phone rang. It was Karen Berger. She said, "You have some very influential friends." Earlier that day both Neil and Dave had rung her to rave about my inks and suggest she give me the job. I wouldn't have been given the chance without their help.

I'd only inked three issues when Neil landed me my first full art job for DC, pencils and inks for his "Pavane" story, the secret origin of Poison Ivy. Strongly influenced by having inked Richard for three months, I used a photo-realistic style, which worked to my advantage a few months later, when Richard left *Hellblazer* and I was able to convince Karen I could continue the story in a comparable style.

Neil's help had astonishing results. In the space of twelve months he had helped me establish a career in American comics as both a penciler and inker. When *Miracleman* finally got under way in the summer of 1989, he had made sure I'd be ready for it.

Q: *What are the things that strike you about Neil as a creator, and a collaborator?*

MB: Working with Neil, right from the very first moment, has always been a pleasure. He's an incredibly humble and giving person. Sometimes you think he must have just been put on this planet just to help people, and the whole being an exceptionally talented writer thing came as an unexpected bonus. He's been there for me throughout my whole career. When not working directly together he has always been keeping a lookout for me . . . cheering me on when things are going well and helping me pick myself back up again when things go awry. I feel blessed to have him as one of my best friends.

One of my fondest memories of working with Neil is when we first sat down together to plan our three story arcs for *Miracleman*. I went to stay with him and his family for a few days, back when Neil still lived in England, armed with sketch pad and pens. But it wasn't to be a weekend of frantic brainstorming and sketching . . . as soon became apparent as we settled down in front of the TV with a big glass of Drambuie each and old episodes of *The Addams Family* playing in the background. Or going for a long walk in the surrounding woodland. Or driving around with a demo tape from a new talent called Tori Amos playing on the car stereo. And we just talked . . . and talked . . . and without really trying . . . the whole story took shape.

I think that's the secret of success with Neil's closest collaborators. Especially for those of us like Dave McKean and myself who entered into comics with him. Getting to know and understand each other. Building the friendship was as important as the work. We know what makes each other tick. That level of understanding makes the basics of working with Neil effortless. Which then allows Neil to test you and stretch you as a collaborator, based on a high level of understanding of each other's strengths and weaknesses. It also means that we have a high level of trust in each other . . . to the extent that for some of us (again, like Dave and myself) Neil only needs to provide dialogue for the comics we work on together. Stage directions and structure come much more from discussion and intuitive knowledge. It works perfectly.

Q: Miracleman was a watershed moment for you.
MB: Working with Neil on *Miracleman* remains the most precious period in my career. It was like a public sketchbook. With each story Neil would take delight in seeing how far he could stretch me in terms of style and story technique. I took equal pleasure in pushing the art to extremes and encouraging Neil to challenge and surprise me.

Of course . . . even Neil is capable of getting me into trouble sometimes. Like being chased down a street by bottle-smashing tramps screaming, "Give us the camera!" We were working on the original comic strip version of *Feeders and Eaters*, and Neil thought it would be a good idea to go get some seedy London street photo ref . . . until the locals started getting upset.

Q: You got married a couple of years ago, and we understand Neil had a part to play.
MB: Irma and I got married in 2006, and Neil was the best man. The only problem with Neil these days is that he is so in demand from the worlds of comics, books, and film that it can be a little tricky getting to see him. We actually booked Neil before we arranged the rest of the wedding!

I have a videotape of Neil dancing. I'm reliably informed Neil never dances. It's my secret weapon to use against him if he ever turns evil.

THE CHILDREN'S CRUSADE

(1993)

The Children's Crusade was a two-issue Vertigo miniseries that bookended five crossover stories appearing in various Vertigo annuals. It marked the first attempt by the then newly created comic line to do a crossover within its titles. The crossover ran through the titles *Animal Man, Swamp Thing, Doom Patrol, Black Orchid,* and *Arcana/The Books of Magic,* and featured the children who played major roles in these books (Maxine Baker, Tefe Holland, Dorothy Spinner, Suzy, and Timothy Hunter, respectively).

The story is meant to be read in the following order: *The Children's Crusade 1, Black Orchid Annual 1, Animal Man Annual 1, Swamp Thing Annual 7, Doom Patrol Annual 2, Arcana/Books of Magic Annual 1,* and *The Children's Crusade 2.* We will focus mainly on the events that take place in The Children's Crusade issues 1 and 2, as those segments were the only ones written mainly by Gaiman (sections of the second issue were written by Alisa Kwitney and Jamie Delano). Issue 1 was illustrated by Chris Bachalo, and issue 2 by Peter Snieberg.

Historians are not sure whether the story of the Children's Crusade is true. The standard version of events is that in 1212 or 1213, a boy began preaching in either France or Germany, claiming that he had been told by Jesus to lead a crusade to convert Muslims to Christianity. Through a series of supposed portents and miracles, he garnered a considerable following of children, numbering in the tens of thousands. He led his young followers southward toward the Mediterranean Sea, believing that it would part when he arrived so that he and his followers could march to Jerusalem, but this did not occur. Two merchants gave passage on seven boats to as many of the children as could fit. The children were either taken to Tunisia and sold into slavery, or died in a shipwreck. Some accounts have them dying or giving up from starvation and exhaustion even before they reached the sea.

Gaiman references these events, but morphs them a bit, substituting a strange monk/priest for the charismatic young man. In Gaiman's version, the monk also appears to have inspired the stories of the Pied Piper of Hamlin.

The events of the modern-day story begin when the children of Flaxdown, England, mysteriously disappear. A young girl named Avril Mitchell hires two young detectives, Edwin Paine and Charles Rowland (the ghost boys previously seen in issue 25 of *The Sandman* and later in their own miniseries, *The Dead Boy Detectives*) to locate her brother Oliver, who, along with dozens of other children, disappeared from the small village. As the story continues through the crossover issues, key

Neil Gaiman, Stephen Jones, and Dennis Etchison at the 1993 World Fantasy Convention. Photo courtesy of Stephen Jones, from his collection.

child characters of the Vertigo books are recruited to "Free Country" to help aid in the rescue of the children of the "Bad World."

The comics include many references to the works of Robert Browning. One occurs in Chapter 5 of issue 1, when Gaiman departs from the main story for a moment to talk about Browning's poem "The Pied Piper of Hamlin." The chapter, titled "The Piper and the Gate," begins:

> "Hamlin Town's in Brunswick, by famous Hanover City." That was how Robert Browning began his poem The Pied Piper of Hamlin. The tale of the Piper was an old story, based on events that happened on the 26th of June, 1284. Afterward the town dated its published documents from the event. Browning embroidered, redated, and retold the story in rhyming couplets, written to cheer a sick child.

Gaiman adds a coda to that story, as he tells of a child who approached Browning and, for a coin, tells him a tale of how the Pied Piper came to the town of St. Cecile, in the Italian Alps. In this story, as in Browning's, the piper rids the town of rats, but the town refuses to pay, and so the piper plays his song and leads the children from their beds and into the mountains, where they disappear forever.

Later in the story Charles Rowland visits a dark tower in a dream, where he glimpses the visages of the five children who are destined to play a role in the story that's unfurling. The chapter in which this occurs is titled "Charles Rowland To The Dark Tower Came," an obvious play on the title of Browning's poem, "Childe Roland to the Dark Tower Came," a work also utilized by Stephen King as inspiration for his Gunslinger books.

PEOPLE, PLACES, AND THINGS

CHARLES ROWLAND AND EDWIN PAINE. Having set out into the world to find adventure, the two ghosts have set up shop as private detectives, something they think would be right up their alley based on their extensive knowledge of mystery novels and films. The boys are visited in their offices (122B Butcher's Street, echoing Sherlock Holmes's address of 221B Baker Street) by Avril Mitchell, a young girl who finds their flyer ("Private Detectives. Rowland and Paine. No case too small. Masters of Disguise"). After questioning their credentials, she enlists them to search for her younger brother, Oliver, who, along with all the other children of Flaxdown, has gone missing.

The boys learn that the children have been spirited away to Free Country; a mystical haven for abused children, it's currently being used for more sinister purposes. After gaining access to Free Country by playing a game of hopscotch and chanting a spell, the detectives find Oliver in the company of Suzy/Black Orchid and Tim Hunter. Summoned to the council's presence by Maxine Baker, the children face off against the council.

Charles, possessed by an envoy of the Dark Tower, sets things to rights, allowing Free Country to return to normal. The envoy also reveals that Jack Rabbit, instrumental in bringing about the crisis in Free Country, is actually the evil monk.

Having saved the day without really knowing how they did it, the boys return to Earth to await their next case.

FREE COUNTRY. Free Country is a place where children never grow old, and are free from the abuse and tyranny of the adults in the Bad World (i.e., our world). It is a place that has obviously inspired stories about many magical places, like Wonderland and Neverland.

Free Country's first citizens were twelve survivors of the Children's Crusade, who ritually sacrificed one of their own to obtain passage there (the rite involves a pattern, drawn in blood, that certainly inspired the game of hopscotch). These pioneers, known as the Crusaders, have made it their mission to create thresholds, or gates, wherever and whenever they're needed to facilitate the rescue of abused children.

Free Country is run by a council of children who have lived there for hundreds of years. Under the advice of Jack Rabbit, the council is attempting to bring all the children in our world to Free Country. Unfortunately, the magical land is having trouble supporting them all. To help bolster Free Country's power, the council seeks the assistance of five innately powerful Earth children. As long as they remain in Free Country, the land can sustain all the children they have brought there.

Jack Rabbit, however, has not told them the real reason he wants Earth's children to be brought to Free Country. Their trusted adviser is actually an evil cleric in disguise; this monk has been selling children for profit for millennia, and wants to use Free Country as a staging ground for his activities.

THE COUNCIL. The governing body of Free Country, it consists of Daniel, Kerwyn, Joan, Wat (the subject of the wishing poem that begins "What comes out of the chimney?"), Aiken Drum (out of Scottish folklore), Mary/Peter/Puck (who obviously inspired the legend of Peter Pan), and Junkin Buckley (an ally of the monk). It is they who implement the grand plan of bringing all of Earth's children to their haven; they do not realize, however, that they are being manipulated by the monk, in the guise of Jack Rabbit.

JACKALARUM, AKA JACK RABBIT. As adviser to the Council, he convinces them to pursue a plan to bring all Earth's children to Free Country. Because Free Country cannot sustain such a huge population, he is forced to seek alternate power sources, in the form of five powerful Earth children. Jack Rabbit is really the monk in disguise.

MAXINE BAKER, TEFE HOLLAND, DOROTHY SPINNER, SUZY/BLACK ORCHID, AND TIMOTHY HUNTER. The five Earth children from whom the Council seeks assistance. Maxine is the daughter of Buddy Baker, aka Animal Man; Tefe is the daughter of the Swamp Thing; Dorothy is a member of the Doom Patrol; Suzy is a young incarnation of the Black Orchid; and Timothy Hunter (of *Books of Magic* fame) is said to be the world's most powerful magician.

THE MONK. The despicable monk has been involved in the slave trade for millennia, kidnapping children and selling them for profit. After his disguise has been penetrated, members of the council comment that they have seen him only infrequently in the Bad World (their term for Earth, where they were victims of child abuse). One says he was a monk, another comments that he was a piper, and a third says, "He ran a carnival." (A reference, perhaps, to Mr. Dark of Ray Bradbury's *Something Wicked This Way Comes*?).

The monk had hoped to use Free Country as a holding pen of sorts for children he would sell to the highest bidder. Disguised as Jack Rabbit, he attempted to trick the council into unwittingly implementing his scheme. His plans were thwarted by an emissary of the Dark Tower. After his disguise was penetrated, the monk escaped from the council's chambers. His present whereabouts are unknown.

TRIVIA

- In issue 1, Gaiman does an amusing riff on the old Abbott and Costello bit "Who's On First?"

Avril: Except I think maybe that foreign kid had something to do with it.
Charles: What foreign kid?
Avril: The one up at Flaxdown manor. I never liked him.
Edwin: What was his name?
Avril: Wat.
Charles: What?
Avril: Wat.
Charles: What was his name?
Avril: Yes.
Edwin: What was?
Avril: His name.
Charles: Look, I'm sorry, but can we try this again?
Avril: He told us his name. His name was Wat. W-A-T.
Charles: Oh, I see.

- Maxine Baker, who chooses to remain in Free Country at the end of the story, makes her home with the wild animals that inhabit the land. Her friendship with the animals, and especially with a large brown bear, is certainly intended to evoke Mowgli, of Rudyard Kipling's *The Jungle Book*.

- The Children's Crusade wasn't the last time Gaiman provided an explanation of the origins of J. M. Barrie's *Peter Pan*. In *The Eternals,* he suggests that the character Sprite, an Eternal stuck in the body of an eleven-year-old, may have inspired Barrie to write his novel.

- "Aiken Drum" is a popular Scottish folk song, which goes: "There was a man lived in the moon, lived in the moon, lived in the moon, there was a man lived in the moon and his name was Aiken Drum." Aiken Drum was a man who played his music upon a ladle, possibly the Man in the Moon, whose clothing was said to be composed of various food products.

THE QUOTABLE GAIMAN

About the origins of this comic book crossover:

There was a Vertigo retreat of a day, and someone (Alisa? [Kwitney]) came up with the suggestion that one thing that all the Vertigo titles had was children, and we could do something with that: the idea was that the story would spill through all the annuals that year. I think I was handed the short straw of starting it, mostly because Sandman wasn't going to be part of it. Mostly I just threw everything I was interested in about children's games, the work of the Opies, hopscotch, and the Pied Piper and all that into the mix.

—During an interview conducted for this volume

SPAWN #9 AND 26;
ANGELA #1–3

(1993–95)

In 1992, seven well-known artists—among them some of the top talent of the era's comic book industry—bolted from Marvel Comics to found their own company, Image Comics, dedicated to publishing comics that were owned by their creators rather than by the publisher. Image consisted of six individual studios in those days, among them Jim Lee's Wildstorm Studios (which would one day become part of DC Comics) and Todd McFarlane's eponymous Todd McFarlane Productions.

McFarlane launched his flagship series (and character), *Spawn,* with the first wave of Image titles. The series starred Al Simmons, a dead CIA agent who went to Hell, where he made a bargain with a demon named Malebolgia, so that he could return to Earth and see his wife. In exchange, Simmons became a "Hellspawn," an agent of that demon.

Shortly into the series' run, McFarlane announced an extraordinary series of upcoming guest writers—Alan Moore, Neil Gaiman, Dave Sim (creator of *Cerebus*), and Frank Miller would each write a single issue of the series, and each, according to interviews conducted at the time, would (in the spirit of Image Comics) own whatever new material they introduced.

Gaiman's issue, *Spawn* issue 9, appeared in 1993, illustrated by McFarlane. In that script, Gaiman created three new characters: a medieval-era Hellspawn who would come to be known as Medieval Spawn; the angelic warrior Angela (who killed Medieval Spawn); and a mentor/adviser figure to the modern Spawn, Count Nicholas Cogliostro. Despite the claims made at the time, the ownership of these characters would become the subject of much angst and litigation in subsequent years (see below), but for the moment, our focus is Gaiman's work.

Angela is an angel who is also a hunter of Hellspawn, such as McFarlane's title character. She made her first appearance in *Spawn* issue 9, feigning helplessness to draw the medieval version of Spawn into her trap. Dropping her disguise as a damsel in distress, she appears as her true self, a fearsome, chain-mailed warrior angel, and slaughters the surprised Hellspawn with her lance after a brief skirmish.

Cut to the modern day, where the latest Spawn, Al Simmons, is in conversation with a strange old homeless man, one Count Nicholas Cagliostro (later Cogliostro), who seems to know more about the Hellspawn than he should. Their palaver is interrupted by the appearance of Angela, some eight hundred years older than when we first saw her, but apparently retaining all the vigor and strength of her younger self. A pitched battle between Angela and Spawn ends when the angel flees the scene.

Gaiman later wrote an uncredited sequence that McFarlane incorporated into the pages of *Spawn* issue 26 in which Spawn speaks with Angela's associate Gabrielle to form a bridge to the then upcoming *Angela* miniseries, the first issue of which was dated December 1994.

In the three-issue miniseres the warrior angel is celebrating her one hundred thousandth birthday by hunting a dragon, when the hordes of Heaven descend upon the scene and place her under arrest. She's put on trial in Elysium, home of the angels, for hunting a Hellspawn without proper authorization (an untruthful version of the events of *Spawn* issue 9), leaving it up to her comrades to help her by convincing Al Simmons/Spawn to travel to Elysium to testify on her behalf. Angela eventually is cleared of the charges.

The most interesting facet of Gaiman's work on Spawn and Angela, however, will always be the legal fallout that ensued, and the entanglements that still persist to the present.

In relating this difficult and ongoing chapter in Gaiman's writing career, we will necessarily refer to existing public accounts and records of the case history—and we do mean case history. Given the 2002 trial and 2004 U.S. Court of Appeals decision on Todd McFarlane's appeal and Gaiman's cross-appeal, and the Court of Appeal Circuit judges Posner, Kanne, and Rovner's access to all relevant testimony and court documents in making and articulating their decision, we will quote extensively from that document, as it is the most comprehensive and impartial standing record of the facts in this case.

BACKGROUND

Evaluation of the defense requires us to consider a chain of events running from 1992—when the contact was made and *Spawn* No. 9, which states on its inside cover that it is copyrighted by McFarlane (actually by one of his companies, but that is immaterial), was published—to 1999."[1]

In 1992, Todd McFarlane and several other prominent, popular, and successful freelancers left Marvel Comics to form Image Comics, a publishing imprint under which the creators would own, publish, and merchandise their own creations. McFarlane launched *Spawn* in 1992, quickly establishing it as one of the comic book direct-sales market's bestselling titles and, via Todd McFarlane Productions, Inc., helming his own merchandizing of the character via action figures, statues, video games, an animated TV series, a feature film, etc.

As related in the United States Court of Appeals for the Seventh Circuit document, "The early issues in the series [*Spawn*] were criticized for bad writing, so McFarlane decided to invite four top writers each to write the script for one issue of Spawn. One of those invited was Gaiman."[2] The issues were *Spawn* issue 8 (scripted by Alan Moore), issue 9 (scripted by Gaiman), issue 10 (scripted and co-illustrated by Dave Sim), and issue 11 (scripted by Frank Miller), all published between February and June of 1993.

[Gaiman] accepted the invitation and wrote the script for *Spawn* issue No. 9. Their contract, made in 1992, was oral. There was no mention of copyright, nor, for that matter, of how Gaiman would be compensated for his work, beyond McFarlane's assuring Gaiman that he would treat him "better than the big guys" did. The reference was to two leading comic book publishers, Marvel Comics (not to be confused with Gaiman's company, Marvels and Miracles) and DC Comics, for which Gaiman and other writers write on a "work made for hire" basis. . . . This means that the publishers own the copyrights on their work. . . .

In his script for *Spawn* No. 9, Gaiman introduced three new characters—Medieval Spawn (as he was later called by McFarlane—Gaiman had not named it and in the issue he is just referred to as a Spawn, with no further identifier), Angela (no last name), and Count Nicholas Cogliostro. . . . *Spawn* No. 9 was a huge success, selling more than a million copies. McFarlane paid Gaiman $100,000 for his work on it. Gaiman testified that this was about what he would have expected to receive from DC Comics had he written the script of *Spawn* No. 9 for that company as a work made for hire. Because Angela was a big hit with *Spawn*'s readers, McFarlane asked Gaiman to do a "mini-series" of three issues starring her, which he did. He also wrote several pages for *Spawn* No. 26 to form a bridge to the *Angela* series. Because Angela hadn't appeared in *Spawn* Nos. 10 through 25, Gaiman was concerned that readers would not realize that *Angela* was an offshoot of *Spawn*. McFarlane paid Gaiman $3,300 for his contribution to *Spawn* No. 26 and more than $30,000 (the exact amount is not in the record) for the *Angela* series. Only one of these four issues (the second *Angela*) contains a copyright notice; the notice is similar to the one in *Spawn* No. 9.

The *Angela* series was first published in 1994. The following year, having created a toy company to manufacture statuettes ("action figures") of *Spawn* characters, one a statuette of Medieval Spawn, McFarlane mailed Gaiman a check for $20,000 designated as royalties, presumably on sales of the statuette, though the record is unclear.

McFarlane subsequently licensed the publication of paperback books that reprinted the comic books to which Gaiman had contributed. The books carry a copyright notice similar to the one in *Spawn* No. 9 and *Angela* No. 2 except that it adds that "all related characters" are also copyrighted by

McFarlane. Besides inserting the copyright notices that we've mentioned, McFarlane applied to the Register of Copyrights for, and received, copyright registrations on these issues and books.[3]

As noted in Gaiman's testimony during the 2002 trial, he was unaware of these published copyright notices.

At this point in the chronology, Gaiman's concerns about the increasing activity of the characters introduced in *Spawn* issue 9, with the lack of a formal signed contract between McFarlane and Gaiman, and about rumors of a possible sale of McFarlane Productions, prompted him to act. The USCA document defines this decisive turn of events as follows:

> In 1996, learning that McFarlane might sell his enterprise, Gaiman decided that he needed the protection of a written contract and he asked McFarlane for one. McFarlane agreed to give him a written contract and also to pay him royalties for a statuette of Angela that McFarlane's toy company had manufactured and sold. After desultory negotiations, Gaiman's lawyer wrote a letter to McFarlane's negotiator stating that Gaiman had created the characters of Medieval Spawn, Angela, and Cogliostro not as work for hire but "pursuant to the terms of an oral agreement under which Mr. McFarlane agreed that Mr. Gaiman would be compensated on the same terms as set forth in Mr. Gaiman's DC Comics Agreements dated August 1, 1993." . . . The letter goes on to "demand" that McFarlane "immediately forward all monies which are currently owed to Mr. Gaiman in accordance with the terms of the DC Agreement." We'll call this the demand letter.[4]

To understand what happened next, the reader must now reference the earlier chapter concerning Gaiman's collaborative work on Miracleman; McFarlane's purchase of Eclipse's assets in bankruptcy auction; and the ongoing confusion over proprietary rights to Miracleman.

> Direct negotiations between Gaiman and McFarlane ensued. A tentative agreement was reached that McFarlane would pay royalties on the statuettes on the same terms as Gaiman would have gotten from DC Comics but that Gaiman would exchange his rights in Medieval Spawn and Cogliostro for McFarlane's rights in another comic book character, Miracleman. Once the exchange was made, Gaiman would no longer receive royalties on Medieval Spawn and Cogliostro. For the rest of 1997 and 1998, McFarlane sent Gaiman royalty checks totaling about $16,000, presumably on account of the statuettes and the paperback books, together with royalty reports that referred to Gaiman as a "co-creator" of Medieval Spawn, Angela, and Cogliostro.[5]

This wording on the royalty statements would become significant during the 2002 trial, and in the 2004 rulings on the appeal and cross-appeal.

Also note the additional details offered in ICV2.com's analysis, posted after scrutiny of the lawsuit filed in January 2002.

In 1997, Larry Marder of Image started to try to clean up the paperwork by getting Gaiman to sign a written agreement governing his work on *Spawn* and *Angela*. This initiated a period of negotiation, which culminated in an exchange of faxes between Gaiman and McFarlane that are reproduced in the complaint. Those faxes appear to indicate that a deal was struck for the exchange of Gaiman's rights in the characters and work he created for the *Spawn* and *Angela* comics for McFarlane's *Miracleman* rights, after payment of money owed to Gaiman. The transfer was supposed to happen on July 31, 1997. Shortly after that date, Gaiman got paid and received the "tangible property" related to *Miracleman*'s Eclipse days from McFarlane. But in October of 1997, according to the complaint, McFarlane filed trademark applications for the *Miracleman* name, and subsequently has filed an additional "intent to use" application for *Miracleman*. Gaiman alleges in the complaint that McFarlane never intended to honor the agreement to swap rights and lists "breach of contract" and "fraud" as two of the nine counts in his complaint. The chain of events that included the "swap" and McFarlane's subsequent *Miracleman* trademark applications appears to be the crux of the matter. Was there a deal or wasn't there? And if there was, why did McFarlane later make application for rights to *Miracleman*?

Continuing the USCA document's account:

On February 14, 1999, however, Gaiman received a letter from McFarlane announcing that McFarlane was "officially rescind[ing] any previous offers I have placed on the table." The letter offered Gaiman the following deal on a take-it-or-leave-it basis: Gaiman would relinquish "all rights to Angela" in exchange for "all rights to Miracle Man," and "all rights to Medieval Spawn and Cogliostro shall continue to be owned by Todd McFarlane Productions."[6]

In 2001, Gaiman moved to address the situation publicly. In an October 24, 2001, Marvel Comics press conference in New York City, Gaiman and Marvel editor-in-chief Joe Quesada announced a six-issue miniseries to be scripted by Gaiman (see "1602" chapter), and that Marvel was to donate all of its profits from the miniseries to Gaiman's company, Marvels and Miracles, LlC. Marvels and Miracles had been specifically created to work on clearing up the rights to the Miracleman property, and furthermore, "Gaiman pointed out that when he is finally able to clear the rights and publish *Miracleman*, he will donate all the profits, beyond those needed to make sure that the original creators are being properly paid, to the Comic Book Legal Defense Fund and ACTOR."[7]

Marvel's sudden involvement was a curious turn of events. Publishing any new work by Gaiman, and its obvious interest in reprinting and continuing the Miracleman series was arguably motive enough (and reports of the press conference noted that Marvel would allow the original name, "Marvelman," to be used), but this was also a significant gesture from "the new Marvel" as a "more creator-friendly company than its past incarnations, and this change in perception could pay big dividends down the road."[8]

THE LAWSUIT

In January 2002, "Neil Gaiman brought suit under the Copyright Act against Todd McFarlane and corporations controlled by him . . . seeking a declaration that he (Gaiman) owns copyright jointly with McFarlane in certain comic-book characters. . . . Gaiman described, named, and wrote the dialogue for them, but McFarlane drew them. Gaiman contends that he and McFarlane are joint owners of the copyrights on the three characters by reason of their respective contributions to joint (indivisible) work. . . . McFarlane concedes Gaiman's joint ownership of Angela, but not of the other two."[9] The nine-point lawsuit also cited breaches of agreements between Gaiman and McFarlane in 1992 and 1997, and a portion of those disputes involved Miracleman.

In an accompanying January 26, 2002, press release, Gaiman wrote, "This suit is not about the money, it's about respecting the rights of the creator and keeping promises." Kenneth F. Levin, a key member of Gaiman's legal team, was quoted at the time as saying that the suit was "being filed reluctantly, after other avenues proved fruitless. . . . We did everything we could to get this solved outside the courts."[10] The suit went to trial in October 2002 in federal court in Madison, Wisconsin.

It's important to note much had happened in the interval between the 1999 letter from McFarlane and October 2002.

> By the time of the trial, *Spawn* was up to issue No. 120 and had spawned a large number of derivative works, including posters, trading cards, clothing, the statuettes, an animated series on HBO, video games, and a motion picture. Many of these derivative works include all three characters to which Gaiman contributed, so that the financial stakes in the case are considerable.[11]

The statute of limitations was also a possible motive in the filing of the lawsuit at that time. As noted by Judge Posner in his portion of the USCA document, the filing was brought in "a month short of three years after Gaiman's receipt of the [February 14, 1999] letter from McFarlane to rescind any previous offers I have place on the table." According to the three-year copyright statute of limitations,[12] the clock would have run out in February 2002.

Also note the added wrinkles of Miracleman. This additional character, with extensive prior history, legal baggage, and the involvement (and proprietary claims) of many other creators, further confused the issues by dragging in another character (one which McFarlane had never worked on as a creator, collaborative or otherwise). What, precisely, McFarlane actually purchased and owns of the Marvelman/Miracleman property has never been publicly defined. Given the many parties involved in Miracleman, whatever McFarlane owns (or believes he owns) can only be a portion of any proprietary legal interest in the character, trademark, property, and extant published body of work that Gaiman already owns a part of, having written Miracleman from 1990 to 1992.

THE TRIAL

The trial began on October 1, 2002, in federal court in Madison, Wisconsin. Presiding over the jury trial (an all-female jury, in their twenties to fifties) was Judge John Shabaz; for a full account of the trial, see ICV2.com's coverage (see Trivia, below). Shabaz's reputation for presiding over "one of the fastest courts in the country to complete trials"[13] was borne out by this trial, which was over (including jury deliberation and damages) in less than a week.

In his opening statement, McFarlane's attorney defined this as a case about "two realities, Neil's reality and Todd's reality." Accordingly, though each side was represented by a sizable legal team, both creators testified on their own behalf. McFarlane was on the stand "considerably longer" than Gaiman; each became emotional at certain points in their testimony, but remained composed enough to complete examination and cross-examination. By all accounts, the basic facts were never in dispute, and were as described above by the USCA document. However, "[i]t was the secondary uses and trade paperback reprints that were actually the source of much of the dispute. As those uses became more important, Gaiman asked for a written agreement spelling out his rights and compensation."[14]

Some additional facts emerged:

* As noted, there were no written contracts between Gaiman and McFarlane or any of his companies. As reported, "The $100,000 payment amount was decided upon by McFarlane later, who decided to pay each of the writers the same amount because he expected them to compare notes and didn't want any of them upset at being paid less than another. Neither side appears to dispute that that amount represented the highest amount ever paid to Gaiman to that point (and probably ever) for a single issue of a comic. Sales responded, and issue #8 sold 1.1 million copies and #9 around 1 million copies, compared to the 600,000 copy sales on *Spawn #6*."[15]

* The ICV2.com report on the first day of the trial noted that the Medieval Spawn and Angela toys reportedly "generated over $5 million (wholesale) in revenue."[16]

Also as noted earlier, Gaiman's attorney's 1996 letter, asserting that McFarlane pay Gaiman royalties comparable to the "DC Comics Agreements dated August 1, 1993," played a critical role in the testimonies. ICV2.com's report on day one of the trial noted that sometime after August of 1997,

> McFarlane came to believe, based on his conversations with DC VP-Managing Editor Terry Cunningham about DC's handling of royalties on derivative characters, that Gaiman had overstated the terms of his DC contract and stopped trusting him. And Gaiman ultimately came to believe that McFarlane was attempting to claim ownership of his work and use it without the compensation and credit he deserved. Although negotiations continued into 1999, the parties would never again be as close to a resolution as they were in August of 1997. As Larry Marder, who was attempting to negotiate an agreement on McFarlane's behalf, put it, the dispute then became a situation in which "a jury will have to decide whether to believe an Englishman or a Canadian."[17]

After a little over twenty-four hours, the jury returned with their verdict on phase I of the trial around 4:15 P.M. on October 3, awarding a complete victory to Gaiman. As ICV2.com reported:

The jury held that:

1. Gaiman has a copyright interest in Medieval Spawn, Cagliostro, and Angela, the three characters he created in his script for *Spawn* #9.

2. A reasonable person would not have deduced from the copyright notices in the books that McFarlane was claiming copyright ownership in the characters and the scripts (meaning that the statue of limitations had not expired on the copyright claims).

3. There was a contract in 1992 (when McFarlane promised that he would treat Gaiman "better than the big guys").

4. McFarlane breached the 1992 contract.

5. There was a contract in 1997 (this was the rights swap of Gaiman's interests in Medieval Spawn and Cagliostro for McFarlane's interest in Miracleman, plus setting royalty percentages for all uses of Angela and allowing "one-off" projects using the characters).

6. Image's failure to identify Gaiman as a writer on some of the books in question caused damage.

7. Image had no right to use Gaiman's name and biography without his permission on its recent reprint of the Angela series in trade paperback format.[18]

Judge Shabaz thereafter instructed the attorneys to begin opening arguments in the damage phase almost immediately, despite McFarlane's attorneys' attempts to delay. At this point Gaiman had the option of deciding if he wished to get breach-of-contract damages related to the 1997 and 1992 contracts, or to determine damages using solely his copyright interests in the characters. This was resolved quickly: "Gaiman decided to keep his copyright interest in characters he created for Todd McFarlane's *Spawn* comic—Medieval Spawn, and Cagliostro—rather than seeking breach of contract damages from McFarlane. . . . Under the option Gaiman chose, the rights for Miracleman that McFarlane purchased from Eclipse remain in McFarlane's hands."[19]

Thereafter, the only award left for the jury to decide was for the unauthorized use of Gaiman's name and biography on the back cover of the Angela trade paperback. Gaiman's attorneys had asked for $45,000; "[t]he jury found for Gaiman in precisely the amount requested . . . due from Image Comics."[20]

Note, too, that subsequent to this verdict, Todd McFarlane Productions continued to exploit the Miracleman property (see the chapter on Miracleman).

THE APPEAL AND CROSS-APPEAL

McFarlane's attorneys of course appealed the verdict, and Gaiman's attorneys filed a cross-appeal. The appeals were argued on January 5, 2004, and decided on February 24, 2004, by Seventh Circuit Court judges Posner, Kanne, and Rovner.

The verdict was affirmed: "To summarize, we find no error in the district court's decision, and since the decision gave Gaiman all the relief he sought, there is no need to consider the cross-appeal."[21]

As Judge Posner writes:

McFarlane contends that a reasonable jury would not have rejected his statute of limitations defense . . . [And] that in any event two of the comic-book characters at issue are not copyrightable."

[Gaiman's cross-appeal] is from the dismissal of his auxiliary claim for breach of contract. The cross-appeal is contingent on our reversing the copyright judgment, since Gaiman seeks no additional relief on his contract claim; it's just a backstop to his copyright claim. . . .

It might seem that when McFarlane told Gaiman that he would treat Gaiman "better than the big guys" did, he just meant he'd compensate him more generously for work made for hire. But McFarlane rightly does not argue this. Gaiman's work for him was not work for hire . . . There was no written agreement between Gaiman and McFarlane, and Gaiman was not an employee of McFarlane.[22]

One or both of these conditions would have to exist were work for hire to apply legally. Judge Posner goes on to articulate and dissect how work-for-hire language does and doesn't apply to the case and the verdict, ultimately finding it not at all applicable: "[T]here is nothing to suggest that Gaiman ever became a de facto employee of McFarlane. And while Gaiman could have assigned to McFarlane his copyright in any work he did under the oral contract, copyright assignments must be in writing . . . and there was no written agreement."[23] This fact weighed heavily in both the jury's verdict and the Court of Appeals' affirmation of that verdict.

As to the statute of limitations portion of the McFarlane appeal, Judge Posner notes, referring to McFarlane's February 14, 1999, letter, that "[t]he statement 'all rights to Medieval Spawn and Cogliostro shall continue to be owned by Todd McFarlane Productions' was an unambiguous denial of Gaiman's copyright interest and therefore is the last date on which his claim could have accrued and the three-year copyright statute of limitations . . . thus have begun to run. This suit was brought in January of 2002—a month short of the three years after Gaiman's receipt of McFarlane's letter."[24]

Posner goes on to weigh other aspects of the statute of limitations issues, including applicable interpretations of state and federal law: "The parties . . . rightly agree that the copyright statute of limitations starts to run when the plaintiff learns, or should as a reasonable person have learned, that the defendant was violating his rights . . . in this case by repudiating Gaiman's ownership of copyright." Posner cites McFarlane's assertion that Gaiman "knew, or certainly should have known of McFarlane's copyright claim, no later than 1997"—the date of Gaiman's attorney's 'demand' letter—or "in 1993 when *Spawn* No. 9 was published with a copyright notice that did not mention Gaiman." Judge Posner notes that this reflects "a misunderstanding of both the function of copyright notice and the nature of the copyright in a compilation," and succinctly addresses both points: "the function of copyright notice is to warn off copiers," and the copyrighting of a work "formed by the collection and assembling of preexisting materials . . . in such a way that the resulting work as a whole constitutes an original work of authorship," as in *Spawn* #9's inclusion of covers, story, text and letters pages, advertising, etc. "Therefore the compiler's copyright notice is not adverse to contributors' [individual] copyrights and so does not put them on notice that their rights are being challenged." For these reasons, and others Posner goes on to discuss for six more pages, he says that though this aspect of the case "was not open and shut . . . all this is just to say that it was a close case [and] the jury found his claim did not accrue more than three years before he sued."[25]

Considering "McFarlane's alternative ground for [partial] reversal—that

Medieval Spawn and Cogliostro are not copyrightable"—Posner's assessment is worth quoting at length.

> This . . . may seem inconsistent with McFarlane's contention that the "all related characters" copyright notice established that he, not Gaiman, owned the copyrights on Medieval Spawn and Cogliostro. If they were not copyrightable, McFarlane had no copyright in them. In fact, it became apparent at argument that McFarlane thinks that he owns copyright on them but that Gaiman doesn't. His theory seems to be that they became copyrightable, after *Spawn* No. 9 was published, as a result of further work done on them by him. We think they were copyrightable from the start, and that Gaiman owns the copyrights jointly with McFarlane.[26]

Posner goes on to articulate their reasoning. He quotes extensively from Gaiman's script pages (in which Medieval Spawn was referred to as "Olden Days Spawn"), and cites Gaiman's considerable characterization of "Olden Days Spawn," "Count Nicholas Cagliostro (later spelled Cogliostro)," and Angela; he also proposes possible scenarios in which McFarlane's argument might be valid.

> Had someone merely remarked to McFarlane one day, "you need a medieval Spawn" or "you need an old guy to move the story forward," and McFarlane had carried it from there, and if later a copyeditor had made some helpful editorial changes, neither the suggester nor the editor would be a joint owner . . . Otherwise almost every expressive work would be a jointly authored work, and copyright would explode. But where two or more people set out to create a character jointly in such mixed media as comic books . . . and succeed in creating a copyrightable character, it would be paradoxical if though the result of their joint labors had more than enough originality and creativity to be copyrightable, no one could claim copyright. That would be peeling the onion until it disappeared.[27]

After further consideration of various relevant possible arguments, Posner considers McFarlane's second argument which "appeals to the confusingly named doctrine of 'scenes a faire.' . . . McFarlane argues that even as dolled up by the penciler, the inker, and the colorist, Cogliostro is too commonplace to be copyrightable," an argument Posner efficiently dissects and demolishes.

> Gaiman's contribution may not have been copyrightable by itself, but his contribution had expressive content without which Cogliostro wouldn't have been a character at all, but merely a drawing. The expressive work that is the comic-book character Count Nicholas Cogliostro was the joint work of Gaiman and McFarlane—their contributions strike us as quite equal—and both are entitled to ownership of the copyright.[28]

Posner also compares these questions to the various arguments involving Medieval Spawn, which "may seem to present a closer case than Cogliostro so far as copyrightability is concerned," only to conclude: "A Spawn who talks medieval and has a knight's costume would infringe Medieval Spawn, and if he doesn't talk medieval and doesn't look like a knight then he would infringe Spawn."[29]

Thus, judges Posner, Kanne, and Rovner affirmed the verdict in Gaiman's favor. The verdict, and damages awarded, stand and are due.

WHAT NOW?

It's necessary at this juncture to mention the fact that Todd McFarlane was also sued in 1997 by professional National Hockey League player Tony Twist, who took issue with a McFarlane character in *Spawn* named Anthony "Tony Twist" Twistelli. Twist sued "for misappropriation of his name and for defamation. The court dismissed the defamation count but allowed the misappropriation of name count to go to trial. The jury awarded Twist $24.5 million dollars" in 2000.[30]

There was an appeal and a second trial, and a final decision rendered on McFarlane's appeal in 2006 affirmed the judgement "against Todd McFarlane and Todd McFarlane Productions, Inc. ("TMP") on Tony Twist's right of publicity claim involving the use of his name in a comic book."

In short, as reported by Matt Brady on Newsarama.com:

The jury found for Twist in 2000, awarding him $24.5 million in damages. That decision was tossed out on appeal, but then in 2004, a second trial ordered by the Missouri Supreme Court saw a $15 million award go to Twist, which was also appealed, but upheld in June of 2006. In December of 2004, with the $15 million verdict looming, McFarlane Productions (the only arm of the McFarlane businesses named in the Twist complaint) declared Chapter 11 bankruptcy to protect the company, and allow it to continue operation.[31]

What does this have to do with Gaiman and McFarlane?

As Gaiman himself puts it, "Todd declared bankruptcy (and is still bankrupt). Currently I'm his biggest creditor."[32]

So, as to the question "what now?" we can only say: Time will tell.

TRIVIA

- Full accounts of the trial are available online.[33]

- The October 2002 trial ended happily for at least one young fan.

The trial ended with a bizarre, almost surreal scene of camaraderie between the two adversaries, who both comported themselves with great civility and showed considerable mutual respect, at least in a creative sense, throughout the entire proceedings. After Judge Shabaz dismissed the jury and adjourned the court, McFarlane caught up with Gaiman outside the courtroom. With one of the *Spawn* comics that had been used as an exhibit in the trial in his hand he asked Gaiman to sign it for a young boy who was in the courtroom with one of McFarlane's attorneys. McFarlane signed the comic and handed it to Gaiman saying, "I saved you the sweet spot." Gaiman signed and posed for a picture with McFarlane and the boy, providing a fitting coda to a case about a medium that is, after all, about entertainment and fun.[34]

- Note that Gaiman made concessions throughout the period under consideration and contention. For instance, in the 1996 letter from Gaiman's lawyer to McFarlane's negotiator, the oral agreement was interpreted as Gaiman being compensated by McFarlane "on the same terms . . . set forth in Mr. Gaiman's DC Comics Agreements dated August, 1993."[35] Judge Posner's portion of the ruling comments, "This was a surprising interpretation of the oral agreement, since in it McFarlane had promised to treat Gaiman *better* than DC Comics treated him; but as nothing turns on this interpretation we'll ignore it." We won't; Gaiman was already making concessions in the spirit of negotiation and possible resolution in 1996.

- Note that Gaiman wasn't the only one of the four guest writers on *Spawn* issues 8 to 11 to do subsequent work with McFarlane in 1993–94. *Spawn* issue 8 writer Alan Moore went on to script the three-issue miniseries *Violator* (1993), and Frank Miller scripted the Image/DC Comics crossover Spawn/Batman (1993), which was illustrated by McFarlane. Dave Sim had previously contributed a pinup page featuring Cerebus to *Spawn* issue 4 (September 1992), and a Frank Miller inset poster was published in *Spawn* issue 8.

- Hardly trivial, this, but—what is the moral for other creators? As ICV2.com pointed out in their analysis of the January 2002 suit,

  The nature of the deals cited in the complaint indicate that the Gaiman/McFarlane relationship was informal and was undocumented in many cases. From the beginning, when Gaiman apparently turned in work that was published under an oral agreement, all the way to the "swap," which appears to have been documented only with the exchange of faxes, there's not a single formal contract cited that lays out the rights and duties of the parties. From our vantage point, it appears likely that the lack of documentation was a contributing factor to this litigation.

That this same core issue—the lack of clear contracts and documentation—has also been a consistent characteristic of the entire Marvelman/Miracleman debacle only hammers home the point. The ill-defined nature of what rights to Marvelman/Miracleman existed, when, and to whom they belong or belonged plagues this situation to the present.

> According to the complaint (and our recollections), *Miracleman* in the US consisted of 24 comics, with the first sixteen written by Alan Moore, and 17–24 by Neil Gaiman. Those comics were published by Eclipse, which eventually went bankrupt. Todd McFarlane bought the assets of Eclipse in the bankruptcy. According to the complaint, the *Miracleman* assets purchased by McFarlane included "... tangible property which ... had been used by Eclipse in its publishing of *Miracleman*," presumably films, but did not include any publishing rights, which had lapsed.[36]

That the cumulative weight of this decades-long legacy falls currently on the back of Gaiman is not his fault, and he is to be commended for taking up the challenge on behalf of all the involved Marvelman/Miracleman creators as he has—and does.

|||||||||||||||||||||||||||||||||||||||||||||||||||||||||||||||||||||||||

THE LAST TEMPTATION

(1994)

In 1994, Gaiman was contacted by Bob Pfeifer of Epic Records, calling on behalf of Alice Cooper, to see if he might be interested in working with the legendary rock star on a concept album. After meeting with Cooper in a Phoenix, Arizona, hotel room, Gaiman agreed. Together they began, in Gaiman's words, to collaborate on a story about "a boy named Steven, and a strange theater, and a showman with a strange resemblance to Alice Cooper—part Machiavellian ghost, part commentator, part demon. It was the story of a deal Steven is offered; of a theatrical performance he attends; of his parents, his school friends, his teachers, and, ultimately, his temptation." Cooper then took the concept, and, with some input from Gaiman, wrote the songs that eventually appeared on Cooper's 1994 album, *The Last Temptation* (which, incidentally, sported an album cover by Dave McKean).

The album contains ten cuts: "Sideshow," "Nothing's Free," "Lost in America," "Bad Place Alone," "You're My Temptation," "Stolen Prayer," "Unholy

War," "Lullaby," "It's Me," and "Cleansed by Fire." Probably one of Cooper's most underrated albums, it was produced by Andy Wallace, Don Fleming, Duane Baron, and John Purdell. Cooper's last recording on the Epic label, it's basically an exploration of the musician's faith. It also reprises Cooper's Steven character from his *Welcome to My Nightmare* days. Other guest writers on the album include Chris Cornell (from the band Soundgarden); Tommy Shaw (Styx, Damn Yankees); Jack Blades (Damn Yankees); and Brian Smith (Beat Angels).

Gaiman doesn't recall exactly when, but at some point, someone suggested doing a comic book adaptation of the material. Echoing the title of Nikos Kazantzakis's classic novel about the final moments of Christ, the story was titled *The Last Temptation*. Illustrated by Michael Zulli and edited by Mort Todd, it was first published by Marvel Music, an imprint of Marvel Comics, as a three-issue miniseries in 1994. In 2005 it was collected and published as a graphic novel by Dark Horse Books.

Containing "chunks of plot" that didn't make it onto the album, *The Last Temptation* is a visually arresting, utterly engrossing tale of a young man who through no fault of his own finds himself drawn into a surreal world, where he is forced to make a difficult decision. Zulli's art is full of disturbing touches, from the overt nature of the realistic Halloween displays that decorate Steven's hometown to the appearance of the back of the seats that populate the Theatre of the Real, which resemble row upon row of tombstones from behind.

Set in a generic American town "in the middle of nowhere," the story opens on the day before Halloween, evoking Ray Bradbury's classic *Something Wicked This Way Comes* (Steven is shown with a copy on his desk). The illustrated bildungsroman unfolds in three acts, detailing Steven's dark right of passage.

PEOPLE, PLACES, AND THINGS

STEVEN. Plucked off the street by an aggressive barker named the Showman, Steven witnesses a bizarre show in a theater that doesn't exist. The show purports to show him his bleak future, after he becomes an adult. Steven is offered the choice of never leaving the theater; of never growing old; of living in an environment where he can't ever be hurt, physically or emotionally. Over the course of hours following his visit to the Theatre of the Real, Steven is shown several disturbing visions, all designed to tap into his fear of what the future holds in store.

Finding the courage to confront the demonic Showman, Steven rejects his offer, angering the soul stealer, and forcing him to reveal his true visage. Steven fends off the demon, but his victory is bittersweet; although he resists temptation, he will be forever marked by the experience.

THE SHOWMAN. The proprietor of the Theatre of the Real, who bears an uncanny resemblance to Alice Cooper. He repeatedly tries to tempt Steven into surrendering his potential. Following the *Something Wicked This Way Comes* analogy, he's Mr. Dark. Steven later learns that the Showman has been active in his town for over 150 years, stealing the souls of children.

The Showman appears to Steven in several guises, taking the forms of one of Steven's friends, his mother, his teacher, his coach, a lunch lady, a janitor, and as his romantic interest, Nancy. When Steven defies him, he reveals his true identity as a serpent, the proverbial Father of Lies.

Although Steven wins this battle, the Showman makes it quite clear that the war is not yet over.

MERCY. The Showman's assistant, she appears as an usher, and later as a striptease artist. Although she's a creation of the Showman, she's no longer able to force herself to participate in his evil schemes. Steven tries to rescue her but ultimately fails; his realization that he cannot save her gives the story a bitter coda.

THE THEATRE OF THE REAL. The Showman's showcase, the theater purports to "tell you what it's really like, out there in the world of growing up and getting even." In reality it shows the Showman's prey whatever it takes to cajole them into abandoning their potential.

BILL AND PAULINE. Steven's parents: his mother, who is practical and down-to-earth, and his father, who seems filled with fear.

TRIVIA

- Look carefully in the background of a couple of panels featuring Steven and his friends in their Halloween garb, and you might discern a child dressed as Dream.

THE QUOTABLE GAIMAN

And the album came out, and the comic came out, and Alice and I stumbled around Europe promoting it. I fulfilled a childhood dream and found myself backstage on BBC TV's *Top of the Pops,* as Alice and the band performed "Lost in America" in front of Michael's double-page splash from part one. We were treated a little like kings in Germany, and a little like gods in Scandinavia.

—Introduction, *The Last Temptation*

NEIL GAIMAN'S MIDNIGHT DAYS[1]

(1999)

By the end of the 1990s, the ongoing success of all the collected Vertigo Neil Gaiman works—the *Sandman* graphic novels primary among them—made the notion of gathering the previously uncollected Gaiman one-shots, guest issues, and single stories as a self-standing trade paperback an inevitability. The resulting volume, *Neil Gaiman's Midnight Days*, also provided the opportunity to showcase a previously unpublished *Swamp Thing* story. We've saved discussing the individual works in their initial publications in order to cover them here. In order of their appearance in *Midnight Days*, they are:

SWAMP THING: "JACK IN THE GREEN" (1999, ORIGINAL TO *MIDNIGHT DAYS*)

This ten-page story was originally written by Gaiman in 1985, one of two trial scripts he wrote immediately after mentor and friend Alan Moore had shown him the template for writing comic scripts—on a notebook page at a pub during the British Fantasy Convention. His first attempt, "The Day My Pad Went Mad," involved "John Constantine going home after [the Swamp Thing serialized saga] 'American Gothic,' and the things he found growing in his fridge," according to Gaiman's introduction to the story in *Midnight Days*. His second script, "Jack in the Green," "was about a 17th Century Swamp Thing. Nothing much happened in it, but I liked it." He submitted it to *Swamp Thing* editor Karen Berger in 1986 after meeting her for the first time at a UK comics convention, but nothing came of it until the summer of 1999, when work was under way on the *Midnight Days* compilation.

"Jack in the Green" is narrated by the medieval incarnation of Swamp Thing, the titular "Jack in the Green." Jack is shown caring for and conversing with a plague-infested man named Simon up to the moment of Simon's death. After burying his friend's body (as only a plant elemental can), he explores the neighboring village; finding all of its residents dead, Jack torches the village and watches as it burns. The meat of this melancholy, anecdotal tale is Jack's description of his journeys around the world, meditating on the vast diversity of life while trying to comfort Simon in his final moments.

The inclusion of a new story, of course, made the volume essential to Gaiman fans who may have already owned the individual comics and annuals collected in it. Gaiman and editor Karen Berger took full advantage of the situation by approaching Alan Moore's original art collaborators on *Swamp Thing*, Stephen Bissette (pencils), John Totleben (inks), Tatjana Wood (colors), and John Costanza (letters). The team completed the story, with John Totleben illustrating the ninth-page solo, and this remains the only publication of the story to date. Bissette and Totleben based Jack's likeness on a seventeenth-century Celtic sculpted face of the Green Man, the elemental archetype Gaiman (and, in the *Swamp Thing* series, Alan Moore) had used as a basis for his characterization.

"BROTHERS" (ORIGINALLY PUBLISHED IN SWAMP THING ANNUAL #5, 1989)

Springboarding from both the Alan Moore–scripted and Rick Veitch–scripted and–penciled issues of Swamp Thing, Gaiman's single *Swamp Thing Annual* opens with "Brothers," featuring Moore's kindhearted aged hippie character, Chester, and his significant other, Liz. In this tale, Gaiman introduces the reviled DC character Brother Power, The Geek, into the series, positing that The Geek's animated mannequin nature—a human simulacrum animated by some supernatural spiritual force—as an elemental force, is an unstable companion to the plant elementals central to the entire Swamp Thing universe and Gaiman's proposed "vegetable theology." In many ways, "Brothers" is concerned with what sets natural elementals apart from aberrations like Brother Power, thus elaborating on the vegetable theology Gaiman began to articulate in *Black Orchid*. At one point, an "ambassador" from the Parliament of Trees (an ancient ruling force of the vegetable realm, introduced by Alan Moore during his *Swamp Thing* tenure) explains, "In times of trouble . . . the Earth . . . our mother . . . brings forth champions . . . Sometimes . . . elements are missing . . . sometimes . . . things go wrong. . . ." Thus, Brother Power is "a failure . . . one of the Earth's mistakes . . . a doll god . . . a puppet elemental . . . like others before it. . . ."

The plot mechanics involve a downed satellite that crashes in Tampa, Florida, releasing its captive, Brother Power, the Geek. A covert U.S. government operative tracking the spacecraft, identified only as "Steel," assigns a cynical Bu-Intel-Sec/Defense Department Intelligence (hereafter D.D.I.) agent to deal with the problem, which leads Steel, a "man who lied, and betrayed, and murdered his countrymen, for his country's good" to Chester Williams, Liz Tremayne, and Abby Cable/Holland, all characters from Alan Moore's *Swamp Thing* run. As the havoc and panic inadvertently caused by the renegade Brother Power escalates, it turns out to be Chester's gentle hippie roots and philosophy that mesh perfectly with Brother Power's mind-set, saving the day and averting catastrophe.

Via the characters of Brother Power and Chester, Gaiman mounts an ultimately affecting meditation on the mythic sixties counterculture, its remnants and its relevance (and irrelevance) to the 1990s. Via the constant disdain expressed by agent Gideon Endor (who only refers to Chester insultingly, as "Hippie")—a character who embodies the flip side of postsixties mind-sets—Gaiman also explores what becomes of those who lose their ideals and retreat into cynicism, bitterness, and nihilism.

But the heart of Gaiman's script is really the dynamic between Chester and Liz: Chester's realization that his caretaking of Liz defines their relationship, and that it is finite, and that he can live with this, knowing Liz will one day leave him once she has regained her confidence and courage, is very touching.

PEOPLE, PLACES, AND THINGS

BROTHER POWER, THE GEEK. Like Prez (from *Sandman* issue 54), Brother Power, The Geek, was created by writer Joe Simon. Gaiman revived both characters after decades of fan ridicule and obscurity. Note the fleeting appearance of a Prez campaign poster in Chester's collection on page one of "Brothers," anticipating Gaiman's revival of Prez in Sandman.

Simon and artist Jerry Grandenetti cocreated the hippie-era oddity *Brother Power, The Geek* (1968, 2 issues), which crashed and burned in short order. "Here is the real-life scene of the dangers in Hippie-Land!" the cover of the debut issue shouted. The origin was Frankensteinian, as was much of the adventure that follows: Brother Power was a blood, oil, and water–soaked tailor's dummy (see possible sources, below) given life and superhuman strength by a lightning bolt. Once animate, he was "adopted" by a group of hippies who indoctrinated him into their "flower power/peace and love" philosophy. Defending his newfound friends, The Geek wielded his strength to fend off the Hell's Angels; tried to go to school; and was abducted by the Psychedelic Circus and displayed as a freak. He escaped and ran for Congress until the police chased him into a river, where he apparently drowned—until the second and final issue of his series.

Gaiman's incarnation of Brother Power is engagingly childlike, and expands considerably upon the powers Simon and Grandenetti had eluded to in 1968. Like Swamp Thing, Gaiman's Brother Power seems to be an elemental being, his life-force not confined to the ragged mannequin body he inhabited in the sixties. Brother Power grows multiple bodies from debris in "Brothers," one of them gigantic, and at one point speaks from an animated doll. His sensibility, though, remains that of a harmless, benevolent "flower child," cast adrift from all he knew (he asks Chester at one point, "Like where did the beeeautiful people go?"), and any harm he causes is entirely accidental. Like the bikers and gangs in the original 1968 series, whose own violence caused Brother Power to lash out, the only real threat emerges from the provocation by the U.S. military and covert government agencies trying to contain Brother Power's eruption in the rubble of the crashed satellite. Fortunately, Chester's flower power pacifist intervention defuses the situation, and Brother Power departs to "find the heart of America," like the Beats of the 1950s and the bikers Captain America and Billy in the counterculture classic *Easy Rider* (1968).

LIZ TREMAYNE. A longtime figure in the Swamp Thing series, Liz is a former television journalist and author of the book *Swamp-Man: Fact or Myth?* She became involved with Chester after escaping an abusive relationship. As Gaiman presents Liz, she is further along in healing from the psychological and emotional trauma she suffered. Though still dependent upon, and attached to, the kindly Chester, her growing sense of self, security, and independence is manifest in ways that Chester is beginning to struggle with.

CHESTER WILLIAMS. Chester Williams was one of the Swamp Thing's and Abby's best friends throughout the run of the 1980s–1990s incarnation of *Swamp Thing*. When introduced, Chester discovered a strange-looking yam, actually one of the hallucinogenic potatolike growths that had fallen from Swamp Thing's back. Later he joined a loose-knit Swamp Thing–worshipping cult that called themselves "Swampies." With Chester's participation (and passive leadership), the Swampies evolve into an ecological activist group, and it is in this capacity we meet Chester anew in "Brothers." Ever open to alternative lifestyles, realities, and life-forms, it is also Chester (who by this time has had a good deal of experience with such matters) who brings the mounting conflict with Brother Power to a peaceful resolution. His conversations with Brother Power—amusingly surreal and yet peer to peer, like the old hippies and survivors of the sixties they both are—allow him to also find some peace with the knowledge that Liz will likely one day leave him.

"SHAGGY GOD STORIES" (ORIGINALLY PUBLISHED IN SWAMP THING ANNUAL #5, 1989)

This succinct, atmospheric ten-page story represents Gaiman's only collaboration to date with comics artist Mike Mignola (*Hellboy*), and is the most extensive published articulation of Gaiman's vegetable theology.

"Shaggy God Story" finds Jason Woodrue, aka the Floronic Man, aka "Floro," wandering the Brazilian swamps with a potted Venus flytrap he has named Milton, and talking to himself. Hoping to sort out his mounting bafflement about the relationship between plants and humans, Woodrue converses with a member of the Parliament of Trees, who cryptically warns him to avoid the Forest Lords, to "beware . . . the corruption of . . . Matango" (a fungus manifestation that subsequently menaced Swamp Thing), and curtly concludes, "Now leave us, Woodrue . . . your place is . . . not here." Woodrue drops Milton and departs, fuming, "I want to be a God too! . . . If you . . . won't make me a god, then . . . maybe other people will!" In the final panel, toothy smiles form on Milton's three flytrap mouths.

PEOPLE, PLACES, AND THINGS

JASON WOODRUE/THE FLORONIC MAN. Jason Woodrue was the first of DC Comics's Silver Age vegetable-human hybrids, introduced in 1962 as a foe of the Atom. Known as the "Plant Master" until transformed into a plant-human hybrid, the Floronic Man, Woodrue had lashed out at humanity repeatedly in the past. His first clash with Swamp Thing had been in Alan Moore's first story arc in 1983–84 (*Saga of the Swamp Thing* issues 21–24), which left Woodrue defeated, mad, and imprisoned, adrift from both mankind and the Green. Gaiman's Woodrue is depicted as yearning for a more meaningful connection with the Green, a vegetable "fallen angel" (an association evoked via the name he gave the flytrap he carries with him, "Milton") unhappy with being essentially spurned by the Parliament and driven by fresh aspirations of power, which will turn him against the powers that be.

Gaiman had plans to bring Woodrue back as a primary nemesis for his planned run on *Swamp Thing* had that come to pass. "I was going to bring him back as a villain. He was getting back to being Woodrue, the Rue of the Wood, and probably on a much bigger scale, a much nastier scale. It would have been fun, but again it didn't happen. I probably would have brought back Black Orchid in there. I don't know, because as I said, it never got that far."

"HOLD ME" (ORIGINALLY PUBLISHED IN HELLBLAZER #27, 1990)

"This is probably my favorite of all my short stories," Gaiman wrote in his introduction to this reprint in *Midnight Days*. It is as affecting and concise a ghost story as any ever published, in comics or any form; it is scripted and illustrated with a potent economy of atmosphere, emotion, and impact. It also anticipates themes that inform Gaiman's later efforts, primary among them *Neverwhere*.

A trio of homeless adults seek shelter in an abandoned fourth-floor flat, where they freeze to death. Two of them, Fat Ronnie and Sylvia, die wrapped in a blanket in each other's arms, but Jacko dies alone, and his restless spirit (and body) lingers, seeking warmth. When occult detective John Constantine bolts out of a taxicab due to the cabby's offensive chatter, he drops into a commemorative party for the one-year anniversary of a friend's death and walks a woman named Anthea home. She manages a shelter for the homeless, and happens to live in the tower estate where Jacko died almost a year earlier. En route, noting the smell from the abandoned apartments, Anthea tells Constantine of the "two dead tramps underneath a curtain" found by the police months before; the reader realizes Jacko's body was never found. Constantine follows Anthea into her flat, neither knowing that Jacko watches from outside, moments after inadvertently killing a single mother by embracing her, leaving her young daughter alone with her mother's body. When Anthea tries to seduce Constantine, he leaves, after realizing she's a lesbian hoping to use him to make her pregnant ("You could have bloody asked, you know"), and he stumbles upon the crying little girl. Turning her over to Anthea for safekeeping, Constantine investigates, finding the frigid and still animate Jacko asking, "Hold me." Embracing the spirit, Constantine releases the haunt, but returns to Anthea's door. "Just hold me," he says.

Other horror comics have offered variations on this theme, usually as grim variations on the classic Robert Service poem "The Cremation of Sam McGee" (1907). However, Gaiman brings unprecedented immediacy, empathy, passion, and pathos to his spare tale.

In his introduction Gaiman cites McKean's art as "some of the finest I ever got in mainstream comics," noting that McKean was hired for the job only after the scheduled artist had to decline the job (due to his marriage and honeymoon). McKean dropped "one page of obligatory scary stuff from the story I'd written (which improved it to no end)," and even traveled to DC's office in New York City to computer color a few pages, to establish the approach colorist Danny Vozzo adhered to in completing the task. However, McKean was dissatisfied with the art he'd created. "I was barely using the line to do anything that I wasn't doing in paint. . . . Some of the drawings, I think, underneath all that crosshatching and stuff . . . are okay," he later said. "But they just lost it with that treatment. It was a big problem I was trying to fight my way through at that point." Whatever McKean's reservations, the story and art are indeed outstanding, and Gaiman's affection for this Hellblazer "fill-in" issue is understandable.

"SANDMAN MIDNIGHT THEATRE" (ORIGINALLY PUBLISHED AS THE ONE-SHOT SANDMAN MIDNIGHT THEATRE #1, 1995)

This one-shot crossover between Gaiman's Morpheus, the Lord of Dreams, and Matt Wagner's Vertigo revival of the Golden Age Sandman character—the gas mask–wearing crime fighter introduced in *Adventure Comics* issue 40 (1939)—offers an inspired conjunction of characters and pulp origins. It is also posited as a prequel to the entire Gaiman *Sandman* series, set during Morpheus's captivity in the glass prison before the events of *The Sandman* issue 1.

The original *Adventure Comics* Sandman was clearly modeled on pulp heroes of yore, like the Shadow and the Green Hornet: Apparently idle wealthy gent Wesley Dodds transcends mere detective status when he dons hat, coat, and gas mask and wields his gas gun, whose chemical vapors prompt criminals to tell the truth and/or renders them unconscious. Though he was never portrayed as a superhero, the Golden Age Sandman served on the All-Star Squadron and Justice Society of America. It was this version of the character Matt Wagner resurrected for the Vertigo series *Sandman Mystery Theatre* (70 issues, 1993–99). "What fascinated me," Gaiman writes in his introduction to the reprint in *Midnight Days,* "was the way Matt would take 1930s pulp motifs and retell them with contemporary sensibilities."

Whatever the catalyst was for teaming up the Vertigo Sandmans in "Sandman Midnight Theatre," Gaiman admits he cannot recall. However, he was intrigued with the conceit of an interaction between the two characters—not so much for what they could do interactively, since the chronology of both Sandman continuities required that Morpheus remain imprisoned throughout the narrative—but for the opportunity to play with the British contemporaries of the American 1930s pulp fiction. Gaiman cites Leslie Charteris (creator of *The Saint*) and Dennis Wheatley as inspirations.

Gaiman also had a character he wanted to introduce in this idiom: "I had an idea for a Saint-like master burglar called the Cannon," he says in his introduction. He used the 1939 setting to send the original Sandman, Wesley Dodds, off to visit Great Britain. Plunged by a friend's suicide into a murderous blackmail plot, which is nestled amid a posh hotbed of aristocratic vipers, satanists, and occultists, Dodds tries to protect his girlfriend, amateur sleuth Dian Belmont, from the worst. Both Dodds and Dian inadvertently trip over the parallel secret investigation and activities of the Cannon, with each detective unsure of the other's true role or motives. Amid the intrigue, Dodds encounters the imprisoned Morpheus, Dream incarnate, in a striking three-page sequence. Morpheus is imprisoned and secreted away in a subterranean chamber by the coven magus Roderick Burgess.

Nothing that transpires impacts Morpheus's plight, and Dodds is in fact left remembering nothing of the encounter. Gaiman uses one of Dodds's dreams to frame the story itself, overtly placing Dodds in Morpheus's place via the point of view of these panels. Thus, Gaiman slyly implies that Dodds's chosen Sandman identity might be explained by Dream's absence from the Dreaming, and furthermore, that Dodds's prophetic dreams embody a link between the gas mask–wearing mortal and the supernatural realm of Morpheus.

TRIVIA

- Though *Midnight Days* provides welcome access to four of Gaiman's previously uncollected Vertigo/DC works, it falls short of the volume Gaiman had in mind. A number of short Gaiman Vertigo/DC works that remain "orphans" would have been welcome; precious few of these have since been sandwiched into subsequent editions of other volumes. But the greatest absence here, by Gaiman's own admission in his introduction to the Swamp Thing Annual issue 5 reprint herein, is "Pavane," Gaiman's secret origin of the Batman villainess Poison Ivy (originally created by Bob Kanigher), an evocative fourteen-page tale illustrated by Mark Buckingham and published in Secret Origins issue 36 (January 1989). Gaiman notes that this was written during work on his first DC project, *Black Orchid*, and was his "first DC Comics short story," and it is integral to *Black Orchid* and Gaiman's "vegetable theology."

- Another tantalizing tidbit of "what might have been" surfaces in Gaiman's introduction to the Swamp Thing Annual issue 5 reprint in *Midnight Days*. Noting that he and Jamie Delano were originally slated to take over scripting Swamp Thing after the completion of Rick Veitch's tenure as writer/penciler on that series—a plan abandoned when DC abruptly refused to publish Veitch's *Swamp Thing* issue 88—Gaiman writes that the annual "was to have been my first issue," and his "Shaggy God Stories" Jason Woodrue/Floronic Man story "would have set up for a huge and strange storyline, that has, instead, found its home in the comics boxes in Lucien's Library, I'm afraid." Gaiman offers an evocative snapshot of his planned opening Swamp Thing story: "It began with the Wolves of the Woods padding out of the forests, thorns on their feet instead of claws."

- "Jack in the Green" penciler Bissette felt the purgative story perfectly reflected his own current view of the comics industry he had worked in for over two decades. He lettered "Farewell" above his signature on the final page, asking editor Berger to make sure the sign-off remained intact in the printed version. She did, and the story indeed remains Bissette's last published new work in the mainstream American comics industry. He announced his retirement from the industry that same year.

- Brother Power, the Geek, was brought into the Vertigo fold with Gaiman's Swamp Thing Annual issue 5 reprinted in *Midnight Days*, and returned in *Vertigo Visions: The Geek* issue 1 (June 1993), to date the last hurrah of The Geek. Scripted by Rachel Pollack and illustrated by Michael Allred, this one-shot tapped Gaiman's concept of the character to present him as a sort of elemental toy spirit, and resurrected elements of the original series.

- Like many of Dennis Wheatley's villains in his Duc de Richleau novels, the "Sandman Midnight Theater" coven magus Roderick Burgess is based in part on real-life occultist, author, and philosopher Aleister Crowley (1875–1947). So notorious was Crowley in his day that he was dubbed by the press "The Wickedest Man in the World," and he indeed fueled the twentieth-century pop culture archetype of satanism and occultism, until the 1969 arrest and subsequent trial of Charles Manson supplanted the Crowley archetype with a more contemporary incarnation.

- The metal-handed Steel character appearing in Swamp Thing Annual issue 2 and reprinted in *Midnight Days* wasn't originally a DC Comics character. Sarge Steel was a character created by Pat Masulli for Connecticut-based Charlton Comics. DC Comics purchased the Charlton characters in the mideighties, hence his appearance here. The character of Sarge Steel starred in his own comic, *Sarge Steel* (8 issues, 1961–66), starting as a steel-handed private detective and engaging in an ersatz fusion of

Mickey Spillane hard-boiled action and Ian Fleming James Bond–like espionage.

THE QUOTABLE GAIMAN

The voice in the caption boxes in "Brothers" is me doing a good-natured if not entirely successful Alan Moore impression. It seemed appropriate: it had been his comic, and he had given it a voice.

—Introduction to "Jack in the Green" in
Midnight Days

I was very pleased with "Jack in the Green," because Steve and John drew it in precisely the style they were drawing *Swamp Thing* in the mid-1980s. You often see artists return to a comic they are most associated with, and it rarely works. They've moved on and simply cannot capture the flavor so unique to their earlier work—but Steve and John caught it, spot on. I was so happy about that, and still am.

—from an e-mail to Stephen R. Bissette

||||||||||||||||||||||||||||||||||||||||||||||||||||||||||||||||||||||||

GREEN LANTERN/SUPERMAN: LEGEND OF THE GREEN FLAME

(1988—2000)

L egend of the Green Flame" is a fascinating artifact in the Gaiman library. Written after *Black Orchid* (but prior to its publication) and before *The Sandman*, it is more entrenched in existing continuity than anything else Gaiman has written. Though brief, it reveals the author's love for the DC universe, while also serving as precursor for a number of elements that he would develop more prominently in *The Sandman*.

As he states in his introduction to the 2000 one-shot publication, Gaiman was approached by Mark Waid—at the time an editor at DC—to write a story that would conclude an experimental comic book series called *Action Comics Weekly*. *Action*—the venerable DC title in which Superman had made his debut—had become a weekly anthology book, with each issue showcasing several different characters in separate, ongoing stories. But that experiment proved a failure, and DC intended to transform the book back into a monthly title, focused once again on Superman. Waid hoped for a wrap-up story that would involve all of the characters who'd been featured in the individual serials in the weekly, and approached Gaiman.

Though known for his love for—and reinvention of—mythology, unlike many people Neil Gaiman never seems to have made a distinction between the myths of the ancient Greeks and the four-color DC comics gods he grew up reading about. Literate and ambitious as a storyteller, at heart Gaiman was also a comics geek. He loved not only the heroes themselves but the entire universe, together with its tangled web of continuity. Over the years he has shown evidence of this love time and again, but *"Green Lantern/Superman: The Legend of the Green Flame"* is that love incarnate. Gaiman gleefully accepted the assignment, and the challenge of working with the various stars of the weekly *Action Comics* and working with the continuity of the DC universe at the time, and being able to include older stories and very recent revisions that had been made to the characters. When he finished he had a story that pleased both himself and editor Mark Waid.

Then it began to unravel.

Gaiman had already been given several editorial mandates during the process. Unable to use the Jack Kirby creation Etrigan the Demon, the writer kept the sequence he'd planned in Hell, but replaced Etrigan with a new demon character. When Waid asked Gaiman to accomplish certain ends regarding the Phantom Stranger, the answer was a resounding yes. The story had been tailored to fit DC's editorial needs, but it retained the heart that would become Gaiman's trademark.

But one final change needed to be made. On a trans-Atlantic call from Mike Carlin, Gaiman learned that continuity changes had caused the powers that be at DC to determine that Hal Jordan (Green Lantern) no longer knew the secret identity of Superman. Since the story revolved around the personal relationship between Hal and Clark Kent, Gaiman felt that the only choice was to step away.

The script was not only shelved, it was lost by both DC and Gaiman.

More than a decade later, Neil remembered the story and asked DC editor Mike Carlin if publishing it as a stand-alone, out-of-continuity story would be a problem. With blessings from Carlin, and a phone call to new DC editor Bob Schreck, Gaiman played detective until he managed to find an extant copy of the script. Schreck brought together an amazing team of artists—including Mike Allred, Terry Austin, Mark Buckingham, John Totleben, Matt Wagner, Eric Shanower, Arthur Adams, Jim Aparo, Kevin Nowlan, and Jason Little—and twelve years after its intended publication *Green Lantern/Superman: Legend of the Green Flame* finally appeared in print.

Though the central story—of Hal Jordan seeking out Clark Kent for advice, trying to sort out his life, only to have them both imperiled by an encounter with an artifact from Green Lantern history—is warm and well told, the most intriguing elements to this story do not involve Superman and Green Lantern. Other characters appear in supporting roles whom Gaiman would later utilize in his Vertigo (and pre-Vertigo mature readers) titles. Some of the concepts that form the core of his comics work are also prevalent.

The enigmatic Phantom Stranger plays a role in the story, coming to the rescue in the end. Gaiman would use the Stranger to wonderful effect later on in the pages of *The Books of Magic*. Likewise, Deadman (aka Boston Brand) appears, even using a quip that Gaiman would have the character repeat later in *The Books of Magic* (though, of course, given its twelve-year publishing delay, readers would have encountered Brand's joke first in that title). The Hell that Gaiman employs here is clearly, as he notes in his introduction, the version Alan Moore introduced in *Saga of the Swamp Thing*. In addition, he opens with the aftermath of the Justice Society of America's World War II battle over the Spear of Destiny, a subject that would be touched upon again in the pages of the Sandman story *Season of Mists*.

Even more interesting, however, are the comments that Superman makes on page thirty-one, talking about the damned souls he and Green Lantern had encountered in Hell. As powerful as he is, Superman could not help them. But what bothers him far more than that is that he could sense that they did not want his help, that they were there by choice. "They were creating that place themselves," Superman explains. This is, of course, the central conceit upon which Gaiman built his own version of Hell in the pages of *The Sandman* and its various spin-offs and derivatives, already a major part of his ideology.

"*Legend of the Green Flame*" is an oddity in the Gaiman canon, but one that should not be overlooked.

PEOPLE, PLACES, AND THINGS

GREEN LANTERN. Hal Jordan, a former test pilot, is also Green Lantern, member of a universal corps of daring heroes who—with rings of extraordinary power—keep order in the universe. Troubled and feeling alone, the Green Lantern Corps decimated, Jordan is seeking to define the purpose and direction of his life, and he goes to visit his friend Clark Kent for advice. Attending a museum exhibit, they see a familiar-looking green lantern, but it doesn't belong to Jordan; it looks strangely like the one that once belonged to the very first Green Lantern, Alan Scott. A member of the Justice Society of America, Alan Scott had vanished with the rest of the JSA several years earlier. Unbeknownst to Hal Jordan, however, the JSA traveled back in time to battle Hitler over the Spear of Destiny (helping to end World War II), and Alan Scott's lantern was left behind in the rubble of Berlin.

When he attempts to recharge his ring with Alan Scott's old lantern—but using his own oath, which differs from Scott's—Jordan causes himself and Superman to be killed by the magic within the lantern. (Jordan's ring and lantern, created by aliens called the Guardians from the planet Oa, operate on technology, while Scott's was based in magic.) Using his ring, Jordan manages to get himself and Superman out of the limbo of death, but only succeeds in transporting them to Hell. Finally, they seem trapped as tiny spirits inside Alan Scott's lantern, but the Phantom Stranger manages to free them. Once free, Jordan discovers that Alan Scott's old lamp is actually a magical, sentient being that seeks to corrupt and control him, but by saying Alan Scott's oath instead of his own, Jordan is able to use his fearlessness to tame the wild magic of the lantern. With the Phantom Stranger's help, they return fully to life, after which Jordan is filled with new purpose.

SUPERMAN. Upon a visit from his troubled friend Hal Jordan (Green Lantern), Clark Kent (Superman) takes the time to try to lift the other man's spirits. When Lois Lane persuades Kent to cover a museum exhibit in her place, Kent brings Jordan along, and the two encounter a very different sort of green lantern. Superman is with Green Lantern throughout this adventure, but when the two are briefly in Hell, the Man of Steel is deeply troubled by the suffering of the damned.

BLACKHAWK. In 1949, Janos Prohaska, leader of the Blackhawks (a squadron of World War II ace pilots), and Weng Chan, another member of the team, paid a late-night visit to debris-strewn ruins unearthed in Germany. There they found the corpse of a man who was apparently Wesley Dodds (once, ironically, the Sandman) and other evidence that suggests that this was the location of the final battle for which the Justice Society of America traveled back in time to defeat Hitler. In the rubble they found the green lantern that once belonged to Alan Scott, the original Green Lantern.

THE PHANTOM STRANGER. One of the most powerful mystic figures in the universe, the Phantom Stranger is also one of the most mysterious. Though there are many theories about his origins, no one seems to know the true story. Some say he is an angel who remained neutral when Lucifer rebelled, but there are other stories.

Leaving behind an apartment where he has resided briefly, apparently sensing a mystical disturbance, the Phantom Stranger arrives at the museum exhibit just in time to lend a hand to Green Lantern and Superman.

DEADMAN. Former circus acrobat Boston Brand cannot go on to whatever afterlife awaits him. Instead, he greets souls newly departed from the flesh, and sometimes offers them counsel and comfort. When Superman and Green Lantern appear, presumably dead or nearly dead, he is the one who informs them of their situation.

WENG CHAN. A member of the Blackhawk Squadron, in 1949 he accompanied the leader of the group into the unearthed debris of the JSA's battle against Hitler.

CATWOMAN. Skilled thief Selina Kyle makes a brief appearance, bumping into Hal Jordan at the museum exhibit. She is dismayed to find that an item called the

Catkin Pearl is not to be a part of the exhibit. It has gone missing. Presumably, she is perturbed because she hoped to steal the pearl for herself.

TRIVIA

- Recalling the previously rejected *Action Comics Weekly* script, Gaiman sought Carlin's approval to see if the story might now be published apart from established continuity. Carlin agreed, but one further obstacle remained: Neither Gaiman nor DC had a copy of the script anymore. Gaiman remembered making a copy of the script for Brian Hibbs, but he no longer had it; however, he had previously copied it for his friend James Barry. Gaiman acknowledged both men in his introduction to the book.

THE QUOTABLE GAIMAN

On his love of obscure DC characters, the Phantom Stranger in particular:

I have a huge fondness for strange and stupid stuff. *Metamorpho*, from the 60's, is a title I love. The 60's run of *Plastic Man, Brave and Bold* from the 60's, y'know, because they had these incredible covers—Batman and Hawkman in the air, trying to rip each other's masks off for no apparently discernible reason. The *Time Commander* stories—Green Lantern trapped in a giant metal bat! Those were the kind of comics I loved. *Swamp Thing.* I loved the Phantom Stranger—the Len Wein/Jim Aparo run on *Phantom Stranger* in the 70's was absolutely stunning at the time. Nobody else, apart from Alan Moore very briefly, has ever done the Stranger right.

> —Interview with Brian Hibbs, owner of
> San Francisco's Comix Experience,
> October 26, 1989

‖‖‖

1602

(2004)

In 2002, Gaiman filed a lawsuit against Todd MacFarlane that involved the ownership rights of Cogliostro, Medieval Spawn, and Angela, three supporting characters he created back in 1991 when he, at the request of MacFarlane, did some work for the creator of Spawn at Image Comics.

The lawsuit was funded in part by Marvels and Miracles LLC, which Gaiman created to assist in untangling the legal copyrights surrounding the characters above, and those of another character he had written about, Miracleman. Gaiman directed that all of the profits from a new miniseries he was writing be used to fund Marvels and Miracles; that miniseries was called *1602*.

The concept driving *Marvel:1602* is simple, but intriguing: What if the Marvel Comics Universe came into being at the beginning of the seventeenth century, rather than at the end of the twentieth century? Assisted by artist Andy Kubert and colorist Richard Isanove, Gaiman concocted an original and intriguing answer.

The series began as a simple love letter to the Stan Lee/Jack Kirby/Steve Ditko comics of Gaiman's youth. But it soon grew unwieldy, almost unmanagable in scope, with nearly three dozen speaking characters. Another problem was that Gaiman had begun work assuming that the early Marvel history was common knowledge, only to discover that many modern comics readers had no knowledge of the stories of that era.

His idea had been to shift the Silver Age Marvel characters back, from 1962 to 1602, setting his story in Elizabethan England rather than the environs of modern-day New York City. Queen Elizabeth the First sits on the throne.

Bizarre weather patterns are manifesting across the globe. Many believe that the End Times are near. Meanwhile, King James of Scotland and Count Otto Von Doom (also known as Otto the Handsome) of Latveria are separately planning on conquering England. James wishes to become king, while Doom hopes to steal a secret weapon from the Knights Templar for use in his conquest of Europe.

Advising the queen in these turbulent times are her Intelligencer, Sir Nicholas Fury, and her court magician, Doctor Stephen Strange, *1602* versions of mainstay Marvel heroes Nick Fury and Dr. Strange.

Other players in this drama include:

Carlos Javier, who provides shelter and training to a group of uncanny
  teenagers who manifest strange abilities (*1602* versions of Professor X and
  the X-Men)
Peter Parquah, a confused but well-meaning teenager with an affection for
  arachnids (*1602*'s Spider-Man)
Blind Irish minstrel and spy Matthew Murdock (*1602*-era Daredevil)
Four uniquely powered crew members of the sailing vessel *The Fantastick* (the
  Fantastic Four, obviously)
Donal, who by striking his wooden cane on the ground transforms into the
  Norse God of Thunder (*1602*'s version of Marvel Comics's version of Thor)

And many, many others.

How much you enjoy this tale really depends on your knowledge of and affection for the core characters of the Marvel universe. The brief moments of frisson that occur each time an iconic figure is introduced are alone worth the price of admission. Gaiman incorporates almost all the early characters into the tale, with the notable exceptions of Tony Stark (Iron Man) and Hank Pym (Ant-Man); the fact that he has managed to tell an engaging story is gravy.

Longtime Marvel fans may recall the series *What If*, which told "imaginary" stories outside accepted Marvel continuity (something the editors there used to prize). *1602* however, is not that type of story. Rather, it represents a very original mystery with an excellent twist that makes sense—as such, it can comfortably exist within normal Marvel continuity.

Gaiman was ultimately happy with the way the book turned out. In the afterword to the hardcover collection, Gaiman talks about rereading the individual issues of the series in June 2004: "I just re-read *1602*, for proofreading purposes, this afternoon, in a small boat, drifting across a lake on a sunny day, and I found, to my relief, it was very much the kind of comic I had wanted to write: something for summer, to be read under a porch or in a treehouse; or up on a roof; or in a small field, a long time ago, beside the bulrush patch."

PEOPLE, PLACES, AND THINGS

QUEEN ELIZABETH THE FIRST. The historic Elizabeth I (1533–1603) was queen of England and Ireland from 1558 until her death. Also known as the Virgin Queen, Gloriana, or Good Queen Bess, Elizabeth was the last monarch of the Tudor dynasty. Playwrights William Shakespeare, Christopher Marlowe, and Ben Jonson flourished during the Elizabethan era; Francis Bacon wrote philosophical and political works; Francis Drake became the first Englishman to circumnavigate the globe; and the first English colonies in North America were founded. Like her father, Henry VIII, Elizabeth was a writer and poet.

KING JAMES OF SCOTLAND. The historic James (1566–1625) was king of Scots as James VI, and king of England and Ireland as James I. He ruled in Scotland as James VI from July 24, 1567, when he was only one year old, succeeding his mother Mary, queen of Scots. He succeeded Elizabeth I in 1603, ruling England, Scotland, and Ireland until his death some twenty-two years later.

SIR NICHOLAS FURY. The queen's Intelligencer (replacing spymaster Sir Francis Walsingham), he is *1602*'s equivalent of Nick Fury, director of SHIELD.

DOCTOR STEPHEN STRANGE. Master of the queen's medicines (replacing Elizabeth's personal mystic, Doctor John Dee), Strange is, of course, Dr. Strange, Master of the Mystic Arts.

MATTHEW MURDOCH. A blind musician gifted with great agility, he serves as a spy for Fury. Matthew is called Sir Devil by Fury; in the Marvel Comics universe he is better known as Daredevil, the Man without Fear.

PETER PARQUAGH. Young aide to Fury, Peter is the equivalent of Peter Parker, who, due to the bite of a radioactive spider becomes the Amazing Spider-Man. The joke built into Gaiman's story is that, although he comes close several times, Parquagh is not bitten by a spider until he reaches the New World at the conclusion of this tale.

COUNT OTTO VON DOOM. Otto the Handsome. In modern times he is better known as the malevolent, armored genius Dr. Doom.

THE GRAND INQUISITOR. Father to Petros and Sister Wanda, he is his time's equivalent of Magneto, evil master of magnetism, leader of the Brotherhood of Evil Mutants, sworn foes of the X-Men.

PETROS AND SISTER WANDA. 1602's version of Pietro Maximoff, better known as the mutant speedster Quicksilver, and Wanda Maximoff, aka the Scarlet Witch.

ROJHAZ. Pronounced "Rogers," which gives away his identity as Captain America. Here he's a white man dressed in Native American garb who zealously protects a young mutant girl named Virginia Dare.

THE WITCHBREED. In the world of 1602, witchbreed is another name for mutant.

SCOTTIUS SUMMERISLE, JOURNEYMAN ROBERT TREFUSIS, APPRENTICE JOHN GREY, WERNER, MASTER MCCOY, CARLOS JAVIER. The 1602 version of the X-Men; Cyclops, Iceman, Marvel Girl, the Angel, the Beast, and Professor X, respectively.

NATASHA. A spy against the crown, she is this era's equivalent of Natasha Romanoff, the Black Widow.

MASTER BANNER. An agent of James, he becomes a rampaging monster in the New World as a result of energies unleashed when all is restored to normal. The monster Banner is transformed into is that era's Incredible Hulk.

SIR RICHARD REED, MASTER JONATHAN STORM, MISTRESS SUSAN STORM, BENJAMIN GRIMM. Four seafaring adventurers, they are the first heroic family of any era they inhabit. They are, of course, the stars of what Marvel has called the World's Greatest Comic Magazine, the Fantastic Four, consisting of Mr. Fantastic, the Human Torch, the Invisible Woman, and the Thing.

THE WATCHER. The only character who retains his identity, he is Uatu of the race known as the Watchers, sworn only to observe the rise and fall of species throughout the universe.

DONAL. An old man, he is the human vessel for the Norse God of Thunder, the mighty Thor.

TRIVIA

- In 2004, *1602* was the best selling comic book series of the year.

- In 2005, *1602* won the Quill Award for Graphic Novel.

- The series spawned two spin-off miniseries: *1602: New World*, written by Greg Pak and illustrated by Greg Tocchini; and *Marvel 1602: The Fantastick Four*, written by Peter David and illustrated by Pascal Alixe.

- *1602* is much like the alternate histories perpetrated by close Gaiman friends like Kim Newman, Eugene Byrne, and Alan Moore, such as *Back in the USSA, Anno Dracula,* and *The League of Extraordinary Gentlemen*. All such revisionist fantasies owe a debt to the innovative science fiction/fantasy of Philip Jose Farmer (born 1918), whose taboo-busting novels often involve revisionist fusions. Farmer tied his own pantheon of characters and concepts to popular pulp and pop culture icons, and wove them all into a unified (and ever playful) mythology.

Such cross-fertilization of known genre "pocket universes" has become a mainstay in contemporary pop culture, but it was Farmer who blazed the trail, with his audacious, often satiric, riffs on revered literary heroes. The so-called Wold Newton Family novels propose that a meteorite that crashed in eighteenth-century Yorkshire, England (near Wold Newton), irradiated local pregnant women, who gave birth to mutant superhumans, spawning a family tree that included Lord Grandrith (Tarzan), Doc Caliban (Doc Savage), and others. This pantheon of novels eventually incorporated characters, concepts, and settings from Jules Verne, Edgar Rice Burroughs, H. Rider Haggard, Sir Arthur Conan Doyle, and others, and embraced King Kong, Phileas Fogg, Jack the Ripper, Sherlock Holmes, and even Kurt Vonnegut's fictional SF author Kilgore Trout.

The most popular of Farmer's work in this vein is undoubtedly the Riverworld series (8 novels, 1965–83), an epic fantasy featuring Samuel Clemens (Mark Twain), Jack London, Sir Richard Burton (the explorer, not the actor), and others, exploring their newly conjoined lives amid the resurrection of all mankind on the banks of a many-million-mile river on another planet. Clearly, Moore's *League of Extraordinary Gentlemen*, Newman's *Anno Dracula* novels, and some examples of Gaiman's work, including *1602,* owe debts to Farmer's pioneer creations, which forged what is now a genre in and of itself. These tales are extraordinary treats for fans with a broad knowledge of popular culture, allowing them to see different facets of familiar characters by placing them in extraordinary situations they normally wouldn't be seen in, or by exploiting historical oddities and happy coincidences.

I viewed the Marvel Universe as a real place. Everyone knew everyone. Everyone had mistakenly fought everyone, everyone had rescued everyone. The midsixties American Marvels I was able to find confirmed this impression: I delighted in the Inhumans, in the arrival of the Silver Surfer (not to mention Galactus). I caught up with Daredevil and Spider-Man. I found out what these characters looked like in color.

It was magic.

—Afterword, *1602*

|||||||||||||||||||||||||||||||||||||||||||||||||||||||||||||||||||||||

THE ETERNALS

(2006—2007)

After completing *1602*, Gaiman was asked by Marvel Comics editor-in-chief Joe Quesada if he'd be interested in working on another project for the company, this time writing a miniseries about the Jack Kirby–created Eternals. A devoted Kirby fan since childhood, and perceiving a worthy challenge to more firmly and logically integrate a group of godlike creatures into the Marvel universe, Gaiman readily agreed.

Anyone who was into comics in the sixties and seventies knows the name Jack Kirby. Kirby, who had cocreated Captain America in the forties for Timely Comics, was one of the chief architects of the so-called Marvel Age of comics in the sixties; he cocreated such iconic characters as Thor and the popular superteams the Fantastic Four and the Avengers. He is generally considered the most influential comic book artist of all time.

Although mostly (and justly) famous for his work on *Fantastic Four*, Kirby soared as an artist when he and Stan Lee worked on The Mighty Thor, a reworking of Norse legends. Kirby poured a lot of attention and love into his drawings of the God of Thunder and his fellow Asgardians, such as Odin, Loki, and Balder. He also seemed to relish drawing the lavish landscape of Asgard itself, often devoting wildly detailed two-page spreads to depicting the home of the gods, in an attempt to capture its majesty and wonder.

After departing Marvel Comics in the early seventies, Kirby spent several years at DC Comics, during which time he continued to pursue his interest in mythology, now through the vehicle of his Fourth World epic, in which he told tales of the New Gods, a race of powerful beings who arose from the ashes of the old gods. Although these titles were interesting and lovingly rendered, they failed to generate sufficient sales, disappointing both Kirby and his new employer. Kirby was perhaps a little bit ahead of his time, as the characters he created in the seventies have become cornerstones of the current DC universe.

After problems at DC led to his return to Marvel in the midseventies, Kirby created the Eternals, and again embraced themes he had started to pursue in his Fourth World series (for instance, the series is populated with many characters with variants on mythological names, i.e., Ikaris, Makkari, and Sersi in The Eternals, and Orion and Izaya in The New Gods).

The Eternals proposed that there had been two races of nonhumans dwelling on Earth since prehistory, unknown to mankind: the godlike Eternals, wellspring of the Greeks' mythic pantheon of gods, and the hideous, subterranean Deviants.

But the inspiration behind the Eternals differed from that which had sparked the creation of the New Gods. While the stories set in the Fourth World had dealt with creating new myths for a new era, The Eternals sought to provide an explanation for enduring myths and legends. Always prone to wonderful excess, Kirby, drawing on then popular books like Erich von Daniken's *Chariots of the Gods* and his own fevered imagination, threw a dizzying number of concepts into the series. During the course of its troubled run, the series delved into lost civilizations, apocalypse, secret superhuman relatives of man, godlike aliens, and genetic manipulation. Alas, the series never really caught on with Marvelites, and was canceled after a run of nineteen issues. Attempts to integrate the quirky characters were made over subsequent decades, all unsuccessful.

After the cancellation of Kirby's series, Marvel tried to resolve the uncomfortable union of the Eternals mythos and the Marvel universe in *The Mighty Thor* (issue 272 and up). A twelve-issue limited *Eternals* miniseries followed in 1986, adding little to the premise, though it was superior to subsequent one-shot efforts that introduced a bevy of new Eternals to its resurrection of Kirby's cast, to no good end.

Enter Neil Gaiman.

Gaiman described the challenge of revitalizing Kirby's characters on a panel at the 2007 San Diego Comic-Con:

> The problem with folding the Kirby characters into the Marvel universe is that the entire rationale for the Eternals is that these are the people who inspire the tales of the gods. The Deviants are what people believe to be demons. Which is all very well, except you're in a universe that really does have demons, and really does have gods. So how could you make these characters interesting, and seeing that pulling them back out of the Marvel universe was not an option, because over the last thirty years the things

that Jack created in The Eternals have become part and parcel of the Marvel universe?

Ably assisted by artist John Romita Jr., Gaiman proved equal to the task.

As the seven-issue miniseries opens, the superrace collectively known as Eternals is now scattered and amnesiac, having forgotten their powers and immortality, living normal, mundane, human lives. Meanwhile their age-old enemies, the Deviants, stalk the shadows, intending to awaken the Dreaming Celestial, who they feel is the key to a return to their former glory and power.

It is easy to recognize Gaiman's imprint on this modern-day clash between ancient forces. Shying from Kirby's *Chariots of God*–style alien mythologizing, he focuses more on his protagonists' struggle with coming to grips with the enormity of their identities and subsequent loss of their recently acquired humanity. Gaiman treats his source material with love and respect, revitalizing the franchise without sacrificing the least of Kirby's delightful and outrageous characters and concepts (he even manages to reference current Marvel continuity). Romita's storytelling is strong and compelling, capturing the grandeur of Kirby's art without slavishly imitating it.

It's interesting to note a Sandman connection here: The first page of issue 6 shows a number of individuals sharing a collective dream provoked by the waking of the Dreaming Celestial. This haunting scene recalls similar situations in the *Sandman* series, such as from Gaiman's first story arc, especially the pivotal story "24 Hours."

PEOPLE, PLACES, AND THINGS

THE ETERNALS. A race of "about 100" powerful beings created by the godlike Celestials to protect Earth. Shortly after the reappearance of the Celestials in the 1970s (the Third Horde), this race lost its collective memory and went out to live anonymously among the humans they had nurtured and protected over the centuries.

THE DEVIANTS. Also created by the Celestials, every member of the Deviant race was "a fresh roll of the genetic dice." The Deviants, who number in the thousands, would use their powers to subjugate the human race. Their current plan is to awaken the Dreaming Celestial, who is imprisoned under the crust of the Earth in California for reasons known only to him and his fellow Celestials. His awakening may bring the next Horde of Celestials to Earth, resulting in a cleansing of "this part of the galaxy of the disease called life."

THE CELESTIALS. An enigmatic, unimaginably powerful race of space aliens, they seeded the Earth eons ago with Eternals, Deviants, and the progenitors of modern human beings, then departed. It is known, however, that they will one day return to judge their creations, either allowing them to continue on, or merely wiping them out, perhaps to start their experiment over again.

MARK CURRY. An ER doctor, he dreams of having another identity, that of Makkari of the Eternals. His dreams are confirmed as reality when he is visited by Ike Harris, who tells him that he is actually an immortal, indestructible being, placed on Earth by aliens to preserve and safeguard the planet. Makkari has the power of superspeed. Over the centuries he's had an on-again, off-again relationship with fellow Eternal Sersi.

IKE HARRIS. Ikaris of the Eternals, he is the first to recover his memories. He travels the Earth seeking out his old companions, such as Makkari, who, like him, have forgotten their past lives. Besides having impressive strength, Ikaris, as you might expect, can fly.

SPRITE. Star of *It's Just So Sprite,* a popular television show. An Eternal trapped in a body equivalent to that of a human eleven-year-old (Gaiman reveals that he inspired J. M. Barrie to write *Peter Pan*), he longed for a normal life. His quest for mortality warped him, and led him to pursue an ambitious plot that altered the very nature of reality. Gifted with the power of illusion, he wiped the memories of his fellow Eternals, giving them human identities while securing fame, fortune, and, most important, humanity, for himself. Due to his actions, the Eternals are not ready to fend off the plans of the Deviants to awake the Dreaming Celestial. Sprite ultimately perishes at the hand of Zuras.

SERSI. This flighty, irresponsible party planner was formerly a member of the Avengers, one of the premiere supergroups of the Marvel universe. As the story begins, however, she has no memory of the Eternals or the Avengers. Sersi is a sorceress, with the ability to transform creatures and things from one form to another.

THENA. Daughter of Zuras. Along with her father, she acts as a tactician for her race. In human guise she is known as Dr. Thena Eliot. Thena is the ultimate huntress and warrior.

TONY STARK. Billionaire industrialist playboy, he is also Iron Man, the armor-clad Avenger. His interest in the Eternals is political, as he has sided with the current administration in its effort to force all superhumans to register with the U.S. government. When he asks whose side the Eternals are on, he is given the answer: "If you saw two groups of children arguing over which of them could play in some waste ground, would you choose sides?"

ZURAS. The mightiest of the Eternals, he is their leader, the rock their race was built on. Because of Sprite he has spent the last thirty-plus years wandering the streets of New York City—homeless.

AJAK. An Eternal who can speak to the Celestials, mind to mind.

DRUIG. Deputy prime minister of Vorozheika, he is, like his fellow Eternal Sersi, a transformer. He also has the power to reach into minds and pluck out unpleasant memories that he uses to manipulate his victims. His ambitions are limited, however, as he uses his abilities merely to seize control of the Eastern European country he used to serve.

OLYMPIA. Situated in Antarctica, Olympia, the home of the Eternals, is the location of the alien technology that grants the Eternals their immortality. It also contains their collective memory.

THE UNI-MIND. The "greater consciousness" formed by the collective minds and life-forces of the Eternals. "It has no gender. It has no race. It is made of light and mind and of pure energy. It is composed of will and of intelligence."

MORJAK AND GELT. The two Deviants (although they prefer to call themselves members of the "Changing People") behind the plot to wake the Dreaming Celestial, they call to mind other gruesome antagonists in the Gaiman canon, like Brute and Glob (from *Sandman*), Mr. Vandemar and Mr. Croup (from *Neverwhere*), and Mr. Stone and Mr. Wood (from *American Gods*). The two Deviants use Makkari to wake the Dreaming Celestial.

THE DREAMING CELESTIAL. Imprisoned on Earth, this entity slept until it was awakened by the emissaries of the Changing People. Although its awakening did not trigger the next coming of the Celestial Horde, it did result in a message being delivered by this massive and majestic creature to the Eternals via Makkari: When it has seen enough, it will judge the Earth.

KRA. Military leader of the Deviants of Lemuria, he leads an attack on Olympia, only to relent after realizing that Makkari is in fact the Skadrach, whom the Deviants believe to be a prophet of the Celestials.

THE QUOTABLE GAIMAN

A really cool thing about *The Eternals* is that Jack (Kirby) never really got to finish it, and then it got badly incorporated into the Marvel universe. The guys at Marvel came to me to ask if I could fix it, could I at least try to take what Jack did and incorporate it slightly better into the Marvel universe so that these characters had value. I thought, that's a fun challenge, sure!

—Rain Taxi, Vol. II, No. 4
(raintaxi.com), Winter 2006/2007

TEKNO COMIX

Between 1995 and 1997 a company called Tekno Comix was formed by Laurie Silvers and Mitchell Rubenstein (also known for developing the Sci-Fi Channel) as a division of their publicly traded company, Big Entertainment. Seeking to carve out a piece of the comic book market, the company published titles conceived by well-known creators, such as fantasy author Tad Williams (*Mirror World*), Gene Roddenberry of *Star Trek* fame (*Lost Universe*), Isaac Asimov, author of the science fiction classic *I, Robot* (*I-bots*), John Jakes, creator of *The Kent Family Chronicles* (*Mullkon Empire*), Leonard Nimoy, *Star Trek*'s Mr. Spock (*Primortals*), and Mickey Spillane, author of the legendary *I, The Jury,* featuring the iconic Mike Hammer (*Mike Danger*). Although exploiting characters and situations created by these people, the comics were for the most part scripted and illustrated by hired comic book professionals.

Gaiman himself contributed characters and concepts to the line, including Lady Justice, Mr. Hero, the Newmatic Man, *Phage: Shadow Death* (a six-issue limited series), Teknophage, and *Wheel of Worlds* (two one-shots). Though they aren't technically Gaiman's own writings, the creator was more involved than most people think.

"What most folks don't realize about Teknophage was how deeply involved Neil was in the whole creative process," says Rick Veitch, writer for Teknophage, in reply to an e-mail query for this volume. "After he created the basic character, he and I worked closely to flesh out Teknophage. And, even though I don't think he was being paid, Neil was hands-on story editor for all six issues that I wrote for Bryan [Talbot]. It was a terrific creative experience for me, with Neil gently pushing me to make my human protagonists more soulful and nuanced. Bryan, of course, turned in a brilliant art job and I'm extremely proud of our run on that series."

Because these weren't actually written by Gaiman, we won't discuss them issue by issue. We are pleased, however, to present, with the author's permission, the original proposal he prepared for these comics.

Enjoy.

OUTLINE FOR TEKNO COMICS, BY NEIL GAIMAN

If this is 2049, why does it look so much like 1994?

There is an Earth that's a lot like ours. Too much so perhaps, considering that as far as the inhabitants are concerned they're living in the 1990s.

And the world certainly looks a great deal like the one we know. Cars, CDs, crime, famine, war, rock 'n' roll, America, Japan . . . it's here all right.

But there are a few slight differences.

Most of these have to do with people.

On this Earth, the era we think of as "Victorian" went on for another forty years. Branches of science were explored in new (or old) and very different ways. It was a grimy past, a place of steam and coal and miracles, in which Edison—The Wizard of New Jersey—actually practiced a form of steam-driven alchemy, in which all the excesses and cruelties of the Victorian world were magnified, in which all the hypocrisies were made even deeper and more divisive, in which the advances made in science instead of lessening the boundaries between rich and poor only enlarged them, made them more terrible. Huge gritty smoky unpleasant cities covered the Earth, in which child prostitution and begging became the norm. In which the Germany of Hitler was closer to the world of METROPOLIS, and even more deadly . . .

The Victorian Age became the Victorious Age.

And then—somehow—the past was changed. Something happened. Fifty years were as if they'd never been. It was no longer 1939: it was 1888 once more.

The fifty-odd years were swallowed by time and almost forgotten. The river of time had rushed through in 1888, leaving the Victorious Era behind. (Look at a geography text on the formation of an ox-bow lake. That was what happened here. Sort of. Those fifty years sort of unhappened.)

This time, the second time, Time flowed properly, and followed much the same path as it did in our own world.

However, it means that while the rest of the multiverse sees the world as 2049, for us, we're in the 1990s.

The Victorious Age has also left a few fossils, as it were, behind.

Some of these are in the form of people.

THE RECOMBINANT

He has no clear memory of his birth or early life. He is the closest thing there is to a "Super-hero" in this world. If he is, in fact, for that matter, a "He."

Created in the laboratories of the Victorious Age by a combination of experimental science and alchemy, the Recombinant has, sometimes, strange powers and abilities; at others times, crippling disabilities. The Recombinant is a genetic experiment gone horribly wrong—or right.

The Recombinant cannot die.

Or rather, the Recombinant does die, but as soon as its heart stops breathing, it recombines, into something new and, always, strange (although sometimes strange in ways it doesn't figure out until they happen).

The Recombinant's entire bodily structure changes on death—sometimes even size and sex change. Skin color isn't constant either. It's a fast process—as soon as the Recombinant dies, it simply recombines. It's thrown up a number of variants over the years—there was the time the Recombinant turned into a wolf when the moon was full, there was the recombinant with wings, there was the time the Recombinant had a body that people simply did not focus on or think about, rendering him effectively invisible; there have been supermen, there have been monsters; there have been times he was male, times he was female, times he was neither.

It tends to recombine into a form that will help the Recombinant at death—killed by a fall, the next Recombinant body might well be able to fly, for example. It's one long, losing game of catch-up.

Of course, the Recombinant doesn't know how much longer this will go on. Killing yourself to get out of a tight spot is not an easy thing to do: you simply don't ever get used to it. Or like it. Or trust it.

And he does die. Each time he dies, it's for real.

Very few people have realized over the last 100+ years that the various humanoid biological anomalies, the strange heroes who have cropped up in various parts of the world, were in reality only one person. Who dies a lot. Who doesn't die. The Recombinant.

The Recombinant seeks a normal life. Normally circumstances don't give it one for very long.

MISTER HERO, THE NEWMATIC MAN (PUGILIST AND RATIOCINATOR)

Mister Hero, the Newmatic Man, was named after Hero of Alexandria, discoverer of steam power, and his *Pneumatica,* the original book on the power of steam. Mister Hero was created a hundred years ago by an unknown amateur scientist, and sold to British magician and conjurer John Maskelyne, who improved and named him.

Maskelyne was a magician, famed for his illusions, such as Psycho, a torso on a glass pillar that picked out cards and fortunes for the audience.

Mister Hero was one better than that. He was a metal, steam-driven "pugilist and ratiocinator." A robot, before the term was coined. Coal-fueled, steam-driven.

He's the height of a tall man. When he's naked you can see the little door and gauge on his chest. When he's naked he has a Victorian bathing costume painted on.

At Maskelyne and Devant's Conjuring Emporium in London, Mister Hero would, first of all, box one round with anyone in the audience. Then Maskelyne would apparently replace its head with another, and it would answer questions from the audience, making Holmes-like deductions.

An unfortunate incident, when a man from the audience suffered a broken jaw, and the public outcry that followed, led Maskelyne to retire Mister Hero. He went into a box.

He's been in mothballs for a century, in the basement of a museum of Conjuring; or most of him has. Over the years, many of the bits have been separated.

A young amateur magician finds one of the packing cases, in the museum basement, and reads the legend "MISTER HERO, THE NEWMATIC MAN—PUGILIST

AND RATIOCINATOR" on the side. She decides to try and rebuild the Newmatic Man, and see if she can figure out how the trick was done.

She rebuilds Mister Hero—some of him. There's a hand missing, and no head. It doesn't seem to work—there's a rudimentary steam engine boiler inside, some flexible pipes inside. It's very heavy. She's coming to the conclusion that Mister Hero must have been a string puppet and a ventriloquist act when . . .

She finds a cast-iron head in an art gallery. It's the head of a Victorian gentleman. The paint's scratched in places, and the gloss has gone. It's cast in one piece, so you can't open it. It's on sale as a rather ugly example of antique kitsch, redeemed as modern art. But there's a bolt-and-screw unit around the neck that looks familiar. There are other potential buyers. It's crazy, but . . .

She blows her savings on the thing. It's a wild guess, and it's the money she was going to use to buy a car. (The head's been welded to a bicycle frame, and she needs to chip off the frame without damaging it too much.)

She takes the head back to the museum. Screws it on . . .

And it fits. A puff of steam comes from the pipes in his back. The gauges swing around. His eyes open.

"Allow me to introduce myself," he says, in a voice like Basil Rathbone's. And Mister Hero, the Newmatic Man, Pugilist (and, if they can find its thinking head, Ratiocinator) lives again. It looks like a slightly stiff Victorian prizefighter, mustachioed and clean-jawed.

Motivated by the best Victorian ideals—honesty, sympathy, "fair play" and so forth, Mister Hero is a fish out of water in the here and now, as, accompanied by its new friend (the amateur magician who rebuilt our coal-fired, steam-driven hero) it sets off to find its other heads, and the truth of its existence, to right wrongs and fight for decency and modesty.

Once it gets its ratiocinating head (which has a pipe, out of which clouds of steam are emitted) it is able to deduce and ponder. One of the things it points out is that there were several other heads.

THE TEKNOPHAGE

Tecnophage, or Teknophage (you can spell it both ways) is an old word. It means "child eater."

The Teknophage is the last of the dinosaurs.

Sixty-five million years ago, in the last days of the dinosaurs, there was, briefly, an intelligent race of dinosaurs. A little more than man-high. There weren't many of them—only a few hundred. They kept their numbers down by eating their young. They were intensely territorial—there would be one of the Teknophages to an area of thousands of square miles.

The nastiest, largest of the 'phages (He's gorilla-sized or bear- sized, not T. Rex–sized) gradually began to expand its territory, which it did by killing off the other 'phages around it. Each life it ate added to its own life span.

Eventually there was only one of them left: him. The last Teknophage. A slightly telepathic, immensely powerful, wise, cruel old reptile.

When a giant meteor hit the Earth, however, the 'phage was powerless. The mental powers of the 'phages together might have turned it away. But they were gone. There was only one left.

What killed the Dinosaurs?

The Teknophage did.

He went into hibernation, then, emerging for a few brief programs of genetic experimentation, some of which bore fruit, some of which didn't. His last one may have produced humanity—or so he claims.

The Teknophage was the serpent in the garden.

He's watched as mankind has grown and expanded. He's still territorial. He considers himself the owner of Earth, and in some senses anyway, he's right.

The Teknophage knows part of what happened to the mysterious, lost Victorious Age, and this Earth's lost fifty years.

It has discovered, now, that there are other dimensions, other versions of Earth, accessible through the Wheel of Worlds. It wants them as its own territory.

The Teknophage is the ultimate crime boss, behind-the-scenes dictator, mad scientist, big business boss. It makes Josef Mengele look like a kid in a science lab. It does not eat often, but it needs to eat live food when it does—predators for preference.

It does not look human, although it is humaniform. It has huge, sharp, carnivorous teeth in a wide mouth, reptile eyes, grayish-crocodiley skin.

It wears immaculate suits.

ADAM CAIN

He's twenty thousand years old, more or less, one of the very first Homo Sapiens. The basis for every legend of the wandering Jew, of Cain and Abel.

He was born in Africa, the birthplace of mankind. He's black, with a thin black tribal tattoo down one side of his face. He walks everywhere, with the aid of a long staff. He looks perhaps in his forties, although his eyes are much older. He dresses appropriately, if shabbily, to wherever he is, but favors a long coat.

He says he's walking to forget, or until he is forgiven, but the nature of his crime is unknown.

He has come in conflict with the Teknophage several times in the last twenty thousand years. The 'phage, however, has not had Adam Cain killed—possibly he can't.

There is nothing overtly remarkable about Adam Cain, other than his long years. Cut him and he bleeds, although he also heals fast. He has learned many things over the years, and speaks most languages. He's wise, and as he walks he tries to right wrongs around him. There are dark depths to him, though; memories of old sorrows, of lives he's seen, of cities and places that have been swallowed by time and to which he can never return.

He comes out of nowhere, gets involved in people's lives, does his best to help, and then leaves again. Sometimes it's a small thing—it's reuniting a shattered family, restoring someone's confidence, getting a kid off crack, introducing two people who'd make a perfect pair; sometimes it's a bigger thing—rescuing Jews from Germany, occasionally bringing down an evil government or organization.

All of it, though, is done in a sense of expiation—as if only by doing good, but doing all that one man can do to improve a world, he will at last be able to stop walking, to rest and find peace.

LADY JUSTICE

There may or may not be gods and occult powers in this version of the Earth.

There is, however, Lady Justice.

It could be a ghost, a power, a strange form of mass hysteria. What it is doesn't matter. It's what it does . . .

Lady Justice is a force that possesses women—only ever women. Only one woman at a time, and then, only when the scales of Justice need to be tipped back, in a place where the law can do nothing.

It could be the president of a corporation. It could be a welfare mother. It could be a doctor, a secretary, a stripper, a TV newscaster, a homemaker, a truck driver. The power picks a woman to right the injustice . . .

She ties on a blindfold. As long as she is blindfolded, she is Lady Justice. Her senses become supersharp. She becomes able, somehow, to perceive on a level that isn't seeing. She takes on abilities that, in real life, she doesn't have. She becomes an implacable enemy of a specific injustice, and remains Lady Justice until either the wrong is righted, and the blindfold comes off—leaving her with no memory of the time she was Lady Justice—or until the host body is killed.

If the host body is killed, the Lady Justice entity will choose another woman to wear the blindfold, until whatever it went after is finished.

The Lady Justice phenomenon is recognized in the world. It isn't understood.

It's a start.

THE QUOTABLE GAIMAN

I've never had a very high opinion of people who talk loudly in comic stores. I'm not talking about the customers, and I'm not talking about the staff. It's the other ones—the ones who hang around the front counter—normally really irritating the staff and getting in the way of the customers—talking loudly about the secret world of comics. Because these guys know the secrets. And they tell everyone. That they know nothing is no impediment to them talking . . .

Jo Duffy, a very nice lady, overheard one of them claiming intimate knowledge of a number of writers, ending with "Now that Jo Duffy—that guy is a bastard. Let me tell you about *him* . . ."

My cousin Adam Gaiman told me about listening to one of them telling a comic shop in Newcastle everything he knew about me. Adam thought it was particularly hilarious, because none of it was even remotely true. At the point where the gentleman announced that it was common knowledge in the industry that "Gaiman" was a pen name chosen to proclaim my sexual preferences to the world, Adam went over and showed him his bus pass, with his name on it.

Sometimes I worry that the Internet is in danger of giving the loud guy at the front of the comic-book store an audience rather larger than a couple of kids and the manager.

—journal.neilgaiman.com

||||||||||||||||||||||||||||||||||||||||||||||||||||||||||||||||||

RARITIES, DABBLINGS, AND JAMS

Over the course of his career Neil Gaiman has penned dozens of comic book stories that have not garnered the attention lavished upon his more famous works. In the preceding pages we have drawn special attention to those of particular length or merit or interest or significance in the Gaiman canon. But the author's other comic book work—the rare appearances, dabblings in other people's universes, and artistic and creative jams with other writers and artists—must not go without mention. And, honestly, some of our favorites are on this list.

Have we covered them all? Almost certainly not. Some readers will doubtless point out a scribbled sketch accompanying a letters page comment, a few panels of dialogue, or even an entire story we've left undiscovered. But we think we've got them all . . . and we'll stick to that belief until the first conclusive e-mail commentary arrives.

Of course, by the time this book is published, Gaiman will surely have added to the list.

"A BLACK AND WHITE WORLD" FROM BATMAN: BLACK AND WHITE #2 (1996)

Published in the second issue of *Batman: Black and White*, a four-issue 1996 miniseries featuring Batman stories in, surprise, black and white. Illustrated by Simon Bisley, the story brings to mind those old Looney Tunes shorts where the sheep dog and Wile E. Coyote punch in at the beginning of the cartoon, do battle, then punch out at the end, another day at the office concluded. In this tale it's Batman and the Joker, who run through their lines, engage in pitched battle, then retire to a film studio's commissary.

"CELEBRITY RARE BIT FIENDS" (1994)

Comic book writer and artist Rick Veitch spent years chronicling his dreams in illustrated form in the series *Rare Bit Fiends*. In 1994, Gaiman provided three of his own dreams to Veitch, who illustrated them as backup sections in the second and third issues of the series.

"THE CIGARETTE AD" FROM THE TRUTH #6 (1988)

The sixth issue of British magazine *The Truth* included an amusing article called "Kid's Stuff," co-authored by Gaiman, Eugene Byrne, and Kim Newman. Within the article was an amusing four-panel comic book "story" (really a faux cigarette ad) written by Gaiman, with art by Mark Buckingham, in what was apparently their first collaboration.

"COMIX ECSPERIENSE" FROM COMIX EXPERIENCE FIFTH ANNIVERSARY ASHCAN (1994)

A short strip written and illustrated by Gaiman to celebrate the fifth anniversary of Comix Experience in San Francisco, California, one of the most prominent comic book retailers in the United States.

"THE COURT," FROM IT'S DARK IN LONDON (1996)

This brief tale, illustrated by Warren Pleece for editor Oscar Zarate's noir collection *It's Dark in London*, would eventually be incorporated into Gaiman's short story "Keepsakes and Treasures." (See the short stories section for more information.)

"COVER STORY" FROM A1#5 (1991)

Gaiman worked with frequent Sandman illustrator Kelley Jones on "Cover Story." A1 was an anthology series published by UK-based Atomeka Press, which frequently published work by the superstars of that era's British comics scene, including Alan Moore.

"DEADY AND I" FROM THE BOOK OF DEADY (2006)

ART BY VOLTAIRE

The Book of Deady collects the first three issues of artist/writer Voltaire's series about an evil teddy bear. Though that description alone is pure genius, there is a bit more to it. "What do you get when the galaxy's greatest evil escapes confinement on its home world and possesses the body of a discarded teddy bear here on Earth? An adorably evil teddy bear that eats cats, chases skirts, and torments children," declares promotional copy for the collection.

Gaiman's four-page tale, "Dead and I," comes from the third issue, *Deady the Evil Teddy.* Illustrated, of course, by Voltaire, the story concerns an "unfortunate meeting with Voltaire and Deady in an all-night noodles joint in New York City!"

Longtime comics publisher Sirius put out the collection in 2006. Voltaire is best known as the artist/writer/creator of such series as Oh My Goth! and Chi-Chian. Other guest creators in the collection included Clive Barker, James O'Barr, Daniel Brereton, Roman Dirge, Ted Naifeh, and Gris Grimly.

"THE FALSE KNIGHT ON THE ROAD" FROM THE BOOK OF BALLADS AND SAGAS #1 (1995)

"The False Knight on the Road" is an eight-page story written by Gaiman and illustrated by the series creator (and through his company, Green Man Press, publisher) Charles Vess. Vess, of course, is best known to Gaiman fans as the artist/collaborator who created Stardust with Gaiman.

Based on a work collected in Francis James Child's *The English and Scottish Popular Ballads,* this 1995 adaptation tells of a young lad who has a potentially perilous encounter with a knight with a flaming skull, a specter with whom he engages in a brief battle of wits before the False Knight, in reality the Devil, abruptly disappears, leaving the boy to resume his trip to school. It is collected in 2004's *The Book of Ballads.*

"FEEDERS AND EATERS" FROM ASYLUM #2 (1993)

A comic book adaptation of Gaiman's short story of the same name, "Feeders and Eaters" was illustrated by Mark Buckingham and first appeared in the anthology comic book *Asylum* issue 2. The issue also included work by others of Gaiman's friends including P. Craig Russell and John Bolton. (See the short stories section for more information.)

"FRAGMENTS" FROM REDFOX #20 (1989)

Originally debuting in *Dragonlords* magazine, the tales of the woman warrior Redfox led to the creation of Valkyrie Press, which would also later publish Bryan Talbot's groundbreaking *The Adventures of Luther Arkwright*. In this, the final issue, Gaiman scripted five pages to help out, because the series writer, Chris Bell, was busy preparing for the arrival of her baby. When the creator/god of the Redfox universe appears, he bears a striking resemblance to Gaiman.

"FROM HOMOGENOUS TO HONEY" FROM AARGH! (1998)

The title of this anthology graphic novel is an acronym for Artists Against Rampant Government Homophobia. It was the brainchild of Alan Moore, who formed his own publishing company, Mad Love, to publish the book as a reaction to Clause 28, a British law meant to outlaw the promotion of homosexuality. The book included work by such comics industry stars as David Lloyd, Frank Miller, Dave Gibbons, Bill Sienkiewicz, Art Spiegelman, Dave Sim, Robert Crumb, Jamie Delano, and Brian Bolland. Moore contributed a story, "The Mirror of Love," illustrated by his *Swamp Thing* collaborators, Steve Bissette and Rick Veitch.

Gaiman's tale, "From Homogenous to Honey," was illustrated by Bryan Talbot and Mark Buckingham, two of his most frequent collaborators. It featured a figure covering his face with a mask, discussing the efforts of his society to go back in time and eradicate any trace of influence by homosexuals. While this begins with entertainment—television and film and radio and music—it goes back through books, and then into society and civilization. When their efforts are complete, modern society is filled with faceless, featureless, indistinct drones.

"Everybody is exactly the same," the no-longer-masked, blank-faced man concludes. "Isn't it sweet?"

"THE GREAT COOL CHALLENGE" FROM BLAAM! #1 (1988)

A giveaway by Titan distributors in the UK, BLAAM! issue 1 was a September, 1988 experiment that contained several stories, including "The Great Cool Challenge" by Gaiman, illustrated by Shane Oakley. According to Gaiman himself, "Other than some great Shane Oakley art, you aren't missing anything."

"HARLAN AND ME" (1994)

This free chapbook was a small comic book given away at the 1994 Chicago Comic-Con, a tribute to the convention's guest of honor, Harlan Ellison, written *and* drawn by Gaiman.

"AN HONEST ANSWER" FROM SOU'WESTER: EASTERCON 1994 PROGRAMME BOOK *(1994)*

Later reprinted in *Ex-Directory: The Secret Files of Bryan Talbot*, "An Honest Answer" is Gaiman's response to the question writers most dread, and are most frequently asked: "Where do you get your ideas?" Drawn by Talbot, it is a humorous four-page comic book story in which Gaiman goes to visit "the Infinite" to ask for an idea and becomes frustrated with customer service.

"THE INNKEEPER'S SOUL" FROM CHERRY DELUXE #1 *(1998)*

Cherry was a pornographic comic book series that debuted in 1982 as *Cherry Poptart*. The title was changed in an effort on the part of creator and publisher Larry Welz to avoid a lawsuit from Kellogg's over their Pop-Tart trademark. Originally published by Last Gasp, the comic was later produced by Cherry Comics. Though there would always be detractors because of its adult content, the series was much loved for its charm, humor, politics (and, of course, sex), and for the winking irony of Welz's art style, a deliberate play on the house style of Archie comics.

In Gaiman's story, drawn by *Cherry*'s creator, Larry Welz, an angel version of Cherry struggles with a demon version for the girl's soul.

"IT WAS A DARK AND SILLY NIGHT" FROM LITTLE LIT: IT WAS A DARK AND SILLY NIGHT *(2003)*

An anthology of comic book stories for children, *Little Lit* was published by HarperCollins in the United States and edited by Maus creator Art Spiegelman and Françoise Mouly, and it featured contributions by authors and artists including Lemony Snicket and Richard Sala, William Joyce, J. Otto Seibold and Vivian Walsh. Each of the stories is entitled "It Was a Dark and Silly Night."

For his own "It Was a Dark and Silly Night," Gaiman teams up with legendary *Playboy* and *New Yorker* cartoonist Gahan Wilson. The review from *School Library Journal* puts it better than we could: "Neil Gaiman's creepy saga of a ghouls-just-wanna-have-fun cemetery party derives much of its goofiness from Gahan Wilson's trademark goggle-eyed, lumpish kids and creatures."

Gaiman and Wilson are delightful together, and this story leaves the reader wishing for more collaborations between the two.

"THE LIGHT BRIGADE" FROM TRIDENT #1 *(1989)*

This 1989 comic book anthology from short-lived, UK-based Trident Comics featured a two-part tale entitled "The Light Brigade." Part 1 was written by

Gaiman, with Nigel Kitching (who illustrated both parts of the story), and Part 2 was written by Gaiman alone. Also featured in this issue was Eddie Campbell's "Bacchus."

In a 1989 preview book announcing Trident Comics, the story is described as "SF adventure in a computerized world, as four young people enter cyberspace. Created by Neil Gaiman (*Sandman, Black Orchid, Violent Cases*) and Nigel Kitching, continued by Nigel with Neil's help."

"LUTHER'S VILLANELLE" FROM THE ADVENTURES OF LUTHER ARKWRIGHT: THE CRYSTAL PALACE EXHIBITION OF 1991 *(1991)*

In 1989, Gaiman wrote this poem as a birthday present for Luther Arkwright creator Bryan Talbot. This is a comics adaptation of the poem, illustrated by Ali Clark. (See the poems section for more information.)

"MR. X: HEARTSPRINGS AND WATCHSTOPS" FROM A1 #1 *(1989)*

Illustrated by Dave McKean, this was one of three Mr. X stories that appeared in the first issue of UK publisher Atomeka's A1 anthology series. Created in 1983 by writer/artist Dean Motter, the series Mr. X revolved around the mysterious title character, apparently the architect of Radiant City, a twisted, Fritz Lang–inspired city. Shortly before publication of "Heartsprings and Watchstops," Gaiman told interviewer Steve Whitaker, "I'm doing some Mr. X stuff with Dave [McKean]. We're doing three short stories now, which will be appearing as the backups for Mr. X 15–17. Another story by Dave and I will appear in *A1*, and then in colour as a backup in Mr. X."

Only the *A1* story ever appeared.

"ON THE STAIRS" FROM SOLO #8 *(2006)*

In 2005, DC Comics launched a new experimental title, Solo. Each issue showcased a different artist, illustrating various stories, often provided by multiple writers. *Solo* issue 8 focused on Danish artist Teddy Kristiansen, who first worked with Gaiman on the *Sandman Midnight Theatre* one-shot in 1995. Gaiman wrote one of the five stories in this issue (Kristiansen wrote three of them himself). Longtime DC and Vertigo character Deadman is featured in Gaiman's story having a conversation while sitting "on the stairs," and talking about love and death, and the relative merits of one when faced with the other.

"ORIGINAL SINS" FROM SECRET ORIGINS SPECIAL #1 (1989)

This story, illustrated by Mike Hoffman, is a framing device for the *Special,* detailing the behind-the-scenes action of a crew filming a segment for the television show *Steve Jones Investigates,* about Batman, his villains, and Gotham City. The story acts as an introduction to the three main stories in the *Special,* about the origins of the Penguin, the Riddler (see "When Is a Door?"), and Two-Face. The Joker has a cameo at the end of the story, killing Steve Jones on camera with his Joker venom, leaving him with a demented smile on his face.

"'ORRIBLE MURDERS" (1992)

In 1992, Gaiman plotted this 24-hour comic, a fundraiser for the London Cartoon Centre, which provided classes in comic book illustration during the early nineties UK comics scene. Four different writers contributed to the script, though Gaiman only provided the plot, and a long list of artists each drew a single page to create the finished product, including Mark Buckingham and David Lloyd.

"PAVANE" FROM SECRET ORIGINS #36 (1989)

Illustrated by frequent Gaiman collaborator Mark Buckingham, "Pavane" is a tale of Batman nemesis Poison Ivy, and is quite significant in relation to Gaiman's work on Black Orchid, and his intention to take over the reins of Swamp Thing. (See the essay "Notes Towards a Vegetable Theology.") In it Ivy plays games with Prison Inspector Stuart, a man who is making an attempt to understand her psyche. The story establishes the connections between Ivy and Jason Woodrue, later the Floronic Man.

"ROMITA—SPACE KNIGHT!" FROM JOHN ROMITA, JR. 30TH ANNIVERSARY SPECIAL (2007)

Second-generation Marvel artist John Romita Jr. celebrated his thirtieth anniversary in comics in 2007. This sixty-four-page special included a reprint of the first story Romita ever drew at Marvel, as well as a host of covers and pinups, and interviews, and one brand-new story, "Romita—Space Knight!" a humorous riff written by Gaiman and illustrated by Hilary Barta. The title of the story is a play on an old Marvel series, *Rom—Space Knight,* itself based upon a 1970s Parker Brothers toy line.

"SLOTH" FROM SEVEN DEADLY SINS (1989)

Another of the anthology trade paperbacks that Gaiman contributed to for UK underground comics publisher Knockabout, *Seven Deadly Sins* featured seven tales, each focusing on one of the titular sins. Gaiman's story concerned "Sloth," and was illustrated by Bryan Talbot; it was later collected in *Ex-Directory: The Secret Files of Bryan Talbot*. The book included other well-known UK comics creators of the era, including Alan Moore (on "Lust") and Dave Gibbons (on "Gluttony").

"THE SPIRIT: THE RETURN OF MINK STOLE" FROM THE SPIRIT: THE NEW ADVENTURES #2 (1998)

Writer/artist Will Eisner—one of the greatest figures in the history of comics and widely considered the father of the modern graphic novel—created The Spirit for newspaper comic sections in 1940. At its height, "the Spirit section"—which also featured other Eisner-created characters—reached a circulation of more than five million. The original series has been reprinted many times over the decades, most notably in the hardcover *The Spirit Archives* series by DC Comics. New adventures have also been produced, first by Kitchen Sink Press in the midnineties, and then by DC Comics in 2007.

"The Return of Mink Stole," Gaiman's one Spirit story, appeared in the second issue of the Kitchen Sink Press revival; it was illustrated by Eddie Campbell, an artist best known for his work with Alan Moore on *From Hell*. Gaiman's story—about a screenwriter who encounters the Spirit and Mink Stole while brainstorming ideas for a new film—is unusual for the series in that it appears to be set in the present day.

"SWEAT AND TEARS" FROM BLOOD CHILDE #4 (1995)

Despite its inclusion here, this story was not written by Neil Gaiman. Millennium Publications produced writer/creator Faye Perozich's short-lived series Blood Childe in the midnineties. The series was originally meant for DC Comics, and Perozich wanted to have Death of the Endless appear. Gaiman apparently gave his blessing, leading to a long phone call with Perozich, which inspired the story of this issue 4 significantly enough that the writer gave Gaiman costory credit when it was published. Reportedly, Gaiman was unaware of this credit for years after publication.

THE TOTALLY STONKING, SURPRISINGLY EDUCATIONAL AND UTTERLY MINDBOGGLING COMIC RELIEF COMIC *(1991)*

British comedy writer Richard Curtis founded Comic Relief in 1985 as a charity to raise money to combat famine, prompted by the dreadful situation at that time in Ethiopia. The organization has become more and more active each year, with television specials and various products, and in particular with Red Nose Day, during which people around the UK wear clownlike red noses that they have purchased from shops around the country, with the proceeds going to Comic Relief. A telethon is held on Red Nose Day as well. As of this writing Comic Relief has reportedly raised over £300 million since its inception.

Produced by Fleetway as a benefit for Comic Relief, this single issue featured contributions by a who's who of UK comics stars, including Simon Bisley, Mark Buckingham, Jamie Delano, Garth Ennis, Melinda Gebbie, Dave Gibbons, David Lloyd, Grant Morrison, Mark Millar, Peter Milligan, Bryan Talbot, and many more.

Gaiman coplotted with Richard Curtis and Grant Morrison and co-edited with Curtis and Peter Hogan. As to what he actually wrote, according to Gaiman himself—in a reply to a fan question on his blog: "Yes, I wrote the [Teenage Mutant Ninja] Turtles two pages, mostly because my son Mike, who was about 6 at the time, was a huge Turtles fan and also because no-one else wanted to. Other than that, I did an awful lot (along with Peter Hogan and Richard Curtis) to keep the book more or less consistent (ha!) and there are lines by me all the way through. Dick Curtis and I wrote the credits on the back page, because I'd always wanted to write some Baldrick stuff."

Along with television characters from series like *Dr. Who* and *Blackadder* (hence the Baldrick reference above), the comic book featured characters from many different publishers, who loaned them for this project. Unfortunately, the comic wasn't available for long. On that same blog post, Gaiman explained why: "The comic sold out in minutes. The reason it never went back to press is because DC gave permission to use their characters but only if they were traced from the Standard Poses that they had, and we couldn't figure out how to do that without looking silly, so we drew the characters in action, figuring DC would realise that we had saved them from embarrassment, but they didn't see it that way."

"TRUE THINGS" FROM THE EXTRAORDINARY WORKS OF ALAN MOORE *(2003)*

Not a story so much as a commentary, *True Things* is a two-page strip illustrated by Mark Buckingham, in which Gaiman provides an affectionate tribute to longtime friend Alan Moore. TwoMorrows Publishing produced the book in honor of Moore's fiftieth birthday.

"VIER MAUERN" FROM BREAKTHROUGH (1990)

Catalan Communications published *Breakthrough* in 1990, which collects stories by various comic book creators relating their reactions to the fall of the Berlin Wall. Dave McKean illustrated Gaiman's two-page tale, which laid some of the groundwork for their landmark *Signal to Noise* graphic novel (and was, in fact, later included in a hardcover edition of that book). In a May 1992 interview with *Comics Scene,* Gaiman reflected that he wrote the text of the story "while Dave McKean looked over my shoulder in a little French hotel room."

"WHEN IS A DOOR: THE SECRET ORIGIN OF THE RIDDLER . . ." FROM SECRET ORIGINS SPECIAL #1 (1989)

Gaiman's ten-page "When Is a Door: The Secret Origin of the Riddler . . ." was originally published in *Secret Origins Special* issue 1, with ingenious art by 1980s independent comics creators Bernie Mireault (pencils) and Matt Wagner (inks). Appropriate to the character of the Riddler, aka Edward Nigma (E. Nigma), this "secret origin" is essentially a "nonorigin" tale. Told via a staged Q & A session between a group of journalists and the Riddler in a warehouse filled with worn, gigantic props from the Riddler's crime career, the clever exchange yields elusive, inconclusive answers: "[M]aybe I was a carnival barker . . . the Puzzle King, Conundrum Champion, Wizard of Quiz . . . maybe I decided to turn my talents to crime . . . maybe that isn't it at all."

The heart of the tale is a meditation on the way comics themselves had changed since the 1960s, expressed via the Riddler's remorse over the critical change in "the rules": "Batman and Robin were part of the fun—they were the straight men, but we were the stars. No one ever really hurt anybody. Not really. Nobody died. You look around these days—it's all different. It's all changed. The Joker's killing people, for God's sake!"

When the reporters finally vent their exasperation with the Riddler's nonanswers, he replies, "Understand me: you don't come to the Riddler for answers . . . you just come for the questions."

Indeed.

"WORDSWORTH" FROM HELLRAISER #20 (1993)

Marvel published this anthology series based on Clive Barker's popular *Hellraiser* film series through its Epic Comics imprint. Many of the stories published over the course of the series focused on people obsessed with finding and/or solving—and thus opening—an infernal puzzle box, sometimes known as the Lament Configuration. This fifteen-page story, illustrated by Dave McKean, focused on the titular character, Wordsworth, another in a long line of such obsessed individuals. In this case, however, the story follows the man's descent into insanity—and then Hell—while struggling to solve a crossword puzzle.

||||||||||||||||||||||||||||||||||||||||||||||||||||||||||||||||||||||||

P A R T   F I V E

THE NOVELS

I occasionally wonder—most often when I'm reading something by Neil Gaiman—what it must be like not to be able to dream.

Ideas come from dreams—or mine do, anyway—but mostly they fizz away like cemetery mist when you wake up, and you just can't remember what they were. Neil doesn't seem to have that problem. In fact, I reckon that Neil has actually tapped into dreams better than pretty much anybody else (which, of course, is appropriate, considering that Dream is one of his most enduring and endearing creations).

After all, who can possibly forget the rickety old wooden gate through which the magical lands of Faerie may be accessed? Or, conversely, the door through which Coraline finds a not-quite-as-it-should-be version of Everyday Earth? Or even the just-short-of-laughable convention for serial killers held in an American motel? Or maybe the embattled Shadow and his search for/flight from what constitutes godhood in the twenty-first century? I could go on—and will do, when, in another minute or two, you and I have gone our separate ways. These are things that can really only come to you in a dream . . . in that strangely Ditko-esque off-kilter four-color landscape where the familiar just isn't there while all the oddness that is there seems perfectly natural.

Neil is a wonderful writer—nobody would dispute that. But, more importantly, he's one of our most talented and versatile imaginists (is that a word? Let's make it so!)—a true storyteller . . . one of those talented people who make you feel like a kid at camping cookout, sitting there cross-legged, safe within the circle of the fire's glow while Unca Neil spins you another yarn. In short, he's a "once upon a time" writer. That fact is obvious in Sandman and it's obvious in his short stories. But it's most obvious in his novels.

On the long haul, Neil really takes advantage of the extra space. You can hear those joints flexing as he stretches out . . . in Good Omens, of course, his collaboration with Terry Pratchett; in Anansi Boys and Neverwhere; and in the relatively short Coraline and Stardust (which some folks would have you believe are kids' stories—trust me: don't accept candies from those people) but mostly you can hear it—so loud, it's almost deafening—in American Gods, a truly epic road trip that reads like a blissed-out collaboration between Homer and Ken Kesey.

Getting back to how we started out here—three days ago, as it happens (during which time I've reread whole slabs of Neil's long hauls), but just a few words here on the printed page—here's the bottom line: With Neil's books, you don't actually need to

*dream—he does it for you. Every novelist ought to be able to say that about themselves,
but very few can do it honestly. Here's one who can.*

—Peter Crowther

When you look at Neil Gaiman's career as a novelist with the benefit of twenty-twenty hindsight, it seems almost inevitable that his books would someday find their way to the *New York Times* bestseller list. But, of course, that was never a certainty. Rather, it was the old combination of preparation, perspiration, happenstance, and, yes, talent.

The preparation began in childhood, as the future author ravenously consumed the written word, reading, in his own words, omnivorously and indiscriminately. All grist for the creative mill, his wide, constant reading was giving him the tools he needed for his chosen profession (indeed, he aspired to be a writer from an early age, often fantasizing of the day he would become a famous wordsmith, either by hard work, or a change in reality, or by kidnapping all his famous writing heroes and forcing them to churn out stories that he would publish under his own name).

As he matured and actually began writing, he began to be more practical about his goal, realizing that he still had much to learn; pragmatically, he became a journalist, to learn about the way the world he wished to inhabit worked, and also, as a way of honing his skills and paying his dues.

Now, if you're going to be a novelist, a good way to do so is to learn from the best, as Gaiman certainly did when he collaborated with the more experienced Terry Pratchett on *Good Omens*. Gaiman himself has described the team-up as an apprenticeship. The work he did with Pratchett, the popularity of the novel, and his ever growing reputation from his work in comics (*Sandman*, remember, was only three years old at the time), laid the groundwork for his next novel-length work, *Neverwhere*.

Based on his television scripts, *Neverwhere* might more properly be characterized as a novelization rather than a novel, but his efforts to tell the story he set out to tell (the BBC version was not totally satisfying to him) proved invaluable to his development as a novelist, forcing him to work his vision into something that he himself might describe as "novel-shaped." The benefits of the experience certainly show in *Stardust*.

Conceived in 1991, *Stardust* was finally realized as a novel (albeit a short one) in 1998. Here Gaiman took a story that had been bubbling in his subconscious for many a year and delivered a work that, like much of his output, was simultaneously a throwback and something fresh, at least in terms of genre fiction. It was also starting to become more personal, which is perhaps the secret of Gaiman's subsequent bestsellerdom—Gaiman was tapping something deep inside, something that helped him forge deeper connections with his existing audience, and capture the attention of those who had not yet seen his work in other genres.

That personal aspect of his work is nowhere more evident than in his next novel, the justifiably celebrated *American Gods*. Besides its commercial and critical success (it spent two weeks on the *New York Times* list and garnered several major genre nominations and awards), it cemented Gaiman's status as a pop culture icon. By dint of his talent and hard work, his growing popularity, and changes in the reading public's perceptions (most important, the increasing willingness of modern audiences to follow an author from genre to genre, media to media, and subject matter to subject matter), Gaiman was building a worldwide reputation as a modern master of fantasy.

Not one to rest on his laurels, or to take success for granted, Gaiman set out to write something totally different from the very dark *American Gods*, something light, something funny. Even though there are still dark elements in *Anansi Boys,* they only serve to enhance the funnier, lighter sections of the book. Here Gaiman proved he was as adept at writing outright humor as he was at straight fantasy or horror. The pinnacle of his novelistic success so far, *Anansi Boys* didn't merely land on the *New York Times* bestseller list; it debuted at number one.

Why are these books so popular? Perhaps the secret is that Gaiman has one foot in the past, and one very much in the present, and he acts as a link to classic literature for modern audiences who, because of the pace of today's world, and because they are not as deeply read, see much of what Gaiman does as new. Which isn't to suggest that any of his work is redundant—the furthest thing from it, in fact. Neil Gaiman looks back to the pre-Tolkien fantasy of the nineteenth and early twentieth centuries, which influences his style and storytelling sense, but he infuses those elements into original ideas and speaks to a twenty-first-century audience in a fresh voice that has made him one of the preeminent fantasists of the modern age.

Gaiman's audience is likely split into two camps: readers experiencing the fantasy tropes he uses for the first time, and the more widely read, who can appreciate the influences he so lovingly embraces. It certainly doesn't hurt that, word for word, sentence for sentence, and paragraph for paragraph, he's one of the most agile and skilled writers of modern times.

Although he has not discussed plans for a new "adult" novel as yet (as this is written, he is wrestling with the writing of *The Graveyard Book,* ostensibly a young adult novel), you can be sure that, somewhere in the recesses of the literary catacomb that is his mind, the germ of a new work exists. When he decides to develop that idea into a full-blown novel, you can also be sure that it will be eagerly gobbled up by his ever-growing legion of fans, and be the subject of much critical attention. Oh yes, and that it will probably end up on the *New York Times* bestseller list.

GOOD OMENS:
THE NICE AND ACCURATE PROPHECIES OF AGNES NUTTER, WITCH

BY NEIL GAIMAN & TERRY PRATCHETT (1990)

The literary world has changed a great deal since the 1990 publication of *Good Omens*. While it was not uncommon in those days for the occasional novelist to dabble in comic books, the reverse journey—from comic book writer to novelist—was far rarer. When it happened, as it did that same year with Jim Starlin's *Among Madmen* (a nasty, well-executed tale), such novels were often overlooked. Publishers, and the reading public, seemed to operate on the presumption that scribes who had achieved their initial success in comics were somehow less sincere or less worthy or . . . less *something*. Even after all of the attention that his groundbreaking work on *Sandman* had already garnered him (and no matter his background in journalism), Neil Gaiman came to publishers and to bookstores as a "comic book writer."

Within the comic book industry itself there was then—and among many creators there remains to this day—a prejudice against their own medium. Almost unaware of it, some comic book creators still refer to novels as "real books," novelists as "real writers," and the companies that produce them as "real publishers." Yet this is fast becoming an outmoded attitude. Presently, writers such as Mike Carey and Warren Ellis emerge from the world of comics to garner huge attention as novelists. Writing comics—or "graphic novels," as many refer to them, in order to accept certain works as serious while keeping open the option of dismissing others as "comics"—now has a level of cool attached to it among certain publishing and reading circles. Certainly the Hollywood fascination with comics and graphic novels has much to do with this.

But Neil Gaiman was the trailblazer, the first to shatter the preconceptions of people both outside and within the industry. And it began with *Good Omens*.

Gaiman met Terry Pratchett in 1985 when the former—then a freelance journalist—interviewed the latter to promote the release of Pratchett's novel *The Colour of Magic*. The interview took place in a Chinese restaurant in London and began a friendship that continues, through the present day. In 1988, the two wrote

Good Omens together, beginning with a few pages of a short story that Gaiman had begun but could not decide how to continue.

In a short essay at the end of the 2006 paperback reissue, Gaiman described the book as "a funny novel about the end of the world and how we're all going to die." A nice and accurate summary, but *Good Omens* is far more than that. It is wonderfully plotted, silly, and ironic, and full of the sort of wisdom about human nature, politics, and the world that seems so obvious and right to those who read and nod in agreement and yet apparently never seems obvious to those for whom such wisdom could do the most good. In the midst of their good time, Gaiman and Pratchett take on government, but more frequently challenge the behavior of human society where war, poverty, and especially the environment are concerned. Particularly of note are the pair's observations about global warming, addressed with an unusual clarity for 1990, so many years before most of the world lent any credence to such theories.

There exists a wonderful dichotomy in *Good Omens,* a split between wistful, weary, Swiftian archness on the one hand and indefatigable hope and faith in basic human decency on the other. Perhaps that—and laughter—are the things that made the book a worldwide success, and a cult classic in the mold of William Goldman's *The Princess Bride.* Time has passed, and Gaiman and Pratchett have both gone on to greater and greater success. And yet *Good Omens* remains a singular achievement. There is Neil Gaiman, writer, and there are his myriad works for page and screen. There is Terry Pratchett, writer, and there are his many novels, including his popular Discworld series.

And then there is *Good Omens.*

Which isn't to say that somehow this novel is better than those the two have written separately. That is almost certainly not true. *Good Omens* is, however, unique. It is an old friend to many readers, now, embraceable and with its own . . . ineffable . . . personality.

So, what's it all about?

Why, the end of the world, of course. Or, at least, God's plan for the apocalypse, and the way Heaven and Hell interpret that plan and the intentions behind it, and how a small error by a harried demon screws the whole thing up, leading to moments of wry humor and general silliness and a hysterical bit of farcical running around that may actually prevent Armageddon.

Good Omens begins with the birth of the Antichrist—or, more accurately, with the attempts by a much put upon demon named Crowley to place the infant doom-bringer with the family destined to nurture him into a proper Antichrist. This family is seen little in *Good Omens,* but the resemblance to the Thorne clan of *The Omen* is amusing and obviously intended. The title of Gaiman and Pratchett's novel is no coincidence. The premise, at its heart, is, "What if Damien Thorne had been raised in an idyllic environment with an ordinary, loving family and good friends, with whom he had many wonderful adventures."

A Satan-worshipping nurse makes a fateful error, delivering the infant son of the Devil into the hands of the wrong family. It isn't until eleven years later, as the Four Horsemen of the Apocalypse begin to gather in a preamble to the end, that Crowley and his opposite number—an angel named Aziraphale—discover his error, and the relationship that unfolding events have with a book called *The Nice and Accurate Prophecies of Agnes Nutter, Witch*.

PEOPLE, PLACES, AND THINGS

CROWLEY. Formerly known as Crawly and best known for his participation in the temptation of Eve—he was the serpent, you understand—the demon Crowley does his part to tempt humanity, to corrupt souls, and generally to make life as hectic and frustrating as possible for people. The trouble is, he genuinely likes people, and sees this as his major failing.

The demon drives an old Bentley that he has kept running for years through care and regular service rather than the use of supernatural power. The Bentley's cassette player has the rather infernal habit of only playing songs by Queen, no matter what was on the cassette before it was placed into the player.

Crowley believes there is little he can do as a demon that could be worse than the things human beings do to themselves and each other. Evil never sleeps, but Crowley enjoys sleeping, as one of the pleasures afforded by the human world, and so slept through most of the nineteenth century.

Around A.D. 1020, Crowley had entered into an "arrangement" with his opposite number, the angel Aziraphale. Under the terms of this arrangement, the two make their best efforts at pleasing their employers with various acts of Good and Evil, respectively, but only in careful harmony with one another. Thus, if Crowley plans some particularly evil act, he informs Aziraphale, so that the latter can provide a benevolent counterpoint.

The day upon which Crowley delivered the infant Antichrist to the hospital was not his proudest. The plan called for the baby to be swapped with the child of the American cultural attaché, who also had just been born. In the care of that family—the Dowlings—the baby would be surrounded by teachers and governesses who were devout satanists, all intent upon rearing the son of the Devil properly, to grow up and bring about the Apocalypse.

Unfortunately, Crowley left the actual swapping of babies in the hands of Sister Mary Loquacious, a nurse who also was a satanist in service to demons—one of several in on the conspiracy. In a series of miscommunications, the infant Antichrist ended up in the care of a couple from Lower Tadfield, who presumed him to be their own and named him Adam, while their actual baby ended up going home with the Dowlings under the unfortunate name of Warlock. The Dowlings' actual child, on the other hand, eventually was put up for adoption, and in time becomes known as Greasy Johnson.

Thus, by pure happenstance (or as part of God's ineffable plan—the ineffability of which frustrates Aziraphale and Crowley to no end), the Antichrist is given over to a particularly ordinary life in an almost idyllic environment.

Eleven years later, when Crowley realizes that the Apocalypse is imminent, he enlists the aid of Aziraphale in averting it due to their shared interest in the human world; he then at last discovers the mistakes in the swapping of the babies. A search ensues during which Crowley avoids destruction at the hands of his fellow demons—who want to go to war with Heaven—and his precious Bentley is burned.

In the final confrontation, when the Four Horsemen of the Apocalypse, the Antichrist, and Beelzebub all gather—along with a number of more ordinary witnesses—Crowley serves mainly as an observer and a voice of reason. Acting as the voice of reason is new to him. When the Antichrist decides not to bother with the Apocalypse after all, the ground begins to shake, and it seems Satan will appear at any moment to punish his son. Crowley and Aziraphale take up weapons to fight against the Devil in order to protect the humans who are gathered there.

Fortunately, Adam Young—the Antichrist—uses his power not only to send his father away, but to repair some of the damage already wrought—and to restore Crowley's Bentley.

AZIRAPHALE. One of the order of angels called Principalities, Aziraphale is also referred to as the Angel of the Eastern Gate, a reference to one of the gates to the Garden of Eden. When Adam and Eve were driven from the garden, Aziraphale gave them his sword of fire. In the eons since he has come to love humanity in all its chaotic glory. Aziraphale has an arrangement with the demon Crowley that keeps their conflicting efforts in balance, so that when each reports to his superiors they both seem to be doing an excellent job without ever actually winning.

In addition, Aziraphale owns and operates a shop specializing in antiquated books, though he only nominally sells books, and the shop is actually more of a storage space for his own unique collection.

When Crowley informs Aziraphale that the Antichrist will soon rise to power, and that the Four Horsemen of the Apocalypse are on the move, the angel is distraught. He and Crowley enjoy the world too much to allow it to end without at least attempting to avert its destruction. The idea of living without antique shops and bookshops and crossword puzzles and "fascinating little restaurants where they know you" is appalling to him.

In the course of the search for the Antichrist, Aziraphale's physical form is accidentally destroyed, but the angel's essence manages to take up residence in the body of Madame Tracy. With the aid of Madame Tracy, and the reluctant accompaniment of Sergeant Shadwell, Aziraphale continues on the trail of the Antichrist, eventually (with help from Crowley) discovering the mix-up that occurred eleven years earlier, learning that Adam Young is the boy they seek.

Aziraphale's main participation at the climactic moments of the book is to ask pointed questions, but in a Neil Gaiman novel this function cannot be underesti-mated. In the end, Aziraphale and Crowley attempt to puzzle out the mystery of God's plan, only to be distracted by a rather ineffable figure feeding the ducks at a pond as they walk by. Their agreement remains in force, but now that the Antichrist has refused to serve his purpose and the Apocalypse has been averted, and without further prophecies from Agnes Nutter to hint at what's to come, there is no telling what the future may bring.

ADAM YOUNG. The Antichrist, also affectionately known as the Adversary; De-stroyer of Kings; Angel of the Bottomless Pit; Great Beast That is called Dragon; Prince of This World; Father of Lies; Spawn of Satan; and Lord of Darkness.

Apparently born in Hell, Adam is delivered to this world by a pair of demons called Hastur and Ligur, who then assign the demon Crowley the mission of mak-ing certain that the son of Satan will be raised in the right environment. The baby is supposed to be swapped with the newborn child of the American cultural attaché, but instead he is accidentally swapped with the newborn son of an entirely ordinary family from Lower Tadfield, in England.

Adam is raised by Mr. and Mrs. Young in an environment that is almost idyllic, and he subtly influences the world around him to make it even more to his liking. Adam has several close friends, and they think of their gang as "the Them," because no matter what cool name they might come up with for their gang, the locals just referred to them as "Them," forcing them to adopt "Them" as a moniker. This group includes a girl named Pepper and two other boys, Wensleydale and Brian. They share adventures and daydreams, wander Lower Tadfield, and often run afoul of the only other gang of kids in town, a bunch of ruffians led by a boy named Greasy Johnson.

For his first eleven years Adam experiences a blissful childhood, so that when things begin to change, he does not approve. The sole exception is the arrival of Dog (see below). When the Four Horsemen of the Apocalypse seriously begin to get their work under way, and the End Times are nigh, Adam's innate power grows, and his infernal nature begins to rise and take control of him, driving him instinc-tively to want to destroy humanity and take over the world. But the part of him that is Adam doesn't want the world to be destroyed. He doesn't want to make his friends sad or frightened. In fact, he wants Lower Tadfield—and his life there—to remain completely untouched.

With parents who love him, a playful dog, and the camaraderie of his friends, Adam has been raised to be ordinary—to be human. In the end he eschews his legacy and power, and refuses to bring about the Apocalypse, thwarting the Four Horsemen and the plans of both Heaven and Hell, much to the delight of Crowley and Aziraphale.

DOG. A hellhound sent by the forces of Hell to do the bidding of the Antichrist, this beast has the remarkable quality of its taking true form only when given a name by its master. The name gives it purpose and shapes its nature. While the demons who sent it no doubt intended it to be some fierce monstrosity, the hell-hound instead overhears Adam talking to his friends about his desire for "the kind of dog you can have fun with," a dog small enough to go down rabbit holes, with one "funny" ear that always looks as though it has been turned inside out.

And when the Them ask Adam what his dog will be called, he decides the only proper name is simply "Dog." From which point on, the hellhound becomes an adorable, playful little dog who loves his master dearly and protects him at all costs.

PEPPER. Though her given name is Pippin Galadriel Moonchild, Pepper will in-stantly assault and damage anyone fool enough to address her by any other than her chosen name. The only female member of the Them, and probably the most sensible.

WENSLEYDALE. One of Them, Wensleydale's friends seem aware that he might actually have been christened Jeremy, though like Pepper he is never called by his given name. Wensleydale gives the "impression of having been born with a mental age of forty-seven."

BRIAN. One of Them, Brian is endlessly fascinated by things that are supposed to be secrets of the world: conspiracy theories; witches; and all manner of other things that adults deny exist. The Them often debate such subjects, but always look to Adam to be the arbiter of such debates. As leader of the group, Adam has the final word.

AGNES NUTTER. A witch, Agnes Nutter was also the author, oddly enough, of *The Nice and Accurate Prophecies of Agnes Nutter*, which was published in September 1655 by a firm called Bilton & Scaggs. It sold horribly, and became remarkably rare, but the greatest distinction afforded *The Nice and Accurate Prophecies of Agnes Nutter* is that out of the plethora of books of alleged prophecies published since the invention of the printing press, it is the only one whose predictions are 100 percent accurate. The only trouble is that Agnes's spelling was atrocious, and her visions were often unclear, so that her vague prophecies often require so much in-terpretation that they cannot be confirmed until the events predicted have actu-ally taken place.

Killed by a witchfinder major called Thou-Shalt-Not-Commit-Adultery Pulsifer, Agnes managed to eradicate all those responsible for her execution by concealing eighty pounds of gunpowder and forty pounds of roofing nails beneath her clothes. When she was burned alive on a pyre, the result was explosive.

For all the generations since, Agnes's descendants have followed her prophecies, attempting to decipher them before the events actually occurred, or otherwise in hindsight.

ANATHEMA DEVICE. The last surviving descendant of Agnes Nutter, Witch, Anathema Device is also a witch. It has fallen to her to track the prophecies of her ancestor, but she also has a part to play in the events Agnes predicted. When

Crowley and Aziraphale give her a ride after she has trouble with her bicycle, she accidentally leaves her copy of *The Nice and Accurate Prophecies of Agnes Nutter* in Crowley's Bentley. Aziraphale discovers it there and instinctively appropriates it. As a dealer in antiquated books he recognizes its value instantly. As an angel he understands the truth of the visions detailed within.

Anathema serves as a positive influence on Adam Young through her kindness and exemplary open-mindedness. When Witchfinder private Newton Pulsifer (Newt) tracks her down—the descendant of Agnes Nutter confronted by the descendant of her killer—things don't go quite as Newt had planned, but rather precisely as Agnes had predicted. Anathema and Newt become lovers, decipher notes Anathema has kept about the end of the world, and manage to put themselves in the midst of the final confrontation between the eleven-year-old Antichrist, Crowley and Aziraphale, and the Four Horsemen of the Apocalypse.

Though she has spent her entire life enslaved by her commitment to the prophecies, in the end Anathema is free. The world did not end. When a mysterious delivery arrives—held by a law firm since the early seventeenth century—she opens it to discover a second volume of prophecies by her ancestor, Agnes Nutter. Crestfallen, she goes to open the book but Newt stops her. Whatever the future holds for her and Newt, they both want it to be a surprise.

NEWTON PULSIFER. A witchfinder private—and one of only two living members of the Witchfinder Army (though the payroll books show entire regiments)—Newt Pulsifer is an earnest young man with an enthusiasm for the job. His enthusiasm wanes, however, when he is sent on his first solo assignment and meets Anathema Device, an actual witch. Utterly disarmed by her frankness and the fact that she is female, Newt quickly loses the focus of his investigation. When Anathema shares with him her own history, and that of *The Nice and Accurate Prophecies of Agnes Nutter,* as well as his ancestor's involvement in Agnes's death, he eventually must accept that his meeting with Anathema was foretold centuries earlier. Together they work out the meaning of several prophecies and, as the Apocalypse approaches, manage to embroil themselves in the final conflict. When all has been set right again, Newt and Anathema remain together and plan to explore the unknown future together.

WITCHFINDER SERGEANT SHADWELL. The senior member of the Witchfinder Army (there are, at present, only two members, though the accounting books claim far greater numbers), Sergeant Shadwell is a curmudgeonly old fellow with a great passion for the history of his occupation, a talent for shady bookkeeping, and a dogged persistence in the pursuit of witches, though he has never actually discovered one.

Shadwell maintains a cordial yet verbally abusive relationship with his landlady, a supposed medium named Madame Tracy whose occupation he presumes is that of prostitute. As a result, he regularly refers to her as a whore and harlot, and a seemingly endless stream of other disdainful nouns. Actually, in spite of the disgust he pretends to feel, Shadwell is rather fond of the kindly and tolerant Madame Tracy.

When Shadwell overhears a conversation that makes him believe Aziraphale is a demon, he attempts to destroy the angel with nothing but his pointed finger and the power of his righteousness. Coincidentally, at that moment Aziraphale's corporeal form is destroyed through an accident unrelated to Shadwell's finger, but Shadwell believes it was divine power working through him.

Later, however, when Aziraphale's essence has taken up residence in Madame Tracy's body, and both angel and landlady explain that the Apocalypse is approaching and must be averted, he reluctantly allies himself with them, grumbling all the while.

Shadwell and Madame Tracy agree, eventually, to retire together to a little bungalow in the country, happily (and somewhat grumpily) ever after.

MADAME TRACY. Every afternoon except Thursdays, Madame Tracy provides her services as a medium to those wishing to speak to their dearly departed. For the most part, she fakes it. Every evening except Thursdays, she is available for strict discipline and intimate massages. This latter occupation turns out to be somewhat misleading, as no matter what services Madame Tracy provides to her evening clients, they don't seem to involve prostitution—though you couldn't convince Sergeant Shadwell of that. Shadwell, Madame Tracy's tenant, treats the woman abominably, yet the ever patient Madame Tracy evidently thinks Shadwell's discomfort with her evening assignations is charming.

When Aziraphale's corporeal form is destroyed, his essence takes up residence within Madame Tracy, sharing access to her voice and recruiting her in his efforts to avert the Apocalypse. Madame Tracy, in turn, attempts to convince Shadwell that Aziraphale is not a demon. Eventually, the three of them (well, two plus one angel riding in Madame Tracy's head) manage to make it to the final showdown riding Madame Tracy's motor scooter.

Madame Tracy has a bit of money put aside, and would like to move out to the country someplace, to settle down with someone. Though Shadwell is slow on the uptake, she manages to make him realize that she'd like that someone to be him.

WAR. War has been many things since time began, most recently an arms dealer called Scarlett and a war correspondent named Red Zuigiber. When the International Express delivery man arrives with a package for her, which lets her know that it is time for the Four Horsemen to ride, she welcomes it. Although the Four Horsemen do gather and eventually make their way to Lower Tadfield, they're prevented from bringing about the Apocalypse by Adam Young, the eleven-year-old Antichrist.

FAMINE. Like the other Horsemen, Famine is still far too active in the world. At the moment he is Dr. Raven Sable, creator of a new diet supplement containing no actual food, who makes it fashionable and seemingly healthy to wither away to nothing. When the International Express delivery man arrives with a package containing a set of scales, Famine knows the End Times have arrived, and he is so pleased he bursts into song. Although the Four Horsemen do gather and eventually make their way to Lower Tadfield, they're prevented from bringing about the Apocalypse by Adam Young.

POLLUTION. Pollution has only been one of the Four Horsemen since 1936, when the invention of penicillin caused a frustrated Pestilence to retire, although perhaps, truly, they are one and the same. Also known as Mr. White, or Chalky, he is brought a crown by the International Express delivery man and soon rides to join the others of the Four Horsemen. It should be noted that the Horsemen actually ride motorcycles. Although the Four Horsemen do gather and eventually make their way to Lower Tadfield, they're prevented from bringing about the Apocalypse by Adam Young.

DEATH. Not the cheeriest of fellows, he speaks in all capital letters. Although the Four Horsemen do gather and eventually make their way to Lower Tadfield, they're prevented from bringing about the Apocalypse by Adam Young.

THOU-SHALT-NOT-COMMIT-ADULTERY PULSIFER. A witchfinder major and ancestor of Newt, he was responsible for the burning of Agnes Nutter as a witch, and he died in the ensuing explosion.

THE INTERNATIONAL EXPRESS DELIVERY MAN. The unfortunate man responsible for traveling the world to deliver certain items and messages to the Four Horsemen of the Apocalypse. His final message is to Death, and he kills himself in order to deliver it. Death's address: everywhere.

HASTUR AND LIGUR. Demons of Hell, Hastur and Ligur are the ones who deliver the infant Antichrist to Earth and into the hands of the demon Crowley.

THE YOUNGS. The unknowing adoptive parents of the Antichrist, Adam Young, and the biological parents of Warlock Dowling.

THE DOWLINGS. The unknowing adoptive parents of Warlock Dowling, and the biological parents of Greasy Johnson. Mr. Dowling is the American cultural attaché.

SISTER MARY LOQUACIOUS. Born Mary Hodges, Sister Mary Loquacious is a member of the Chattering Order of Saint Beryl. The sisters of the order take vows to emulate their patron saint at all times—and chatter incessantly about whatever is on their minds—with the exception of a single half-hour break every Tuesday afternoon.

Sister Mary is also a nurse and a satanist and, through a series of miscommunications, she is the person responsible for swapping the infant Antichrist with the Youngs' rather than the Dowlings' baby.

THE *OTHER* FOUR HORSEMEN OF THE APOCALYPSE. A quartet of roughhousing bikers who try to menace the Four Horsemen but end up following them, calling themselves the *Other* Four Horsemen, or the Four Bikers of the Apocalypse. Pigbog, Greaser, Big Ted, and Skuzz, though already having nicknames, decide they ought to have names more in line with their new status, such as Grievous Bodily Harm, Cruelty to Animals, and Things Not Working Properly Even After You've Given Them a Good Thumping. Sadly, all four are buried beneath an avalanche of fish, and only Skuzz survives.

Yes, we said fish. Go read the book.

TRIVIA

- A film version of *Good Omens* has often been discussed, most frequently with Terry Gilliam attached as director.

- Note the caveat on the copyright page: "Bringing about Armageddon can be dangerous. Do not attempt it in your own home."

- According to Leo Breebaart and Mike Kew's online Annotated Pratchett Files, "the United States edition of *Good Omens* had numerous alterations to the text. The most significant of these is the addition of an extra 700-word section just before the end, dealing with what happened to the character of Warlock, the American diplomat's son, who was swapped with Adam."

THE QUOTABLE GAIMAN

On working with Terry Pratchett:

I felt very much at the time like a journeyman, getting to work with a master craftsman, because even at that point, I forget how many novels Terry was into Discworld, seven or eight, maybe more. Terry could build a novel like a fine Chippendale chairmaker could make a piece of furniture. He knew how they were crafted.

—Interview in *Locus*, February 2006

NEVERWHERE

(1997)

Neil Gaiman's first solo novel, *Neverwhere* was born of a strange coalescence of factors, and has matured into a true oddity in the world of publishing. Prior to his success as a comic book writer, Gaiman spent years as a journalist, mainly in the field of entertainment. During that era of his life he began establishing relationships across many mediums, including film, music, publishing, and television. In time, his efforts would touch upon all of those mediums, and beyond.

In the mid-1990s, Gaiman began developing an idea for a television series for the BBC. A conversation with writer, actor, and comedian Lenny Henry proved a springboard for the author's creativity, and Gaiman began work on the scripts for *Neverwhere,* which would become a six-part BBC television series.

Used to the creative control that his work as a comic book writer had provided, it did not take long for Gaiman to become disenchanted with the television process. According to an interview with *SFX* magazine, the author has said that he found himself to be "a small voice in the background." The series became something other than what he had imagined.

Gaiman soon determined that the only way for him to solve this problem was to write, as quickly as possible, a novel version of *Neverwhere*. Published in 1997, the novel has gone on to become far more successful than the BBC series. Those readers familiar with *Neverwhere* are unlikely even to be aware that the BBC series exists, or, if they're aware of it, most undoubtedly believe the series an adaptation of the novel rather than the other way around.

This is a singular achievement on Gaiman's part, made possible by the unique creative arrangements that the BBC makes when it enters into a format agreement with a creator. Had *Neverwhere* been an American television series, its fate would likely have been very, very different, and chances are we would not ever have had the pleasure of reading Gaiman's now classic urban fantasy novel. This is unquestionably a bizarre path for any author to have taken for his first solo novel, even more so for a writer who has become one of the most read, best paid, and most well-respected fantasy authors in the world.

A great many influences are on display in *Neverwhere*, particularly classical fairy tales featuring an ordinary man who encounters a being from a magical, parallel world, and who is intrigued enough to be lured from his own realm into that other world. Gaiman's love of folklore, mythology, and legend show throughout the novel, which also features a hero's journey: An ordinary man discovers that he has a greater significance than he ever imagined, is transformed by experience into a hero, and proves his worth to a princess, who then returns his love.

These elements are woven with far more modern conceits, including the mundane life of a London office worker, an urban environment, and a dry wit and ironic self-deprecation inherent in a great deal of British entertainment across a variety of mediums, from the novels of Douglas Adams to the iconic BBC television series *Doctor Who*.

Neverwhere's origins as a television series and Gaiman's experience as a comic book writer are evident in the episodic structure of the novel, and in the way the narrative pauses to paint a picture of each new character as they are introduced. Yet perhaps its greatest strength—and what has made it such an enduring example of urban fantasy—is the charm of its nebbishy central character, Richard Mayhew.

Gaiman readers will find that in addition to being a wonderful tale in its own right, *Neverwhere* provides the foundation for elements the author continues to explore in subsequent novels, particular the folkloric elements and world-behind-the-world conceit that crop up later in *American Gods* and *Anansi Boys*. By the time of *Neverwhere*'s publication, however, Gaiman had already been charting this territory every month in the pages of *Sandman* and other comics, so that it has become a kind of trademark, and it is not unusual to see certain works of urban fantasy referred to as "Gaimanesque." Indeed, when an author's style has become an adjective, clearly he has made such a lasting impression that critics and fans are more likely to discuss his influence rather than those things that influenced him.

The homeless and lost of London have a world all of their own, where magic and monsters exist, and all sorts of oddities have created a society with its own rules. There are angels and vampires and parallel dimensions, inhuman killers and ancient beasts. Yet though this alternate world—London Below, as its denizens call it—is a fantasy realm, it is also umbilically connected to London Above in myriad but inextricable ways.

Fantasy involving the homeless—and/or alternative colonies of the perceived homeless who are in fact members of an invisible society living undetected amid the nooks, crannies, or subterranean underworld of urban centers of activity—emerged anew in the 1980s and 1990s. *Neverwhere* is part of that re-emergence, which has deep roots in myth, legend, fairy tales, and folklore, and in popular fantasy works like T. H. White's *Mistress Masham's Repose* (1946), which features a secret community of Lilliputians surviving after Gulliver carried them back to England; the parallel lives of store mannequins in John Collier's short story "Evening Primrose" (1941), which Rod Serling reworked for a memorable episode of *The Twilight Zone*; and the definitive classic of the genre by Mary Norton, *The Borrowers* (1952).

Similar ground is covered, in various inventive ways, in Phyllis Eisenstein's short story "Subworld" (1983); Tim Powers's novel *The Anubis Gates* (1983); the "invisibles" of Christopher Priest's *The Glamour* (1984); and others. Many of Clive Barker's key works, including early efforts like his screenplay for the botched *Underworld* (1985, aka *Transmutations*), and the novel *Cabal* (1988), which Barker himself adapted to film as *Nightbreed* (1990), tapped very similar concepts and imagery. So did Christopher Fowler's *Roofworld* (1988), with London gangs dwelling above; Stephen Elbox's *The House of Rats* (1991), with exiled humans literally living between walls and under floors; like the wolves in Gaiman's *The Wolves in the Walls*; and various strains of fantasy/SF/horror involving hidden races (and race wars) of witches, sorcerers, vampires, werewolves, shape-shifters, faerie folks, aliens, angels, demons, and others too numerous to detail, in all media: novels, short stories, gaming, movies, television, etc.

Despite the hugeness of the fantasy ideas Gaiman brings to life in *Neverwhere,* perhaps the signature element here is that London Above and London Below really aren't that far apart after all. The quest that Richard Mayhew and the Lady Door and their companions undertake leads them through sometimes oddly literal versions of Underground stations on the London Tube. There is an actual Earl at Earl's Court station, and friars at Blackfriars station, and Night's Bridge at Knightsbridge station, or at least the alternate world versions of them.

In the London he's always known, Richard is a nobody, defining himself through a boring job and a distant fiancée who barely tolerates him as a necessary accessory to go along with her individual life's ambitions. It takes erasure from his own life and a trip to London Below for Richard to discover that there are far more valid and noble ways to define his identity.

When Richard nearly stumbles over an injured, bleeding girl named Door, he cannot pass by without acting the part of the Samaritan, though his kindness costs him his future with his brittle fiancée, Jessica. Soon he learns that Door is the last (she believes) surviving member of the family of Lord Portico, and that she is being hunted by inhuman hired killers who will stop at nothing to fulfill their contract. Richard would like nothing better than to go on with his life and forget all about Door, but after she has gone, he discovers that his brush with her—and other figures from London Below—have magically caused him to be deleted from the world he has known. No one seems to remember him, or even to be able to focus on him for more than a moment. His job, his flat, and his relationship have all, essentially, evaporated. If he wants to get them back, he must find answers in London Below, and he begins an adventure that will eventually enable him to return to his normal life, though by then he may no longer wish to do so.

Full of unforgettable characters, ideas, and betrayals, as well as a charming sincerity, *Neverwhere* has become yet another of Gaiman's modern classics, far surpassing the television series that provided its origin, and spawning a comic book adaptation and discussion of a feature film version.

On January 21, 2008, in the midst of the strike by the Writers Guild of America that caused a massive shutdown of television operations and the development of new films, Gaiman wrote the following on his blog:

> The Writer's Strike continues. I was delighted that the Weinstein Company has just made a deal with the WGA, agreeing to all the terms, as that means I can now go back to work on the *Neverwhere* movie. (A short history—I wrote about eight drafts of *Neverwhere*-the-movie between 1997 and 2000, and then retired. Other people came in and wrote scripts, some of which were hated and some of which weren't, but it died. Last year my agents sent someone who asked about it the version of the script they had, which was the last draft script I did in 2000, and people read it, got excited and suddenly it came back to life, with the Hensons producing and doing it with the Weinstein Company. It needs to find a director, but at least I can work on it now.)

Whether a new film version of *Neverwhere* will emerge from these developments remains to be seen.

PEOPLE, PLACES, AND THINGS

RICHARD MAYHEW. Among his friends from home, Richard Mayhew might be considered both courageous and successful when he leaves his birthplace behind and starts a new life in London. But once in the capital city Richard is swallowed by the bustle of things, becoming just another nondescript worker drone. He's got a small flat, a mundane job, and a demanding fiancée who keeps him around only because she sees in him a certain amount of potential—not in what Richard can become, but in what she can manipulate him into becoming.

On a night when Jessica's boss, Mr. Stockton, is supposed to be taking her and Richard out to dinner, Richard forgets the one element of the arrangements that was meant to be his responsibility—reservations. Desperate, he attempts to fix the situation, and has to endure Jessica's disdain and impatience. She's made very clear how important this dinner is to her career, and when the two of them encounter a wounded young woman who lies bleeding on the sidewalk, she is determined to ignore the girl's plight. Richard won't leave her, however, even when Jessica threatens to break off their engagement.

Richard brings the injured girl home and soon discovers that her name is Door, that she heals rather quickly, and that she claims to be from London Below, a parallel version of London that occupies the lost corners and hidden places of the Underground. Door reveals that the homeless and lost inhabit London Below, which is full of magic and monsters and things Richard doesn't understand or believe in. She tells him that her family has been murdered, and that she is being hunted, though she knows not why.

When a pair of frightening men—Mr. Croup and Mr. Vandemar—pay him a visit, Door vanishes and reappears after they've left. Richard has no choice but to believe at least some of her tale. All he wants is to get back to his own life, and so when Door asks him to go and recruit help for her—someone who owes her family a favor—Richard agrees. If that will get her out of his apartment, he's happy to help.

In a dark alley he locates the Marquis de Carabas, who agrees to help. The marquis convinces Richard to descend with him into the sewer—only to find himself on a ladder far above the streets of London, and then on a rooftop talking to a seemingly insane, bird-obsessed old man named Old Bailey.

Soon Richard returns to his flat with the marquis, and Door takes her leave, thanking him for his help. Expecting his life to return to normal, and worrying about how to repair things with Jessica, he quickly discovers that things could not be any less normal. No one knows who he is. Most people don't even seem to see him. Jessica doesn't remember him, and his employers behave as though he never existed. Realtors show his flat to potential buyers—while Richard is naked in the bathtub, apparently invisible to them. He has been touched by London Below, and is no longer a part of his own world, which Door calls London Above.

Richard pursues his only option, which is to find a way into London Below and search for Door, hoping she has a solution. Along the way he meets Hunter, a professional warrior, hunter, and bodyguard. She helps him find the Floating Market, where he is told he will find Door. The marquis is holding auditions for someone to be Door's bodyguard, and Hunter easily gets the job.

Door, who doesn't have a clue how to get Richard back to normal, reluctantly agrees to have him accompany her, promising to help figure it out once she has dealt with her own troubles. She needs to find out who killed her family, and why, and believes the only one who can provide those answers is the angel Islington.

The angel gives them a quest to retrieve a certain key, and it's back into the strangeness of London Below. At the Abbey of the Black Friars (having parted ways with the marquis), Door, Hunter, and Richard must each undergo a trial in order to earn the key. Hunter passes the trial by combat and Door the trial by conundrum, leaving Richard to attempt the third, called "the Ordeal." No one has ever survived the Ordeal (though the friars are kind enough to provide a nice cup of tea to those who attempt it).

The Ordeal is an hour—though it seems an eternity—locked in a room where Richard's mind is toyed with; he believes he is back in London Above, and he is made to question his sanity over and over again. Fortunately, he survives, and is given the key, which he turns over to Door.

Upon returning to the angel Islington, Richard and Door discover that Hunter is a traitor; that Croup and Vandemar are in the angel's employ; and that Islington wants the key to escape from Heaven-commanded imprisonment—so that the angel can wage war against Heaven itself. When Hunter is killed by the Great Beast of London, Richard kills the beast in turn.

The angel's plans are thwarted (see listing for Door), and Richard is able to use the key to return himself to London Above, and to get back to the life for which he has yearned. Soon, however, he realizes that his experiences in London Below have changed him, that he is not the same man and no longer fits in the mundane world. In a darkened alley he uses a knife given to him by Hunter to scratch a door in a wall. At first nothing happens, and he is dejected. But, at last, the door he has drawn opens, and the Marquis de Carabas is there to welcome him back below.

DOOR. The Lady Door, a noble of the House of the Arch, daughter of Lord Portico, comes from a family of Openers. An Opener has the ability not only to open doors, but to open nearly anything that is in some way closed, and to open a channel or pathway to another dimension when necessary.

When Door's family is slaughtered (with the possible exception of one sister, whose fate is never clearly delineated), she barely manages to escape. On the run, she is pursued by a pair of inhuman killers, Mr. Croup and Mr. Vandemar, and a third brutal murderer called Ross, whom they have hired. When Ross catches up to Door, he stabs her. She fights back, instinctively "opening" his chest, causing his heart and other organs to spill out.

Fleeing from Croup and Vandemar, Door manages to open a way into another reality. She collapses on a sidewalk in the world she knows as London Above—the ordinary, modern-day city of London. There she is discovered by Richard Mayhew, who takes her to his flat and provides a place for her to rest and recover. Fearful and yet determined to discover who is responsible for her family's murder, she begins to take action. With Richard's aid, she recruits the Marquis de Carabas, a mysterious figure who trades in favors. He has a debt of obligation to the family of Lord Portico, and so agrees to help.

Thanking Richard—and apologizing, for she knows what helping her will cost him—she and de Carabas set off. In her father's study, Door and the marquis find his holographic journal, in which he hints that only the angel Islington can provide the answers she needs to find his killer. But to get to the angel before Croup and Vandemar can catch up, they will need protection, and they go to the Floating Market, seeking the services of a bodyguard. Door eventually engages Hunter to protect her while she is on her quest.

While they are at the Floating Market, Richard catches up with Door to ask for her help. Touched by the magic that makes London Below unnoticed by those in London Above, Richard himself has become almost invisible in his own world, erased from his life. At first, Door goes along with a suggestion from the marquis and Hunter that she leave Richard behind. They cannot help him. But guilt makes her retrieve him, and she promises to do whatever she can to help solve his problem, once she has dealt with her own situation.

Though the marquis leaves them for other errands, Door reaches the angel Islington, who assures her that if she retrieves a certain key from the Black Friars, it will be able to tell her the identity of the one responsible for her family's murder. With the aid of Richard and Hunter—and pursued by Croup and Vandemar—she manages to acquire the key. Upon her return to Islington, however, she learns that the angel itself is responsible.

Islington hired Croup and Vandemar. The angel destroyed Atlantis thousands of years before and has been punished by imprisonment on Earth. The key will allow Islington to open a particular door, to escape confinement, and to return to Heaven, where it plans an assault on God. To escape it has always needed an Opener, and had asked Lord Portico for help. Understanding the angel's madness and malice, Portico refused, so Islington had the family murdered, allowing Door to live so that it could manipulate her into performing the task her father refused. Islington even had Croup and Vandemar alter Portico's holo-journal.

After Hunter betrays her, and with the marquis unable to help, and Croup and Vandemar threatening Richard—whom she has come to have feelings for—Door has no choice but to comply. She takes the key and opens the door—or so Islington believes. Door has had an old friend make a copy of the key, and she uses that copy instead of the original. Using her power as an Opener, she opens up a passage to the most horrible, distant, burning world or dimension that she can reach, and once Islington begins to step through, it is dragged off into that world—and Croup and Vandemar are swept up in the angel's wake.

With Islington gone, Door intends to follow in her father's footsteps, and she attempts to unite the various tribes that comprise London Below. She wishes that Richard would stay and help, as she's grown fond of him—though whether as friend or romantic interest is unclear—but he returns to London Above. In the end, Richard does return to London Below, but we can only postulate regarding Door's reunion with him, for there the story ends.

THE MARQUIS DE CARABAS. A mysterious figure in London Below, the marquis trades mostly in favors, but also barters items of particular—and peculiar—value. Though considered far less than trustworthy by most of those acquainted with him, the marquis honors his debts. When he is approached by Richard Mayhew on behalf of the Lady Door, he immediately assesses the situation and goes to her aid, both to satisfy an old debt to her family, and in exchange for some future favor she promises to provide. Before he links up with her, however, the marquis leaves his life (in a small box) in the safekeeping of an eccentric old man known as Old Bailey.

The marquis accompanies Door to her home, witnesses the aftermath of the murders that took place there, and with her watches the holographic journal of her father, Lord Portico. From there the two attend the Floating Market to hold auditions for a bodyguard to protect Door. Once they have engaged Hunter in that capacity, the marquis takes his leave of the group to pursue a different approach to the mystery. He tracks Croup and Vandemar to their lair, and forestalls any violence by tempting Mr. Croup with an antique ceramic of extraordinary value and delicacy, and he threatens to destroy it if they do not answer his questions. His conversation gains him some hints as to their employer, but clever as he is, he cannot escape them afterward and is killed, his body dumped in the sewer.

After his corpse is found by the Sewer Folk, they put it up for sale at the Floating Market, where it is retrieved by Old Bailey. Using the small box containing the marquis's life, de Carabas is resurrected with full memory of his final confrontation with Croup and Vandemar. But by the time he can rejoin Door's quest, she has been betrayed by Hunter and taken by Croup and Vandemar to face the angel Islington, who was their enemy all along.

In a labyrinth in London Below, the marquis and Richard hold Hunter captive and make their way through, following the guidance of a talisman that is soon broken. They get lost in the maze, and with the Great Beast of London lurking about, they are out of options. When they are attacked by the Great Beast, Hunter attempts to kill it using the one weapon in the world that can do the job; but, she fails, and it falls to Richard to finish the beast.

The Marquis and Richard find their way to the chamber where Croup and Vandemar have brought Door to face Islington, but they can do little but become witnesses to the final act.

When Richard attempts to return below after his return to London Above, it is the Marquis de Carabas who comes to fetch him.

HUNTER. A warrior, hunter, and personal bodyguard, Hunter is engaged by Door to protect her from Croup and Vandemar, and from any other enemies who might attempt to harm her. However, she does all of this under false pretenses, having already accepted a commission from the angel Islington to protect Door—and to make sure she is safely delivered into the angel's presence with the key from the Black Friars.

Hunter has killed many of the iconic mythical beasts beneath the great cities of the world, and now she wants to hunt the most intimidating prey of all—the Great Beast of London. There is only one weapon that can kill the beast, a spear that she accepts as part of her payment for her services to Islington when she hands Door over to Croup and Vandemar.

Her attempt to kill the beast is unsuccessful, and instead the Great Beast of London kills Hunter. She passes the spear on to Richard with her dying breath, instructing him in how to finish the job.

MR. CROUP AND MR. VANDEMAR. Insidious, brutal killers whose deeds are notorious in a variety of realms, they are hired by the angel Islington to murder the family of Lord Portico; to deceive the Lady Door; and to eventually drive her to the angel's doorstep. Mr. Croup is a small, vulpine man with a love of priceless, ancient, delicate antiques—which he eats, apparently only for the sheer pleasure of destroying them. Mr. Vandemar is a larger, more brutish man, who has a greater appreciation for inflicting physical pain and eating flesh (hearts included). In the end they suffer the same fate as the angel Islington, sucked away through a portal Door has opened into a distant world.

ISLINGTON. Once upon a time Islington was meant to look after the civilization of Atlantis. Unfortunately for them, the Atlanteans apparently got on Islington's nerves, so the angel destroyed it, killing millions, and then pretended it was all a terrible accident. As punishment, God imprisoned Islington in a single chamber in London for thousands of years, with the promise that one day, with proper penance, it might return to Heaven.

But Islington is impatient. The door to Heaven can be opened with a special key, but only if it is turned by an Opener. When it attempts to persuade Lord Portico to help retrieve the key so that it can return to Heaven, Portico refuses, perhaps sensing that Islington intends to wage war on Heaven. The angel arranges for Portico and his family to be murdered, except for his daughter, Door, who he manipulates into providing the services that her father would not.

However, in the end, Door is more cunning than the angel. She uses a replica of the key rather than the genuine article and uses her abilities as an Opener to open a passage into a realm as distant as hostile as she can reach. Islington and his lackeys are sucked through the door, gone from the world—and likely from Heaven—forever.

THE GREAT BEAST OF LONDON. A giant monster, complete with horns and hooves, that guards a terrible labyrinth in London Below. Richard Mayhew has had dreams about it, and when Hunter fails to kill the beast, Richard must do the deed. By tasting its blood and smearing it on his eyelids, he is able to navigate the labyrinth with ease.

JESSICA. Richard's remarkably shallow fiancée, she breaks up with him when he stops to help the wounded Door, thereby ruining her plans for the evening. He believes that he wants to be reunited with her, but later, when he returns to London Above, realizes that isn't what he wants at all.

OLD BAILEY. An eccentric old man with a love of birds (and they seem to love him back), Old Bailey owes the Marquis de Carabas a favor, and repays it by holding on to a small box that contains the man's life, sort of a backup disk of his mind, soul, and life-force. When de Carabas is murdered by Croup and Vandemar, Old Bailey uses that box to bring him back to life.

LORD PORTICO. Door's father and the head of the House of the Arch, Portico refuses to aid Islington with his escape plan. He and most of his family are murdered for this refusal.

ANAESTHESIA. When Richard descends into London Below, he is aided by rats—Door's friends—and, reluctantly, by a group of people who apparently venerate them. Anaesthesia is assigned to accompany Richard to the Floating Market, but to get there they must cross Night's Bridge. While crossing the bridge she is swept up by the ominous force of darkness—perhaps Night itself—that surrounds the bridge. Presumably, she is dead. Richard grieves for her because she showed him kindness, and he keeps a bead from her necklace to remind him of her.

During his Ordeal, he finds that bead in his pocket, and he realizes that he is not insane after all.

THE LORD RAT-SPEAKER. Leader of a tribe of people in London Below who venerate rats—and the one able to understand their language—he briefly menaces Richard Mayhew, before a rat instructs him to see that Richard reaches the Floating Market safely. The Lord Rat-Speaker assigns Anaesthesia to guide Richard there.

THE EARL. A half-mad, aging noble, he is the Earl of "Earl's Court," which in London Below is a train that travels along Tube lines. Inside the train car is a vast, noble court, complete with guards, servants, and courtiers. An old ally of Lord Portico—and an enemy of the Marquis de Carabas—the Earl helps Door reach the angel Islington.

NIGHT'S BRIDGE. Though it echoes the Tube station Knightsbridge, the Night's Bridge of London Below is actually a terrible crossing, whereupon one risks attack by a living darkness. Crossing can take a terrible toll, as it does when Richard Mayhew's companion Anaesthesia is swallowed up by the Night.

THE FLOATING MARKET. A marketplace where the various tribes and denizens of London Below set up shop to sell various goods and services. The market is held in a different location every time, hence the "floating" moniker.

THE BLACK FRIARS. In the abbey of the Black Friars, in a remote area of London Below, the friars guard a powerful key. Richard, Door, and Hunter visit the abbey to retrieve it for Islington, and must undergo three trials. Hunter passes the trial by combat, Door the trial by conundrum, and Richard survives the Ordeal. With dread at what it may bring, the Father Abbot of the Black Friars hands over the key. He is also the one who later helps Richard recover from injuries sustained in his struggles against Croup, Vandemar, and the Great Beast of London. The Father Abbot also informs Richard that the key is the key to all reality, and with it he can return to his old life.

THE SEWER FOLK. A tribe who live in the sewers of London Below, and who dredge things from the Thames to be sold at the Floating Market. They are the ones who retrieve the corpse of the Marquis de Carabas and sell it to Old Bailey at the market.

HAMMERSMITH. A magical metalsmith and friend to the family of Lord Portico. At Door's request he makes a chain, so that she can wear the key around her neck; he also secretly forges a duplicate key that has none of its extraordinary properties.

LAMIA AND THE VELVETS. The Velvets are vampirelike creatures who live in London Below. Lamia takes a liking to Richard Mayhew at the Floating Market, at the same time that Door is having Hammersmith make her duplicate key. When

Lamia offers to guide them, Richard agrees, only to have the marquis drive her away when it becomes clear that the price for Lamia's services is Richard's blood.

SERPENTINE AND THE SEVEN SISTERS. After Door and Richard visit the angel Islington and drink a brew that makes them both very drunk, Hunter takes them to Serpentine's lair to recover. Door is initially very afraid, explaining to Richard that Serpentine is a sort of bogeyman in London Below; when parents want their children to behave, they say that if the kids are naughty, Serpentine will get them. However, Serpentine shows them nothing but hospitality, perhaps because she and her sisters (the Seven Sisters) were once Hunter's employers. No other information about Serpentine's sisters has yet been revealed.

TRIVIA

- In 2005 and 2006, DC Comics's Vertigo imprint published a comic book adaptation of *Neverwhere*, written by Mike Carey, who also penned the long-running comics series Lucifer, a spin-off from Gaiman's *Sandman*.

- Gaiman has acknowledged that he has ideas for a sequel to *Neverwhere* entitled *The Seven Sisters*, presumably centered around Serpentine and her siblings.

- In the pages of his short story collection *Fragile Things*, Gaiman confirms that a novella-length work set in the world of *Neverwhere* is half written. It is entitled *How the Marquis Got His Coat Back*.

- The concept of the Floating Market returned several years later in Gaiman and Charles Vess's illustrated novel, *Stardust*, and its film adaptation.

- A second season of the BBC series was contemplated, featuring Richard Mayhew as a wandering hero in London Below, but when Gaiman could not persuade the BBC to commit to doing forty-five-minute (rather than thirty-minute) episodes on film (rather than video), the idea was shelved.

- As a teenager, Gaiman began his first novel, about a boy attending a school that taught magic. Though the novel was never completed, some of the central ideas eventually became the DC/Vertigo miniseries *The Books of Magic*, and its spin-offs. The novel also featured the first appearance of *Neverwhere*'s Mr. Croup and Mr. Vandemar.

- While the relative low budget of television production compromised some elements of *Neverwhere*'s fantasy elements, by far the most self-evident compromise was manifest when the Great Beast of London appears on-screen. Despite assurances Gaiman was given by the production staff, he couldn't help but register his dismay when the Great Beast of the labyrinth was represented by—a black angus bull! Neil's comments on this "special effect" for the DVD commentary track are diplomatic, to say the least.

THE QUOTABLE GAIMAN

On recording his commentary track for the *Neverwhere* DVD release:

I sat in front of the screen in a studio in Minneapolis today for the entire afternoon, while all six episodes of *Neverwhere* played, and talked about whatever
came into my head while *Neverwhere* ran, as a sort of stream of consciousness
thing. It's been a long time—I'd forgotten, on the one hand, how much I disliked
the way the first episode came out, and the edit of the last few minutes of the last
episode, and on the other, how much I enjoyed large chunks of episodes 4 and 5,
particularly the Croup and Vandemar and De Carabas bits.

And I really, really kept wishing that we had all the footage that was shot, and
could edit it all back together the way it was meant to be, missing scenes and all.

—journal.neilgaiman.com

||||||||||||||||||||||||||||||||||||||||||||||||||||||||||||||||||||||

STARDUST:

BEING A ROMANCE WITHIN THE

REALM OF FAERIE

(1997)

There once was a young man who wished to gain his Heart's Desire.

And while that is, as beginnings go, not entirely novel (for every tale
about every young man could start in a similar manner) there was much
about this young man and what happened to him that was unusual, although
even he never knew the whole of it.

Thus begins *Stardust,* which began life in 1997 as a four-issue miniseries under
DC Comics's Vertigo imprint. Yet, though published in comic book format,
Stardust was not a comic book at all. Each edition contained forty-eight pages and
featured Gaiman's text story accompanied by Charles Vess's ethereal art. This presentation seemed particularly apt, given that the story is set in the era during
which Charles Dickens was serializing *Oliver Twist.*

Those four issues were then gathered together into a handsome hardcover collection in 1998, which had the advantage of showcasing Vess's work in a larger

format (for instance, his two-page spread of the Faerie market is simply dazzling). In 1999, HarperCollins issued a new, text-only version of the story under its short-lived Spike imprint. Finally, in August 2007, *Stardust* reached the big screen, in a film version starring Michelle Pfeiffer, Robert De Niro, and Ricky Gervais. Many different incarnations, all driven by Gaiman's charming, witty narrative.

Stardust is a short novel, and its author suspects that is because he wrote it in longhand, using a fountain pen. This method, he has said, forced him to think more about sentence structure before he wrote. He also wanted to write the book as if he were writing eighty years earlier, to get the kinds of sentence and storytelling rhythms absent from much of modern literature.

The story is, of course, a fairy tale, but one that can be enjoyed by adults. Gaiman dusts off old tropes in a refreshing manner, carefully walking a tightrope between appealing to younger and older audiences. For the young there is magic, and unicorns, and wonder; for adults there is knowing humor and a lot of sexy banter and sexual tension.

Set in the aptly named English town of Wall (there is a wall on the edge of town that marks the border between the real world and Faerie), it tells the story of Tristran Thorn, who while seeking what he believes is his heart's desire, finds something entirely different and unexpected, something he was searching for all along without knowing it. Romantic and funny, yet also a real nail-biter at times, *Stardust* is quintessential Gaiman, a fusion of the old and the new, a traditional sort of tale powered by modern sensibilities. It is those very qualities that make it, like any good fairy tale, timeless.

PEOPLE, PLACES, AND THINGS

THE TOWN OF WALL. Wall is located in England, right on the border of the Faerie kingdom. There is a wall on that border, which is meant to keep humans and Faerie folk from mingling.

DUNSTAN THORN. As *Stardust* begins, eighteen-year-old Dunstan is told by a man in a tall, black, silk top hat that the next day he will attain his "Heart's Desire." At Faerie Market the next day, Dunstan meets, and is seduced by, a very beautiful maiden. After their one night together, Dunstan returns to his life in Wall. Time passes, until one evening, some nine months later, a basket containing a small child is found at the entrance to Faerie. On the basket is a piece of parchment with the name Tristran Thorn written on it.

THE FAERIE MARKET. Held every nine years, it is the only time that humans can freely visit Faerie. Many things are available at the market, including new eyes for old, bottled dreams, salves, ointments, philters, and nostrums. At one stall Dunstan Thorn encounters a beautiful girl, one of the folk from Beyond the Wall.

THE GIRL AT THE STALL (AKA LADY UNA). The personal slave of a witch woman, she is tending the stall when Dunstan Thorn passes by. In selling him a pure white glass snowdrop from her wares, she also claims his heart. The two have one night of passion together before going their separate ways. The girl, who later in the book takes the form of a bird, is none other Lady Una, daughter of the lord of Stormhold. After being held in slavery by a witch woman named Ditchwater Sal for more than sixty years, she is freed through the intervention of her son, Tristran. She returns to Stormhold afterward, and rules there in her son Tristran's stead until he is ready to take the throne.

TRISTRAN THORN. Found in a basket at the entrance to the Wall nine months after his father Dunstan's tryst with Lady Una, Tristran grows up in Wall unaware of his heritage. Madly in love with the beautiful but distant Victoria Forester, he secures a shaky and untrustworthy promise from her: She will give him what he desires if he can secure a star for her that they see falling to earth in Faerie. Tristran's promise is prelude to a strange but wonderful journey in Faerie, where he comes into his own and finds true love in the form of Yvaine, the evening star. He also discovers that he is the last living heir to the throne of Stormhold. After marrying Yvaine, he rules it wisely for many years before his passing.

VICTORIA FOSTER. The apple of Tristran's eye, it is a promise from her that triggers the events described in *Stardust*. Her subsequent marriage to the villager Mister Monday (breaking that promise), which occurs in the same week in which Yvaine falls from the sky, helps fulfill the conditions that result in Lady Una's release from slavery, as she is bound to Dishwater Sal until the day that the moon loses her daughter, if it occurs in a week when two Mondays come together.

YVAINE. The fallen star that catches Tristran and Victoria's attention one fateful evening. An evening star, Yvaine is the moon's daughter. When she falls to earth in Faerie, Yvaine is thrown together with Tristran Thorn, who originally arrives on the scene eager to claim her as the prize he needs to win the hand of Victoria Foster. At first standoffish toward the young man, she finds herself falling in love with him as they travel across the entire length of Faerie toward Wall, encountering many obstacles. Yvaine eventually marries Tristran, and they live happily ever after in Stormhold. After his death she becomes the lady of Stormhold, and "proved a better monarch, in peace and in war, than any would have dared to hope."

THE UNICORN. Shortly after they set out, Tristran and Yvaine come across a unicorn engaged in a fierce battle with a lion. Due to Tristran's quick thinking, the unicorn is saved from death at the lion's claws. After befriending the unicorn, Yvaine uses it to make her escape from Tristran. After they travel for a day, they end up at the Lamia Inn, which, in reality, is an elaborate trap laid for Yvaine by the witch queen. Shortly after Tristran arrives at the inn, the witch queen reveals herself as their enemy. The unicorn buys Tristran and Yvaine time to escape by charging the sorceress, spearing the witch's shoulder with his horn. Unfortunately, the beast is slain by the witch in retaliation.

STORMHOLD. A kingdom of Faerie, Stormhold has had, as of the time this tale begins, eighty-one lords. The chance to be the eighty-second lord of Stormhold drives the current lord's sons to great extremes.

THE SEVEN SONS. The eighty-first lord of Stormhold once had seven sons, all of whom coveted his throne. Four—Secundus, Quintus, Quartus, and Sextus—are dead when we first encounter them, having been murdered by their brothers Primus, Tertius, and Septimus; they still haunt the living, however. Before his death, the eighty-first lord hurls a topaz, the Power of Stormhold, out the window, telling the surviving brothers that whoever finds it shall be the new lord.

LORD SEPTIMUS. Outlasting Tertius and Primus (who become spirits, and join their siblings in haunting Septimus), Septimus seeks the Power of Stronghold so that he may become its new lord. Septimus is killed by the witch-queen when they square off late in the story.

THE TOPAZ. Known as the Power of Stronghold, he who holds it will be lord of that kingdom. When the eighty-first lord hurls it from his keep, it strikes Yvaine in the side, knocking her from the sky. Because she decides to carry it with her, she soon finds the Lords of Stormhold on her trail.

THE THREE HAGS. Seeking the power of the fallen star, these three ancient sisters, the Lilim, send one of their number (really an aspect of themselves, the witch queen) to find the fallen star Yvaine so that they may feed on her heart and so regain their own power and youth.

THE LITTLE HAIRY MAN. Tristran's guide in Faerie, he dresses the young man in the style of the land, then provides him with a magic candle stub that when lit enables Tristran to travel great distances in a short period of time.

MADAME SEMELE (DITCHWATER SAL). A witch, she holds Lady Una captive for more than sixty years. Being a witch, she also considers the heart of a star to be of great interest for the power it holds. She is, however, bested in a battle of wits by the Witch Queen, who casts a spell on her so that she is unable to see, perceive, touch, taste, find, or kill the star.

Sal encounters Tristran and Yvaine as they travel back toward Wall. Tristran bargains with her (remember, the witch cannot see Yvaine) and secures her promise to transport him to Wall in exchange for the glass flower he carries (a gift from his father). He also makes her promise that she will not harm him. Upon gaining the flower, she promptly transforms him into a dormouse, keeping her promise to him, albeit in her own way. Thus Sal, who would have gladly consumed Yvaine's heart had she known she was near, unwittingly transports the star to Wall as a stowaway.

THE TREE. Actually a nymph, transformed into a tree by a magician. The "magnificent" copper beech is told by Pan, Lord of the Forest, to give Tristran and Yvaine all possible aid and succor. "I will tell you three true things," the tree says to Tristran, and it informs him that the star Yvaine is in great danger, a carriage is coming, and to listen to a leaf she gives him when "you need it the most."

CAPTAIN JOHANNES ALBERIC. Captain of the Free Ship *Perdita*. The *Perdita*, which sails the skies rather than the seas, is bound on a lightning-hunting expedition. The captain rescues Tristran and Yvaine from a predicament caused when Tristran uses the magic candle to escape from the Witch Queen, unexpectedly ending up on a cloud. Looking back, Tristran considers the time he spent on the *Perdita* as one of the happiest of his life.

STARDUST: THE MOVIE (2007)

A film version of *Stardust* premiered in the United States in August 2007. It was directed by British filmmaker Matthew Vaughn, director of 2004's *Layer Cake* (and a producer on *A Short Film About John Bolton*), and the screenplay was penned by Vaughn and Jane Goldman (the wife of Gaiman's longtime friend Jonathan Ross). Apparently the film happened because Vaughn's spouse, model Claudia Schiffer, was a big fan of the book. Fortuitously, Vaughn had just pulled out of directing *X-Men 3,* and felt like making a film in the UK.

There are many differences between *Stardust* the novel and the film adaptation, both major (gone is the eloquent red-leaved tree, modeled on Neil's friend Tori Amos) and minor (the hero Tristran is renamed Tristan). The movie, of course, is not entirely faithful to the book. Characters were omitted, and parts of the story are compressed so as not to lose the audience's attention (for instance, in the novel Tristran takes months to find Yvaine; in the movie he's instantly transported to her side). Gaiman had mixed feelings about these departures and differences, but overall enjoyed the film. In a November 2007 interview with bookslut.com, he noted, "Some of those things I liked, and some of those things I don't particularly like, and some of those things lead to moments like the amazing Ricky Gervais/Robert DeNiro scene which is improvised and absolutely one of the funniest things I've ever seen and wouldn't have given up for the world."

The movie was well received, for the most part. Although *Entertainment Weekly* gave it a B, stating that the film "evokes a hundred other things you've seen before," and *The Village Voice* said it was "less an adaptation of Neil Gaiman's 1999 novel than of its jacket copy," other reviews were far kinder. *USA Today,* for instance, said *Stardust* lit up the screen "with a splendid tale of heroism and romance," and the *Hollywood Reporter* said it was "diverting and pleasurable to watch."

Most likely due to a lackluster job on publicity, the movie was not a big hit in the United States, with an opening weekend of only $9 million. But true to Paramount's predictions, the fantasy made up for its disappointing performance domestically ($38.4 million) at the overseas box office. Paramount, which put up half of the film's $74 million budget, had contended from the outset that *Stardust* would be a strong international player because of its whimsical story line and ensemble cast, which includes Charlie Cox, as Tristran; Claire Danes, as Yvaine; Sienna Miller, as Victoria Foster; Robert De Niro, as Captain Alberic, here called Captain Shakespeare; Peter O'Toole, as the eighty-first lord of Stormhold; Michelle Pfeiffer, as the Witch Queen; and Rupert Everett, as Septimus. Through early December 2007, the film's international take stood at approximately $95 million, nearly two and one half times its North American haul. It was the number one film in the UK for many weeks, only giving up that spot in November when, ironically, it was supplanted by *Beowulf.*

TRIVIA

- In 1999, the illustrated version of *Stardust* won the Mythopoeic Fantasy Award for Adult Literature.

- Gaiman's friend Tori Amos lent the author a house to write in; he wrote the first chapter in it. All she asked in return was that he make her into a tree. He did.

- Gaiman got the idea at a party held at a friend's home n the Arizona desert (he and Charles Vess were celebrating winning the 1991 World Fantasy Award for "A Midsummer's Night's Dream"). He saw a saw a shooting star, there and began a game of "what if?" What if someone were to go after that star? And what if that star wasn't a star, but a girl?

- As noted, *Stardust* has an unusual publishing history. *Stardust* was originally published by DC/Vertigo in 1997 as a four-issue "prestige" miniseries—illustrated novella chapter books, not comics or a serialized graphic novel—and it did well, winning solid sales, good reviews, and many awards. DC/Vertigo collected and repackaged the whole in 1998 in complete hardcover and a trade paperback editions; thus, *Neil Gaiman and Charles Vess' Stardust (Being A Romance Within The Realm of Faerie)* (the full title) spilled beyond the boundaries of the comic book direct-sales marketplace. The hardcover was bound in faux leather and featured all four of Vess's covers and many sketches; the paperback and all subsequent trade editions featured new covers by Vess. Eight years later, DC/Vertigo published a new hardcover edition of *Stardust*, sporting over fifty pages of new material.

- When Charles Vess's beloved wife, Karen, suffered terrible injuries in an auto accident, Gaiman and Vess and a bevy of artists (William Stout, Mike Mignola,

Terri Windling, Bryan Talbot, Jill Thompson, Paul Chadwick, P. Craig Russell, Michael Zulli, Terry Moore, Linda Medley, Dave McKean, Jeff Smith, Trina Robbins, Steve Leialoha, Gary Gianni, Stan Sakai, Mike Kaluta, Moebius, Geoff Darrow, Brian Froud and more) contributed to a special Green Man Press fund-raiser portfolio, *A Fall of Stardust* (1999), which contained a wealth of art plates, and two chapbooks, one by Susanna Clarke, featuring the short story "The Duke of Wellington Misplaces His Horse," and the other by Neil Gaiman, containing a short story titled "Wall: A Prologue," and three poems, "Septimus' Triolet," "Song of the Little Hairy Man," and "The Old Warlock's Reverie: A Pantoum."

- It's important to note the steady collaborative solidarity Gaiman and Vess maintained over the decade, a rare bond between author and illustrator that continues to the feature film adaptation. Notably, the film credits—on-screen and in all its promotional materials—list its source as the book written by Neil Gaiman and illustrated by Charles Vess. This is an almost historically unprecedented screen credit. Of late, DC/Vertigo film adaptations have reverted to screen and advertising credits more anonymous than those that adorned serial and movie adaptations of Golden Age comic books, a reversion unfortunately fueled in part by the highly publicized decision of Alan Moore to exile himself from—and refuse credit on—any further Hollywood productions. With the notable exception of David Lloyd's credit on *V for Vendetta,* Moore's decision relegated the rest of his collaborators to the limbo of "based on the DC/Vertigo Graphic Novel" on relevant film adaptations.

- Gaiman had, in fact, sanctioned the publication in 1999 of both UK and U.S. editions of *Stardust* sans Vess's illustrations. It's standard practice in the book industry to relegate illustrators to interchangeable, disposable components of the author's realm, a practice that is utterly pragmatic and firmly established as a fair and legal precedent. In spite of this, Gaiman recognized, fought hard to retain (amid the legal negotiations with the studios), and properly honored Vess's intrinsic importance to *Stardust.* As Gaiman noted, "It actually took a lot of work to get Charles his credit (and 1/3 of the money). Seeing how happy he was made it all worth it."

THE QUOTABLE GAIMAN

I owe an enormous debt to Hope Mirrlees, Lord Dunsany, James Branch Cabell, and C. S. Lewis, wherever they currently may be, for showing me that fairy stories were for adults too.

—Afterword, *Stardust*

A CONVERSATION WITH
CHARLES VESS

(JANUARY 8, 2008)

Question: How did you meet Neil?

CHARLES VESS: Years ago, *Amazing Heroes*, a monthly magazine on comics, would do a special swimsuit issue each summer, featuring drawings of scantily clothed superheroines. I would submit pinups that appealed to my sense of humor, depicting various obscure comic book or comic strip characters with scarcely a buxom beauty in sight, and, one year, 1988 or 1989, I did a pinup featuring the Warriors Three, with the enormous Volstag molding a fine figure of himself out of sand, a play on a humorous element of James Branch Cabell's fantasy novel, *Jurgen*. I signed the art with the addendum, "With apologies to James Branch Cabell."

Amazing Heroes misconstrued that as Cabell being an artist, rather than a writer. In a subsequent issue, a letter appeared from one Neil Gaiman, correcting that misconception. Thus, I was already aware of Neil when I met him months later at the San Diego Comic-Con, where we quickly bonded over, among other things, our mutual admiration of Cabell. We had a great conversation in the middle of an aisle. Mind you, this was before Neil morphed into the fan magnet that he is now, so we could do that.

Q: And that conversation led to your work on Sandman?

CV: At the end of that conversation, he mentioned that he was doing a comic called *The Sandman*, and that if I wanted to do an issue, to let him know. I thought to myself, I would never say yes to that, because, at the time, I perceived *The Sandman* as a horror comic. The first five issues or so were centered around modern horror, which wasn't anything I'd ever want to draw. Then I saw issue twelve, with the story "Tales in the Sand," the African folk tale, and then I thought, of course, *The Sandman* can tell any story, any time, anywhere, and Neil's a really good writer, so I called him up, and said yes, I'd love to do an issue with him, any time he wanted.

Q: In the meantime, Neil had started thinking about "A Midsummer's Night's Dream"?

CV: Yes. He had seen my work on the illustrated Donning edition of the play, and was playing with the idea of retelling the story in the series, so he asked if I was interested in doing that, of course interpreting it in an entirely different way. At that point it became a matter of what to do with the characters. I think it was

Neil's idea to make Puck into a vicious monkey creature, and it was my idea to make Oberon a nine-foot figure with horns and red armor. Because of the similarity in our tastes regarding fantasy literature, the whole process was simplified; we had kind of a shorthand communication, where we would get where the other was coming from. We didn't have to explain some obscure bit of fantasy matter because we both were familiar with it.

Q: *What were Neil's scripts like?*
cv: Very funny, full scripts, always with the acknowledgment that if you've got a better idea, please do it. All sorts of funny asides, what he was thinking about at the time, what he was watching on TV.

Q: *So the collaboration was untroubled?*
cv: Very much so, it was more like the two of us together became a third distinct entity, whose work was better than each of us could have produced on his own.

Q: *And it garnered you a World Fantasy Award.*
cv: Yes, and other awards, and a level of notoriety. As an aside, it was probably the only thing I ever turned in before it was due. [Laughter] I surprised myself, and I especially surprised [the editor] Karen Berger.

Q: *And afterward?*
cv: There was the issue of Books of Magic that was set in Faerie, which felt as if it were written for me. That went really well.

Q: *Then you did an eight-page "insert" in the sixth chapter of* The Kindly Ones.
cv: Yes, which to me was the entire story of The Sandman told in eight pages.

Q: *And the last issue, "The Tempest"?*
cv: Which was the bestselling comic that month, but it was a sad thing, because it only sold a bit more than one hundred thousand copies. This was during the down market in comics, mind you.

Q: *But your work is still reaching new readers through the collections.*
cv: Yes. It's interesting—at the time, DC had a policy that you could either be paid once for your work, or you could take royalties. [Pauses] I took the royalties, which can be characterized as a gift which keeps on giving.

Q: *Whew. Thank goodness. When you paused there, I thought you might be about to say that you took the one-time payment . . .*
cv: [Laughter] No, I made the right decision. And now there's the *Absolute Sandman,* which is just stunning.

Q: When did you do "The False Knight on the Road"?

cv: 1995. We had agreed to do *Stardust* in 1991 at the World Fantasy Convention, but it took a while for Neil to start writing that. In the meantime, I had had an idea for a new comic, and I knew it would be a good thing to have Neil's name on the cover of the first issue, and I knew he loved ballads. It turned out well.

Q: Stardust *was originally conceived of as a graphic novel?*

cv: Yes. But I was tired of drawing panel-to-panel continuity, so I suggested to Neil that we do it as an illustrated book. And, being an agreeable sort, he said, "Yes, let's do that." And off we went. And 175 paintings later, we were done. It still bothers me a little that people often refer to it as a graphic novel, though.

Q: What was it like to see the movie?

cv: I got to go to a screening that Robert De Niro hosted of the film at the Tribeca Film Festival, accompanied by my friend Michael Kaluta. I got to sit in the same theater with many of the actors in the movie. Sitting right in front of me was Lorenzo di Bonaventura, the producer of the movie. After it was over, he turned to me and asked how I'd liked it. Now, I can't lie, I'm really bad at it, but, happily, I was able to tell him I had a ball, I really loved it. After seeing it, oh, about ten times now, there are things I'd change, but that's always the case. And the film has spurred sales of the source material.

Q: Stardust *is a beautiful book, you should be very proud of it.*

cv: Thanks. I'm very, very happy with it.

Q: And you secretly placed Neil in a scene, as you had done previously in a two-page spread in the third issue of *The Books of Magic*?

cv: In quite a few scenes, actually. In the original issues, Neil can be seen in the Faerie Market; he's the shifty-looking gent in an overcoat and the dark glasses way over to the left, in the bookstall. Because of the way it's printed, the format, he can't be seen in the original hardcover edition, though. In the re-issue, for which I painted several new pieces, he's joined by his daughter Maddy.

Q: Who else appears?

cv: My wife and I. The Lilim. Kiki and Totoro, from the Miyazaki films. Herobear is in there. Gandalf, because I figured he'd certainly show up. Lots of stuff like that.

Q: Any upcoming projects with Neil?

cv: I just finished the art for *The Blueberry Girl*; it should be out early in 2009.

Q: Any final words on your working relationship with Neil?

cv: In any relationship, you should be learning from your partner. I think, with

Neil, one of the strengths of our collaboration is that I soften some of his edges, and he puts some hard edges on some of my soft spots. We get to play in a special playground where we have lots of fun. We've never had any issues; it's really been a blissful experience.

||||||||||||||||||||||||||||||||||||||||||||||||||||||||||||||||||||||||

AMERICAN GODS

(2001)

Although obviously not his first work in novel form, Gaiman has been known to describe *American Gods* as his first novel. The much loved *Good Omens* was his collaboration with longtime friend Terry Pratchett. *Stardust* was written as an illustrated story, almost in the style of pulp magazines, and serialized in four issues, as though it were a comic book. *Neverwhere,* he reminds interviewers, was a novelization, an adaptation of television scripts. As such, it was "not really novel-shaped."

American Gods more fully explores themes that Gaiman had only previously touched on in *The Sandman*; specifically, thoughts voiced by the character Ishtar in his *Brief Lives* story arc, and by the trickster Loki in *The Kindly Ones*. Gaiman was inspired to further pursue these ideas by an incident that occurred while he was in Iceland for a twenty-four-hour stopover. Figuring he'd play it smart, he thought he'd try to stay awake until it got dark; he failed to reckon with the fact that the sun wasn't about to go down in Iceland at that time of the year. Thus, awake for thirty-six hours straight, he began to explore Reykjavik. Wandering into a tourism office, he had just started looking at little maps of Viking incursions into Newfoundland and back, and was struck by the thought, "I wonder if they left their Gods behind?"

Gaiman wrote the first draft in fountain pen, in several five-hundred-page, leather-bound sketchbooks that he purchased in a close-out sale. "I really wanted a second draft," says the author. "It's my experience with computers that they do not give you a second draft. Computers give you an ongoing, ever-improving first draft."

Exploring the topic of people carrying their gods with them to the New World, Gaiman also realized that he wanted to write about America, and, more specifically, about the immigrant experience in America. Penning several sections labeled "Coming to America," which described the struggles of several foreigners trying to adjust to life on American soil, he also explored the way that America tends to consume and digest other cultures, turning them into something different.

Another thing that is featured importantly in this novel is the uniquely American phenomenon of the roadside attraction, those places that dot the American landscape, designed with one purpose: to give you the illusion that you've seen something out of the ordinary while making you part with your hard-earned money. Places like South of the Border, or the Cadillac Ranch, or, to name a site that plays a prominent role in *American Gods,* the House on the Rock, places that feature enormous balls of tin or string, or mouse circuses, or even mummies, places that you can read about in magazines like *Weird New Jersey.*

It's a novel steeped in Americana, a picaresque, a book so rich in incident and characters that we'll hardly be able to scatch the surface in our attempt to describe it further below. It's a uniquely American road novel ("America is one huge road novel," says Gaiman, "You have to get into a car and you have to go places."). Although he doesn't consciously evoke them, you can be sure that the spirits of Tod Stiles and Buzz Murdock of *Route 66* fame accompany Gaiman's hero, Shadow, on his strange odyssey across the United States. It's an America that is both comfortably familiar and exceedingly strange—Gaiman describes the geography as fairly accurate, but warns readers he took some liberties ("This is a work of fiction, not a guidebook").

American Gods is also a novel that only Gaiman could have written: Given his "outsider" status (having settled in the United States after spending his formative years in England), and his refined powers of observation, he could be part of America but remain removed, "in it, but not of it." The novel reflects his deep fascination with and love for his adopted country, but also subtly reflects its harshness, and strangeness, and flaws.

Besides its obvious merit as a work of literature (it was critically well received, and won several major genre awards for best novel, including the 2002 Hugo, Nebula, and Bram Stoker awards), this also was a significant book for Gaiman in terms of his career arc, in that it firmly cemented his status as a major figure in the fantasy field, granting him the freedom to pursue whatever subject matter he saw fit. He had successfully avoided one of the chief fears he had had early in his career, that of being typecast, of being relegated to a narrow niche.

Based, in the author's words, on "forty years of cumulative research," this *New York Times* bestseller (it debuted at number ten on the list on July 8, 2001) follows the adventures of the ex-convict Shadow, who is released from prison a few days early upon the death of his wife, Laura, in a car accident. Hired by the mysterious Mr. Wednesday (think Odin's [Woden's] Day) to act as an escort and bodyguard, he travels across America visiting Wednesday's colleagues and acquaintances. Wednesday is on a mission to recruit the American manifestations of the so-called Old Gods (whose powers have begun to wane as their believers have decreased in number) to make a stand against the New American Gods, which are manifestations of modern life and technology.

All you need to know from there on is that a fierce battle is coming, and it's not going to be pretty . . .

PEOPLE, PLACES, AND THINGS

SHADOW (AKA MIKE AINSEL, AKA BALDER MOON). Three years in prison have changed Shadow very little; other than learning a few magic tricks, and gaining an appreciation for Herodotus's *Histories*, he's pretty much the same huge, strong, soft-spoken fellow he was when he first entered stir. With only a few weeks left to his sentence, he's looking forward to being reunited with his beloved spouse, Laura.

Fate, alas, has other things in store for Shadow, who is released early after his wife is killed in a car accident. On the way home to her funeral, he meets an old man named Wednesday who offers him a job as a bodyguard, an offer he initially rejects. But after learning the truth behind his wife's death, and wishing to make a clean break with his past, he eventually agrees, little knowing that he's just become one of the most important people alive.

Working for Wednesday brings Shadow into contact with many gods and other creatures of myth. Although it should be intoxicating, it is really very serious business, as Wednesday is a general preparing for war. Shadow learns bits and pieces about the coming battle and the stakes at risk along the way, and comes to realize that he is destined to play a key role in the conflict—and reluctantly accepts that role out of his overdeveloped sense of duty.

When Wednesday is murdered by his enemies, Shadow is the one to claim the body, and the one who holds a vigil for the leader of the Old Gods, by hanging in a tree for nine days and nights, without food or water. Shadow's death on that tree and his subsequent resurrection prepare him for his role in the god war (he also learns that he's actually Wednesday's son, by a human mother). Traveling to the battlefield on the back of the Thunderbird, he single-handedly halts the carnage.

After fulfilling his destiny, Shadow returns to the sleepy town of Lakeside, Wisconsin, and solves the mystery of a local girl who has gone missing. As we learn in "Monarch in the Glen," he doesn't stay there long afterward.

DREAMS. Dreams and dreamlike experiences play a key role in American gods. Early on, Shadow is warned of trouble aborning from the Buffalo Man, who appears to him in a dream. He also dreams of the Thunderbird, who plays a key role later in the book. He also takes a dreamlike journey after he "dies" (recalling Max the Wizard in *A Princess Bride*, he's told, "There's dead, and there's dead, and there's dead. It's a relative thing.") on the World Tree, and gains insight into his situation.

LOW-KEY LYESMITH. This fellow's name might give his true identity away to most, but not to Shadow, at least until it's almost too late. Shadow's cellmate in prison, he's described as a "grifter from Minnesota." In reality he's the Norse God of Mischief, Loki. Wednesday's secret ally, he works under the alias of Mr. World to further their goals.

Loki is killed by Laura Moon.

LAURA MOON. Although she's quite dead at the beginning of the story (she died while performing oral sex on Shadow's best friend in a moving car, causing an accident that killed them both), Laura plays a key role in events after being resurrected by a magical gold coin that Shadow throws in her grave. Visiting her "widower" periodically, in increasingly disturbing states of decay (vignettes inspired directly by Gaiman's nightmares), she's got his back, saving his skin more than once.

In the battle of Rock City, Laura kills Loki with the Odin spear, dedicating his death to Shadow.

MR. WEDNESDAY. After a mix-up puts Shadow in first class on his flight home for Laura's funeral, he finds himself sitting next to an older man with reddish gray hair and one eye ("Didn't lose it. I know exactly where it is"). The man says, "I've got a job for you, Shadow."

The man, who introduces himself as Wednesday, wants to hire Shadow as a bodyguard. At first resistant, Shadow eventually agrees, serving the old man faithfully, even going so far as to hold a vigil (it's tougher than it sounds) for him when he dies.

Wednesday is actually Odin, the All Father of Norse mythology. One of the first gods to be transplanted to the new world, he's one of the most powerful. Despite that, he's fallen on hard times. In recent decades he's been reduced to the status of a con man, using his powers to swindle suckers and seduce women. The secret of his success, according to Wednesday, is "charm."

Assisted by his son Loki (his other son, Thor, killed himself in Philadelphia in 1932. "He was a whole lot like you," Wednesday tells Shadow. "Big and dumb."), Odin is presently working on perhaps the greatest con of all time. Using a variation of the grift known as "the Bishop's Game," he's manipulating the Old and New gods into a battle royal, during which he plans to harvest the power that conflict will inevitably release.

THE OLD GODS. The gods that every explorer and every immigrant brought with them to America, led by Wednesday and his lieutenants, the Slavic god Czernobog and the West Indian god Anansi (aka Mr. Nancy). Numerous deities make appearances in this wide-ranging novel, including Eostre, Ibis, Thoth, Anubis, and Kali. It's also worth pointing out here that creatures of myth and legend also make appearances in *American Gods,* including a real live djinn and American folk hero Johnny Appleseed.

THE NEW GODS. Uniquely American gods who despise the Old gods, their ranks include the gods of technology, of the credit card and the freeway, and the deities of the Internet, telephone, radio, television, plastic, and neon. It's a basic premise of this novel that gods emerge and evolve with the culture of their believers.

THE WORLD TREE. Located in Virginia, it is an ancient tree upon which Shadow is hung while he holds a vigil over Odin's body.

THE BATTLE OF ROCK CITY, GEORGIA. Located just southwest of Chattanooga, Tennessee, on Lookout Mountain, it is the location of the apocalyptic battle between the Old and New gods. The battle, the result of the enmity between Old and New gods, and of the machinations of Loki and Odin, will release great energy into the surrounding area. Loki, aka Mr. World, plans to throw the legendary Odin spear over the ongoing battle, dedicating said conflict to Odin, thus allowing him and the All Father to absorb the released energy, ensuring their survival at the cost of the lives of all the other gods. The duo's plans are thwarted by the appearance of Laura Moon and Shadow.

LAKESIDE, WISCONSIN. A small, clean, peaceful, prosperous town located in America's heartland, Lakeside provides a safe haven for Shadow in between his trips with Wednesday. Shadow, living there under the name Mike Ainsel, grows very fond of the town and its denizens during his time there. The perfect little oasis harbors a dark secret, however, one which Shadow uncovers at the end of the novel.

TRIVIA

- The book is prefaced by a "Caveat, and A Warning for Travelers," which concludes: "Furthermore, it goes without saying that all of the people, living, dead, and otherwise in this story are fictional or used in a fictional context. Only the gods are real."

- The book's dedication reads as follows: "For absent friends—Kathy Acker and Roger Zelazny, and all points in between."

- *The Wizard of Oz?* Yes, it's mentioned in *American Gods;* when Shadow arrives at Marguerite Olsen's house (in Lakeside, Wisconsin) for dinner one evening, the movie is playing on video.

- Gaiman's subsequent novel, *Anansi Boys,* was actually conceived before *American Gods,* and shares a character, Mr. Nancy. It is not a sequel, but is a part of the same fictional world.

- The novella *Monarch of the Glen* (in which it is acknowledged that Shadow is actually Balder of Norse myth), collected in *Fragile Things,* continues Shadow's journeys. This story also features Mr. Alice and Mr. Smith, a dubious pair who also appeared in a Gaiman short story called "Keepsakes and Treasures," suggesting that this tale is a part of the *American Gods* universe as well.

- According to Gaiman's blog, *American Gods* is *not* based on Diana Wynne Jones's *Eight Days of Luke,* "though they bear an odd relationship, like second cousins once removed or something." When working on the structure of a story linking gods and days of the week, he came to realize that a similar structural idea had already been used in *Eight Days of Luke*. He abandoned the story, but later used the character Wednesday in *American Gods*.

- Besides winning the 2002 Hugo, Nebula, and Bram Stoker awards, this book was also nominated for the British Science Fiction Association (BSFA) and the International Horror Guild Award.

- Two signed and numbered editions of *American Gods* have been released by Hill House Publishers. They are advertised as being twelve thousand words longer than the mass-market editions, and as representing the author's preferred edition. When asked about the import of the preferred edition, and how it differed from the mass-market one, our subject replied, somewhat facetiously, somewhat modestly, and very succinctly, "It's longer."

- Once again, groups of three women play key roles in one of Gaiman's novels. Czernobog has three sisters, the Zorya, and three strange women, the Norns, bind Shadow to the World Tree. In Norse myth the Norns are the equivalent of the Fates, which is one manifestation of the three witches used throughout *The Sandman*.

THE QUOTABLE GAIMAN

In America, the journey is the destination. And with Shadow, the journey really was the destination.

—Interview, June 29, 2001,
bookreporter.com

On contemporary British authors who have influenced his work:

There was an author named Roger Lancelyn Green who wrote these wonderful books for kids on mythology. They're enormously fun—*Tales of the Norseman, Tales of the Egyptians*, etc. I loved that stuff as a kid, I couldn't get enough of it.

—Interview, June 29, 2001,
bookreporter.com

‖‖

ANANSI BOYS

(2005)

In an interview with Chris Bolton of Powells.com, in August 2005, Gaiman described *Anansi Boys* (his first number-one *New York Times* bestseller) as a "magical-horror-thriller-ghost-romantic-comedy-family-epic." While we wouldn't want to argue with the author, who certainly knows best, we also perceive *Anansi Boys* as a story about ancient feuds, brotherly love, gods, and murder.

Running beneath all of this is another theme: embarrassment. In an interview with 10 Zen Monkeys, with R. U. Sirius on October 4, 2005, Gaiman noted that the novel was "pretty much a comedy of embarrassment, which is why I wanted to do a character that was English. Because the English do embarrassment better. We have raised it to some kind of slightly awkward apologetic art form."

In *Anna Karenina,* Tolstoy wrote, "All happy families resemble one another, each unhappy family is unhappy in its own way." *Anansi Boys* humorously echoes that sentiment, illustrating the many ways in which one's family can be responsible for squirming embarrassment. Gaiman drew on his own life for inspiration, recalling his feelings about his own father, and his daughter Maddy's insistence that he park around the corner from her school when dropping her off, embarrassed by his car and the music he listened to. As he notes in the acknowledgments for *Anansi Boys,* "I don't think I could have written Fat Charlie without having had both an excellent but embarrassing father and wonderful but embarrassed children. Hurrah for families."

Gaiman found that part of his motivation for writing the book was to "get a novel right," in the sense of writing a book that was classically structured, what he considered "a proper novel." (He certainly didn't write the book to garner more awards—despite receiving enough votes for a Hugo nomination, Gaiman declined it.) The author has explained in interviews that in his mind, at least, his prior solo novels don't meet that standard; he points out that *Neverwhere* and *Stardust* had their origins in other media, and confesses that he doesn't feel confident about *American Gods,* despite its favorable critical and commercial reception.

Just as *Stardust* was his attempt to write in a style popular some fifty years before his birth, *Anansi Boys* represented a resoundingly successful attempt to re-create another voice: the one he uses to write his popular blog, which he considers more humorous than his normal voice. In that he was successful. The narrative, related in a breezy, almost chatty manner, evokes both the artists he mentions in his dedication (Zora Neale Hurston, Thorne Smith, P. G. Wodehouse, and Frederick "Tex" Avery),

||||||||||||||||||||||||||||||||||||||||||||||||||||||||||||||||||||

Juliet E. McKenna, Clive Barker, Neil Gaiman, and Ramsey Campbell at the British Fantasy Awards in 2006. Photo by and © Peter Coleborn

||||||||||||||||||||||||||||||||||||||||||||||||||||||||||||||||||||||

and those he might have forgotten to list, such as writer S. J. Perelman and film-maker Preston Sturges. Writing in this manner helped him come to a conclusion about the fundamental difference between comedy and horror: In comedy, people tend to get what they need, and in horror, people tend to get what they deserve.

His hero, the hapless Fat Charlie, certainly needs something. Like Richard Mayhew of *Neverwhere* fame, his spirit is being crushed by the life he leads; he just doesn't realize it. The death of his distant but high-spirited father, Mr. Nancy, and the appearance of his long-lost brother, Spider, change everything, throwing his life into turmoil and causing him no end of trouble. Charlie's life is turned upside down, but he can't decide whether that's good or bad.

Readers must decide for themselves whether Fat Charlie gets what he needs, or what he deserves. (Though, for our money, we'd say he got *exactly* what he needed.)

PEOPLE, PLACES, AND THINGS

MR. NANCY. Mr. Nancy is the human aspect of Anansi, the spider, a trickster god that readers first met in *American Gods* (Gaiman "borrowed" him from *this* novel, unwritten at the time he began *American Gods*). After taking a human wife, the charming Mr. Nancy fathers a son, Charlie, whom he later tags with the unfortunate nickname Fat Charlie. It is Mr. Nancy's "death" (he dies while singing a karaoke version of "I Am What I Am") that provides the impetus to the main action of *Anansi Boys*.

Anansi is a West African / West Indian spider/trickster god, a deity who owns all stories (sounds like a certain Dream Lord we know, doesn't it?). Gaiman tells several hilarious Anansi stories throughout the novel, all detailing the trouble that the charming trickster causes and brings upon himself.

Mr. Nancy's favorite movie, apparently (he can't remember the title), is *Carrie*.

CHARLES "FAT CHARLIE" NANCY. Charles Nancy had the misfortune of having a larger-than-life father, the indomitable Mr. Nancy, who had a knack for giving nicknames that stuck. Unfortunately, he nicknamed his son Fat Charlie, and it stuck, even though the boy was not, nor would he ever be, fat.

Charlie is imprisoned by the trappings of his existence but doesn't know it. He has a so-so apartment, and a dead-end job at the Grahame Coats Agency. He's engaged to Rosie Noah, a nice enough girl, but there's no passion in the unconsummated relationship. As to family, he only has his father, whom he hasn't spoken to in years.

One evening Charlie receives a phone call from an old family friend, Mrs. Higgler, informing him that his father has died. Traveling from his home in the UK to the funeral in Miami, Florida, Charlie learns from Mrs. Higgler that he has a brother, Spider. She also tells him that if he needs his brother, "just tell a spider. He'll come running."

Charlie is more amused by this than anything else. After returning to the UK, he finds a spider in his apartment. Rather than killing it, he takes it outside. Just before releasing it, he says, "If you see my brother, tell him he ought to come by and say hello." Shortly thereafter, Spider enters his life, and, as they say, hijinks ensue.

Charlie spends most of the novel laboring under the assumption that Spider is his twin brother, the one who got all of their father's godly attributes. The truth, having to do with starfish, is far stranger. In a riff on a classic doppelganger plot, Spider and Charlie were once one and the same. Whereas Stephen King wrote about *The Dark Half*, Spider might be considered Charlie's "fun half," born out of a childhood accident.

Spider's abrupt appearance in Charlie's life turns it upside down. Now stepping into his brother's life whenever he feels like it, Spider romances Charlie's fiancée and antagonizes Charlie's boss, Grahame Coats. At first Charlie is upset by the turmoil his brother causes, but his hardships start to forge him into a better, more competent, more confident person. By story's end, it is Charlie, rather than Spider, who takes control and saves the day. Most important, he overcomes his fear of singing in public.

ROSIE NOAH. Fat Charlie's ultrachaste fiancée. Her life is dominated by her mother, the intimidating (at least to Charlie) Mrs. Noah. Wooed by Spider in the guise of Charlie, she discovers a passion that she didn't know she possessed. Although upset when she discovers that she's been ravished by another man, she grows to accept the situation, and professes her love for Spider.

MRS. CALLYANNE HIGGLER. A friend of the Anansi family. She informs Charlie that he's the son of a god, Anansi, and that he has a twin brother who was driven away by a neighbor, the irascible Mrs. Dunwiddy, when Charlie was young.

MRS. LOUELLA DUNWIDDY, MRS. ZORAH BUSTAMONTE, MRS. BELLA NOLES. Three old ladies from Charlie's childhood neighborhood. Growing up, Charlie believed Mrs. Dunwiddy was a witch, which turns out to be true. Mrs. Dunwiddy is in fact the leader of a group of witches. When Charlie seeks help in getting rid of Spider, Mrs. Dunwiddy and her "coven" are there to help, by sending him to another realm, where Charlie communicates with his father's associates/rivals, animal totems such as Lion, Snake, Tiger, Hyena, Monkey, and, finally the Bird Woman.

GRAHAME COATS. Unscrupulous owner of the eponymous Grahame Coats Agency, described at one point (somewhat prophetically, it turns out) as "an albino ferret in an expensive suit." Overly fond of clichés, this villain (one of Gaiman's best, a truly repellent, repugnant reprobate) embezzles funds from his clients and frames Charlie. He also murders Maeve Livingstone when she questions him about her deceased husband's royalties.

In the end, fortunately, Coats gets what he deserves.

MAEVE LIVINGSTONE. Widow of comedian Morris Livingstone, whom Grahame Coats has been bilking for years. She is murdered by Coats (using a hammer) when she questions some oddities in her husband's account. Much like Laura Moon in *American Gods,* she lingers on (in spirit) to see that justice is done.

SPIDER. Fat Charlie's twin, he appears to have gotten the better of the bargain as far as inheriting their father's godly powers; where Charlie is decidedly ordinary, Spider is decidedly extraordinary (Gaiman has said Charlie is a reflection of him on a normal day, and Spider is him when he's "cool").

Since being separated from Charlie, Spider has spent his time traveling the world, living the high life by exploiting his godly gifts. When his brother tells a spider he'd like to see him, Spider is intrigued, and pays him a visit. Although he's upset that he didn't feel his father's passing, he quickly embraces his new circumstances.

As his father's son, he can't help causing mischief, at one point impersonating Charlie and interfering in his love and work lives. Spider's meddling has grave consequences, and sets off a chain reaction that forces a breakup between his brother Charlie and Rosie Noah, and causes a panicked Grahame Coats to frame Charlie for embezzling company funds.

Encountering his brother works changes in Spider's life as well. For instance, he falls in love with Rosie, something that's never happened to him before. He also finds himself fighting for his life, as his father's old enemies surface to take their revenge on his bloodline. Luckily, his presence has changed his brother for the better. Together they overcome the obstacles facing them, living, as is often the result in fairy tales, happily ever after.

DAISY DAY. After a night on the town with Spider (they're celebrating/mourning their father with wine, women, and song) Charlie wakes up the next morning to find a beautiful girl named Daisy Day in his apartment. Daisy brought him home and put him to bed after he passed out. They part, little knowing how fateful their meeting was.

Daisy, you see, is actually Detective Constable Day of the police fraud squad. As such, she investigates Charlie's alleged illegal activities at the Grahame Coats Agency. Although she arrests Charlie, she doesn't really believe he is guilty, which may have something to do with the truth, and may also have something to do with the fact that they're falling in love with each other.

SAINT ANDREWS. As the story builds to its amusing climax, all the major players in *Anansi Boys* end up on this Caribbean Island. It is here that relationships are sorted out, justice is served, and Charlie, coming into his own as a person, reconciles with his brother, Spider.

TRIVIA

- Gaiman originally had no plans to kill off Maeve Livingstone. In fact, he didn't know she was going to be murdered *until* he found her on a staircase going up to Grahame Coats's office. This realization virtually paralyzed him for the next four months. In his interview with Powells.com, Gaiman states: "It was all the most fun I've had writing a novel except for the four months in the middle, when not a word got written. I was at the very moment when Maeve Livingston was going upstairs to see Grahame Coats in the lift, and I suddenly thought, 'If she goes in to see him, he's going to kill her.' It was one of those absolute moments of, 'Oh my God, that isn't in the plan, that's not meant to happen at all.'"

- *Anansi Boys* won the Mythopoeic Fantasy Award for Adult Literature in 2006.

- At one point in the novel Charlie, concluding that his brother Spider might not have his best interests at heart, stands up to him, stating, "Of course, you realize, this means war." Fans of famous cartoon trickster Bugs Bunny might remember the hare making this declaration to several of his enemies. Groucho Marx also used the phrase in movies like *Duck Soup* and *A Night at the Opera*.

- While it should come as no surprise to find allusions or references to Shakespeare in *any* literary work, it would be surprising to find *none* in a work penned by Neil Gaiman. *Anansi Boys* contains several lines from Hamlet, and Charlie's situation is compared to Macbeth's on a couple of occasions.

- *Anansi Boys* is a punning title on the English phrase of abuse "Nancy boys," which implies that a man is girlish or feminine.

- *Anansi Boys* was adapted into a radio play by Mike Walker for the BBC World Service. It starred Lenny Henry as Spider and Fat Charlie; Matt Lucas as Grahame Coats and Tiger; Rudolph Walker as Anansi; Dona Croll as Mrs. Noah and the Bird Woman; Tameka Empson as Mrs. Higgler; Petra Letang as Rosie; Jocelyn Jee Esien as Daisy; and Ben Crowe as Cabbies and other voices. It was broadcast on the November 17, 2007. It was directed by Anne Edyvean (who also worked on the Radio 3 adaptation of *Signal to Noise* in 1996).

THE QUOTABLE GAIMAN

The thing I think I love best about tricksters is that they lose from time to time. Gods and heroes win. Tricksters are just like the rest of us. They win sometimes; they lose sometimes. They screw up every bit as often as people do, only with more style.

On Grahame Coats:

I loved writing him. I took enormous joy in writing a character who was everything I could hate. He's every crooked agent that I have ever encountered.

—Interview with R. U. Sirius,
October 4, 2006, 10zenmonkeys.com

||||||||||||||||||||||||||||||||||||||||||||||||||||||||||||||||||||

TIME IN THE SMOKE

(SOMEDAY)

Perhaps it's a bit unfair to include *Time in the Smoke,* since it is entirely possible that Gaiman will never actually get around to writing it. And yet it exists, both in the author's brain and in a small snippet of prose that might one day blossom into a full-fledged novel. Like many of Gaiman's works, it has been floating about in his consciousness for quite some time.

"It was the book I was going to write after *Neverwhere* and *Stardust,*" Gaiman told us, in reply to an inquiry for this book, "a temporal fantasy set in London. And then one day I thought, 'If I write this, I'll be that guy who writes fantasies set in England, and mostly in London,' and so I wrote *American Gods* instead.

"It's a lovely idea, and I may still write it. I just went looking on the hard drive and found the opening . . ."

Thus, we are pleased to present the previously unpublished opening to *Time in the Smoke.*

Sometimes, Lord Rochester would believe himself to be a-dreaming, and a-dreamed. It was a conviction that would steal over him in the quiet times, when the servants were a-bed, and the world was still, and he would be peering at some document of state or another in the flickering candle's light, and he would suddenly find himself overwhelmed by the improbability of his life, and the suspicion that this was all a dream would come to him. He even knew when he was dreaming it: thirty years earlier, when he was a young rakehell, and he bumbled and jumbled and strutted his way through the world in a mean and misty winish haze, one night after whoring and boozing, when his cock and his liver were still his to command, he would have slept and dreamt a whole lifetime filled with little tragedies and littler triumphs, and it would have ended, with him here, as his majesty's chief minister, his youthful indiscretions forgotten with his poetry, and the next morning, or early afternoon, he would have wakened with his head all full of the dream, until the discovery that his purse had been picked would have jerked him into full wakefulness, and the whole life of John Wilmot would have swum back into the nature of a forgotten dream, as meaningless and foolish as any other.

As for whether *Time in the Smoke* will ever grow into the novel Gaiman imagined, the author says only, "I might write that book one day, you know. I like that bit, and I know what happens before it and what happens next . . ."

P A R T S I X

THE CHILDREN'S BOOKS

I may not be the first children's book editor who saw promise in Neil's work, but I think I was the first to make an offer for Coraline. *Alas, the Suits above me didn't get it, and said no I couldn't buy it—and then phased me out as well. Actually, this turned out to be a great blessing for both of us. I took huge delight in Neil's phenomenal success with the book thereafter.*

What the Suits didn't get then is the brilliance of the horror in that book: it is family turned into monsters, which the feisty girl manages (finally) to control. Just as Wolves in the Walls *is the family home becoming monstrous.*

Of course, don't ask Neil where he gets his ideas from. He might just tell you. And then, of course, he'd have to kill you. It's always the way with the greatest writers. Would I lie?

—Jane Yolen

Somewhere in Neil Gaiman's attic there is a typewritten manuscript for his first novel, *My Great Aunt Ermintrude*. Written in 1981 (or '82) by a twentyish Gaiman, *My Great Aunt Ermintrude* represents the Holy Grail of Gaiman fandom, but it remains unpublished and likely shall remain so during the author's lifetime. And, if he has his wish, the novel won't even be published when he's gone. (Note: Gaiman discusses the book at length in our interview later in this volume.)

The author submitted *My Great Aunt Ermintrude* to publishers at the time, but never managed to find one willing to publish it. And now, in a time when any publisher in the world would be thrilled to publish his merest scribble, it is Gaiman himself who has decided that the young man who wrote that book wasn't ready, and the manuscript simply isn't good enough.

Yet for the purposes of any discussion of Neil Gaiman's evolution as a writer, the book is vital. It was written in a time before Gaiman's initial success as a comic book writer, before his renown as an author of short stories, and before he became a *New York Times* bestselling fantasy novelist. *Coraline* may have been the book that made the publishing world—and readers—stand up and take notice of Gaiman's talent as a children's author, but his love for children's literature and his efforts in that arena began much, much earlier.

As a writer, he began on an old typewriter, with *My Great Aunt Ermintrude*.

Neil Gaiman's first novel was a children's book.

|||||||||||||||||||||||||||||||||||||||||||||||||||||||||||||||||||||||||||||

Gaiman's description: "Mr. Punch territory. My paternal grandfather, me and my cousin Sara, on the seafront in Southsea. July 1963." Photo courtesy of Neil Gaiman, from his collection.

|||||||||||||||||||||||||||||||||||||||||||||||||||||||||||||||||||||||||||||

The author's love of children's literature began from the moment he could read, and as you will see in the aforementioned interview, is fascinating in itself. The odd little English boy who always had his nose in a book, who read while walking to school, and who explored every page of every book in the children's section of his local library seems like a character straight out of great children's literature himself. It's the perfect setup, isn't it? That "bookie" kid, as Gaiman calls himself, would then be dragged off on some grand adventure. And in so many ways, he has.

But as his extraordinary work as a children's author has proven, he has still never left that library. It's in his heart and head, now, all of those words and pages. Gaiman's work as a children's author is almost a chart of his boyhood growth as a reader. And though this section of our examination of the author comes after those about his work in comics, graphic novels, and novels, it is no less important.

In fact, an argument could be made that a children's author is what Gaiman has always been. And that argument would begin with *My Great Aunt Ermintrude,* his first novel. Shortly afterward, as Gaiman began to sell short stories successfully, he penned tales that work perfectly well for both children and adults, including, "The

Case of the Four and Twenty Blackbirds" and "How to Sell the Ponti Bridge." In 1986, he and Stephen Jones cowrote the poem "Now We Are Sick," a humorous play on the classic A. A. Milne children's poetry collection *Now We Are Six*.

In 1991, within the pages of the comic book series Miracleman, Gaiman and artist Mark Buckingham produced what can arguably be considered the author's first children's book. In an issue entitled "Winter's Tale," one of the series' characters reads a book to a pair of children, and fourteen pages of that issue were designed, written, and illustrated in the style of a children's book.

In 1997, Gaiman and longtime collaborator Dave McKean partnered up for *The Day I Swapped My Dad for Two Goldfish,* an almost Seussian tale whose title is self-explanatory. Published originally by an imprint of White Wolf, a gaming company, its initial reception seemed like pleased bemusement to the outside observer. Gaiman and McKean were still mostly known for their comic book work, and White Wolf for its role-playing games. It may well have been perceived as a lovable oddity at the time.

Then, in 2002, there came *Coraline*. Gaiman's love for children's literature had always informed his work, but his ambitions in that regard came to full bloom in that dark, troubling adventure. *Coraline* spent more than a month on the *New York Times* bestsellers list, and the paperback edition hit the list the following year. Yet sales are only one benchmark by which to gauge success. Gaiman's work as a children's author is a landmark in the field, harkening back to a time before "children's literature" was separated from other books. *Coraline* is so wonderfully and elegantly written, and so full of the kind of fear only children feel and adults too soon forget, that with its publication Neil Gaiman reminded the rest of the publishing industry what children's literature *could* be, that not every story had to be a series.

Just as his adult fantasy novels touch upon pre-Tolkien wanderings and tropes, *Coraline* erased the tendency of modern children's fiction toward safety. In the flights of fancy from the late nineteenth and early twentieth century that Gaiman spent so much time reading as a child, the young protagonists were never safe. Also undermining that sense of security, *Coraline* is deeply unsettling, and yet ultimately reassuring as well. In ages past children were supposed to be afraid. Original bedtime stories and fairy tales—back to the Brothers Grimm and earlier—were cautionary tales. *Don't go into the woods alone, at night.* This subject is addressed in greater detail in the section on *Coraline,* but suffice to say that the fear and wonder that great children's literature can produce are useful and necessary. There is catharsis for children in such works. The fears they read about—the harrowing or disturbing adventures they take within the pages of books—can distract them from genuine fears, but they also can help children process their fears and emerge less fearful.

Coraline and—for younger readers—*The Wolves in the Walls* (both illustrated by McKean, and both *New York Times* bestsellers) are perfect examples. With such work, and the upcoming *The Graveyard Book,* Gaiman has provided a service to children and to literature. For that young English "bookie" boy, it must be a great pleasure to be able to give even a single child the kind of pleasure in literary journeys that had such an extraordinary influence on his own life. A perfect illustration of his desire to bestow that gift is *Odd and the Frost Giants,* written for free for the UK's World Book Day, during which kids can purchase books for a single pound, an enormous event promoting the love of reading.

Children today may not commonly read the things that he read, but perhaps if they read Gaiman, they might be led to seek out such works, or at least provide—in spirit—the fright and excitement and quality and emotional involvement that the author so loved in his own treasured books.

THE DAY I SWAPPED MY DAD FOR TWO GOLDFISH

(1997)

Listed by *Newsweek* as one of the best children's books of that year, *The Day I Swapped My Dad for Two Goldfish* was published in 1997 by Borealis, an imprint of the now defunct White Wolf Publishing. The book, now featuring an afterword from Gaiman, was reissued by HarperCollins in 2003.

The story's essential elements should feel familiar to anyone who's been a member of a family: bickering siblings; oblivious parents; and kids acting like, well, kids. Somehow, it manages to feel a lot like a *Little Rascals* short written by Roald Dahl. Gaiman's absurd but knowing tale is perfectly complemented, once again, by Dave McKean's offbeat art and book design. The text, looking like a child wrote the whole thing out by hand, also adds to the book's unique look.

As in *The Cat in the Hat,* the trouble begins when a little boy's mother goes out and leaves her family at home. The boy's father sits in front of the television, reading the paper. The little boy, who is also the narrator, tells us that his dad "doesn't pay much attention to anything when he's reading his newspaper."

The narrator, who delights in harassing his little sister, is visited by his friend Nathan, who arrives carrying a glass bowl containing two goldfish. The little boy instantly desires the fish, and offers to make a trade for them. He offers Nathan all sorts of boyish riches, which Nathan dismisses.

The boy sits and thinks, and muses: "Some people have great ideas maybe once or twice in their life, and then they discover electricity or fire or outer space or something. I mean, the kind of brilliant ideas that change the whole world.

"Some people never have them at all.

"I get them two or three times a week."

Then the boy gets, as Dr. Seuss's Grinch might say, "a wonderful, awful idea."

"I'll swap you my dad," he says.

Although initially reluctant, Nathan eventually agrees. Then, the fun begins.

In the end, *Goldfish* is a charming tale about a deal with unexpected consequences, not unlike classic fairy tales such as *Jack and the Beanstalk.* The events depicted within are sometimes absurd but make perfect sense when a child's logic is applied. The book makes some acute observations about family, and about how children perceive the world. Oh, and also about how Moms are the secret masters of the family universe, always there to restore order.

PEOPLE, PLACES, AND THINGS

THE BOY. The narrator of this tale, the boy lives to make his sister's life miserable, and for his own pleasure; in other words, he's a normal little boy of about nine or ten. Wanting to possess two goldfish that his friend Nathan has shown him, he looks for things to trade, eventually settling on his father. The boy's trade triggers a day-long adventure, as the boy and his sister try to locate their father, who has been traded several times within a few hours.

HIS MOTHER. Like most moms, the boy's mother represents order. In fact, the adventure begins merely because she has to go out of the house for a moment, leaving her precocious son to his own devices. Upon returning, however, she insists that the boy find her husband and bring him back home.

HIS DAD. Like his son, the boy's father is in his own little world: Engrossed in his paper, he isn't aware of anything going on around him. Thus, he's barely cognizant of the fact that's he's been removed from his home and been traded several times during the day.

HIS SISTER. The boy's target and foil, she has the patience and endurance of a saint. She's also quite the pain in the . . . well, she's a nuisance to the boy, but, heck, she's only doing her job.

NATHAN. The boy's friend, Nathan, can't wait to show his pal his two goldfish, a present from his aunt Violet. When the boy proposes a trade, he initially rejects offers of Transformers, baseball cards, books, a punching bag, a pennywhistle, a spaceship, a puppet, and Clownie the Clown. Although he thinks his friend is getting the better of the deal, Nathan eventually agrees to accept the boy's father in exchange for his two goldfish, Sawney and Beaney.

VASHTI SINGH. A young lady who swaps Nathan a big, white, electric guitar for the boy's father.

BLINKY. A young man who trades Vashti a realistic gorilla mask for the boy's father.

PATTI. A young lady who trades Blinky a fat white rabbit named Galveston (certainly an *Alice in Wonderland* reference) for the boy's dad. Patti is the end of the long chain of trades. The boy and his sister rescue their oblivious father from a rabbit hutch "with chicken wire all around it" and bring him home. Order is restored (although Dad is now especially fond of carrots for some reason).

THE PROMISE. At the story's end, the boy promises his mother that he would "never-ever-swap" his dad "for anything ever ever again." But, he reminds us gleefully, he never promised anything about his little sister . . .

TRIVIA

- Gaiman has been known to inscribe the book with the phrase "With Love and Best Fishes."

- The original Dave McKean cover art for *The Day I Swapped My Dad for Two Goldfish* (the 1997 White Wolf edition) was also used on the 1999 Counting Crows album *This Desert Life*.

- An audio version, read by Gaiman, appears on the *Neil Gaiman Audio Companion*. The CD also features the author reading *The Wolves in the Walls, Crazy Hair,* and *Cinnamon.* Topping off the package is a charming interview with Gaiman conducted by his younger daughter, Maddy.

- Gaiman's afterword states that the story reflects the very real and bitter hostility that existed between two of his children, and between himself and his own sister. This bit of background gives the two-page spread that closes the book, which most will initially see as humorous, a new, more malicious, resonance.

- Speaking of malice, the names of the two goldfish are most certainly a playful reference to Alexander "Sawney" Bean(e), the infamous patriarch of a forty-eight-member clan in sixteenth-century Scotland, who was executed for the mass murder and cannibalization of over a thousand people. The story appears in *The Newgate Calendar,* a crime catalog of the notorious Newgate Prison in London. While historians tend to believe that Sawney Bean never existed, his story has passed into legend and is part of the Edinburgh tourism industry.

THE QUOTABLE GAIMAN

On writing books for children:

I think having *been* a child, and having been a certain sort of child, is probably the thing that made me the most interested. But it's certainly been incredibly useful for my credibility at home, doing children's books. Especially from my youngest, Maddy—it's been fun doing things like *Coraline,* and having a daughter to try them out on. It's simply lovely having somebody who thinks this stuff is fun. From Maddy's point of view, really, the cool thing is the fact that I know Lemony Snicket, that she got to have dinner with Daniel Handler, the fact that R. L. Stine says hello. I am now cool.

—AV Club interview with Tasha Robinson,
September 28, 2005 www.avclub.com

CORALINE

(2002)

In 2002, Gaiman, ably assisted by frequent collaborator Dave McKean (who provided the arresting cover and interior illustrations), published a thoroughly creepy, thoroughly strange but totally satisfying dark fairy tale called *Coraline*. Judging by its overwhelmingly favorable critical and commercial success (it won the Hugo, Nebula, and Bram Stoker awards), it's a work that seems destined to stand the test of time and become a classic of children's literature. As no less a light than Phillip Pullman (author of the *His Dark Materials* trilogy) said in his review in *The Guardian,* "Ladies and gentlemen, boys and girls, rise to your feet and applaud: *Coraline* is the real thing."

Like many of his works, the idea had been in his consciousness for several years before he finally got around to committing it to writing. As noted in his dedication, it was a book that he began some ten years before its publication, for his then five-year-old daughter, Holly, and finished for his then eight-year-old daughter Maddy.

Coraline lives with her parents in a section of a huge old rooming house, which is also home to former actresses Miss Spink and Miss Forcible and a mustachioed old man who claims to be training a mouse circus. Because her parents seem to have little time for her, Coraline contents herself with exploring the vast garden and grounds, and counting the things she finds. She counts everything blue (153), the windows (21), and the doors (14). Thirteen of those doors open and close normally. One door, however—a big, carved, brown wooden door at the far corner of the kitchen—contains a doorway to another reality, a distorted version of the world she knows. At first that reality seems to be perfect, complete with attentive parents and delicious food. But Coraline soon comes to realize that horror hides behind the façade of that world, and she struggles to return home.

Although it sounds a little like *The Lion, the Witch, and the Wardrobe,* or *Alice's Adventures in Wonderland,* or *The Wizard of Oz,* Gaiman's novella is far darker, far stranger, and far more threatening than those books; it is, in fact, a work that many adults find too scary to read. As Gaiman states on the Harper-Collins Web site, "It was a story, I learned when people began to read it, that children experienced as an adventure, but which gave adults nightmares. It's the strangest book I've written, it took the longest time to write, and it's the book I'm proudest of."

PEOPLE, PLACES, AND THINGS

CORALINE JONES. After nine-year-old Coraline and her parents move into an old house that's been converted into an apartment building, she asks her mother about a mysterious locked door. Her mother unlocks it to reveal that it leads nowhere; apparently, when the house was remodeled, the door was bricked up.

Intrigued by the doorway, Coraline later pinches the key and unlocks it, and finds that the bricks have vanished. Passing through the doorway, she enters a dark corridor leading to another world that, on the surface, resembles her own, but with sinister differences. In that Other world, she encounters her "Other Mother," a woman who looks like Coraline's mother, except "her eyes were big black buttons." The Other Mother has lured Coraline to her world, hoping to trap her there forever.

Coraline eventually makes it back to her real home, only to find that her parents have been kidnapped, and are now imprisoned in the shadowy other world; only she can save them. Relying on her wits, and a bit of luck, Coraline challenges and defeats the Other Mother at an exploring game, a "finding things game," rescuing her parents and the souls of other children who have been trapped in the other world for centuries.

Perhaps *only* a child could have coped with the overwhelming menace of the Other Mother—adults would either be too scared, or tend to overthink the situation. Coraline simply does what she must to set things right, trusting in her innate ability to see things through.

MR. AND MRS. JONES. Coraline's mother and father, they treat her with a sort of benign neglect, allowing her a lot of time to herself. Both work from home, "doing things on computers." They are later kidnapped by Coraline's Other Mother, and held hostage to prevent Coraline's departure from the other world.

MISS SPINK AND MISS FORCIBLE. Two old ladies, retired actresses, who live with their three Highland terriers in the flat below Coraline's, on the ground floor. These kindly old women enjoy Coraline's company, primarily because she listens politely to their stories about the good old days when they trod the boards.

The two spinsters also seem to have a mystical side, as they sense danger gathering around Coraline. Miss Spink gives Coraline a stone with a hole in it, which proves to have magic properties in the other world. When Coraline puts it up to her eye in that world, it allows her to see things not visible to the naked eye.

MR. BOBO. A "crazy" old man who lives on the floor above Coraline. He also enjoys the little girl's company, because it means the eccentric old man can talk about the wonders of the mouse circus he is training. Early on in the story Mr. Bobo tells Coraline (who he mistakenly refers to as Caroline) that his mice have a message for her: *"Don't go through the door."*

THE OTHER MOTHER. The creator of the world behind the door, Coraline's malevolent Other Mother resembles the real Mrs. Jones in most ways—except for her black button eyes and her horrific plans for Coraline. According to the Other Father, she made the house, the grounds, and the people in the house: "She made it and she waited."

Although outwardly pleasant, once she has Coraline in the other world, she doesn't intend to let her go. To force the girl to cooperate, the Other Mother kidnaps Mr. and Mrs. Jones and imprisons them in a mirror.

Even when Coraline bests her in a lopsided battle of wits, she still persists. After Coraline escapes, she is stalked by the Other Mother's hand in the real world. Coraline outsmarts the spiderlike appendage, trapping it in the depths of an old well near the boardinghouse.

THE OTHER FATHER. Like the rest of the occupants of the Other World, the Other Father, a poor man's doppelganger of Mr. Jones, is the creation of the Other Mother. Although created to assist the Other Mother in her quest to seduce Coraline, the sympathy he feels toward the bright little girl keeps him from being effective.

THE CAT. A large, black, nameless feline who hangs around the apartment building where Coraline lives, this creature can travel between the two worlds. He tells Coraline that the reason he has no name is, unlike people, cats know who they are, and thus don't *need* names. In our world he is a normal, everyday house cat, with no voice. In the other world, he can speak. He proves to be a staunch ally and guide to Coraline in her struggles with the Other Mother.

THE OTHER MISS SPINK AND THE OTHER MISS FORCIBLE. In the other world, the actresses are still active on the stage, performing for an audience composed of dogs.

THE OTHER MR. BOBO. In the other world, Mr. Bobo trains rats instead of mice.

THE RATS. Menacing rodent denizens of the other world, these servants of the Other Mother haunt Coraline's dreams even before she visits the other world. Described as "Little black shapes with little red eyes and sharp yellow teeth," they sing:

> We are small but we are many
> We are many we are small
> We were here before you rose
> We will be here when you fall.

THE CHILDREN BEHIND THE MIRROR. Returning to the other world to rescue her parents, Coraline confronts the Other Mother, who, in a rage, locks her in a dark space behind a mirror that opens like a door. In that space Coraline encounters three ghostly children who have been there for "Time beyond reckoning." The three children, who have been there so long that they have forgotten whether they are boys or girls, beg her to "win free" their souls, which the Other Mother has taken and hidden after feeding on them, to the point that they have nothing left of themselves. Coraline agrees to try.

After defeating the Other Mother, Coraline encounters the three children in a dream. Reunited with their souls, their identities are now more distinct. One of them is a little boy wearing red velvet knee britches and a frilly white shirt. Another is a tall girl wearing a brown, shapeless dress. The last is a pale girl, dressed in "what seemed to be spider's webs." Coraline could swear that this creature also had "dusty silver butterfly wings" coming out of her back.

The children tell Coraline that they are setting out for uncharted lands, and "what comes after, no one alive can say . . ." They warn her that her difficulties with the Other Mother are not over, since the evil creature, who they call "the beldam," had lied to her when they made their wager.

TRIVIA

- At the time of this writing, Henry Selick is in production on a film adaptation of *Coraline,* in the style of Selick's famed *The Nightmare Before Christmas.* The film is set to star Dakota Fanning, as the voice of Coraline, and Teri Hatcher, as the voice of her mother and the Other Mother.

- A graphic novel is also in the works, to be illustrated by frequent Gaiman collaborator P. Craig Russell. The lettering will by done by Todd Klein, whose innovative style enhanced Gaiman's work on *The Sandman.*

- The epigraph to *Coraline,* from Gaiman favorite G. K. Chesterton, reads: "Fairy Tales are more than true: not because they tell us that dragons exist, but because they tell us that dragons can be beaten."

- Yet another reference to William Shakespeare: Miss Spink once played Portia and Miss Forcible once played Ophelia.

- The house in that book is one where Gaiman lived circa 1965:

  What my mum wanted was a modern two-up, two-down house, but they couldn't afford that so they wound up getting the servant's half of an old manor house, with ten acres of grounds, because in 1965 that was significantly cheaper than a two-up, two-down. We got one good room, the drawing room. We weren't often allowed in there, but through the door leading out of one end was a bricked wall, because that's where the other family lived. My mother gets a kick out of the fact that I borrowed the bricked wall behind the door for Coraline.

- In his review in *The Guardian,* Phillip Pullman notes similarities between *Coraline* and Catherine Storr's 1958 novel, *Marianne Dreams,* which tells the story of a young girl trapped in a sickbed by a long-term illness. Drawing pictures to pass the time, she discovers that she can visit the world she draws in her dreams. As her illness deepens, she spends more and more time within her fantasy world; her attempts to improve that world by modifying her drawings only make things worse. In our interview, Gaiman noted that he "would have read it as a boy, but it made much less impression than you'd think (Margaret Storey, the next author along on the library shelves, made a bigger splash). I think that the *Paperhouse/Marianne Dreams/Mirrormask* connection is really interesting though—most of that was brought along by Dave McKean, who had somehow missed out on *Paperhouse* completely, but dreamed it . . ."

THE QUOTABLE GAIMAN:

[*Coraline*] is about a nine-year-old girl learning a lot about bravery. It's not about growing up, but it's definitely about taking those first steps toward independence.

—Neal Conan's interview with Gaiman on
National Public Radio's *Talk of the Nation,*
December 5, 2006

On the name, Coraline:

It started for me as a slip of the fingers—I was typing to a Caroline, and it came out wrong. Larry Niven wrote an essay collected in the Bretnor book on writing science fiction where he talks about treasuring your typos as ways to name characters or alien races, and that's the only time I've ever done that. I loved the name—the way it was like, but not like, the name Caroline, the way it reflected, that it was about coral, which is both beautiful and hard and hidden.

The first time I noticed it as a real name, I was reading the memoirs of Casanova, and at one point, at a ball in Venice, if I remember correctly, he met a young lady named Coraline. "It's a real name!" I thought.

—journal.neilgaiman.com

I suspect the parents in *Coraline,* and all the books, are much more me—my nose in a book, my head somewhere else. It's more me taking all the worst bits of me, than it is my parents.

—"A Writer's Life: Neil Gaiman" *Telegraph,*
December 12, 2005

THE WOLVES IN THE WALLS

(2003)

This followup to 1997's *The Day I Swapped My Dad for Two Goldfish* reunited Gaiman and illustrator Dave McKean, each borrowing elements of their own parenting and respective children—Neil and Mary Gaiman's younger daughter Maddy, whose nightmare about hearing wolves scratching around within their home's walls inspired this book, and Dave and Clare McKean's son Liam, who loaned the images of his beloved "Pig Number 1" to his father's illustrations—to create a singular children's book.

The impetus for the book came not only from Maddy's nightmare, but from Gaiman's telling of stories to (and with) Maddy, plotting their escape from the feral menace behind the wallpaper, and then working through the potential consequences and methods of dealing with the imaginary wolves. As a loving paternal storyteller working through his daughter's primal fears with her, via the weaving of bedtime stories, Gaiman helped Maddy deal with her fears, and eventually coalesced their improvizations into this book, after a number of false starts. The mantralike "if the wolves come out of the walls, it's over"—derived from an overheard non sequitur about something else entirely—became the catalyst for the book's final form.

The protagonist is a young girl named Lucy, who lives in a large old house with her video game–playing brother, jam and preserve–jarring mother, and tuba-playing father. Lucy alone hears the wolves lurking behind the wallpaper, and her family's attitude about the pending threat is off-putting, as each family member both dismisses and acknowledges Lucy's fears. Her brother mocks her and the adults don't believe her, but all agree on the unverifiable but fundamental common-sense folk wisdom that "when the wolves come out of the walls, it's over."

Initially, the wolves embody every childhood dread of the unseen: darkness; hidden fears; strange sounds amplified by unknown causation. The dread of their eruption into day-to-day reality, and the prospective disruption of the security of the home, becomes all-pervasive, the ignorance of every family member Lucy tries to warn only adding to her mounting concern. The worst happens—the wolves indeed plunge out of the walls, taking over the house and forcing Lucy and her family to live outside—and it is Lucy who thinks through the repercussions of the home invasion, and convinces her family they can seize control of the situation to reoccupy and reclaim their home.

Lucy's initial determination to re-enter the wolf-infested house is prompted by her concern for her stranded Pig-Puppet. Once inside, after rescuing her beloved

Pig-Puppet by moving within the now abandoned inner walls, she is able to get past her initial abject fear and the cryptic fatalism of "it's over" to reconsider the new paradigm: "They are in the house, not the walls." From that realization, a new strategy emerges.

The Wolves in the Walls gleefully springs from the classic wolf-inhabited cautionary fairy tales and children's literature of yore, from Little Red Riding Hood to the boy who cried wolf, and to anecdotal folk wisdom of "the wolf at the door," and parallel roots in H. P. Lovecraft's classic horror tale "The Rats in the Walls."

But at its core, *The Wolves in the Walls* is about a child's frustration with a family's fragmentation and lack of communication. Each family member is focused on their individual obsession to the detriment of the unit, and shuts out the home reality (the wolves are in the walls). It is significant, of course, that Lucy alone recognizes the initial threat; silenced, ridiculed, and ignored, she is unable to protect her family from the disaster she alone sees coming. Once uprooted, it is Lucy alone who conceives of how the interlopers must be dealt with, mobilizing the family as a unit to oust the canine invaders and repossess home and hearth. By prompting communication—getting the family members beyond their obsessive, isolated behavior and finally working as a family unit—Lucy restores that which was lost, though the concluding image reminds the reader (and Lucy) that she must remain ever vigilant: Bigger things than wolves now lurk behind the walls.

Though *The Wolves in the Walls* is a slight tome (Gaiman's text is barely over two thousand words), its primal, playful power is not to be underestimated. This deals with basic stuff—the loss of home, the loss of control, the abdication of parental power, and the need for reunification of the family, and so on—and does so brilliantly, with inviting clarity, wit, and humor. Without overtly tapping anything but common fears and venerable children's literature imagery and themes, Gaiman also offers a timely parable about dealing with fear itself in post-9/11 society, in which an ounce of recognition and reason is worth a pound of cure. The fatalism of the "everyone knows that" mantra resonates with this subtext, as does the open-ended final image. It expands the escalation of the "unseen" threat while ridiculing its enormity (tapping the age-old playground joke about how one knows there are elephants in the refrigerator). In every way, *The Wolves in the Walls* is an exemplary twenty-first-century children's book.

PEOPLE, PLACES, AND THINGS

LUCY. The protagonist and utterly pragmatic center of the story, she is initially shrugged off as "the girl who cried wolf" until her belief that wolves are inhabiting the walls is proven true. Lucy is the most communicative of her family, expressing herself clearly and without guile, never ridiculing her family though they dismiss her fears until it's too late. Lucy wants to protect her home, and, once she and her family are ejected, she is intent upon reclaiming it. She rescues her Pig-Puppet and unites her family in the effort to get their house back.

HER MOTHER. Like most moms, Lucy's mother embodies domestic order. She is seemingly perpetually involved in "putting homemade jam into pots" until the wolves emerge from the walls. She listens and interacts with Lucy more than either her husband or son, but still dismisses her daughter's fears as soon as they are spoken, and she is the first to assert, "If the wolves come out of the walls, it's over." Mother believes mice are in the walls. Once the wolves emerge, her first inclination is to move the family to "the Sahara Desert" to live in a tent, and later suggests, "a hot air balloon," leaving it to Lucy to assert, "we could go back and live in our house again."

HER FATHER. Like Lucy's mother and brother, Lucy's father is in his own little world, constantly "at his job, playing the tuba," or practicing the tuba, otherwise unaware of anything going on around him. Like the father in *The Day I Swapped My Dad for Two Goldfish,* Lucy's father seems barely cognizant of his children's concerns or the threat to the household until it's too late, dismissing her fears ("you have an overactive imagination") and offending Puppet ("Why am I asking you to tell her anything?"). Her father believes rats are in the walls, and defers dealing with the problem. When the wolves eject the family from the house, her father initially suggests moving to "the Arctic Circle" and into an igloo, or to "a desert island," still skirting his parental responsibilities. Note, too, that when the wolves do invade the home, Lucy's father rescues Lucy—and "his best tuba."

HER BROTHER. Lucy's brother, like all brothers, is a pain in the neck more often than not, but he has an active imagination that moves in a different direction from Lucy's. Like their parents, he isolates himself with his activites—playing video games, drawing, doing his homework—and acts as if every interaction with Lucy is an intrusion. He makes jokes at her expense when she asserts that the wolves are in the walls, calling her "bats," which is what he believes are in the walls. Her brother's imagination is evident here: He, in fact, hopes one of the bats turns him into a vampire. Once the family is pushed out of their home by the wolves, he wants to "live in outer space" or "in a tree-house."

PIG-PUPPET. Lucy's beloved Pig-Puppet is a passive player in that he is inactive, as all children's toys, but active in that he is loved by Lucy, and she speaks to him and he replies. It is her remorse over abandoning Pig-Puppet when she and her family flee that drives her to brave returning to the house when no one else will. Terrified that the wolves may have eaten Pig-Puppet, Lucy is relieved to find the toy safe, and together they retreat and hide behind the walls to watch the wolves and scheme about how to reclaim their home.

THE WOLVES. The wolves, when unseen and malingering behind the walls, are glimpsed only as canine eyes peeking from knotholes, heard only as a furtive "scrambling, rambling, rustling in the walls." Once they erupt from the walls, though, and are visible, they cease to be as mysterious or threatening. They are initially scary and savage, ravenous, all-devouring creatures, all fur, claws, teeth, and jaws with mad eyes. Once they take over the house, however, they become increasingly ridiculous, in short order assuming the stations of Lucy's family members in their respective places. They sleep snoring on their backs with socks stuck on their paws, watching television and eating popcorn, playing her brother's video games and her father's "second-best tuba," eating and smearing the walls with her mother's jam, running up stairs and sliding down banisters, wearing the family's clothes (with holes cut for their tails) and partying like teenagers. These antics are what fire up Lucy's family enough to act at last.

MR. WILSON. Lucy's brother's teacher, one of the authorities cited as a reliable source for the three facts about wolves. "He teaches us about wolves and things," Lucy's brother says. "Firstly, there are no wolves in this part of the world . . . Secondly, wolves don't live in walls, only mice and rats and bats and things," and "thirdly," the oft-repeated phrase "if the wolves come out of the walls, it's over." When asked how Mister Wilson knows, the inevitable answer is, "Everybody knows."

THE QUEEN OF MELANESIA. The queen of Melanesia just "dropped by to help with the gardening," in time to express dismay at Lucy's suggestion that the family move back into their home, but plays no other part in the drama.

THE HOUSE. Lucy's large home invites and supports the fragmentation of the family, as each member except Lucy seems consigned to their respective rooms and places: Mom is forever in the kitchen, jarring jams; Father is in his studio, playing the tuba; her brother is in the living room, laying on the floor in front of the TV, either drawing, doing homework, or playing video games. Only after they are forced out of the house do they come together by night, around the fire; by day, Lucy's mother goes to work, Lucy's brother goes to school, and Lucy's father "practiced his tuba and read travel brochures" in "the bottom of the garden."

This prescribed fragmentation codified by the House is reinforced by the idea of the walls as barriers—between the domestic safety of the rooms themselves and the hidden, threatening nature of the realm behind the walls. Once this barrier is breached, however, the behind / between the walls realm becomes Lucy's entry back into the home, through which she is able to move with relative freedom to rescue her Pig-Puppet, and then to spy on the wolves. Though the House is depicted as an inanimate object, it is portrayed as a living, breathing environment, the walls both permeable (when the threat of the wolves are within) and impregnable (once the wolves have burst through, and the behind/between the walls offers Lucy and her family a means to frighten the wolves away).

THE ELEPHANTS. We've already said too much.

TRIVIA

- The book won the *New York Times* Best Illustrated Book Award for Children's Literature, the IRA/CBC Children's Choice Award, and the British Science Fiction Association Award for Short Fiction (2004).

- *The Wolves in the Walls: A Musical Pandemonium* was presented on stage by the Improbable Company and the National Theatre of Scotland, a production spearheaded and codirected by Julian Crouch and National Theatre of Scotland artistic director Vicky Featherstone. It was "conceived and made for the stage by Julian Crouch, Vicky Featherstone and Nick Powell," with music by Powell and lyrics by Neil Gaiman, under the musical direction of Martin Lowe, with choreography by Steven Hoggett. This seventy-five-minute play premiered at the Tramway in Glasgow on March 22, 2006, and enjoyed a lengthy run throughout the UK, until the end of November 2006. That production won the 2006 TMA Award for Best Show for Children and Young People.

- Two items of interest involving the theatrical adaptation: The play presents Lucy as an artist scrawling portraits of wolves on the walls, which is suggested by Dave McKean's cover image to the book, though never otherwise made explicit in the book illustrations themselves. Unfortunately, when the play was performed in the United States, it was revised to minimize Lucy's role, and to present her parents as the pro-active characters who rescue the family—thus undermining the entire point of the book!

- Gaiman has been known to inscribe the book with a sketch of a wolf and a word balloon saying "—It's all over!"

- An audio version, read by Gaiman, appears on the *Neil Gaiman Audio Companion.* The CD also features the author reading *The Day I Swapped My Dad for Two Goldfish, Crazy Hair,* and *Cinnamon,* and a bonus interview with Gaiman conducted by his younger daughter, Maddy, who at the time of this writing is thirteen.

- Note the 1931 case history of reported poltergeist activity in the home of the Irving family on the Isle of Man. What began with the family hearing disturbing noises of something scratching, barking, growling, and gurgling behind the walls evolved into what seemed to be speech, and in time the Irving family claimed to be able to communicate with the poltergeist. The poltergeist that lived between the walls was named Gef, and claimed to have been born in 1852 in Delhi, India, and only the youngest daughter claimed to be able to see it. Like all poltergeists, Gef's behavior was disruptive and destructive of property and the family's peace; whenever the Irvings threatened to move away, though, Gef would whine and beg them to stay. This continued until 1937, when the Irvings finally sold the house and moved away. The subsequent owner reportedly shot a "mongoose-looking animal" in 1947. This case history is among the most unusual in paranormal activity history.

THE QUOTABLE GAIMAN

Upon seeing an early preview of the Improbable Company's theatrical adaptation:

So, yesterday I saw a dress rehearsal of WOLVES IN THE WALLS, and the very first preview. It's got some amazing stuff going on—the cast are fantastic, the musical arrangements are wonderful, the technical wizardry is wizardy. The kids laughed, held their breath, and, in the case of one small girl in the seats behind us, announced "I'll have nightmares, I know I shall" proudly and loudly to all of her friends during a scary bit.

—journal.neilgaiman.com

And on the morning the show finally opened . . .

It's WOLVES IN THE WALLS today! And how could anyone feel grumpy on a day like that?

—journal.neilgaiman.com

Drove home from Chicago through the night, last night, and was woken this morning by my assistant handing me the phone. Merrilee, my literary agent, wanted to tell me that THE WOLVES IN THE WALLS has gone in at #2 on the children's picture book bestseller list at the *New York Times*. I croaked something appreciative, then went back to sleep.

—journal.neilgaiman.com

INTERWORLD

(WITH MICHAEL REAVES)
(2007)

The wonderful thing about fairy tales is that with a single twist in one direction or the other, such stories can instantly become darkly, gruesomely adult, or wistfully, joyfully aimed at the hearts of children. Throughout his career Gaiman has shown a remarkable ability to skate smoothly from one to the other.

In books such as *The Day I Swapped My Dad for Two Goldfish,* Gaiman showed his talent for speaking to younger readers, long before the publication of his landmark young adult novel, *Coraline.*

But *InterWorld* existed before either of them. Though the book was not published until 2007, Gaiman and Michael Reaves had conceived of it as early as 1995. Reaves's background was as both a novelist and a television writer (*Star Trek: The Next Generation* and *Batman: The Animated Series,* among others), and while Gaiman was in London working on *Neverwhere,* they concocted the basic story of *InterWorld* as a potential television series.

When it seemed they could not persuade television executives of the potential of their idea, the two decided to turn *InterWorld* into a novel—not for publication, but as a selling tool for their TV series concept. Getting television executives to read the book, however, seemed an even greater challenge than explaining its central conceit. The book lay fallow for several years, until the authors returned their attention to it.

Though Gaiman is known primarily as a fantasist, he has on occasion dabbled in science fiction (as in his script for the TV series *Babylon 5*). It could be argued that *InterWorld* is more science fantasy than science fiction, but its premise certainly veers far from the typical Gaiman tale. The combination of Gaiman and Reaves is a fruitful one, however, as *InterWorld* proves a thrilling mixture of the two writers' strengths and a perfect foundation for a television series, despite the failure of executives to recognize its potential.

About collaborating on the book with Gaiman, Reaves told us:

> The actual, physical writing of *InterWorld* took place during a fevered week about ten years ago, which was all the free time he had, and we had to wait six months for that much to become available. He's a busy boy.
>
> I don't remember too much. We sat at computers and pounded out chapters, then swapped and critiqued, then did it again. After eight days we had a manuscript, which then took us ten years to get around to publishing. Still not quite sure why . . .
>
> It was a lot of fun. I remember that, even in his house, he still always went for the Johnny Cash look. I told him, "It's just you and me here on this—go crazy, wear plaid. I'll never tell."
>
> He never did. Love his writing, but I can't say much for his fashion sense . . .

The setup of *InterWorld* is not unfamiliar, at least on the surface. A teenage boy with a quirky favorite teacher, and a crush on a girl who barely knows he exists, discovers that he has a greater purpose. He must sacrifice his own needs in order to fulfill his destiny and protect his world, and in this case, the multiverse. Yet the fundamental familiarity of teen fantasy adventure stories is immediately superceded by the sure hand, the authors' obvious pleasure in the telling, and the ironic tone of the writing.

The television pitch origins of *InterWorld* are evident in the swiftness of the story. The central character, Joey Harker, is barely introduced before he is thrust into an alternate reality and then spirited through the multiverse, dropped into perilous scenarios, and then trained to be an interstellar, intra-universal agent provocateur.

Gaiman and Reaves share a certain frame of reference in decades' worth of comic books, and the sensibilities of those stories resonate in the pages of this novel. Joey Harker meets myriad versions of himself from different worlds across the multiverse, many of whom are different enough (wings, wolfish appearance and ferocity, cybernetic mind) that they could be considered superheroes, in a sense. DC Comics's Legion of Super Heroes, in particular, comes to mind. Though the members of the legion are not all variations on the same character, they are all teenagers from different worlds with varying superpowers. The multiverse concept is also familiar from a variety of sources, but perhaps most famously in the Eternal Champion stories of Michael Moorcock and in DC Comics's *Crisis on Infinite Earths*.

Within the pages of *InterWorld*, the multiverse is comprised of a potentially infinite number of planets arrayed on an arc. One end of the arc consists of planets whose cultures function entirely upon magical foundations, while the planets on the other end are focused on science. Toward the middle of the arc are planets where the two are balanced. While science fiction and fantasy stories often center around the balance and/or conflict between science and magic, Gaiman and Reaves' approach is original.

As always, it is in the way in which the elements are woven together, the skill of the writer, and the uniqueness of the voice that make a work of fiction successful. Although many facets of *InterWorld* may be familiar, Gaiman and Reaves crafted something unique out of them.

PEOPLE, PLACES, AND THINGS

JOEY HARKER. High school kid Joey Harker has no sense of direction. Once, he even got lost inside his own house, which is located in a small town called Greenville. When Mr. Dimas, his social studies teacher, separates Joey and his class into small groups and strands each group in a different part of town with instructions to find their way back to school—an unorthodox experiment to be sure—Joey quickly gets lost. Unaware that he has crossed over into an alternate world, Joey manages to get a bus home, but when he arrives at his house he finds it occupied by a slightly different Harker family, including a girl named Josephine, who is this Earth's version of Joey himself.

Panicked and confounded, he again walks between worlds and ends up visiting an alternate version of his teacher, Mr. Dimas, in a parallel Earth where Joey Harker died by drowning some months earlier. While in this version of his life, he is set upon by attackers with electrical nets, riding on flying disks. He is saved by Jay, a mysterious figure in a reflective silver suit.

Soon Joey learns the truth: He is a Walker, a person who can move between parallel Earths as well as through the In-Between, a bizarre limbo space between realities. There are a nearly infinite number of Earths, increasing all the time as timelines splinter. The collective universes are called the Multiverse, and the slice of the Multiverse containing all possible Earths is the Altiverse. The Earths are arrayed in a kind of arc, with the worlds at one end based on magic and those at the other end based on science, while the center is an equal balance between the two.

The cultures at the science end of the Altiverse have created a group called the Binary, which wants to conquer the magic worlds and turn them to science, while the cultures on the magic end have a group called HEX who have the opposite goal. Joey's attackers were from the Binary.

When he is briefly parted from Jay, Joey is abducted by Lady Indigo, a representative of HEX, and her minions, Scarabus and Neville. Lady Indigo puts him under a spell so that he adores her and is willing to do whatever she says, but soon Jay arrives, tricks her into dropping the spell, and escapes with Joey in tow.

They slip into the In-Between, where Joey learns about Mudluffs (MDLFs or multidimensional life forms). Soon they rest on a strange world. Passing an odd creature that seems to be nothing more than a sentient bubble, Joey cannot escape the feeling that it is trapped by whatever tethers it to the ground. But when he attempts to free it, he discovers that this thing is a Mudluff, and that a terrible, intradimensional monster is using it for bait. Joey manages to free the Mudluff—which seems to communicate by altering its color—but Jay is fatally wounded by the monster.

Jay manages to scrawl into the dirt a mathematical formula that works in Joey's mind almost like a magical spell. When he focuses on the formula, it takes him immediately to Base Town, the floating headquarters of InterWorld, an organization of Walkers devoted to thwarting both HEX and the Binary, to maintain the balance in the Altiverse.

The Mudluff, which he has named Hue, cannot follow.

Joey brings Jay's dead body to Base Town, where he meets the leader of Inter-World, whom everyone calls "the Old Man." The Old Man recruits Joey to join InterWorld and help battle HEX and the Binary. Joey learns the secret of Inter-World, which is that all of its agents are alternate world versions of himself, all Joey Harkers of other realities.

On Joey's first mission, something goes horribly wrong. A magical spell has been cast that redirects his efforts to Walk through the In-Between, and they end up on the wrong Earth—one fully controlled by HEX. Thanks to Hue's timely assistance, Joey escapes, but he has to leave his team behind.

Determined to prove himself and save his team, he tracks them down and—with Hue's assistance—helps them to escape. They scuttle HEX's grand plans for an assault on an entire cluster of Altiverse Earths, destroy Lord Dogknife's flagship, and return to Base Town in triumph.

Joey knows that his Walking can be traced, and that if he ever returns home, his enemies will be able to track him back to his family. He will never be able to go home. It saddens him deeply, but it is a sacrifice he must make to protect his family and the entire Altiverse, and he dedicates himself to InterWorld.

HUE. Hue is a bubble-shaped Mudluff (MDLF, or multidimensional life form). Joey encounters him first with Jay, in the In-Between. Hue is tethered to something in the ground, stuck, and when Joey tries to free him he discovers that the tether is actually connected to a huge, underground monster that is using Hue as bait. Joey manages to free Hue, but Jay is killed.

After this, Hue—who communicates only by changing colors—follows Joey throughout the Altiverse, saving his life more than once, and it is his image that triggers the return of Joey's memory after it has been wiped. In the end, Hue helps Joey and his team to defeat HEX and destroy the *Malefic,* and it becomes an official part of Joey's InterWorld team.

JAY. An alternate Joey, Jay comes to recruit him for InterWorld just in time to save him from an attack by the Binary. Later Jay rescues him from the clutches of HEX commander Lady Indigo. But while traveling through the In-Between with Joey, Jay is accidentally killed, and Joey must bring his body back to Base Town.

MR. DIMAS. Joey's unorthodox social studies teacher. Mr. Dimas breaks Joey's class up into teams and drops them at spots all over town, in an experiment to see who can find their way home. It is during this experiment that Joey gets lost and wanders into an alternate Earth.

One alternate world version of Mr. Dimas thinks the Joey he sees is a ghost, since in that Greenville, Joey Harker had drowned.

When Joey gets his memory back, he struggles with the choice of staying home, making sure his world and his family are safe, or going back out into the Altiverse to rescue his team and help InterWorld against the forces of HEX and the Binary. Mr. Dimas and Joey have a hypothetical conversation that the teacher quickly realizes is more than hypothetical, and the teacher gains new respect for Joey.

ROWENA DANVERS. Rowena is Joey's classmate, and he's had a longtime crush on her. When Mr. Dimas conducts his experiment, Rowena is part of Joey's group. They start off together, with Joey certain he (for once) knows how to get home, but soon Rowena becomes disheartened. She waits while Joey tries another direction, but he doesn't return, having Walked into a parallel world. He also meets the Rowena of that parallel world, but she doesn't know him.

When Joey returns briefly without any memory of his time with InterWorld, Rowena doesn't believe that he has amnesia and becomes angry that he won't tell her the truth about where he went.

JOSEPHINE HARKER. The first time Joey Walks into an alternate Earth, he goes to his house and discovers it is inhabited by a female version of himself, Josephine Harker, and her family.

BASE TOWN. The headquarters of InterWorld. It floats inside a sphere that shifts regularly between one alternate Earth and another, moving at regular intervals to avoid discovery by HEX or the Binary.

THE OLD MAN. The leader of InterWorld. He recruits Joey to the cause after Jay is slain, believing Jay's reports that Joey is one of the most powerful Walkers they've ever discovered. When Joey bungles a mission, leaving five of his fellow agents in peril, the Old Man has his memory wiped, and has him returned to his own world. But when Joey regains his memory and returns to rescue them and stop an enormous HEX armada, the Old Man reconsiders, allowing Joey to stay and the team to remain together as a unit.

THE ALTIVERSE. The slice of the Multiverse that contains all of the myriad Earths.

THE IN-BETWEEN. The area between realities, a place of weird geometry, floating shapes, sensory shifts (tastable colors, odorous sounds), and Mudluffs (multidimensional life forms).

HEX. A group of would-be conquerors—ruled by the Council of Thirteen—from the magical planets at one end of the arc of the Altiverse. They want to conquer the entire Altiverse and crush all scientific thought and development, turning all societies into worlds founded on magic. The presence of their scouts on Earth is responsible for many legends of fairies and goblins.

LADY INDIGO. A mysterious, witchlike woman who works for HEX, and who, at one point, magically enslaves Joey. She is defeated by Joey and his team in the end, but it is not known if she survives the explosion of the *Malefic*.

LORD DOGKNIFE. Supreme commander of the forces of HEX and captain of the flagship *Malefic*. He orders Joey and his team to be rendered down to their spiritual essence, that he can use to power his ships, but they manage to escape and destroy the *Malefic*. Lord Dogknife barely escapes the explosion.

SCARABUS. One of the minions of Lady Indigo and a part of HEX, Scarabus is covered with tattoos that can come to life with a touch, or even transform his body into whatever is represented in the tattoo. He helps to capture Joey more than once, and torment Joey's team, but in the end, when the team manages to blow up the HEX flagship, the *Malefic*, Scarabus escapes.

NEVILLE. A minion of Lady Indigo's, Neville has transparent skin through which his inner workings are visible, almost like a jellyfish. He can also shift his flesh to envelope his victims. He escapes the destruction of the *Malefic* with Lord Dogknife and Scarabus.

THE BINARY. Ruled by an artificial intelligence called 01101, the Binary is a group of would-be conquerors from the scientific end of the Altiverse arc. They want to conquer all of the Earths along the Altiverse and eliminate all traces of magic, moving all societies into a scientific culture. The presence of their scouts on Earth is responsible for stories of alien abduction and "gray men" aliens.

INTERWORLD. An organization attempting to keep magic and science in balance throughout the Altiverse, its members and field agents are variations of Joey Harker from alternate Earths, who can Walk between realities.

JAI. A male alternative version of Joey, Jai looks a great deal like him except that he has walnut brown skin. Jai becomes a member of Joey's team. He has a huge vocabulary and loves using long words.

JO. A female alternative version of Joey, Jo has wings and comes from a world of magic that allows her to fly against probability. She doesn't like Joey at first, but becomes part of his team.

JAKON HAARKANEN. A male alternative version of Joey, Jakon comes from an Earth where humanity evolved from lupine ancestors, and so has a wolfish body and appearance. He becomes a member of Joey's InterWorld team.

JOSEF HOKUN. A male alternative version of Joey, Josef is huge and strong, hailing from a denser Earth with a higher gravitational pull that gives him denser bones, wider tendons, and other physical traits that contribute to his size and power. He is twice Joey's height. He becomes a member of Joey's InterWorld team.

J/O HRKR. A male alternative version of Joey, but around eleven years old. J/O is half computer. He becomes a part of Joey's InterWorld team. Though he is annoying, he eventually proves himself in battle.

TRIVIA

- The title was, according to Gaiman, "one of those placeholder names that stuck."

- Though it began life as a pitch for an animated television series or film, Gaiman and Reaves shopped *InterWorld* around to no avail. Years later, after the publication of the novel, it has actually been optioned and is in development as an animated film from Dreamworks—the first studio to have turned it down years earlier.

THE QUOTABLE GAIMAN

On irony:

A decade later, I'm delighted and slightly bemused to report that it's just been optioned by Dreamworks Animation, who want to make it into a movie. . . .
There's a moral there somewhere, you know, but I have no idea what it is.
—journal.neilgaiman.com

ODD AND THE FROST GIANTS

(2008)

Gaiman wrote *Odd and the Frost Giants* as his personal contribution to World Book Day in the United Kingdom, which exists purely to inspire children to read. It is an annual event in which a group of authors write books for nothing, and publishers publish them for nothing. These books are then sold for £1 each to children who have been given £1 book tokens. On its Web site, the World Book Day organization (worldbookday.com) describes it as "the biggest annual event promoting the enjoyment of books and reading."

The tradition was started by Unesco, inspired by a custom from Catalonia Spain, in which roses and books were given as gifts on April 23 (St. George's Day, Shakespeare's birth, and death, day, Nobokov's birthday, and Cervantes's death day). As of this writing, the 2008 event is scheduled to take place in the UK and Ireland on March 6.

The bad news, at least for U.S. citizens, is that there are no current plans to publish this 14,500-word novella there. The good news is that the book is available through Amazon.uk. It's only £1, but be warned, there's a hefty shipping charge.

The story, enhanced by several illustrations from frequent Gaiman collaborator Mark Buckingham, is delightful. As you may have guessed, *Odd and the Frost Giants* deals with characters from Norse myth, a subject the very young Gaiman became entranced with after reading Roger Lancelyn Green's 1909 collection, *Myths of the Norsemen: From the Eddas and Sagas*. As such, it features mainstays like Odin, Thor, and Loki, characters that Gaiman has woven into his fiction before, in the *Sandman* story arc contained in *Season of Mists,* and as pivotal players in his 2001 novel, *American Gods*. Although he is consistent in his treatment of them in all three venues, his use of them here is by far the most affectionate and amusing.

The novella tells the story of the disabled Viking boy Odd, who befriends a group of forest animals—a fox, a bear, and an eagle—who are far more than they seem. In truth, they are the Norse gods Loki, Thor, and Odin, respectively. Hoodwinked by a crafty and vengeful Frost Giant, they have been transformed into animals and exiled from Asgard. Odd offers his help, and travels with the gods to their homeland, where he parlays with the Frost Giant in attempt to save the day.

Of course, you're probably wondering: Is Odd, in fact, odd? Well, no, not really (unless you asked one of his fellow villagers). Like many of Gaiman's younger protagonists, he seems to possess a maturity, fortitude, and fearlessness beyond his years. In fact, as a little research will prove, Odd is not even that odd a name, at least if you're Norwegian. As Gaiman relates early on in the narrative: "There was a boy called Odd, and there was nothing strange or unusual about that, not in that time or place. Odd meant *the tip of a blade*, and it was a lucky name." And how did Odd come to have the meaning it has in the English language today? As is common in his blog, Gaiman provides an answer to his readers' questions: "According to etymonline.com/index.php?term=odd points of weapons were triangles, and the three-sided-ness gave us the concept of *odd* versus *even*, and from there we probably got *odd* versus *normal*."

We're tempted to finish by saying "How odd," but we won't.

Whoops.

PEOPLE, PLACES, AND THINGS

ODD. The hero of this tale, Odd is an eleven-year-old boy who has certainly seen his share of suffering. His biological father is dead, and his mother has remarried to a witless oaf. He has endured a terrible injury to his leg, which forces him to use a crutch. Despite these tragedies, Odd is a confident, optimistic boy, as stubborn as he is quick-witted.

During a time of great troubles for his village, Odd runs away from home to try his luck at his father's abandoned cabin, deep in the woods. While there he makes the acquaintance of three animals, a fox, a bear, and an eagle, who turn out to be the three Norse gods, Loki, Thor, and Odin, who have been trapped in their present forms by a cunning Frost Giant.

Teaming up with the beastly trio, the clever Odd travels from Midgard (Earth) to the legendary Asgard (via rainbow, of course) to face the Frost Giant. Discovering that the giant's main goal in taking over Asgard was to obtain beauty, Odd convinces him to accept a beautiful carving (some claim it was a wooden key, others a carving of Thor's hammer, but it was really a carving of Odd's mother at the moment his father first laid eyes on her) he has crafted in return for restoring things to normal.

Odd thus restores order to the world of Loki, Thor, and Odin. To show her gratitude, the goddess Freya uses her powers to substantially heal the damage to Odd's leg. When he returns to his village, the newly assertive, now strapping (for he has grown in stature on his quest) young man seeks out his mother; he would like to take her on a trip to visit her native Scotland, which she hasn't seen since Odd's father kidnapped her years before.

ODD'S FATHER. Two years before the events described in the novella, Odd's father was killed on a sea raid. As Gaiman states, he wasn't "killed by a Scotsman, dying in glory in the heat of battle as a Viking should." Rather, he died from exposure after he dove into a raging sea to save a pony that had fallen overboard.

ODD'S MOTHER. After being kidnapped from her village in Scotland by Odd's father on a sea raid, his mother settled down to life with him in their village.

Seemingly content, she does admit to missing people who spoke her native language. Gifted with a beautiful voice, she sang ballads to the young Odd, relating stories of high adventure.

After her husband's death, she married the oafish Fat Elfred, becoming stepmother to his four sons and three daughters from a previous marriage.

When last heard from, Odd's mother had just left Elfred and retreated to her deceased husband's cabin in the woods. She is overjoyed to see her long-missing son at the cabin door; she is made even happier when he asks if she'd like to take a trip to her native Scotland.

fat elfred. Odd's stepfather, described as "amiable enough when he had not been drinking."

the fox. Also known as Loki, the Skywalker. Seduced by a Frost Giant disguised as a beautiful woman, a lustful Loki brings "her" Mjollnir, the hammer of Thor, to secure her favors. Apparently granted new power over the gods and Asgard through possession of the hammer, the giant transforms Loki, Thor, and Odin into animals, and brings eternal winter to Asgard.

the eagle. Also known as Odin, the All-Father, this eagle has only one eye.

the bear. Also known as Thor, the God of Thunder.

asgard. The home of the Norse Gods, it has been captured by a Frost Giant.

the frost giant. Seeking beauty and revenge (for a past offense committed by Loki and Thor toward his brother, who built a wall around Asgard), the unnamed Frost Giant tricks the trickster Loki into bringing him the hammer of Thor. Once in possession of the hammer, he takes over Asgard and exiles Loki, Thor, and Odin.

Although one of his goals was to possess the beauteous goddess Freya, he realizes that he should have been careful what he wished for, because the strong-willed Freya yells at him constantly. When offered an out by the industrious lad Odd, he seizes it, and departs Asgard to tell his fellow giants of his triumph over their enemies.

freya. Also known as "the Lovely." Freya, according to the Frost Giant, is one of the three most beautiful things in the world, along with the sun and the moon. Although beautiful, she does, in the giant's words, "have a tongue on her," constantly berating her captor and making him very reluctant to bring her back with him to Jotunheim.

After Odd strikes a bargain with the Frost Giant, Freya returns Loki, Thor, and Odin to their normal states. She also partially heals Odd's leg, which was injured when the youth stubbornly tried to fell a huge tree.

TRIVIA

- At one point, Gaiman was considering renaming the book *Odd and the Frost Giant,* because only one member of that ancient race plays a prominent part in the story. But the title remains plural because one of the Asgardian gods in the tale was born a Frost Giant—only to be adopted as Odin's son. The one who is not what he seems? Loki, of course.

- Gaiman references *The Wizard of Oz* many times in his work. Though Bifrost—the rainbow bridge—is a mainstay of Norse mythology, there is certainly a comparison to be drawn between the stories of L. Frank Baum and that of Odd and his three strange companions traveling "over the rainbow" to Asgard.

THE QUOTABLE GAIMAN

On how he chose the name "Odd" for his protagonist:

Before I started writing, I called my favourite Norwegian, Iselin Evensen (last seen on this blog taking me to a tomb in Oslo, I think), and she put several lists of old Norse names and nicknames and what they meant and suchlike together for me, and Odd jumped out from the list and started waving.

—journal.neilgaiman.com

||||||||||||||||||||||||||||||||||||||||||||||||||||||||||||||||

THE DANGEROUS ALPHABET

(2008)

From time to time, at Christmas, Gaiman creates and sends stories and oddities to those on his Christmas card list. In 2001, those few fortunate (four hundred total) received an odd scroll, bearing the title *The Dangerous Alphabet: A Piratical Ghost Story in 13 Ingenious but Potentially Disturbing Couplets, Conceived as a Confection Both to Amuse and to Entertain This Festive Season, by Mr. Neil Gaiman, Scrivener.*

What follows is as promised in the lengthy title.

As of this writing, HarperCollins had announced that a version of *The Dangerous Alphabet* would be released at the end of April 2008, fully illustrated by Gris Grimly, who also created a stunning cover for the book.

In February 2008, Gaimain wrote in his online journal about having received the first copies, hot off the press.

Elise Howard, my editor at Harper Children's, phoned one day to say that she had it framed on her wall, and kept reading it, and what would I think about turning my Christmas Card into a book. Many phone calls with Gris Grimly later, it's a book.

If it works, it'll be a sort of interactive book. The pictures tell a story, the words amplify it, but really, what actually *happens* in the book will be something for each reader to decide. I hope.

TRIVIA

- The Christmas scroll version of *The Dangerous Alphabet* came with the following notation and caveat:

This entertainment, as educational as it is concise, was conceived in the year 2001, executed with a blunt instrument, and the copyright on it is held by Neil Gaiman, who has, out of love for his fellow creatures this Holiday season, caused it to be issued, in his name and that of his family, in a limited edition of 400 copies, to be sent through the mail and personally given to friends, loved ones, and close associates. Please note: the alphabet, as given in this broadsheet, is **not to be relied upon** and has a dangerous flaw.

||||||||||||||||||||||||||||||||||||||||||||||||||||||||||||||||||||||||||||

THE GRAVEYARD BOOK

(2008)

A s of this writing, Neil Gaiman has three very unique book projects on tap for 2008, all of them for younger readers. We've already discussed *Odd and the Frost Giants* and *The Dangerous Alphabet*. This third work will be a bit trickier to discuss than others, mainly because, as of this writing (late December 2007), it is still very much a work in progress. Although Gaiman may indeed have finished it (he "fell off the world," as he puts it, just before Christmas to work on it), it is probably still only a first or perhaps second draft in his mind, and has yet to be seen in its entirety by an editor. That said, we'll soldier on, discussing what Gaiman has said publicly (mostly at a reading and a talk he gave at the University of Minnesota on November 17, 2007), and referring to what's already been published. We'll also omit our usual People, Places, and Things section, as we have no finished text to work with.

Gaiman first mentions *The Graveyard Book* on his blog in July 2004, citing it as the next thing he planned to work on after completing *Anansi Boys*, which was published in 2005. "Plan" is a key word here, because although he mentioned it intermittently over the course of the next two and one half years, it's obvious that other projects came to occupy his time.

What we do know is this: *The Graveyard Book* is, in part, Gaiman channeling Rudyard Kipling's 1894 story collection, *The Jungle Book*, particularly the story of the boy, Mowgli, who was raised in the jungle by animals, specifically by his mentors, Baloo, the bear; Kaa, the snake; and Bagheera, the panther. Gaiman's take on the story involves a boy, Bod (short for Nobody), who is raised by the denizens of a graveyard. Like many ideas he's developed, it is one that occurred to Gaiman a long way back, and stayed with him over the years.

> Around 1985 or 1986, we lived in a house with no garden, but we had a graveyard just over the run, so that was where my son Michael (three or four at the time) rode his little tricycle. And I remember watching him, and thinking it would be fun to do *The Jungle Book,* only set in a graveyard instead of a jungle, and that was the start of it. Because I tend to be fairly slow about these things, it's taken me . . . twenty-two years to get to it.
>
> —journal.neilgaiman.com

Gaiman first experimented with some of the book's concepts in his short story "October in the Chair," which was written for an issue of *Conjunctions* magazine edited by Peter Straub. There the embodiment of the month of October tells the tale of a boy named Runt, who runs away from home and befriends a dead boy named Dearly, to his fellow months during one of their regular gatherings (see our Short Story section for more details).

In the first half of Chapter 1, which we were fortunate enough to hear Gaiman read at a gathering at the University of Minnesota, he describes how a man named Jack enters a house and kills its occupants, except for an infant, a boy, who manages to escape the killing zone, and ends up in a graveyard. There, the denizens of the graveyard reach a momentous decision, and decide to raise the boy as a member of their extended family. After much humorous and heated debate, they name him Nobody, because he's like nobody else in the cemetery. Bod, as he comes to be known, is still in danger, however, as Jack (like the lethal and murderous tiger Shere Khan in *The Jungle Book*) is still looking for him, hoping to finish killing Bod's family.

Gaiman elaborated on the remainder of the book after he finished his reading (to, we might add, enthusiastic and sustained applause from a grateful audience).

> That's the first half of Chapter 1, it's going from there, and it's rather nerve-wracking, because it's not done yet, so it could all go terribly wrong.
>
> I'm writing it. I thought it might be fun to write something that structurally was a novel, but was also a set of short stories. So I'm writing short

stories, set roughly two years apart. So the next chapter, called "The New Friend," is when Bod is around four years old, when a family starts bringing their daughter to the graveyard, and how they become friends, and how the two of them encounter the very oldest inhabitants of the graveyard.

Chapter 3 was meant to be, it was one of those things, it was obvious I was riffing on *The Jungle Book*. Chapter 3 was my version of Chapter Three of *The Jungle Book*, when the monkeys, the Bandar-Log, steal Mowgli away. . . .

But it turned out to be a version of a P. L. Travers story. Something she did in every *Mary Poppins* collection, a story called "Bad Tuesday," or "Black Thursday," where one of the children would get grumpy, and get in incredibly deep trouble and Mary would have to rescue them.

Here, Nobody starts hanging out with three ghouls. One is named the Bishop of Bath and Wells, one is the Duke of Westminster, the third is the Honorable Archibald Threeput (you get the distinct impression that the ghouls took the name of the first person they ate after becoming ghouls). These three end up taking him through a ghoul gate—every graveyard has one grave that's scary and spooky and different from the other graves, and that's the ghoul gate—and he has to be rescued.

Chapter 4 has already been published; it's called "The Witches Headstone." [Again, see our Short Story chapter for details.]

Chapter 5 is called "Danse Macabre." It's about the one day every hundred years when the living and the dead can dance together.

And that's the stuff I've written so far. I have the last three chapters to go, where you'll find out who the man Jack was, what he was doing, and, of course, the very last chapter, where the boy will hopefully survive what happens in the graveyard.

It's exactly eleven months late at this point, and I promised it wouldn't go later than twelve months; they (my publishers) are nervously and patiently waiting for it, with an eye on publication dates, schedules, and illustrators, all that.

—journal.neilgaiman.com

At one point, Gaiman mentioned in his blog that *The Graveyard Book* would probably be about sixty thousand words long, making it approximately twice as long as his classic 2002 children's novella *Coraline*. Having heard him read the first chapter, and having read the fourth, and knowing that it is that substantial a book, we can hardly wait to read the finished product.

TRIVIA

- To support the First Amendment Project, Gaiman promised to place the high bidder's name on a gravestone that would be mentioned in *The Graveyard Book*.

THE QUOTABLE GAIMAN

I decided it was time to rewrite *The Jungle Book* all set . . . in a graveyard, so it's called *The Graveyard Book*, . . . about a kid whose parents are killed, and who gets brought up by dead people.

—Talk at the University of Minnesota,
November 17, 2007

||||||||||||||||||||||||||||||||||||||||||||||||||||||||||||||||||||||||||||||||||||||

PART SEVEN
THE SHORT STORIES

Although Neil Gaiman is perhaps best known for his comics work and novels, it is easy to overlook his significant contribution as a writer of short stories.

When reading these works, you get the feeling that Neil definitely enjoys working in the shorter form—perhaps more so than at novel length. This may be due to his comics background.

Most of his short stories are perfectly crafted gems, with rarely a word wasted. You only have to read "Snow, Glass, Apples," "Murder Mysteries" or one of my all-time favourites, "October in the Chair," to understand how much time and effort he must lavish on these shorter works.

Along with the more serious stories, there are also fan favourites such as the award-winning "Shoggoth's Old Peculiar" or "A Study in Emerald," where he is obviously just having fun with his material. These stories connect with readers in a way that simply says that he wants to share that sense of frivolity or exuberance with them. And there's nothing wrong with that.

I think that the first story of Neil's I published was "Foreign Parts" back in 1991 in Fantasy Tales. *Since then I've reprinted quite a number—including the memorable "Harlequin Valentine" and "The Problem of Susan"—in my annual anthology series,* The Mammoth Book of Best New Horror. *I've also used his work in various other books, such as* The Mammoth Book of New Terror; The Mammoth Book of Vampires; Dark Terrors 3 *and* 4; Keep Out the Night; *and* Shadows over Innsmouth.

Neil has always been very supportive when I've asked him for a story, and he's a delight for an editor to work with, because he is always such a consummate professional.

I don't think that Neil's expertise as a short story writer has been properly recognized yet. This may be because he works in so many different genres—fantasy, comic fantasy, science fiction, horror.

The majority of the stories found in Neil's collections Angels & Visitations, Smoke and Mirrors, *and* Fragile Things *are good enough to stand alongside the best work of authors such as Ray Bradbury, Gene Wolfe, or Harlan Ellison, whose own writings so many of them are obviously inspired by.*

You get the feeling that, if given the opportunity, Neil could quite happily spend the rest of his creative life turning out these little short pieces. However, all those award-winning comics projects, bestselling novels, and blockbuster Hollywood movies somehow just keep getting in the way.

—Stephen Jones

Stephen Jones and Neil Gaiman: a portrait of the starving artists. Photo by and © Peter Coleborn

Gaiman's short story collections have shown the same trajectory as his novels—straight up. From relatively humble beginnings (his first two collections, *Angels & Visitations* and *Adventures in the Dream Trade,* were published by two small presses, Dream Haven and NESFA, respectively), Gaiman moved on to substantial success with his three follow-ups, *Smoke and Mirrors, Fragile Things,* and *M is for Magic.*

How significant is this success? Well, it's a truism (perhaps self-fulfilling) in publishing that short story collections and anthologies do not sell. So it's probably astounding to Gaiman's publishers that his do, and in substantial numbers. Evidence of this can be found in the success of *Smoke and Mirrors* (by our reckoning, the trade paperback version of this collection is in its twenty-second printing), and *Fragile Things,* which spent a week on the *New York Times* bestseller list, a place few short story collections of any kind, much less genre-oriented, ever land.

Like his novels, Gaiman's short stories show the wide range of his reading, tastes, and talents. Although many stories were crafted merely because it entertained him to do so, the majority, reflecting the nature of today's publishing world, were written because someone asked him to write something for one of the ubiquitous theme anthologies that dominate the market. It's a tribute to his talent that the work he does for these anthologies, which lend themselves to a kind of paint-by-numbers analogy, often stand the central themes of those books on their respective heads, and are recognized by sharp-eyed editors and included in many of the "best of the year" anthologies for their quality and depth.

While Gaiman's legions of fans—and those who've heard of him but never read him—are likely more familiar with his novels and his work on *The Sandman,* the author is often at his finest in the short story form. A reader who discovers Gaiman for the first time in the pages of such short stories as "Snow, Glass, Apples" or "Murder Mysteries" will never forget the encounter.

Gaiman's short work has been collected in five volumes thus far: *Angels & Visitations* (1993); *Smoke and Mirrors* (1998); *Adventures in the Dream Trade* (2002); *Fragile Things* (2006); and *M Is for Magic* (2007). Besides short stories, these volumes also contain poems, essays, reviews, journalism, and introductions. In this chapter we will confine ourselves to discussing the short stories.

Short stories were an integral part of the fabric of *The Sandman* saga: "A Tale of Two Cities"; "Ramadan"; "A Dream of a Thousand Cats." Indeed, they were so numerous that they filled three of the ten volumes of collected Sandman stories, namely *Dream Country*; *Fables and Reflections*; and *Worlds' End.* The last three stories in the series—"Sunday Mourning," "Exiles," and "The Tempest"—were all self-contained short stories. Let's not forget the most famous short story in the entire saga, "A Midsummer Night's Dream," which won the World Fantasy Award in 1991 for Best Short Story, the first and last time a comic book story garnered that honor: After Gaiman's victory, the organization that presents the awards changed the rules to prevent it from ever happening again.

Gaiman has penned several dozen more traditional short stories over the course of his career, garnering several awards for best short story from a variety of organizations. Many were written because someone asked him to, as in the case of numerous themed anthologies; if the premise intrigued him, and time permitted, he forged ahead. Others were written simply because they had to be, because ideas he was mulling over in his head had developed into full-blown stories. Like any other writer, those were written because the time had come for him to write them, or merely because he had to get them out of his head.

How do the short stories differ from the longer works, the comics, the films? Aside from the obvious differential in form, the answer is: not very much. Gaiman shows the same inventiveness and thoughtfulness in crafting these tales as in the rest of his work, delivering up gems like "Chivalry" and "A Study in Emerald," which are just as rich in language and allusion as his novels and comics. Of course, we're not intimating that every story is a masterpiece, but they all seem to stand up to rereading. Each contains its own rewards, regardless of how it fares when ranked against his others.

You can see glimmers of other great short story writers (and Gaiman favorites) in several of his stories, including such luminaries as Harlan Ellison, Robert Sheckley, R. A. Lafferty, Saki, and John Collier, to name a few. Comparisons to the great Ray Bradbury are also warranted. If there is any doubt, read something like "October in the Chair," which was dedicated to Bradbury, or refer to *Fragile Things,* which was dedicated to "Ray Bradbury and Harlan Ellison, and the late Robert Sheckley, masters of the craft." Also, consider the title of Gaiman's most recent short story collection, *M is for Magic.* The title was inspired by Bradbury's collections *R is for Rocket* and *S is for Space.* In fact, Gaiman states in his introduction to that book that he actually wrote and asked permission from his childhood favorite to riff on those titles in creating his own.

An observation or two about each collection:

Angels & Visitations (1993) is subtitled *A Miscellany,* because that's exactly what it is: a gathering of short stories, poems, essays, even a book review. *Angels* was published by DreamHaven Books of Minneapolis, a firm with which Gaiman has had a long and steady relationship. Owned by Greg Ketter, DreamHaven has also produced a handful of CDs featuring Gaiman reading his short stories, including the cleverly titled *Warning: Contains Language, Telling Tales, and Speaking in Tongues.*

Smoke and Mirrors followed in 1998. Containing many of the tales presented in *Angels & Visitations,* it is convincing evidence of Gaiman's rising power and stature as a creator. In its introduction, the author makes the following very candid statement: "Most of the stories in this volume have that much in common: The place they arrived at in the end was not the place I was expecting them to go when I set out. Sometimes the only way I would know that a story had finished was when there weren't any more words to be written down."

Adventures in the Dream Trade was a two-thousand-copy edition published in 2002 by NESFA Press. Besides the short stories it features, it's also notable for the numerous introductions it reprints, and for presenting the first year of Gaiman's successful blog in its entirety. The blog, created in conjunction with the appearance of *American Gods,* is still running strong today, recently (i.e., in 2007) going over the million-word mark.

Fragile Things was published in 2006 by William Morrow. As you might have guessed, the theme of fragility permeates the entire package, from the design of the dust jacket (transparent paper with a picture of a broken egg over the hardcover, which features a heart, a butterfly, and two snowflakes), to the introduction, to the stories within. It also contains a blown-up panel from Windsor McKay's *Little Nemo* comic strip, across from the title page, that depicts Nemo delivering the line of dialogue which Gaiman had originally wanted to use for the title of this collection: "These people ought to know who we are and tell that we are here."

Finally, there's the most recent collection, *M is for Magic.* Intended for a younger audience, this collection features several delightful illustrations by the Danish comic book artist Teddy Kristiansen and Gaiman stories that might be considered child-friendly, such as "Chivalry" and "Troll Bridge," possibly his most reprinted stories. As Gaiman notes in his introduction, "Stories you read when you're the right age never quite leave you. You may forget who wrote them or what the story was called. Sometimes you forget precisely what happened, but if a story touches you it will stay with you, haunting the places in your mind that you rarely ever visit." The beauty of these stories is that the "right age" can be anywhere from six to one hundred and six.

In this section, each of Gaiman's short stories, collected and uncollected, will be addressed alphabetically. For collected tales, we'll let you know where you can find them (many, like "Chivalry," make more than one appearance) by appending initials to the heading of each entry. The key is as follows:

- *Angels & Visitations*: AV
- *Smoke and Mirrors*: SM
- *Adventures in the Dream Trade*: ADT
- *Fragile Things*: FT
- *M is for Magic*: MM

Several of these tales have been produced as audio stories, so we'll note that as well. The key for those projects is:

- Warning: Contains Language: WCL
- Speaking in Tongues: SIT
- Telling Tales: TT
- The Neil Gaiman Audio Collection: NGAC

If we discuss a tale that hasn't yet been reprinted in a collection or produced on audio, we'll try to point you to an independent source where you might experience it for yourself.

"BABYCAKES" (1990). AV SM WCL

Written for a publication to benefit People for the Ethical Treatment of Animals (PETA), this short, Swiftian, cautionary tale is truly disturbing, positing a world where, a few years back, the animals went away, presumably because of the abuse they received at the hand of man. To replace those animals, which provided many necessities, humanity turns to . . . babies.

Yes, babies.

Gaiman emphasizes in an introduction, "For the record, I wear a leather jacket and eat meat, but I am quite good with babies."

"Babycakes" was adapted to comics by artist Michael Zulli for *Taboo* issue 4 in 1990.

"BEING AN EXPERIMENT UPON STRICTLY SCIENTIFIC LINES" (1990). AV

This is a very funny piece about an author who experiments with alcohol as he writes, trying to prove that drinking has no efff . . . noifkt . . . well, it doesn't hurt his wrtinng att oll.

Check out the extras on the DVD of *A Short Film About John Bolton* for an uproarious live reading of this story by the author himself.

"BITTER GROUNDS" (2003). FT

This zombie story was written for Nalo Hopkinson's anthology, *Mojo: Conjure Stories.* Gaiman has said that of the four short stories he wrote in 2003, he "suspects" this was the best.

As the story opens, the narrator has decided to give up his life and hit the road. Drawing as much money as he can from his accounts, he does so, driving until he realizes he could really use a bath. At a hotel he meets another customer, who needs a ride back to where his is car has broken down. Offering him transportation, he learns that his passenger, Jack Anderton, is an anthropology professor on his way to give a lecture. The professor tells him about the coffee girls of Haiti, little girls who knock on your door to sell you coffee, who some believe are zombies.

Arriving on the scene of his breakdown, Anderton realizes he has left his wallet at the hotel. The narrator offers to go back and get it while his passenger waits with the car. When he returns, Anderton is gone, most likely the victim of a robbery. His tickets and itinerary have been left behind, however. The narrator thinks this has happened for a reason. Taking the papers and tickets, he decides to assume the professor's identity.

As Anderton, the narrator travels to the conference in New Orleans, where he meets a woman while bar hopping with a "colleague," described only as having a red ribbon in her hair. She tells him she is a priestess of Santeria. He spends some time with her, and they chat about the living and the dead.

After he does a surprisingly credible job of delivering a paper that he hadn't written (the real Anderton's paper, "The Zombie Coffee Girls"), he sleeps with a female colleague, reflecting that after all that's happened to him, "People come into your life for a reason." The next morning, he wakes to find a coffee girl at his door; the story ends as the pair walks off together "into the misty dawn."

"THE CASE OF THE FOUR AND TWENTY BLACKBIRDS" (1984). AV MM

Gaiman has called it "juvenalia," but this hard-boiled fairy tale certainly has its moments. It was the third piece of fiction Gaiman wrote to be published in a mass circulation magazine (*Knave*), following "Featherquest" and "How to Sell the Ponti Bridge." The former has never been collected; the latter, like "Four and Twenty," is contained in *M is for Magic*.

The narrator and hero of this piece is Jack Horner, who is hired by Jill Dumpty to investigate the alleged murder of her brother, Humpty, and to obtain some photographs that have gone missing. Humpty, known as "the Fat Man," had "his finger in most of the crooked pies in town." Contrary to popular belief, Dumpty didn't fall off a wall; he was pushed.

Cock Robin is a stoolie who is killed before he can reveal who killed Humpty Dumpty. His death raises the question, "Who Killed Cock Robin?" A tip from Old Mother Hubbard sends Horner in search of the Queen of Hearts, whose real identity provides the answer that Horner seeks.

"CHANGES" (1998). SM

"Changes" was written for Lisa Tuttle's anthology about gender *Crossing the Border*. When Gaiman first had the idea for this story, "it was a set of linked short stories that would have formed a novel exploring the world of gender reflection." What ultimately resulted was a number of vignettes and insights into the work and life of a geneticist named Rajit.

Rajit is the inventor of a "set of chemical instructions" called "Reboot" that resets the body's genetic code. The process that Rajit conceives has one drawback—in order to cure diseases like cancer, the patient has to accept the fact that the "instructions" might result in changing his or her gender entirely.

"CHIVALRY" (1993). AV SM MM WCL

Having written this in one weekend, Gaiman has called this story "a gift from the gods, easy and sweet as anything." A tale of a knight on a quest, and a wise, sweet old lady who finds the Holy Grail in a secondhand store, it's easily one of Gaiman's most charming (and most reprinted) short stories. In *Angels & Visitations*, it's accompanied by an illustration by longtime Gaiman collaborator Michael Zulli.

Mrs. Whitaker is a widow who haunts secondhand shops in search of bargains, like cheap paperbacks, and knickknacks for her parlor. One day, she finds the Holy Grail and purchases it, as it will look good on her fireplace mantel. Her purchase brings the knight Galaad into her life. A genuine Knight of the Table

Round, Galaad is on a "Right High and Noble Quest" for the Sangrail. Realizing that Mrs. Whitaker has the Grail in her possession, he tries to entice her into trading it to him. He offers her many wonderful items in trade; Mrs. Whitaker eventually settles for the Philosopher's Stone and Egg of the Phoenix. He also offers her one of the apples of Hesperides, which she wisely rejects.

"CINNAMON" (2004). NGAC
NEILGAIMAN.COM

This is a charming fable of a princess named Cinnamon who refuses to speak. As of this writing, there are only two places to get this story: you can listen to Gaiman reading it on the *Neil Gaiman Audio Collection* CD, or you can read it on his Web site, where the text is enhanced with some lovely illustrations from Jill Schwarz.

Cinnamon is the beautiful, blind princess of "a small hot country, where everything was very old." Cinnamon did not talk. Her father and her mother—the rajah and rani—offered great treasures to anyone who could get their daughter to speak. Many tried, but only a tiger succeeded. The tiger gets Cinnamon to speak by teaching her lessons about pain, fear, and love. Her first word is "Love?"

"CLOSING TIME" (2002). FT

First published in *McSweeney's Mammoth Treasury of Thrilling Tales*, edited by Michael Chabon, "Closing Time" turned out to be a combination of an M. R. James ghost story and a Robert Aickman strange story. Like the Worlds' End inn from Gaiman's *Sandman* series, the Diogenes Club (a gentlemen's club that originated in the Sherlock Holmes stories of Sir Arthur Conan Doyle, and about which Gaiman friend and collaborator Kim Newman has written an entire volume of stories) is a place where people gather together to share a pint and tell some stories.

The narrator of this tale—a journalist—tells of a tale he told at the Diogenes Club, of the strange experience he had as a boy at the Swallows, a sprawling, run-down manor that had been shut when its owner, the Earl of Tenterdon, died. Dared by three other boys to enter a playhouse on the property, he tricks them into entering instead. None of them, as far as he knows, ever came out.

"THE DAUGHTER OF OWLS" (1996). SM SIT

This brief piece, recounting the legend of a woman known as "the daughter of owls," purports to be from *The Remaines of Gentilisme and Judaisme* by John Aubrey. It's actually an instance of Gaiman writing as Aubrey, the seventeenth-century collector and historian, whom the author greatly admires for his voice and erudition. "I tried writing this story in a couple of different ways, and I was never satisfied with it," writes Gaiman in his introduction. "Then it occurred to me to write it as by Aubrey."

Incidentally, a John Aubrey quote, from his "The Minutes of Lives," serves as the epigraph to *The Sandman* collection *Brief Lives*.

"The Daughter of Owls" was adapted to comics by artist Michael Zulli for the two-story 2004 graphic novel *Creatures of the Night*, published by Dark Horse Comics.

"DECEMBER 7, 1995" (1995). ADT

This story was written for Gaiman's friend, singer/songwriter Tori Amos, after she sent him a CD of the album that would eventually become *Boys for Pele*. When Gaiman played it, he imagined the songs as people, and their stories, and he wrote them down for her, sending them to her as a thank-you.

"DISEASEMAKER'S CROUP" (2002). FT

Written as an entry in a book of imaginary diseases called *The Thackery T. Lambshead Pocket Guide to Eccentric and Discredited Diseases*, edited by Jeff VanderMeer and Mark Roberts, this piece purports to take a look at the imaginary disease of making up imaginary diseases. Gaiman wrote it with the aid of a computer program called babble and a "dusty, leather-bound book of advice to the home physician."

"DON'T ASK JACK" (1995). SM MM

This story, inspired by a Lisa Snellings sculpture of a demonic jack-in the-box, tells of a malevolent toy that sits in a huge old wooden toy box. None of the children who live in the house knows how it came to be there, but most instinctively avoid it. Those who do play with it, sneaking up to the nursery in the middle of the night to do so, meet bad ends.

"ESSAY FOR PATTI" (1996). ADT

This is a brief piece on writers and their faces done for Patti Perret's *Faces of Fantasy*, a book of photographs of fantasy writers.

"THE FACTS IN THE CASE OF THE DEPARTURE OF MISS FINCH" (1998). FT SIT

Asked to write a story about a Frank Frazetta painting of a woman flanked by two tigers, Gaiman couldn't think of a story, so "I told what happened to Miss Finch instead."

The narrator of the piece speaks with a voice that feels as though Gaiman himself is telling the tale, and all the references point in that direction, but . . .

The narrator is a writer, a "liar by trade," who doesn't expect anyone to believe the story he has to tell. In England on business, he receives a call from Jonathan, an old friend, asking if he'd like to accompany him, his wife, Jane, and his wife's friend on a night on the town. Not exactly a blind date, but . . .

The narrator gamely agrees, and goes on to witness a strange transformation. The narrator's married friends share the same first names of Gaiman's close friends, Jonathan Ross and his wife, Jane Goldman. The couple convinces the narrator to accompany them and Jane's straitlaced friend, Miss Finch, a very dour, very prim person.

Miss Finch finds herself part of the act at the Theater of Night's Dreaming, a circus sideshow. After traveling through six rooms, she is pulled from the crowd in the seventh room, despite her feeble protests. By the time the narrator and his friends see her again in the ninth of ten rooms, she has been totally transformed: "Her black hair was down. The spectacles were gone. The costume, what little there was of it, fitted her perfectly. She held a spear, and she stared at us without emotion. Then the great cats padded into the light next to her. One of them threw its head back and roared."

The last time her companions see her, she is coolly corralling one of the cats that has lurched toward the audience. She never emerges from the sideshow, and they never see her again.

In 2007, Gaiman's frequent collaborator, Michael Zulli, illustrated Gaiman's adaptation of "The Facts in the Case of the Departure of Miss Finch," published by Dark Horse Comics.

"FEEDERS AND EATERS" (1990/2002). FT.

Gaiman writes, "This story was a nightmare I had in my twenties." First written as a comic (published in *Revolver Horror Special*), Gaiman later tried re-imagining it as an outline for a pornographic horror film he'd never make (working title: *Eaten: Scenes From a Moving Picture*). Then Stephen Jones asked Gaiman if he had a story for his *Keep Out the Night* anthology; Gaiman remembered this piece and "rolled up my sleeves and began to type."

The story begins: "This is a true story, pretty much. As far as that goes, and whatever good it does anybody."

Late one night the narrator enters an all-night café and finds an old acquaintance, Eddie Barrow, inside. Barrow, who looks terrible, is waiting for his girlfriend to show up and, while he waits, tells a story about his strange relationship with another tenant in the boardinghouse where he resides, the elderly Effi Corvier.

After winning his trust with a few small gifts, Miss Corvier, who had fallen ill, had made a strange request of Eddie: She asked him to being her meat, raw meat. This seemed to help her. Soon, a cat owned by the landlords went missing. One night, Eddie entered Miss Corvier's apartment and found the cat, looking as if something had been consuming it piece by piece, even though it was still alive.

Eddie, who looks drained to the narrator, finishes his story as his companion,

Miss Corvier, arrives. The narrator thinks it's odd how Eddie looks older than he should and Miss Corvier looks so much younger than he expected.

"FIFTEEN PAINTED CARDS FROM A VAMPIRE TAROT" (1998). FT

Fifteen shorts about some of the characters of the Tarot, first published in *The Art of Vampire*. Gaiman has promised artist Rick Berry that he'll write seven additional tales about the Major Arcana one day. "Then," he writes, "he can paint them."

"THE FLINTS OF MEMORY LANE" (1997). ADT FT

This eerie tale was written by Gaiman for Stephen Jones's anthology *Dancing with the Dark*, a book of true ghost stories, and is, as Gaiman has stated, "as true as recollection allows." In it Gaiman tells of a strange, terrifying encounter he had with a woman who was dressed "like a gypsy queen in a stage play, or a Moorish princess," at the age of fifteen. The woman was standing beneath a lamppost on the street in front of his house, staring up at his home; her looks and her silence frightened the young Gaiman, who quickly walked away. When he turned to look back, she had vanished.

"FORBIDDEN BRIDES OF THE FACELESS SLAVES IN THE SECRET HOUSE OF THE NIGHT OF DREAD DESIRE" (2004). FT

Gaiman started writing this amusing tale at the ripe old age of twenty-two. Upon completing it, he showed it to a couple of editors he knew; both reacted negatively. Discouraged but trusting in their judgment, he put the story away, only to unearth it some twenty years later, when asked for a story for an anthology called *Gothic!* As he read it he smiled, deciding the story was "pretty funny, and it was smart, too, a good little story." The story, about a writer who lives in a reality where every Gothic cliché is actually a part of everyday life, was voted Best Short Story in the 2005 Locus Awards.

"FOREIGN PARTS" (1990). AV SM

Although this could be seen as a story about the AIDS epidemic, Gaiman says that that is only partly true; in his mind, it's "mostly about loneliness, and identity, and, perhaps, it's about the joys of making your own way in the world." "Foreign Parts" was originally published in Steve Niles's *Words without Pictures*.

Simon Powers is a twenty-six-year-old man who works in a large London bank.

Simon, who is not promiscuous, wakes up one day having difficulty in urinating. His pain, which a doctor diagnoses as "non specific urethritis," continues to worsen; Simon eventually concludes that his penis is not his own anymore. That turns out to be the least of his problems, as something is literally consuming him from the inside out, taking him over.

"THE GOLDFISH POOL AND OTHER STORIES" (1996). SM

This story, about a writer's odyssey in Los Angeles, was written for an anthology edited by Janet Berliner and David Copperfield, called *David Copperfield's Beyond Imagination*. "Some of this story is true," writes Gaiman. Filled with melancholy and longing and nostalgia, this tale also gives some insight into a writer's mind, as he deals with other people's visions and conceives a new one of his own.

As he arrives in Los Angeles, the writer/narrator of this story, author of the novel *Sons of Man,* tells readers he feels surrounded by a "hundred old movies." On the cab ride over his driver tells him that John Belushi died at the hotel he is staying at, and that Robin Williams and Robert De Niro were with him at the time. Later, he's told that it was Meryl and Dustin. Still later, that it was two big Hollywood directors, and finally, a hotel employee, Pious Dundas, tells him that Belushi died alone.

The writer tells of Hollywood's interest in his novel, *Sons of Man,* a sort of take on Ira Levin's *The Boys From Brazil,* except that the children involved are actually the sons of Charles Manson. This being a Hollywood story, he's told many times how wonderful his novel is, and, in almost the same breath, how it's going to have to be reworked to make it into a film. As the story progresses, the script of *Sons of Man* morphs into something entirely different.

"GOLIATH" (1999). FT

When he was asked to write this story, Gaiman was told that it would appear on the Web site of a film that hadn't come out yet. The filmmakers sent a script to him, which he read with interest. That script convinced him to write this story, about a man who learns firsthand about the nature of reality. The story went up about a week before the movie came out, and is still up as of this writing. The movie? A little film called *The Matrix.*

"GOOD BOYS DESERVE FAVOURS" (1995). ADT FT

This story, Gaiman writes, "walks that twilight place where fiction and memory collapse gently into each other, and demonstrates that while things need not have happened to be true, by the same token just because something really happened, it is still not to be relied upon." It was, like several other Gaiman works, inspired by a Lisa Snellings-Clark statue, this one of a man holding a double bass, just as Gaiman did when he was a child. The story tells of a boy who has a brief mystical, magical experience with a musical instrument.

"HALLOWE'EN" (1996). ADT

"Hallowe'en" is an excerpt of a larger story, the final part of a round-robin Halloween ghost story written for London's *Time Out* magazine. Portions were written by his friend Kathy Acker, Peter Straub, and Christopher Fowler, among others. Gaiman wrote in *Adventures in the Dream Trade* that when he read the published story, he was astonished at how much sense it all made, "more or less."

"HARLEQUIN VALENTINE" (1999). FT

Gaiman's inspiration for this story came from a Ferris wheel that Lisa Snellings designed and made that had been featured in a book called *Strange Attractions*. A number of writers wrote stories based on the passengers in the cars. Gaiman asked if he could write a story inspired by the ticket seller, a grinning harlequin. The harlequin, of course, is the trickster figure of the commedia dell'arte, and is the pathetic but sinister narrator of this story ("Oh, Harlequin in love is a sorry creature"). His narrative details his every movement as he pursues (stalks?) a young woman named Missy, whom the Harlequin refers to as "My Columbine," on Valentine's Day. As proof of his love, the magical trickster literally removes his heart and affixes it to her front door.

Surprisingly calm at finding an organ pinned to her door, Missy takes the object to her old place of employment, the coroner's office, and has it identified as, in fact, a heart. Consuming her strange suitor's heart, she becomes a harlequinade. As the story ends, she goes out into the world: "I have things to do," she tells the former harlequin, now transformed into a mere human being. "Tickets to take. People to dream."

Gaiman and artist John Bolton adapted "Harlequin Valentine" into a graphic novel, which was published by Dark Horse Comics in 2001.

"HOW DO YOU THINK IT FEELS?" (1998). FT

This story came about when Gaiman was asked to contribute to *In the Shadow of the Gargoyle,* an anthology about gargoyles. Here Gaiman explores the notion of having a personal gargoyle to guard one's heart from guilt and pain.

As a young man, the narrator meets and becomes enamored of a girl named Becky; they have a fling, which ends badly, at least from the narrator's point of view. In a fit of self-pity, the narrator crafts a crude gargoyle out of plasticine, and magically imbues it with his anger and frustration at his ex-lover. After the narrator makes the gargoyle, he falls asleep with it on his chest. When he wakes the next morning, he doesn't take notice of where it's gone.

Becky enjoyed her time with the narrator, but realizes at one point that it is time to move on. Years later the two meet again, and find that there is still a strong attraction between them. Without much prelude, they steal off to a private room to make love, which both find satisfying. Afterward, the narrator has a dream about the gargoyle emerging from his chest; he also half remembers waking to see the gargoyle, clenching black hair in its fists, re-enter his chest. When he wakes fully, Becky is gone.

"HOW TO SELL THE PONTI BRIDGE" (1985). MM

A story Gaiman wrote when he was very young, this is a fantasy inspired by a man named "Count" Victor Lustig, who really did sell the Eiffel Tower in much the same way the character in the story claims he sold the Ponti Bridge to a tourist.

The story unfolds in the Original Rogues' Club, the oldest and most exclusive Rogues' Club "in all the Seven Worlds," which is located in the city of Lost Carnadine. The club was formed by a "loose association of rogues, cheats, scoundrels, and confidence men almost seventy thousand years ago."

Stoat, an apparently long-lived con man of immense talent, tells his colleagues of his brilliant scheme to sell the Ponti Bridge for immense riches.

"HOW TO TALK TO GIRLS AT PARTIES" (2006). FT MM

According to Gaiman, this story, which first appeared in the *Magazine of Fantasy and Science Fiction,* began life as two different and failed attempts to write an account of a tourist holiday on Earth. In its final incarnation, it took the form of a science fiction tale where two horny teenagers, Enn and Vic, crash a party, only to find its guests are not of this world.

At the insistence of his friend Vic, Enn, the narrator of this tale, allows himself to be dragged to a party, where he overcomes his shyness and actually talks to three girls. Because they are so peculiar, he slowly starts to realize that he and Vic are the only denizens of Earth attending the affair.

Vic tells his friend not to be nervous about talking to the opposite sex, because, after all, "[t]hey're just girls. They don't come from another planet." Well into the evening, Vic suddenly realizes that the party he has crashed is far different from any he could have imagined, and that the "girls" he has been talking to do, in fact, come from other planets. He collects his friend Enn and flees, quite shaken by the whole experience.

"I, CTHULHU, OR WHAT'S A TENTACLE-FACED THING LIKE ME DOING IN A SUNKEN CITY LIKE THIS (LATITUDE 47 DEGREES 9'S, LONGITUDE 126 DEGREES, 43' W" (1987)

If you can't find the first appearance of this as yet uncollected story (in *Dagon* 16), you might still be able to read it on Gaiman's Web site, under the tab labeled "Cool Stuff." It's not very long, but it is very droll, a humorous "autobiography" of H. P. Lovecraft's "big bad," as dictated to his human stenographer, Whateley. We won't go into detail, because it's really not advisable to invoke his name. We will say, however, that the joke about the parrot and the magician cracks us up every time.

"IN THE END" (1996). FT

In this short, short story (a little over 220 words), Gaiman says he was trying to imagine the very last book of the Bible. In short, it's a rewind of the story of the Garden of Eden.

"KEEPSAKES AND TREASURES" (1999). FT

Subtitled "A Love Story," this tale began life ("or part of it did") as a comic, as part of Oscar Zarate's noir collection *It's Dark in London*. Gaiman later expanded it when Al Sarrantonio asked him for a story for his *999* anthology. It's notable for being the first story to feature Mr. Smith and Mr. Alice, who also appear in the *American Gods* novella, "The Monarch of the Glen." Gaiman has intimated that he has more Mr. Smith and Mr. Alice stories to tell, particularly the one in which the pair come to a parting of the ways.

The corpulent Mr. Alice has his fingers in many a sordid pie. Rich (one of the ten richest men in the world), powerful, influential, and private, he usually gets what he wants. When he decides he wants the Treasure of the Shahinai, he moves heaven and earth to obtain it.

Mr. Smith is Mr. Alice's amoral, loyal, lethal right-hand man, who has done things for his boss that would break a lesser man, all without a twinge of guilt.

Bred and raised by what amounts to a cult, the Treasure is actually a young man, whose beauty and attractiveness surpasses that of any other human. Upon seeing him for the first time, Mr. Alice falls deeply in love with him, and decides he must have him. He purchases the boy from his keepers for an enormous sum, takes him home, and surrounds his lover with the best of everything. The Treasure is a delicate being; after only eight months in the outside world, he catches the flu, sickens, and dies, leaving Mr. Alice heartbroken.

"LOOKING FOR THE GIRL" (1985). AV SM

Written for *Penthouse* for their twentieth-anniversary issue, this story deals with men's attitudes toward beautiful women, models in particular. Who, Gaiman, asks, is being exploited? It finally occurred to him that *Penthouse* and magazines like it had absolutely nothing to do with women and absolutely everything to do with photographs of women.

The narrator tells of a model who first caught his eye when she appeared in a 1965 issue of *Penthouse* he purchased when he was nineteen. Charlotte, who somehow stood out from the other girls in that issue, was nineteen, too. Charlotte appeared in a subsequent issue of the magazine in 1969, only this time named Melanie, her age again listed as nineteen. Four years later she shows up again, this time as Belinda, still nineteen. This occurs again and again, with the girl appearing under different names over the years, but never aging. The narrator, a photographer himself, tries to track her down, but there is an air of mystery about the girl—her real identity remains unknown.

One day, some two decades after he saw her for the first time, she comes into his studio, offering to pose for him, looking no different than she did in 1965. He realizes that the ageless "Charlotte" has been exploiting her looks for ages, that "Charlotte is there, in all places, all times, sliding through our fantasies, a girl forever."

"THE MONARCH OF THE GLEN" (2004). FT

This novella, first published in *Legends II,* edited by Robert Silverberg, marks the third time that Gaiman has worked with concepts found in the epic poem *Beowulf.* The first time was the script he wrote with Roger Avary; the second, in his poem "Bay Wolf." The third time is just as entertaining: Set two years after the events of *American Gods,* it features the hero of that dark novel, Shadow.

Incidentally, a copy of *The Monarch of the Glen,* the 1851 oil-on-canvas painting depicting a majestic stag created by the English painter Sir Edwin Landseer, actually appears in the novella, hanging on a wall in a castle's library.

PEOPLE, PLACES, AND THINGS

SHADOW. AKA BALDUR, AKA BALDER MOON. Having been on the road for some eighteen months, Shadow finds himself in Scotland, where a local convinces him to take a lucrative job as a security guard at a fancy party held on the premises of a nearby castle. Unknown to him, however, his employers have a hidden agenda—they have hired him to take part in an age-old ritual, a battle between man and monster. Although Shadow defeats his opponent, he refuses to allow him to be slaughtered by the partygoers, displeasing those who hired him.

JENNIE. A barmaid who befriends Shadow, she is also a being of great power who aids Shadow at the conclusion of his battle with the young man/monster.

THE SON AND HIS MOTHER. If Shadow can be seen as a stand-in for the hero Beowulf, then this huge, hairless, misshapen but sharp-eared young man and his fiftyish mother are certainly Grendel and his mother. Shadow finds himself locked in mortal combat with the young man.

As Gaiman writes: "This fight was old, Shadow thought . . . It was the fight of man against monster, and it was old as time: it was Theseus battling the Minotaur, it was Beowulf and Grendel, it was the fight of every hero who had stood between the firelight and the darkness and wiped the blood of something inhuman from his sword."

Because Shadow spares her son, the mother places him under her protection, promising Smith that there will be great trouble if Shadow comes to harm.

SMITH. An employee of the enigmatic Mr. Alice, he's in charge of security at the castle.

MR. ALICE. Mr. Alice is the prime mover behind the events that occur in this tale, the host of the party at the castle. A very powerful, very rich man who keeps to the shadows, he first appeared in Gaiman's story "Keepsakes and Treasures."

"MOUSE" (1993). AV SM

Written for Peter Crowther's *Narrow Houses II,* an anthology dealing with superstitions. In "Mouse," Gaiman writes, he is operating in Raymond Carver mode. It seems to be a reflection on killing, and the relative importance of life across species; someone, or something, is always killing someone or something else.

Regan begins this story looking for humane mousetraps. He finds some, and sets them in his apartment. Catching a mouse after a few days of trying, he sets it free in his garden, only to watch it be killed by a cat.

"MURDER MYSTERIES" (1992). AV SM

When Gaiman first began writing this story about the first crime of passion, it was called "City of Angels," for reasons which will become obvious. Its appearance in *Angels & Visitations* is accompanied by an illustration from P. Craig Russell. An audio adaptation of "Murder Mysteries," starring Brian Dennehy, can be heard on *two plays for voices.*

In 2002, Dark Horse Comics published Gaiman's graphic novel adaptation of "Murder Mysteries," illustrated by P. Craig Russell.

PEOPLE, PLACES, AND THINGS

THE NARRATOR. Visiting Los Angeles, the narrator finds himself talking to a homeless man who claims to be the angel Raguel, also known as Vengeance of the Lord. In return for a cigarette, Raguel tells him a story of the first murder, which took place in the original City of the Angels, the Silver City.

LUCIFER. The captain of the Host, and the chief servant of The Name. Lucifer often takes walks in "the Dark," the darkness which surrounds the Silver City, home of the angels.

RAGUEL. The Vengeance of the Lord, he is created by The Name to investigate the murder of his fellow angel, Carasel.

THE NAME. The Creator. God.

CARASEL. An angel, he was murdered by his lover in a crime of passion; the murder is the first that has ever occurred. Carasel worked on the details of Creation, on some of the basics, like Dimension and Sleep, for instance.

PHANUEL. The angel who discovered the body of Carasel. Like Carasel, Phanuel is a designer working on the details of Creation.

SARAQUEL. Carasel's coworker, cocreator of Love, and, sadly, Death. The pain he feels when his lover Carasel ignores him to concentrate on his work leads him to commit a horrible crime, the first of its kind.

"NICHOLAS WAS" (1989). AV SM WCL

Written for one of Gaiman's much coveted Christmas cards, it was calligraphed "elegantly" by none other than Dave McKean. Exactly one hundred words long, the short, dark, disturbing piece first saw print in *Drabble II*. Here Gaiman posits that Nicholas is not a jolly old elf but someone being punished, on a scale exceeding the punishments doled out to Prometheus, Loki, Sisyphus, and Judas.

"OCTOBER IN THE CHAIR" (2002). FT MM

This story was written for Peter Straub for a volume of *Conjunctions* magazine (number 39) that the author of *Ghost Story* edited in 2002. The story is interesting in that Gaiman, who wanted to write a story about a dead boy and a living one, penned it as sort of a dry run for his upcoming *The Graveyard Book*.

Dedicated to Ray Bradbury, this tale won the Locus Award in 2003 for Best Short Story. The story features the months of the year as distinct entities who meet periodically to tell stories. In this particular meeting, October has the chair, and presides over the gathering. October tells the haunting story of Runt, an emotionally abused little boy who runs away from home.

Runt (given name Donald) is befriended by the dead boy Dearly (he used to have another name, but he "can't read it anymore") and enjoys the time he spends playing with Dearly so much he decides he wants to stay with him forever.

"ONE LIFE, FURNISHED IN EARLY MOORCOCK" (1994). SM

When Gaiman was twelve, Moorcock's stories were "as real to me as anything else in my life and a great deal more real than, well, geography, for a start." This story, whose title riffs on the title of a Harlan Ellison story, "One Life, Furnished in Early Poverty," features a thirteen-year-old would-be writer named Richard, whose experiences seem to echo those of Gaiman's as a young man.

In 1996, Topps Comics published a single-issue comic book adaptation of "One Life, Furnished in Early Moorcock," illustrated by P. Craig Russell. The adaptation is exquisitely crafted in every department, vividly delineating Gaiman's introspective autobiographical story about his teenage years and awakening sexuality (at a time when he was a year younger than his classmates, due to being "bumped up" a year in school), and the importance of Moorcock's Elric stories to this phase of the young writer's life. Russell's sensitive, expressive fusion of naturalistic characterizations, rich fantasy imagery, and unflinchingly candid depiction of young male sexuality still places this among the best of all possible comics adaptations of Gaiman's fiction to date.

"ONLY THE END OF THE WORLD AGAIN" (1994). SM

Once again, this is Gaiman writing for a Stephen Jones anthology, this time *Shadows Over Innsmouth*. Larry Talbot would make another appearance in the Gaiman poem "Bay Wolf." A werewolf, Larry maintains an office in the village of Innsmouth. On the door of the office, it reads:

LAWRENCE TALBOT
ADJUSTOR

In his travels around town, Larry receives several hints that someone intends to raise the Deep Ones from the sea. Little does he realize that he's an integral part of that plan; those who wish to resurrect the Deep Ones plan to sacrifice the wolfman as part of a ritual. Larry doesn't play ball, however, and interrupts their rites, spoiling their plans.

In 1998, P. Craig Russell adapted the short story into a two-part script for Oni Press. The story was illustrated by Troy Nixey, and appeared in *Oni Double Feature* issues 6 and 7.

"OTHER PEOPLE" (2001). FT

In his introduction to *Fragile Things,* Gaiman labels this a "little Mobius story," for reasons that become obvious upon reading. Originally called "Afterlife," this story of a man condemned to Hell and an eternity of reliving his sins was given its current title by noted editor Gordon Van Gelder after he bought it for the *Magazine of Fantasy and Science Fiction.*

"PAGES FROM A JOURNAL FOUND IN A SHOEBOX LEFT IN A GREYHOUND BUS SOMEWHERE BETWEEN TULSA, OKLAHOMA AND LOUISVILLE, KENTUCKY" (2002). FT

This piece chronicles the day-to-day experiences of the anonymous narrator, who is "looking for Scarlet." First published in 2002 as part of Tori Amos's *Scarlet's Walk* tour book, the story was eventually chosen for inclusion in *The Year's Best Fantasy and Horror Sixteenth Annual Collection,* edited by Ellen Datlow and Terri Windling. In the introduction to *Fragile Things,* Gaiman says he was trying to write something about identity and travel and America, "like a tiny companion piece to *American Gods,* in which everything, including any kind of resolution, hovered just out of reach." We'd say he succeeded.

"THE PRICE" (1997). SM MM SIT

"The Price" is the story of a cat that acts as a guardian angel to a family. Gaiman said in the introduction to *Smoke and Mirrors* that he wanted to thank his family for letting him put them in this story, and, "more importantly, both for leaving me alone to write, and for sometimes insisting I come out to play."

A family man, the narrator tells the story of a stray cat who turned up at his house one day. The narrator and his family adopt the male cat, who always seems to be getting in tussles with other animals, suffering noticeable injuries over the course of his stay. One night the narrator spies the cat's real nemesis, the Devil; the cat has come to protect his family from evil.

The story ends on a somber note, as the narrator wonders what the family did to deserve the Black Cat. He wonders who sent him. And, selfishly, he wonders how much more the cat has to give.

In 2004, Michael Zulli adapted "The Price" as part of Dark Horse Comics' two-story Gaiman collection, *Creatures of the Night.*

"THE PROBLEM OF SUSAN" (2004). FT

In this story an elderly woman, Professor Hastings, is depicted as dealing with the grief and trauma of the deaths of her entire family in a train crash. The woman's first name is not revealed, but she mentions her brother "Ed," and it is strongly implied that she is actually Susan Pevensie of Narnia fame.

Gaiman's story, about a problematic moment in the *Narnia Chronicles* that has long bothered him, has been seen by some as a critique of C. S. Lewis's treatment of Susan in those books. Gaiman himself has said in interviews that those who read that story that way are missing the point; people who talk about it in terms of how readers process children's literature are closer to understanding it, according to the author.

The story was originally published in *Flights: Extreme Visions of Fantasy Volume II,* edited by Al Sarrantonio.

"SHOGGOTH'S OLD PECULIAR" (1998). SM

This tale, which was nominated for a World Fantasy Award in 1999, had its origins in a conversation Gaiman had with John Jarrold in 1985 in a bar at a science fiction convention (the same night, coincidentally, that he had a conversation with editor Richard Evans that, six years later, became *Neverwhere*). It was originally published in *The Mammoth Book of Comic Fantasy,* edited by Mike Ashley.

Touring the British coastline, Benjamin Lassiter comes to the north of Bootle, to the village of Innsmouth. The village has a bed-and-breakfast named Shub Niggurath, and a pub called The Book of Dead Names, whose proprietor is listed as A. Al-Hazred.

Entering an establishment called The Saloon Bar, he starts a conversation with two locals, Wilf and Seth, over pints of a beer called Shoggoth's Old Peculiar. They talk about the fact that there's also an Innsmouth in the United States, which was, in fact, named for their village. "He wrote about it all the time," they say. "Him whose name we don't mention."

The author they're speaking of turns out to be none other than H. P. Lovecraft. They have a lively conversation about the merits of his writing. Lassiter, however, forgets the latter portions of their talk, waking up in the countryside the next day to find that nobody knows of the village or its inhabitants.

"SIX TO SIX" (1990). AV

Written for *Time Out,* London's weekly listings magazine, for a special issue on London's nightlife, "Six to Six," is the story of the adventures of a journalist who hangs around the West End streets of London for twelve hours. It is "all true," except that the garrulous taxi driver who appears at the end of the story "wasn't the one on the way to Victoria, but the one from Gatwick Airport" to Gaiman's house, an hour later.

The story, presented only in *Angels & Visitations,* is accompanied by an illustration by Bill Sienkiewicz.

"SNOW, GLASS, APPLES" (1994). SM

Another story which was inspired by Neil Philip's *The Penguin Book of English Folktales,* this story tells the tale of Snow White from a decidedly different angle, that of the "wicked" stepmother. Snow White here is no innocent waif; rather, she is a demon whose heart continues to beat, even after it has been excised from her body.

This story was originally published by Dreamhaven Press in a limited-edition booklet that benefited the Comic Book Legal Defense Fund. It also was converted into an audio drama starring Bebe Neuwirth, which can be heard on the CD collection, *Two Plays for Voices.*

"STRANGE LITTLE GIRLS" (2001). FT

This piece, inspired by Tori Amos's album of the same name, contains twelve short "pen portraits" of fictional women. The idea for the piece stemmed from Gaiman's idea for Amos to emulate creator Cindy Sherman. (Sherman works in series, typically photographing herself in a range of costumes. For example, in her landmark sixty-nine-photograph series, the *Complete Untitled Film Stills,* Sherman appeared as actresses clothed in B-movie, foreign film, and film noir style.) Amos, who knew exactly "who" was singing each song on the CD, took photos of herself as each character, and Gaiman wrote accompanying text.

"A STUDY IN EMERALD" (2003). FT

Hugo Award winner "A Study In Emerald" (2004) is a delightful, atmospheric homage to both Arthur Conan Doyle and H. P. Lovecraft, successfully combining elements of Doyle's Sherlock Holmes and Lovecraft's Cthuthlu mythos. Written for *Shadows Over Baker Street,* which was edited by Michael Reaves and John Pelan, the creation of this tale of murder and conspiracy also played a part in Gaiman's induction into the Baker Street Irregulars.

As an aside, the advertisements that open each chapter of the story are alone worth the price of admission, pitching products and services such as Victor's Vitae (Do Your Limbs and Nether Regions Lack Life?); V. Tepes—Professional Exsanguinator; and Jekyll's Powders (Release the Inner You!).

PEOPLE, PLACES, AND THINGS

THE CONSULTING DETECTIVE. This master of deductive reasoning is asked by the bumbling Inspector Lestrade of Scotland Yard to solve the murder of a member of the royal family. As of a result of his inquiries, during which he repeatedly displays his intellectual brilliance, the detective determines that the killing was committed by Restorationists, humans who resist the rule of the Old Ones. He also determines that there were two killers, a tall, pipe-smoking man accompanied by a medical practitioner.

THE NARRATOR. Just back from military duty in Afghanistan, the narrator becomes the roommate and boon companion of the Consulting Detective.

THE QUEEN. One of the Old Ones who conquered the Earth some seven hundred years before the events described in this story, she is a being whose appearance has been known to drive mere mortals to madness. Sensing the Consulting Detective is just the man to find out who murdered Franz Drago of Bohemia, Gloriana, as she is known, gives him her full support. She also reaches out a tentacle and heals the narrator's war wound.

SHERRY VERNET. Believed to be the killer by the Consulting Detective, the actor Vernet (leader of the Strand Players), also known as "Rache," outwits the Consulting Detective when he sees through one of the great man's disguises. Knowing that his alias has been compromised, he flees London in the company of his good friend, John (or James) Watson, a former military surgeon who, like the narrator, also recently finished a tour of duty in Afghanistan. As the story concludes, Vernet is still at large, leading the Restorationist fight against the tyranny of the Old Ones.

"SUNBIRD" (2007). FT MM

Written for his daughter Holly's eighteenth birthday, Gaiman calls this his R. A. Lafferty story. First published in a "book with an extremely long title, often abbreviated to *Noisy Outlaws, Unfriendly Blobs, and Some Other Things That Aren't as Scary,* as a benefit for the literacy program 826NYC," he's described it as a story about people who like to eat things.

The tale concerns the Epicurean Club, whose members number only five, and who take great pleasure in eating exotic dishes. As the story opens they lament the fact that they have probably consumed every exotic food imaginable. Then one of them mentions the Sunbird. The five members of the Epicurean club embark on a mission to capture and consume the Sunbird, unaware that one of their number has a hidden agenda.

"THE SWEEPER OF DREAMS" (1996). SM

This story began with a Lisa Snellings statue of a man leaning on a broom. Gaiman concluded that the man was obviously some kind of janitor. He wondered what kind, "and that was where this story came from."

The opening lines of this short, short story say it all:

> After all the dreaming is over, after you wake, and leave the world of madness and glory for the mundane day-lit daily grind, through the wreckage of your abandoned fancies walks the sweeper of dreams.

"TASTINGS" (1998). SM

Gaiman says that this oftentimes erotic story took four years to write—he would write a page, stop, and exit with his ears burning and his face red, and then it would be another six or eight months before he'd go back and write another page. That could be because it describes a couple having a conversation while making love. The twist is that, while both have almost telepathic experiences during sex, one is more powerful than the other, and actually absorbs the memories of their partner.

"Tastings" first appeared in Ellen Datlow and Terri Windling's *Sirens,* a collection of erotic fantasy stories.

"TROLL BRIDGE" (1993). AV SM MM WCL

This 1994 World Fantasy Award nominee was written for *Snow White, Blood Red,* an anthology of fairy stories retold for adults; Gaiman chose "The Three Billy Goats Gruff." Here, the narrator, Jack, tells of his encounters with a troll as a child, a teenager, and an adult. Poignant and surprising, it is arguably one of Gaiman's most memorable and haunting tales. In *Angels & Visitations,* the text is accompanied by an illustration by Charles Vess.

Jack first encounters the troll at the age of age of seven, when he ducks under a bridge. The Troll wants to eat him, but Jack talks his way out of trouble, convincing his captor that he should defer eating him until he is older. The next time Jack encounters the Troll he is a teenager, and the meeting is shortly after he has broken up with a girl. Jack once again convinces the Troll to wait.

The last time Jack meets the Troll he is an adult who, having made a mess of his life, is tired and ready for his fate. When Jack returns as an adult, the Troll swaps places with him, taking over Jack's life. Assuming the Troll's body, Jack lives contentedly under the bridge.

In 1998, artist Colleen Doran adapted "Troll Bridge" and published it in the pages of her regular Image comic book series, *A Distant Soil.*

"WEBS" (1990). AV

According to Gaiman, this is a very long science fiction story, "although nobody seems to believe that except me." He says that this tale, published in 1977 in *More Tales From the Forbidden Planet,* edited by Roz Kaveney, is the third or fourth story in a sequence of tales that exist somewhere in his head, and tells the overall story of its heroine, Lupita, a guest in the web-covered halls of the King of Spiders. Lupita takes revenge on the two huge spiders who have killed her cat, killing them with her knife. The two spiders turn out to be the King and the Lord Chamberlain.

"WE CAN GET THEM FOR YOU WHOLESALE" (1984). AV SM

A story that, upon rereading it several years after he wrote it, Gaiman characterized as a "John Collier story," "We Can Get Them for You Wholesale," is a tale of murder and excess.

While looking for an assassin to murder his rival, one Archibald Gibbons, Peter Pinter makes a call to the firm of Ketch, Hare, Burke and Ketch. The firm, all too glad to take his business, tells him of a two-for-one offer that is considerably cheaper. Since he appreciates a bargain, Pinter accepts, only to be told that he could obtain a bulk rate, and have ten people killed for the same amount of money. The situation escalates until Pinter, a truly miserable human being, finds himself asking, "How much would it cost to kill everybody? Everybody in the world?" The firm's representative tells him that they'll do that for nothing—they've been ready for a long time, they've only been waiting to be asked.

"Burke" and "Hare" are references to two of the most infamous serial killers in history, men who worked as a team. Burke and Hare killed at least seventeen people in 1827 and 1828 in Scotland, and sold the bodies of their victims to the Edinburgh Medical College—which was short on teaching cadavers—for dissection.

"Ketch" is a reference with several meanings, and Gaiman was undoubtedly aware of them all. Jack Ketch was a seventeenth-century English executioner in service to King Charles II. So famous—and reviled—was Ketch that his name, "Jack Ketch," became one of many synonyms for death and, sometimes, for Satan, as well as shorthand for the gallows. It is significant to note that in traditional Punch and Judy shows, which Gaiman famously wrote about in *Mr. Punch,* Jack Ketch is the name of the hangman.

In 1994, writer Joe Pruett adapted the story with artist Ken Meyer Jr. for Negative Burn issue 11.

"WHEN WE WENT TO SEE THE END OF THE WORLD BY DAWNIE MORNINGSIDE, AGE 11¼" (1998). SM

One day, Gaiman and Alan Moore sat down and began talking about a place that they would want to set stories. This story is set in that place.

Dawnie Morningside is the eleven-and-one-quarter-year-old narrator of the story, which describes a family outing that she embarks upon with her sister, Daisy-daisy, and their parents. Full of her observations, it reads like any young girl's writing, except for several things she describes so matter-of-factly: for instance, a unicorn that she wants to feed an apple.

"THE WITCH'S HEADSTONE" (2007). MM

This story is actually a part of Gaiman's as yet unpublished children's novel, *The Graveyard Book,* his take on Rudyard Kipling's *The Jungle Book.*

PEOPLE, PLACES, AND THINGS

BOD. A living boy adopted by the denizens of a graveyard. Meeting the spirit of the supposed witch Liza Hempstock, young Bod determines that he will obtain a headstone for her to properly mark her resting place.

MR. AND MRS. OWENS. Bod's adoptive parents.

SILAS AND MR. PENNYWORTH. Another of Bod's deceased guardians, and his teacher, respectively.

THE WITCH. Drowned and burned, Liza Hempstock was buried in the potter's field of the graveyard, among the suicides and other undesirables. Everyone who watched Liza die was subsequently murdered, presumably by one of her suitors.

ABANAZER BOLGER. The unscrupulous owner of a pawnshop, he becomes intrigued by Bod when the boy brings in a priceless brooch he found in a grave. Learning that no one knows that Bod has come to his shop, he imprisons the boy. Bod escapes, however, with the assistance of Liza Hempstock.

THE MAN JACK. Jack murdered Bod's family and has spent the ensuing years searching for the boy, presumably to kill him as well.

TRIVIA

- Much like CDs that contain hidden tracks, two of Gaiman's introductions to his short story collections contain hidden stories. "The Wedding Present," a bracing tale of what might have been, can be found in the introduction to *Smoke and Mirrors*. "The Mapmaker" (originally published by Hill House Press as a Christmas card to subscribers) is secreted within the introduction to *Fragile Things*.

- "October in the Chair" won the 2003 Locus Award. "Closing Time" took the same award in 2004.

- *Angels & Visitations* contains the following dedication: "For my parents, who taught me to read, and gave me the run of the shelves, and who never minded what I read: with affection, love, and gratitude."

- *Smoke and Mirrors* is dedicated to Ellen Datlow and Steve Jones, two of the top editors in the horror genre.

- Several of Gaiman's short stories have been adapted as comics and published in a handsome hardcover format by Dark Horse Comics. In 2001, "Harlequin Valentine" appeared, written by Gaiman, illustrated by John Bolton. An adaptation of "Murder Mysteries" by P. Craig Russell came out in 2002. Finally, *Creatures of the Night*, featuring "The Price" and "The Daughter of Owls," both illustrated by Michael Zulli, was debuted in 2004. Zulli also will be illustrating the forthcoming "The Facts in the Case of the Departure of Miss Finch."

THE QUOTABLE GAIMAN

Short stories are tiny windows into other worlds and other minds and other dreams. They are journeys you can make to the far side of the universe and still be back in time for dinner.

I've been writing short stories for almost a quarter of a century now. In the beginning they were a great way to begin to learn my craft as a writer. The hardest thing to do as a young writer is to finish something, and that was what I was learning how to do. These days most of the things I write are long—long comics or long books or long films—and a short story, something that's finished and over in a weekend or a week, is pure fun.

—Introduction to *M is for Magic*

Stories, like people and butterflies and songbirds' eggs and human hearts and dreams, are also fragile things, made up of nothing stronger or more lasting than twenty-six letters and a handful of punctuation marks. Or they are words on air, composed of sounds or ideas—abstract, invisible, gone once they've been spoken—and what could be more frail than that? But some stories, small, simple ones about setting out on adventures or people doing wonders, tales of miracles and monsters, have outlasted all the people who told them, and some of them have outlasted the lands in which they were created.

—Introduction to *Fragile Things*

Neil Gaiman with dark-fantasy author and pop culture journalist Les Daniels in 1988.
Photo by and © Peter Coleborn

Gaiman in 1995. Photo by and © Kelli Bickman. All rights reserved.

Gaiman and Princess the Cat, hard at work on *Stardust* in 1996. Photo by and © Kelli Bickman. All rights reserved.

Gaiman in New York City in a photo taken at a shoot for the "Pop Tartz" cable access show. "The monitor worked well for dramatic effect," says photographer Kelli Bickman. The photo was used for *Smoke and Mirrors*. Photo by and © Kelli Bickman. All rights reserved.

Gaiman in the Patagonian town of Gaiman, 1998. Photo
courtesy of Neil Gaiman, from his collection.

Gaiman, Jo Fletcher, Joe Hill, and Graham Joyce at the British
Fantasy Awards in 2006. Photo by and © Peter Coleborn

Neil Gaiman and his old friend, editor Stephen Jones, at the British Fantasy Awards in 2006. Photo by and © Peter Coleborn

Left to right: John Bolton, Geoff Ryman, Stephen Jones, Paul McAuley, Neil Gaiman, Kim Newman. Neil's forty-seventh birthday, London, November 10, 2007. Photo courtesy of Stephen Jones, from his collection.

Puppet designs in progress at Rogue puppet designer Joyce Hutter's workshop. Photo taken by Simon Edelman

THE TRAGICAL COMEDY OR
COMICAL TRAGEDY OF
MR. PUNCH
SET DESIGN BY JOEL DAAVID

Set rendering for *Mr. Punch* by Joel Daavid, Scenic Designer

Puppet designs in progress by Rogue Ensemble member, Joyce Hutter. Photo credit Joyce Hutter

A giant nightmarish Mr. Punch (Thomas Ashworth) haunts the boy's (Dalton O'Dell) nightmares. Photo taken by Simon Edelman

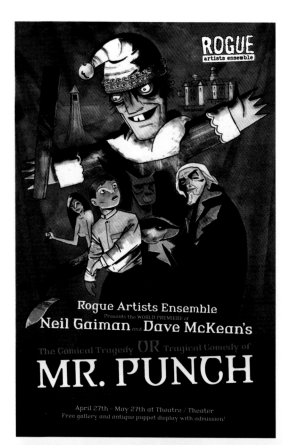

Mr. Punch production postcard designed by James White and inspired by the images originally created by Dave McKean for the graphic novel.

Left to right: Punch, The Doctor, and Dead Judy (dead), Puppets designed by Joyce Hutter. Photo taken by Simon Edelman

"My Sisters and I Would Sing," ©
and ™ Neil Gaiman and Charles
Vess' Stardust

"The False Knight on the
Road" Pg. #2, © 1995 Neil
Gaiman and Charles Vess

happy birthday [to] neil-dave & clare

"This is a drawing for Neil's fortieth birthday. It was added as a plate in the front of an old edition of *Arabian Knights* that I picked up from an antiquarian bookshop."—Dave McKean. Image courtesy of Dave McKean.

"This is the rejected cover for *Endless Nights*."—Dave McKean. Image courtesy of Dave McKean.

"This page is from the book *The Day I Swapped My Dad for Two Goldfish,* with warm-up sketches that I tend to do to get into the style of a particular project."—Dave McKean. Image courtesy of Dave McKean.

"Here's a drawing that I did for my daughter's birthday card, after we'd read the advance manuscript of *Coraline* together. It also convinced *Harper's* that I could draw a kid's book."—Dave McKean. Image courtesy of Dave McKean.

ONCE UPON A TIME THERE WAS A *HUGE* BLOOD MONSTER. AND IT SAW BEN AND LUCY IN TOWN, AND IT THOUGHT --*MMM-MMM*, DELECTABLE, DELICIOUS!

SO IT FOLLOWED THEM HOME...

IT KNOCKED ON THE DOOR. LUCY AND BEN LOOKED THROUGH THE LETTERSLOT AND SAW IT WAS A BLOODMONSTER. WERE THEY SCARED?

YES.

NO, YES.

"NO! THEY DIDN'T LET IT IN. BLOOD MONSTERS CAN'T GET IN IF YOU DON'T INVITE THEM. SO THE BLOOD MONSTER WENT AWAY AND KILLED A POLICEMAN AND SUCKED OUT HIS INSIDES, AND CLIMBED INSIDE THE EMPTY SKIN."

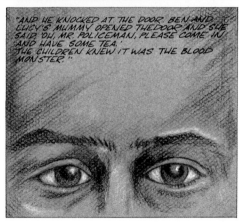

"AND HE KNOCKED AT THE DOOR. BEN AND LUCY'S MUMMY OPENED THE DOOR AND SHE SAID 'OH, MR. POLICEMAN, PLEASE COME IN AND HAVE SOME TEA.' THE CHILDREN KNEW IT WAS THE BLOOD MONSTER."

THEY WARNED HER, BUT SHE WOULDN'T BELIEVE THEM. SHE MADE THE BLOOD MONSTER A CUP OF TEA. SHE THOUGHT IT WAS A POLICEMAN.

OH, *GODDAMM*IT! I TELL YOU, IF *EITHER* OF THE KIDS HAVE NIGHTMARES TONIGHT *YOU* CAN DEAL WITH THEM!

I'M NOT GOING TO!

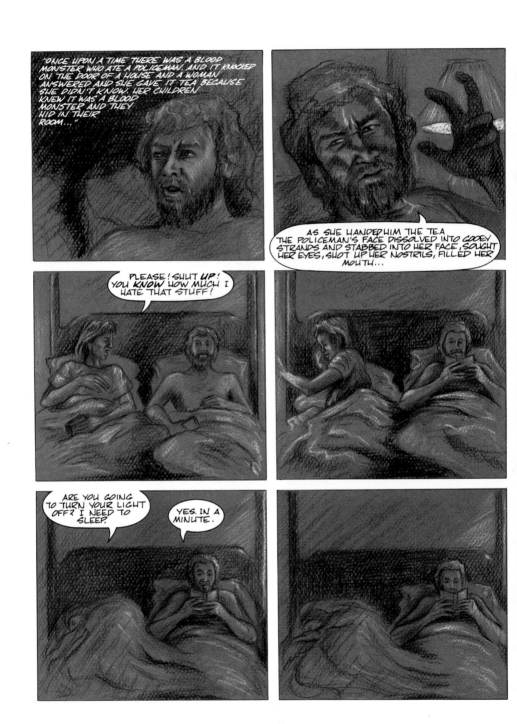

||||||||||||||||||||||||||||||||||||||||||||||||||||||||||||||||||||||||||||

PART EIGHT
THE POEMS AND SONGS

Neil Gaiman is well known for his fiction, introducing the world to Dream, Death, and a whole family of aspects of existence, but what of other methods of writing? Peek into his collections and you'll find hidden in plain sight: poetry. Not just a few lines here and there, rhyming or not, but verse in elegantly named formats like villanelle and sestina.

Neil's work is piercing, bright, and breathless, like his tales. "Locks" is a retelling of "Goldilocks and the Three Bears," told through the heart of a father (growing older and cynical) and a daughter, quirky and imaginative in her determined way. In this poem, he expertly uses repeated word cycles and a turn at the end that is often a distinguishing point in poetry.

A poet uses such things as style and repetition to spin songs, turn words into patterns, to move us out of our chair into the authenticity of the poem. He tells fables, unveils pain and love through shapes unique in his imagination and at the same time accessible to everyone.

One of my favorites is from Neil's book Angels & Visitations. "The Song of the Audience" speaks to the storyteller soul deep in me and ends with: "They make the images. / We give them flesh."

Even his fiction sings poetic. In "The Sound of Her Wings," from The Sandman: The Doll's House, Dream says of his sister, Death:

> I walk by her side, and
> the darkness lifts from
> my soul.
> I walk with her, and I
> hear the gentle beating
> of mighty wings . . .

Indeed, we walk in the many forms of Neil's dreams and delight in the shadows of mighty wings.

—Linda Addison

As if further proof of his versatility was needed, Gaiman has also been known to pen a poem or two. While he makes no claims as to their quality or worth, he does seem fond of the form, seeing it as one more way to express himself, or, on occasion, a challenge to himself, as when he chooses to experiment with certain forms.

As evidenced by this passage from the poetry section of *Adventures in the Dream Trade,* Gaiman seems to be almost bemused by his work in this area, but also seems to realize that some of it has struck a chord with his readers.

> There's poetry, and then there's "poetry," and then there's *poetry.*
>
> And then there's the stuff in this section, which is none of the above. This section is a small ragbag of what might be called occasional verse, if it weren't for occasional verses all over the world writing in to complain.
>
> One day I'll collect together all the real poetry I've written. The stuff that got awards and made it into Year's Best collections. The immortal, deathless words I'm proud to have penned.
>
> None of them are here (well, except possibly for "A Writer's Prayer"). This is the other kind.

Intuition seems to be the tool Gaiman uses to determine whether an idea will become a prose story or a poem. When we asked what can be achieved in poetry that can't be done in prose, his reply seems more about gut instinct than function.

"Sometimes, when it works, you can encapsulate something in the perfect words for it in a way that means that the words and the rhythms combine to make something more than it would have been as prose," he says. "I tried writing 'Daughter Of Owls' as a poem, and it died on the page. I tried reformating 'Cold Colours' as prose for a London anthology that specifically asked, and although it's in print, it doesn't work."

Asked whether he would enjoy having his poems collected all in a single volume, Gaiman replies: "I'd quite like it. The trouble is rounding them up, and some kind of quality control. Quique Alcatena offered to illustrate a book of poems years ago, but even Hill House decided it was a bit too out there."

Of course, some of what we refer to as his poems are actually the lyrics to songs he has written. But in many of those, Gaiman has written the music as well.

"I like writing songs more than I like writing lyrics, I think," he told us. "There's a to-and-fro there—things I wrote as poems sometimes turn into songs (both the sonnets for example). I think 'Post-Mortem On Our Love' was a poem first.

"When I was a teenager I was in bands, and I carried on playing and singing into my early twenties, when I stopped. It's nice to write songs and lyrics, although I have to have someone waiting."

For instance, Gaiman says that the first songs he wrote for the Flash Girls were "just ones that I'd written over the years and would play for friends at parties and so forth."

His poems have appeared in each of his collections, so we will handle them in the same way we did his short stories. Thus, they will be discussed in alphabetical order, and a note will be made of where they appeared.

The key is as follows:

- *Angels & Visitations*: AV
- *Smoke and Mirrors*: SM
- *Adventures in the Dream Trade*: ADT
- *Fragile Things*: FT
- *M Is for Magic*: MM.

Several of these tales have been produced as audio stories, so we'll note that as well. The key for those projects is:

- Warning: Contains Language: WCL
- Speaking in Tongues: SIT
- Telling Tales: TT
- The Neil Gaiman Audio Collection: NGAC

"ALL PURPOSE FOLK SONG (CHILD BALLAD #1)" (1994). ADT

At once an instruction manual and a send-up of folk songs, this piece is, like many of Gaiman's poems, just what its title suggests. Use it the way you want, the refrain even suggests, "You can cross out or forget about the bits that don't apply."

This poem was adapted and sung by the Flash Girls, Lorraine Garland and Emma Bull.

"BANSHEE" (1995). ADT WCL

According to Gaiman, this piece started out as an attempt to write a song that was also a pantoum, "but then it reconfigured into a new form, all of its own." As suggested by its title, it deals with the harbinger of death, the banshee.

"BAY WOLF" (1998). SM

"Bay Wolf" was written at the request of editor Stephen Jones, who called Gaiman looking for a piece for his anthology *Dark Detectives*. At the time the request came in, Gaiman had just finished cowriting the screenplay for the film version of *Beowulf* with Roger Avary, and was struck by the number of people who misheard this as him having written an episode of *Baywatch*. This misunderstanding inspired this retelling of *Beowulf* as a futuristic episode of *Baywatch*, starring the Wolfman, Larry Talbot. Talbot (the Wolfman of Universal Pictures fame) had previously appeared in Gaiman's short story "Only the End of the World Again."

"BOYS AND GIRLS TOGETHER" (2000). TT

A poem about the fundamental differences between boys and girls (Boys "would prefer not to be princes," Gaiman writes, while girls "are secretly princesses."). Writing about this poem (first published in the 2000 anthology *Black Heart, Ivory Bones*) in the liner notes to the *Telling Tales* CD, Gaiman stated, " 'Boys and Girls Together' was written in a hotel room in Boston. It rained outside, and I was certain I was telling the world something very important."

"COLD COLOURS" (1990). AV SM WCL

According to his introduction in *Angels & Visitations*, here Gaiman is trying to say something about computers, black magic, and the London he observed during the late eighties, which he labeled a period of "financial excess and moral bankruptcy." As he also wrote, this piece "didn't seem to be a short story or a novel, so I tried it as a poem, and it did just fine."

"CRAZY HAIR" (2004). NGAC

Read by Gaiman on the *Neil Gaiman Audio Companion,* this delightful little poem deals with eleven-year-old Bonnie's attempt to comb the narrator's "crazy hair," home to dozens of creatures and people, "pools and carousels and water slides," and various other entities.

"THE DAY THE SAUCERS CAME" (2006). FT

Written for Rain Graves's spiderwords.com Web site, "The Day the Saucers Came" deals with alien invasions, zombies, Ragnarok, and various others forms of Armageddon, both large and small. But the person this poem is addressed to did not notice any of this because they were waiting for the poet to call.

"DESERT WIND" (1998). SM

This poem was written at the request of Robin Anders, drummer for the band Boiled in Lead, about one of the group's songs, called "Desert Wind." Telling of a man who has a strange experience while lost in the desert, it calls to mind Gaiman's Sandman tales "Soft Places" and "Exiles."

"THE FAIRY REEL" (2004). FT

Gaiman himself writes of this poem, describing one man's longing to reach the realm of Faerie, "Not much of a poem, really, but enormous fun to read aloud."

"A GIRL NEEDS A KNIFE" (1995). ADT

An edgy (forgive us) poem about a girl and her . . . knife, this was written for the Flash Girls.

"GOING WODWO" (2002). FT

This piece was written for Ellen Datlow and Terri Windling's anthology, *The Green Man.* A wodwo, or wodwose, is a wild man of the woods, a half-man, half-animal spirit of the forests that appears often in English poetry.

"THE HERRING SONG" (1993)

A song from the debut album from the Flash Girls, *The Return of Pansy Smith and Violet Jones,* this piece, about a woman with a fondness for herring, was cowritten by Gaiman and his personal assistant, Lorraine Garland.

"THE HIDDEN CHAMBER" (2005). FT

This piece was written at the request of "the Nancys Kilpatrick and Holder" for their anthology, *Outsiders.* Gaiman responded by writing a Bluebeard poem set in the almost empty house he was staying in at the time.

"HOW TO WRITE LONGFELLOW'S HIAWATHA" (2001). ADT

The title says it all.

"INSTRUCTIONS" (2000). SM FT SIT

One of Gaiman's personal favorites, this is literally a set of instructions to follow should you find yourself in a fairy tale. The author is in the habit of sending out stories, poems, and sometimes even whole books (*Melinda*) as his "holiday card," and "Instructions" was among those works.

"INVENTING ALADDIN" (2003) FT

Ending with the phrase "We save our lives in such unlikely ways," this poem tells of Scheherazade's creation of the tale "Aladdin and the Magic Lamp."

"LOCKS" (1999). FT

Gaiman's riff on "Goldilocks," written for his then two-year-old daughter, Maddy.

"LUTHER'S VILLANELLE" (1989). AV

Written as a birthday present for Bryan Talbot, this piece was loosely inspired by the comic Talbot wrote and drew, *The Adventures of Luther Arkwright,* considered by many to be the first British graphic novel.

Per Wikipedia, a villanelle is

> a poetic form which entered English-language poetry in the 1800s from the imitation of French models. A villanelle has only two rhyme sounds. The first and third lines of the first stanza are rhyming refrains that alternate as the third line in each successive stanza and form a couplet at the close. A villanelle is nineteen lines long, consisting of five tercets and one concluding quatrain.

In 1991, artist Ali Clark illustrated an adaptation of the poem for *The Adventures of Luther Arkwright: The Crystal Palace Exhibition of 1991.* Three years later, it was adapted again by arist Tommy Berg for *Wiindows: The Anthology of the Bizarre.*

"A MEANINGFUL DIALOGUE" (2001)

A song from the 2001 Flash Girls CD, *Play Each Morning Wild Queen.* All we have to say is, you know a relationship is probably on the skids when your lover shrieks:

> *I've got my fingers in my ears I'm going lalalalalalalalalala,*
> *I can't hear you*
> *I got my fingers in my ears I'm going lalalalalalalalalala*
> *Going la la la la.*

"MY LIFE" (2002). FT

This "odd little monologue" was written to accompany a photograph of a sock monkey, one of two hundred photos contained in a book called, oddly enough, *Sock Monkeys: 200 Out of 1863.*

"NEIL'S THANK YOU POME" (2001). ADT

A poem Gaiman wrote to express his joy upon receiving a copy of Diana Wynne Jones's *Hexwood*, which the author dedicated to him.

"THE OLD WARLOCK'S REVERIE: A PANTOUM" (1995). ADT

Again looking to Wikipedia, the pantoum

is a form of poetry similar to a villanelle. It is composed of a series of quatrains; the second and fourth lines of each stanza are repeated as the first and third lines of the next. This pattern continues for any number of stanzas, except for the final stanza, which differs in the repeating pattern. The first and third lines of the last stanza are the second and fourth of the penultimate; the first line of the poem is the last line of the final stanza, and the third line of the first stanza is the second of the final. Ideally, the meaning of lines shifts when they are repeated although the words remain exactly the same: this can be done by shifting punctuation, punning, or simply recontextualizing.

This piece relates an older wizard's reflections on his youth, and one of his lovers, a fellow shape-changer.

In 1997, artist Guy Davis adapted the poem for the comic book anthology *Negative Burn* issue 50.

"PERSONAL THING" (2001). ADT

Written for the Flash Girls, this piece tells of a lover's pride and regret, summed up by the final words of its refrain: "I want you back but I'm too proud to say it out loud—it's a personal thing."

"POST-MORTEM ON OUR LOVE" (1993). ADT AV

Another song for the Flash Girls, this poem tells of someone reflecting on the wreckage of a love affair gone wrong.

"READING THE ENTRAILS: A RONDEL" (1997). SM

Per Wikipedia, a rondel

is a variation of the rondeau in which the first two lines of the first stanza are repeated as the last two lines of the second and third stanzas, thus a rhyme scheme of ABba abAB abbaA(B). (Sometimes only the first line of the poem is repeated at the end.)

The rondeau is a form of verse also used in English language poetry. It makes use of refrains, repeated according to a certain stylized pattern. It was customarily regarded as a challenge to arrange for these refrains to contribute to the meaning of the poem in as succinct and poignant a manner as possible.

The lines repeated in this piece, written for Lawrence Schmiel, who asked Gaiman for a poem to introduce his anthology of stories about foretelling the future, are:

They'll call it chance, or luck, or call it Fate—
The card and stars that tumble as they will.

"QUEEN OF KNIVES" (1995). SM

Gaiman says of this piece, "This, like my graphic novel *Mr. Punch,* is close enough to the truth that I have had, on occasion, to explain to some of my relatives that it didn't really happen. Well, not like that, anyway."

"THE SEA CHANGE" (1995). SM SIT

Like several of his short stories, "The Sea Change" was inspired by a Lisa Snellings statue, and by the memory of a beach at Portsmouth from his childhood. Gaiman was writing the last installment of The Sandman, "The Tempest," when this was written, so bits of that play can be found in here as well.

"THE SONG OF THE AUDIENCE" (1993). AV WCL

This poem seems to be commenting on the symbiosis/synergy between a creator and his audience. Not quite as cynical as the Rolling Stones's "It's Only Rock and Roll," but close.

"SONNET" (2001). ADT

A sonnet about sonnets.

"SONNET IN THE DARK" (1993)

Another collaboration between the songwriting team of Gaiman and Garland from *The Return of Pansy Smith and Violet Jones.*

"TEA AND CORPSES" (1993)

Another song from the 1993 Flash Girls album *The Return of Pansy Smith and Violet Jones,* it tells of a couple who work out their romantic problems by poisoning each other.

"VAMPIRE SESTINA" (1989). AV SM

Gaiman describes this as the only piece of vampire fiction he's ever completed.

Once again looking to Wikipedia, a sestina is

a highly structured poem consisting of six six-line stanzas followed by a tercet, for a total of thirty-nine lines. The same set of six words ends the lines of each of the six-line stanzas, but in a different order each time; if we number the first stanza's lines 123456, then the words ending the second stanza's lines appear in the order 615243, then 364125, then 532614, then 451362, and finally 246531.

"VIRUS" (1990). AV SM

Of this piece, written for David Barrett's *Digital Dreams,* a computer fiction anthology, Gaiman writes, "I don't play many computer games: when I do, I notice they tend to take up areas of my head. Blocks fall, or little men run and jump, behind my eyelids as I sleep. Mostly I'd lose, even when playing with my mind. This came from that."

"THE WHITE ROAD" (1995). SM WCL

This long poem, which first appeared in *Ruby Slippers, Golden Tears,* was inspired by variants on the tale "Mr. Fox" Gaiman found in *The Penguin Book of English Folktales,* edited by Neil Phillip. Here Mr. Fox's fiancée recounts all the horrors she saw him commit in a dream, including the dismemberment of his victims. At the end she throws down a bloody digit, or a finger, which proves that everything she said she saw while "dreaming" was actually true.

"A WRITER'S PRAYER" (1999). ADT

A plea to a higher power to be a better writer, it could be dissected and turned into a list of rules for good writing, boiling down to: "Don't overwrite, don't underwrite, and be brave."

"A Writer's Prayer" is another of those works Gaiman has sent as his "holiday card" over the years.

"YETI" (1995)

Another song written by Gaiman for the Flash Girls, which appeared on their 1995 CD, *Maurice and I*. The cover to this CD, as well as that of *The Return of Pansy Smith and Violet Jones,* contains an illustration by frequent Gaiman collaborator Michael Zulli.

TRIVIA

• The epigraph to The Sandman collection *The Wake* is "The Bridge of Fire," from poet James Elroy Flecker (1884–1915). The sailor girl "Jim" misquotes from another Flecker poem, "The Golden Road to Samarkand," in "Hob's Leviathan," from issue 53 of *The Sandman*. According to Gaiman, the play that poem appears in, *Flecker's Hassan,* was an important inspiration for the Sandman story "Ramadan," from issue 50.

THE QUOTABLE GAIMAN

Although I put several poems into *Smoke and Mirrors*, my last collection, I had originally planned that this collection would be prose only. I eventually decided to put the poems in anyway, mostly because I like this one so much. If you're one of the people who doesn't like poems, you may console yourself with the knowledge that they are, like this introduction, free. The book would cost you the same with or without them, and nobody pays me anything extra to put them in.

—Introduction, *Fragile Things*

||||||||||||||||||||||||||||||||||||||||||||||||||||||||||||||||||||||||||

P A R T   N I N E

THE SCRIPTS

Not too long ago, Neil and I were on the phone together having a friendly debate as to whether or not I'm a writer. Neil's point was that I'm a director who writes out of necessity, just as he's a writer who occasionally directs out of necessity. According to Neil, he will never really be a director, and I will likely never really be a writer. Perhaps this is why our collaborations are so rewarding to the both of us. I conceded the debate and agreed with him because of one important truism: My writings are usually just blueprints for what will ultimately be a finished film—a means to an end. Then, not a week after the conclusion of our debate, I experienced a terrible tragedy which plunged me into the darkest period of my life. At the nadir of my despair, when I wanted to run away from the world out of grief and shame, Neil called me up and suggested that there was one thing I could do to alleviate my grief—he suggested that I write. So I did. And it's only now, as I write this, that I realize that his prescription for my misery was the only thing that could have lifted me during that darkest of times. Writing isn't a means to an end, it's the act of peeking into one's own soul—it's a process of discovery. None of my director colleagues could have given me the same insight. It took a writer. It took a friend.
—Roger Avary, February 18, 2008,
Ojai, California

Over the course of his career, Neil Gaiman has written in a wide variety of creative mediums, each of which is a separate discipline following a unique process. Writing novels and short stories—and oftentimes, nonfiction—is usually solitary work, but the greatest benefit of such endeavors is the certainty that (aside from editorial suggestions and influence) the author is entirely in control of the outcome.

Comics (and their younger yet somehow more mature brother, the graphic novel) are a far more collaborative art form. The writer colludes with the pencil and ink artists, the colorist, the letterer, the cover artist, and the editors to create a single work of art. The dynamic of such a creation is dependent upon any number of factors, including talent, personalities, and levels of success. From the beginning of his career, Neil Gaiman has shown enough talent—and achieved enough success—that he has usually been able not only to write whatever he wished and see it published, but exert enough influence to be certain his vision ended up on the page. Of course, anyone paying attention will note that many of Gaiman's projects have been with artists, such as Dave McKean, with whom he has formed fruitful collaborative partnerships. But that doesn't eliminate the fact that when working with other artists this author has enough influence to essentially control the final product if he so desires.

By and large, if you have a team able to complete a comic book, enough money to pay for printing, and the force of will to see it through, anyone can publish a comic book of their own. Turn the control of that same project over to an existing comic book company, and the fate of your work might be less certain. But when Neil Gaiman wants to do a comic book, it's going to happen. (There were exceptions during the early days of his career—things he pitched to DC, many of which are mentioned in these pages—but otherwise this is a truism.)

If Neil wants to write a novel, a short story, a poem, a graphic novel, or a comic book, he can, and readers will have the opportunity to, and the pleasure of reading it.

But, alas, then there's Hollywood.

Children and teenagers and other hopeful sorts around the world dream of going to Hollywood, of becoming famous actors or directors. Some of them, poor souls, even dream of becoming Hollywood screenwriters, of putting words in the mouths of actors on television and in film. But screenwriters and novelists are different breeds. They may be cousins, certainly, but the average working novelist seems to find satisfaction only when the work appears in print and ends up in the hands of a reader. A working screenwriter can make an excellent living writing their own screenplays (or, often, rewriting somebody else's) without ever having a film actually made. Even if a film is made, chances are good that the script has been rewritten by two or three other people, and changed by producers and the director, and arbitration is necessary to determine whose names will appear on screen as the "authors" of the screenplay.

Most screenplays end up on a shelf somewhere, the property of the studio that commissioned or purchased it, never to be seen by the public in any form. So, writing screenplays—even earning a good living doing so—can translate into writing not for readers but for an audience of dust mites.

Not always, of course.

But even in the best case scenario, the vision of the screenwriter cannot remain undiluted. The director and producers demand changes based on budget or whimsy or their own creative vision. Actors alter lines, or deliver them differently from what the writer had imagined. The set design changes the atmosphere completely. The performances are lacking or the music overwhelming. The screenwriter has no control over the finished product, either in story or in quality. This is the nature of film and television.

Even for someone with the success, magical talent, and reputation of Neil Gaiman.

Gaiman has been writing TV and film scripts in various forms for most of his career, yet the nature of that business means that, unlike the other mediums in which he works, the audience gets to see only a fraction of the work he's done. The result, of course, is that to the general populace, "screenwriter" is not the first thing to come into one's mind when Neil's name comes up.

Disappointed with the quality of the BBC's production of his original scripts for *Neverwhere,* Gaiman wrote the novel of the same name. Yet, in spite of the low-budget production, much of the Gaiman magic shines through in the quirky dialogue and characterizations and wild fantasy of the BBC miniseries.

As a gun-for-hire on the English translation for Miyazaki's *Princess Mononoke,* Gaiman went through a grueling process with producers and directors, attempting to keep the original creator's message and story intact and simultaneously fulfill demands for simplification. But this was not a Gaiman story to begin with.

Perhaps the screen work he has written that has been least tampered with was "Day of the Dead," the episode Gaiman wrote for *Babylon 5.* And yet, left alone or not, the script is still a story set in a universe he did not invent, featuring characters he did not create.

For *Mirrormask,* Gaiman collaborated with director Dave McKean from the beginning, and on *Beowulf* he wrote the script with Roger Avary, both incredibly talented creators in their own right. Both films are wonderful achievements of which the writers can be very proud, and both served to elevate Gaiman another rung up the Hollywood ladder.

For an author whose name has become an adjective ("Gaimanesque") to describe dark, magical, sometimes whimsical, emotionally resonant storytelling, Gaiman has yet to see a full-length work of film or television produced from one of his scripts that truly captures those qualities. Fortunately, we have the 2003 short film he wrote and directed, *A Short Film About John Bolton.* How ironic that, with the exception of that short film (Gaiman's sole directorial effort), the film that is the most Gaimanesque—as of this writing—is the charming adaptation of *Stardust* written by Jane Goldman and director Matthew Vaughn.

With Gaiman's star still rising in Hollywood, driven by *Stardust* and *Beowulf* and the upcoming Henry Selick adaptation of *Coraline,* momentum is building that should allow the author to at last bring his signature storytelling voice to film undiluted. A new film version of *Neverwhere,* scripted by Gaiman, may be on the horizon. And there has long been talk of the author writing and directing an adaptation of his Sandman spin-off series *Death: The High Cost of Living.*

Time will tell. One thing is certain, however. Hollywood can only benefit from letting Gaiman be Gaiman, by capturing the magic that has made him one of the best-loved fantasists of the modern age.

NEVERWHERE

(1996)

Please see the chapter on *NeverWhere* in Part Five: The Novels.

PRINCESS MONONOKE

(1997; U.S. VERSION, 1999)

In 1998, Neil Gaiman was engaged by the Miramax and Disney studios to adapt the screenplay for Hayao Miyazaki's new feature, *Mononoke-hime*, for the English language–dubbed version, *Princess Mononoke*. On the heels of the ongoing interest in adapting Sandman into a feature film, which had thus far led to naught, this project marked Gaiman's official entrance into the American and international film industry.

It was, however, a less than harmonious experience, through no fault of Gaiman. Though *Princess Mononoke* isn't a significant part of Gaiman's creative canon, his involvement indeed launched his film career, and is hence deserving of attention and some analysis. It should also be noted that *Princess Mononoke* is compatible with much of Gaiman's own work. Like *Black Orchid*, *Princess Mononoke* is essentially "a pacifist fable," to use Gaiman's term. Essentially, the film is an ecological parable, an adult fairy tale deeply rooted in mythology and fused with invented elements concocted by its creator (Miyazaki). Thus, the selection of Gaiman for the task of converting Miyazaki's Japanese script to an English translation that would preserve the poetry of the language was a well-informed choice, grounded in Gaiman's oeuvre.

Hayao Miyazaki's *Mononoke-hime (Princess Mononoke)* was the seventh solo anime feature by the most internationally revered of all Japanese anime directors and manga artists since Osamu Tezuka (creator of *Mighty Atom/Astro Boy*, etc.). Building upon the bedrock of his prior features—*Lupin III: Castle of Cagliostro* (1979); *Nausicaä of the Valley of the Wind* (1984); *Laputa: Castle in the Sky* (1986); *My Neighbor Totoro* (1988); *Kiki's Delivery Service* (1989); and *Porco rosso* (1992)—Miyazaki conceived *Princess Mononoke* as his most ambitious ecological fantasy fable to date.

Essentially a *jidaigeki* (period drama) in the style of many popular manga, anime, and live-action *daikaiju-eiga* (giant monster movies) set in the middle ages (e.g., *The Magic Serpent*, the *Majin* series, etc.), *Princess Mononoke*—which takes its name from a Japanese term for a nonhuman elemental deity/being in nature—is set in the late Muromachi period of Japan, at the end of its medieval era. Miyazaki's exotic, complex parable defies synopsizing, just as it defied distillation to the dualistic "good versus evil" scenario Miramax/Disney hoped to offer in dubbed form to family audiences.

A young prince named Ashitaka is exiled from his village after he is infected by a virulent contagion contracted from a monstrous boar he had killed to save his village. Seeking the source of the disease, he stumbles into a simmering conflict between a mining, iron-forging militaristic community named Irontown, led by Lady Eboshi Gozen, and the supernatural beings that guard the surrounding natural environment, led by the feral teenage girl San, the Princess Mononoke, and the wolf goddess, Moro, and her offspring, who raised San from infancy. The struggle between these feral forest guardians and the technologically advanced human village ravaging the landscape for raw materials has already upset the balance of nature, causing the infection carried by the diseased boar (its catalyst an iron bullet) and now spreading in Ashitaka's blood. At the heart of this war is the mysterious and magnificent Forest Spirit—by day, it is the elk-like Shishigami, by night the humanoid giant Daidarabocchi. The Forest Spirit's head is coveted by those who believe it can make them immortal. The mercenary monk Jogi, eager to collect the ransom on the creature's head, convinces Lady Eboshi to decapitate the Spirit when it is most vulnerable—at twilight, midtransformation between its day and nocturnal forms.

She decapitates the being, which does not kill it. The headless forest god instead transforms into a malignant, cancerous magmalike ooze that envelopes the countryside, threatening to consume the forest, Irontown, and all living beings.

Mononoke-hime was the most expensive anime feature ever produced. It debuted in Japan on July 12, 1997, and enjoyed instant acclaim and phenomenal box-office success. It was, in fact, the highest-grossing movie in Japanese history until the opening of *Titanic* several months later, and it remained the most popular theatrically released anime feature ever, until it was eclipsed by Miyazaki's subsequent anime features, *Spirited Away* (2001) and *Howl's Moving Castle* (2004). It was also a major box-office hit in almost every other world market, throughout Asia and Europe and elsewhere—except North America.

Princess Mononoke did not open in the United States until its debut at the New York Film Festival on September 26, 1999. It opened afterward in select cities on October 29, and in November 1999, with a rather lackluster campaign, nevertheless enjoying extended runs in those venues until it was withdrawn in early 2000. Bypassing first-run mainstream theaters, *Mononoke* was instead inexplicably dumped into short (sometimes daylong) runs in third- and fourth-place venues, matinees, and colleges—despite rave reviews and placement on many top ten lists (Roger Ebert placed the movie sixth on his top ten movies of 1999; other U.S. critics ranked it similarly). Disney executives subsequently complained about the film's poor box office showing, fulfilling a self-imposed prophecy of failure.

It is hard to reconcile the numbers: According to numerous online sources (including Wikipedia), total admissions for *Mononoke* in Japan were over 13 million, and more people saw it in France than in America (over half a million in France, less than 470,000 in the United States). During this same period, Warner Bros. opened the first *Pokemon* feature theatrically, to record-breaking box office, paving the way for the wider release of *Mononoke*—which never followed.

How could as powerful a corporation as Disney/Miramax so resoundingly fail to sell the film? The studio's planned release of the rest of the Miyazaki and Studio Ghibli (Miyazaki's anime studio, a body of work including the work of other anime directors) on DVD and video was similarly compromised: By 1999, the studio had only released one English-language title on video, *Kiki's Delivery Service,* sans fanfare, and featuring a trailer for *Laputa: Castle in the Sky*—a release that did not follow. The videocassette release of *Princess Mononoke* was inexplicably botched, announced and delayed no less than four times in early 2000. The DVD release was further delayed, from August to December 2000, and both VHS and DVD packaging downplayed the film's imagery, featuring only a drab picture of a sword-wielding Ashitaki, suggesting the film might be a fantasy pastiche of *Star Wars.*

Whatever the reasons for Disney's initial cold feet about their obligation to release the Miyazaki/Studio Ghibli catalog, everything had changed by 2002, thanks to the active participation of John Lassiter of Pixar, who took it upon himself to promote the Miyazaki canon within Disney, followed by the enormous critical success of the limited release of Miyazaki's *Spirited Away.* The film eventually earned the coveted Academy Award for Best Animated Feature, despite the studio's apparent indifference. Only after the Oscar win was *Spirited Away* rolled out for wider theatrical release. Soon afterward, the initial DVD release of three titles from the Miyazaki/Studio Ghibli catalog was launched with proper promotion and great success.

What happened in the two-and-a-half years between the Japanese and American debuts of *Mononoke*? This is a point of much contention, though it must be noted that Miramax/Disney originally intended to treat *Mononoke* as many U.S. distributors before them had handled import features, especially those targeting general audiences. This was traditional. As far back as showman Joseph Levine's acquisition of the Japanese *Gojira* (in 1955, and released in the United States in 1956 as *Godzilla, King of the Monsters*) and the Italian *Le Fatiche di Ercole* (in 1958, and released in the United States in 1960 as *Hercules*), import fare intended for wide release to family audiences was shorn of any adult content, via edits and dubbing.

The first anime features from Japan to make it to American theaters had been extensively recut and dubbed, often to remove religious content as well as to tone down violence. Buddhist mythology was shorn of its context in the U.S. release of *Saiyu-ki* (1960), which was adapted by Osamu Tezuka from his own popular manga classic to become *Alakazam the Great* (1961), with voices and singing by Frankie Avalon, Jonathan Winters, and other name stars further altering the original work to suit children. Miramax and its subsidiary Dimension Films habitually re-edited and dubbed imports like the Jackie Chan films, often imposing significant cuts and alterations, claiming such changes were "necessary" to make the films palatable/presentable to American audiences.

Initially planning such treatment for *Mononoke,* including cuts for time (the complete feature runs 134 minutes) and violence, to earn a PG rating rather than the more restrictive PG-13, Miramax/Disney quickly drew the ire of Miyazaki, who refused to permit such manhandling of his epic. Few of Miyazaki's anime (features and TV episodes) had landed U.S. venues prior to the Miramax/Disney acquisition of the Miyazaki/Studio Ghibli catalog. *Nausicaä of the Valley of the Wind* (1984) had been shorn of thirty-two minutes and crudely dubbed by New World Pictures for a 1985 theatrical release, and on video as *Warriors of the Wind.*

Subsequently, however, there came a very limited release of a complete, English-dubbed version of *Laputa: Castle in the Sky,* and a direct-to-video release of *My Neighbor Totoro* by 20th Century Fox, likewise intact and dubbed nicely. Miyazaki had no intention of allowing his work to be altered in any significant way, and his contractual arrangements with Miramax/Disney protected that right. Conceding to necessity, Miramax/Disney contracted staff writers to see to the translation for dubbing a definitive English-language version, working from the literal translation from the Japanese original. Eventually it was decided to employ freelancer Neil Gaiman to preserve (and perhaps impose) a more poetic reading of the script. Though Gaiman had not yet scripted a feature film, the leap of faith seemed justifiable, given his body of published work and its growing popularity. The studio was sparing no expense in the vocal talent involved: Billy Crudup (voicing Ashitaka), Claire Danes (as San), Gillian Anderson (Moro), Minnie Driver (Lady Eboshi), Billy Bob Thornton (Jigo), and others were engaged, lending considerable talent and celebrity weight to the dubbing process.

To begin with, much of the cultural context of *Mononoke* was simply impossible to communicate to the targeted "average" American audience. Sans any knowledge of the Japanese history the film is rooted in, American viewers would undoubtedly take *Mononoke* as an out-and-out fantasy. Set in the Muromachi period, historically the transition phase between Japan's medieval Dark Ages and the early modern period, as mining, forging, blacksmithing, and crude firearms transformed the culture, *Mononoke* was arguably as grounded in reality as Akira Kurosawa's live-action classics *The Seven Samurai* and *Yojimbo* (set roughly during the same transitional period).

Furthermore, the young protagonist, Ashitaka, is portrayed as the last prince of an exiled renegade faction of the Emishi, an actual tribe that successfully resisted the rule of the Japanese emperors for centuries; after their defeat by the Yamato clan, which subsequently ruled the empire, the Emishi retreated to a remote corner of Japan's largest island, Honshu, until they were eventually absorbed into Japanese society by A.D. 1300. Furthermore, much of Miyazaki's rich invented mythology defied translation, and the expected confusion of American audiences with the many Japanese names resulted in the simplification of key elements—for instance, the night guise of the Forest Spirit (itself a rough translation of Shishigami, which has no literal translation in English), Daidarabocchi, was changed to "the Nightwalker" for the dubbed version. "Jibashiri" also has no correlation in English: the rough approximation of "Mercenary" was used in its place, though this only added to the confused nature of Jigo's character for most American viewers, who remained unsure just what Jigo was supposed to be. Typical in such transitions, character names were changed, too: Jiko Bou became Jigo, and so on. In other cases, cultural orientation resulted in confusion that simply was allowed to stand: As he leaves his village after his self-exile, Ashitaka is bid farewell by only one person, a young woman named Kaya, cited as his "little sister." As Miyazaki noted in subsequent interviews, Kaya was actually Ashitaka's fiancée, and the line "little sister" was intended as a term of endearment.

This may all seem very arcane, but in a narrative as steeped in ancient history, culture, and lore as *Mononoke,* every alteration contributed to a cumulative impact on the whole. To many attentive critics and fans, that impact was negative, obfuscating and diminishing Miyazaki's complex, truly adult eco-parable. Furthermore, the growing American audience devoted to manga and anime were passionate about the minutiae of, and fidelity to, the original Japanese-language film, so much so that when Miramax/Disney announced the pending August 2000 DVD release of *Princess Mononoke* in the English-dubbed-only version, a fan-propelled letter and Internet campaign gained such momentum that the studio postponed the DVD release for months (December) until the release could also include the original Japanese version with English subtitles.

Adapting another author's work is always a difficult process under the best of circumstances. The requirements of lip-synching, timing, and delivery along with these extensive cultural issues weighed heavy on the process. Gaiman wrestled with all of this throughout the writing and rewriting of his adaptation, frustrated by the studio's frequent requests to alter material due to their own reworking of Gaiman's initial drafts. Each revision was subsequently retooled "by committee," after Gaiman's delivery of a coherent draft, often incorporating elements that had been discarded earlier.

In an e-mail to the authors, Gaiman explained the final steps:

> After I wrote the scripts and they were approved, and after Gillian Anderson's dialogue from my script was recorded, someone else wrote a new script, which was meant to have been a clean up on my script to make sure it

matched the mouth movements. But he didn't like my script, so went back to the subtitles and wrote a script based on them, which was what they re-corded, without clearing it with me (at the point they approved my script I was cut out of the process). Then it got booed off [the screen] when it was previewed. THEN, to salvage something from the wreckage, I was pulled back in, allowed to talk to the director the first time, and the director got to read the various scripts for the first time, and we had to try and put as much as we could of the original script back in. But we couldn't re-record the whole thing (which is where things like the "Little Sister" or the description of the guns as "rifles" come from).[1]

Unfortunately, many critical of the English-language dub blamed Gaiman for its erratic quality. In the end, he was completely unsatisfied with the script eventu-ally used for the final dubbing sessions, feeling it represented neither his nor Mi-yazaki's voice or vision, or their best work.

Still, *Princess Mononoke* opened many doors for him. His diplomatic handling of a potentially volatile studio situation, his aplomb in dealing with the politics of the Miramax/Disney bureaucracy, and his persistent attempt to deliver his best work despite resistance meant his credit on *Mononoke* was ultimately rewarding, however compromised the final product.

||||||||||||||||||||||||||||||||||||||||||||||||||||||||||||||||||||||

DAY OF THE DEAD
(BABYLON 5)

(1998)

This script represents another example of Gaiman working with someone else's characters, themes, and situations, and doing it well. This time, he was playing in the sandbox known as *Babylon 5,* a science fiction television series cre-ated by his good friend J. Michael Straczynski (who went on to write numerous comic books, and has since found a great deal of success as a screenwriter).

Babylon 5 was an epic project, designed by Straczynski from the outset to run for five years, telling many different stories all contained under the umbrella of one major story arc. Set in the latter half of the twenty-third century, the show centered on a space station called, you guessed it, *Babylon 5.* Uniquely positioned in space, the station became a focal point for stories scrutinizing politics, diplomacy, conflict, intrigue, and religious fanaticism. Many described the series as an unusually complex novel for television.

The show's pilot, which appeared in February 1993, set the stage for the regular series, which began its run in January 1994, running, as planned, for five full seasons. Straczynski reportedly set a number of goals for the show. In his mind the show had to be both good science fiction and good television, achieving for science fiction television what *Hill Street Blues* had done for police dramas. It would also observe strict budgetary restrictions, even as it strove to look unlike anything ever seen before on TV.

It was Straczynski's ultimate goal, however, to take science fiction seriously; to present stories and characters that would appeal to mature audiences; and to incorporate real science but keep the characters at the center of the story. He seems to have succeeded, as the series went on to snag two Hugo awards for best dramatic presentation, and a pair of Emmys for its varied makeup and innovative special effects.

In order to achieve his vision, Straczynski maintained tight control over his baby; *Babylon 5* was largely written by its creator, who scripted every episode in the third and fourth seasons. Other writers to have contributed scripts to the show included Peter David, D. C. Fontana, David Gerrold, and a fellow named Neil Gaiman.

Appearing in the fifth season of the series, the episode (a break from the show's continuing story arc, though some events do have relevance to the rest of the series) tells of an alien religious festival in which the dead actually reappear for one night every two centuries or so. This celebration is different from prior celebrations, however, because it affects not only the alien race, but also many residents of the Babylon 5 station.

Gaiman seized on the Jewish concept of an *eruv,* a shared physical domain that allows Jews to carry objects from one household to another on the Jewish Sabbath, to drive this powerful story. Rabbinic literature records the development of the *eruv* as a legal device that allows Jews in a community to merge their separate domains into one shared domain, thus allowing for easier travel on the Sabbath. The idea of sharing distinct domains for a religious purpose piqued Gaiman's interest, who expanded upon it a bit by asking the classic writer's question: "What if?" What if one could "borrow" a domain far from their home? And, what if this merging of domains was made manifest in a literal and physical sense? The episode poses the following scenario: an alien race known as the Brakiri symbolically buy a portion of Babylon 5 for a night, allowing them to celebrate their holiday, which involves the dead coming back to visit with the living. These visits seem to have a purpose mainly in putting the living's minds to rest about troubling events of the past.

PEOPLE, PLACES, AND THINGS

BABYLON 5. A space station in neutral space, it's more or less central to all five of the different alliances, human or alien. To travel to one or the other, you're forced to pass through this sector of space. Babylon 5 has been created as a way station for travelers, statesmen, emissaries, traders, refugees, and other, less savory, characters. Five miles long, Babylon 5 is divided into separate, discrete sections that rotate at differing speeds to provide different gravities to accommodate those who come to the station.

THE BRAKIRI. A significant number of this "night dwelling" race reside on Babylon 5. Approximately once every two centuries, a comet approaches the Brakiri home world, signaling the Day of the Dead, during which, for one night, people can interact with those who've died. On this particular occasion the Brakiri arrange with the authorities on the station to "buy" a portion of Babylon 5 for a night in order to celebrate this solemn holiday. Those who live in this section of the station experience visits from the dead, whether they be Brakiri or not.

PRESIDENT JOHN SHERIDAN. A key character in the series with an awesome destiny to fulfill, he plays more of a supporting role in this episode. He does receive a message (written into the script by Straczynski at the request of Gaiman) from one of the dead, however, through Captain Lochley. Lochley passes along the following, purporting to be a message from the deceased ambassador Kosh Naranek (Ardwright Chamberlain): "When the long night comes, return to the end of the beginning." This shapes Sheridan's future decision to travel to the site of the last battle of the Shadow War, where the Shadows, Vorlons, and remaining First Ones, with Lorien, left the galaxy.

CAPTAIN ELIZABETH LOCHLEY. The commander of the station, Lochley is a hard-edged, no-nonsense type of leader. As teenagers, Lochley and her friend Zoe spent much of their time strung out on drugs, living in squalor. Zoe eventually committed suicide, something that has haunted Lochley her entire life (Zoe's suicide had been so traumatic for Lochley that she uses the phrase "Zoe's dead" as a password). After Zoe's suicide Lochley put her old life behind her and entered the military.

MICHAEL GARIBALDI. The station's security chief, he has a troubled past, bouncing from position to position and trying to overcome alcoholism. Garibaldi is a smart-aleck, always ready with a quip, but given to bouts of self-doubt and introspection when alone. In this episode, Chief Garibaldi is visited by a woman named Dodger, with whom he almost had a romantic fling three years before.

REBO AND ZOOTY. Famous throughout the galaxy, comedians Rebo and Zooty have starred in a variety of shows and movies. Zooty (whose catchphrase is "Zoot! Zoot!") speaks via a small handheld device. Both are serious students of their craft, having studied Minbari, Narn, and myriad other races' forms of humor. Their visit to Babylon 5, which coincides with the Day of the Dead, causes quite a stir.

LONDO. The representative of the Centauri republic. A war hero in his younger days, he has since grown decadent and indulgent. Londo can often be found in one of the station's bars or casinos, drinking himself into a stupor. In this episode, Londo has a touching encounter with his lost love, Adira Tyree.

LENNIER. This episode is significant to Babylon 5 aficionados because its events foreshadow Lennier's eventual betrayal of President Sheridan. In the episode, the Minbari is confronted by the ghost of Mr. Morden, the human who worked with the Shadows. Lennier, who had returned from training hoping to speak to a spirit as part of the alien religious observance, makes the mistake of seeking counsel from Morden. The traitor predicts that Lennier will one day betray the Rangers.

TRIVIA

- In 1998, Gaiman's original script for this episode was published as a trade paperback by Minneapolis's Dreamhaven Books, which is run by the estimable Greg Ketter. A portion of the profits from the book went to the Comic Book Legal Defense Fund. The heavily footnoted script contains scenes not actually filmed, and some which were filmed but later cut. It was introduced by J. Michael Straczynski, and sported color art by John Berkey. Dreamhaven has also worked with Gaiman on several other projects, including the collection *Angels & Visitations*, and three audio presentations, including the cleverly titled *Warning: Contains Language*.

- The episode contains a reference to the well-known "fact" that all of Emily Dickinson's poetry is capable of being sung to the tune of "Yellow Rose of Texas." One of the examples Dodger sings is:

My candle burns at both ends;
It will not last the night;
But ah, my foes, and oh, my friends—
It gives a lovely light!

It's been pointed out that this isn't Dickinson; it's actually "First Fig" from Edna St. Vincent Millay.

- The episode featured Penn and Teller, who portrayed the famous comedians Rebo and Zooty. Famous fantasist Harlan Ellison provided the robotic voice of Zooty, portrayed by Teller, who characteristically remained silent while on-screen. Ellison's voice issues forth from a voice box that Zooty carries with him (Gaiman actually did not write it this way, but the casting of Teller dictated this change).

- All the people who returned in the episode had suffered untimely or violent deaths: Morden was decapitated on Londo's orders ("Into the Fire"); Adira was poisoned ("Interludes and Examinations"); Zoe committed suicide; and Dodger was killed in combat ("GROPOS").

THE QUOTABLE GAIMAN

Rebo and Zooty were played by Penn and Teller, who are my two favorite magicians in the whole world. I danced around the room when I'd heard they'd been cast, only I danced very quietly, as it was a hotel room in Lucia, Italy, and my wife was fast asleep.

—Annotated "Day of the Dead" script book
(Minneapolis: Dreamhaven Press, 1998)

THE QUOTABLE STRACZYNSKI

When asked how much he got involved in outside scripts:

It varies, I get involved to different degrees with different writers; with Neil, it was more "What do you want to write?" He noodled around with some ideas, ran one past me that he liked, and I liked it . . . he asked for a truckload of scripts for reference, picked the characters he wanted to use, researched them, we talked on the phone and via email a number of times as he refined his ideas further, then wrote the script. I tucked and nipped a little here and there, but pretty much left it alone.

—The Lurker's Guide to *Babylon 5* Web site

||||||||||||||||||||||||||||||||||||||||||||||||||||||||||||||||||

A SHORT FILM ABOUT
JOHN BOLTON

(2003)

Those familiar with Gaiman's work probably know the name John Bolton, most likely because he illustrated part of Gaiman's *Books of Magic*. Fans of horror and fantasy art certainly know of him, as exposure to his sexually charged art is almost unavoidable. John Bolton was the first of the British comics professionals to land work with mainstream U.S. comics publishers in the 1980s, initiating the British New Wave in comics that led to Gaiman's quick acceptance by U.S. publishers and readers. Bolton was employed by Marvel Comics to illustrate sword-and-sorcery stories for the short-lived Marvel black-and-white newsstand comics magazine *Bizarre Adventures,* predating the U.S. publication of his immediate contemporaries, including Brian Bolland, Alan Moore, David Lloyd, and many others.

For his debut as a film director, Gaiman conceived a story revolving around a fictionalized version of Bolton titled, somewhat plainly, *A Short Film About John Bolton.* Although many pieces of his art are featured, John Bolton only appears in the film as an extra in a crowd scene. Produced in association with Ska Films, *A Short Film About John Bolton* is indeed a short film, but about a fictional character, one who is only *inspired by* John Bolton.

The plot of the movie is simple: It follows a young journalist who is working on, you guessed it, a short film about John Bolton. In the tradition of *The Office,* the journalist has recorded several interviews with Bolton's associates and various talking heads, interspersing bits and pieces of them throughout larger scenes, such as Bolton arriving at an art gallery, and the public exhibition of his art later that evening.

The journalist becomes intrigued by the artist, and wants to interview him more extensively, and thus wrangles an invite to Bolton's remote studio. It's there that the journalist discovers the truth behind Bolton's statement that he paints what he sees.

Produced by Matthew Vaughn, who wrote and directed the hard-hitting crime movie *Layer Cake* (an early vehicle for Daniel Craig, who would later succeed Pierce Brosnan in the role of James Bond), and who would later direct *Stardust, A Short Film About John Bolton* is short and sweet, a winning combination of humor and horror that makes some telling observations about art and artists as it builds to its *Blair Witch*–style shock ending. Thoroughly enjoyable, the end product bodes well for future Gaiman-helmed film projects.

A Short Film About John Bolton is deliberately reminiscent of the classic 1960s and 1970s portmanteau films produced by the British production firm Amicus Studios. Inspired by the classic British anthology feature *Dead of Night* (1945), Amicus Studios launched their multiple-story features in 1965 with the popular *Dr. Terror's House of Horrors,* and followed with seven more, from *Torture Garden* (1967) to its final film, *The Monster Club* (1980), including the first adaptation of the pre-Comics Code EC Comics to film with *Tales from the Crypt* (1972).

PEOPLE, PLACES, AND THINGS

CAROLYN DALGLEISH. As played by Carolyn Backhouse, she is the fawning proprietor of a posh London gallery (named The Gallery Upstairs). Dalgleish frets incessantly over a showing of the latest works by John Bolton, which includes strange, disturbing, erotic paintings of nude female vampires.

JOHN BOLTON. As played by John O'Mahoney, Bolton is an eccentric British artist who creates highly charged portraits of sensuous creatures of the night. The slight, distracted, middle-aged Bolton first appears in the film as he arrives at Dalgleish's art gallery to insure that his paintings are placed in the optimum positions.

Appearing to suffer from agoraphobia, Bolton is clearly uncomfortable with being the center of attention. Surprised that he's expected to make a speech that evening, he utters a comment that seems clichéd but seems to satisfy his audience: "I paint what I see."

MARCUS. As played by Marcus Brigstocke, he is a journalist who gets deep into his subject matter, and thus wangles an invite to the studio of the reclusive and secretive artist John Bolton. The day after the showing, Marcus and his crew arrive at the artist's home to film their interview. Bolton seems distracted throughout, rarely offering concrete answers to Brigstocke's questions. When pressed, he reluctantly agrees to allow Marcus (and only Marcus) to film his creative process.

As dusk approaches, Bolton takes the journalist to his studio, located in the basement of an ancient monastery and graveyard. As time passes, Bolton shows no signs of getting started; this frustrates the journalist, who decides to leave. Filming himself with a handheld camera as he walks out of the graveyard, the interviewer spots two ghostly women (one with zebra stripes running up her leg) moving toward him. The camera catches only fleeting glimpses of what happens next, but viewers can certainly draw their own conclusions about the fate of the journalist.

TRIVIA

- Noted anthologist and journalist and Gaiman friend Stephen Jones appears in Gaiman's twenty-seven-minute mockumentary as one of the guests at Bolton's showing. Another Gaiman friend, Jonathan Ross, appears as himself, describing Bolton's work as "beautiful, and yet terrifying."

- The DVD of *A Short Film About John Bolton* is notable for its extras. One of these is Gaiman's and actor Marcus Brigstocke's candid commentary on the film. Another highlight is *Live at the Aladdin,* a recording of Gaiman conducting a lengthy reading and question/answer session to benefit the Comic Book Legal Defense Fund. If you have not yet seen Gaiman in a public forum, this is the next best thing.

- Without giving too much away, the denouement of the film is reminiscent of the ending of the famous H. P. Lovecraft 1927 short story, "Pickman's Model." We'll also reveal that the ending is a quite hilarious answer to the interview question that most authors have come to dread, namely, "Where do you get your ideas?"

THE QUOTABLE GAIMAN

I loved doing *A Short Film About John Bolton,* though I'm not entirely sure how I feel about it now being commercially available. From a point of view of learning new skills, I'd love to do it again. I've discovered that I love the auditioning process. I love working with the technical guys. I absolutely love the editing room. That was completely fascinating to me, working with an editor in crafting the thing into something you had in your head. I really like being able to laugh at my own jokes. And so it was absolutely fascinating seeing it all, being involved. And I loved the fact that I didn't quite know what I was doing. There was a desperate terror going on. I'm pretty much better when I'm not cocky.

—Interview with Tasha Robinson,
AV Club. com September 28, 2005

|||||||||||||||||||||||||||||||||||||||||||||||||||||||||||||||||||

MIRRORMASK

(2005)

This visually stunning film represents the end product of yet another collaboration between Gaiman and his frequent coconspirator Dave McKean. In the summer of 2001, the pair was approached by Lisa Henson on behalf of the Jim Henson Company, which was looking to create a new film in the tradition of their own elaborate fantasies, *The Dark Crystal* and *Labyrinth*. In return for unlimited creative control, the company offered Gaiman and McKean a $4 million budget.

Agreeing, the pair set to work, little knowing that this collaboration would not work as smoothly as prior partnerings. As Gaiman wrote in his introduction to the illustrated film script: "Dave McKean and I had worked together very happily for about sixteen years at that point. It had always been easy. This wasn't."

Gaiman subsequently concluded that most of the difficulty lay in the way they approached writing. McKean liked to outline, needing to lay everything out before the first word of the script was written, whereas Gaiman liked to talk about it to the point when he was ready to start writing, and find out the rest as he went along. The other part of the problem was that while McKean appreciated the limitations that the medium and budget imposed on them, Gaiman did not. In an interview with Tasha Robinson of the A.V. Club (avclub.com) on September 28, 2005, Gaiman described the conflict as follows:

For instance, I wanted to do a school scene, and Dave said, "We can't *afford* it. We'd have to have at least 10 kids, we'd have to have chaperones, a teacher, locations, this, that, and the other, and it will cost." And he'd see my expression and he'd say, "But look, if you wanted the world crumpling up like a piece of paper and turning into a flower, I can do that for nothing." So we had this very, very strange and testy series of days on the thing. And I think a lot of it was just a shock of discovering that this wasn't as easy and pleasant as everything else in our collaboration had ever been.

In the end they were able to work through their difficulties, delivering a first-rate piece of film, with the following credits:

Screenplay by: Neil Gaiman
Story by: Neil Gaiman and Dave McKean
Designed and Directed by: Dave McKean

Gaiman was quick to point out, however, that McKean had more to do with the success of the final product than he did. Again from the Tasha Robinson interview:

> This is Dave's movie. Dave came in knowing the movie he wanted to make, and I felt like at the end of the day, really, I was hands, I was dialogue, I wrote some scenes, but Dave knew a lot of the big scenes he wanted to do. The stuff I brought to the table was things like the anti-Helena storyline, and the stuff that sort of complicated things and roughed them up. If you look at the *MirrorMask* script book, where you can see us writing backward and forward, I think of this very much as Dave's movie. I was just helping.

The film premiered at the Sundance Film festival in January 2005, and was released on DVD by Goldwyn/Sony on September 30, 2005.

MirrorMask focuses on a sullen teenage girl named Helena (played by Stephanie Leonides) who is at odds with her circus performer parents (Rob Brydon and Gina McKee). Shortly after a careless insult appears to send her mother into a coma, Helena has a dream where she travels to the Dream Lands (think Oz, by way of Salvador Dalí). There the Queen of Light (McKee again) is dying; she can only be awakened by the power of a mysterious talisman, the *MirrorMask.*

Much like Dorothy in Oz, or Lucy, Susan, Edwin, and Peter in C. S. Lewis's Narnia books (or, for that matter, Coraline in the other world), Helena, accompanied by the flighty juggler known as Valentine (Jason Barry), embarks on a strange and perilous journey through the terrain of the surreal landscape of the Dark Lands, a fantastic landscape populated by floating giants, monkey birds, and dangerous sphinxes. Helena searches for the MirrorMask, an object of enormous power that represents her only hope of escaping the Dark Lands, waking the Queen of Light, and returning home. But the Queen of Shadow (again, McKee) is after her, too, because she thinks Helena is her daughter (the selfish, rebellious princess who stole the MirrorMask in the first place).

Helena is captured by the Queen of Shadow, who remakes her into a pliable, mindless daughter. Meanwhile, the queen's real daughter (the anti-Helena, also played by Leonidas) is in Helena's world wreaking havoc. She fights with Helena's dad, smokes, makes out with boys in her bed, and threatens to destroy the Dream Lands by tearing down and burning the drawings Helena has made and hung all over the walls of her room. Helena must escape the control of the Queen of Shadow, find the MirrorMask, figure out how it works, and reverse the magic that the anti-Helena has worked so she can return her and her twin back to their own lands before the Lands of Light and Shadow are forever destroyed.

In addition to comparisons to Narnia and Gaiman's own *Coraline* (not to mention the Sandman arc *The Dream Country*), the influence of Stephen King and Peter Straub's novel *The Talisman* is woven into the underpinnings of *MirrorMask*. In *The Talisman,* a boy whose mother is ailing must travel to a parallel fantasy world in which the queen, also ailing, is his mother's alternate reality twin. The only way to save both his mother and her royal twin, and restore the dying fantasy world, is to recover a magical talisman.

Of course, McKean and Gaiman's story differs greatly from the tales that influenced it, and the execution is extraordinary and unique, but those influences are evident throughout. As in *Coraline*, with the presence of the dual queens (of Light and Shadow), Gaiman plays upon the common childhood fear that our parents (particularly mothers) will turn out to be something else entirely, either secretly evil or not our parents at all.

People, Places, and Things

HELENA CAMPBELL. A teenager, Helena spends most of her time in her room drawing; the rest of her time is spent performing as a juggler in her parent's circus (aptly named the Campbell Family Circus). Helena feels trapped, and resents her parents' attempts to control her.

After a nasty fight with her daughter, Mrs. Campbell falls ill. Helena feels guilty about this, having uttered some particularly hateful words during the argument ("You'll be the death of me," said Mrs. Campbell. "I wish I was," said Helena). Adding to the pressure of having a sick mother who is about to have surgery, she discovers that her father is having problems keeping the circus going.

After experiencing a strange dream, in which her reflection in the mirror is laughing at her, Helena wakes up in a strange world, where she meets fellow juggler Valentine. Like everyone else in this world, he has a mask for a face. Due to a case of mistaken identity, she winds up before the prime minister (who bears an uneasy resemblance to her father). Realizing his mistake, he explains to her why she was brought to him: a girl who looks a lot like her has been the cause of much tribulation in the City Of

Light, where they now stand. The girl, it seems, caused the ruler of this kingdom, the White Queen, to fall into a coma from which no one can wake her, and then disappeared. Since then dangerous black birds and shadow clouds have started coming out of the adjoining Shadow Lands, tearing the White City apart.

Volunteering to wake her up, Helena learns that she must obtain a certain charm to do so. Thus, she embarks on a strange journey to find the charm and awaken the White Queen.

MUM/THE WHITE QUEEN/THE DARK QUEEN. These are all aspects of Mrs. Campbell. Helena's mom loves her daughter, but constantly clashes with her, as parents and teenagers are wont to do. Stricken by a malady that is never identified (presumably a brain tumor), she lays dying in a hospital bed in our reality.

The White Queen also lays in a coma after an encounter with the Dark Queen's daughter, the anti-Helena, and only Helena can save her.

The Dark Queen rules the other kingdom in the other world, known as the Dark Lands. Her reason to live, it seems, is to have a daughter whose life she can totally dominate. When Helena enters her domain, she seizes the girl and tries to remake her into another anti-Helena, this time "perfectly passive and perfectly pathetic."

THE DARK QUEEN'S DAUGHTER. The anti-Helena, or the "Not Me," as Helena refers to her. Her plan to escape the clutches of her controlling mother using the MirrorMask is the root cause behind all the mayhem in the Dream Lands (as the girl states in her letter to her mother, "Of course, if I use the MirrorMask it may upset things a bit. But you can't run away from home without destroying somebody's world"). Using the powerful object to switch places with Helena, the rebellious anti-Helena begins destroying the pictures that Helena has drawn of the other world. The destruction of the pictures in our world is causing the other world to collapse.

DAD/THE PRIME MINISTER. These are both aspects of Mr. Campbell.

VALENTINE. Helena's companion and comrade in the other world, he helps her on her quest to find the MirrorMask. Valentine, a juggler, is a bit of an eccentric, and tells Helena he is a "Very Important Man" and that he "Owns a Tower." Although he betrays her to the Dark Queen, he later repents, and is instrumental in frustrating the plans of the Dark Queen and her daughter, the anti-Helena. His tower plays a key role in their success, rescuing them from the Dark Queen.

Ending up in Helena's reality at the end of their adventures, the juggler seeks Helena out. He doesn't remember much, but he does know he doesn't want to be a waiter.

THE DREAM LANDS. A world created by Helena through her art, and divided into two kingdoms known as the City of Light and the Land of Shadows, it faces destruction because of the actions of the anti-Helena.

THE MIRRORMASK. The charm Helena seeks, used by the anti-Helena to escape to our reality, it is Helena's only means of restoring order.

THE HISTORY OF EVERYTHING. A book that Helena reads to discover what she must do in order to awaken the White Queen.

A REALLY USEFUL BOOK. A little red book that comes in handy. Each page contains a sentence, "odd things like MOST GHOSTS ARE AFRAID OF WHISTLES and TRY DANCING."

THE GRYPHON THING. A creature that confronts Helena and Valentine as they approach the park where the Orbiting Giants reside, barring their way until Helena stumps it with a riddle (Q: What's green, hangs on a wall, and whistles? A: A herring. No the answer didn't make sense to the Gryphon either).

THE ORBITING GIANTS. Two enormous creatures that look as if they were carved out of stone a long time ago and weathered down. Although they are pressed together, one can discern that they are a man and a woman. They are unique because they float in the sky. Acting as an oracle, they reveal to Helena that the charm she seeks is known as the MirrorMask.

THE CAT THINGS/THE SPHINXES. A deadly winged species that inhabits the other world, they present challenges to Helena and Valentine at crucial points of their journey. The key thing in dealing with these odd-looking carnivores is, as *The Really Useful Book* says, DON'T LET THEM SEE YOU'RE AFRAID. If that fails, the creatures can be distracted by throwing a book at them (they seem compelled to attack books).

TRIVIA

- Amid a plethora of arresting images in this film, there is one that stands above the rest. We won't go into detail, but believe us when we tell you that the scene where Helena is transformed into the Dark Queen's anti-Helena is both stunning and unsettling.

- Once again we need to mention Catherine Storr's 1958 novel, *Marianne Dreams* (see chapter on *Coraline*). The fact that it deals with a girl who visits a world that she draws is particularly relevant to a discussion of *MirrorMask*, though the film's concept, according to Gaiman, is based largely on McKean's own dreams.

- In 2005, HarperCollins published a book version of *MirrorMask,* replete with illustrations by Dave McKean, while sister publisher William Morrow put out *MirrorMask: The Illustrated Film Script,* which contained the complete script, plus photos and interviews, and more than seventeen hundred storyboards created for the film. A third book called *The Alchemy of MirrorMask*, published by Collins Design, detailed the history of the project and the production of the film.

THE QUOTABLE GAIMAN

Sure, MirrorMask is fantasy. Dave McKean—who directed it and co–came up with the story—I suspect thinks it's not fantasy because it's a dream and because of various other things, and because Dave is not terribly comfortable with the idea of fantasy. I'm perfectly comfortable with fantasy, so I think it's definitely fantasy.

—"Geek Gods," *Time*.com, September 25,
2005, interview by Lev Grassman

On collaborating with Dave McKean:

Oh, it was horrible. It was absolutely dreadful. It wasn't as much fun as everything else has been, partly because we'd worked together very happily for about 17 years, and suddenly we actually had to collaborate. Normally, the way we'd worked on most of our things is that I would do the story and then Dave would do the imagery. With *MirrorMask,* we both came into it with stories—bits and ideas. And when we sat down to plot our movie, we discovered that we had two completely different points of view on absolutely everything, which probably wouldn't have come as a surprise if we hadn't worked together happily for so long. But suddenly we were actually sort of facing each other and discovering we had different points of view on fantasy, and story, and creating movies.

—Interview with Tasha Robinson, AV Club,
September 28, 2005

||||||||||||||||||||||||||||||||||||||||||||||||||||||||||||||||||||

BEOWULf

(2007)

As coscripted by Neil Gaiman and veteran filmmaker Roger Avary (writer/ director of *Killing Zoe* and *The Rules of Attraction,* and story author of *Pulp Fiction,* etc.), the animated feature film *Beowulf* presents a contemporary revamp of the classic heroic epic poem.

The original *Beowulf* was scribed by an unknown Anglo-Saxon author, and historians disagree on the date of its origin. Some date the tale as originating around A.D. 700–750 as an oral poem, while others mark the story's inception as the composition of the only extant manuscript, circa A.D. 1010. The untitled manuscript has been called *Beowulf* since the early nineteenth century, and Gaiman and Avary retained that title for their adaptation. Though derived from Scandinavian history and myth, *Beowulf* has been adopted by Gaiman's native country as "England's national epos" (per H. Munro Chadwick's *The Cambridge History of English and American Literature,* Volume 1, 1907), and was the wellspring for J. R. R. Tolkien's career as an academic—and as the renowned author of *The Lord of the Rings* novels.

In the original epic poem, warrior Beowulf travels to the northern Denmark kingdom of King Hrothgar, where Hrothgar's mead hall Heorot has been ravaged for months by the carnivorous monster Grendel. Beowulf battles and slays three monstrous beings: Grendel, Grendel's vengeful mother, and—after an older Beowulf has become the reigning king in his native country, Geatland (now Sweden)—a dragon, which mortally wounds the fierce warrior before their fateful struggle is over.

Just as the original poem has survived via numerous translations, *Beowulf* has also endured many adaptations to other media, including novels, comics, graphic novels, and film (surprisingly there were no feature film adaptations of this most venerable of all epic heroic tales prior to 1998). The most famous adaptation remains John Gardner's novel *Grendel* (1971), which presented the tale from the monster's point of view, and was adapted into the Australian animated feature film *Grendel Grendel Grendel* (1981), with Peter Ustinov voicing the sympathetic monster. Shortly after the initial rumors surfaced concerning Gaiman and Avary's project, the UK/Canadian/Icelandic coproduction *Beowulf & Grendel* (2005) opened, directed by Sturla Gunnarsson. In fact, by that time Gaiman and Avary had been working on their *Beowulf* for over half a decade.

Like many, Avary first encountered Gaiman's work via reading Sandman, beginning in 1989. Among the projects Warner Bros. studio head Lorenzo DiBonaventura offered to Avary after the release of his film *Killing Zoe* (1994) was a feature film adaptation of *Sandman* under producer Jon Peters, which Avary abandoned over a year later.

Working from his own 1982 notes on a possible adaptation of *Beowulf,* Avary prepared a treatment in the spring of 1995, proposing many of the concepts retained in the final 2007 screen version. However, the two-act structure of the epic poem—with a fifty-year gulf between Beowulf's slaying of Grendel's mother and his fatal battle with the anonymous dragon in his native land—remained problematic. It was in a phone conversation with Gaiman in 1996 that Avary's *Beowulf* treatment came up, and Gaiman proposed a solution to that dilemma, and a link between Beowulf and the dragon that followed logically from Avary's concept of a link between Grendel, King Hrothgar, and Grendel's mother. Avary immediately invited Gaiman to join forces on the script, with Avary directing.

Though *Beowulf* became an animated feature, it was originally conceived of as a live-action fantasy film, to be directed by Avary on a modest budget. On his online journal, Gaiman explained:

> Roger Avary asked me to co-write a script for *Beowulf* for him to direct. We went off to Mexico together and wrote it as a sort of Dark Ages *Trainspotting*, filled with mead and blood and madness, and we went all the way from the beginning of the poem, with Beowulf as a hero battling Grendel, to the end, with Beowulf as an old man fighting a dragon. Robert Zemeckis really liked the script, and his production company, ImageMovers, bought it, for Roger to direct. [ImageMovers had a deal with Dreamworks at the time.] Dreamworks, for whatever reasons, didn't want to make it, and—eventually—the rights to the script reverted back to me and Roger.

By 2005, the project had coalesced around Robert Zemeckis as director, expanding the original scope of the project and, to that end, orchestrating the motion-capture computer-generated imagery (CGI) animation Zemeckis had showcased in his adaptation of Chris Van Allsburg's popular illustrated children's book, *The Polar Express* (2004). Impressed with Zemeckis's plans to refine and expand considerably upon that film's CGI techniques, to create a film for adult audiences (though its final MPAA rating was PG-13), Avary and Gaiman agreed to this new synthesis of energies.

Gaiman and Avary remained as executive producers, and actively engaged with the necessary rewrites. The final draft of the screenplay reflected the mutation of the project from live action to animation, and amplified the climactic dragon battle to suit Zemeckis's sensibilities, building climax upon climax, while retaining the key narrative elements and set pieces that had distinguished Avary's original treatment and Avary and Gaiman's deft reinterpretation of the epic heroic poem.

Though *Beowulf* is an animated feature, it is not a traditional animated film by any means, nor a typical CGI-animated feature. Zemeckis's ongoing experimentation with performance-capture animation reaches its current zenith in *Beowulf;* he fuses the human attributes of live-action performances with the almost infinite possibilities of CGI. Performance-capture animation draws from live-action performers with far greater fidelity and flexibility than traditional "rotoscoping" techniques, demanding much more interaction between the actors and creative filmmaking team than any prior dynamic between animation and vocal performances. Thus, *Beowulf* was cast to provide vivid visual (via facial and body language) as well as vocal performances, settling upon Ray Winstone (Beowulf), Anthony Hopkins (King Hrothgar), John Malkovich (Unferth), Robin Wright Penn (Queen Wealtheow), Crispin Glover (Grendel), and Angelina Jolie (Grendel's mother).

Gaiman and Avary's ingenious revision of the epic poem links King Hrothgar and the hero Beowulf with the three monstrous foes in ways no prior adaptation had considered. Here Grendel's mother is a shape-shifting amphibious seductress, and Grendel is in fact the offspring of her mating with King Hrothgar. Thus, Grendel spares Hrothgar during his savage attacks on Herot, and Hrothgar is unable to kill the monster because Grendel is his son. As in the epic poem, Beowulf arrives in Hrothgar's kingdom to slay Grendel, and this he does by severing Grendel's arm. However, Grendel's mother's immediate retribution against Beowulf involves not only her brutal slaying of his men, but also seduction: When Beowulf enters her subterranean aquatic den, she confronts him in her golden woman guise, seducing him and demanding a new son ("You took a son from me. Give me a son, brave thane"). Thus, Beowulf does not slay Grendel's mother, he only claims to—and the dragon that descends upon Beowulf's own kingdom half a century later is the offspring of Beowulf and Grendel's mother, a creature also capable of shape-shifting and filled with hatred for the father that sired and spurned him.

Furthermore, Gaiman and Avary imply that Beowulf himself is more than human: not merely a hero, but perhaps the offspring of some prior coupling of human and nonhuman parents. This remains an enigmatic proposition, never explicitly clarified. Grendel's mother recognizes Beowulf's true nature before seducing him in her lair: "Are you the one they call Beowulf? The Bee-wolf. The bear," she says. "I know that underneath your glamor you're as much a monster as my son Grendel. Perhaps more."

In an earlier passage, when the Danish thane Unferth questions how Beowulf lost a swimming race with a warrior named Brecca, Beowulf explains that he rescued Brecca from an attacking sea creature; he was then delayed by an onslaught of more monstrous sea serpents. He claims to have slain them all, but we see, via flashback, that Beowulf was seduced by a golden mermaidlike creature that resembles Grendel's mother. This sequence serves to provide a possible earlier link between Beowulf and Grendel's mother (though it is only implied they are one and the same), while also revealing an unnatural affinity between Beowulf and other mythic humanoid creatures of his era, one he suppresses and denies. In both this sequence and his subsequent claim to have killed Grendel's mother, Beowulf's boasts of slaying monsters are juxtaposed with imagery of his seduction by the same creatures. This is a radical reimagining of the oldest of all Anglo-Saxon heroic epics, but it does not betray its source.

Though its original conception was Roger Avary's, *Beowulf* fits neatly into the whole of Gaiman's body of work, specifically in its imaginative reworking of a revered mythic text. Per usual, Gaiman's skillful reimagining of the primary motives and links within the context of a venerable cultural myth—enhancing and subverting without altering the essence of that myth—maintains uncanny fidelity to its source material. As amply demonstrated throughout the entirety of Gaiman's career thus far, this is among his greatest strengths as a fantasy writer, and Avary's collaborative venture with Gaiman on *Beowulf* embodies a perfect union between like-minded creative spirits.

TRIVIA

- During a period when Roger Avary believed he would not be directing *Beowulf*, Gaiman wrote another screenplay. At the time of this writing, neither Gaiman nor Avary has discussed this script publicly.

THE QUOTABLE GAIMAN

So when people have asked me about the *Beowulf* movie I've said, honestly, that I really don't have any idea what to expect. As of today I have the beginnings of some idea what to expect, and it's rather significantly cooler and stranger and more like a Real Movie than I ever dreamed. And what I've seen is just the early stages.

—journal.neilgaiman.com

||||||||||||||||||||||||||||||||||||||||||||||||||||||||||||||||||||

PART TEN
THE ODDITIES

Neil Gaiman simply cannot stop writing, the way some people are compulsive readers and will read anything—even the backs of cereal boxes over breakfast. In addition to his comics, scripts, novels, poems, songs, short stories, nonfiction books, and graphic novels, all of which we hope we've covered within these pages, he has written an apparently endless stream of articles, essays, introductions to other people's work, letters to editors, and a million words in his online journal.

In this section we'll focus on a handful of oddities—things that don't really fit under any of the definitions that encapsulate Gaiman's other work, but that we would be remiss in leaving out.

||||||||||||||||||||||||||||||||||||||||||||||||||||||||||||||||||

A WALKING TOUR OF
THE SHAMBLES

(2002)

Debuting at the 2002 World Horror Convention in Schaumberg, Illinois, *A Walking Tour of the Shambles* purports to be a travel guide to an old Chicago neighborhood known as the Shambles, famous for having survived the Great Fire of 1871 ("Ya can't burn Hell," as a local politician is rumored to have remarked). The fifty-eight-page book was written by Gaiman in collaboration with fellow convention guest Gene Wolfe, who, among many other well-deserved honors, received the World Fantasy Life Achievement Award in 1996.

The authors cover a distance of approximately three city blocks, namely Old Street, Meat Street, and Canal Street, describing interesting Destinations of Note in each and happily channeling macabre humorists Charles Addams and Edward Gorey all the way. The book sports a cover by Gahan Wilson (described as "America's reigning King of Whimsical Terrors"), that features caricatures of Wolfe and Gaiman; surrounded by all sorts of strange beasties, the hapless pair make their way through the Shambles, accompanied by Alice in Wonderland and the White Rabbit. Interior illustrations of Shambles's locales are handled by Randy Broecker and Earl Geier, "two daring Chicagoans."

To quote from the back cover copy:

Uniquely Chicago, the Shambles offers an array of delights for the intrepid sightseer: Cereal House with its terribly Strange Bed (be sure to fill out the next of kin form if you stay the night: a quaint touch adding to the fun of an overnight visit); the House of Clocks boasts a collection of 20,000 time pieces—make sure you arrive on the hour for an unforgettable moment; the historic H. H. Holmes' House with bars on his children's windows still intact; Saunders Park, a soothing respite from the city streets (if one is careful), with its gardens, statuary, ornamental lake and the infamous Petting Zoo (a favorite with children, but it's best not to bring your own); plus many more intriguing sights.

An excerpt from the book's preface will provide a little taste of its dry humor.

We bring this book back into print now only as a service to collectors of the Little Walks for Sightseers series. There are, after all, many good reasons why the initial printing was removed from bookstores, libraries, and, where necessary, bedrooms, by law enforcement agencies and employees of the Chicago Tourist Commission.

First, the area described herein does not exist.

Secondly, should the area described herein actually exist, any journeys, expeditions, or visitations to, from, or in the Shambles would be strongly and actively discouraged by the Greater Chicago Chamber of Commerce and the Chicago Tourist Commission.

Thirdly, both Gene Wolfe and Neil Gaiman . . . now both deny having written any part of this book.

And so on.

TRIVIA

- The book is dedicated to author R. A. Lafferty, "who would have remembered all the tall tales he heard in Gavagan's." Gavagan's Irish Saloon is one of the fine drinking establishments the collaborators visited during the extensive research phase of this book; Gaiman and Wolfe note in the book, "It is unfortunate that neither of your authors has yet made it out of Gavagan's without a badly beer-soaked notebook, or with much in the way of hard facts."

- The book is also interesting for its "By the Same Authors" section. Wolfe's titles include *Thirteen Months in the Desert* and *I Was a Werewolf for the CIA*. Gaiman's titles are *Several Interesting Bus Journeys; Common Cucurbitae and How to Identify Them (Illustrated)*; and *Little Walks for Sightseers Numbers 8, 11 and 24*. Your humble authors have made every attempt to track down copies of these works, which we refer to as "the Lost Gaiman" (the author himself vehemently denies they exist), but, as of this book's publication date, have been unsuccessful. We are pursuing one lead, though: a private collection maintained by one Mr. Lucien has informed us that they may have copies.

- The book has two versions, one where Wolfe gets top billing, and one where Gaiman does. Gene Wolfe was the subject of one of the very first interviews a young journalist named Neil Gaiman ever conducted.

- The book was published by American Fantasy Press, Woodstock, Illinois.

THE QUOTABLE GAIMAN

The best idea in (*A Walking Tour of the Shambles*) we stole, happily, from what may be the only place it's ever been done (which is Charles G. Finney's *The Circus of Dr. Lao*): the list of unanswered questions. He has a list of questions which were not answered in the book. We actually went one step further, because we provide not only a list of unanswered questions but a list of answers, which Gene did. The acid bath one always gets a horrified laugh at readings: "What kind of man would kill a woman and dissolve her body in acid, and how could that safely be done today?"

—from "The Wolfe and Gaiman Show,"
Locus, September 2002.

||||||||||||||||||||||||||||||||||||||||||||||||||||||||||||||||||||

GAIMAN CONCEPTIONS

W hile Gaiman has been involved in various projects as concept creator (*Teknophage,* other Tekno Comix series, etc.), editor, packager, and even consultant, his most unusual credit to date may be those on books he "devised" and/or "codevised."

Five books were "devised/codevised" by Gaiman between 1991 and 1993, and these were primarily anthologies of original short fiction by a variety of authors. The titles were *Temps* and its sequel *Eurotemps,* both "codevised" with Alex Stewart; *The Weerde: Book I* with Mary Gentle and Roz Kaveney and *The Weerde II* with Gentle, Kaveney, and Stewart; and *Villains!* with Gentle. The *Weerde* anthologies chronicle the misadventures of a shape-shifting alien elite in different periods of history. *Villains!* presents various antagonists from popular works of fantasy as the protagonists of their tales—taking the enemy's side, so to speak—and stands as a companion volume to Mary Gentle's solo turn with the satiric *Grunts!* (published in 1992), which presents the points of view of "the losing side" of famous fantasy epic battles as the nominal heroes, such as the orcs of *Lord of the Rings* fame.

PART ELEVEN
THE WORLD OF NEIL GAIMAN

THE INTERVIEW[1]

FAMILY HISTORY, NOSES, AND MR. PUNCH

Stephen R. Bissette: How did your family end up in England?

NEIL: My great-great-grandfather—whose name I don't recall—owned what I believe was the largest department store in Lodz. The family name at that point was Chaiman, or Haiman; it wasn't even a Polish name, it was a Jewish name. The few people who had survived the Holocaust were looking for my side of the family after the war, and they were looking for "Haiman."

My great-grandfather was the black sheep of the family. I don't know an awful lot about him. I know that he was married to an older woman in the hope that it would cause him to settle down. I know that they left Poland and came initially to Belgium, where my great-grandfather worked on the diamond force as a diamond courier. I think he lost a diamond and went to England because he was in big trouble. A diamond went missing, and he went on the run.

As far as I understand it, he more or less abandoned his family for a while. My grandfather, who at that point was about eleven, wound up as the sole support for his mother and younger brothers and sisters. This was about 1914. He didn't speak much English, but he wound up getting a job in a London hotel, initially as a bus boy. During the First World War he apparently had a thriving trade in furnishing American servicemen with black market whiskey. He was more or less self-supporting the family. I don't know a lot about my great-grandfather after that. He crops up from time to time in photographs.

My aunt Betty, who is currently in her nineties, talks about how one day there was a knock on the door, and there was a very good-looking man with a distinguished beard who said, "I am your father," and she had no memory of ever having seen him before. Whether he was in prison, whether he abandoned them for long periods, or quite what happened, I don't know, and I don't think anybody is quite sure.

My father tells the story of being in, I think, the Dorchester Hotel with my grandfather, in what I assume must have been the late 1940s—and seeing my great-grandfather dining across the road with an attractive young blond woman who was definitely not my great-grandmother. He may have been a con man—he was definitely a black sheep.

SRB: There was definitely something odd—

NEIL: There was something odd there. My grandfather's [name was] Morrie, Morris, or Moishe Gaiman. Morris is what would have been on his passport, if he'd ever had a passport. But he didn't have a passport; he was a stateless person and he remained so. If I had known it at the time I wrote *Mr. Punch,* it would have gone into *Mr. Punch.* Pretty much everything—all the weird little anecdotal stuff in *Mr. Punch*—is true, except the things I made up. Mostly it's true, [including] the fact that he owned the amusement park with the mermaid in it—it was sold long before I was born. It was something that cropped up that I learned when I was asking about him, and it seemed to fit beautifully into this thing that I was putting together.

The name "Gaiman" happened when they came over to England; the "ch" sound was hardened to "g." It was spelled "Gaeman," and then my grandmother changed it to "Gaiman," because she liked that better. The only reason I know that is because I remember as a boy seeing the engagement announcements of my grandparents, and it was "Mary Parsons and Morris Gaeman," and then the wedding announcement was "Gaiman," and I asked, "How did it change?" and she said, "Oh, I just liked that better." And I said, "Did you have to do it legally?" and she said, "No, we just printed what we did up there."

She was East End Jewish. All my family were. Then again, the East End of London was where the Jews went, and then spread out from there.

SRB: So, her family had been in London for a time.

NEIL: Longer than the other part—she was born in England, in Rothschild buildings, which were these buildings put up by some rich Jews for the poor ones—you know, the Rothschilds put them up. It sounds fairly nightmarish. I talked to her younger sister, my aunt Lottie, a few years ago. I said, "What was it like?" She said, "It was very hard, dear, especially when you'd come home from school and you'd find someone had hung themselves in the stairwells from hunger. You never forgot that, and it happened too often."

You're talking the first decade of the century, and you're talking poor Jews, Jewish immigrants—you're talking the guys who, if they'd had any more money, would have made it to New York.

SRB: London was as far as they could get.

NEIL: Exactly. They were trying to get out of Eastern Europe. I mean, all of my background is Russian Jewish, German Jewish, Polish Jewish, White Russian Jewish, which is what is now Belarus—they're all from that part of the world, and everybody fleeing west, and nobody making it any farther than the East End of London.

My grandfather became, by a series of long and amusing anecdotes, a grocery magnate, though he never moved beyond Portsmouth. Gaiman's was the grocer's in Portsmouth. He remained stateless through his life. Apparently—again, according to family legend—because Sir Percy Pink, his wonderfully named business rival, who was also a magistrate. At the time when (in 1938 or '39) my grandfather applied for British citizenship, Percy Pink objected. He pointed out [that] my grandfather had a criminal record; he was arrested in the very early 1920s. If you were foreign in the 1920s, and my grandfather technically was foreign, you had to register your location with the police, and be there. You were not allowed to go anywhere else. Because my grandfather's family lived in one room in the East End, and my grandmother's family lived in two rooms in the East End, my grandfather had taken to sleeping over there. And this was a crime. He was actually arrested for not being in his registered place of residence. My grandmother had to bail him out before the engagement party. Mr. Pink used this, and objected [to his application for citizenship]. My grandfather refused ever to appeal, never applied again, and to the end of his life was a "stateless" person. He carried a document stating he was a stateless person.

SRB: How did this impact on your father?
NEIL: Not at all, as far as I know. I think it impacted only insofar as my grandfather was an unstable sort of person. It did not give him any stability or security. My dad has talked about how my grandfather tended to go mad when confronted with the tax people and stuff—he would actually go into these depressions, and go barking mad and stuff. He was quite terrified of, and did not deal well with, authorities.

The family anecdote—which I believe is true, I should say—about how he became a grocer is that he'd started out as an itinerant soap seller, selling cheap carbolic soap pretending it was "Sunlight Soap." [This was] something that he apparently abandoned after he got turned around on a mountain road in Wales, and had gone back to a town he'd already visited, where they beat him up and left him with soap in his mouth. He abandoned that, then went on the road doing some other stuff, and then at one point was doing the market, selling china. I remember hearing that they'd found a barge loaded with tin goods that had gone down in the Thames, and they rescued all the tin goods and relabeled them, printed new labels—

SRB/Hank Wagner: [Laughter.]
NEIL: My great-uncle Monty was a hunchback, which I thought was really cool, because when you're six years old and can actually look an adult in the eye, that was great. And Monty—whose name I changed very slightly—is in *Mr. Punch*, too. Everybody looks a little bit more English than they actually were, because Dave went out and found models of people—

SRB: We were going to ask if Dave had used Gaiman family photos for reference.
NEIL: No, which actually is in some ways a slight pity, because one of the great things about my family is, you've got this great Jewish nose running through the family. You have a bunch of people who all do look rather like *Mr. Punch*. I don't

actually have it anywhere near as much, but my dad's got a great "Punch beak," my grandfather had it—you had that sort of visual thing.

SRB: Did your dad grow up working for your grandfather's grocery chain?
NEIL: Yes, yes, he began as a grocer. But it goes back to Monty. Monty sold broken bits of chocolate in a market; offcuts and seconds. According to family legend, a lorry, a truck, loaded up with groceries of various kinds, set up at the other side of the market, selling stuff cheaply. One of the things they sold cheaply was broken-off chunks of chocolate. They sold them cheaper than Monty did, and than Monty could afford to. Monty went and talked to my grandfather, which he always did when he was in trouble. And my grandfather went to the guys in the truck, and said, "Look, my brother's a cripple, selling his chocolate; sell anything else you want, just stop selling the chocolate while you're here." According to family legend, the reply was basically, "Fuck off, Jew."

So my grandfather took his life savings, which amounted to about fifty pounds, went up to London, hired a truck, went to see the Lord Cohen—though he was not Lord Cohen then, he was just Cohen—who was a mate of his, who later founded Tesco's. In England and around much of the world, Tesco's is the largest supermarket (I think it was named after his wife, Tessa). So he went to see Cohen in Tesco, and said, "I've got fifty quid, can you loan me another fifty quid?—and I want to buy groceries from you." So he basically bought a hundred quid's worth of groceries. He went back down to Portsmouth, scoped out the other lorry, checked out all of their prices, went back to his lorry, and simply priced everything they had a little bit below the other guy. Set up at one end of the market, and after four days of this, the other lorry moved on, waved bye-bye, and drove to Southampton.

That was all my grandfather was planning to accomplish. The entire purpose of this was simply to get the other guy out of the way so Monty could go back to selling chocolate offcuts. Except at the end of the week, they totted up what they had made, and he realized he had made more in that week than he had in the previous year. So for the next three years, first in one, and then with a couple of lorries, that was what they did. They sold groceries off lorries. And then, it became shops. Then it became a chain of shops. My grandfather was the grocery king of Portsmouth.

My daughter Holly told me an anecdote that I didn't know recently. The trouble with family anecdotes is [that] they're never handed over in any organized fashion. Sometimes, somebody just doesn't tell you things. Holly had been off with my parents to the place where I was born—

SRB: Which is?
NEIL: Portchester, White Hart Lane in Portchester, above a grocery shop.

SRB: The Gaiman grocery shop?
NEIL: No, it wasn't a Gaiman grocery shop, because my father had left, walked off in a huff—well, not in a huff, but he'd just broken off with my grandfather,

but all he knew was groceries, so he went off and set up his own little grocery. For a year after I was born, or the year of my birth, he worked in this grocery shop which he owned, worked long days, and then sold it. Much like the serendipity that made my grandfather a grocer, when he sold it my father realized that he'd just made more by selling the shop than he had from a year being a grocery person, and my father went off into property. So that was the end of my father's grocery career.

SRB: And that's why you didn't grow up a grocer.

NEIL: Now, Holly's anecdote—she said, "You know, our family could have been incredibly rich." What was interesting is that my grandfather was fairly rich, and he went mad slowly and lost it all. He alienated my dad, he alienated his son Ronny, and they were both basically saying, "You need to become supermarkets." It's the late 1950s, early 1960s, supermarkets are the thing of the future. "Let's turn our grocery shops into proto-supermarkets," my dad would do this stuff, Ronny would do that stuff—and my grandfather was having none of it. Lord Cohen at Tesco's, now, I believe, the single largest supermarket chain in the world, went to my grandfather and said, "Look, Morrie, I've not gone into Portsmouth, I've always left Portsmouth alone, it's always been Gaiman territory with my little supermarket thing." He said, "But I'm going to go in now, I can't have one town in England where there's no Tesco's. So what I'm going to do is, I'll give you shares—I'll give you shares in Tesco's." Now, my grandfather, being my grandfather, said, "I can't—I don't want anything I can't see; what's a share anyway?" So he took some kind of cash payment.

SRB: He sold it off to Cohen for a one-time property sale.

NEIL: Yeah, having no interest in shares. It was just funny, Holly's saying, "We could have been wealthy!" and I said, "I'm perfectly happy, Holly, I've known too many rich people who are too screwed up." [Laughter.]

BATMAN AND THE "BOOKIE" KID

SRB: So what did you grow up with, Neil?
Hank Wagner: What do you think you got from your father, what do you think you got from your mother?

NEIL: My background is one of those things where you think two things at the same time. One, you think everybody else in the world is normal, and your family is weird. I think that's automatic, that's pretty much the human condition. So, obviously I thought that. But also, I thought I was normal. The first inclination I had that I wasn't normal was actually about six years ago—that would be right, because Maddy was seven. I'd now raised three children, so I thought I could begin to generalize. And I thought, "OK, here is the third of my children who has not carefully alphabetized their bookshelves." I thought, "You know, thinking about it, I might have been a weird child." It was that sudden moment of going—

SRB: *I alphabetized my bookshelf, thanks—*
HW: *I alphabetized my books, too.*
NEIL: At what age?

SRB: *Ten or eleven. And I alphabetized my records.*
NEIL: It was part of this weird breed. I remember, at [the] age of seven, [wondering] whether Roger Lancelyn Green belonged in the Ls or the Gs. I was a "bookie" kid. I could sort of put my life together by books. I know what I was reading, I know what was being read to me. I can remember the teachers and the first books I ever read. Books, more than anything—TV and movies, to a lesser degree, but books were this huge, important—they were like places, they were somewhere you went—

SRB: *—and that you could revisit.*
NEIL: And control.

SRB: *When we were kids, it wasn't easy or possible to revisit a movie or a play.*
NEIL: Exactly—but it was also illegal. One of the things that fascinates me in England, in 1972, '73, there was this huge legal case where Bob Monkhouse, the English comedian, was raided and arrested because the police knew there had to be something illegal going on, because he owned lots and lots of sixteen-millimeter films.

HW: *Blue movies, or—*
NEIL: No, it was mainly "solid" movies. He had a famous collection, but I believe the legal status of owning film back then was sort of a gray area. Those things belonged to the studio or distributor or whatever; he said he'd bought all this stuff legally, but had he? But really, what was suspicious was just private ownership of watchable entertainment material.

SRB: *Books never had that stigma.*
NEIL: They never did. So—what was I like? My first memories, I was being walked by my grandmother to go and see the steam trains. I was twenty-three months, nearly two, because my grandmother was looking after me, and my mum was off having my sister. I was born at home, and my younger sister was born at home, but my middle sister was born at hospital, because she was a "breacher." So I can just remember my grandmother walking me down to see the steam trains. Then we moved to Purbrook—Purbrook Garden, in Purbrook, number thirty-two or thirty-three. My favorite book was about a little mermaid. Not *the* little mermaid,

it was *a* little mermaid, at that point there was also a *Sooty Annual*—in which PC Plod in a striped bathing costume was carried out to sea—and *Playhour,* various comics in which woodland creatures got into trouble. Sooty and Sweep were English glove puppets; Sooty was sort of a little bear.

I loved those comics. My youngest memories were of various things that crossed one's path: *TV 21, TV Comics,* so on and so forth. At the time we were living up at Sussex but my dad was working in Portsmouth, and he would bring me back comics every week, as a sort of—it wasn't exactly an apology for working away, but it was a kind of thing that he'd bring every week, it became a rhythm—it also became very important to me because I was a *Batman* freak.

HW: Batman, *being the TV show—*
NEIL: The *Batman* TV show went just as huge [in England] as it did over here. In fact, huger in an odd way, because in America, to the best of my knowledge, nobody thought Batman could fly, but in England it was widely and erroneously believed that Batman could fly.

HW: Huh? Because?
NEIL: I don't know, but kids kept getting killed.

HW: The same thing with Superman—
NEIL: There was a special opening, recorded for the UK, that I do not believe was shown over here, in which Adam West and Burt Ward actually said, "Remember, kids, don't try and do what Batman and Robin do," and I just remember going [smacks fist into palm of his other hand], "Holy broken bones, Batman!"

SRB: What year did that run in England?
NEIL: Sixty-seven?

SRB: So, the year after the program debuted in the U.S.—
NEIL: Maybe, '66 or '67. I'll see if I can find you [a] copy of a *Smash!* comic downstairs, because it'll give you some context on what we're talking about. *Smash!* reprinted the American newspaper strips, in which people looked and acted like they did in the TV show. That was the thing that got me hooked. Once you got inside, *Smash!* Comics, you then got some Leo Baxendale strips, including *Grimly Feendish,* which was sort of a Charles Addams knockoff. Grimly Feendish was actually drawn to look like Uncle Fester—

SRB: I always wondered if [Alan Moore and Steve Parkhouse's] Bojeffries Saga had come out of Grimly Feendish.
NEIL: I always thought Bojeffries came more or less completely from Henry Kuttner's Hogben Saga. I remember saying to Alan, when I first met him,

"Bojeffries—Hogben Saga?" And he said, "Yes! In fact, Uncle Hog Ben-Henry will come in one day," and I even saw a drawing of Hog Ben-Henry, but I don't think he ever cropped up in the actual comic—well, there you go.

I started getting *Smash!*, which had a superhero comic in it called the *Rubberman*. Cursed by an Indian fakir—whatever that was, I didn't know—he could stretch, he was stretchy, like rubber; and I think "The Legend Testers" were in there. They used to go back in time and find out if something was Excalibur or whatever. *Smash!* had a mixture of humor and adventure strips, with Batman on the covers. But then they announced very excitedly that they were bringing out more comics. There was actually a whole line of them: There was *Wham!* and *Smash!*—which was the one I got hooked on—*Pow!*, *Fantastic!*, and *Terrific*. *Pow!* was a mixture of Marvel reprints and English humor strips; *Fantastic!* and *Terrific* were simply Marvel reprints. They were reprinting Marvel stuff from the beginning, right from '62 and '63, which meant when I encountered the X-Men for the very first time, it was Marvel Girl turning up at Professor Xavier's college and meeting the X-Men for the first time. When I encountered Spider-Man and the Hulk for the first time, that was how I encountered them.

HW: Did you see American DC or Marvel comics?
NEIL: Not at that point, but I did almost immediately after that. Now, at this point, I'm hooked and excited by this stuff.

SRB: Are you buying them at your own at this point, or are these still gifts your father is bringing home?
NEIL: One of the things I'm doing at this point—if you check Wikipedia or something, you could probably find out what the first date of publication of *Smash!*, *Wham!*, *Pow!*, *Fantastic!*, and *Terrific* was, and you can date this—but we're into '67, early '68, I'd say, so I'm six or seven years old.[2]

The next thing that I remember that is huge and important in my life was a box of American comics. Oddly enough, I mentioned it to my dad, and he said, "Yes, I know who those comics came from, I can tell you about those comics," and I said, "Oh, good!"—and he never did. I should really bring it up before he dies. Circa late '67 and early '68, I was given a box containing, at a guess, a hundred comics from the faraway land of America. These included that issue of *Brave and the Bold* where Batman and Hawkman are trying to rip each other's masks off; it included the Green Lantern *Brave and the Bold* where Batman is trapped inside a giant metal bat and Green Lantern is using his power ring. It included the *Hawkman* issue where the guy turns into the giant lion monster, with the beautiful Murphy Anderson art. It included loads and loads of *Fantastic Fours*: The Inhumans stuff was all there, the Silver Surfer stuff, the Galactus stuff—we're in the number 40s or so. I'm pretty sure this was six months or a year old, so it was probably 1968 when I was given all this stuff. And it was all in color—

SRB: Yes, the British reprints were in black and white—

NEIL: One- or two-color: Black and white and blue, or black and white or green, or whatever. Also in '66—it may have been '65, but I'm pretty sure it was early '66—I bought one of my proudest possessions, that I still have, although I no longer have the cover, which was *Dalek World,* the *Dalek World Annual.* I loved my *Dalek World Annual.* I read that over and over.

SRB: These were the English annuals, with comics and text pieces and illustrations, hardcovers—

NEIL: With comics, illustrations and stuff, and hardcovers, published for Christmas, the annual nature of it was, they came out before Christmas for the Christmas market.

MATURING TASTES

SRB: Now, those were the comics that were hitting you; what books were you into?

NEIL: The first point that I remember going mad for a book was C. S. Lewis. In about 1965—again, you'd have to do a search—sometime in, I think, '66, the ITV did an adaptation of *The Lion, the Witch, and the Wardrobe.*[3]

NEIL: I saw either the first or the second episode at my grandmother's house we'd just moved up to Sussex. We'd been living with my grandmother for about a year before that—sold the house in Purbrook—but I remember being down at my grandmother's and watching this *Lion, the Witch, and the Wardrobe* thing, and just going, "That's amazing!" Even though Aslan was a guy in a lion suit, standing up on his hind legs, and all that kind of stuff. I remember the beavers, I remember Aslan, I remember going home and getting hold of a copy—and I would have been six at this point.

SRB: To remind people, the "reality mind-set" then for TV fantasy was quite different than it is now. I mean, Dr. Who's monsters were very convincing when I was a kid (we saw it on Canadian TV), because that was the norm—

NEIL: That was the norm; you accepted a guy in a lion suit.

HW: How did you find out there were books out there, too?

NEIL: I remember buying myself a *Lion, the Witch, and the Wardrobe,* I bought a *Voyage of the Dawn Treader*—those were the first two that I owned. I may have realized they were books because the kids up the road, the Harrises, who I used to occasionally go and play with, had copies of the books. I read everything, so I discovered their copies of the books, and went, "Ah, *The Lion, the Witch, and the Wardrobe.*"

SRB: *Prior to that, what had you enjoyed? What other books had played a key role in your early years as a reader?*

NEIL: Enid Blyton—the madness of Enid Blyton was something that never made it across to the U.S. Enid Blyton is very [hard] to describe. One of the sets of books I remember learning to read on were the Noddy books by Enid Blyton, these stories of this strange little creature with a pointed hat with a bell on, who drove this little car around with his best friend, a gnome—he looked like a garden gnome—called "Big Ears". When Noddy nodded, his little bell would ring. One of the weird and interesting things about Enid Blyton is, she's one of the very few authors who is almost unreadable at the wrong age. She would write books for two-year-olds, that two-year-olds would like, but three-year-olds would disdain as "kid's stuff," and books for three-year-olds that the four- and five-year-olds would laugh at; books for six-year-olds that, by the time you're eight or nine, you try and read again, but can't remember what the spark was. Incredibly, nightmarishly prolific, and a very, very odd author. I remember thinking at the time, if only she'd written books for forty-four-year-olds that fifty-year-olds would disdain—

SRB/HW: *[Laughter.]*

NEIL: It was just, you'd find the right ones for you. There were the Secret Seven mysteries. I'd loved Noddy stories when I was two and three, and by the time I was four I'd found her stories about elves and pixies, and strange little magical stories in which some naughty elf would decide to steal a "do the housework" spell from an old wizard, and then everything would go wrong.

HW: *Was this a house author name, or just one writer?*

NEIL: This was all one person who wrote incredible quantities of stuff. She wrote this remarkable series called The Faraway Tree books, about a large tree at the bottom of this garden that was filled with elves and gnomes and whatever, and if you climbed the tree, you'd get a different world at the top of the tree every week, or every couple of days a new world would arrive. One day it would be the Land of Dreams, and that would be followed by the Land of Toys, and that would be followed by the Land of Evil Spanking, or whatever—

SRB/HW: *[Laughter.]*

NEIL: I don't think I'm joking on that one. I've got distinct memories of somebody with a name like Mistress Spanks Academy or whatever—Enid Blyton was definitely . . . these were books I owned, stole from school, or borrowed. I think the Famous Five series was big—the much parodied Secret Seven. She was very good at doing series. I remember, years ago, sitting down and going, "You know, if you want to be a successful children's author, the way to do it is to do a series." And that never happened. As a children's author, I've completely failed. You do realize that really works.

HW: *Do you find yourself doing riffs on her once in a while?*
NEIL: No, not really. She's a very odd writer—she has no discernible prose style, and most adults find it really hard rereading her. She's an author I've studiously not gone back to, because I'm fond of her. I even tried reading one of her books to Maddy, and found it was not working. Even though I knew how good it was, it really wasn't written for me. As opposed to someone like P. L. Travers. I bought a copy of *Mary Poppins* when I was about five.

It's probably worth pointing out [that] I was an early and obsessive reader. I'd got the copy of *Mary Poppins* in 1964 or '65, because I'd loved the film, and had not of course been able to go back and rewatch the film because you couldn't—

SRB: *To go more than once to a film back then was rare.*
NEIL: The thing was, I would have gone to see *Mary Poppins* as many times as anyone would take me. The only thing that anybody took me to that was around for-fucking-ever—it was around for years, and people kept taking me, and I hated it, every time I'd hate it worse—was *The Sound of Music.* It was around forever, and adults would take you to see it as if they were doing you a favor, and I would shoot off my fingers rather than go again. What I really wanted to see was *Mary Poppins,* but *The Sound of Music* wasn't any good: There was kissing, and Nazis, and those awful children.

There were other books: Hugh Lofting and *Doctor Dolittle* were hugely important. Actually, there is one other writer I haven't mentioned, somebody who was incredibly important to me from more or less the age of three on, which was W. S. Gilbert, from Gilbert and Sullivan, which I actually talk about in [the 24-Hour comic *Being An Account of the Life and Death of the Emperor*] *Heliogabolus.* My aunt Diane, who died of leukemia, took me to see *Iolanthe* when I was about three, and I loved it. It just went into my head, and it was important to me. I would make my parents buy me the records. For both my birthday and Christmas, my presents would be [producer Richard] D'Oyly Carte Theatre Company "Best Of" selections. I would read the biographies, and I subscribed to the Sadler's Wells Theatre, and my mother would take me, normally once a year, to go and see a Gilbert and Sullivan play. These were important to me. In my head, I cast these things, I'd put them together, I'd restage them—

SRB: *This brought theater front and center for you.*
NEIL: Well, yes, because they're all about words. I loved Gilbert because I got words from him, and I got to see what words did, and I wanted to use them. Everything that Gilbert was about, in many ways, is about the magic of words, even all the questions of identity that Gilbert's plots so improbably hinge on are always word-based. I used to love learning the songs—I learned all the patter songs. They were what I learned, and what I loved, and they were the things that went through my head when I would walk, or when I needed company or whatever. You know, "The Nightmare Song," or "It Really Doesn't Matter" from *Ruddigore,* or whatever. These were

the sort of things that were touchstones for me, as important as C. S. Lewis was, probably more so in some ways: my obsession and fascination with musical theater, and what you could do with a song, how incredibly funny they were—

HW: *Did this lead you into Shakespeare at an older age?*
NEIL: No, no, Shakespeare I got accidentally because I was bar mitzvahed. Shakespeare I got when I was thirteen. Shakespeare I didn't discover in a theatrical way, but in a literary way. As a bar mitzvah present, a friend of my father's gave me a dozen of the New American Library Penguin Shakespeares, with the Milton Glaser covers, and I read them, because I loved reading. I would read the preliminary essay, read the play, read the ancient criticism at the back, I would read the ads as stories—I read them as books. I'd been given them, so I read them. That was what I did when people gave me books. I read an enormous amount of very strange stuff when I turned thirteen, because it was all bar mitzvah stuff. Somebody gave me *The Complete Works of Oscar Wilde,* so I sat down and read the complete works of Oscar Wilde. Looking back, I still have no idea what I thought "The Portrait of Mr. W. H." was about, or "The Ballad of Reading Gaol," because there's nothing in *The Complete Works of Oscar Wilde* to tell you what his crime was: I'd had no idea what he'd done!

SRB: *Nobody was going to explain it to you at that time; you might not have even been able to articulate the question.*
NEIL: No—I was just trying to figure it out. I remember even getting a copy of *Son of Oscar Wilde,* by his son, Vyvyan [Holland], and reading that, hoping it would explain it somewhere, and it never did. So, that was the odd way that I discovered Shakespeare: not theatrically. I don't think I saw Shakespeare until I was about sixteen, and I'd been taken to *Romeo and Juliet.*

PORTRAIT OF THE WRITER AS A YOUNG MAN

SRB: *Let's get back to your chronology, then. What spark did C. S. Lewis trigger that was unlike all these earlier books you'd grown up with?*
NEIL: First, you've got an authorial voice, beautifully written. Lewis's prose style is faultless. I admired his use of parenthetical statements to the reader, where he would just go talk to you. Suddenly the author would address a private aside to you, the reader. It was just you and him. I'd think, "Oh, my gosh, that is so cool! I want to do that! When I become an author, I want to be able to do things in parentheses." I liked the power of putting things in brackets.

HW: *Were you thinking that way—"When I become an author"—at six and seven?*
NEIL: I was definitely thinking, "Oh my god, I love the power of putting things in brackets; I wonder how you make them put things into italics?" I remember, for

my seventh birthday, my parents got me a boxed set of the Narnia books, all seven of them, and I lay on my bed and read them. That's what I did on my seventh birthday: I read my way through the complete set. I already had *The Lion, The Witch, and the Wardrobe* and *The Voyage of Dawn Treader,* but I didn't have the others. I actually covered the set in cellophane. I made my parents get me cellophane, and we wrapped my Narnia books in them, like books were wrapped in the library. Actually, I only remembered about this because, just curiously, about three or four years ago I went down into my library and pulled out dozens of books, and I pulled off the cellophane—and you could see the colors had not faded. I just wanted to see what the colors were like underneath.

SRB: *Let's walk through, say, five writers who were that kind of touchstone.*
NEIL: Roger Lancelyn Green.

HW: *You were reading Green when you were five?*
NEIL: No, that was when I was six or seven. My friend Steven had a copy of the Lancelyn Green *Tales of the Norsemen,* which I read a lot. I went out with my own money and bought *Tales of Ancient Egypt,* which was his retelling. When I was seven years old, it was C. S. Lewis, P. L. Travers, Enid Blyton, Roger Lancelyn Green, and whatever I found in the library. There's things I would find as a kid that would just be incredibly important to me, but hard to explain why—the novelization of [the TV series] *Bewitched.*

HW: Alice in Wonderland?
NEIL: *Alice in Wonderland* was a favorite title forever. Alice was default reading to the point where I knew it [by heart]. It's hard to talk about Alice, because I don't remember a time when I didn't know Alice. If you want to stick Lewis Carroll down as the fifth—put it this way: when I was seven, one of the things we had to do in English class, we would win a something-or-other, a gold star, if you learned anything from Lewis Carroll. And I remember getting up there and reciting in one breath—

> Fury said to a mouse that he met in the house "Let us both go to the law: I will prosecute you. Come, I'll take no denial: we must have a trial: for really this morning I've nothing to do." Said the mouse to the cur, "Such a trial, dear sir, with no jury or judge, would be wasting our breath." "I'll be judge, I'll be jury," said cunning old Fury: "I'll try the whole cause and condemn you to death."

Which I could do back then in one breath. I was six and a half, seven. I got a gold star for knowing that. And I knew that already. That's one of those things you almost don't mention because you can breathe it.

Also, you have to include all my parents' books, because they were all around. Any books that were around—Rudyard Kipling, I was big on Stalky and Co. when I was about eight—but nine was Moorcock.

SRB: Michael Moorcock?

NEIL: When I was nine, everything changed, in two completely different ways. When I was nine, I bought a copy of Michael Moorcock's *Stormbringer*. And [age] ten was Tolkien. Now, I discovered Tolkien in a sort of weird, upside-down way. The first Tolkien thing I read wasn't *The Hobbit,* and wasn't *Lord of the Rings*—it was a book called *The Tolkien Reader,* edited by Lin Carter, mostly consisting of a long essay by Peter S. Beagle called "Tolkien's Magic Ring." The first thing I read was actually the essay "Tolkien's Magic Ring," a bunch of poems, "Leaf by Niggle," and his essay "On Fairy Stories." I was seven or eight—I don't know what I gleaned from it, other than there's this really cool thing out there that you have to fight.

When I was nine—I know I was nine, because I know what school I was at—I was at a school called Ardingly, and they were doing a book sale my first term there; and again, I know it was my first term because I only did one term in that class, and then I got bounced up a year. And I bought two books which both proved very important. I bought *The Hobbit,* which they sold off. And I bought *Stormbringer,* and [Michael] Moorcock became an enormous touchstone. I would buy everything, and probably from 1969 through to about 1974 was the period when everything Mike Moorcock had ever written came into print in the UK, and I bought it all.

SRB: Did that include his work as an editor? That would have exposed you to many, many more writers.

NEIL: No. The thing that really was the giant head-fuck—which was, again, around the age of nine—was Judith Merril's book, which in America was published as *SF 12* [1967], that was republished in England as just *SF.* I remember discovering Samuel R. Delany, William Burroughs, and R. A. Lafferty from that. "The Primary Education of the Camiroi" is in there, so is "Narrow Valley"—it's astonishing.

HW: Was that the "new wave" stuff? It didn't even have a name yet, probably.

NEIL: I'd never have known that it was "new wave" at that point. [Regarding] Moorcock as editor—the thing is, I wasn't really discovering *New Worlds,* because that was a magazine, and I was [reading] books.

SRB: So, Jerry Cornelius, all the Elric stuff.

NEIL: I remember spending my own money, and getting my dad to write a check or some kind of postal money order, and sending off the money. There was a thing with publishers back then, where you clip out the order form in the book and send off for the books, and I got *Breakfast in the Ruins* [1972].

HW: Was this stuff going over your head at that age, when you were nine and ten years old?

NEIL: You get what you get from it. I do remember the realization that I wasn't going to be able to ask a teacher to explain to me what was happening in *A Cure for Cancer,* [1971] while Bishop Beasley was buggering his daughter Mitzi with a strap-on while eating a Mars bar. You were taking stuff out from it. I remember the rape scene in *The English Assassin* [1972] as being the first hard-core sex scene I'd ever read, and I was about eleven. I remember when I was twelve and reading [William Peter Blatty's] *The Exorcist* [1971], which was being passed around the school.

So, Moorcock became incredibly important to me around age nine, ten, eleven, twelve—those years. It grew and spread: I read an Elric book and liked it, and I bought *The Singing Citadel* [1970], and I liked that, too, and then I got *The Sleeping Sorceress* [1970, aka *The Vanishing Tower*], which I bought on holiday in Scotland, and discovered while reading that at one point Elric meets Erekosë and Corum. They were all the same thing, they were the Eternal Champions, so now I had all these other Moorcock books that I had seen but wasn't buying because they weren't Elric books. Now that I'd discovered they were all the same thing, I had to find them. But quite what I made of things like *Breakfast in the Ruins,* I have no idea to this day, but I remember reading it.

SRB: Now, were you writing in those styles as well?

NEIL: Sure, I ripped off Moorcock continually. But, you know what's interesting, I ripped off anything I found that I liked. I remember some Kenneth Bulmer sword-and-sorcery things that I loved as much as everything else, but the difference would be, you couldn't go back to it. I remember finding some short story I'd written which is filled with, you know, elements of the Kenneth Bulmer world with, I think, Conan in it, and Elric as well.

SRB: Were you writing this for yourself, or friends, or school?

NEIL: For school, mostly. [I loved] the idea that you could write something for pleasure [and for credit], you know? I could write anything as an essay. What I tended toward was serial fiction, but then you had to end that when you changed classes. You could write for a teacher, but once there was a new teacher—

HW: —just like different editors and publishers!

NEIL: Exactly. It's an anecdote I've told before, but it's true. In the school library, they had volume one and volume two of *Lord of the Rings,* which I would take home with me and read and bring back, and take home and read and bring back, and take home with me and read, and I eventually gave up the bring back part. I took it home with me and would read and read and read.

It lacked the third book. When I was twelve, I won the school English prize, and I also won the school reading prize. They said, "What would you like for your English prize?" And I said, "Well, what I would really like, I'd like *The Return of the King,* because I'd like to find out how it ends." They did this thing: "You know, because you won the reading prize and the English prize, we'll lump them in with the total value, and then we'll get you a cheaper volume." I was given a Penguin book of modern English verse, which again, was incredibly useful and a book I loved and read.

It's hard to explain now in any way that's easily comprehensible: I was a reader. I loved reading. Reading things gave me pleasure. I was very good at most subjects in school, not because I had any particular aptitude in them, but because normally on the first day of school they'd hand out the schoolbooks, and I'd read them—which would mean that I'd know what was coming up, because I'd read it. They'd give you this history book; I would have it read that day! I was an incredibly fast, incredibly enthusiastic reader who loved reading. This was what I got the most pleasure from of anything. I retained information fairly well, for I was young and had not as yet ruined my mind with cell phones. I didn't read to get something from it, but because it was pleasurable—whatever it was, it was pleasurable.

When I was seven, if someone asked who were my favorite authors, I could list four or five people. By the time I hit eight, Lewis Carroll was definitely a favorite, and I remember reading *Sylvie and Bruno* [1889] and trying to make a movie of it in my head, trying to figure out how you would shoot this thing as a movie. Which I look at now and go, "I must have been weird!" I remember, at roughly the same age, doing the same with *King Solomon's Mines*—

SRB: *H. Rider Haggard.*
NEIL: —and those books, thinking, "How would you make this? This should be a film, I think it would be more interesting." As far as I could tell, the school library really had some money to spend about 1910, and they got another bunch of money about 1935, another bunch of money about 1958. So life became: G. K. Chesterton, absolutely, everything. Baroness [Emmuska] Orczy—yes.

SRB: *Lovecraft?*
NEIL: Ah, H. P. Lovecraft, which I discovered—I think *Dagon* was the first of these I discovered in 1973, so I would have been twelve. Which is exactly the right age. Kurt Vonnegut was hugely, hugely important to me.

DARK HE WAS AND OPEN-EYED

HW: Did you find an author and just read everything right through?
NEIL. Yes. I'd go around everything. Edgar Wallace, and so on. You got all the kind of stuff. Plus, at the same age, there was a little bookshop they started, a

school bookshop; it would come through the school once a year. But what was really good is that they were not kid's books. That was where I found [Ray] Bradbury. The first Bradbury I read was *The Silver Locusts,* which is the English version of *The Martian Chronicles* [1950], but I remember buying *Dandelion Wine* [1947], buying *The Golden Apples of the Sun* [1950], those were the ones that I bought. *Dandelion Wine* I didn't like because I was eleven going on twelve when I read it, and I remember going, "Your picture of what it is to be twelve is hopelessly wrong, sir. It is nothing like this at all!"

I was voracious. I was an incredibly fast reader who got everything from the books. I was reading more than a book a day, because I would always have a book with me that I read at any down point; also, when I was meant to be doing anything else. I'd have the book you'd read during class, the book behind the thing. After lunch, we had to go lie down quietly for half an hour, forty-five minutes or whatever, and at that point you'd read a book: James Bond, or the Man from U.N.C.L.E. series, or *The Pan Book of Horror Stories* [1959], the stuff that was around when we were laying in these back bunks. Dennis Wheatley, I remember the school was into Dennis Wheatley in a big way, and everyone was passing these books around.

SRB: When and how did you get deeper into the genre—James Branch Cabell and so forth?

NEIL: Cabell I found thanks to the James Blish reprints when I was about thirteen. The year would have been 1972, maybe '73. In America, Lin Carter brought a bunch of that stuff back into print as Ballantine editions. In the UK, James Blish brought three of them back into print: *Figures of Earth* [1921], *The Silver Stallion* [1926], and *Jurgen* [1919]. I bought *Figures of Earth* and loved it, and bought the other two. *Jurgen* for me was slightly problematic, in that it was the first time in my life I'd ever bought a book that was badly misprinted, so I got three-quarters of the way through it, and then the previous signatures began again. I had to take it back to the shop, and they didn't have another copy, so I wound up actually taking it out of the library to find out how it ended. Even at the time, I found something slightly sort of sly and snickery about the treatment of sex. Probably, to be honest, because I'd grown up—even at that age, prepuberty—I'd been reading enough "new wave" stuff, the science fiction had become more explicit, descriptive, comfortable with sex, that there was something very schoolboy, in the worst sense, about Cabell. But I loved everything else.

When I was about eighteen, nineteen, in [the bookshop] Dark They Were and Golden-Eyed, I bought enough Cabell in paperback reprints to know that I really, really liked him. They'd brought back all the fantasy into print, and I really wanted to read more. I went up to the British Museum, and I talked them into giving me a British Museum reader's card. How, I do not know, but I did. And I mostly read James Branch Cabell, and also began writing a radio play about Kaspar Hauser, which I've forgotten about until this moment.

SRB: The fellow who turned up in a small German town in the 1820s, a mysterious shut-in who was essentially nonverbal, carrying two letters, and with no apparent prior contact with society.

NEIL: I was putting together a science fiction thing about Kaspar Hauser.

SRB: Let's not jump ahead too quickly; let's back up just a bit. Dark They Were and Golden-Eyed was a science fiction bookshop in London, yes? Is that the venue that got you deeper into science fiction as a preteen?

NEIL: There was a shop called Dark They Were and Golden-Eyed—at that point I was about fifteen, sixteen. I'd been able to go up to London on my own. One of the things that was amazing for me, and for science fiction and fantasy, was the decimalization in England. England used to be on pounds, shillings, and pence; twelve pence to the shilling, and stuff like that. In 1971, when I was ten, it went over to ten pence, you know, a hundred pence to the pound. You immediately got a period of very hefty inflation that my pocket money could not keep up with, but—and there is a but—I would go to the Wilmington Book Shop, our local bookshop, where John Banks worked. Very nice guy, dead now, which is really sad; at the time, young university graduate, science fiction fan, long hair and a beard. He liked it that this smart young ten- or eleven-year-old would come in, and what I would do is, I would go through the shelves, looking for the books published around the time of decimalization, because books were now thirty-five to forty pence, and I would find all of these authors, because they were cheap. That was how I found Thomas Disch—*Echo Round His Bones* [1967], "Look, a twenty p book!" It was frugality that drove me initially. I would just find all these authors because they were published in 1971; that's when they were affordable, and they were still on the shelves. After a while John would start pointing me at things: "Have you read such and such? I think you'd like such and such."

It was the first time I actually had an adult pointing me at books with a sense of what I liked. It's also worth mentioning that, by this point, in my school holidays, I would get my parents to drop me off at the library first thing in the morning. They would drive me up to the town library, and they would drop me off, and I would go in, and I'd read my way through the children's library, which was very easy. You could start at A and go all the way to Zed. When I'd finished, I tried that with the adult library. You got up to Brian Aldiss, and went, "You can't do this with an adult library, there are too many books, too many bad—too many things that I'm not interested in." So, after that, once I was loose in the adult library, it really was much more science fiction and fantasy, whereas in the kid's library it was everything; I just read everything in the children's library until I was done. What was really interesting about that is that, for reasons I still do not understand . . . there is no particular reason a small Sussex library should have had a fairly complete R. A. Lafferty collection. [Laughter.] A better R. A. Lafferty collection than dedicated science fiction collections.

I had a lovely moment recently that made me feel my existence was not a useless and wasted thing. I had a cup of tea with Bill Hader, who is now on *Saturday Night Live,* a very fine young comedian and actor. He's from Oklahoma, and he reads my blog, he reads my stuff. In *Fragile Things* I do a story called "Sunbird," which is my R. A. Lafferty pastiche, and I'd written about Lafferty in there, and said, "Comes from Oklahoma, great unsung genius of American literature." Because of that, Hader had gone out and found all this Lafferty stuff. He's from Oklahoma—he's from Tulsa—and at one point he got interviewed by his local newspaper, and they asked, "Who really would you consider the great Oklahoman, the great Tulsan?" "R. A. Lafferty!" he said, and I felt great—I was spreading the word: Look, an Oklahoman has now learned of one of his own—

SRB: —*because of that little Sussex library*—
NEIL: —because of a little Sussex library that had this—they had these, uh, Dobson Books, I think they were called. Some tiny English publisher who I learned later basically were publishing for the library trade, and would do things in editions of about a thousand copies. My library bought Laffertys.

Anyway, there's a point where what I'm doing is reading everything. I've joked about the fact that my parents would frisk me for books before family functions—

SRB: —*to make sure you weren't bringing things along.*—
NEIL: Absolutely. If I was going to a bar mitzvah or a wedding or whatever, I would be reading in the car until I got out of the car, and they would frisk me for a book. It normally wouldn't do any good, because I would find something to read there. I'd just go sit underneath the table, or in a corner, or wherever. I got a phone call the other day from my sister Lizzie, who is my younger sister—

HW: *Who are your sisters?*
NEIL: Claire, who's one year, eleven months and five days younger than I am, and Lizzie, who is about six years younger. Actually, what's really weird is that Mike and Holly are the same distance apart to the day that Claire and I are, which actually made it (a) in some ways very easy parenting, because it was really familiar territory, this age difference, and also, (b) it makes it really easy for me to remember their birthdays, because I can do the same sums—I know that sum apart.

Anyway, Lizzie was saying—and it was very odd, one of these very weird "seeing yourself through somebody else's eyes" things—she was saying how proud she was of me at the *Beowulf* premiere. She said, "I saw you come on, and they brought you up with Anthony Hopkins and Angelina Jolie and Crispin Glover, and you got as much applause from the audience as they did, and I thought, 'My brother is cool'; and I remember dropping you off at school, when you were eleven or twelve, and I would have been five or six, and you got home from school, reading, and you would walk down the path from the school, reading, and I just thought, 'My brother is so embarrassing.'" [Laughter.] She said, "And finally, thirty-two years later, I'm seeing you up on the thing, and thinking, 'He's not actually embarrassing and weird, he's somehow become cool.'"

HW: You mentioned making movies in your head earlier. Why were you thinking cinematically?

NEIL: I don't know. I used to read things and translate them into my head into other forms. Let's put it this way: My fantasies were writerly fantasies. By the time I was eleven, twelve years old, my fantasy was that I [would] be in a universe in which I had a copy of *The Lord of the Rings,* and would enter a parallel universe—exactly the same as the one I had left, except nobody had written *Lord of the Rings,* I had the only copy. And I would give my copy of *Lord of the Rings,* to an adult, who I would get to type it out, and I would hand over that typed script to a publishing house, with my name on the front, and I would be the person who'd written *Lord of the Rings.* That was my little—

SRB: —early plagiarism fantasy. [Laughter.]

NEIL: —early plagiarism fantasy. But it wasn't plagiarism; I wanted to be the person who'd written *Lord of the Rings.* By the time I was about thirteen, my next fantasy—because that one didn't take you very far. It only gets you the first one, but what about after that? You're not creating anything—so then I made up this huge story in my head about a precious stone that gets split into thirteen different pieces, that gets sent off across time and space, and then has to be rounded up. And every book would be in a different genre as well. You'd have the Western one, the Atlantean one, you'd have the Conan one, but what was important was how they were going to get written. How they were going to get written is, I was then going to kidnap all of my favorite writers, living and dead, imprison them together in a huge castle, including myself as one of their number. So there would be this thirteen-year-old kid, and then they would all be told they had to collaborate on these novels, and two of them were to take a novel each. So, you know, G. K. Chesterton and Len Wein had to work together, and Chip Delany and Hope Mirelees or whatever—but I wanted to be one of their number, I didn't want them to know I had done this to them. I also wanted to learn; that was the thing of putting all my favorite writers together—to see how they did it!

HW: What was your social life like at this point?

NEIL: It was easier when I was at the school I was at from ages nine to thirteen, because even though I was slightly odd, I was *their* odd. I was an odd that belonged to them, that they had grown up with. Neil was the kid you went to when you wanted to know what a word meant. I had my skill set, and the biggest problem I had was when, after a term, the school bumped me up a year. That was really weird, because I went from the kids my age to kids a year older, which, as you're heading through puberty, was really, really weird. All these kids would go nipping off to the woods to start masturbating or whatever, and I thought, "I have no idea what's going on here." So that was weird. And then, when I got to be twelve, and all the kids then went into the upper school, they decided to keep me down a year. It was a very odd sort of thing. Then I changed schools, from Ardingly to Whitgift; one in Sussex, one up in Croydon, in South London.

HW: *Is that like going from junior high to high school in America?*
NEIL: Well, nothing matches exactly, but—essentially, yeah. It would probably be easier if you think of it as me going to middle school in Sussex, and then going to a high school in South London. I had to go by train every day. That was much harder: I'm suddenly thirteen and a half, and I'm walking through a class, and someone says, "Gai-man? Are you gay?" Which wasn't the first time that gag had been made.

fINDING THE PATH

SRB: *When did the reading as a focal point become writing as the focal point? And when did the community, however vestigial, of reading become a community of writers that you felt part of?*
NEIL: I did it all upside down. I was about—twenty-one, maybe? I had a really bad night, and all I remember is, it was the very first night of my life that I had not been able to sleep, just couldn't sleep. That [possibility] hadn't occurred to me before. I remember lying there in bed, and I had this sort of vision, this train of thought. And the train of thought went, "OK, let's say I'm eighty years old, and I'm on my death bed. And I say to myself, as my life ends, 'I could have been a writer. I could have actually been a writer.'" And I would die not knowing if I was lying to myself or not—and I found that unbearable. I found the idea that I would die thinking maybe I was kidding myself, a terrible thing. It would be better to go and try and be a writer, and to fail, and to at least know that no, I was put on Earth to be a hotel manager or executive or whatever. It would be better to do that. The worst thing that I could think of for myself in the world, at that point, was just the idea of not knowing if I was lying to myself or not. Because in my heart, I'd think I was a writer.

HW: *Had you put things to paper?*
NEIL: Yeah, but I would never finish anything. Maybe I had a few short stories. I'd corresponded occasionally with R. A. Lafferty. I'd write things, I wouldn't finish them—I thought I was brilliant. Luckily, I had no idea how crap I was. I had a certain facility for doing other people's voices, but absolutely nothing to say, which is of course the hardest part of anything for most writers in their late teens, early twenties.

I saw something a writer wrote online—I wish I could remember which one—when he was saying that he came to me and asked me for advice when he was a very young writer. He said, "Look, I'm good, I can finish things, I can write. I don't really have anything to write about, I'm not really selling anything. What would you suggest?" And apparently I told him to "go and live." I said, "Go do things, and everything else will sort itself out." That's the biggest problem that most nineteen-twenty-twenty-one-year-old writers have.

Bear in mind that I was setting myself up, standards-wise: Samuel R. Delany, at nineteen, writes *The Fall of the Towers* book [1963–65, collected 1971]. At twenty, twenty-one, he's writing *The Einstein Interception* [1967]. "Fuck, look at me, I haven't written *Fall of the Towers* yet"—the truth was, I had nothing to write, really. I could do other people's styles, I could do pastiche—I'd handwritten things, I couldn't type yet—and then, after my awful night, things started changing. I started writing. I started thinking of myself as a writer. I bought an old manual typewriter, and a book on teaching yourself typing, and I started writing my first book—unfortunately, I finished the book before I finished the typing course. Which meant I got three or four letters in, and was quite good, and then I started hunting and pecking. Now I am probably the fastest hunt-and-peck typist you've ever seen. I'm not a two-fingered typist, but I'm not a ten-fingered typist, I'm a sort of in-between—maybe if I'd written a longer novel, or finished the course, but I'm a five-fingered typist, or whatever. That was a book called *My Great Aunt Ermintrude*, which is upstairs in the attic. That would have been 1981 or '82, somewhere in there.

By way of a footnote, *My Great Aunt Ermintrude*—it was a children's book—I used to read to Maddy, from more or less the age of three until more or less the age of ten and a half. I would read to her every night, and would do it from pretty much anywhere in the world I was as well. I would call home and read to her. Somewhere in there, shortly after *Coraline* and *Wolves in the Walls* was published, I was suddenly looking around, and went, "I seem to be a children's author. I have that children's book in the attic! I will go and pull it out," and I thought, "Wouldn't this be great! I can just send it in, and I have a book going in." So I pulled it out, and over the next five nights I read it to Maddy. There was one page, about three-quarters of the way through, that actually felt like me, and that I delighted in. You could see, if you knew what I later turned into, that this page was absolute pure quintessential Neil Gaiman. [Laughter.] One page, out of about one hundred and eighteen. I keep the manuscript in the attic, and I'm sure I'll hand it over to some university with my papers and whatever, and I really hope nobody decides to publish it after my death. There is a reason authors don't publish stuff during their lifetime; we have a quality-control thing. Especially with the posthumous stuff: if Tolkien had wanted *The Father Christmas Letters* [1976] published, he would have published them.

HW: Back to 1981. Were you in university at this point?

NEIL: No, at this point, I'm still living at home. I'm just off trying to write. I'm failing. I'm sending stuff out, and it's coming back. I'm writing short stories, and sending them out, and they're coming back.

SRB: *What was your perception of a writer's life, at this point?*

NEIL: It's probably worth mentioning here, just as a weird little oddity, because it contradicts all facts, that while I wanted to be a writer, what I thought I probably was was a hard science-fiction writer, like Larry Niven, despite the fact that I had no particular interest or expertise in the hard sciences. The place that my head went was automatically fantasy or horror. My favorite authors were Moorcock, a fantasist, and [Roger] Zelazny. This was the place my head went. Pretty much everything that I'd written at school for myself for pleasure, or as essays or whatever, was fantasy. I have no idea why I thought that I was going to grow up to be a hard science-fiction writer when I got good, when I got confident.

I think part of it was actually because the people who talked about the nuts and bolts of writing—this is actually the first time I've ever thought this one through, and I could be wrong—but the people who talked about the nuts and bolts of crafting a story and selling fiction, the books that I had on how you did this, were all science fiction, and all fairly hard science-fiction. People like [Isaac] Asimov would actually talk about the background and the editors and the circumstances under which these were written. People like Larry Niven wrote wonderful essays, where he'd talk about telling people stories to find out whether they'd work or not. I had the Reginald Bretnor book *The Craft of Science Fiction* [1976], twenty-five essays by really good writers: [Harlan] Ellison, on writing TV drama and film; Larry Niven, on crafting names and alien communities. [In another book] Andrew J. Offutt [wrote about surviving as a writer]—the idea that you could put your carbon paper in the oven and heat it up and reuse it, which honestly is the kind of thing that was incredibly useful. It's very hard to understand right now, in these days, where the information and the physical object are different, the idea of a world in which the cost of producing the physical object—the cost of photocopying, the cost of typing, the cost of—

SRB: *It was a trip into town to get photocopies—before that, it was carbon paper or nothing.*

NEIL: —you had to go down somewhere and get it photocopied. It was a different world; ten p a copy.

SRB: *Of course, the availability of that nuts-and-bolts information to the current generation is far beyond anything that was available to an aspiring writer in 1969, '70, '71—*

NEIL: I think that may have been why I thought I was going to be a science fiction writer, because that was the only information out there. If I'd had a good book on writing horror or fantasy . . . also, the other thing, truthfully, is if I'd seen a market for it, if I'd known where I could sell the stuff . . . I sort of knew there were science fiction magazines.

I had a very odd attitude—well, not odd, actually. I had a perfectly understandable, if erroneous, attitude to and conception of how finances worked for a writer. I think how I figured it worked was more or less like this: You are a writer. You announce to the world that you are a writer. You sit down and you write a perfect sonnet. Somebody draws up at your door, and knocks on your door, and says, "We understand that you have written a perfect sonnet." And you say, "Yes," and they say, "May we publish it?" And you say, "Yes," and they say, "This is a check for everything you will ever need financially for the rest of your life, and you may keep the car that I drove up in; we will publish your sonnet, and it will be in books that will be read in schools, and now, forever you are at peace in your sonnethood."

SRB: When did you hit the hard wall of reality?
NEIL: Oh, I think probably at the point when I got my first check for whatever it is I wrote. But there was this sort of point where I figured, if you're a writer, you must live in this special world—

HW: —and now you do.
NEIL: —and now I do. And yet I still live in this strange world, this peculiar world, where I get called a whore for having done stuff in Hollywood. On the one hand, it's really hard to credit people with, "Now I have sold out and I am a whore for work that I did in 1997, before I wrote all those things that you like," so I'm not quite sure how that one works. It's an odd place. But it's also the place that pays my health insurance. I live in America, I have a family. If I write one movie every eighteen months, whether it gets made or not, I have health insurance. So I try and make a point of writing one movie—

SRB: It's also the perverse economy of people's projections, which are not that far from the fantasy of what a writer was to be that you harbored yourself, before you were writing professionally. It's this la-la land that most people project onto any person who has any visible success—meaning, they know what your name is, so you must be rich, wealthy, comfortable, you know—
NEIL: That is why I always remember that Andrew J. Offutt essay in *The Craft of Science Fiction,* and why it was cool and important for me: Just this guy writing basically about how to be a writer while starving. How to eke the most out of . . . What are you typing your rough draft on the back of? It was a wonderful salutary essay for an eighteen- or nineteen-year-old who always wanted to be a writer. That was really good, because that was the world I was in for the first few years of my life as a writer.

FELLOW TRAVELERS

SRB: What was the initial community of writers you were in?
NEIL: I was twenty-two years old when I found everybody. It was September; I had been writing fiction unsuccessfully, and I'd been sending it out. Nobody wants to

buy anything, I've sent out *My Great Aunt Ermintrude,* I've sent out short stories. Stuff had been coming back with letters to me. Very little had been coming back with "not quite right, does not meet our requirements" slips; most of it had been coming back with, you know, "There's some good stuff in here, but you're not ready," and whatever. Which, looking back on it, is because there was good stuff in there, but I wasn't ready. However, luckily, I did not choose to believe that. Luckily, I went, "Either I have no talent, or I'm doing this wrong. Therefore, I'm going to understand the world." And I got up and I said, "I'm a journalist. As of right now, I'm a freelance journalist specializing in science fiction, fantasy, and horror in the world of publishing, because that's what I want to understand."

HW: Was this naïveté, or faith in yourself, or arrogance, or just being twenty-two?
NEIL: I think it was a giant cake, and all of those things were ingredients. [Laughter.] The arrogance was in going, "I am good enough, therefore I'm going to find out how this thing works." I'm writing stuff, I'm sending stuff out, stuff comes back—I have no control over this. I do not understand the system; I do not know these people. I have to understand it; I need to know how it all works, because I cannot make the system work in a world in which I write story, I put it in the post, it comes back. And while I just said the stuff wasn't very good, it would also be true to say that that stuff included things like "The Case of the Four and Twenty Blackbirds" and "We Can Get Them for You Wholesale," stories that have since been published. That was all being written around this time. There was a lot of rubbish, too. If there was one thing I had, it was time. I was writing. I had that bit down.

So I got on the phone. I picked up a copy of a very short-lived magazine called *Ad Astra,* and I noticed in the small ads in the back, it said, "Fantasy Con: Guest of Honor: Gene Wolfe." And I thought, "I'm a big fan of Gene Wolfe, I love Gene Wolfe, Gene Wolfe is a genius." So I just started phoning editors, I had a copy of the *Writer/Artist Yearbook,* it had the phone number and features editor name for most of the newspapers in England, and I just started phoning, and saying, "Hello, I'm a journalist, I've got an interview with Gene Wolfe, would you like it." And they'd say, "Who's Gene Wolfe?" and at some point in there, I found somebody who said, "Oh, yeah, Fantasy Con, Gene Wolfe is there with Bob Silverberg." So at that point, my spiel became, "I'm doing an interview with Bob Silverberg and Gene Wolfe, would you like it?" Mainly, people said no. I got someone who said, "What would your angle be, what would your hook be?" It hadn't occurred to me that one would need an angle or a hook, so I said, "Oh, Bob Silverberg's the guy who put sex into science fiction," and they said, "Oh, why don't you pitch it to *Penthouse?* They like anything that's arty with a sex angle." And I said, "Oh, okay." So I go to *Penthouse,* talked to the editor: a nice Australian. And I say, "I've got an interview with Bob Silverberg, the man who put sex into science fiction," and they said, "Sounds great! Oh, we've got a science fiction angle, we love that good ol' Silverberg. I'll tell you what: If you could ever get an interview with

Douglas Adams, whoa, that'd be great." So then I phone the publisher, I phone Gollanz, and I say, "Hello, Bob Silverberg; want to do an interview for *Penthouse*." And they say, "Great." So I went up to the New Imperial Hotel—which is no longer there, I think—in Birmingham, and did an interview with Bob Silverberg for *Penthouse*.

[At the same time] I did an article called "Fantasy Time at the New Imperial," which was done for some London listings magazine. The editor commissioned it, and then, when I went and handed it in, the editor was putting the furniture from the office on the truck that her dad was about to drive away—the magazine no longer existed. But, because I had to do that article that had already been commissioned, I'd spoken to Peter Nichols and Gene Wolfe and to Steve Jones. I'd gone around, and I'd really forced myself—and I'm kind of shy—to actually mingle more and talk to people, and had the experience, because it was for the article. I met Steve Jones, Jo Fletcher. I met Ramsey Campbell there—I mean, Ramsey and Jenny, when their kids were one and two, and I was twenty-two. Steve Jones said, "Come along to BFS"—the British Fantasy Society—"it's open night." So I went to that, and Jo Fletcher introduced me to Kim Newman. She said, "You'll like him, he's another aspiring author," and Kim and I hit it off. It was very much him as the elderly, sage one, and me as the bouncy, enthusiastic one.

SRB: Kim always carries himself as a gent.

NEIL: It's strange, right now, encountering Kim, aged forty-eight, because Kim was a forty-eight-year-old twenty-three-year-old. He had that thing from when I first met him: He had the mutton chops. He's become more Chestertonian, and has grown into it, but yes, he had that thing going on from the word "go." I tried copying, and failed: I bought a hat. Kim wore these dapper trilbies and things, and I thought, "I can do that," and I bought a hat. A lovely sort of gray hat, but I'm so not a hat-wearing person: I'd leave it in restaurants. All over London I would go, knock on restaurant doors at eleven o'clock when they first opened: "I left a hat here last night." Eventually one day I didn't go back for it.

SRB: *You and Kim collaborated as writers early on, including some pieces written under pen names.*

NEIL: We did. Oh, God—Dr. Sigmund von Doppelganger, Paul Lobkowitz—I was writing at the time under at least three pseudonyms: Gerry Musgrave, Richard Grey, and W. C. Gull, maybe others. I did a *2000 AD* story about a man who gets his pen names surgically removed. Kim and I had pseudonyms when it was the two of us, and then sometimes with Stefan [Jaworzyn], and Eugene Byrne. In the beginning it was just Kim and me. Later on, Stefan Jaworzyn drifted into and out of the mix again.

The thing was, we were freelancers. We made money by writing things and selling them. Kim and I and sometimes other people would get together for weekends.

I'd stay over, sleep on the floor. We would buy cheap white wine, cheap bread, cheap pâté; we'd get a few bad videos, for when things flagged. We would sit there—one of us would write things down and take notes. We tried once writing fiction together, it didn't work, and we never did it again. It was obvious that did not work, but we could do humor articles, and any kind of nonfiction humor articles. We would just sit there and make each other laugh while writing stuff down. I've got tubs filled with this stuff in the attic: articles on "Whatever happened to . . . ?" Interviews with imaginary people, an interview with Santa Claus, and whatever. We called ourselves the Peace & Love Corporation, which was the name on the bank account, and Eugene Byrne still annually sends Kim and I statements about how much money is in the Peace & Love Corporation bank account, and what we propose to do with it. I think it's something under the order of ten pounds, and Eugene will send these hilarious e-mails: things like, "Okay, this is what we will do with it," how we will put the money in a compound-interest account and own the universe eighteen thousand years from now, at which point the entire destiny of the human race will have run its course, and we will have all the real estate.

SRB: *About your early work with Kim: I loved* Ghastly Beyond Belief. *Despite the typos and flaws in the published version, that was a really cool project to step out with.*

NEIL: So Kim Newman and I had just met at BFS—Jo had introduced us—and I'm chatting with Kim, and I say, "Yeah, I've had stories accepted by *Interzone*," and he says, "I want to do a big Guy N. Smith kind of novel about a huge badger [laughter] that terrorizes the south of England, and I'm going to call it *The Scent*." And I said, "I think one could do a science fiction fantasy book of quotations and call it *Beam Me Up, Scotty*," and Kim said, "I'll do the film half, you do the rest." And being Kim, two days later, in the post—back then you used things like post—I got a sample chapter, and Kim's outline of what he wanted to do. So I wrote my sample chapter and proposal, and sent it off to three publishers, one of whom never replied, one of whom said it was too close to something else, and one of whom was Faith Brooker, who I had met at Fantasy Con. She was looking after Gene Wolfe; she was basically sort of a secretary back then for a respected editor. Faith liked the thing. She took me and Kim out to lunch, and we were the first authors she'd ever been allowed to take out to lunch, which meant that her boss had to come in at the end of the meal and actually pay the tab. She basically said, "Yeah, we'll do it, what we like best is the emphasis on the bad stuff, so let's go for that," so *Beam Me Up, Scotty* became *Ghastly Beyond Belief*.

Nobody had told me at that point that authors weren't supposed to get involved with cover designs, so I just designed a cover on a napkin, indicating the word "ghastly" had to be green, the girl has to be running away, and here's the brain monster behind her, and we need Saturn in the sky, and a rocket ship. She didn't know authors didn't do that either, so she gave it to an art director, who gave it to an artist, and that's why we got that cover. And it was published to much enthusiasm. It was only ever published in the UK. We sent it to a U.S. publisher, who wrote back telling us they loved it, and they couldn't send the copy back because so many people were reading it in the office, and how everyone was laughing over it, and that they didn't think they could publish it.

I look back on it with a certain amount of relief, just as I had a certain amount of relief on the failure of the Duran Duran book. I wrote *Duran Duran* for Proteus. I was offered three choices—Barry Manilow, Def Leppard, or Duran Duran. I chose Duran Duran. My plans were, I would eventually do things like the Velvet Underground, things that I wanted to do. I did it, it came out at the height of Duran Duran mania, sold out in a week, that was it, first printing gone, I thought, "Oh my God, I've earned back my advance, I'm now into royalties, this will be amazing." Plus, I know this has been happening in America. Two weeks later, Proteus Books was sued by its American distributor and taken into involuntary liquidation. As a result of which, I never saw anything past that initial advance. I looked back on it and saw that I had spent three or four months of my life on a book that I really had no desire to read. I did it for the money, it bought me an electric typewriter, and paid the rent for the next year, but I had sort of learned a lesson there, because I didn't have a book I could be proud of.

And it was a good thing. If that book had paid royalties . . . I was hungry, I was out there on my own in London, a freelance journalist, feeding myself with my pen, which is what I've been doing for the past twenty years—it was that terribly simple. And if I'd made a lot of money from it, and if Proteus had still been there, I would have written the next one, and I could see my life—

I tried to explain to Holly, recently, because Holly is off in London right now. She wants to be in film, film production, and she gets offered jobs, and sometimes, she genuinely doesn't know which job she should pursue. The only thing I can tell her is that I was in her position, wanting to write comics, and wanting to write fiction, now making a living as a freelance journalist. I say to her, look, I used to think it was a mountain, a thing I wanted to do, a thing I wanted to be, and as long as I was walking toward the mountain, it was okay. I told her she needs to figure out what her mountain is, and you can sort of judge these things by—does it take you toward the mountain?

The scary thing is, within a few months of declaring that I was a journalist, I'd now had two books out. I found a quote from Muddy Waters which I tapped out and taped to my typewriter. It was, "Don't let your mouth write no check your tail can't cash." I'd found I'd had this ability to persuade people, convince people, to charm them. But, if Proteus hadn't gone down, I might have found myself walking away from what I really wanted to do.

The first real job offer I got was in 1985. Here I am, married, with two children, Holly is a newborn, Mike is a toddler. We don't have a mortgage, my dad's given us a space, we're not paying rent at the time, which was a good thing, but we were barely paying the bills, and I get a call from *Penthouse,* saying we'd like you to be the features editor—a real job, paying real money—at a point where we were having petty squabbles about money. I chose not to take it, because I was somehow smart enough to know that I was walking away. I had this amazing, complete confidence in my ability, totally unjustified—

SRB: You also did Don't Panic.

NEIL: I had interviewed Douglas [Adams] a few times, for *Penthouse,* and I had more interview than I could use, so I sold the extra material, first to *Knave,* then to *Fantasy Empire.* We sort of now knew each other, and Richard Hollis, who was going to do the book, couldn't, for reasons I was never told, and I was asked to do it. I interviewed him more; he gave me the run of his archives. What I walked away with from the writing of *Don't Panic* was the sense that "I can do this."

I wrote the five-thousand-word [opening] scene of *Good Omens,* and then sort of abandoned it. Another weird "walking toward the mountain" moment. A lot of stuff is being written at this point: *Violent Cases,* the [Knockabout] bible book, more, from there—I wrote *Good Omens,* the first chapter, and I stopped, because I had the thought that "Terry Pratchett is the guy who writes funny fantasy novels, I will be [considered] the guy who writes funny horror novels, and that is not where I want to live." I knew enough about myself to realize I would be doomed if I was that one thing. Already I'd seen friends of mine, moderately successful, talking about the book they wanted to do that their publishers wouldn't let them do, because it wasn't like the last one, it didn't fit some preconceived notion.

The important thing is that, at that time, I was writing a lot. It's that old Chuck Jones line, that you've got a million bad drawings, and the paraphrased Ray Bradbury line, that you've got a million lines of shit, and you've got to get it out of your system. I'm writing, and that's important. Most of it isn't prose, but I'm getting the words out.

I just put that first *Good Omens* chapter away. Later, Terry Pratchett called and asked if I wanted to sell him the idea, or if I wanted to do it with him. Terry is already the guy who writes funny novels, so I won't get typecast. I wrote the first draft, which is actually called *William the Antichrist.*

fOUR-COLOR DREAMS

SRB: Jean-Marc Lofficier mentioned to me that during these early years you once walked up to him and told him he was the reason you didn't get to do Boy Commandos for DC Comics. This was before Black Orchid, before Sandman.[4]

NEIL: True. I had such a great pitch for Boy Commandos. [It] was very much 1987, but the truth is, you could do it now and it would work. What I was going to do was, you'd meet the original Boy Commandos all grown up. The fat English kid would be a newspaper editor. Brooklyn, with the derby . . . they've all grown up. The idea was that Captain Rick Carter, who was the boss of the Boy Commandos, was basically court-martialed during the Korean War for taking boys into combat zones. He is now essentially a mercenary who is doing the same thing: He's getting these kids out of orphanages and taking them out into combat zones. In 1987, I forget where we were: Lebanon or wherever. If you were doing it now, it would be Iraq. But the idea is, you've got these four old men, and their lives were ruined, because it's never as good as it was when they were twelve. When they were twelve, their posters were up on the walls, they were heroes, they were loved, and it was all an adventure. They're now these old men going into a battle zone, in order to stop Carter from this thing that he'd been doing—and that was my *Boy Commandos* plot. And I thought it was really good.

SRB: And what killed it was that Jean-Marc had already done something with them—
NEIL: —or had dibs on them. It was that weird thing at DC, or he put in a proposal that had been accepted, but it was never published? I'm not sure. I don't even think Jean-Marc was using them, but he had dibs on them. Anyway, I don't remember the other unsuccessful pitches.

SRB: What led to Black Orchid being accepted? When I first met you, I recall you had a parcel of pitches for DC.
NEIL: I once pitched a Phantom Stranger, and they sat there and said, "That's weird, Grant Morrison pitched us a Phantom Stranger, too; unfortunately, Paul Kupperberg's got it, so there'll be no Grant Morrison and no Neil Gaiman Phantom Stranger." Kupperberg's ended up being one of the most beautifully drawn Phantom Stranger stories there's ever been. But I did actually get to write a couple of pages and a few lines of dialogue for the Phantom Stranger in my little Action Comics special. So, they said, "No, well, who else would you like to do?" "Well, the Demon?" They said, "No, because Matt Wagner's got that." So I said, "What about the Forever People." At one point, I don't think I had a plan, I just started listing things—and somewhere in there, I said, "Black Orchid."

SRB: What was their reaction?
NEIL: Karen actually said, "Black Hawk Kid, who's he?" [Laughter.] Which actually is the thing that made me the happiest, and then Dick Giordano said, "No, Black Orchid, great costume, do her!" And Dave [McKean] and I walked out, and Dave said, "They didn't mean it, they didn't actually want us to do Black Orchid?" And I said, "Well, they said they did." And he said, "Well, what have you got me into? You know, a hundred and eighty pages of cheesecake?" And I said, "No!" He said, "Well, I liked that stuff you were talking about, with doing

something with the Amazon rain forest." I said, "Okay, I'll do it, I'll put the Amazon rain forest in there." And I had no idea what I was doing, and I plotted Black Orchid on the train home. I phoned Dave the next morning at art college. He very famously tells the story about how people in the art college thought it was some kind of bizarre practical joke, because he's standing there on the phone, the line getting longer and longer behind him, people waiting to use the phone—there weren't cell phones in those days. And he's not saying anything, because I'm telling him the story of Black Orchid. We got to the end, and he did four paintings, four character study paintings, they were gorgeous—they've never been seen since. They went into DC and they were never seen again. They never got returned.

I did an outline, and dropped it off on the Saturday. We had the meeting on the Thursday, they had a party on the Saturday, and they left on the Sunday. Several years later I learned from Karen that the thing that actually meant they took us seriously, and the thing that impressed them was, Thursday they gave us the pitch, and by the time they flew home on Sunday they had four big paintings and the outline, the treatment. I try to impress that on people, that sometimes it's pretty good to do it, even if it's not perfect. You're much better off striking when the iron is hot. The Black Orchid thing I proposed to them wasn't Prestige Format. I think I proposed a four-issue miniseries. It ended the middle of issue two or three, and Karen suggested roughing it up a bit more.

SRB: So it would have ended with Orchid in the jungle with the new seed; the rest was a new coda, with the villains arriving.

NEIL: Yeah, exactly. I think that was added on. And then they suddenly told us it was going to be in the Prestige Format, and that was terrifying, because the only thing that had been in the Prestige Format at that point was [Frank Miller's] *The Dark Knight Returns.* And then I got that phone call from Karen—we're halfway through the whole thing—and she says, "Look, we've just been sort of thinking about this thing, and you're two guys no one's heard of doing a character nobody remembers, and it's a female character, and female characters don't sell, and we think this is a huge problem, so we want you to do a monthly comic book, and we're going to give Dave a Batman comic to do." Grant Morrison had written this thing called *Arkham Asylum,* and she said, "Well, we want Dave to do this first, and we want you to start writing a comic, so pick a monthly comic." The idea of me writing a monthly comic was something that they hit upon as a sales buttress for *Black Orchid.*

Of course, then, what happened is, Dave got grumpy enough about the idea of doing *Arkham* first, and then having Black Orchid come out, because people would see it as a step back. Also, I think we all got a bit more confident about Black Orchid. But I also think there was a level on which they didn't want a hundred and eighty pages or whatever it was of fully painted art that they'd paid quite a lot of money for sitting in inventory—we were just starting out, but it was still fully painted art, and they're paying for it.

SRB: *That was also a point at which a painted comic alone was a sales point.*
NEIL: What wound up happening, in the way my life always works, is things happen together; suddenly, *Sandman* issue one is coming out the same time that *Black Orchid* issue one is coming out, or three weeks later, or something like that, despite the fact that they were written a year and a half apart. In terms of what the initial strategy was meant to accomplish, it never actually happened, but it was still a cool thing.

HW: *When you started Sandman, were you just scripting issue to issue, or did you have that longer arc in mind?*
NEIL: Yes.

SRB: *You did? Because we actually had ongoing arguments—*
NEIL: We had arguments?

SRB: *"Neil, they are never going to let you kill Sandman." We argued about that for years.*
NEIL: Actually, the way the arguments would begin with me and Steve—I think Steve was one of the very, very few people that I briefed on the giant—I think you were the only one! In some restaurant or something.

SRB: *We went out and ate, and it was on the same scale as when Alan [Moore] laid out the whole of From Hell in one phone conversation—you laid it all out, this entire tapestry, beginning, middle, and end.*
NEIL: Yes, I remember briefing you on it.

SRB: *I didn't believe DC was going to let you bring it to a close.*
NEIL: Well, you also didn't believe they were going to stop the comic—so, yeah. It's so strange, the arguments I used to have with you, and with Dave Sim. Dave was forever on me to leave DC, because they would put this stuff out of print the moment my back was turned. The moment that I stopped doing a monthly comic, [he thought] they would automatically put this stuff out of print, despite having a "created by" royalty, because I didn't own it, I couldn't control it.

SRB: *Well, it was a different era. I was coming from my experience with DC in the eighties, which was an obsolete view.*
NEIL: Well, no, it wasn't obsolete, and you weren't wrong, but what I was essentially trying to do was play chess with them. I floated my little trial balloon along about issue twenty-two, twenty-three. We'd been doing this for a couple of years,

and I remember saying to Karen somewhere in there, "I think I'm going to want *Sandman* to stop when I stop." And she said, "You know that will never happen," and so on. A few months later, I was having dinner with [DC publisher] Jeanette Kahn, and during the course of the dinner, I said, "I think I'm going to want Sandman to stop when I stop," and she said, "Oh, sweetie, you know, that's not the way we do things in comics," and so on. And I said, "Okay, not a problem." And I just carry on with my grand plan, and everything keeps going. And then people started asking me in interviews what I'm going to be doing, and how it's going to work once Sandman stops. And I said, "DC will stop *Sandman* when I'm done, which I would really like, or they'll carry on, and I don't really have any control of it. Although obviously, if they did carry it on, I would not do any further work ever for DC. If they stop it when I stop it, I will maintain a very cheerful business relationship with DC." And that's basically what they did. Whether those interview quotes did any good or not, I don't know, but it is very true that round about issue sixty-ish, well over two years away from the end of *Sandman,* I remember Karen just saying to me at some point, "We really aren't going to be able to continue this when you're done, are we? We should just end this," and I said, "Yes." And it was never more complicated or big or grandiose than that. Years had gone by, and honestly, it was now obvious. No one was thinking, "We have to bring Paul Kupperberg in to take over." It wasn't that thing.

SRB: You were the linchpin in the transition of the comics market to collections, trade-paperback-collected editions, and in the book market's adoption of the graphic novel format. Others were critical there, too, but Sandman really was one of the linchpins, paving the way for the graphic novel market as we know it today.

NEIL: I was the linchpin, hugely accidentally. It was one of those things that if you look back on it, you think, "My God, wasn't Gaiman a brilliant career strategist," but the way that it happened was that DC had heard that in *Rolling Stone*'s "Hot Issue" of 1989, they picked Sandman as the hot comic. Bruce Bristow decided to take out an ad. The economics of taking out an ad meant that they had to have something to sell. The sudden idea was, we're going to do a graphic novel collection of *The Doll's House,* the book we were already on. Which meant that suddenly, issue sixteen is hitting the stands and *The Doll's House* collection is coming out at exactly the same time, looking like it had been designed over a couple of days. Which is exactly what happened, because they only had two days to put it together, no corrections really of any kind at that point got made. We're bugging out. Bristow is convinced it's an enormous failure, because only a dozen people have called the number off the ad to order it, and he's wasted fifty thousand dollars of DC's money, or whatever, except that because we had this book, actually, it seemed to be selling, and Bruce wanted to stand behind this thing, and he and

Bob Wayne had this idea of "Sandman month," because now we had the book after and the book before—we had *Preludes & Nocturnes* and we had *Dream Country*. They came up with various things, a poster, and a watch, a T-shirt, and I'm the one going, "Why are you guys trying to bring all this stuff out in one month? For God's sakes, spread it out!"

They said, "No, no, no, it's going to be Sandman month!" And I thought they were stupid. And they did it, and it went huge. It worked, and I had to apologize. Statues! It was the first statue. These days—it was the first. Suddenly, we had a line of books, and part of Sandman month was that you got a slipcase.

SRB: It was the accidental conjunction of a marketing scheme and the right books at the right time.

NEIL: And the timing was right, and it propelled us to a new level. So we had three books out, and then we had *Season of Mists*. Up until that point we had been in paperback, and suddenly, I somehow got to talk us into hardback. I don't remember how. I did say it would look like an old family bible, and I think the fact that the Science Fiction Book Club was ready to order some hardbacks had something to do with it. And now we've got a hardback, and again, it made things happen, in terms of the way we were looked at, and we got Norman Mailer to give us a quote.

SANDMAN: KEYSTONES AND ARCS

SRB: Let's back up a bit, to the early years of Sandman. While your collaborative novel Good Omens was taking shape, you were scripting other comics at this point.

NEIL: In the same period, I was writing Sandman and *Books of Magic*. *Books of Magic* was another inherited thing. It was meant to be a Marc DeMatteis project, drawn by Kent [Williams] and John [Bolton], about the DC magic universe. The brief was, it had to be a guide, a who's who of the DC magic universe. I turned that down; I didn't think it was a tenable brief. I went to bed that night, lay in bed, almost drifted off, and I thought, *A Christmas Carol*! I got up and wrote it down to avoid losing the idea forever, saw it the next day, thought, "It works," and phoned Karen [Berger] up.

I loved doing *Books of Magic,* I thought it was a great children's story. My one problem with it was when the series became a Vertigo title, and was labeled "for mature readers." I never thought that was right. I consulted on the book initially, but my involvement fell off. The biggest problem I had with being a consultant was being consulted. "Do you like this?" "No." "Okay, you were consulted, bye." I would have loved to continue it. I know where I would have taken it. It would have been a story about him trying to cope with being twelve or thirteen, trying to cope with life, very YA [young adult], while trying to cope with the fact that you're something bigger.

SRB: An aside, if you'll indulge me: You riff on the old Abbott and Costello "Who's on First?" routine in Children's Crusade, *and I happily noted that you have a complete Laurel and Hardy DVD collection in your home. How big a fan of such classic postvaudeville comedy are you?*

NEIL: I love silent movie comedy—ever since the Bob Monkhouse series *Golden Silents*, which I watched as a kid—and vaudeville and music hall comedy too. The English stuff and the American stuff (I love Jack Benny and Phil Silvers as much as I love Will Hay or Frankie Howard). I think Laurel and Hardy were geniuses. (I have a Charlie Chaplin–shaped blind spot, though. Harry Lloyd or Harry Langdon or dozens of others were comedy geniuses. Chaplin I watch and think, it's very clever and well done, and it just doesn't make me smile.) I'm a bigger fan of radio comedy than I am the filmed stuff, though.

SRB: I'd like to talk about some structural things here, about the transition between comics as periodicals and comics as graphic novels. I've told you that I think you, either consciously or unconsciously, came up with a very elegant solution to address the problem inherent in longer serialized works. It's what I call a "keystone story." You would come up with a story in the midst of a longer arc that stood on its own, and was very satisfying as a story, that would perfectly summarize the entire thematic arc of that particular segment.

NEIL: I stopped doing that, because I was afraid it would become a cliché. But when I first did it, it definitely was a solution to certain problems. It brings to mind a problem that occurred in Sandman issue twelve, the issue right before "Men of Good Fortune," which I was only just able to fix in the *Absolute Sandman*, Volume 1. At the end of issue twelve, he says, "I can't stay with you, I have a prior engagement." I wrote the caption below as "Next: The Prior Engagement." They changed that to "Next: Men of Good Fortune," and I kept trying to get them to change that. So initially, it was a solution to a problem.

No, it wasn't. I had a double issue coming up, and the idea of getting Michael Zulli to do [the art for] that story was appealing. It was probably the oldest story script I had I my head, I was sixteen or seventeen when I first had it, a story of two men meeting in a pub every hundred years.

HW: Was Shakespeare in the story as well?

NEIL: No, all of the stuff that showed up in that issue was happenstance. The year was 1989, so I started there, and looked back to what was happening in '89s, from 1289 onwards. So, 1589, there's Shakespeare, which was wonderful. I've got a young Shakespeare, who's a wannabe, like I was at the time, with an older Christopher Marlowe, who is the coolest thing in the world at the time, like a Clive [Barker] or an Alan [Moore] to me. That's good. And I loved the idea of Shakespeare in the pub, he's a fanboy, with all the ambition and none of the skill, sitting there with Marlowe. And, because it amused me to do so, I wrote their entire conversation in iambic pentameter. If I happened to be writing it in 1965, I would have done it in '65s, and Shakespeare wouldn't have been in there at all. I was always going for structure and failing.

SRB: Failing how?
NEIL: "24 Hours." Sandman issue six. I went, "Oh my God!" I had a twenty-four-page comic, and thought, "Hey, each page could be an hour in a day," and I started writing it, and the first thing I need is four pages just to set everything up, so I'm already screwed.

SRB: So was it after that story was completed that you realized that that using the keystone would be functional for future narrative arcs as well?
NEIL: Yeah, I realized that. It was less problematic than in early Sandman stories. I built *them* with [Alan Moore's Swamp Thing arc] "American Gothic" as my model [Saga of the Swamp Thing issues 37–50, 1985–86]. They were all short stories, except for that three-parter. The first was done as a Dennis Wheatley. The second, as EC meets old horror hosts. Third, [Ramsey] Campbell and [Clive] Barker. Fourth, as like *Unknown Worlds,* [John W.] Campbell, a rich fantasy. In my mind, it owes a lot to Heinlein's *Magic Inc.,* where I shamelessly stole the idea of lining up every demon in Hell and finding the one causing trouble. The [Sandman issues] five, six, and seven was its own little arc.

I went into *The Doll's House* with the idea of a specific narrative arc. Realized that "Men of Good Fortune" encapsulated everything I was trying to say in *The Doll's House.* Which meant that by the time I was halfway through *Season of Mists,* I had an idea: I was going to do a story halfway through that apparently has nothing to do with the arc, but actually sums everything up.

SRB: One other aspect: Was this also being shaped by the graphic novel concept? Was there any conception of shaping the serialized arcs into the graphic novel editions?
NEIL: Not then. We had no idea that anything was going to be collected at that point. If we had, *Dream Country* would have been five, or maybe six issues rather than four. We're in a universe where, by the time we get to *The Kindly Ones* I know that I'm writing a series of stories that will be collected. By that time I'm no longer hiding a flashback or a recap within the first three pages. I'm actually doing the no-holds-barred, take-no-prisoners kind of storytelling that I learned from watching Dave Sim in Cerebus. It was peculiar in that if you talk to people who read them monthly, as they came out, they will tell you that was the point when I lost the plot. If you talk to those who read the graphic novel, it was brilliant, they loved it. It points out the problem with Marc Hempel's art, that it's not "normal" comic art, like you've been reading elsewhere. As a great big book, it builds and builds, and pulls you in, and doesn't let you go. That was a thirteen-issue arc that was

published over eighteen months. That was the only time I had to do a prose recap, story-so-far piece partway through, something that we haven't included in the collection.

SRB: People forget what it was like back then, particularly regarding Dave Sim and Cerebus. Dave broke the ceiling by self-publishing his five-hundred-page Cerebus phone books, and did so at a time that the market initially rejected his expansion of the format: the size of the books, the twenty-five-dollar price tag. Before that, nobody was publishing that expansive a graphic novel; they were like glorified giant annuals, at best. Dave changed everything.

NEIL: It's frustrating. Sim wrote me a letter challenging the value of a blog, and suddenly, over two thousand people are writing to him, nice handwritten letters, asking for things from him. These days, even he blogs.

SLINGS AND ARROWS

HW: What was it like to see your work parodied in Cerebus?

NEIL: It was lovely. One of things Cerebus was from the beginning, it was Dave's ongoing commentary and parody of what was going on in the world of comics at the time, starting with Barry Windsor Smith's Conan, then he did Bernie Wrightson, Wolverine, X-Men, Punisher, Batman, Moon Knight, a wonderful Dark Knight thing. The idea of Roach becoming Swoon [the Sandman parody], it was flattering. Sim was the only one who got the idea that Dream had certain rhythms in his speech, and re-created them accurately, accentuating them for purposes of parody. Other people's caricatures just weren't very good. I ended up suggesting to him that he should do a naked Mrs. Henrot-Gultch as a naked Despair. He said, "Oh my God, I do!"

I keep meaning to do an essay on Cerebus, immediately after I do a giant re-read of the entire series from beginning to end. Someday. The line I keep thinking about is what G. K. Chesterton said about Charles Dickens, the aesthetics of Dickens, is that the problem, if it is a problem, with *The Pickwick Papers,* is that the kind of book it is changes halfway through. We can forgive the character changing; we can't forgive the author changing during the course of a work. That, I think, is the problem that Cerebus has; the author changes so hugely during its course, the kind of book it is changes so much, it's hard to see it as one work.

That's the problem I think I managed to avoid by stopping Sandman after ten years, I was no longer the twenty-six-year-old who began Sandman. When I ended, I was still more or less him. I can write things that are cooler or smarter, but I can't write them with the sheer sense of exuberance, the sense that I was breaking new ground, that he did.

SRB: You enjoyed Dave's satire of your character, but what do you make of the reviews of your work? Does that impact you, or your creative path? For instance, the movie Beowulf you coscripted received pretty split reviews, and those who didn't like it really didn't like it.

NEIL: What is interesting to me is that—I have the same phenomenon with *American Gods*, where eighty percent of the people loved it, and twenty percent of the people hated it. There wasn't much of a middle ground; it felt like they were reading a different book. With *Stardust*, people like it, people hate it, but I understand why the people who hate it, hate it.

SRB: Really?

NEIL: Well, yeah. Because mostly, the people who hate *Stardust* don't like the fact that it's essentially a fairy tale. They're trying to read it as an epic fantasy, but it's not. It starts off with a rather dry description of a little English town, he goes over the border, and it does things where it mentions really interesting adventures that it never goes off and describes, and it has a completely anticlimactic ending, as far as they're concerned. There are people who love it, and there are people who hate it, but I understand the people who hate it hate it for more or less for the same reasons, and I really do understand why—you know, they're trying to read it as something else.

SRB: They're after another book altogether.

NEIL: An anecdote that I've told before, which is true, is the first bad review we ever got was *Violent Cases*. We were very excited about what the review was going to say, the first people to review it—pretty much the only place that really bothered to review it was *Speakeasy* magazine—and they reviewed it, and they said it was too expensive. [Laughter.] Dave McKean and I took this very seriously. We took reviews of this book very seriously, and they said that it was too expensive. So we went to Titan Books and said, "You have to lower the price on the next printing." And we were so insistent that they did; they lowered it from four pound ninety-five down to three pound ninety-five for all subsequent printings. And we expected some kind of outcry or applause, to be lifted up on the people's shoulders—and all that had actually happened was, we'd cut our royalty. Nobody noticed, nobody appreciated what we'd done. That was my first real experience with reviews. It was also more or less the last time I ever took a review seriously. Well, partly because, as a reviewer, I knew how often I was wrong. Five years on, ten years on, I'd run across a review I'd written, and go, "Oh my God, I was a moron." Sometimes it was seeing things as works of genius that weren't. For example, I remember, I was flipping through some magazines a few years ago, and I ran across my review of *Fright Night* [1985], which was just the most enthusiastic rave for "a film of such brilliance and subject," and all this sort of stuff—and I'm reading it, and I remember, "*Fright Night* is a fairly average kind of little film."

SRB: *Now it is, but that was a radical film in its day; that hadn't been done with vampire films at that time.*

NEIL: I think that was also what was so interesting. When I wrote it, yes, it was playing on the subtext of the vampire films that had been done, and now every second-rate vampire film has the same subtext—well, okay, point taken.

SRB: *Well, your point taken, as well.*

NEIL: Do I read reviews? Yes, more or less—I tend to weigh them, I guess—which is going all the way back to reader's letters on *Sandman.* I would weigh them, in the sense, I mean, by weight. I was much more interested in, "Okay, are they asking about this yet?" The point where, by issue five, the letters start coming in saying, "When are we going to see the Sandman's big brother, Death?" Okay, that's working. So it's weighing on them. It's sort of the Rotten Tomatoes [Web site] thing. They have about a hundred and twenty *Beowulf* reviews up right now. Do I want to read all of them? No. Am I interested in knowing roughly what the consensus is? Yeah. I can look over and see that the ones that hate it hate it for the same reasons, the ones who like it mostly like it for the same reasons. Some like it because they think it's a stupid popcorn movie, and it's really good. Some like it because they think it's a really smart, satirical movie, and it's really good.

SRB: *Have you ever changed anything that you were working on—as it was being serialized—because of reader response, where you either accelerated a plot point or disposed of a plot point?*

NEIL: A couple of times I changed things, occasionally delayed things or whatever, because Karen [Berger] asked me to—

SRB: *That's different. Karen was your editor on Sandman. That's your relationship with your editor.*

NEIL: —and I once saved—I didn't kill Matthew the Raven in *Sandman,* who was meant to be killed in *The Kindly Ones,* because Alisa Kwitney had just given birth to a son who she named Matthew. She got quite upset, and she loved the character, and I think the character might have somehow influenced the name of her son.

SRB: *Was she familiar with Matthew's prior incarnation as a character in Swamp Thing?*

NEIL: I guess; she was a collector.

SRB: *What was that leap, with Matthew Cable, from Swamp Thing to Sandman?*

NEIL: I just wish you'd asked me eighteen years ago, when I could have said, "Oh, well, this is the chain of thought . . ." [Laughter.] I loved *Swamp Thing.* Alan's

Swamp Thing was very much the start of what I was doing, and I was trying to re-create the pleasure that I had with *Swamp Thing*. Probably the starting point with Matthew was gathering together all the images I could of the various [DC Comics] horror hosts. I was fascinated by Eve, because there was Eve, the old crone in *Plop!*[5], and there was either an Eve or somebody else with a different name, a beautiful woman drawn by [Mike] Kaluta who was a horror host, who had a huge black raven [Madame Xanadu in the short-lived *Doorway to Nightmare*, five issues, 1978]. She had a black raven, and I liked the idea, and I decided, "Okay, she's going to be Eve," except she had this raven knocking around. Alan had this thing of the horror hosts existing in dreams in the Ron Randall–illustrated issue of *Swamp Thing*,[6] and that gave me something to hold on to. So, I went, "Okay, I've got a raven," and just the idea that he was Matt Cable was really cool. I don't actually remember the details of Rick [Veitch]'s issue of *Swamp Thing*[7] where Sandman turned up. Morpheus shows up—I'm trying to remember if it was some kind of transitional issue? I think I just phoned Rick and said, "I want Matt Cable," and we worked it out.[8]

I liked Matt. I was from the first round of *Swamp Thing*, I was from Len [Wein] and Berni [Wrightson]'s *Swamp Thing*, and I loved the death of Matt Cable. He seemed a nice character to bring back. I also liked the fact that it was like a little Easter egg. It was there for people who wanted to notice it. I don't know that it was ever spelled out.

So anyway, I didn't kill Matthew because Alisa named her son after him. But I don't remember anything changing because of any letters or any reviews.

SRB: Were you seeing reader response or letters as a journalist, or with your short fiction?
NEIL: I don't remember getting one letter—there was no reader response in the short stories, either. It wasn't until comics, because comics had that tradition. The letters came in, and that was interesting; every now and then I'd reply to some. I did less and less as the thing went on, just because there was less and less time.

SRB: Your complete Sandman run has just been reissued in a durable, expansive new format from DC/Vertigo, The Absolute Sandman sets. What's your involvement been with these reprint editions, which are represented as "definitive," and are you happy with them?
NEIL: Lots of proofreading and color input. On issues one through eight I talked the whole thing through with Danny, panel by panel, to try and get it really good. Occasionally little corrections [on things] that had slipped through the cracks over the years. (I'm hoping that the sign in *The Kindly Ones* will now actually say "Do not feed the pigeons" in good Hungarian.)

SRB: Folks only think of your collaborations with artists in terms of your comics and graphic novel works, but you've had ongoing creative collabora-

tions with other cartoonists in other venues. For instance, you and renowned **Playboy** *cartoonist Gahan Wilson worked together on "It Was a Dark and Silly Night" for* **Little Lit**, *and he did the cover for* **Now We Are Sick**. *Gahan is a grand fellow, so I'm curious if you had some fun with that, and if you and Gahan are planning or hoping to do anything else?*

NEIL: He also illustrated *M is for Magic* for Subterranean Press, and did the cover of the Gene Wolfe/me collaboration *A Walking Tour of the Shambles*. I believe that they're animating "Dark and Silly Night" for a documentary on Gahan.

SRB: *One other vital aspect of your comics career we haven't touched on: You've contributed extensively to the Comic Book Legal Defense Fund [CBLDF] over the years; more, I believe, than anyone, other than founder Denis Kitchen, and perhaps Dave Sim, and those actually in the organization. The 1990s was rough—lots of prosecutions, of artists, of retailers, and so on—but that kind of prosecution and persecution seems to have settled down over the past few years. What is your current reading of the climate in the U.S. regarding comics censorship, now that the market has shifted so heavily toward bookstores instead of comic shops—and what new fronts do you see in the CBLDF's active role in this new environment?*

NEIL: Overall, I think things are really good. The trouble is, it just takes one nasty prosecution like the Gordon Lee case to set everything back twenty years. And I measure the success of the CBLDF by the number of things that don't get prosecuted.

NIGHTMARES, STARS, AND AMERICAN GODS

HW: Let's shift gears and talk about your writing process. Is your work fueled by your dreams and nightmares?

NEIL: I used to have nightmares, and they were really scary and really troubling. And then, once I started writing *Sandman*, I'd wake up from a nightmare thrilled; I would wake up happy and excited from a terrifying dream. I'd think, "Oh, God, I can use that," and I would grab a pen and write that down—and if there really were little demon creatures making sure that I had bad dreams, I think they retired, they gave up. They decided that the whole thing was a completely bad job, an embarrassing mistake, because I just wasn't playing. I loved bad dreams at that point. They made me amazingly happy.

SRB: If you had to choose a sequence in Sandman that was fueled by one of your dreams—

NEIL: Okay, in *A Game of You,* in Hazel's dream, where she's on a train, and she goes into the basement of the train, which is really weird, because she didn't know that trains had basements. There's a dead baby that looks like it's already undergone an autopsy, and she picks it up, and then it sort of starts attacking her with sharp teeth, and it's a real thing—that was straight out of my head. That was, like, standard Neil-issue nightmares. As I say, the trouble was, now I'd wake up and say, "That was really good! Get that straight down!" I remember having dreams where I was pursued by things that looked like spaghetti; you know, sort of faces like giant saucepans filled with boiled spaghetti.

SRB: Have your dreams also fueled your novels or short stories?
NEIL: *American Gods* had a lot of things in it, but one of the things was a dream. I had this dream in which my wife—and the wife wasn't Mary, it was "a" wife—was some kind of dead vampire/zombie creature, who was sort of following me around across America, at a distance. At one point I remember looking for her in a motel, and finding every bathtub in the motel with a corpse in it, filled with water, like it came out of—I was going to say, less *The Shining,* and more Steve and John [Totleben] and Alan [Moore's] *Swamp Thing* underwater vampire story—and knowing the moment that it got dark, they would come out. They would rise up from the bathtubs, looking out, and my realizing it was dusk already. That bit never got into *American Gods,* but the idea of sort of a zombie wife following him around at a distance keeping him kind of safe, but also being a strange, unresolved plot point, was definitely a dream thing. I don't think there was anything else that was particularly dream-driven in that. There's nothing very dream-driven that I remember from either *Coraline* or *Anansi Boys.*

HW: I was curious about Wolves in the Walls.
NEIL: That was Maddy's dream. That absolutely was a dream. That was me going upstairs, Maddy age four, just really being upset. She said, "Dad, we have wolves in the walls, and they came out, and they took over the house," and she showed me the place in the wallpaper they came out from. It was really bad, I mean, these wolves were terrible, and they were monstrous and dangerous, and they did really bad things. Initially, I would just tell her stories about wolves, and just try to defuse this thing, because it was very upsetting for her. She just had it once, but I was smart enough to say, "This is something." The other thing is that Mary said that she had that dream when she was a girl, and I thought, "How odd."

HW: In the book, the characters would say, "Everybody knows it's all over when the wolves come out." Is that something you took from—
NEIL: What was weird about that—you know that way that writers are honestly the last people that you should listen to when you actually ask important questions about the process of having written, because we misremember. We half remember things; we go, "I think it must have occurred like this," and we think of things. There are interviews in which I say that I tried writing *Wolves in the Walls* at least twice, and it wasn't until I had the idea of the line "when the wolves come out of the walls, it's all over," it suddenly clicked into place, and I had the voice, and I had the whole thing.

I believed that was true when I said it. Except when we were moving stuff up to the library I brought up lots of notebooks with things handwritten there. And one of the things I found there was either the third or the second version of *Wolves in the Walls*. They weren't really drafts, in the sense that when you've written something that's two thousand words long, and you don't get it right, it's easier to put it away and do it again six months later, or whatever. But what was interesting was that, even though it didn't quite work, and it wasn't deep enough, that phrase is actually in it. So, I actually got it wrong. I'd remembered that as being the big key that opened it up for me, but actually that wasn't it. It was just getting it right when I did it.

I do actually know where I stole that from, and I wrote him a letter and told him. He'd told me how much he liked it, and I said, "Actually, I think I got the key phrase from you." That was Daniel Pinkwater's book *The Snarkout Boys and the Avocado of Death* [1982]; there is a character in it who's his uncle; he's a famous wrestler who complains about the terrifying thing about having to wrestle orangutans, and who says words to the effect of, "you have to watch out when wrestling orangutans that they don't get you by your feet, because when an orangutan gets you by your feet, it's all over." That phrase just sort of stuck with me, and it just sort of came out right as, "when the wolves come out of the walls, it's all over." And so, yeah, that was where that phrase started.

HW: It sounds almost folksy—"everybody knows that!"
NEIL: Well, that was what I liked about it. I've even had people say, "So, that is an old English expression, then, when the wolves come out of the walls, it's all over." And I say, "No, that's in my head, I cobbled it together."

SRB: I'm also curious about the fantasy archetypes you embrace from time to time, that seem to have a personal resonance for you. For instance, Stardust, Sol in Sandman—in a few stories, you've used the star that is a humanoid being. It's a concept that you've returned to.
NEIL: It probably dates back to age six, reading C. S. Lewis's *The Voyage of the Dawn Treader*, where there is the Island of the Star, and Prince [now King] Caspian marries the star's [Ramandu's] daughter, and the idea that stars are people. I approach it in different ways. It was nice doing it in very different ways. In *Stardust*, it's very metaphorical; you've got Faerie, you've got a fallen star. I did read a review of *Stardust* which explains the entire thing is nonsensical, because stars are hundreds of millions of light years away, and a thing thrown would not reach here, and she could not come down on the same night. And you go, "You're kind of missing it." Whereas the joy of having Sol and all of these suns in *Sandman* was much more hard "universe"—and it was also fun to me. I wanted to do something that was a weird little thing filled with Easter eggs for DC Comics fans. I loved the fact that Killalla of the Glow [in *Sandman, Endless Nights*: "Dream—The Heart of the Star"] was a blue-skinned Oan [a reference to the DC Comics character Green

Lantern], and that you were millions and millions of years before what was going to be the Green Lantern Corps; they were just figuring out what this green stuff is, I mean, I liked it.

SRB: Circling back to American Gods, would you have written that novel if you hadn't moved to America?

NEIL: No, I couldn't have done it. The first three-quarters of *Sandman* was written before I moved to America, and even with the last part, that was written here, I'd only been here a couple of years. What I used to say to people who would say, "Well, you're English, how can you write America?" was, "Well, I'm probably not going to write New York as good as a New Yorker, but I can write a New York that's probably as good as that of a San Franciscan who's never been to New York but had seen it on TV and is now setting something in New York," which to some extent was true. But it is also true that the America of *Sandman* is a sort of delirious America of the imagination. It's constructed from films and from TV; it's constructed from the imagination; it's a composite. It's not actually America; it's a sort of strange, communal Americanish place. There are places in it that I look at—and some of them are artist failures as well as "me" failures. It would be fair to say, for example, that with the Florida in the *Doll's House,* being written by me, and being drawn by Mike Dringenberg, Mike is basically, I think, drawing Utah, and I think I'm writing San Francisco. Were I to write the stuff set in Cocoa Beach, Florida, in *The Doll's House* now, it would read like Florida, and damn it, I would make the artist draw it like Florida. But, I don't worry about it, because it's a place in the head.

SRB: It's also a factor of the process; you two were writing and drawing a serialized story in a periodical, and it had to come out within a certain period of time.

NEIL: Well, it was also that you couldn't find the information. Honestly, if I were doing it now . . . it's hard to explain to people that information used to be a commodity. It's hard to explain to people how difficult it would be to find the reference to anything. When you guys were doing *Swamp Thing,* you went down there.

SRB: Yep, I went down. It required my going to Louisiana and the city of Houma and traveling around—

NEIL: —and making photographs, and then sending what you found to Alan. Now you'd go to the Web, you'd go to Google and Houma.com and look around at photos of their fair city. You'd at least be in a different world. I would go to Cocoa Beach on the Web, and I would look at what it looked like, and I would find houses on the realtor sites, and I'd say, "Mike, I think they're living in one that looks a lot like this." That was not an option then, that information simply wasn't there, and you couldn't have gotten it in time if you needed it.

Which is my loopy way of [getting back to] *American Gods*. I'd moved to America in 1992. In '97, my movie agent, John Levin, said to me in the course of a casual phone conversation, something like, "[actor Robert] De Niro's looking for something, let me know if you think of anything for De Niro." And I didn't, really. I started thinking about two people meeting on a plane. I made one of them Rip Torn, and one of them a much, much younger De Niro, initially. He wasn't De Niro as he was in '96, he was De Niro as he was in *Taxi Driver*. And Rip Torn, because I'd met him in '91, and he had these really strange speaking patterns, which actually they pretty much used in *The Larry Sanders Show*, that's more or less his speech patterns. I just sort of imagined these two people meeting on a plane. I didn't really know who they were, except that I knew one of them shouldn't have been there, and the other one basically turns to him and says, "You're late, I've got a job for you."

I tried writing a story about the car parked on the ice, gathering the town together, and it didn't really work.

SRB: *That's a local [Midwestern U.S.] event, the car on the ice.*

NEIL: Oh, sure. Not just here; it occurs up into Canada. I did see it here, on the lake, but it happens where there's ice, and cars, and someone with an imagination. Having that kind of writer's mind, my immediate thought upon seeing the car parked on the ice every day, waiting for it to sink in, well, obviously you would hide a body in the trunk. It makes it more interesting, and nobody's ever going to check the trunk. Amusingly enough, though, there was a car parked on a lake near a restaurant that the local kids used to use as a diving board. It had been there for ten years, and then it got hauled out, and they did open the trunk, and they did find a body. It was true, so there you go.

So, *American Gods*, it was sort of accumulating; it's more and more of this conversation that's happening in my head before I go to sleep, but I don't really know who these people are or what's going on. Then, I was sleepless in Iceland. My travel agent had pointed out to me, since I was going to Norway, I could take advantage of a free stopover in Iceland. I think this was in '98. I flew to Iceland, it was around July the Fourth; I left at seven o'clock in the evening, got in around six thirty in the morning, local time there, and hadn't slept on the plane because it was too quick—you hop over the Pole—and said, "You know, I'm not going to bed now." I never did. The room that I was in didn't have curtains, and it was daylight. So, the following afternoon—Sunday, my twenty-four-hour-day in Iceland—I hadn't slept in a long time. I wander into the corridors of this building, I buy a little piece of scrimshaw, and then I see a little diorama showing the voyages of Leif Ericson across Iceland to Vinland [in North America], and the timeline: This is when they got in, they fought the Indians, they got driven out again. And I just thought, "I wonder if they left their gods behind."

I was still working on [the] *Princess Mononoke* [translated script] at this point in time, and I think the way that I tell people about this is, "I went back to my hotel, and I wrote this letter to my editor saying I have a new book, this is the plot, this is what it is, and it's called *American Gods*." I think in reality, I worked on *Princess Mononoke,* and then a day later, in Norway, once I'd actually slept—because [when] I got to Norway, they gave me this tiny little room, but it had curtains pulled and darkness, and I slept, and it was magic, and I was in such rough shape when I left Iceland—I wrote the letter. The letter was, "This is the book and this is what it's going to be about and this is how it's going to happen, and I'll call it *American Gods* until I come up with something better."

I sent it in to my publisher, and within a month or two, they sent me a mockup of the cover, which *was* the cover. This was a really odd thing, and suddenly it was called *American Gods,* because that was what it said on the cover. And it had this road heading out, and this lightning bolt, and I thought, "Okay, this is the book I'm writing." It was really helpful, and it wasn't like they sent me a bunch of things to choose from—they sent me this cover. I could choose a typeface or something, or whatever, but it was like, "Here's the cover we'll use." Then I wrote the first chapter—I think I might have written it on the way to San Diego, in the summer of '99, and I may be wrong on this. I know I wrote the first draft of the first chapter in the first person.

SRB: Would it have been a different book after September 11?
NEIL: Yes. It wouldn't have been completely different, but it would have changed.

SRB: I imagine your relationship with America changed after that as well.
NEIL: No, my relationship with America changed in 2003, at the time when America went into Iraq. I was standing there going, "This is fucking madness. It's not that I'm unconvinceable, but I'm unconvinced, and nobody is convincing me." I thought, "You don't do this thing; you don't go out there and invade other countries. That's not what America is designed to be about. You have a huge fund of goodwill; you have a world in which you could get out there right now, and for a fraction of the cost of a war, you could have the entire world loving you and being your friend and eating out of your hand. You're about to declare a war that, from my perspective, seems unwinnable for reasons that are not articulated and unproven."

The war was happening because people wanted a war. I was talking to—you know, I have friends in the White House, you would be surprised at the places people read my books. I remember having a conversation with my friend in the White House, and saying, "Why are you doing this?" And he said, "Well, we're doing it for this and this," and a lot of the stuff he told me I didn't believe. The weirdest thing about this: They believe it because they want to believe it. I remember at one point he was saying, "and they have this technology to launch airborne botulism spores, we've got this thing that they've got airborne botulism! But, how? We can't do that!" Actually, they didn't have it. Somebody lied, somebody said,

"Oh, no, they've got airborne botulism spores!" But anyway, that was definitely the point where my emotional relationship with America changed, after that.

SRB: How did the process of writing American Gods reflect your relationship with our country?
NEIL: I don't think *American Gods* could have been written by someone who was American. A lot of that is because, if you're a goldfish in the water, you don't go, "This water tastes odd." You go, "This is what water tastes like." I, at least, have to come in and go, "This water is really—excuse me, guys, explain that House on the Rock thing [in Spring Green, Wisconsin]. Tell me why five million people go to the House on the Rock." They go, "Uhhhhhh . . ."[9]

HW: That's not a European experience, all these little roadside attractions.
NEIL: No. The idea of the roadside attraction was part of it. The experience of driving through America. I started driving down to Florida, and I wouldn't drive on the thruways. I just stayed with—you can do the same drive that you do on the freeway in thirty-six hours in thirty-eight hours. It doesn't add in incredible amount of time, except now you're driving through places that look interesting. Some of it fell in my lap: I remember Rock City. I actually had the proper experience of encountering Rock City. I'd never heard of it. I'm driving to Florida, I'm driving through Tennessee or Kentucky, and I'm driving on some mountain road, and I see painted on the side of a barn, "See Rock City: The World Wonder!" I thought, "Oh, that must be somewhere around here." Little did I know it was two hundred miles away!

SRB: It's like the South of the Border signs as you're heading through the Carolinas.
NEIL: Exactly! I love South of the Border, because South of the Border has that exact thing: It exists because it exists. And its existence generates more things around it. I found a copy of *Roadside America,* which proved very useful. I had a couple of editions of that, which had different lengths of essays and stuff, and as I started writing *American Gods,* the Web sort of became functional enough that I could sometimes use it for a little bit of research, but not really.

PROSE, POETRY, AND SONG

SRB: Let's talk a bit about your short stories and poetry. What was your first published short story?
NEIL: I think it's "Featherquest," from late '83 or early '84, in *Imagine* magazine.

SRB: What are your personal favorites among your short stories?
NEIL: "Chivalry" is really fun to read aloud. Every sentence in it does something. I quite like "A Study in Emerald." I think "Bitter Grounds" is a really smart story

that doesn't get as much love as it should.[10] Christ, I dunno. The ones that work, once they're done I tend to forget about. The ones that don't work I chew over in the back of my head and wonder how they could have worked.

SRB: We discussed your influences in novels and short stories and comics, but not short story writing. Which writers influenced you in terms of your short stories? "Everyone?" Harlan Ellison, R. A. Lafferty, Saki [H. H. Munro], John Collier? Italo Calvino? Jorge Luis Borges?
NEIL: All of those (Calvino not so much; in my head he's a novelist). And [Roger] Zelazny, [Samuel R.] Delany, P. L. Travers, Judith Merrill anthologies, especially *SF 12*, Lou Reed, Gene Wolfe, Ray Bradbury, Rudyard Kipling, [Philip K.] Dick, Angela Carter, Raymond Carver, Lord Dunsany, [J. G.] Ballard—the list goes ever on.

SRB: Will we ever see your collaboration with Harlan Ellison? Care to talk about what it is, or may become?
NEIL: It's a story about movies, called "Shoot Day for Night." We wrote four pages back in 1998. In 2002 we got back together, and by the time we were finished it was down to three pages. I have no doubt that before we die we will get back together and work on it once more, and probably get it down to a page and half.

SRB: I'm curious, too, if Harlan asked you to be part of The Last Dangerous Visions.
NEIL: Sure.

SRB: Let's get into your poetry. What inspires you to write poetry, and who are your favorite poets—as a younger man, and now that you're a seasoned writer?
NEIL: e.e.cummings, John Wilmot Earl of Rochester; Don Marquis; Hugh Sykes Davies; Wendy Cope—favorite poets then and now. Robert Graves. *The Penguin Book of Surrealist Verse* is wonderful. I like [Charles] Bukowski more than I suspect I should.

SRB: That could be said about all of us in terms of Bukowski. Any favorites among your poems?
NEIL: I think I'm a worse poet as I get older. I tend to make things story shaped, and perfect poems aren't. I liked "Poem" and "The Day The Saucers Came," though.[11]

SRB: What can you say/do with poetry that you can't do with prose?
NEIL: Sometimes, when it works, you can encapsulate something in the perfect words for it, in a way that means that the words and the rhythms combine to make

something more than it would have been as prose. I tried writing "Daughter of Owls" as a poem, and it died on the page. I tried reformatting "Cold Colours" as prose for a London anthology that specifically asked, and although it's in print, it doesn't work.

SRB: How did you get involved with writing songs for Lorraine Garland, and have you found this a pleasurable venue? Any personal favorites?
NEIL: It was Guy Fawkes Day 1992, and she and Emma had been playing songs, and I played them the "Tea" song, and it all started from there. I tend not to write songs if there's no one waiting for them. If there is, I write them pretty fast—with Folk Underground, I remember thinking that they should have a song with their name in, and it should be more literal, and I wrote it in about ten minutes.

My favorite song is probably "Unresolving," the lyrics of which I wrote to a piece of music by Chris Ewens that I'd already used in *A Short Film About John Bolton,* sung by Claudia Gonson. In my head it's about a bad relationship, and a girl who died in a car crash, and she's singing about what she remembers.

fUTURE TENSE

SRB: Before we wrap up, what are your now adult children doing these days? Maddy's still at home, but what are Mike and Holly up to?
NEIL: Mike's a senior software engineer at Google. Holly's working in film production in the UK, and today is happy to report that she's assistanting on *Quantum of Solace* and not on *Bond 22.*

SRB: Thanks for that. Let's look ahead, for you. What projects are you working on that may reach fruition over the next two years?
NEIL: It's never really a one- or two-year thing; it's always like a ten-year thing.

SRB: Well, for example, when did The Graveyard Book *begin to take shape in your mind? What was the catalyst?*
NEIL: That was 1986, maybe '85. I did actually start it a couple of times, but I wasn't good enough. Each time I put it away, and I thought, "You know what, I'm going to have to be good enough to write this." It's eight chapters, which are short stories set two years apart, that form into a novel, of which the first five are written. Six, seven, and eight aren't. It has the scariest and most disturbing first couple of pages I've written of anything.

SRB: You had a new Sandman project you proposed to DC Comics, which isn't going to see the light of day. Would you care to talk about it?
NEIL: Well, there's not really a lot to talk about. The Sandman's twentieth anniversary is coming up, and I wanted to do—there's a story line I've thought about

doing for years, which I've always called Sandman issue zero. It's the story of what happens before Sandman issue one. We learn in *Brief Lives*—we also learn it in the text piece in Sandman issue eight—that he was on his way back from halfway across the universe, and was exhausted, and that is how he was captured; he is easy to capture because he is exhausted. So I wanted to do that story, because it is really cool, I sort of know it, and it has some great scenes in it, and bits, and it would have been fun. I wanted to do it as six months of comics, then as a big book.

SRB: Why was it passed on? It would have been a bestseller for DC for years.

NEIL: It was passed on because I wanted a larger royalty than I got. I passed on it largely because I couldn't afford to do it at 1987 rates and May 1987 royalties. There's sort of a level on which it would take me about as much time to do it as it would to write a novel. I know what I get for writing novels, and I get a fifteen percent royalty, and an incredibly healthy advance. I did *Sandman: Endless Nights* as my charity project; *Sandman: Endless Nights* was a favor to Karen [Berger], it was done at the four percent royalty I've had since the beginning, for a twenty-thousand-dollar advance, and I found the time, I fitted it in, and I did it. It got them onto the *New York Times* bestseller list for the first time ever. For this one, I said, "Look, I can't afford to do it. I can't actually afford to drop everything." And I said, "But, I also know you're not going to turn around and pay a million-dollar advance for a Sandman book, nor would I force you to. So my suggestion would be that you up my royalty on the entire Sandman line by two percent." Which, according to my calculations, in sixteen years would bring me up to what I would have made if I'd written a novel. And they said, "Wooo, we'll tell you what: Because we love you, we will give you that two percent for eighteen months, and then you're back to your normal rate." And I said, "But that doesn't do it. It doesn't do very much. Why would I do that? I'm saying, it would actually take me sixteen years to make that up. I'm not saying, give me more money now, I'm saying, look, over sixteen years—"

Mostly, it was just sort of a pride thing. Pride isn't even the right word—a sort of saving-face thing. I thought, "Well, okay, this way, it barely appears on their balance sheet." I get to go, "Well, even if it's sixteen years, I haven't actually really done this for free." In a world in which I make eleven percent more just straight royalty—I get a larger royalty on a single copy of *Anansi Boys* being sold in hardback than I do on *The Absolute Sandman*, which is a one-hundred-dollar book. And they said, "No," and I said, "Okay," and that was it. And I genuinely don't understand; I'm going, "But this would have been international news."

SRB: It would have been a money machine!

NEIL: It would have burst the whole thing up; it would been a money machine. It would have rebooted the sales on everything, and it would have—yeah.

HW: Plus the movie interest—

NEIL: I don't care about the movie interest. On a weekly basis, Warner Bros. gets contacted by stars and directors, and have been for roughly seventeen years. People wanting to make Sandman movies, and they have no idea how to make the Sandman movie. A Sandman movie, as a proposition, is something that's five hundred dollars million up front, because you'd have to look at it as a three- to four-movie sequel thing, and the movie interest is neither here nor there. You know, Warner options its own rights, which means every five years I get ten thousand dollars or something. So it's irrelevant on sort of a cosmic scale. But the point is—I would have thought it would have been a sensible thing [to do *Sandman* issue 0], and I would have thought it would have been sensible from a financial point of view. I know that there was a very, very large contingent of people within the offices of DC who thought it made sense. I know there was a very very small number of people who vetoed it, with whom I'm still friends, because it's a business decision. Whatever. I'll write another book.

One of the reasons that I have survived emotionally in the world of comics, when I have seen my friends and loved ones chewed up and spat out, emotionally destroyed or put through the wringer . . . In many ways, for me, it goes back to the conversation you, Steve, dramatized in the little "roast" comic [from the 1996 Chicago comic book convention], where you and I are driving, and I'm saying, "You can't take it personally." They're a company, they make business decisions. Some are good, some are bad. I personally do not consider that a terribly wise business decision. On the other hand, from a financial point of view for me, not having to find the time to write six issues of *Sandman* this year in 2008 is great. I will write a novel, and it will be good, and I will own it, and I will own the film rights.

The film rights to *Sandman* are nothing. They don't matter to me. In a world in which DC Comics ever turns around and makes an amazing *Sandman* thing, and the option gets exercised, I'll see not much money from that under the terms of the 1987 agreement, and that's fine. It doesn't really—I don't control it. Whereas, *The Graveyard Book* is mine. I own it, I've already got about five major film companies sniffing round it, and saying, "When you finish it, it is ours, right?" I'm going, "Well, let me finish it first, and we'll see what happens when it's done." But I own it. I try to get that bit, and that's so important to me. That level of ownership, the level of noncompromise, and the amount of the thing that you get—the slice of the pie, I like.

HW: This is a bit morbid and premature, but—well, let's go to the big picture. How would you like to be remembered as a writer? With the recent passing of Ira Levin and Norman Mailer, I'm just curious.

NEIL: The truth is, in terms of opinion, in terms of the stuff you're doing, the critical and epicurial opinion at the point that you die is always the least helpful and the least relevant. The stuff when you're doing it, and the reaction of the people to what you're doing when you're doing it, is interesting and relevant. The opinion twenty years after you're dead, eighty years after you're dead, one hundred years after you're dead—that's interesting and relevant, because at that point you've sort of shaken down, and you have context. Any books of yours that are going to survive are sort of dropped into this Darwinian fight for survival, for which there are always more books than survivors. At the point when I die, it may not be apparent that *The Day I Swapped My Dad for Two Goldfish* is the only thing that will outlive me. [Laughter.]

SRB: For instance.

NEIL: Yes, for instance. Like A. A. Milne, being remembered for *Winnie the Pooh*. A. A. Milne, probably the most successful playwright of his time, editor of *Punch*, adult humorist—you know, very successful, very popular writer. I remember going to Google in about 1999, because I wanted to find a book called *The Holiday Round* [1912], which was a collection of A. A. Milne's humorous essays, and going onto amazon.com, and typing in A. A. Milne, and getting 650 books back, and going through them. What was interesting was every single one of those books was a variant on the two Winnie the Pooh and two books of poetry; it was a different edition, or chapbook, but that was it. You do not get to choose. G. K. Chesterton, at the time of his death, was regarded as a slightly cranky essayist who did lots of potboilers to support his cranky essay habit. Thirty years after his death, he was regarded as the author of the Father Brown stories, but nothing else. Now, he's actually attained much, much wider currency once more as a cranky essayist.

SRB: Then there's the phenomenon of incredibly popular contemporary authors who fade from cultural memory as soon as they're gone. They feed the publishing machine while they're alive, and reach and please a massive audience, but once they pass away, it all evaporates.

NEIL: For example—the death of Stephen King, which has not happened yet, and hopefully won't for a very, very long time. When Steve dies, what the critics will say about him will depend on (a) whether his last book was one of the big, respectable ones, or (b) whether it was something like *Cell*. Whatever the last one was that he wrote, he will be that thing, because that's the way that it always is with King. He writes the serious one— "Oh, yeah, King, serious writer, yeah, he used to be a popular writer." He writes a potboiler, "Ah, King, the potboiler man!" Whereas my own theory on King is, if he is remembered—which I think he will be, and I think he will last—but I think it will be the point where, a hundred years from now, they realize [that] probably the best portrait of America from 1974 to whenever is King. That actually you can pick up a King book written in 1978 and get a really good portrait of what people were doing, wearing, speaking, how things sounded, what the world looked like. I suspect that may well be what people think of King, how people relate to King, and what people do with King a hundred years after his death. But I could be completely wrong. Or—and it's just as possible—that in a hundred years' time Stephen King will be absolutely forgotten, chiefly remembered as a cultural phenomenon. You can't decide what's a literary classic.

But I'm just saying, in terms of—in answer to your question, I read the Ira Levin reviews, and thought, "They're pointless." You actually have critics sitting there, grasping—with Norman Mailer, at least you had some interesting personality stuff. With Levin, really all they had to do is grouse, with a certain amount of puzzlement, over the fact that he'd never really done enough in any one genre for them to be able to comfortably put him in a box. The tone of the reviews, when you actually boiled it down, was that he was an inconvenience. "He wrote a really good science fiction novel, a really good gothic, a really good thriller, a really good techno-satire, which means he's—puzzling. But he was obviously very successful, because they filmed a lot of his stuff." [Laughs.] Which is the strangest criteria for success. It's been the criteria since the 1930s, or more.

MOVIES, MASTER PLANS, AND THE REAL MAGIC

HW: How do you feel about that aspect of the films made from your work?
NEIL: The only thing about—I don't know, I'm just experiencing this myself. I remember when I first saw the film of *Stardust,* thinking, "Oh, they made a really nice film. It's not the film I would have made, but then, I didn't make it." I don't know. I have this strange point of view on these filmic things, which is, I generally feel the same way about them that I feel about stage plays of my stuff. I just think, "Whoa, the book is the thing; you've done a nice adaptation. Twenty years on, maybe someone will come along and do a different *Stardust* film. Yours is very nice." But I don't look at it and go, "That was *Stardust*." I look at it and go, "Your film of *Stardust* is cool."

HW: They're never going to be what's in your head.
NEIL: Well, they may be. I mean, Roman Polanski's *Rosemary's Baby* is pretty much Ira Levin's *Rosemary's Baby*—there's almost nothing between them.

SRB: In the cinematic phase of your career, from Princess Mononoke to Beowulf and beyond, what has been gaining momentum for you? What's next?
NEIL: The movie version of *Neverwhere* has come back to life. It's controlled by Crucial Films; it's come back to life because it's owned by [the Jim] Henson [Company]. I quit—I was going to be writing the script for it, and I did a bunch of drafts between 1998 and 2000.

SRB: *In terms of mainstream theatrical feature films, what are your current projects and plans as a writer for cinema?*

NEIL: To carry on, and enjoy myself.

SRB: *What comics projects are simmering on any burners of your keyboard, inner stove, or brain?*

NEIL: Only one, right now. But I cannot talk about it until it is announced.

HW: *A consistent aspect of your work is how you touch more on the mythic themes that transcend culture, working with themes that reflect the human condition. Is that something you deliberately set out to do?*

NEIL: I think Jerry Garcia said, "Style is the stuff you get wrong." My tendency to go mythic, it's not something I really think much about; it's not like I sit down and say, "I think I'll go mythic today." You just try to follow the story wherever it will go, try to write something you'd like to hear. The places where Sandman worked, worked because I thought, "I have to write a monthly comic, and I'd better create a storytelling framework where I can do absolutely anything, a machine that would allow me to tell stories." The fact [that] I created this rather peculiar late-twentieth-century uber-myth was more of a by-product of that; it wasn't intentional. It's like the Hero's Journey. I got twenty percent through Campbell's book, *The Hero With a Thousand Faces,* and thought, "I shouldn't know this. Because if he's right, I'll be doing it anyway, and if he's wrong, it doesn't matter"—and I stopped reading it, and I never felt the urge to pick it up again. Not even when in meetings, where Hollywood executives were apt to say, "Well, according to Campbell, you really need the reconciliation with the father here." They haven't read it either, by the way, they just heard about it.

SRB: *From George Lucas and his devotees, no doubt. The powers that be in Hollywood are always seeking proven templates and formulas, which are actually anathema to a writer. What is your inclination when working with the tropes of fantasy and myth and the classics? Do you want to challenge them, or amplify them, or reject them in some way? What do you see yourself doing when you write?*

NEIL: I tend to think of it as "having a conversation with." It's partly a conversation, partly a stew. When you turn up as a young writer, there's a stew that's already been bubbling for a while, and you just sort of ladle from it, you know what it tastes like, there's a whole slew of things in the stew (something I recommend you don't say fast). There are different kinds of stew. As you proceed, you realize that you've been ladling stuff back in. The first time I saw something labeled "Gaimanesque," it was terrifying. Then I realized that I had been adding to the stew, and new writers were ʰaving conversations with me. You can add to the stew, embrace the recipe.

SRB: *Like you and Roger [Avary] did with* Beowulf—

NEIL: I've now done at least three different variants of *Beowulf.* "Bay Wolf," my peculiar poetic mash up of *Baywatch* and *Beowulf,* set in the future, starring the Wolfman. My favorite riff is in "The Monarch in the Glen," an *American Gods* short story, where the monster is not terribly bright, and actually quite sweet, but his mother is one of those terrifying Scottish ladies, wielding a purse as a weapon. The third is the actual film. Ever since I was a kid, I loved the idea of Grendel and his mother, a monster and his mother.

SRB: *The synthesis between your comics work and your fiction looks like a brilliant strategy. Looking back, it's almost like there was an ingenious master plan, Neil.*

NEIL: I have a brilliantly strategized career as long as you look at it in hindsight. As long as you stand here and look back on it, there is a level of brilliance, and you go, "Now, how did he ever—?" *Stardust* was, I believe, number one in the UK box office last week, and will be dislodged this week from the UK box office by *Beowulf* at number one. And you go, "How the hell did he arrange that?" You know, the clout that gives me in the UK—which is where I really want to go and do stuff right now anyway—is amazing. I can go back and be taken seriously anywhere I want to go in the UK, and you go, "The level of brilliance and organization it must have taken me to do that—" and it's complete, bizarre happenstance.

HW: *Why did* Stardust *do better in the UK than here?*

NEIL: Oh, it was marketed better. The marketing in America was crap—well, calling it crap was unfair. It was marketed incorrectly. What was being advertised on television looked like sort of *Pirates of the Caribbean* "lite." What was being advertised in posters, in those places that had posters, looked kind of like *Ella Enchanted.* There was nothing to tell the kind of people who would have liked to have seen *Stardust* that it was a funny, smart, romantic fantasy comedy. *"Princess Bride"* is what people who saw it said; *"Princess Bride,"* those two words were forbidden to use, because they kept saying, "Well, *Princess Bride* didn't make any box office." *"Princess Bride"* was what the reviewers said, and the people who went to see it said; it was not anything they [the studio] ever did. In fact, they worked very hard to get away from the idea of *Princess Bride.* So, it was badly mismarketed. In the UK, we took over the marketing, and we marketed it as funny, and we got Tom Baker doing the voiceover.

SRB: *You also had Ricky Gervais, who has a higher profile in the UK.*

NEIL: Yes, but people also hate Ricky in the UK, so what they really loved was that he got killed [laughter], which the *Sun* newspaper described as "giving the people what they want!" And I love Ricky—but it was, well, good marketing in the UK. Well, what it is—it's accurate marketing. My biggest problem with the *Beowulf* marketing is that it looks like *300*. I keep going, "Don't sell it to people as *300*, because if they go and see it, it's not that, and they will be disappointed. Sell it to them as what it is." I would have loved to have seen a poster for *Beowulf* that looked like the posters you used to see in the sixties and early seventies, with big, lush, historical, magical things.

SRB: *"See! Beowulf Battle Grendel! See! The Cave of the Monster! Witness!—"*
NEIL: Yes! Absolutely.

SRB: **How do you even deal with that aspect of Hollywood at this point?**
NEIL: At this point, I don't. Although, with *Coraline* I seem to be getting listened to a lot more.

SRB: *That preview was amazing; it was haunting and tantalizing, though it didn't tell me any detail of what it was—*
NEIL: You know, I loved that. I loved what Henry [Selick] made, and I fought for it to be done like that. I had them change a couple of shots in the middle, and they said, "Yes," and it got better. And I said, "Okay, just promise me one thing. Do not do a *Coraline* preview eight months from now where you spend thirty seconds giving people the impression they've seen the movie, and have some character say, 'and now things get exciting!' or 'and now, it starts,' and then a moment of silence, a drum bang, and loud rock music followed by a lot of clips from all the action sequences." What I learned watching some of the bad trailers for *Stardust* . . . I saw trailers that made me feel like I'd seen the whole thing that were about different movies completely. I saw a really bad trailer that was all about Tristan's search for his mother, and saw trailers that were all about witches, and trailers all about pirates. The worst thing is, you can give someone the impression they've seen the entire movie when actually they have no idea what they're seeing.

HW: **At the University of Minnesota fantasy symposium today [November 17, 2007], you talked about a prepared lecture you intended to give; you discussed a bit of it during the final Q and A session with the audience. What was that talk going to be about?**
NEIL: I've been traveling an awful lot over the past few weeks, due to *Beowulf,* which wasn't really planned. I had expected to get *Stardust*ed this year, but didn't expect I had to do too much regarding *Beowulf.* Somewhere on my trips, rather sleeplessly, I made a lot of notes on fantasy, and it was really, really good, all the notes made a lot of sense, when I wrote them.

I've got this sort of mad bee in my bonnet right now that started with notions that arose when talking to journalists about *Stardust,* in reaction to their strange questions: "Why do you write fantasy? Why don't you write real literature?" Frustrated with this attitude, I was polite for a short while, but I came to a point where

I started basically to say, "Look, literature *is* fantasy." Throughout most of humanity's history there is a direct one-to-one correlation: Homer, Apollonius, *Beowulf,* the good bits in Petronius that aren't about sex, [Geoffrey] Chaucer, [Giovanni] Boccaccio, *The Journey to the West,* large chunks of Shakespeare, the Bible, the Arabian Nights—you look at world literature, and it's fantasy, what we would consider to be fantasy today. Magical, wonderful things happen. I never convinced anyone, but it was incredibly satisfying as a position to take. The existence of a special fantasy section in a bookshop, somehow different from the rest of the bookshop, is such an astonishingly recent development; it would have been unheard of in the past.

Stardust was very consciously written, trying to put myself in a pre-Tolkienian mind-set. Tolkien is the bowling ball in a rubber sheet; Tolkien changed things. Before him, things weren't published, regarded, or reviewed as fantasy. They were reviewed in the *New York Times* by W. H. Auden. We live in a world where the idea of fantasy as being "something else" is prevalent, where its success means it has to be replicated to keep it commercial. *Stardust* was intended to be a throwback to the time where a novelist would simply write a fairy tale, and nobody felt it was anything different, it wasn't an aberration, any more than they would look at Dickens and say, "Ah, it's got a miser and three ghosts in it." That would have been the first half of the talk.

The second half was something I began to realize was important on my recent travels. I was in China at a science fiction convention, which didn't resemble anything you might imagine an SF convention to be. The last science fiction convention in China was ten years ago. China is a country in which SF and fantasy are read and enjoyed, but, until very, very recently, have been officially disapproved of. Not on the level that crime fiction was disapproved of, for instance, under Mao, because there was, of course, no crime in China. In China, science fiction was disapproved of because it was considered trivial.

Things have been changing over the past few years. The Chinese leaders looked around, noticed they were good at a lot of things, but they weren't creative—they didn't invent; they did their own riffs on things that already existed. They looked further, at creative people in other cultures, and noticed these people were fond of fantastic literature. So they began to look at fantasy differently, more approvingly. I watched these guys, I talked to these really smart, really nice Chinese writers, and it was obvious to me that all they still thought about was utilitarian; it all had to have a purpose. I tried to explain to them that what was important was the imagination; everything you see around you had to be imagined first; somebody had to daydream, ask themselves the big question of fantasy, "What if?" At the point where I explained to them [that] they had to daydream more, it was very odd; it was as if I had told the denizens of a monastery that they had to get laid more often. It was something both terrible and thrilling for them. That was going to be the other part, only far more exhaustive and brilliant.

SRB: But that's the magic—imagining, inventing. Still, the real magic is in the writing, isn't it?
HW: Michael Chabon once described writing as—I'm paraphrasing here—passion for the idea, then persistence and problem solving. Is that how it works for you?

NEIL: Well, that's a perfectly adequate description. It's interesting the illusions people have about writing. The fact is, once you are writing—really writing—you probably can't remember why you thought it was a good idea, all the characters are flat. Meanwhile, your family are starting to get grumpy with you, because while this was exciting and fun in week one, it's been three weeks since they've seen you. You're preoccupied and irritating, and irritated, and this whole thing seems pointless. I say, "Welcome to the club." Okay, this is how you write a novel: You put one word in front of another word a hundred thousand times. It's like watching a guy build a dry stone wall: He picks up a rock, and puts it in the right place, and has to pick the right size rock for the right size place, and then put another one in, and you do that fifty to a hundred thousand times. At the end of the day, you know, it's all about putting that one word after another. It's not romantic, it's not clever, it's not brilliant, it's just—the process of doing it. But, yeah, it's problem solving, that's one of the things it is. It's starting out with an idea that's going to keep you enthusiastic enough to get you so far into it that at the point where you realize this whole thing is stupid and pointless and want to give up, you've already written half a book, so you may as well just carry on.

That's all part of, but it's all part of this whole thing—in terms of, is the idea important? Kind of. But it's nowhere near as important as the people think it is who come up to you and say, "You're a writer; you know, I've got an idea for a book, and I will tell you what: I will tell you my idea, you write the book, and we'll split the thing fifty-fifty." Because people think that writers are these hungry, sad little people who are questing around like squirrels after fallen bird seed, just hoping to find an idea somewhere, and then they will take it away with them and bury it, and it will grow magically and without any work into this beautiful tree. It's not like I'm short of ideas. I could stop having quote unquote "ideas"—in the sense of a big plotlike idea that would drive another novel or drive a major short story—I could probably stop having those tomorrow, and have a lifetime's worth of books still to write. And, of course, I wouldn't be able to write them if I stopped having ideas, because everything that happens in a book—every moment, every branching intersection of "okay, I've got half a page to fill now before the bomb explodes, so I'm going to have to take them into a café," and write about what happens to them in that café before the bomb can go off, and actually, what happens in that café turns out to be more interesting than the explosion of the bomb, but you don't know that before you've sat down and written it.

In many ways, the thing that keeps me going as a writer—the magic thing, about being a writer—is the moment that you find yourself writing something amazing and wonderful and magical that honestly wasn't even in your head the second before it started getting written. And that, for me, is everything. That, for me, is the power, the glory, the delight. It's not the cool bits that you planned ages ago. It's that thing that makes it all worthwhile. And you never know when that's going to happen, you never know when that's going to strike. It's that moment where something that you were doing gives you something else.

|||||||||||||||||||||||||||||||||||||||||||||||||||||||||||||||||||||

THE JOURNAL

June the 19th is the publication date of *American Gods,* a book which despite the many shelves in this office filled with books with my name on the spine, feels an awful lot like a first novel.

Thus began, on February 9, 2001, a Web-oriented journey that continues to this day (specifically, December 30, 2007) and shows no signs of ending soon. Gaiman suggested doing a blog or something like it to his editor Jennifer Hershey about a year prior, while *American Gods* was still being written. Hershey preferred waiting until the book was actually on its way to publication, which explains the actual premiere date.

Up until that time, Gaiman, who loved reading diaries, had never managed to keep one himself. Now, through his online journal, he's kept one for over six years, faithfully updating it at least every couple of days or so, keeping his fans up-to-date on his life, activities, and whatever catches his fancy at a particular moment. Thus, we've experienced his reaction to the 9/11 tragedy, to the deaths of a number of his friends, of his struggles and joys on specific projects, graduations, birthdays, proposals, and even a quest or two, as when he got on his soapbox to urge creative types to make sure they had wills. Readers have also been treated to several delightful guest entries from Gaiman's younger daughter, Maddy.

It's quite remarkable how open and honest he is in his journal, expressing opinions on issues that matter to him and answering all sorts of questions from whoever wishes to write to him. There's a great deal to be learned from the journal about writing, publishing, and the entertainment business; there's also a wonderful opportunity to tap into Gaiman's extensive knowledge of literature, movies, and comics. The added value of his Web presence is that even if he doesn't know something, a friend or a member of his vast audience (hundreds of thousands of individual hits each month) will.

In 2007, Gaiman went over the million-word mark on the blog, celebrating the event as follows. First, acknowledging the momentous event:

Saturday, January 27, 2007
1,014,261 not counting these
And I just got to see some site statistics (courtesy of Dan Guy who has made the Webelf her Clouds—the first is up at http://www.neilgaiman.com/journal/labels/ and is really rather fun. Hurrah for you helpful people out there reading this) and I learned that as of the last post, I'd written One Million and Fourteen Thousand, Two Hundred and Sixty One words on this blog.

I wish I'd known that 14,261 words ago. We would have had a party. With balloons.

—And then, celebrating the event, in real time, and virtually:

Saturday, July 21, 2007
Party Party
So this is the million words party post, and as with all good parties, I already feel faintly sick from devouring too many sweet things. (In this case, big lumps of honeycomb, the first from the hive. The Birdchick (Sharon Stiteler) will tell you all about it, with photos, soon enough.)

(Celebratory Party Art on next page by the Wonderful Web Elf.)

Although Gaiman has spoken in vague terms about ending the blog someday, that day seems, at the moment, to be well in the future. As long as he perceives it as a viable outlet for the issues that concern his restless mind, he seems likely to continue blogging for a long, long time.

||||||||||||||||||||||||||||||||||||||||||||||||||||||||||||||||

THE FABULOUS LORRAINE

Lorraine Garland performs a key function in Neil Gaiman's life: allowing him time to breathe, and to write. That means she has to maintain a figurative wall around her boss, preventing the distractions that come from his success from in-

terfering with his personal life and his writing time. Lorraine accomplishes this task with grace and aplomb, all while pursuing her musical life when she can, as evidenced by her contributions to albums made by the Flash Girls, Folk Underground, and Lorraine a Malena, and as many gigs in the Minneapolis area as time will allow.

So what exactly does Lorraine do for Neil Gaiman? Well, like many other questions, that one is answered on Gaiman's blog, a portion of which we reproduce here with his and Lorraine's permission. We follow that up with a brief Q&A we conducted with Lorraine, who graciously agreed to sit down with us even as she demonstrated her mutant ability for multitasking; she truly earns the title "Fabulous," in all aspects of her life.

Lorraine calls this her "Day in the Life . . ." essay:

Saturday August 12, 2006
What My Assistant Does

Over the years quite a few of you have written in and asked what Lorraine, my assistant, actually *does*. (Whatever it is she does, she's been doing it now for about 14 years.) Today she swung by on her way to go off and do her other job (er, playing violin and singing). "Hey," she said. "Check your email. I wrote about what it's like to be a personal assistant."

I checked my email. I read it. I laughed. I nodded with a certain amount of recognition. (Though I've only sprung a visit to Tasmania that she had to organize on her once, in about 1998, and I didn't bring back any animals at all.)

"Shall I put it up on my blog?" she said.

"Sure," I said. Then, "Would you like me to put it up on mine?"

She said yes, she would actually, so here it is. A Lorraine's-eye view of the world . . .

A DAY IN THE LIFE OF A PERSONAL ASSISTANT

Wake up. Drive to Boss's House. Think to myself "way way too early." Make tea. Get ready to wake Boss for an early morning conference call with foreign editor. Attempt to wake Boss. Find what looks like a corpse. Remember Boss promised to have an "Early Night" and wake upon the dawn like a lark, refreshed and ready for the day. Realize Boss has only been asleep for an hour or so.

Shake corpse. Corpse attempts speech. Corpse fails. *Tea,* I say, over and over, in conversational tones. Boss makes it to tea, which is beside the bed, not a far leap for many, but a large one for Boss. Asks me to find the Last Big Contract for the Last Big Project but I am too smart for that trick. Wait until Boss is actually working thru morning e-mail until I leave the room.

Make more tea. Start to go thru the mail, which comes in a bucket sort of thing every morning. Throw away the junk. Bucket thing still full. Start to open the Mail and sort into piles. Important, Black and Whites of Comics in Progress, Galleys of Books in Progress, Case of Mangos (look, if you want something from me, a case of mangos gets that request right to the top) contracts, requests for quotes, fan mail, gifts from fans and friends, Things From Editors, Publishers, and Studios, CDs people have sent, and really odd things (see essay on "Top Ten Things Never to Send Your Favorite Writer"). Notice one of the CDs. Stop. Impressed. Love her work. Pop CD into the player. Ah, yes. . . .

Time for more tea for Boss. Remind him about the conference call in ten minutes. He asks, *Any chance of breakfast?* Make breakfast. Fast. Get Boss on call, with more tea and go downstairs with tiara for the portion of the day known as "Princess of No."

E-mail. Lots of E-mail. I promise myself I will, today, get it down under 500. I will be patient. I will be kind, as I dash people's hopes and dreams. You have 130 new e-mails, my computer helpfully tells me. Well, it's early I think, not to worry, can't really sink my teeth into it until I get at least 200.

Dear Assistant, we would like to invite your Boss to our Con next month, next year, in ten years time, many of them start out. Can't be done, sorry, he is booked thru the year 2060. When he will be 100. *Sorry,* says the Princess of No.

Dear Assistant, can we interview your Boss for our web-page, fanzine, newspaper, major paper, television show, documentary? "Maybe," I tell the *Washington Post,* David Letterman and the guy doing a documentary on Seriously Weird Un-dead Things who Like Mangos (hey, I like Seriously Weird Un-dead Things and Mangos—rule number one, get the Assistant behind you) . . . . . .

The ones that come thru foreign publishers, I say, "you get *one* major interview, pick it wisely, that's it for you." Boss is published in over 40 different countries. I wonder how we are going to do 40 interviews for his current bestselling book, the one coming out in a month, and the two movies he is working on. Everyone else gets to meet the Princess of No (No one likes her. UN-popular.).

Dear Assistant, I wrote you almost a week ago and have received no reply to my questions, what's the problem?

I have my first good laugh of the day.

Dear Assistant, I am an aspiring writer-publisher-editor-illustrator and desire greatly to get into the field and am inquiring about an internship with Mr. Gaiman, I don't need to be paid, just a couch to sleep on and I feel I could be of great help working with him and his publishers and could learn a lot from an internship. (Hmmm . . . we DO need someone for the garden. But no.)

Receive a letter from my best friend asking what I am up to today. Ruining people's hopes and dreams I say. Oh, she writes back, the usual. Another letter friend asks can we go out sometime. I wonder idly what that means.

(During the E-mail phase I should point out [that] the phone has not once stopped ringing.)

Boss is off the conference call and I give him a list of calls to return. He lets me know the cats have been peeing in inappropriate places. I apologize and take responsibility for the cats' bladders, and go have a talk with the cats. *Look* says I, *you gots these nice litter boxes, why for you peeing around all the doors?* Cats say *because you close the doors.* I say, *Because if we don't you pee in the rooms.* Stand off. Never argue with a cat.

Arrange with Movie People for Boss to go out for Meetings the following week. Arrange car to airport, air, car to hotel, hotel car service to meetings and airport again.

Arrange Meetings: Breakfast, Coffee, Lunch, Coffee, Drinks, Dinner, Drinks for people in order of importance. Wonder that Boss isn't fat and floating away.

In one of the ebbs and flows we find ourselves, Boss and I, able to flee the house and have a walk round the garden. Nice garden, nice walk. Take notebook, always. Now I have things to do if I get bored. Not to complain, I like the garden. Threaten plants with pruning shears if they don't start growing better and making me look bad.

I go to the grocery store, the post office, the bank, the garden center and out for some really weird electronics whose purpose I will never understand.

Back home again I hear Boss on the phone with Friend with Family in Town. I overhear Boss say *Sure, come on out tonight for dinner and spend the night, I have to leave for the UK in the morning, but that's ok.* Wait, I say, leaving out the fact I am completely unaware of this UK trip, first things first, How Many and What do they Eat? Go back to grocery store, find beds and bedding. NOW. . . .

What do you mean, Boss you leave tomorrow? Oh. *Right.* Says he. *Director needs me on the set . . . Just found out. Oh, I need to go via Tasmania. Right.*

Set up airfare from Midwest to Tasmania, find hotel with shuttle, and arrange flights to UK and hotel and back home four days later.

Have short talk with Boss about tomorrow's flight. I tell him again that flights will not wait upon him, they are fixed and firm and WILL leave without him. Boss finds this funny. Again. Remind Boss that he is leaving for LA the day *after* he gets back from the UK.

Boss brings home Tasmanian Devil. Research Tasmanian Devil care. Boss tells me Tas has shredded the couch. Take responsibility for Tas's claws. Shoot Tas. Know that if Boss asks where's Tas, the phone will ring, and he might forget for days.

Phone rings. *Oh,* says I, *he's here. Oh, uh, loved your last movie. Lovely about the Oscar.*

Check e-mail. Ah, that's more like it. Numbers I can really sink my teeth into. Letter from Godlike Writer asking is Boss free to be Grand Master of Everything on April 30th he says he will if he's free. Sure, says I, he has nothing except Easter Weekend when he is Godlike Master of Everything at the Most important Thing in the World. Easter Weekend, I recall from last year, is in early April. Copy Boss. Get mail back from Boss. Find out Easter Weekend Moves Each Year and is now on April 30th. Damn. Write letters throwing myself on my sword.

Being a Personal Assistant is like shooting from the hip. You have to be fast, you have to be ready. If it goes wrong, oh, and it will, you will take the blame. If it goes right, that's good because that's how it should be. I, however, know that I am appreciated. My Boss has the sweetest temper going, and is one of the kindest people I have ever met. I know everything I do is really, really important. He has told me so, many times.

I lay in my bed, wishing I had got everything I wanted to done, and run over my various affirmations for the day tomorrow. I *will* get my e-mail under 500. I *will* get tomatoes staked. I *will* be friendly, funny, and *try* and get to the gym.

Then two very very truthful, simple and profound things occur to me and I smile.

I so love my job. And. . . .

Thank the Gods that I am not as busy as my Boss.

And now our interview . . .

Question: Lorraine, let's talk a little bit about your typical day. How do you function? As a buffer, a facilitator?
LORRAINE GARLAND: A combination of both. I jokingly refer to myself as "the princess of no." I feel bad about that, but if I don't do that, Neil won't be able to get his work done.

Q: In a typical month, how many requests do you field for Neil's time and/or attention?
LG: I never thought about quantifying it, but let's say many, many more requests than he could possibly handle. We're talking about requests for interviews, appearances at conventions and conferences, signings, book tours, movie publicity, etc.

Q: Is it stressful for you to say no all the time?
LG: If I let it, but, in the end, I have to remind myself that the better I am at my job, the more time Neil has to write.

Q: So the more you say no, the more Neil Gaiman product we'll have?
LG: That sums it up. He's constantly being asked to do something. In fact, I said no to two people even before I got here today.

Q: On a Saturday?
LG: On a Saturday. It's not that I say no, outright, either, just that I don't think something might be possible at the moment. How long did it take for us to arrange this, six months?

Q: Yes.
LG: I really believe that Neil would accommodate everyone if he could; that's just the way he is. He loves to talk to people; he loves the fans; and he would probably say yes to most everything. But that would leave him with no time for his family or for his writing.

Q: But you run everything by him?
LG: I tell him about every single request. He gets a summary of every proposal from me; nothing is ever dismissed out of hand. But he can't do everything. He's

either coming off a trip, or embarking on another, or he has a deadline, or he's just plain exhausted.

Q: After all this time, do you feel you know him well?

LG: A personal assistant has to know their boss intimately, to be able to anticipate what they'll say, or how they'll react. But even after sixteen years, I still get surprised.

Q: How did you meet?

LG: I had no clue who he was when I first met him. I was at a convention out East, and we ended up at a dinner together with several other people. He was passing out a black and white of his comic, an early issue of *Sandman*. I didn't know anything about comics at the time. When he moved out here, he needed someone to put his library on the bookshelves, so I did that. Then there was something else that needed tending to. Then something else. Suddenly, I looked up one day and I had been working for him for years.

Q: It's no exaggeration to say that Neil has achieved "rock star" status. Do you have to deal with crazed fans?

LG: Sometimes, but it doesn't happen that often. By and large, Neil's fans are great.

Q: It must be easy to get lost in a job like yours. What do you do to maintain a work/life balance?

LG: I write and play music. I go off periodically to make an album, or to sing with a couple of local bands, and then it's more about me. Neil's good about that; I can take a couple of weeks here and there, and on the weekends I can sing with a pub band.

Q: And you have cut several albums?

LG: Originally, with Emma Bull, in a group called the Flash Girls, then with a band called Folk Underground. My last two CDs were joint efforts with my bandmate Malena Teves. Malena and I did one CD called *Mirror Mirror* as Lorraine a Malena. [The second is] *The Hidden Variable* (which is) both band name and CD title. The Hidden Variable is Malena, me, and Chris Ewen (from the Future Bible Heroes). Chris wrote all the music, and the lyrics were written by a who's who of writers, such as Neil and my former bandmate, Emma Bull. Coming out spring '08. It is the only one of my CDs *not* produced by Adam Stemple (Flash Girls, Folk Underground, and Lorraine a Malena). He's a writer too; he has a couple of books out.

Q: How did you meet Malena?

LG: Neil hosted a show for Fox called *13 Nights of Fright,* which he was very keen on doing because he got to come out of a coffin. Malena played a sexy vampire character in those pieces, à la Vampira. I felt an instant connection with her, so I wrote her a letter. That was the beginning of our creative relationship; we knew within a few weeks that we'd form a band together.

Q: *After sixteen years, do you ever find yourself getting bored?*
LG: Someone asked me a similar question a while ago, and I had to tell them that I didn't understand the question. It's never boring here; every day brings something new to occupy my attention. I love my job, and I think I'm very good at it. I wouldn't want to do anything else.

A LORRAINE DISCOGRAPHY

* 1993 Flash Girls (with Emma Bull), *The Return of Pansy Smith and Violet Jones*

* 1994 Neil Gaiman's *Warning Contains Language* features the song "Banshee" (with Flash Girls)

* 1995 Flash Girls (with Emma Bull), *Maurice and I*

* 2001 Flash Girls (with Emma Bull), *Play Each Morning, Wild Queen*

* 2003 Folk UnderGround (with Paul Score, Adam Stemple, and various others), *Buried Things*

* 2004 Folk UnderGround, *Get Yer Hands Off Me Booty*

* 2005 Lorraine a Malena (with Malena Teves), *Mirror Mirror*

UPCOMING:

* Spring 2008 Paul and Lorraine, *We're Irish Enough For You*

* Spring/Summer 2008 The Hidden Variable (with Chris Ewen and Malena Teves), *The Hidden Variable*. This CD also features, Lorraine says, "a *beyond* cool list of writers."

* Video, Band: Hidden Variable (Lorraine, Malena, and Chris Ewen; directed by Kimberly Butler). Song: "Kindermarchen" (lyrics by Gregory McGuire) available Spring 2008.

CURRENT BANDS:

* Lorraine a Malena: lorraineamalena.com

* The Hidden Variable: hiddenvariable.net

* Paul and Lorraine: paulandlorraine.com

UNUSUAL THINGS THAT HAPPEN
AT SIGNINGS: A MODEST PROPOSAL

There must be a million stories about unusual things that have happened at the book signings of various authors, from rudeness to violence to overexuberance; from breast flashing to flesh signing to broken glass and police sirens and arrest. There's the one about a fan cutting themselves in front of Clive Barker and bleeding onto the open book, asking him to sign in blood. Did it happen? Perhaps, and perhaps not. Many stories about Unusual Things that Happen at Signings are probably apocryphal.

But not all.

Neil Gaiman has undoubtedly had more than his share of such unusual things. And yet, in his journal, under the tag Unusual Things that Happen at Signings, there is only a single entry. It is a recent happening, and rather than something as grim as bloodshed, it is a wonderful thing.

In November 2007, the accommodating Mr. Gaiman took part in the elaborate scheme of Jason Drilon to propose to his lady love, Maui Reyes, during a signing at the Philippine Ad Congress.

Jason began planning the operation weeks before, contacting Gaiman to see if he was game. Of course, the first hurdle he faced was the Fabulous Lorraine, Gaiman's personal assistant. Jason wrote on his blog:

> So one late night, I went to the "Ask Neil" portion of his blog and wrote a rather long e-mail about how I planned to propose, and if he could find some time in his busy schedule and play a small part (understatement of the year) in it. I did this well knowing that the e-mail would probably be discarded along with the thousands of messages he gets every day. But two days later, a reply from his assistant:
>
> Hi Jason, I am sure we can help with this, give me a bit to make sure of his schedule . . .

A day later, while having lunch with Maui, Jason received a call from Jaime Daez, owner of local book superstore, Fully Booked, telling him that Neil had, in fact, agreed to assist him. Jason then hurried to Daez's store to talk to him, so that Daez could meet him and see his face, so that he could signal Gaiman during the event. Jason

What Neil wrote on Maui's *Absolute Sandman Volume 02*. The guy deserves an award for being such a great human being. Photo courtesy of Jason Drilon and Maui Reyes.

I hadn't planned on kneeling, but I found myself with one knee down. Photo courtesy of Jason Drilon and Maui Reyes.

purchased a copy of *Absolute Sandman* Volume 2, which was a key prop in his plan.

The day of the proposal, Jason tried to approach Gaiman after the author had finished giving a talk to the Congress, but had to abort when Maui returned to his side sooner than expected. Thinking quickly, he instead pushed the unbelieving Maui toward Gaiman and took a photo.

Jason was eventually able to contact Gaiman to make final arrangements.

Saturday morning arrived, the day of the signing, and Jason and Maui waited patiently in line for Gaiman to sign Jason's copy of the second volume of *The Absolute Sandman*.

Although Jason knew the fix was in, he remained nervous. And with good reason, it turns out.

Taking Jason's book, Gaiman drew a picture of Morpheus inside in silver ink, signing his name, and adding a P.S.: *Will You Marry Jason?*

Starstruck, Maui closed the book without glancing at the inscription. In fact, Maui had to be asked several times to read it. As Jason recorded the conversation:

||||||||||||||||||||||||||||||||||||||||||||||||||||||||||||||||||||||

Coconspirator Neil Gaiman with Maui Reyes. Photo courtesy of Jason Drilon and Maui Reyes.

||||||||||||||||||||||||||||||||||||||||||||||||||||||||||||||||||||||||||||

Maui (squealing, closing the book): Thanks!!!

Gaiman: Aren't you going to read what I wrote? You have to read it . . .

Maui (opening the book, shrugging, then closing it again): Thanks!!!

*Jason: You **have** to read the dedication . . .*

Maui bent over to give Gaiman a kiss, still not catching on.

Gaiman: You really have to read this . . .

When she finally did, Jason took the ring out of his pocket, knelt, proposed . . . and she said, "Yes," thrilling the crowd, her suitor, and her favorite author.

THE APPENDICES

APPENDIX ONE:
THE GAIMAN TIMELINE

1960   Born Neil Richard Gaiman, November 10, 1960, in Porchester, England. Gaiman was the eldest of three children born to David Gaiman, a director of a company, and Sheila Gaiman, who worked as a pharmacist; he has two younger sisters. He reproduced this pattern when he had children; in fact, his son is exactly one year, eleven months, and five days older than his first daughter, the same as Gaiman and his sister.

1965   Gaiman, who described himself as "a completely omnivorous and cheerfully undiscerning reader," reads *Alice in Wonderland* for the first time. Between the age of five and twelve, it becomes his "default reading."

1967   Buys Roger Lancelyn Green's *Tales of Egypt* with his own money.

1969   Convinces parents to take him to see several Gilbert and Sullivan plays. Discovers the work of Michael Moorcock.

1970   Attends grammar school at Ardingly College (1970–74).

1973   Gaiman studies for his bar mitzvah with cantor Reb Meyer Lev, who introduced him to the stories of Jewish mythology.

1974   Begins secondary education at the Whitgift School (1974–77)

1976   Gaiman plays in a punk band, originally called Chaos. After undergoing a lineup change, it became Exexecs.

1977   The young Gaiman grows disillusioned with comic books, giving them up for several years.

1980   Embarks on a career in journalism.

1983   Gaiman reconnects to comics through Alan Moore's Swamp Thing.

        Michael Gaiman born July 21, 1983.

1984   *Duran Duran: The First Four Years of the Fab Five* is published by Proteus Books.

        Ghastly Beyond Belief: The Science Fiction and Fantasy Book of Quotations, co-authored by Kim Newman, is published by Arrow.

1985   Married Mary Therese McGrath on March 14, 1985.

        Holly Gaiman born June 26, 1985.

1986   *Now We Are Sick* is published privately (later reissued, in 1991, as *Now We Are Sick: An Anthology of Nasty Verse* by Dream Haven Press).

        Writes several stories for *2000 A.D.*

        Gaiman meets DC Comics editor Karen Berger at a convention.

        Gaiman meets art student Dave McKean and the two decide to collaborate on *Violent Cases.*

1987   *Violent Cases* is published by Titan.

1988   In early 1988, Gaiman writes the first four thousand words of what was to become *Good Omens* and sends it off to several friends, among them Terry Pratchett.

        Don't Panic: The Official Hitchhiker's Guide to the Galaxy Companion is published by Titan (UK) and Pocket Books (U.S.).

        The Sandman debuts in December.

1989   DC publishes Gaiman's Black Orchid miniseries.

        DC begins publishing the individual issues of *The Books of Magic.*

1990   *Good Omens,* a collaboration with Terry Pratchett, is published by Gollancz (UK) and Workman (U.S.).

        Gaiman handed the reins of *Miracleman* by Alan Moore; begins writing series with issue 17.

1991   Gaiman and Charles Vess win the World Fantasy Award for Best Short Story for "A Midsummer's Night's Dream."

        Todd MacFarlane asks Gaiman to write one issue of his *Spawn* series. Gaiman obliges him, creating the characters Cogliostro, Medieval Spawn, and the warrior woman, Angela.

1992   *Miracleman Book Four: The Golden Age* is published by Eclipse.

Signal to Noise is published by Dark Horse Comics.

Moves to Minneapolis, Minnesota.

1993   *Angels & Visitations: A Miscellany* is published by Dream Haven Books.

The collected *The Books of Magic* is published by DC Comics.

1994   *The Tragical Comedy, or Comical Tragedy, of Mr. Punch* is published by VG Graphics.

Death: The High Cost of Living, illustrated by Chris Bachalo, is published by DC Comics.

Angela, a three-issue miniseries, is published by Image Comics.

Maddy Gaiman born August 28, 1994.

1995   Marvel Comics publishes the three issue miniseries The Last Temptation.

1996   The TV series *Neverwhere* debuts on the BBC.

Neverwhere is first published in novel form by BBC Books.

The Sandman: Book of Dreams, co-edited by Gaiman and Ed Kramer, is published by Harper Prism.

1997   Gaiman's first children's book, *The Day I Swapped My Dad for Two Goldfish*, illustrated by Dave McKean, is published by White Wolf Publishing.

Death: The Time of Your Life, illustrated by Chris Bachalo, is published by DC Comics.

Neverwhere appears in novel form in the U.S., published by Avon.

Gaiman given the Defender of Liberty Award from the Comic Book Legal Defense Fund.

The first installment of *Stardust,* illustrated by Charles Vess, is published by DC Comics in October.

The last monthly issue of *The Sandman,* number 75, appears.

1998   *Smoke and Mirrors: Short Fictions and Illusions* is published by Avon.

1999   *The Sandman: The Dream Hunters*, with art by Yoshitaka Amano, is published by DC Comics.

2000   *Green Lantern/Superman: Legend of the Green Flame* is published by DC Comics.

2001   *American Gods* published by William Morrow. In February, Gaiman begins his ultra-successful blog to promote its publication.

Harlequin Valentine, illustrated by John Bolton, is published by Dark Horse Comics.

2002   *Coraline* is published by HarperCollins.

Murder Mysteries, illustrated by P. Craig Russell, is published by Dark Horse Comics.

Gaiman wins the Hugo, the Bram Stoker, and the BFSA Awards for *American Gods.*

Adventures in the Dream Trade is published by NESFA Press.

Gaiman writes and directs *A Short Film About John Bolton.*

Gaiman files and wins a lawsuit against Todd MacFarlane involving three *Spawn* supporting characters, Cogliostro, Medieval Spawn, and Angela.

2003   *The Wolves in the Walls,* illustrated by Dave McKean, is published by HarperCollins.

Endless Nights is published by Vertigo.

Gaiman wins the Nebula, the Bram Stoker, and the Hugo Awards for *Coraline.*

2004   The Marvel miniseries 1602 debuts.

Gaiman wins the Hugo Award for his short story, "A Study in Emerald."

2005   *MirrorMask* premieres at the Sundance Film Festival in January.

Melinda published by Hill House in March.

Anansi Boys published by HarperCollins in September.

2006   *Fragile Things* published by William Morrow in September.

The Eternals, a seven-issue minseries from Marvel Comics, premieres.

2007   The short story collection *M is for Magic* is published by HarperCollins.

InterWorld, coauthored by Michael Reaves, is published by Harper Eos.

The film version of *Stardust* premieres in August.

The animated film *Beowulf,* cowritten by Gaiman, premieres in November.

2008   The twentieth anniversary of the first appearance of The Sandman.

Odd and the Frost Giants is published by Bloomsbury Publishing in March.

The Dangerous Alphabet, illustrated by Gris Grimley, is published by HarperCollins in April.

The Graveyard Book, illustrated by Dave McKean, is scheduled to be published by HarperCollins in September.

||||||||||||||||||||||||||||||||||||||||||||||||||||||||||||||||||||

APPENDIX TWO:
THE AUDIO GAIMAN

American Gods, Harper Audio, 2003, unabridged, performed by George Guidall.

Anansi Boys, Harper Audio, 2005, unabridged reading of Gaiman's novel by Lenny Henry.

Coraline, Harper Audio, 2002, Gaiman reading, with original music by the Gothic Archies.

Fragile Things, Harper Audio, 2006, unabridged, with Gaiman reading.

The Neil Gaiman Audio Collection, Harper Audio, 2004, Gaiman readings of *The Day I Swapped My Dad for Two Goldfish, The Wolves in the Walls*, "Cinnamon," and "Crazy Hair." It also contains an interview with Gaiman conducted by his daughter Maddy.

Neverwhere, Harper Audio, 2007, unabridged, read by Gaiman.

Speaking in Tongues, Dreamhaven, 2004, Gaiman reading "Daughter of Owls," "Instructions," "The Price," "The Sea Change," and "The Facts in the Case of the Departure of Miss Finch." Music on the production was handled by Adam Stemple.

Stardust, Harper Audio, 2006, unabridged, read by Gaiman.

Telling Tales, Dreamhaven, 2003, Gaiman read "A Writer's Prayer," "Harlequin Valentine," "Boys and Girls Together," "The Wedding Present," and "In the End."

Two Plays for Voices, Harper Audio, 2002, dramatizations of "Murder Mysteries" and "Snow Glass Apples," starring Brian Dennehy and Bebe Neuwirth, respectively.

Warning: Contains Language, Dreamhaven, 1995, Gaiman reading "The Song of the Audience," "Nicholas Was," "Babycakes," "Cold Colours," "The White Road," "Banshee," "Chivalry," and "Troll Bridge," with music from the Flash Girls and Dave McKean.

ALSO Of NOTE:

Buried Things, Folk Underground, Happyfun! Records, 2003, songs written by Gaiman, including, "Folk UnderGround," "Going Wodwo," and "The Butterfly Road." Folk UnderGround are: Lorraine Garland, Trevor Hartman, and Paul Score.

Get Yer Hands Off Me Booty, Folk UnderGround, Happyfun! Records, 2004, featuring Gaiman's song "Tea and Corpses."

The Last Temptation, Alice Cooper, Sony Music, 1994, concept by Alice Cooper and Neil Gaiman.

Maurice and I, The Flash Girls (Lorraine Garland and Emma Bull), Fabulous Records, 1994 featuring Gaiman's "Banshee," "Yeti," and "A Girl Needs a Knife."

Mirror, Mirror, Lorraine a Malena (Lorraine Garland and Malena Teves), Aranya Records, 2005. Featuring songs written by Gaiman, including, "It's Just Me and Eve," "The Butterfly Road (The Faust Song)," and "Personal Thing."

Neil Gaiman: Where's Neil When You Need Him? various Artists, Dancing Ferret Discs, 2006. From the back-cover copy of the CD: "A collection of exclusive new songs from seventeen top international acts, based on their favorite works of Neil Gaiman. Includes new art from Dave McKean and liner notes written by Neil."

Play Each Morning Wild Queen, the Flash Girls, Fabulous Records, 2001, featuring Gaiman's "A Meaningful Dialogue" and "Personal Thing."

The Return of Pansy Smith and Violet Jones, the Flash Girls, Steel Dragon, 1993, featuring Gaiman's "Tea and Corpses," "Sonnet in the Dark," "Postmortem on Our Love" and "The Herring Song."

APPENDIX THREE: FURTHER READING

Beowulf: The Script Book, by Neil Gaiman and Roger Avary, New York: Harper, 2007.

Ghastly Beyond Belief: The Science Fiction and Fantasy Books of Quotations, by Neil Gaiman, London: Arrow Books, 1985.

Hanging Out With the Dream King: Conversations with Neil Gaiman and his Collaborators, by Joseph McCabe, Seattle: Fantagraphic Books, 2004.

Neil Gaiman, by Steven P. Olson (Library of Graphic Novelists), New York: Rosen Publishing Group, 2005.

The Neil Gaiman Reader, edited by Darrell Schweitzer, Rockville, MD: Wildside
    Press, 2007.
The Sandman Companion, by Hy Bender, New York: Vertigo/DC Comics, 1999.
The Sandman Papers: An Exploration of the Sandman Mythology, edited by Joe
    Sanders, Seattle: Fantagraphic Books, 2006.
Stardust: The Visual Companion, by Stephen Jones, London: Titan Books, 2007.

||||||||||||||||||||||||||||||||||||||||||||||||||||||||||||||||||||||

APPENDIX FOUR:
RELATED WEB SITES

As we said in our introduction, you have only to Google the words "Neil
Gaiman" to find a wealth of information about our subject. Here, however,
are a few choice Web sites that we've encountered in putting this book together.

THE DEFINITIVE SOURCE

If you want the latest information on Mr. Gaiman, the best source would be his
Web site, neilgaiman.com. Contained therein is his ever popular blog (there called
Journal), and sections labeled "Neil's Work," "Cool Stuff and Things," "About
Neil," "Message Boards," "Where's Neil," "Search," "Links and Downloads,"
"MouseCircus.com," and "Frequently Asked Questions." In addition, Gaiman
himself constantly creates links to other sites within his blog that he feels might be
of interest to his readers.

OTHER SITES

A more inclusive list is available under the "Links" section of Gaiman's Web site.

ONLINE STORES

neverwear.net (for Gaiman-related apparel.)
neilgaiman.net
dreamhavenbooks.com (Dreamhaven has had a long association with Gaiman;
they published a story collection and three audio CDs.)

fAN SITES

holycow.com/thedreaming (The Dreaming is a fan site devoted to Gaiman and his works, featuring reviews, insider information and more.)
ninave-lake.tripod.com/ngjump (Referencing the Magian, an extensive fan site.)
geocities.com/Area51/Zone/9923/sandman (The Sandman fan site.)

COMICS

cbldf.com (Comic Book Legal Defense Fund. Founded in 1986, it is dedicated to the preservation of First Amendment rights for members of the comics community.)
dccomics.com (DC Comics/Vertigo Web site.)
marvelcomics.com (Marvel Comics Web site.)
darkhorse.com (Dark Horse Comics Web site.)

REfERENCE

neilgaimanbibliography.com (Neil Gaiman Visual Bibliography, a comprehensive bibliography of Gaiman's works, maintained by Gaiman expert GMZOE.)

MISCELLANEOUS

birdchick.com (Official Web site of Gaiman friend and beekeeper, Sharon Stiteler.)
shettelry.blogspot.com/2007/12/flash-girls.html (For more information on the Flash Girls.)
lorraineamalena.com (For more information on Lorraine a Malena.)

APPENDIX fIVE: NOTES

PART I: THE EARLY YEARS

fANTASYTIME AT THE NEW IMPERIAL

1. A very early Gaiman article, written in 1984 for an assignment, but never before published.

WHO WAS JACK THE RIPPER?

1. *The Truth,* 12, October 20, 1988

PART 4: THE COMICS

1. Veitch, e-mail to authors in response to query for this book.

NOTES TOWARD A VEGETABLE THEOLOGY

1. An unpublished essay.
2. With exceptions. It is implied that Erl-Kings can time travel; it is also possible that something could happen which could stir some of the Parliament of Trees out of their contemplation, and back into the world.
3. I'd like to modify Ivy's origin slightly. As I recall, she was given an ancient poisonous drug that didn't kill her; instead it made her immune to poisons and drove her slightly mad. I'd like to modify this to make it that the drug *did* kill her, very effectively. However, it also brought her back to life. Slowly though it's been transmuting her into a plant-woman. (The main reasons why poisons no longer do anything: Her metabolism is no longer fully animal.) Poison Ivy's origin comes from a Wonder Woman comic, so would need a certain amount of modification anyway.

SWEENEY TODD AND OTHER TABOOS

"Babycakes" (Tabook #4, 1990)
1. Valerie Jones, "Miraclemail," Miracleman issue 22, 1991

BEING AN ACCOUNT OF THE LIFE AND DEATH OF THE EMPEROR
HELIOGABOLUS: A 24 HOUR COMIC

1. This includes Gaiman's introduction.
2. Scott McCloud, *Understanding Comics: The Invisible Art* (New York: Harper Paperbacks, 1994), *vi.*
3. *24 Hour Comics All-Stars,* ed. Nat Gertler (Thousand Oaks, CA: About Comics, 2005), 4.
4. McCloud, *iii–iv.*
5. The complete 1992 edition of "Heliogabolus" is posted, with Gaiman's permission, at "The Dreaming: The Neil Gaiman Page," at www.holycow.com/dreaming/helio/helio04.html

MIRACLEMAN #17—24

1. Gifford, *Happy Days! 100 Years of Comics, 1975/1988* (London: Jupitor), 10–11.
2. Georgy Khoury, *Kimota! The Miracleman Companion* (Raleigh, NC: Two-Morrows Publishing, 2001).
3. This special was eventually reprinted by Eclipse Comics in the United States as *Marvelman 3-D* issue 1.
4. Khoury, 120.
5. Ibid.
6. Ibid.
7 Khoury, 118
8. Ibid.
9. Gaiman, e-mail to authors, January 2008.
10. Khoury, 131.
11. Khoury, 120
12. Ibid.
13. Khoury, 132–136
14. Gaiman e-mail to authors, January 2008
15. Khoury, 123
16. Khoury.
17. "Alan Davis Talks *'Miracleman,'*" November 5, 2001; https://www.comic-bookresources.com/?page=article&id=567
18. "Dueling Miracleman! Gaiman Licenses Randy Bowen" http://www.icv2.com/articles/news/2984.com
19. "Gaiman Keeps Share of Spawn Characters: Gaiman vs. McFarlane Ends," www.icv2.com/articles/news/1890.html
20. Gaiman, e-mail to authors, January 2008.
21. Ibid.
22. Emotiv & Company e-mail to Stephen Bissette, February 1, 2008.
23. Gaiman, e-mail to authors, January/February 2008.
24. Gaiman, e-mail to authors, January 2008.
25. Ibid.
26. Victor Bockris, *The Life and Death of Andy Warhol* *(New York: Bantam, 1989).
27. Khoury, 120.
28. Khoury, 123.
29. Khoury, 120, 123.

SPAWN #9 & #26 AND ANGELA #1—3

1. United States Court of Appeals for the Seventh Circuit, http://www.ca7.uscourts.gov/tmp/EY1FG5C4.pdf, p.6.
2. Ibid. 4.

3. Ibid., 4–7.
4. Ibid., 7–8.
5. Ibid., 8.
6. "Why Gaiman Sued McFarlane: Rights Swap Gone Bad," http://www.icv2
   .com/articles/news/1118.html
7. "Marvel Snags Neil Gaiman: Six-issue Miniseries due in 2002: http://www
   .icv2.com/articles/news/819.html
8. Ibid.
9. http://supreme.lp.findlaw.com/supreme_court/orders/2003/011204pzor
   .html, p. 1.
10. "Miracleman Heads to Court: Gaiman Sues McFarlane," http://www.icv2
    .com/articles/news/1057.html
11. http://supreme.lp.findlaw.com/supreme_court/orders/2003/011204pzor.html,
    p.9
12. Ibid.
13. "Wisconsin Courtroom Drama, Part I: Gaiman vs. McFarlane," http://www
    .icv2.com/articles/news/1878.html.
14. Ibid.
15. Ibid.
16. Ibid.
17. Ibid.
18. "Gaiman Sweep: Wins on All Claims!" http://www.icv2.com/articles/news/
    1883.html.
19. "Gaiman Keeps Share of Spawn Characters: Gaiman vs. McFarlane Ends,"
    www.icv2.com/articles/news/1890.html
20. Ibid.
21. http://www.ca7.uscourts.gov/tmp/EY1FG5C4.pdf, p. 27.
22. Ibid., 2, 5.
23. Ibid., 6.
24. Ibid., 9.
25. Ibid, 9, 11–12, 18
26. Ibid, 18–19
27. Ibid., 21.
28. Ibid., 26.
29. Ibid., 28.
30. See caselaw.1p.findlaw.com/scripts/getcase.pl?court=mo&vol=/supreme/072003/
    &inv01=60729_103)
31. "Over and Done: Twst [sic], McFarlane Settle," http://forum.newsarama.com/
    showthread.php?t=101993
32. Gaiman, e-mail to authors. January 27, 2008.
33. "Wisconsin Courtroom Drama, Part I: Gaiman vs. McFarlane," http://www
    .icv2.com/articles/news/1878.html. "Wisconsin Courtroom Drama, Part II:
    The Jury's Out on Gaiman vs. McFarlane," http://www.icv2.com/articles/

news/1880.html. "Gaiman Sweep: Wins on All Claims!" http://www.icv2
.com/articles/news/1883.html. United States Court of Appeals for the Seventh Circuit document http://www.ca7.uscourts.gov/tmp/EY1FG5C4.pdf
34. "Gaiman Keeps Share of Spawn Characters: Gaiman vs. McFarlane Ends,"
www.icv2.com/articles/news/1890.html
35. Letter from Gaiman's lawyer to McFarland's negotiator, 1996.
36. "Why Gaiman Sued McFarlane: Rights Swap Gone Bad," http://www.icv2
.com/articles/news/1118.html

NEIL GAIMAN'S MIDNIGHT DAYS

1. Including *Swamp Thing Annual* #5, 1990.

PART 9: THE SCRIPTS

1. Gaiman, e-mail to authors. October 13, 2007

PART II: THE WORLD OF NEIL GAIMAN

THE INTERVIEW

1. This interview was conducted by Henry Wagner and Stephen R. Bissette in Mr.
Gaiman's American home on November 16 thruogh 18, 2007, and incorporates
a bit of material from a Q&A session between Gaiman and his audience at the
"Fantasy Matters" symposium at The University of Minnesota, on November
17, 2007, and a procession of e-mail follow-up questions and revisions between
Bissette and Gaiman, December 2007–February 2008. Special thanks to Neil
Gaiman and Lorraine Garland for making this possible and for their gracious
hospitality.
2. The weekly *Wham!* was launched by Odhams Press in 1964, the first *Wham!
Annual* in 1965 for 1966; the weekly *Smash!* in February 1966, its first Annual
in 1966 for 1967; "Simultaneously, Odhams were issuing reprinted stories from
American comic books originally published by Marvel Comics. These reprints
were included in the weeklies *Pow!, Fantastic!* and *Terrific,* all of which were
discontinued after about a year. . . . these titles were issued with annuals: *Fantastic* (1969), *Terrific* (1969) and *Pow!,* which was published for 1968–72 before
being amalgamated with *Wham!* to become *Wham! and Pow! Annual* (1973) . . ."
from Alan Clark, *The Children's Annual: A History and Collector's Guide* (London: Boxtree Ltd.), 150.
3. It was an adaptation by Britain's ABC Weekend Television—no relation to the
U.S. TV network—adapted by Trevor Preston, directed by Helen Standage,
black and white, ten half-hour episodes, first broadcast July 1967; no known
legal video or DVD release extant. As Neil later pointed out, "ABC was one of

the ITV channels; BBC was one entity, ITV was lots of local companies and independents." [Same interview with the authors.]

4. Jean-Marc and Randy Lofficier scripted adult versions of the Boy Commandos into DC's *Blue Beetle* #17–21 in 1987; also note Jack Kirby's tough NYPD cop character Dick "Terrible" Turpin in *New Gods* #5, 1971, which John Byrne reinterpreted as being the adult version of the Boy Commando Brooklyn in Byrne's run on *Superman* in 1987.

5. *Plop: The New Magazine of Weird Humor,* was a DC Comics humor anthology that published 24 issues between 1973 and 1976.

6. "Abandoned Houses," Saga of the Swamp Thing Issue 33, 1985.

7. "Final Payment," Saga of the Swamp Thing Issue 34, 1989.

8. In *Swamp Thing* #84, Matt Cable died and became Mathew the Raven; script and art by Rick Veitch.

9. For more on House on the Rock, go to http://www.roadsideamerica.com/story/2254

10. The story gets as much love as it should from Matthew Cheney at http://mumpsimus.blogspot.com/2004/03/bitter-grounds-by-neil-gaiman.html

11. http://www.spiderwords.com/feature1b.htm

INDEX

Note: Page numbers in italics indicate photos.